G000299538

MOTOCOURSE™

THE WORLD'S LEADING GRAND PRIX & SUPERBIKE ANNUAL

icon
PUBLISHING LIMITED

CONTENTS

AUTOCOURSE 2009–2010

is published by:
Icon Publishing Limited
Regent Lodge
4 Hanley Road
Malvern
Worcestershire
WR14 4PQ
Tel: + 44 (0) 1684 564 511
Website: www.motocourse.com

Printed in the United Kingdom by
Butler, Tanner & Dennis Ltd,
Caxton Road, Frome, Somerset
BA11 1NF

© Icon Publishing Limited 2009,
No part of this publication may be
reproduced, stored in a retrieval system
or transmitted, in any form or by any
means, electronic, mechanical, photo-
copying, recording or otherwise, without
prior permission in writing from Icon
Publishing Limited.

ISBN: 978-1-905334-53-7

DISTRIBUTORS

Gardners Books
1 Whittle Drive, Eastbourne, East
Sussex BN23 6QH
Tel: + 44 (0) 1323 521 555
Email: sales@gardners.com

Menoshire Ltd
Unit 13, 21 Wadsworth Rd,
Perivale, Middlesex UB6 7LQ
Tel: + 44 (0) 20 8991 2439

NORTH AMERICA
Motorbooks International
PO Box 1, 729 Prospect Avenue,
Osceola, Wisconsin 54020, USA
Tel: +1 715 294 3345
Fax: +1 715 294 4448

Dust jacket: Valentino Rossi's legend
grew with his seventh premier-class title
in 2009. He is the most successful
premier-class rider in the history of
MOTOCOURSE.

Title page: Ben Spies took World
Superbikes by storm, with a maiden-
season title win. It was Yamaha's first in
the series.

Left: Hiro Aoyama took the last 250 title
for Honda and Japan.

Photos: Gold & Goose

publisher
STEVE SMALL
steve.small@iconpublishinglimited.com

editor
MICHAEL SCOTT

commercial director
BRYN WILLIAMS
bryn.williams@iconpublishinglimited.com

text editor
IAN PENBERTHY

results and statistics
PETER McLAREN

chief photographers
GOLD & GOOSE
David Goldman
Gareth Harford
Mirco Lazzari
Patrik Lundin
Tel: + 44 (0)20 8444 2448

MotoGP illustrations
ADRIAN DEAN
f1artwork@blueyonder.co.uk

Acknowledgements

**The Editor and staff of MOTOCOURSE wish to thank the following for their assistance in compiling the 2009-
2010 edition: Henny Ray Abrams, Jeremy Appleyard, Katie Baines, Jerry Burgess, Paul Butler, Peter Clifford,
Maria Garcia, Maria Guidotti, Henk Keulemans, Isabelle Lariviere (FIM), Elisa Pavan, David Pato, Julian Ryder,
Mike Trimby, Steve Westlake and Günther Wiesinger, as well as the riders and technicians quoted in this
book, Alpinestars, Marlboro and Repsol hospitality staff, and numerous colleagues and friends.**

Additional photographs published in MOTOCOURSE 2009-2010 have been contributed by:
**Gavan Caldwell, Clive Challinor, Dave Collister, Peter J. Fox, Martin Heath, Tom Hnatiw, Ripton Scott, Neil Spalding,
Mark Walters**

www.motocourse.com

MotoGP Valentino Rossi WORLD CHAMPION YAMAHA RACING 2009

World Superbike Ben Spies WORLD CHAMPION YAMAHA RACING 2009

World Supersport Cal Crutchlow WORLD CHAMPION YAMAHA RACING 2009

British Superbike Leon Camier BRITISH CHAMPION YAMAHA RACING 2009

Yamaha Rules

And you can too

What a year it's been for Yamaha Racing - Championships for MotoGP, World Superbike and Supersport, plus the crown in British Superbike too.
In the words of Motorcycle News, 'Yamaha's Greatest Day' (Sunday 25th October 2009). As we know, racing improves the breed. Look at the technology transfer to our supersport bikes - crossplane crank, YCC-I, YCC-T, engine management just to name a few of Yamaha's innovations. Well all of that and more is available right now on our YZF-R1 and R6, and with the full-sized YZF-R125 for those starting off on their R-Series experience, the choice is clear.
Visit your local authorised Yamaha dealer now - you will find yourself a deal that just can't be beaten, and be part of Yamaha's winning team.

YAMALUBE

R-Series
www.yamaha-motor.co.uk

YAMAHA

FOREWORD by VALENTINO ROSSI

NINE world championships is a great achievement. I would need more than just one page to thank all the people who helped me. My mother Stefania and father Graziano, everyone at Yamaha – especially Jeremy Burgess, who is like my motorcycle father; Uccio and my close friends. Together, we've done a great job. And always with huge enjoyment.

This was a great season – at times, one of my hardest ever. Harder than coming back in 2008 after two bad years. I had a very tough rival: my teammate, Lorenzo.

I think it's been a great duel, and I have to say that he has pushed me to new levels. He did a great job to put so much pressure on us. It is battles like this that make racing fun for the fans. And also very much for the winning rider.

Really, there were four riders, all on a very high level, including Dani and especially Casey. We've been on the limit all season. Even with the mono-tyre rule, we have set new lap records at many tracks. That is why we all made some mistakes.

I crashed at Le Mans and Donington Park; and sometimes we had difficulties getting the settings at 100 per cent. In Portugal, I was third, but too far away. That is sometimes the character of the 800s: with such high corner speed and not so much torque, it is harder for the rider to make a difference.

The worst time for me was crashing at Indianapolis – but we came back to win at home at Misano, so that was a good recovery.

The best was passing Lorenzo on the last corner to win at Catalunya. After such a strong battle, it was a huge pleasure for me. One of my best races ever – out of all 227.

I respect racing history and I watch the statistics. This year, I was proud to win my 100th race. There is still Agostini's total ahead of me – 122 grand prix wins. Will I stay on to try to beat it?

I will decide my future in the middle of next year.

But if you asked me the day after I won the championship, I would have said yes. For sure.

Every championship is special for different reasons; it's unforgettable every time, and this time is no different. I'm world champion once again, and now I want to go and party!

TIME FOR A CHANGE

A YEAR of cataclysmic change was the backdrop to a championship battle of rare depth: old master versus young pretender, on identical motorcycles, with the advantage swinging back and forth.

That Rossi won it was an affirmation of everything we already believed. That Lorenzo challenged so strongly was a challenge to all those beliefs.

It should have been four-strong, but Pedrosa was vulnerable and his Honda unfriendly, while Stoner had his mid-season meltdown. It remained enthralling enough, however, to take attention away from the deep changes happening in the ethos of grand prix racing.

Even the shock at the premature death of the 250 two-strokes – one year sooner than originally expected – was swept aside in the excitement that was Moto2: a series that had independent teams and specialist chassis manufacturers worldwide flocking for a chance to join (in some cases rejoin) the World Championship.

But what kind of World Championship? To traditionalists, the idea of control tyres in MotoGP had been hard enough to swallow. One year later, it is control engines, control airboxes, control electronics – virtually a one-make series, except that there is some free choice (within the rules) of chassis design.

Yet so fast is thinking changing within racing's commercially minded management, that in the same year that Moto2's single-engine rule was mooted and adopted, a similar proposal had surfaced to replace the prototypes in MotoGP, which even gained widespread support.

Current thinking suggests a four-cylinder/1000cc rule, restrictions to revs and electronics, and the freedom for that engine to be anything from a handmade one-off to a series-production motor. In a year when a one-litre Australian Honda Superbike set a faster lap time on the same day than Suzuki's 800cc MotoGP bike, this was an idea that seemed to have reached its time.

This makes a nonsense of any notion that racing is an advanced development tool for the industry. Maybe that is also an idea that has had its day.

After all, the major criterion of a 2009 MotoGP bike was not how powerful the engine could be, but how easily most of the power could be used. That went hand in hand with the need to do so without burning too much fuel, and to run reliably for a period of time considerably longer than before. Criteria not far divorced from those prevailing for a fast road-bike, and with benefits that filter down through the entire range.

Race development would not be leading production engineering. Instead, they would be hand in hand.

This future vision fulfils Dorna chief Carmelo Ezpeleta's original mid-season proposal, for a second tier of private teams able to compete against the factories without having to lease their motorcycles from them. The chances of success would be no higher, but the whole structure would be different. The teams would own their motorcycles.

A future including production bikes sets one big poser. Where do World Superbikes fit in? Possibly better than before. Their 1000cc bikes *must* be production based; MotoGP bikes *may* be production based, but will be full racers in every other respect. This makes a strong link between the two series, whereas until now they have followed separate paths. This could be good for both of them.

World economic problems prompted many changes in the way governments, industries and people thought about themselves and their future plans. Motorbike racing was no different.

Maybe it was time for a rethink anyway.

MICHAEL SCOTT
Wimbledon, LONDON
December, 2009

The two riders who made the season.
Rossi hounds Lorenzo.
Photo: Martin Heath

Photo: Martin Heath

TOP TEN RIDERS

THE EDITOR'S CHOICE

Rider Portraits by Gold & Goose

1 VALENTINO ROSSI

ROSSI'S supremacy was threatened as never before during 2009: his own team-mate proved his toughest challenge yet. There could be no excuses about machine weakness, as when Stoner had defeated his Yamaha in 2007.

It is a measure of his stature, and his unquestionable position as world champion and at the top of this list, that he was able to respond – stylishly and with inflexible resolve.

After 13 GP years, 97 wins, one each 125 and 250 titles, the last 500 crown and then five more in MotoGP, the Italian archangel had already pretty much done it all. He turned 30 in February, but was as ready as ever to do it all again, as Lorenzo pushed him to his limits.

That he was stretched was clear from the low points. A farcical series of crashes and mishaps in France, and a straight error at Indianapolis, were his only no-scores, although he had a lucky escape in Britain, where he was able to get back on. But his worst moment was in Portugal, where failure to find the right set-up left him almost half a minute adrift of his greatest rival.

The high points showed his strength, which ultimately was indomitable. He won six races, usually great races. His margin over Lorenzo in Germany was only 0.099 second. But the definitive win, one of his best ever, was in Catalunya, where he conjured up a last-corner pass that proclaimed sheer genius. The margin there was 0.095.

It was a hell of a ride – and a privilege for his countless fans, and his rivals as well, to have been along

2 JORGE LORENZO

IN 2009, Jorge Lorenzo emerged as a genuine and worthy title contender and rival to the king. Although a title challenge that lasted until the penultimate round was undermined by his own errors, he also matured visibly, as a rider, a personality and as a character.

The mistakes were four crashes, at Jerez, Donington Park, Brno and Australia. He fell also in practice at Laguna Seca, spoiling another chance.

His transformation from notoriously hot-headed teenager to the self-styled gladiator of today has been defined by three stages: first with his father, Chicho, at his side; then with disgraced manager Dani Amatriain; and late in 2008 hiring Brazilian giant Marcos Hirsch as business manager. The former physical trainer brought with him a new-age regime, including the self-awareness discipline of sophrology: the results are obvious, as the ever-polite Lorenzo radiates calm and reason, even at moments of defeat.

It may be a studied and deliberate act, but it seems to work.

Another influence is crew chief Ramon Forcada, highly experienced and on occasion able to out-think his counterpart on the other side of the wall in the pit, Rossi's technical right-hand, Jerry Burgess.

Jorge was as fast as Rossi, and could do the times consistently. As he frequently said, "I am still learning... but I am getting better."

Quite so. Aged 22, he has time on his side.

3 CASEY STONER

THERE was a time during the season when nobody could be sure that we would ever see Stoner return as a force in racing. There were echoes of the end of greatness for Freddie Spencer, at about the same age (he turned 24 in October). And there were critics, notably Kevin Schwantz, who thought that slinking off home mid-season was not the behaviour of a dedicated racer.

Casey silenced them with trademark defiance when he came blazing back from his three-race, ten-week layoff with two wins in four races. Probably would have been three, but for that embarrassing warm-up-lap crash at Valencia.

Stoner's mid-year malaise was puzzling to everybody, not least the rider. Up to that point, he was a serious title contender – and even when fatigue did start to strike, he was still finishing on the rostrum.

Whatever the cause (the current suspect is either sodium imbalance or lactose intolerance), he seemed to have laid it firmly to rest.

Many have assumed that Stoner's success came through his complete trust in Ducati's electronics. Ducati design chief Filippo Preziosi killed that idea, explaining how in fact Stoner had adapted his technique to find ways around the electronic interference and regain more direct throttle response.

Stoner has hidden depths as well as blatant strengths.

4 DANI PEDROSA

LITTLE Dani had another tough year in 2009: blighted by injury, both before the start of the season and again during it. He remained the only rider able to run with the other three superheroes, and on occasion to beat them.

He did so only twice, which exactly equalled his win rate for the previous three seasons. It's intriguing to wonder how many more wins per year a Rossi or Stoner might have added to Honda's rather pitiful recent total, but certainly nobody has been more successful on the ill-favoured RC212V than 24-year-old Pedrosa.

His greatest trick is his lightning start. By far the smallest and lightest on the grid, his technique into the first corner is almost always unbeatable. But to win races, he needs a clear run: once overtaken, he tends to stay overtaken. Would it be different if he were on a different motorcycle? Stardom doesn't sit well on his slender shoulders, and he cuts a morose figure in the public eye. Those who know him better find a wry humorous side. This is kept in check at races, also by the austere presence of his manager/ Svengali, Alberto Puig.

Dani will get another chance to blossom in 2010. But the rise of Lorenzo has toppled him as top Spaniard, and once again he has a lot to prove.

I N his seventh year of grand prix racing, the former double World Superbike champion discovered new levels of inspiration and rode as well as ever in his GP career. Possibly better. One reason was a simmering grudge against team-mate Toseland and crew chief Reynders, who had switched sides of the garage. Edwards owes them a debt of gratitude.

The proof came in a number of runs through from the back, after various misfortunes – none more impressive than that from near last place in the rain in Britain to an eventual second.

That first win continues to elude him, but Edwards did a lot in 2009 to redeem his reputation, and enough to secure a saddle in 2010, when he can oversee the debut of fellow American Spies in the team.

Edwards is not an especially exciting rider to watch. Even his overtakes – and there were many in 2009 – were forcefully smooth rather than boldly aggressive. At 35, he's experienced and professional, and plays the percentages to a very fine margin.

But his character is the antithesis of the antiseptic modern racer: defiantly sexist and exultantly politically incorrect, Edwards affirms old-school racing in a sterile modern world. MotoGP is the better for his presence.

5 COLIN EDWARDS

6 HIRO AOYAMA

H IROSHI Aoyama's capture of the last ever quarter-litre crown was as unobtrusively heroic as it was historic.

In a sustained campaign, he withstood the pressure of the Aprilia/Gilera trio of Simoncelli, Bautista and Barbera. It was accomplished with a finesse that characterises the best 250 riders. His smooth and flowing style made a good marriage with the sweet-handling Honda, and an interesting contrast to the more aggressive riding of his rivals.

Most impressively, Aoyama did it all with only one bike and a minimum of factory support. No wonder he always looked careful: he simply couldn't afford to crash.

He lost composure only once – at the last race, the title in the balance. The way he regained it – saving a crash, then starting out again still cool – was enough.

At 28, Aoyama became the first Japanese champion since Kato in the same class in 2001; this was also Honda's first 250 championship since Pedrosa's in 2005. That it was with a two-stroke instead of that company's favoured four-stroke added piquancy.

Modest and articulate, Aoyama believes his weakness is a lack of aggression. The tactics served him well in 2009.

7 MARCO SIMONCELLI

WITH a personality as big as his Hendrix-style hair, and a full-on riding style that rules out the taking of any prisoners, Marco Simoncelli failed only narrowly to defend his 250 title, and only partly because of racetrack errors. As costly was a motocross crash a few days before the season began, which meant he started the year with a freshly broken wrist and two zero scores.

He did crash out of three races as well, but he also won six – significantly more than any rival. And always in his ebullient style.

Simoncelli made amends to a degree with a single visit to World Superbikes. It was his first four-stroke race, on an Aprilia that was quite unfamiliar to him, and he managed a rostrum finish. In familiar aggressive style. He was pleased afterwards to have got away with a collision with erstwhile team-mate Max Biaggi without censure: he has more than once been hauled up for marginally dangerous riding in the GP paddock, again in 2009 after colliding with Bautista at Mugello.

A prominent member of an extended generation of talent from the Adriatic coastline, 22-year-old Simoncelli counts Rossi among his friends, and is earmarked to follow him to greatness. Much sought after for MotoGP, he was captured by fellow local team chief Fausto Gresini for Honda, and begins his top-class career in 2010.

8 JULIAN SIMON

IT may be populated with inexperienced hotheads and unrefined chargers, but the difficulty of achieving serial success in the 125 class should never be underestimated. The machines are very evenly matched, there is no spare power to make up for any little errors, and corner speeds are significantly higher than for MotoGP.

To win one GP is an achievement. To do so over and over again requires a very high degree of skill, cunning and determination.

Spaniard Julian Simon achieved this feat seven times in 2009 – it would have been eight had he not celebrated one lap early at home in Catalunya.

Back on 125s after two 250 years, more importantly Simon was with the dominant Aspar team. A crash in Spain while chasing the next-best 125 rider, team-mate Bradley Smith, meant a fairly slow start, but as the year wore on he seized control, managing to stay out of trouble in the brawls to impose his authority on race after race.

Simon wore his achievement lightly, winning friends with his good-humoured nature as the year wore on. He turns 23 in 2010, and joins Moto2 with the Aspar team. His progress will be interesting.

9 MARCO MELANDRI

MARCO Melandri was a lost soul in 2008. Unable to find the key to the factory Ducati's speed and unwilling to risk crashing in the quest, the five-time premier-class winner became a sad figure at the back of the grid. Both he and the team were in despair by mid-season, and he was released from the second year of his contract.

He signed for Kawasaki, but the factory withdrew. It was not until testing had begun that he even had a ride.

For the early part of the year, the 27-year-old proved emphatically that he was not the deadbeat he had appeared on the Duke. The crowning achievement was second in the wet at Le Mans, but as impressive were his sixth in Japan and fifth at Jerez.

There were a few more good top tens to come, but sadly for his continued progress Kawasaki was as good as its word, and did not supply any of the hoped-for upgrades and improvements during the season. By the end of the year, he had been outclassed and was struggling to stay on terms.

His comeback meant renewed faith in the former 250 champion's ability, and he returns to the Honda Gresini team for 2010, where he achieved his greatest success in the past.

10 BEN SPIES

SOME might argue that Spies should not be eligible for a list that, in the past, has always concentrated on grand prix riders. He only did one GP after all.

But his debut was so impressive, coming on top of a season in which he had set World Superbike on its ears at his first attempt, that to ignore him would be to pursue exclusivity to the point of absurdity.

Spies underplayed his chances and his achievements, insisting quite plausibly that his previous wild-card rides on a Suzuki had demonstrated that the standard of riding at the front of a MotoGP race was of a different order to that in the second series.

He is correct when he says, "there is still a long way to go". But if you take into account the speed at which he mastered a new machine, new tracks and new rivals in the other series, you have to believe he is capable of making the journey, and at high speed.

After all, at Valencia, in his first ride on the M1 Yamaha, he managed to pass Kallio, de Puniet, de Angelis and Dovizioso (on the factory Honda) on his way through to seventh.

Memphis born Spies is 25, relatively advanced in years for a MotoGP debut. He will waste no time in trying to catch up.

THE STATE OF RACING
A NEW DAWN?

Financial turmoil saw teams disappear from GP racing in 2009, while new rules were drafted in an attempt to cut costs. But was it all doom and gloom? MICHAEL SCOTT ponders the possibility of a new golden age...

Above: Fragmented reflections sum up a year of schizophrenia.

Right: Paddock people peer at the first European Moto2 bike launched, the Suter SRT.

Photos: Gold & Goose

THE conclusion is inescapable: crises are like buses. You wait ages before one comes along, then suddenly a whole lot arrive all at once.

That's how the year felt, anyway. No sooner had racing management issued a whole new series of urgent diktats or looming future plans to address one crisis, than things would get worse in another area, and they'd all have to be changed or renewed once again.

The consequence was a year of sweeping changes in all sorts of areas. Soon everyone was inured to change. In this way, the biggest change of all was at first not exactly ignored, but not taken quite seriously. It was nothing less than a shift in the whole philosophy of motorcycle grand prix racing – the introduction of production-based motorcycles.

What surfaced as an almost humorous or certainly absurd proposal mid-season – the opening of MotoGP to B-grade machines with road-bike-based engines – had by year's end come to be accepted as inevitable. The way is open for production-based bikes to take part in the premier World Championship. No more purists.

This change in perception means that 2009 will surely be seen as pivotal in a process that began with the introduction of MotoGP four-strokes in 2002. The prototypes since then have shrunk to

800cc, and have carried us, helped by world events, to a point where they are themselves expensively redundant. And once the blue-sky prototypes become obsolete, then it really is time to think again.

In fact, basic principles aside, the tenure of the current-generation 800s comes to an end after 2011. It's time to think again in any case.

It is not the role of *MOTOCOURSE* to predict the future. Yet many senior figures in racing were prepared to do so at the end of 2009, including the man with his hand on the tiller: Dorna CEO Carmelo Ezpeleta. The next generation of MotoGP bikes will, it seems, return to full one-litre capacity, and there will be restrictions to electronics and such-like. In both of these respects, they comply with frequent requests from the riders, but that's not the reasoning behind the change. That is to do with rising costs, shrinking grids and fugitive sponsorship. Although the next MotoGP generation will be prototypes, at least nominally, they will be of a technically restricted sort. Most importantly, they don't *have* to be prototypes. The class will be open to and may even positively encourage use of production-based engines.

The basic regulations under discussion as *MOTOCOURSE* went to press specified a four-cylinder engine with restrictions to electronics, rev

but it had the desired effect of scaring the MSMA into a counter-proposal – for the factories to supply engines on lease to private teams, which could then build their own chassis. Much as Team Roberts had done in 2005, using a Honda engine, when Kenny Junior had almost won a GP. But this idea ran out of steam over the coming months as it became clear that the expense would still be prohibitive.

What Ezpeleta had done, however, was to plant a seed, which included the prospect of a return to full-size 1000cc grand prix machines, and it grew steadily.

One event, at the Australian GP, may have contributed, when a Honda CBR1000RR Superbike set a faster race lap time of the circuit than Chris Vermeulen's MotoGP Suzuki had done during qualifying. This proved that 'production-based' need not necessarily mean 'slower', and bore tribute to the continuing close relationship between the best road-bikes and those on the racetrack. A relationship many think should be reinforced.

MOTO2 – ONE YEAR EARLY

Dorna was particularly anxious that the proposed one-litre production-based MotoGP bikes should not be called "Moto1", but what else were they, at least as originally proposed?

By the end of 2008, Moto2 had been defined only in the broadest terms: 600cc production-based engines in prototype chassis. Various electronic, component-weight and rev limits were under consideration, as well as a claiming rule. And the official date for introduction was still 2011. Officially.

Things were to change very rapidly, as it became clear there was widespread interest in the new class from independent racing firms, especially chassis manufacturers, and prototypes were soon to appear in Spanish national championship racing, by special permission.

The first surprise came at the opening round at Qatar, where the MSMA announced that Moto2 would be subject to a single-engine rule. This was ground shaking – certainly a first for any significant

world championship. By the time the circus got to Europe at Jerez, it had been confirmed that the supplier would be Honda, who promised race modified CBR600 engines. In rapid order came confirmation that engines would be supplied free of charge to entrants, sealed; maintenance would be done centrally, and no tuning would be allowed.

Honda promised "at least 150bhp", and chassis designers were given dimensions not only of the engine, but also the airbox, which would also be supplied, along with electronics and dashboard. Gear ratios would be to racing spec, but fixed. By now, the first such chassis had been launched – the Moriwaki at the Japanese GP – while BQR and Harris Performance already had (Yamaha powered) bikes racing in Spain.

From before the start of the year, it was generally accepted that Moto2 would not wait until the official end of the 250 sanction after the 2010 season. This became official before the mid-point, and matters continued to accelerate. Entries were entreated and the list instantly over-subscribed. It was trimmed and refined slightly at the Portuguese round, and then came to at least provisional finality at the last race at Valencia, where teams were required to pay a deposit of US$25,000 per rider by a deadline of 2 November. While Team Roberts was a notable casualty, having failed to find funding, there were 37 entries, a strong promise of close racing and a guarantee of packed grids.

Preference had been given to current 250 teams, and 12 of them signed up, ranging from Ajo Motorsport to WTR San Marino, and including such leading lights as Mapfre Aspar, Scot and Emmi-Caffe Latte. BQR, CIP Moto, Campetella, Cardion AB, Matteoni Racing, Pons Racing, BQR and Viessman Kiefer are also in. MotoGP teams on the list included refugee Hayate and returnee JiR Racing, as well as Honda Gresini and Tech 3. New teams included the Antonio Banderas backed Promoracing and Speedup Aprilia - 250 class losers, also promised to supply five riders, although this decision was abruptly reversed as this book went to press.

Many riders had been finalised. Although the top

ceiling and the number of engines to be used. Production crankcases were not specified, but nor were they banned.

This completely reverses the way of thinking that repeatedly disqualified the WCM Yamaha/Suzuki-based MotoGP entry of 2002. Production-based parts had been mixed and matched with specially made racing internals, but the manufacturers insisted that it was not enough of a prototype. Now the same manufacturers' association had been manoeuvred into accepting the diametric opposite.

In retrospect, this represents some clever footwork by Ezpeleta. MotoGP's constitution had handed technical control to the manufacturers in the form of their association, the MSMA; it was this mainly Japanese committee that steered racing to the unloved 800s. The withdrawal of Kawasaki showed how circumstances had accelerated these machines down a blind alley of increasingly irrelevant technology and expense, and awakened very real fears that Suzuki, or indeed any of the others, might follow suit.

It was on the grounds of expense that Dorna had proposed the B-grade, second-tier privateer machines at the German GP, and at the time it had seemed as though this was a rather red herring,

four in the 250 championship were bound for Mo-toGP, the rest of the top ten were in or very likely to be, plus 125 champion Julian Simon and a couple of others from the smaller class, including Stefan Bradl and Joan Olive. Scott Redding was hunting for a team. Toni Elias and Alex de Angelis were also expected to join the class; there were several new-comers also on the list, promising a good mix of talent and experience.

Enthusiasm from riders goes without saying: where the new rules scored most heavily was in re-connecting the rarefied world of MotoGP with the racing industry in general. Enterprises both old and new leapt at the opportunity. Harris Performance, BQR and soon also a Japanese firm, Burning Blood, had bikes racing in Spain, with a few more to come.

Several machines were also launched at GP races. The next after the Moriwaki was from Suter Racing Technologies, at the Misano GP. Two more appeared at Valencia: the German Kalex and the Italian Rapid Inside. At the end of the year, there were 12 for teams to choose from, the list swelled

by TSR from Japan, FTR (formerly Fabtech) from Brit-ain, Tech 3 from France, and Spanish chassis from Arbizu and Bottpower.

Racing had embraced Moto2, and even original opponents had to fall in line. Principles had been sacrificed, and a semblance of a one-make cup had taken the place of a purist traditional world champi-onship class. The promise of an active rather than a moribund junior class swept these objections aside.

The 250s are dead. Long live Moto2.

THE YEAR THE SPENDING HAD TO STOP

The greatest changes during 2009 were the con-sequence of the world economic situation. This hit the motorcycle industry hard, with sales falling by 30 per cent almost overnight. It also affected every-one else: the pool from which vital sponsorship was drawn was already small, but now it was in serious jeopardy.

The first victim was the Kawasaki team, with Ez-peleta engaged in some frantic shuttle diplomacy

with the factory, which resulted in the support of a single-rider team for just one year. It fell short of the two-rider two-year contract in place, but was better than nothing. Kawasaki removed its name from the enterprise, and the Hayate team was born from the embers of the factory squad.

The next high-profile casualty was the Grupo Fran-cisco Hernando team fielding Sete Gibernau in a comeback year. Hernando's fortune was founded on property development, and a severe slump in Spain (and the collapse of a gigantic deal with the govern-ment of Equatorial Guinea) forced him to cut back on several parts of his empire, including major de-velopments in Spain – and his grand prix team.

In the 250 class, rider Mattia Pasini was again the victim of the financial problems of others. In 2008, his Polaris World sponsorship had melted away; during 2009, his new employer, Team Toth, nearly ran out of cash several times, and finally did so for good at the Portuguese GP. There were oth-ers who suffered without being so noticeable, like the Milar Juegos Lucky 250 team, which came late and left after just two races; a number of teams

experienced sundry privations, Scot Honda being a prime example.

Racing's response was to seek ways to cut expenditure. Urgently. The first move was the cancellation of one of two Sepang tests, as well as the pre-season visit to Australia. Testing during the year was cut back to just two outings.

Track time was also slashed. Where before there had been four full hour-long sessions of practice and qualifying, now there would be just three sessions, each cut to 45 minutes. This left teams severely short of time, especially to set up the increasingly complex electronics. As a result, officials relented to restore sessions to the full hour from the French GP on.

These were just interim restrictions: at Jerez tests, a GP Commission meeting issued a list of new rules. The most controversial would not survive many months – it was a proposal to limit MotoGP riders to a single bike. Deeply unpopular with the existing riders, this was intended to liberate a supply of machines for new riders. The factories could not promise to do this, however, and by late summer the rule had been dropped.

The other important restriction was a reduction in engine use. A try-out was arranged: for the last sev-

Far left: Paddock throng at Valencia. Crowd figures were strong in spite of the crisis.

Below: Switch me on and watch me go-go. Electronics are everywhere in racing.

Bottom left: Bridgestone's add-on whitewall denoted a softer tyre.

Bottom right: For sale, one team hospitality unit, used only on weekends. The Grupo Francisco Hernandez team didn't survive the season.

Photos: Gold & Goose

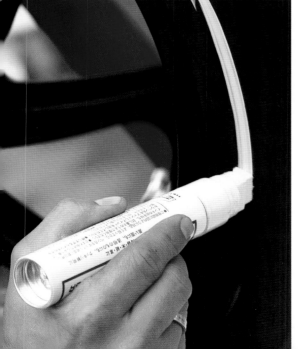

en races of the 2009 season, each rider would be allowed only five engines, which would be sealed to prevent maintenance. The original penalty for exceeding this was the loss of ten points for the rider, but later this was switched to punish the manufacturer's score in the constructors' points table, the rider being sent to the back of the grid.

Only Suzuki and Capirossi fell foul of this rule, but it will really bite in 2010. For the full year, each rider will have only six engines. This counts as some kind of a loss for racing. The long-life engines of late 2009 were already down on power and revs compared with those at the start of the year. In 2010, they are likely to be more so.

Yet the rule does have other benefits. Research into longer-life, lower-friction engines, which last longer and burn less fuel, is of clear benefit to motorcycle engineering in general. If nothing else, this is another argument to persuade factories to stay in racing, rather than to switch their shrinking development and publicity budgets to other areas. At the same time, however, a raft of technical restrictions banning exotic techniques and materials also outlawed electronic damping control (already in production for street bikes by Öhlins), and variable valve timing and exhaust valving (also already in production). Twin-clutch transmissions, in production for some cars, were also banned. Such rules force racing to lag behind street bikes.

There was more of the same to come during the year, with the announcement in late September of yet more cuts as well as some rationalisation in the close-season testing programme. The three days of testing after the last race at Valencia survived, but the showcase pre-season Jerez test – a televised spectacle of increasing importance – was cancelled. Instead there would be two tests at Sepang, at the beginning and the end of February, and just one more at Qatar, three weeks before the race there. Avoiding the return trip to Europe means that teams can save on transport costs, leaving some equipment at the tracks between tests. The Sepang tests would be cut to two days from three, with an extra day available for factory test riders. After the last race, a special concession was made for class rookies, who will be allowed an extra two days for familiarisation.

The savings would be cumulative, and somewhat significant. But the cuts were a shock to the teams, who not long ago enjoyed the freedom to test whenever they wanted to do so.

RIDERS TO THE RESCUE

Grand prix racing lost a lot in 2009. It lost some self-respect – the slightly grubby feeling that came with the single-tyre rule was vastly increased by Moto2's single-engine rule (of course, the new class will also have a single tyre, supplied by Dunlop). It lost speed – long-life engines inevitably must rev less and produce less power. It lost a lot of independence of thought; increasingly restrictive technical rules saw to that.

But it did not lose excitement. The championship contests in MotoGP had more variety and tension than for a number of years; the last 250 battle was memorable. Nor can anything be taken away from the 125s, after a typical year of heart-in-the-mouth racing.

Redemption came from a pool of exceptional talent that continues to grow. That it is predominantly Spanish and Italian is the consequence of aggressive rider development programmes, especially in Spain. That it is so numerous is surely just a gift of history.

It is not too far-fetched to start thinking of a new golden age.

MotoGP had four particularly superior riders in 2009. Rossi, Stoner and Pedrosa were firmly joined by Lorenzo. The prospects for 2010 are even better. Ben Spies joins Yamaha with a pocket full of promise. His maiden title win in World Superbikes was salutary: new tracks, new bike and tough competition, but he still won. His Yamaha debut at Valencia suggested he might do something similar in MotoGP.

Then there are the ex-250 riders, chief among them Marco Simoncelli. He joins the Honda Gresini team for 2010, and while he will need a year to adapt, much is expected from him in the future. Likewise Alvaro Bautista; they are joined by Hector Barbera and 250 champion Hiro Aoyama.

The 800cc MotoGP bikes are not popular with the riders. Exacting and finely balanced, they make overtaking difficult and often yield processional races. Yet the good ones were still able to make the difference.

It is reasonable to hope that if there is a return to 1000cc in 2011, along with some reduction in electronics, that we can talk of a golden age with more confidence still.

Above: Ever-popular American Nicky Hayden will be joined by Edwards and Spies next year.
Photo: Martin Heath

Right: MotoGP rookie Simoncelli will add one more to the Spanish/Italian domination.
Photo: Ripton Scott

TISSOT

SWISS WATCHES SINCE 1853

OfficialTimekeeper

More than a watch

Tissot, Innovators by Tradition.

316L stainless steel, Scratchproof sapphire crystal,
Swiss ETA chronograph movement, Water resistant to 100m/330ft.

TISSOT T-RACE MotoGP
LIMITED EDITION

www.tissot.ch

CHANGE IS FOR THE BETTER

Grand prix racing has changed beyond all recognition in the past decade, and never faster than in 2009. Change meant loss — of speed, of purity, of independence. To find out what has been gained, MOTOCOURSE asked IRTA president and Tech 3 team proprietor Hervé Poncharal just what is good about modern racing.

"MEMORY is always golden...but you have to fit reality. Ideally, this would be a full prototype championship. I remember chatting with Wayne Rainey and Kenny Roberts all those years ago, and they were saying there should be no technical limits. And I agreed.

"But we must live in the present, and we must fit with our time. For example, Moto2 is not a free class, but I think it is the most suitable for our time, because it will have more bikes and it will be more exciting.

"We have seen the new one-tyre rule this year. Valentino and other top riders were against this monopoly, and I was the same. But as it worked out, the racing is closer, and most of the riders are happier.

"We don't live in an ideal world, now even more than before.

"A lot of decisions have been taken recently... I smiled, thinking back on how some paddock guru was complaining: 'You are killing two-strokes.' Now the same person is full of interest for Moto2. As you can see, the Press, the riders and teams...everyone is supporting Moto2.

"In French, we have a saying: 'Only an idiot does not change his mind.'

"The first people we have to think about are the fans. They support the business and pay our wages. We, all of us, the promoters, the federation, the MSMA, IRTA, we all have to think how to be competitive in this area.

"Firstly, we need exciting racing. Secondly, we need big enough grids, Thirdly, it is very important to keep three classes: one to discover the GP world, an intermediate class and MotoGP as the pinnacle.

"We have quite a happy situation now. There is no fight between all the particular bodies, as there often could be in the past, especially when the riders spoke; nobody listened to them.

"We have two missions: to have more bikes available, and for them to be more affordable. Everyone agrees on this.

"Now there are a lot of ideas...IRTA and Dorna had the proposal for...I don't call it Moto1, but for convenience it is like that, with production-based engines. The details and regulations are not clear, but it could be a solution to help the grids get bigger, very soon.

"I understand when people ask, 'Why so many regulation changes?' But the rules have stayed the same for a very long time without changing. It was our plan at first to keep everything the same rule-wise for a five-year period. But unfortunately the credit crunch came, and the whole world is changing. So why should MotoGP remain without change?

"We have to be flexible. It's like the old story of the mighty oak and the slender bamboo. The oak was strong and magnificent, but in the storm it blew down, while the bamboo bent with the wind.

"You must understand that without change, we disappear.

"There are many things about racing that are better now. One is safety. Over the last 20 to 25 years, we have improved safety considerably. Just one example from the German GP: we had two bikes hit the air fence, basically without damage. It would be the same if the riders hit the air fence. Motorcycle is always dangerous. But this is the biggest change.

"And we had to fight for it. But I remember when Daijiro Kato died at Suzuka, Carmelo Ezpeleta said we would never go back there again until they fix that place on the circuit, where there is a wall close to the track. A lot of people thought that Carmelo would bend, that he wouldn't keep his word, because the circuit belongs to Honda, and we needed a Japanese round of the World Championship. I thought then that Carmelo would match his word, and he did.

"Another example is how promoters and race direction sit down for one hour every race weekend, to listen to the riders at the safety commission. Once the attitude was, 'If you don't want to race, then don't race.'

"The paddock is now working in decent conditions. We used to work out in the fields sometimes, with not enough power points, or not reliable. I remember one year at Assen when it rained and rained, and they brought straw to put on the ground to sponge up the mud.

"Now everyone is working in good conditions.

"Also before IRTA, some riders sometimes were not even entered. You had no passes, and you had to

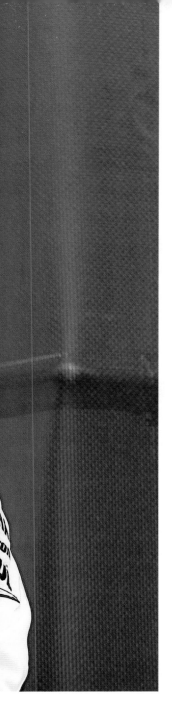

Left: Poncharal – "We must change, or we will die."

Below centre left: New generation Moto2 bikes hit the track at Valencia.

Below centre right: Former 125 champion Mike di Meglio gets his first taste of his new Moto2 bike.

Bottom: The paddock at sunset: "We have not lost our soul."

Photos: Gold & Goose

"The tyre rule has been a benefit, firstly because of cost. The last couple of years have been completely crazy. As a team, we spent two days testing at tracks after races, and tested through the winter. And we were always only testing tyres. You couldn't even adjust the bike to try anything different because you had to keep the same base settings, to compare tyres.

"The riders were obsessed with tyres. Having the right or wrong tyre would make all the difference to his race. Tyres were the essential factor. Now overnight it is all forgotten. Now the essential factor is to find the right setting.

"We do less tests now, and it is a big saving. But we probably actually accomplish more testing of the bikes, because we have forgotten about tyres.

"Now the show is better. It is still the rider that makes a difference, and not everybody is close. But it is more fair, with one big and important variable taken away.

"And people are coming to see an exciting race.

"Moto2 will also be one tyre, and it is good that it duplicates MotoGP in that way.

"You know, I loved the two-strokes, but they are finished. We need to move forward all the time. When we moved from 500 to MotoGP, some thought it would kill GP racing. Can you seriously imagine racing with 500cc two-strokes now? It doesn't matter how good

the past was, we need not to keep it, but to change.

"It is difficult to say that the value of racing for engineering research is over, but if you look at F1, what does that bring to production cars?

"At the same time, we are using always less fuel and longer-life engines, and that is important and valuable for research. And when there was tyre competition, for sure Michelin developed a lot for road tyres, especially in the area of low rolling resistance.

"There are still a few things we can learn from racing...but we must now understand more and more that we are a show. We are the gladiators of modern times. There will be more and more speed and safety restrictions on the road, and motorcycling will be less sporting. You can see already more emphasis on touring and cruising bikes rather than supersports. But riders can still see a race.

"We are a show and we need to produce something exciting. Like when somebody goes to a rock concert, they want to see something to make you dream. We are making a performance, and we must work more on that side. And only then think about R&D.

"I loved the racing of 20 or 30 years ago, but we can't do it now.

"Racing is open now to normal entrepreneurs, where it was not the case before. It can be a career now, and not just a hobby."

go and stand outside the organiser's office, or find your national federation representative and beg for passes and entries. You could go to Austria and find they wouldn't want any French riders this time.

"One of the things that causes a lot of polemic concerns access to the paddock for the public, to see the bikes and the riders. But everyone must understand it is a dream to have the paddock open to everyone. I understand the frustration on the other side of the fence, but there was also a time when a rider might have his gloves or helmet stolen ten minutes before the start.

"But this is something we are working on.

"Another problem is the need for more and more money. We need sponsors to survive. The essence of racing may be a hobby. But it is a business. You need to find a sponsor, to take care of the sponsors, and to behave as you should when you are wearing their colours.

"Some say the paddock atmosphere in MotoGP is getting like F1. But there is still a lot of life in the paddock...late in the evening in the hospitality units. I have friends in F1 who come here and say how different and more relaxed it is here.

"I don't think we have lost our soul.

"MotoGP needs to be professional, but needs to keep contact with its roots. I went to races as a child on a bicycle, before I could go on my moped. People are here because racing is their passion.

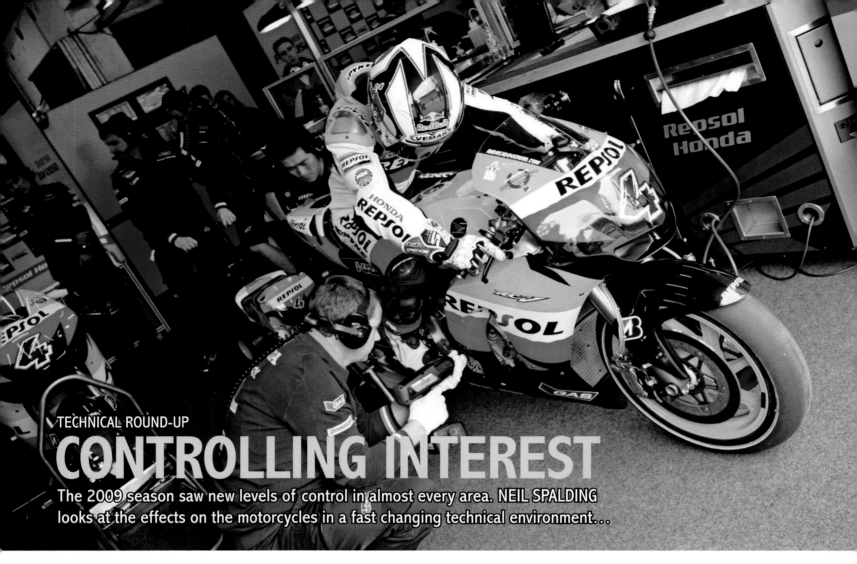

CONTROLLING INTEREST

The 2009 season saw new levels of control in almost every area. NEIL SPALDING looks at the effects on the motorcycles in a fast changing technical environment…

THE control culture really caught up with MotoGP in 2009. Control Bridgestone tyres preceded control engines for Moto2, closely followed by control ECU, datalogging and slipper clutches. All these features have changed the nature of grand prix racing forever.

Given the state of the Western world's finances, perhaps we should be happy that there is any racing at all. The companies that support the circus are walking on very thin ice indeed, after an almost overnight drop of 30 per cent in demand for their products.

MotoGP was created as a class where the factories could play, develop new technologies or build brands. The economic slowdown after September 2008 affected all the manufacturers: in the early part of the season, there was panic, costs had to be slashed, and it didn't seem to matter where from.

The first retrenchment came over Christmas, Kawasaki Heavy Industries withdrawing from GP racing. The reasons were never fully explained, and only some fast footwork by Dorna CEO Carmelo Ezpeleta kept a single-rider team, named Hayate and using the expensively developed 2009 ZX-RR Kawasaki, on the grid.

At about the same time, Honda was reviewing its racing activities: Formula One was dumped, but motorcycle racing, part of Honda's corporate DNA, was retained. At Suzuki, the same questions were asked, and the rally team received the chop.

There would be belt tightening elsewhere. Practice time was cut from four hours to two-and-a-quarter, then relaxed to three hours after some teams ran out of time to set up their electronics. For a couple of months, new rules were introduced ad hoc, mostly banning technologies not yet in use in an attempt to cap future expense. These included control systems that relied on hydraulic pressure (with the belated exception of conventional clutch and brake systems), carbon ceramic brakes and pads, and electronically controlled suspension systems,

as used by Yamaha and Öhlins in World Superbike in 2008. More mysteriously, exhaust gas recirculation was banned, leading to speculation on just how many unburnt hydrocarbons remain in the exhaust gases of engines that are already running lean.

More immediate was the restriction to five engines for the last seven races, a dry run for the much more serious six-engine limit for 2010. Registered engines were sealed with FIM stamps to prevent servicing or maintenance. Inlet and exhaust ports were also sealed at the end of each GP, to prevent motors from being run away from the circuit.

At first, this didn't seem a problem. Most factories achieve between 800 and 1,200 racing kilometres from each engine. Race weekend mileage is about 400km; there seemed plenty of spare mileage available. But retrofitting expensive, race engines with new longer-life parts may be more expensive than using cheaper parts that could be replaced regularly. The more immediate effect was a reduction in power or maximum rpm. Honda limited its customer bikes from the beginning of the year; Yamaha only cut its customer bikes' power from Brno onwards; and clearly neither factory reduced the power or rpm of its works teams.

Testing was allowed using unregistered motors, but all race practice and the racing itself were done using registered and sealed engines. At first, the penalty for using an extra engine was a deduction of ten points from the rider. Signs of concern came at Estoril, where race direction switched the penalty to the less important constructors' championship, the rider merely being moved to the back of the grid. As a result, what had started out as an important rule change aimed at driving a major reduction in costs lost some of its teeth; the dilution of the rule was closely followed by Capirossi needing an additional engine, which only added to the sense of crisis management.

It is obvious that crashes cause problems, and now any assembly mistakes not discovered until af-

ter an engine is registered and used (that is, it has left the pit lane fitted to a motorcycle) are a much bigger headache than expected.

Then there were the control tyres.

Riders who had lobbied hard for this change were surprised to discover that a control-tyre series has quite a few differences. Firstly, without competition, the really high technologies are not necessary, so it was goodbye to most of Bridgestone's multi-compound slicks. Secondly, the total number of tyres per rider was reduced dramatically: 20 each instead of 40. Because all the tyre selection now takes place weeks before the race, Bridgestone only has to provide those tyres that are allocated, and the wet tyre supply. Thirdly, the tyres themselves are designed to be much more tolerant of variations in temperature and track surface. For all that, the quality of the tyres was excellent. Not only race lap records fell, but also some qualifying lap records, a stunning reflection of the development skills of both Bridgestone and the manufacturers.

That's not to say all went swimmingly. Bridgestone based its 'control' carcass on the most successful of its tyre families: that used and developed on the Ducati, which Rossi and Burgess had succeeded in making work on the Yamaha as well. In the past, each manufacturer's chassis had preferred slightly different tyres. The 'Ducati-fit' Bridgestones had been developed about that bike's rearward weight bias, a side effect of the trademark lengthy 90-degree engine vee. Now all manufacturers had to adapt their chassis to suit these tyres, with just one carcass construction and a choice of two compounds per race.

Furthermore, Bridgestone's rear was based on a 'hot-track/long-corner' tyre type that didn't easily overheat, but also lost heat quickly. This was safer for Bridgestone and levelled the playing field, as it meant both Yamaha and Ducati also had to change slightly, to deal with the need to put heat into the tyres and keep it there.

DUCATI

DUCATI'S match with the new control tyres led most to assume that the Desmosedici 09 would be the only bike able to rival the Yamaha. That was not a bad guess, but things didn't turn out exactly as predicted.

For 2009, Ducati debuted a groundbreaking new carbon-fibre 'reinforced-airbox' chassis. Tested in 2008 by Stoner, it worked well from the start, but didn't seem to make any difference to the "only Stoner can ride the bike" situation. As a design, it was brilliantly simple, so simple it was hard to believe that it had taken so long to create. Consider the previous Ducati's construction: a steel-tube lattice frame mounted on the outside of the cylinder heads and containing a carbon-fibre airbox. Now remove the steel tubes, reinforce the airbox and bond in the air intake, bolt the whole lot to the inside of the vee, and you are done! Of course it will have taken much more than that to achieve, but good design always seems beguilingly simple when you see the finished result.

For the first race, the carbon frame was joined by a carbon swing-arm. Most of the bike was 'in the same place', with the same centre of gravity, same swing-arm pivot position and same external bodywork. The major changes were in weight and chassis stiffness.

Stoner won the first race, in spite of suffering front-end slides. New team-mate Hayden couldn't come to terms with the bike. It took several races, and a Melandri podium on a Kawasaki, for Ducati to start looking inwards for answers.

The first parts designed to help Nicky arrived at Catalunya: a kit to raise the seat and foot pegs by 20mm. Other factories raise and lower their bikes for different effects, but apparently Ducati wanted to keep the basic settings unchanged while experimenting. The modifications increased weight transfer under braking and acceleration, working the tyres harder and giving the rider more feeling.

New crew chief Juan Martinez joined Hayden, and new programming techniques were introduced for throttle and traction control. To date, Ducati has sought to save fuel in the twisty parts of the circuit, keeping it for more power on the straights; the resulting throttle feel has been criticised for being remote. The new programming improved feel, but seemingly allowed additional unburnt fuel through the engine. In a limited-fuel class, therefore, it cannot have the same power available as before on the rest of the lap.

Heat shielding under the back of the tank, plus cold-air ducting, was a reaction to the fuel temperatures at lower levels. High temperatures can affect the lighter fractions of the fuel, some of which delay the onset of detonation, something a decent engine management system would protect against by retarding the ignition. Cooler fuel can accept more ignition advance, and therefore should make more power in the latter part of the race.

New bodywork debuted in Portugal was supposed to be far better at dealing with side winds without giving away any top-end efficiency. Stoner proved it, and his return to full health, by promptly winning at Phillip Island.

Opposite: Honda's slipper clutch needed to be locked before spinning the rear wheel to start the motor.

Below: Carbon fibre chassis embraces the steering head.

Bottom: "Reinforced airbox" concept of new carbon-fibre chassis was beguilingly simple

Photos: Neil Spalding

HONDA

Above: Honda's pneumatic valve spring V4, oil radiator attached, was carried over from the end of 2008.

Top: RC212V shows its bones. Honda experimented with swing-arm length and chassis main beam stiffness through the season.

Right: Headstock triple-clamp shows relieved sections to promote controlled flex.

Opposite top: Steering head of Kawasaki did double duty as an air intake.

Opposite bottom: Kawasaki chassis followed convention, but the package was significantly improved.

Photos: Neil Spalding

HONDA started the year with new versions of its pneumatic-valve-spring late-2008 bike. Now with a works rider line-up that shared a desire for 250-style handling, both on the same tyres, great store was put in their ability to take the Bridgestones and move right back to the top of the pile. It didn't happen.

Honda has struggled since the advent of the 800 class. Initially, the RC212V was woefully underpowered, and all attempts to improve power have left the engine very non-user friendly. The 800 era has been characterised by top-quality electronic controls, and clearly Honda still doesn't have them.

The 2009 works bike looked very similar to its predecessor, but from the first test it was apparent that Honda had understood the need for more static weight on the rear wheel, to make the new control Bridgestones work well. Shorter swing-arms were in evidence immediately, but they didn't stay at their shortest settings. Pedrosa soon started to move the rear axle rearwards, citing chronic instability. For a significant part of the early season, both factory riders were quite vocal about Honda's lack of support.

It took until Catalunya before a firm step was made in any direction. A new chassis with cutaway main beams (on the underside, the opposite to Yamaha) and reinforced front engine mounts became standard equipment for both Repsol bikes. There were new swing-arms, too, again re-engineered to work with the revised flexibilities of the new chassis; Dani liked one, Dovi the other. At the same time, Honda dumped its previous and long serving wheel supplier, Enkei, and adopted the same spiral-spoked Marchesinis seen on the Yamahas and Ducatis.

It was clear that the control tyre change was causing Honda some problems, exacerbated by the inability of Dani Pedrosa to transfer weight to the rear tyre at will. New rear linkage choices were a common sight, since the control tyres really exposed the need for a bike to have the right combination of chassis stiffness and spring and linkage rates. These must apply exactly the right pressure to the rear tyre as the bike rolls up from full lean towards full acceleration. Too much pressure, and the rear tyre slips, releasing the pressure and pitching the weight forwards. Too little pressure, and everyone else has just out-accelerated you.

Mid-season, things became even more interesting, Öhlins being invited first to test, then equip Dovisioso's bike for the rest of the year. Apart from the major blow to Showa's pride, the experiment required some seriously hard development work by Öhlins so that its shorter-stroke through-rod rear shocks could be used. All the equipment was similar to that used by Yamaha.

Throughout the year, however, the riders delivered the same message: despite several upgrades, the motor was too aggressive, and the redevelopment needed for the control tyres wasn't complete. New bikes were expected for 2010.

KAWASAKI

TEAM Hayate was formed to allow Kawasaki Heavy Industries off the contractual hook. The remaining two years of the company's MotoGP commitment were cancelled without penalty, in exchange for a single-rider team for a year.

The timing was interesting, for tests of the all-new 2009 bike were already scheduled for Phillip Island in January, and they went ahead. Only later did Kawasaki and Dorna conclude their negotiations, and, in the light of what had been a pretty successful test, the project was given the green light.

The MotoGP technical group in Japan, led by Yoshimoto Matsudo, went into overdrive. It had a month or so to finish the project and supply a number of alternative parts to the team. Guessing at what might be needed, it designed a stiffer-head-stock version of the original chassis, as well as other spares that would keep the team in options as the season unfolded.

The bike was worth saving. In a major redevelopment, several significant changes had been made to the across-the-frame, pneumatic-valve-spring four.

The crank rotation had been reversed, which produced small, but important changes to the way the bike reacted as the throttle was opened and closed, as well as a significant improvement in ability to change direction at high rpm.

The Kawasaki started strongly, proving that Matsudo had finally got to build 'his' bike, and also that Melandri's year in the wilderness at Ducati hadn't been entirely his fault. Constant upgrades by other manufacturers finally got the better of the Kawasaki, but that strong-headstock chassis was exactly what the team needed when it finally got around to testing the frame at Brno, four months after the group that had built it had been disbanded.

SUZUKI

MINOR chassis changes in the middle of 2008 allowed Suzuki to start using the 'right' family of Bridgestones. But for 2009, there were several other modifications, new bodywork and different exhausts with 'mufflers' being the most obvious.

Suzuki has always suffered at circuits with long constant-radius corners. Something doesn't let the bike settle, and 2009 was no exception. Phillip Island and Jerez were especially problematic. Previous chatter problems still hadn't been sorted.

Suzuki quickly worked out that the control tyres were not the same as those it had used in the latter half of 2008. These needed a higher centre of gravity to encourage pitch and to work in more heat. Chris Vermeulen had his bike fitted with extended fork legs for much of the first half of the year, to give him the benefit of adjustability. At Brno, however, there was a new chassis that raised the engine by some 20mm; this, combined with a new shorter setting on the swing-arm and a flatter-rate rear suspension linkage, seemed to help.

Like Honda, Suzuki made an unusual mid-season change of wheel manufacturer, adopting the same Marchesini forged magnesium spiral spoke design. It is hard to believe that there isn't a link between the wheel choice and the tyres.

What was absent from Suzuki's changes of the previous two years was any obvious fiddling with the relative flexibilities of the chassis beams. Given that both Yamaha and Honda introduced well-reported stiffness changes in both main side beams and swing-arms to suit the control tyres, it was quite surprising that Suzuki didn't feel the need at least

to experiment in this area. Tellingly, this would be most apparent when the bike was operating beyond 45 degrees of lean. When everyone has the same tyres, it's reasonable to expect that similar chassis solutions will also be required.

The rest of the Suzuki remained pretty much unchanged: a pneumatic-valve-spring 75-degree V4, with some new engine parts to help maximum power and another new version of its Mitsubishi ECU. As in 2008, however, those electronics were a long way behind the stunningly high standard set by Yamaha. Suzuki had lean-angle-sensitive traction control and throttle systems, but none of the much more complex control systems Yamaha considered normal. The team simply will not catch up until it does

Above: Suzuki raised the engine in the chassis from Brno onwards. Mechanic George Dziedzic is in attendance.

Left: Fuel tank and seat were fitted as a unit – the tank doubling up as subframe support.

Below: Yet another new muffler.

Photos: Neil Spalding

YAMAHA

IT'S a bit difficult to keep improving perfection, but for 2009 Yamaha developed its 'Bridgestone version' bike one stage further. Having Rossi take Ducati's favourite tyres and redevelop his bike to better the Desmosedici was quite a trick in 2008. For 2009, the inevitable short cuts made during such a process were sorted out.

Rossi had used a short swing-arm in 2008, with a deliberately high level of lateral flex. While it was adjusted to give the rearwards weight bias the Bridgestones required, the basic chassis remained the same.

For 2009, the short swing-arm was redesigned for more stiffness and the frame main beams weakened. The modifications were quite obvious: with the mounting points for the rear seat unit unchanged, they left a big gap between the unit and the top of the main beam. The logic was to 'spread' the lateral flex over as long a section as possible, making any movement more gentle and controllable.

At the same time, the rearward weight shift allowed Yamaha to sort out a cooling problem that had been a headache for some time. When Michelins were fitted, the four-cylinder across-the-frame engine was further forward for a front weight bias, but this restricted the scope for incorporating effective hot-air exhaust ducts from behind the radiator. The shift rearward for Bridgestones meant that there was more room between the front tyre and the engine, so it was relatively simple to move the radiator 20mm forward and make a more efficient exit duct.

Rossi also had a new clutch, from major Japanese manufacturer Exedy, as tested at Misano the previous year. Other than that, the rest of the bike was very little changed. It had the same class leading Öhlins 48mm through-rod forks and matching rear shock, and the same pneumatic-valve-spring, irregular-fire, reverse-rotating cross-plane-crank engine.

Yamaha was confident in engine reliability all the way to the start of the restricted-engine-numbers rule at Brno. Until then, satellite team Tech 3's bikes had significantly more power than the equivalent customer Hondas. Afterwards, they were slowed, with lower power levels than the Hondas. We don't know if the works bikes were the same; their performance certainly didn't show any effects of a slow-down, although Rossi did complain somewhat. It may be that Yamaha only invested on uprating the material specs of the two top riders, leaving the others to struggle on with the old short-life engines and less power.

Yamaha's class leading electronics were simplified a little – a necessity with the new practice restrictions. However, the manufacturer continued to dominate the electronics war. At least two, and possibly three, gyros measure the attitude of the bike. Then, factoring in its position on the track and the rider's inputs, the system predicts the best throttle settings and power output to obtain the best grip, acceleration and deceleration characteristics, depending on the levels of slide the rider prefers and the fuel available.

Right now, the Yamaha M1 is the peach of the field.

Left: Yamaha's slotted controlled-flex headstock was given more offset to improve weight transfer under braking.

Below: Lorenzo's bike is festooned with class-leading electronics.
Photos: Neil Spalding

FASTER IS AS FASTER DOES

Progress is integral with racing, and the new electronics are just the latest generation, giving access to the next level of improvement.
KEVIN CAMERON follows the logic from then until now...

Above: Cometh the moment, cometh the mode. A choice of control options for a Honda rider's left hand.

Bottom right: A factory Honda again ... but this one has Öhlins suspension. The quest for improvement invokes constant change.

Photos: Neil Spalding

FOR some spectators and even some within racing, the electronic aids used on all MotoGP bikes are a puzzle – or even a 'moral problem'. An anti-spin system allows faster drives off corners with reduced hazard of high-side accidents – but it takes some responsibility from the rider. A good anti-wheelie system saves rider concentration by preventing time-wasting lifting or traction loss at the front wheel – but it takes responsibility from the rider. Some people imagine an earlier era of 'pure rider control', but riders have been receiving help since the beginning of motorcycling.

Riders go faster when they learn something new, or when machine changes allow a quicker lap time at the same level of security. Over the years, it has been the latter that has brought us improved motorcycles. Electronics have been part of this work for 40 years.

It is relatively easy to build a quick 'one-lap motorcycle', but while such a bike will qualify well, it will finish out of the first rank. The two common reasons for this are that the machine's qualities quickly destroy its tyres, or that marginal machine controllability requires a level of rider concentration that cannot be maintained.

Think back to the days just after World War Two, when the Italian Gilera-4 challenged the British Norton singles. Those early Gileras were actually 25–30lb lighter than the Nortons and had almost a 20hp advantage, yet only tyre failures denied Geoff Duke and the Norton the 1950 500 championship. He went on to win the title in 1951. How does a bike with a superior power-to-weight ratio lose? It lost because it was harder to ride. With a very light frame, the Gilera had built-in control delays, flexing rather than responding promptly, unlike the Norton. This made it slower and more hectic to ride through corners.

Gilera fought back with very smooth, predictable engine power – power that was so tractable that the race bikes were used occasionally for mechanics' jaunts to the smoke shop. Gilera could have made even more power through sharper engine tuning, as Norton had long been obliged to do, but the resulting peakier power would have made the Gilera slower still. When John Surtees began to ride the 500 MV in 1956, he found that this smooth flow of power allowed him to develop a cornering style based upon throttle steering. Had the MV's power been as peaky as that of the Norton, Surtees's method would have been impossible. This is an early example of 'power smoothing' as an aid to lap time.

As the Gileras and MVs were given stiffer chassis, their responsiveness and lap times improved,

for decades – by using needle jets, needles, slide cutaways and idle jets instead of keystrokes and software patches. Shortly before his last win on Yamaha's OW-69 Daytona two-stroke, Kenny Roberts asked for its ignition timing to be retarded slightly. The improved tyre life this made possible, by limiting off-corner wheelspin, contributed to his victory. Although the eras and the tools were different, the goal was the same – to make the motorcycle more easily usable by the rider.

However, making bikes easier to ride has its limits. In 2003, Ducati gave Honda a bad scare with its vast top-end power. For 2004, Honda increased power by the traditional methods, making the RC's torque curve less smooth, which gave its riders a greater workload. More power needs more fuel, leaving less that could be used for the luxury of cancelling engine braking. Honda struggled.

Meanwhile, Ducati addressed the problem of torque smoothing in a new way. The most critical part of racing – the corner exits – takes place on low part-throttle. The 'old method' of torque smoothing, used by most teams during 2002–05, was to trim torque spikes by ignition timing retard, just as had been done manually for Kenny Roberts at the 1984 Daytona 200 – and just as had been done with Aprilia 250s since the mid-1990s with their choice of four ignition maps. Aprilia's 'rain mode' softened the peaks to make wheelspin easier to control.

Ducati, in need of the fuel formerly wasted by ignition retard, however, developed throttle-based torque smoothing. As the rider rolled the throttle on during corner exit, he was merely signalling his torque demand to the engine computer. The computer supplied that torque smoothly by rapidly moving the throttle plates to eliminate the engine's natural torque peaks and dips. In the 1950s, Gilera had achieved this smoothing by use of moderate cam timings and by retaining straight exhaust pipes rather than adding megaphones. It could afford this moderation because its only competition, the Norton, was always 20hp down. Locking 'horsepower horns' with mighty Honda, Ducati needed every scrap of power it could make – and would use electronic means to make it rider-usable. Was this a radical high-tech novelty? No – such controls were familiar to all automotive engineers as developing features of production cars.

Since the first 'oil shock' of 1974, racing organisations have felt it necessary to 'go green' where possible. The 1976 Daytona 200 was shortened to 180 miles, saving possibly 100 gallons of fuel – never mind that the Boeing 747 that flew Dutch fans to Daytona that year burned 65,000 gallons on its round trip. Later, the FIM would reduce, and then in 1998 ban poisonous, metal-based anti-knock agents from race fuel. To show that MotoGP was doing its civic duty, for the 2006 season fuel quantity was cut back from 24 to 22 liters.

This imposed on MotoGP the same stringent economy requirements long faced by the automotive industry, and the solution chosen was the same – electronic fuel management. Ducati, absolutely dependent on fuel economy for its power-based race strategy, gambled on a system that would idle the engine during braking, then pick up the drive smoothly for corner exit. It was a failure. Now every manufacturer began playing the classic game of leaning the mixture on part throttle, compensating for the resulting reduced flame speed by advancing the timing. Fuel injection timing was rewritten to prevent loss of fuel during valve overlap. It was easy to calculate the fuel delivered by the 500 or so measured injection pulses per second, then subtract this from the original 22 liters to compute fuel remaining – my little economy car has this same system. A lap counter then allowed prediction of whether or not the machine could complete the race without running out of fuel. If the answer was no, one or more levels of 'economy mode' would click in, but riders have come to hate the sometimes weaker performance and degraded throttle response that results.

In the early days, Gilera used lower-cost engines for practice, then fitted the expensive version with a German Hirth built-up roller crank for the race. Qualifying engines or set-ups are as old as racing. A camshaft so vigorous that it breaks valve springs

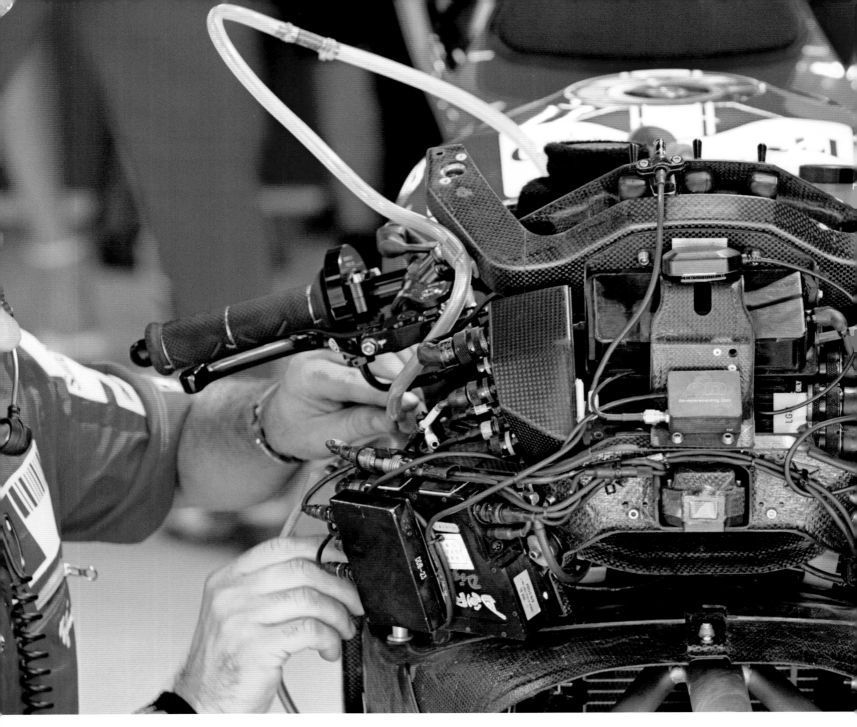

Above: The Desmosedici's nerve centre. Ducati's advanced electronics are an integral part of a high-power strategy.

Top right: Hardware still counts. The factory Dukes used both carbon-fibre and aluminium swing-arms during the season.
Photos: Neil Spalding

Centre right: And so does the rider. Rossi's tyre management skills are as important as his bravery under braking.
Photo: Gold & Goose

Right: All Hondas come with instruction manuals – even the RC212V.
Photo: Neil Spalding

in 50–100 miles can't be used in a race, but may qualify well. So it is that MotoGP engines are sent out in qualifying with their fuel economy measures switched off, and possibly with some of their torque smoothing toned down. Riders concentrate harder in qualifying than they could sustain for a race distance, so added power with added difficulty are tolerable.

Tyres have always been part of the control equation. Those who remember racing on round-profile Avon Green-Dots or Dunlop Triangulars know that those tyres were engineered to forgive error, not to multiply it. Many a bike could be seen 'going around a thrupenny bit' – making the corner line a many-sided polygon with a series of small slides and recoveries. Rubber that behaved in this way was necessary to survive the heavy shocks delivered by the stiff, short-travel suspensions of the pre-1975 era. Then suspension travel doubled, allowing much softer springing and damping. Tyres protected from high peak loads could safely be built with increased grip, but less warning of incipient breakaway.

By 1989, large-section semi-radial tyres had so advanced in grip that they became incompatible with the nature of 500cc two-stroke power. The result was a rash of sudden exit high-side crashes, brought on as steeply rising engine torque momentarily overcame tyre grip. The manufacturers re-

sponded in 1990 with systems that either limited torque in lower gears or actively limited spin. The crisis passed. In 1992, Honda contributed its 'Big Bang' close-firing-order engine as another piece of the puzzle, allowing its riders to safely begin throttle-up earlier.

The central problem with tyres is heat, which causes an overworked tyre to lose its peak properties permanently. This obliges riders to constantly evaluate and conserve their tyres. There is no such thing as 'just goin' for it' in motor racing. Every successful rider is a tyre manager. Technologies such as ultra-strength cord fibres and radial construction allowed tyres to be made thinner, reducing their heat generation so much that rubber compounds formerly useful only in rain could be used on dry tyres from 1992 onwards. Yet below operating temperature, tyres grip poorly. This is why tyre warmers exist: to keep the selection of tyres hot enough to provide some usable grip from the first lap.

As tyres have become thinner and larger in section, they have lost mass and gained great surface area, from which they lose heat rapidly. Keeping a tyre within its temperature zone of best grip depends on choosing the right tyre and riding hard enough to keep it in that zone. In 2009, we saw riders fall during corner entry after being held up by a slower rider

through a few corners. This had allowed the large rear tyre to cool off enough to lose significant grip.

This seems strange, because Bridgestone, the sole MotoGP tyre supplier, is known for the broad temperature operating range of its tyres. But there's also something familiar here. At the introduction of carbon brakes in the late 1980s, there was a difficult season or two when discs could cool enough while running down a straight that their material would lose much of its friction. When the rider applied the brakes again, their rapid heating caused brake torque to rise so fast that a wheel could lock before the rider could sense it. To prevent this, shields were placed over carbon discs to keep them hot – and grippy. Later, improved disc manufacture made this unnecessary. Even so, a standard option in the choice of Öhlins fork bottoms is an integral bracket to hold an infrared brake disc temperature sensor.

Will rider dashboards soon display red/green tyre readiness lights? It could be. For at least ten years, GP and WSB machines have appeared in practice sessions with multiple infrared sensors aimed at their rear tyres.

There is always a solution, and since that first Daimler two-wheeler of 1885, making motorcycles easier to ride fast has employed the best currently available

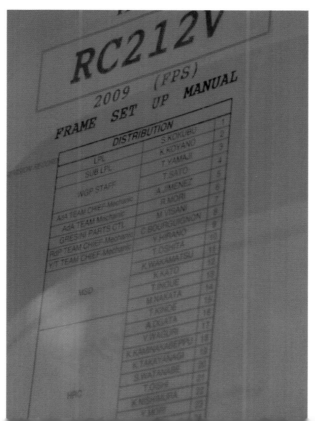

THE MASTER OF REINVENTION

Throughout a long and brilliant career, Valentino Rossi has constantly reinvented himself to meet the needs of the moment. MICHAEL SCOTT considers the factors that may trigger his next incarnation.

Photos: Gold & Goose

L IFE is always looking for renewal. This is true in any sphere: from engineering to dancing, from art to commerce, from smoke to mirrors. And especially in motorsport. The new must always beat the old.

Motorcycle racing is no different, but we have been through a remarkable spell. Since soon after the turn of the century, the renewal has come mainly from the same person, himself apparently constantly renewable. Valentino Rossi's racing has been through as many incarnations as his hairstyles, back in the still-impish 250 days. Almost every incarnation has proved unbeatable.

It was the same in 2009. Events threw a whole new set of circumstances against the Italian: this time a team-mate with a torrid talent. The latest version of Rossi was strong enough once again to deal with the threat, and to come out smilingly triumphant, as ever.

Yet there was a thinning of the lips to that smile,

and a more drawn look to Rossi's face than ever before. Those signs were not just the effects of age, either, although now he is beyond the 30 barrier.

They reflected the novelty of his present position. Not only does time dictate that he must contemplate the end of his career, but also he is confronted with his own humanity. His rivals are six or seven years younger, Lorenzo almost eight. And there are more to come from the 250 class in 2010.

"Valentino Rossi must retire at the top," he told *MOTOCOURSE* late in the season. "When I understand it is too strong, too hard, and I have to fight for fifth place...why? Is better to stop before that."

Yet there is a powerful temptation to keep trying. Rossi has piled up records as his career has progressed. During 2009, he passed the remarkable and historic milestone of 100 GP wins. Only Agostini had done that before, and Ago's total is 122 – a target that is tantalisingly almost within Rossi's reach. He finished 2009 with 103. Only 19 to go.

Previous pages:
Three ages of Rossi:
125 imp with Haru
Aoki; playful MotoGP ri-
val with Sete Gibernau,
and ice-man of 2009.
Photos: Gold & Goose

Above left: Rossi with
Burgess in 2003 – a
crucial partnership.

Left: Rossi gets brutal
attacking Capirossi at
the Corkscrew in 2006.
Two years later the
same move would have
Stoner fuming ... and
also beaten.
Photos: Gold & Goose

Right: Win number
100 – Ago in sight.
As remarkably, Rossi
hasn't missed a single
GP in 14 years.
Photo: Peter J. Fox

Yet the most he has ever won in a year is 11, and at that rate it would take two years. Moreover, he did that in 2001, 2002 and 2005; in 2010, he won six, maintaining the average of the previous three seasons. The arrival of Stoner, Lorenzo and Pedrosa has cut back his win rate quite significantly.

Rossi will be thinking seriously about all this during the winter. About what he has to look forward to: how to steer his career towards its chequered flag. He has already done so much, in a racing history that hardly needs rehearsing, but surely deserves celebration.

Son of glamorous, but somewhat wild former GP winner Graziano, Valentino was in racing from infancy. There is a famous picture of the babe in arms, with his dad wearing his leathers. "I should have run him over when I had the chance," quipped then beginner 'Aspar' Martinez, who later would race against Rossi in the 125 class.

Vale grew up racing karts and minibikes at the many little tracks strung up and down the holiday coast around Rimini – home-town Tavullia is a little inland of the endless line of hotels, beaches, cafes and clubs. This is a heartland of Italian motorcycle racing: the Morbidelli factory is just down the road

– its privately built racing two-strokes took on Japan; one of many past local heroes is double champion and current team boss Fausto Gresini. Valentino was an early pioneer of a current and glittering generation: Melandri, Dovizioso, Pasini, de Angelis, recent 125/250 champion Manuel Poggiali and now Marco Simoncelli are following in his wake. Worryingly, there seems to be a gap behind them.

"We grew up racing so much," recalled Rossi. It was just what they did.

Rossi's career path has always been blessed by good judgement and the best patronage. Not by accident: success in these areas is part of a racer's necessary talent, and while Graziano had the connections within racing, his son's blatant talent did the rest. When Vale arrived in GPs in 1996 as an ebullient and instantly noticeable teen with flowing long hair, he was already a pet of the Aprilia factory, and he remained so over the next four years of vaulting success. One year to learn, one year to win: in this way, he left the 125 and then the 250 classes as champion. Many thought that he would find the same schedule harder to achieve on the big bikes.

Not so. He joined Honda and did it again. It was

at this point that he formed his most crucial alliance – with ex-Doohan crew chief Jerry Burgess. "Jeremy is my motorcycling father," he said, after their seventh premier-class crown together (Burgess' 12th as crew chief).

Rossi's next renewal came with the 990cc four-strokes. He resisted the move at first, but now names the Honda RC211V of 2003 as his favourite bike, supplanting the 500 NSR two-stroke he had loved so much – "so nervous, with a special taste".

The biggest reinvention came in 2004, as a Yamaha rider – the "what if I hadn't tried it" moment. He felt unappreciated at Honda, where engineering is traditionally valued more highly than riding skill; he wanted to prove that it was the rider who made the difference. So he made the great leap to underdog Yamaha, and straight away turned the M1 from problem child into racing prodigy.

His feats that year were unforgettable, riding the still somewhat slower Yamaha to triumph over the best that Honda could muster. The set-up and development skills that he and Burgess brought with them (for he had persuaded his whole crew to move with them) were invaluable. The glamour of the

whole exercise should not overshadow the contribution from the engineers, however: Rossi's move coincided with the advent of the inspired cross-plane-crankshaft engine. He took a big risk with the switch, but in retrospect it turned out to have been very shrewdly timed.

Rossi dominated on the Yamaha, but was beaten to the title in 2006 by Nicky Hayden, more because of mechanical problems – both tyre and engine – that spoiled his fight against a very determined and consistent rival.

The only hiccup came in 2007, the first year of the 800s. Ducati had taken a better shot at the new target than Yamaha, and had found just the rider to make the most of it in young Casey Stoner. Rossi couldn't stop him, but at least he knew why. And he was able to turn the tables in the following year, most emphatically with an epic defeat at Laguna Seca.

Some said they had never seen Rossi ride better – in fact, he was just doing what he had always done, but with a new twist. In the past, he'd been able to run along with his rivals and make an entertaining race of it, then drive his point home in the closing laps, when the tyres had started turning to jelly.

Now, better tyres and a younger generation of rider had changed the ground rules. Pedrosa and, to an extent, Stoner preferred runaway wins to hand-to-hand combat: improved tyre endurance meant that races increasingly were conducted closer to the limit from the first lap to the last.

There were signs, especially at the end of the year, that Stoner might have been able to do it again in 2009, but fortunately for Valentino and all his rivals, the Australian ruled himself out of the contest with his extended mid-season sick break. Stoner's dominance at year's end was that of a man back from a long holiday: his rivals were busy concluding the championship at the end of a long and gruelling campaign. His mid-year absence made his true strength impossible to gauge. For Rossi, it also added considerably to the uncertainty of the forthcoming 2010 season.

But the most troubling presence came from the other side of the wall that ran down the middle of the Fiat Yamaha pit. Jorge embodied everything that Stoner had already shown in terms of speed and ability. And he was on an identical bike. When he beat Valentino, and it happened most notably in Japan and Portugal, there was no excuse. Rossi just

hadn't been fast enough.

And, as Jorge enjoyed repeating, "I am still learning." Showing that in the application of psychological pressure, as well as in post-race pantomime and in lap times, he is a worthy pretender to Rossi's throne.

It was after his Indianapolis crash that Rossi started to make his feelings public: mainly resentment at his treatment by Yamaha. He had been a crucial component in developing the M1 to become the best bike on the grid, "and now they give it to my worst enemy. I think I deserve more respect."

Thus the year closed with a yet another big question mark to add to those already accumulating. Rossi must decide in June 2010 "if I continue with motorbikes, and then if I continue with Yamaha." It goes without saying that if Yamaha does not agree to "let Jorge go" when his contract expires, the threat is that Valentino will walk.

His destination seems almost pre-ordained. Ducati awaits the all-Italian dream. "I have a good offer from Ducati," he confirmed after Valencia. And in the back of Rossi's mind must surely be the same thought, the mantra of reinvention: "What if I hadn't tried it?"

An angle on greatness - Rossi returned to form close to home at Misano.

Photo: Gold & Goose

TEAM-BY-TEAM

MOTOGP REVIEW

2009 Teams and Riders

MATTHEW BIRT

Illustrations

ADRIAN DEAN

FIAT YAMAHA TEAM

TEAM STAFF

Masao FURUSAWA: Executive Officer, Yamaha Engineering Operations
Lin JARVIS: Managing Director, Yamaha Motor Racing
Masahiko NAKAJIMA: Team Director
William FAVERO: Communications Manager
Katie BAINES: Press Officer

VALENTINO ROSSI PIT CREW

Davide BRIVIO: Team Manager
Jeremy BURGESS: Crew Chief
Mechanics:
Bernard ANSIAU
Alex BRIGGS
Brent STEPHENS
Gary COLEMAN (assistant/logistics)
Hiroyami ATSUMI: Yamaha Engineer
Matteo FLAMIGNI: Telemetry
Roberto BRIVIO: Team Co-ordinator

JORGE LORENZO PIT CREW

Daniele ROMAGNOLI: Team Manager
Ramone FORCADA: Crew Chief
Mechanics:
Walter CRIPPA
Javier ULLATE
Valentino NEGRI
Juan Llansa HERNANDEZ (assistant/logistics)
Takashi MORIYAMA: Yamaha Engineer
Carlo LUZZI: Telemetry
Emanuele Mazzini: Team Co-ordinator

VALENTINO ROSSI
Born: 16 February, 1979 – Urbino, Italy
GP Starts: 227 (167 MotoGP/500cc, 30 250cc, 30 125cc)
GP Wins: 103 (77 MotoGP/500cc, 14 250cc, 12 125cc)
World Championships: 9 (6 MotoGP, 1 500cc, 1 250cc, 1 125cc)

Photos: Gold & Goose

JORGE LORENZO
Born: 4 May, 1987 – Palma de Mallorca, Spain
GP Starts: 128 (34 MotoGP, 48 250cc, 46 125cc)
GP Wins: 26 (5 MotoGP, 17 250cc, 4 125cc)
World Championships: 2 250cc

YAMAHA'S factory team was the all-conquering force for the second successive season in MotoGP, securing the triple crown of rider, team and constructor titles with consummate ease. For the second successive season, too, the Fiat backed operation acted more like two separate outfits, its all-star line-up of Valentino Rossi and Jorge Lorenzo split again by a controversial dividing wall.

Many thought the wall would be dismantled with Rossi and Lorenzo no longer battling for supremacy on different tyre brands. But although both were on Bridgestone rubber, the wall was retained at the behest of Rossi.

Yamaha's recent success in MotoGP had been built on stability and a refusal to tinker significantly with personnel, even when things had gone badly wrong in 2006 and 2007.

Masao Furusawa was the executive officer of engineering operations, and he remained the most senior factory figure in the paddock. Lin Jarvis continued in his role of managing director of Yamaha Racing, while former YZR-M1 project leader Masahiko Nakajima was team director.

Nakajima was still a pivotal figure in technical development, and while his role meant that he worked predominantly with Rossi and Lorenzo, he was a fre-

YAMAHA YZR-M1

Sponsors and Technical Suppliers: Petronas · Packard Bell · Yamalube · Bridgestone · Alpinestars · astweb · Termignoni · Exedy · DID · NGK · Magneti Marelli · Beta · 2D · Iveco · Flex · Adidas

Fuel: 21-litres · Wheelbase: 1450mm

Engine: Liquid-cooled 799cc DOHC 16v, In-line four with reverse rotating crank. Machined from solid crankcases and steel crankshaft with titanium rods. Pneumatic Valve Spring operation.

Electronics package: Marelli ECU hardware and Yamaha software to control throttle butterflies, fuelling, ignition timing and traction control.

Chassis: Aluminium beam frame. Aluminium swingarm with Link. Fully adjustable 48mm Ohlins TTx25TR forks and fully adjustable Ohlins TTxTR40 rear shock)

Brakes: 2 x 320mm Carbon front discs with radially mounted four-piston Brembo calipers. 220mm rear disc with a twin piston Brembo caliper.

Tyres: Front 16.5 inch Bridgestone control slick on Marchesini wheel. Rear 16.5 Bridgestone control slick on Marchesini wheels.

quent visitor to the Monster Yamaha Tech 3 garage, and was constantly digesting information fed back from Colin Edwards and James Toseland.

Davide Brivio continued in his role of team manager on Rossi's side of the garage. Daniele Romagnoli, who was a former crew chief to Edwards, continued to oversee Lorenzo's team. At the end of the season, Romagnoli announced that he had found team management to be too removed from the cut and thrust of a MotoGP pit box. He wanted more input into the performance of the bike, as a crew chief. With no room at Fiat Yamaha, he resigned. And with no crew chief roles available in MotoGP, it was announced shortly after Valencia that he would join Hervé Poncharal's new Tech 3 Moto2 squad, crew chief to emerging Italian talent Raffaele de Rosa.

Again, Rossi would rely on the technical expertise of legendary Australian crew chief Jeremy Burgess to propel him to a ninth career world title and seventh in MotoGP.

Only six wins, though, made for Rossi's worst ever tally in a world championship winning campaign. It was more than any other rider, however, and he claimed the most poles and podiums, as well as passing another fantastic personal milestone with a hundredth grand prix win at Assen.

Rossi certainly wasn't as infallible as in previous years, and he crashed in three races. Le Mans bordered on the comical, as he changed bikes three times, crashed out of the lead and received a ride-through penalty for pit-lane speeding, to finish 16th in a flag-to-flag encounter.

The battle between team-mates became much more intense as the year progressed, and the last of Rossi's mistakes, at Indianapolis, gave Lorenzo another title lifeline.

Lorenzo was again partnered with Ramon Forcada as crew chief, and he'd started off at a blistering pace, winning two of the first four races. He took only two more wins in the next 13 races, however, and his season was punctuated with inexcusable mistakes that proved costly. But Lorenzo made Rossi delve deeper into his reserves of talent than any

other rider had previously managed.

Their rivalry had been simmering without ever boiling over prior to the Catalunya race. And despite being forever encouraged to verbally joust in the Italian and Spanish press, they had never previously engaged in all-out warfare on track. What unfolded over 25 pulsating laps will be talked about for decades, Rossi claiming a famous win with an audacious last-corner overtake that left him jubilant and Lorenzo crestfallen.

When Lorenzo crashed out of the lead at Donington Park and Brno, some might say that he had become distracted by the serious interest from Honda and Ducati. He tried to extract more money from Yamaha, suggesting that his performances should give him parity with the astronomical fee commanded by Rossi. Eventually, he signed a new one-year extension during the build-up to the Indianapolis race, which served only to aggravate Rossi.

The 2009 season hadn't finished, but Rossi had to fend off speculation about his 2011 future. Lorenzo's new deal irked him greatly, and at Misano he gave a revealing interview, during which he said that he would have no qualms in quitting Yamaha if Lorenzo was retained beyond the 2010 season.

He reiterated his displeasure at Valencia and whipped the media into a frenzy by suggesting a Ducati move if he walked out on Yamaha. He insisted, however, that his first choice – assuming he did not retire at the end of 2010 – was to remain with Yamaha.

Above: Masao Furusawa: senior industry figure and race boss.

Above left: Crew chief to Rossi, Jeremy Burgess.

Left: Lin Jarvis headed Yamaha Racing.

Below left: : Davide Brivio was on Rossi's side of the garage.

Photos: Gold & Goose

REPSOL HONDA TEAM

TEAM STAFF

Tetsuo SUZUKI: HRC President
Shuhei NAKAMOTO: HRC Vice President
Shinichi KOKUBU: Large Project Leader
Kazuhiko YAMANO: Team Manager
Katsura SHIBASAKI: Assistant
Koshiyuki YAMAJI: Staff Chief

ANDREA DOVIZIOSO PIT CREW

Pete BENSON: Chief Mechanic
Gianni Berti: Crew Chief
Mechanics:
Mark LLOYD (Engine Technician)
Craig BURTON
Katzuhiko IMAI
David GUITTEREZ
Yuji KIKUCHI: Tyres
Ramon AURÍN: Telemetry
Atsushi SHUMIZO: HRC Engineer

DANI PEDROSA PIT CREW

Mike LEITNER: Chief Mechanic
Alberto PUIG: Crew Chief
Mechanics:
Mark BARNETT (Engine Technician)
Jordi PRADES
Christophe LEONCE
Masashi OGO
John EYRE: Tyres
Jose Manuel ALLENDE: Telemetry
Masato NAKATA: HRC Engineer
Marco FRIGERIO: Telemetry

DANI PEDROSA
Born: 29 September, 1985 – Sabadell, Spain
GP Starts: 147 (69 MotoGP, 32 250cc, 46 125cc)
GP Wins: 31 (8 MotoGP, 15 250cc, 8 125cc)

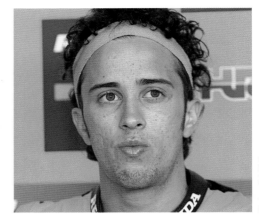

ANDREA DOVIZIOSO
Born: 23 March, 1986 – Forli, Italy
GP Starts: 133 (35 MotoGP, 49 250cc, 49 125cc)
GP Wins: 10 (1 MotoGP, 5 250cc, 4 125cc)
World Championships: 1 125cc

Photos: Gold & Goose

HONDA'S official factory MotoGP squad had fallen on hard times since Nicky Hayden had won the last 990cc four-stroke title in 2006. The august racing factory had not seriously contended for the MotoGP title since, and with only a smattering of race wins in the 800cc era, HRC had been left exposed by the technical ingenuity and riding talent at the disposal of Yamaha and Ducati.

And 2009 was another year of massive underachievement as HRC failed yet again to deliver an RC212V capable of being a consistent race winner to rival the YZR-M1 from Yamaha and GP9 from Ducati.

Recent MotoGP history shows that Honda has lacked strong leadership, and several attempts to resolve the issue have failed dismally. Results were hard to achieve on the track, but certainly were not helped by a gross lack of stability behind the scenes.

HRC has undergone an incredible high turnover of senior management, and 2009 was no exception. The season hadn't even started when Shuhei Nakamoto took up the newly created role of vice president of HRC. A driving force behind Honda's World Superbike project in the late nineties, he had enjoyed a meteoric rise to become senior

HONDA RC212V

Sponsors & Technical Suppliers: Bridgestone · GAS · NGK · RK · Showa · Shindengen · Snap-on · MIVV

Fuel: 21-litres · *Wheelbase:* 1440mm

Engine: Liquid-cooled 799cc, DOHC 16v, 77.5 (est) deg Vee-four. Cast crankcases and steel crankshaft with titanium rods. Pneumatic valve spring operation.

Electronics package: HRC ECU hardware and software to control throttle butterflies, fuelling, ignition timing and traction control.

Chassis: Aluminium beam frame. Aluminium swingarm with Pro Link rear linkage. Fully adjustable 47mm Showa 'Big Piston' forks and fully adjustable Showa rear shock, from Misano Dovisioso used 48mm Ohlins TTxTR forks and a TTx 40TR rear shock.

Brakes: 2 x 320mm Carbon-carbon front discs with radially mounted four-piston Brembo calipers. 218mm HRC rear disc with a twin piston Brembo caliper.

Tyres: Front 16-5 inch Bridgestone control slick on Marchesini wheel. Rear 16.5 Bridgestone control slick on Marchesini wheel.

technical director of Honda's Formula One team, having moved to four wheels in 2000. Just before Honda's bombshell that it would quit F1 in December 2008, Nakamoto's return to his roots was confirmed.

Nakamoto's eight years at Honda's Northamptonshire F1 base meant that he had become substantially Westernised, and he was a much more approachable and affable character than some of the previous robotic Honda senior management.

While Nakamoto brought a more human touch to HRC, he was also brutally honest, admitting early in the season that Honda's engineers had failed number-one rider Dani Pedrosa by supplying a V4 machine that was not capable of mounting a serious challenge.

Managing director Kosuke Yasutake was not seen again, while Mick Doohan's former mechanic, Kazuhiko Yamano, continued as team manager.

Another change came with the departure of HRC president Masumi Hamane. He was replaced by Tetsuo Suzuki, whose first public engagement – at Brno in August – was to (wrongly) declare that Pedrosa and Andrea Dovizioso had agreed new two-year deals.

Eventually, Pedrosa did sign a new deal at Misano, having turned down overtures from Ducati, but it was only for one year. Dovizioso also extended his contract at the same time, with an option for 2011.

The lack of success hadn't dissuaded Spanish petroleum giant Repsol from remaining as backer of the HRC effort again in 2010. When announced at Estoril, though, it was only a new one-year deal, and at a significantly reduced rate, the contract having been renegotiated on the basis of a lack of results and the impact of the worldwide recession.

Pedrosa continued to work with crew chief Mike Leitner, while his personal manager and mentor, Alberto Puig, remained a constant presence at his side, both in and out of the garage.

The Spaniard was badly hampered by yet more pre-season injury misery, though, and he won only twice, at Laguna Seca and Valencia. He snatched

third in the overall standings from Stoner at the last race, but that owed more to the fact that the Aussie didn't score points in four of the last seven races.

Dovizioso was arguably the biggest disappointment of the season. Successive crashes at Assen, Laguna Seca and Sachsenring cost him valuable points, although he mastered the treacherous conditions at Donington Park better than anybody to register an unlikely, but famous first win.

That was his only trip to the podium, however, and in one final blow, he surrendered fifth place in the championship to Colin Edwards with a tame eighth at Valencia.

Before that, it had become common knowledge that the loyal services of Dovizioso's crew chief, Pete Benson, had been dispensed with. Ramon Aurin, who was promoted from the role of Dovizioso's telemetry technician, would replace the New Zealander.

That wasn't the last shake-up either, as HRC adopted an aggressive recruitment strategy at the end of the season. It entered into lengthy discussions with Jorge Lorenzo in the early stages of the season, during which the Spaniard had insisted on bringing crew chief Ramon Forcada and data technician Carlo Luzzi with him from Fiat Yamaha.

Lorenzo's faith in Luzzi alerted HRC to his potential, and he was duly signed to work with Dovizioso in 2010, much to Lorenzo's annoyance.

It wasn't the only swoop on Yamaha. Christian Battagglia and Andrea Zugna were two key components of Yamaha and Valentino Rossi's recent success. Predominantly based at Yamaha Racing's European headquarters in Milan, they were electronics specialists first and foremost. It was a double transfer that sat uncomfortably with Yamaha senior management, particularly considering the intimate knowledge that the pair had of the YZR-M1.

The final piece of the jigsaw was put in place at Valencia, and was easily the most unexpected. Nakamoto had secretly been in discussions with Ducati factory team boss Livio Suppo, and the Italian joined as marketing director.

Above: New ex-F1 team chief Shuhei Nakamoto.

Above centre: HRC's new president Tetsuo Suzuki.

Top: Pedrosa was unbeatable at Laguna.
Photos: Gold & Goose

DUCATI MARLBORO TEAM

TEAM STAFF

Claudio DOMENICALI: Managing Director
Filippo PREZIOSI: Technical Director
Livio SUPPO: Project Director
Christian PUPULIN: Technical Co-Ordinator
Francesco RAPISARDA: Communications Director
Federica DE ZOTTIS: Press Officer
Amadeo COSTA: Team Co-Ordinator
Luigi MITOLO: Asst. Technical Co-Ordinator
Allesandro ZORZI: Warehouse and Components

CASEY STONER/MIKA KALLIO PIT CREW

Cristian GABARRINI: Race engineer
Bruno LEONI: Chief Mechanic
Mechanics:
Roberto CLERICI
Andrea BRUNETTI
Lorenzo GAGNI
Filippo BRUNETTI
Gabriele CONTI: Electronics Engineer

NICKY HAYDEN PIT CREW

Juan MARTINEZ: Race Engineer
Davide MANFREDI: Chief Mechanic
Mechanics:
Massimo MIRANO
Mark ELDER
Lorenzo CANESTRARI
Luciano BERTAGNA
Marco FRIGERIO: Telemetry

CASEY STONER
Born: 16 October, 1985 – Southport, Australia
GP Starts: 126 (65 MotoGP, 31 250cc, 30 125cc)
GP Wins: 27 (20 MotoGP, 5 250cc, 2 125cc)
World Championships: 1 MotoGP

NICKY HAYDEN
Born: 30 July, 1981, Owensboro, USA
GP Starts: 116 MotoGP
GP wins: 3 MotoGP
World Championships: 1 MotoGP

Photos: Gold & Goose

DUCATI'S 2009 season is likely to be remembered more for the tumultuous events off track than some typically explosive performances from enigmatic Aussie Casey Stoner on it.

The Bologna factory and star rider Stoner had a traumatic season to say the least, and at the year's conclusion at Valencia, rumour and conjecture about just how it all had gone so spectacularly wrong were still rife.

Ducati's seventh season in MotoGP got off to a brilliant start, Stoner showing no ill effects from career-saving surgery on his left wrist during the winter with a third straight win in Qatar. It was an immedi-

ate reward for Ducati's typically brave, but creative engineering approach, technical director Filippo Preziosi putting his faith in a new carbon-fibre chassis and swing-arm.

Above Preziosi was Ducati Corse CEO Claudio Domenicali, and on the shop floor, running the squad in the paddock, was Livio Suppo, again in the role of MotoGP project manager.

Again, the project was the best sponsored in the paddock, with that remnant of the good old days, tobacco giant Marlboro.

Once more, Stoner worked under crew chief Cristian Gabarrini, who understood the 24-year-old inti-

DUCATI DESMOSEDICI GP9

Sponsors and Technical Suppliers: Alice · Shell · Advance · Generali · Enel · Riello ups · Bridgestone · Alfa Romeo · Bosch · Breil · Ditec · Gatorade · Guabello Puma · Magneti Marelli · NGK · Regina Chains · SKF · Termignoni · USAG

Fuel: 21-litres **Wheelbase:** N/A

Engine: Liquid-cooled 799cc DOHC 16v, 90 deg Vee-four. Sand-cast crankcases and steel crankshaft with titanium rods. Desmodromic Valve operation.

Electronics package: Marelli MRE ECU hardware and Ducati software to control throttle butterflies, fuelling, ignition timing and traction control.

Chassis: Carbon 'Stressed Airbox' frame attaching in the Vee of the engine. Aluminium/Carbon swingarm with Soft damp rear linkage. Fully adjustable 42mm Ohlins TTx25 forks and fully adjustable Ohlins TTx40TR rear shock,

Brakes: 2 x 320mm Carbon-carbon front discs with radially mounted four-piston Brembo calipers. 200mm rear disc with a twin piston Brembo caliper.

Tyres: Front 16.5-inch Bridgestone control slick on Marchesini wheel. Rear 16.5 Bridgestone control slick on Marchesini wheels.

MIKA KALLIO

Born: 8 November, 1982 – Valkeakoski, Finland
GP Starts: 131 (16 MotoGP 33 250cc, 62 125cc)
GP Wins: 12 (5 250cc, 7 125cc)

Above: Hayden never gave up trying.

Right: Design guru Filippo Preziosi.

Below: Livio Suppo – off to Honda in 2010.

Bottom: : Vito Guareschi, test rider and new technical liaison man.

Photos: Gold & Goose

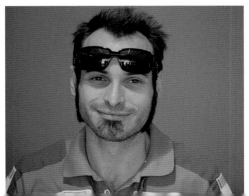

mately. Constant companions in the garage technical scrums were electronics engineer Gabriele Conti and chief mechanic Bruno Leoni.

A second win came in the flag-to-flag clash at Mugello, which was Ducati's first in the Italian MotoGP. By ending Valentino Rossi's remarkable domination of his home race, Stoner sparked jubilant scenes of celebration, giving little indication then that his and Ducati's world title ambitions were about to implode dramatically.

The Australian was ravaged by chronic fatigue at Catalunya, Assen, Laguna Seca and Sachsenring, yet even in his severely weakened state, his worst result was fourth. His decision then to run wet tyres on a damp track at Donington Park seemed bizarre in the extreme – more the gamble of a championship no-hoper than someone still firmly in the chase.

He suffered the embarrassment of being lapped before the halfway stage, but as Stoner left Britain red-faced, nobody realised at the time that he wouldn't be seen again until early October.

He missed the next three races, surrendering his world title hopes and sparking a rumour frenzy that lurched from the ridiculous to the outrageous. Suppo came under siege, and even Phillip Morris boss Maurizio Arrivabene weighed in, saying that Stoner should apologise for his absence.

Stoner returned, as promised, at Estoril, looking somewhat bewildered that his illness and self-imposed exile had provoked such ferocious debate. Without a clear diagnosis though, scepticism was rampant, and Ducati launched big-money raids on Jorge Lorenzo and Dani Pedrosa around Brno and Indianapolis.

What was not in question, though, was his electrifying pace, which had not been diminished by the three-race sabbatical. He was second at Estoril, and then won at Phillip Island and Sepang.

However, a season to forget ended in instantly forgettable fashion. Red-hot favourite to take the spoils at Valencia, Stoner crashed out on the

-warm-up lap.

What is also undeniable is that without Stoner's considerable influence, Ducati is a much less potent force.

For the first time since it had joined MotoGP in 2003, Ducati's factory team didn't field an Italian rider. Nicky Hayden had been dropped by Honda and had arrived at Ducati confident that he could prove that Stoner wasn't the only man who could tame the finicky Desmosedici. He attacked the challenge with typical vigour and determination, but the early races were a mammoth struggle. The Kentucky rider didn't qualify in the top ten until round eight on home soil at Laguna Seca.

By that time, he had already seen a significant change in his pit. He had started the season working with crew chief Cristhian Pupulin, but immediately encountered communication issues that hampered his bid to master the art of riding a Desmosedici.

For the French GP at Le Mans, Ducati instigated the first of two major personnel changes. Pupulin served a dual role at Ducati: as well as a crew chief, he was also the technical co-ordinator. Relieved of his crew chief role with Hayden, he would be left to focus solely on data gathered at the track, and to act as a key liaison with Preziosi and his engineers back in Bologna.

In came Sete Gibernau's former crew chief, Juan Martinez, to take on the role of Hayden's crew chief. He knew how the garage operated from Gibernau's Ducati year in 2006 and, crucially, he spoke good English.

Hayden gradually improved – only three times in the last ten races was he outside the top ten. The undoubted highlight was third at Indianapolis, and his finish to the year would have looked even more creditable had he not been wiped out by Alex de Angelis at the first corner at Misano. He was also rammed off track by Jorge Lorenzo at the first corner at Phillip Island – the third time in 2009 that he had been involved in a first-lap incident.

Despite the big-money approaches made to Lorenzo and Pedrosa, Hayden was retained for 2010 when he agreed a new deal at Misano.

There was still one final twist in a season of turmoil. At the last round, it was announced that Suppo would leave, to join HRC as marketing director. This fuelled speculation, fervently denied by both, that his relationship with Stoner had completely deteriorated.

Alessandro Cicognani would leave his role as marketing manager for Ducati Corse and take over responsibility for the MotoGP project. Test rider Vittoriano Guareschi would become team manager, further strengthening the link between Stoner, Hayden and the factory engineers.

MONSTER TECH 3 YAMAHA

TEAM STAFF

Hervé PONCHARAL: Team Manager

Gérard VALLEE: Team Co-ordinator

Eric REBMANN: Parts Manager

Olivier BOUTRON: Fuel/Tyres

COLIN EDWARDS PIT CREW

Guy COULON: Crew Chief

Mechanics:

Jerômé PONCHARAL

Josian RUSTIQUE

Laurent DUCLOYER

Andrew GRIFFITH: Telemetry

JAMES TOSELAND PIT CREW

Gary REYNDERS: Crew Chief

Mechanics:

Benoît BRUNEAU

Julien LAJUNIE

Sebastien LATORT

Nicolas GOYON: Telemetry

COLIN EDWARDS
Born: 27 February, 1974 – Houston, Texas, USA
GP Starts: 119 MotoGP
World Championships: 2 World Superbike

JAMES TOSELAND
Born: 5 October, 1980 – Sheffield, Great Britain
GP Starts: 35 MotoGP
World Championships: 2 World Superbike

Photos: Gold & Goose

HERVE Poncharal's Tech 3 Yamaha squad looked distinctly different at the start of 2009, even though in reality very little had changed. Firstly, the effervescent French team boss had managed to attract a title sponsor in the shape of American energy drink Monster. The company was keen to invest and gain key brand exposure, but had been left high and dry by the shock departure of Kawasaki's factory team in early January.

In Colin Edwards and James Toseland, Poncharal possessed two of the most marketable riders in the paddock, and a deal was finally signed in early March. Procuring the naming rights to the highest-profile non-factory team in MotoGP came at a fraction of the cost Monster had paid for the signage on Valentino Rossi's AGV helmet and paddock cap.

Secondly, one of the major close-season talking points had focused on Tech 3, about to embark on its ninth MotoGP campaign with Yamaha.

Towards the conclusion of a promising rookie campaign, Toseland had raised concerns about communication issues with Tech 3 co-owner and highly regarded engineer Guy Coulon. Despite his protestations of innocence, Toseland was a pivotal figure in influencing Poncharal to implement a controversial crew chief switch immediately after the

YAMAHA M-1 2009

Sponsors & Technical Suppliers: Monster · Motul · Bridgestone · Pollini · DeWalt

Fuel: 21-litres · Wheelbase: 1450mm

Engine: Liquid-cooled 799cc DOHC 16v, In-line four with reverse rotating crank. Machined from solid crankcases and steel crankshaft with titanium rods. Pneumatic Valve Spring operation.

Electronics package: Marelli ECU hardware and Yamaha software to control throttle butterflies, fuelling, ignition timing and traction control.

Chassis: Aluminium beam frame. Aluminium swingarm with Link. Fully adjustable 48mmOhlins TTx25TR forks and fully adjustable Ohlins TTxTR40 rear shock)

Brakes: 2 x 320mm Carbon front discs with radially mounted four-piston Brembo calipers. 220mm rear disc with a twin piston Brembo caliper.

Tyres: Front 16-5 inch Bridgestone control slick on Marchesini wheel. Rear 16.5 Bridgestone control slick on Marchesini wheels.

Left: The France-based team in pit lane

Below: Proprietor Hervé Poncharal.

Below centre: James Toseland had a tough second year.

Bottom: Veteran Colin Edwards rode as well as ever.

Photos: Gold & Goose

final race of 2008.

Edwards inherited Coulon, while Gary Reynders was shifted to Toseland's camp in a move that, mercifully for Poncharal, failed to disrupt the harmony of his tight-knit team, except between the riders. Edwards felt betrayed, and waged a very public war on Toseland and Reynders through the winter. So incensed was the Texan that he persuaded Poncharal to install a dividing wall in the garage, mimicking the Fiat backed factory Yamaha team pit box.

As the season wore on, Edwards and Toseland would be reconciled, and once again Tech 3 would emerge as the leading independent team in MotoGP, easily defeating Suzuki's factory effort in the coveted constructors' championship.

But while the controversy over the crew chief switch galvanised Edwards, it backfired spectacularly on Toseland and Reynders.

The switch had reignited Edwards's motivation, which previously had been doubted by many as he approached the twilight of his career. He rode harder and better than ever in MotoGP, and only four times finished outside of the top seven. He produced one of the performances of the year, too, by surging through from 15th to second at the British GP, but a maiden victory still eluded him. Only a kamikaze move by homeboy Alex de Angelis at the first corner at Misano prevented a super-consistent Edwards from finishing every race.

He was the top non-factory rider and fifth overall, a feat he revelled in, given that it's no disgrace to finish behind the dominant quartet of Valentino Rossi, Casey Stoner, Jorge Lorenzo and Dani Pedrosa.

Toseland, meanwhile, struggled severely to adapt to Bridgestone tyres, and two spectacular and confidence draining crashes in pre-season tests at Sepang and Jerez set the tone for the year. Weakened by the disappearance of Michelin's qualifying tyres, the British rider qualified in the top ten at only five races. Edwards, however, only qualified outside the top seven once.

Bad grid positions gave Toseland a mountain to climb in the races, and he scored only three top-six finishes, one of which was treated like a victory by Donington Park fans.

With Edwards and Toseland both out of contract, the Tech 3 hospitality unit became a honeypot for a swarm of riders and their representatives, eager for a 2010 ride. Yamaha's YZR-M1 was the best bike, and everybody wanted an opportunity to ride it in the coming season. Some, like Chris Vermeulen, offered themselves for little or no fee; Randy de Puniet, Toni Elias, Alvaro Bautista, Marco Simoncelli, Alex de Angelis and Mika Kallio were all locked in talks at some stage of the year.

Who would be sacrificed was equally tough to decipher. Toseland was the most vulnerable, given his poor results. His position was made all the more precarious by the scintillating performances of Ben Spies in his rookie World Superbike campaign on Yamaha's R1. The Texan was an overnight hit on and off the track with Japanese and European Yamaha management.

Barred by a new rule preventing rookies from joining a factory team, Spies was constantly linked to Tech 3. If he wanted to move to MotoGP in 2010, the ride was his. Yamaha's initial reluctance to have two American riders in the same team, and Dorna's desire to retain British interest in the premier class appeared to leave Edwards out in the cold.

The issue was resolved on the eve of the Estoril race in Portugal in early October. Edwards was in and so was Spies. Toseland was out and taking Spies's place at Yamaha in World Superbikes.

Spies elected also to take a wild-card ride at the final round, racing a Yamaha in the Sterilgarda colours he had worn in World Superbikes, and placing an impressive seventh. The next day, he was with Tech 3 for 2010 tests and continued in the same vein.

Spies won't ride for anybody without long-serving AMA Superbike crew chief Tom Houseworth as his main garage ally. Mechanic Greg 'Woody' Wood would also need to be accommodated at Tech 3, having followed Spies out of domestic racing in the States. This forced Poncharal into a major personnel reshuffle. Fiercely loyal to his crew, he had no option but to move Reynders and mechanic Benoît Bruneau to a new Moto2 effort. Reynders would be crew chief for Yuki Takahashi, and Bruneau one of the mechanics.

RIZLA SUZUKI

TEAM STAFF

Mr H NAKAI: General Manager
Shinichi SAHARA: Technical Manager
Paul DENNING: Team Manager
Katsuhiro NAITO: Technical Manager
Takayuki NAKAMOTO: Engine Development
Akira YAMAJUKU: Engine Builder
Tetsuya SASAKI: Chassis Development
Davide MARELLI: ECU Control Assistance
Tex GEISSLER: Data Analysis
Russell JORDAN: Parts and Logistics
Charlie MOODY: Operations Manager

CHRIS VERMEULEN PIT CREW

Tom O'KANE: Chief Mechanic
Simon WESTWOOD: Crew Leader
Mechanics:
Ray HUGHES
Tsutomo MATSUGANO
Mark FLEMING (assistant)
Renato PENNACCHIO: Telemetry

LORIS CAPIROSSI PIT CREW

Stuart SHENTON: Chief Mechanic
Ian GILPIN: Crew Leader
Mechanics:
George DZIEDZIC
Jeffrey OH
Jez WILSON (assistant)
Gary McLAREN: Telemetry

LORIS CAPIROSSI
Born: 4 April, 1973 – Bologna, Italy
GP Starts: 299 (188 MotoGP/500cc, 84 250cc, 27 125cc)
GP Wins: 29 (9 MotoGP/500cc, 12 250cc, 8 125cc)
World Championships: 3 (1 250cc, 2 125cc)

CHRIS VERMEULEN
Born: 19 June, 1982 – Brisbane, Australia
GP Starts: 72 MotoGP
GP Wins: 1 MotoGP
World Championships: 1 World Supersport

Photos: Gold & Goose

SUZUKI started 2009 fielding two pertinent questions about its future. The first had serious ramifications for MotoGP, and was based on whether Suzuki would honour its contract with Dorna to be part of the World Championship until the end of 2011. The ink was barely dry on Kawasaki's withdrawal announcement when the focus immediately switched to Suzuki and whether it too would succumb to the global financial crisis.

In his new role as project manager, Shinichi Sahara confirmed that withdrawal had been discussed in meetings in Japan, but the answer was an emphatic no. Suzuki would not break its commitment to Dorna and abandon MotoGP.

Sahara was now the figurehead responsible for Suzuki's entire racing effort, World Superbikes as well as MotoGP. It was a role previously filled by Fumihiro Oohnishi. Former technical manager Sahara had a much less hands-on role in the paddock, although that would change as the season wore on.

The other question was how much of a threat would the new factory GSV-R pose, after Italian warhorse Loris Capirossi and Chris Vermeulen had ended the first winter test session in Malaysia impressively fast.

Predictions of a consistent podium challenge

SUZUKI GSV-R

Sponsors & Technical Suppliers: Bridgestone · Beta · 2D · Consultapartecipazioni.it · Crescent · Datapacific · Motul · Mitsubishi · Kokusan · Denki
Toyo Radiator · RK Chain · DID · Shock Doctor · NGK · AFAM · Puig Racing Screens · DAF · Dread · Blue Chip

Fuel: 21-litres · Wheelbase: 1450mm

Engine: Liquid-cooled 799cc DOHC 16v, 75 deg Vee-four. Cast crankcases and steel crankshaft with titanium rods. Pneumatic Valve Spring operation.

Electronics package: Mitsubishi ECU hardware and software to control throttle butterflies, fuelling, ignition timing and traction control.

Chassis: Aluminium beam frame. Aluminium swingarm with Link. Fully adjustable 42mm Ohlins TTx20 forks (Capirossi TTxTR 42mm Forks) and fully adjustable Ohlins TTx40TR rear shock.

Brakes: 2 x 320mm Carbon front discs with radially mounted four-piston Brembo calipers. 220mm rear disc with a twin piston Brembo caliper.

Tyres: Front 16.5-inch Bridgestone control slick on Marchesini wheel. Rear 16.5 Bridgestone control slick on Marchesini wheels.

didn't appear too outlandish, but the answer to that question made painful reading for Suzuki after the final race at Valencia. For the first time since 2004, it finished a MotoGP campaign without a single podium finish, and looked further from posing a threat to Yamaha and Ducati than ever before.

The quiet euphoria of the Sepang test was nothing more than a false dawn. The GSV-R only worked in a narrow range of performance. Veteran Capirossi and experienced crew chief Stuart Shenton did their best to unravel the problems of competing on the machine. But Capirossi had to settle for a best of fifth on four occasions, most notably in hot conditions. Suzuki's GSV-R was a reasonably competitive package in higher temperatures. But cool and cold conditions were its Achilles heel, and he ended the season in unforgettable fashion with a dismal 12th at Phillip Island and 14th at Valencia

Aussie Vermeulen, who remains Suzuki's lone four-stroke MotoGP winner, again worked with crew chief Tom O'Kane, but he struggled more than Capirossi and only saw the top six in three races, with a best of fifth at Assen. He was outside the top ten on seven occasions. The fact that he ended 2009 with the only 100-per-cent points scoring record was scant consolation.

As it became apparent that Suzuki was struggling to convert pre-season promise into solid results, Sahara was fast-tracked back into the fold, and at the final few races he was a permanent fixture in the paddock, desperate to get a handle on the issues and communicate to engineers in Japan.

The team itself remained under the stewardship of Briton Paul Denning, and there was only one change in staff, long-serving operations manager Howard Plumpton moving to the ill-fated Haojue 125GP project. In his place came former Team Roberts co-ordinator Charlie Moody.

Denning was now firmly established at the helm of Suzuki's factory effort, having served his apprenticeship in British Superbikes. In planning ahead for 2010, he managed to pull off a coup by signing a new two-year deal with title sponsor Rizla, whom he had first tempted into MotoGP from British Superbikes in 2006. That deal buried the rumour that Suzuki would quit, which had lingered long after Sahara's pre-season pledge of loyalty.

As always, Denning presented an articulate and powerful defence of what was undeniably a season of disappointment for Suzuki. It was beaten in the constructors' championship by two independent teams, and suffered the ignominy of being the only manufacturer to fall foul of new engine restrictions implemented at Brno.

Capirossi had used all five of his allocated engines by the race at Phillip Island, pursuit of performance having hit reliability. He started from the back of the grid, and Suzuki was docked ten points in the constructors' championship, which cost it fifth to the San Carlo Honda Gresini squad.

Capirossi remained stoic despite the lacklustre results, and he was rewarded with a new contract at Indianapolis, one that would give the evergreen Italian the chance to become the first rider to make 300 GP starts – he finished the year on 299.

Meanwhile, there was a mutual divorce with Vermeulen. He'd grown increasingly frustrated at being hamstrung by the underperforming GSV-R, which made it all the more perplexing when he jumped out of the frying pan and into the fire by signing a deal to join Kawasaki's World Superbike squad.

In his place came one of an exciting crop of rookies set to graduate into MotoGP in 2010. Spaniard Alvaro Bautista signed a two-year deal at Brno, the former 125 champion rejecting the opportunity to stay within Jorge 'Aspar' Martinez's stable.

Aspar planned to move to MotoGP with a fifth Ducati GP10, and he'd made his 250 star, Bautista, his number-one target. Once over his disappointment at Bautista's rejection, he signed Hector Barbera.

Above: Paul Denning ran the team again.

Above centre: Vermeulen at Assen.

Right: In the blue room: riders await the outcome of datalogging.

Top: Rizla Suzuki was the only MotoGP team to operate out of Britain.

Photos: Gold & Goose

SAN CARLO HONDA GRESINI

TEAM STAFF

Fausto GRESINI: Chairman and Managing Director
Carlo MERLINI: Commercial and Marketing Director
Fabrizio CECCHINI: Technical Director

ALEX DE ANGELIS PIT CREW

Antonio JIMENEZ: Chief Mechanic
Mechanics:
Andrea BONASSOLI
Ryoichi MORI
Alberto PRESUTTI
Maurizio VISANI: Spare parts co-ordinator
Diego GUBELLINI: Telemetry

TONI ELIAS PIT CREW

Fabrizio CECCHINI: Chief Mechanic
Mechanics:
Simone ALESSANDRINI
Ivan BRANDI
Marco Rosa GASTALDO
Renzo PINI (assistant)
Francesco FAVA: Telemetry

ALEX DE ANGELIS
Born: 2 February, 1984 – Rimini, Italy
GP Starts: 165 (35 MotoGP, 65 250cc, 65 125cc)
GP Wins: 1 250cc

TONI ELIAS
Born: 26 March, 1983 – Manresa, Spain
GP Starts: 162 (79 MotoGP, 48 250cc, 35 125cc)
GP Wins: 10 (1 MotoGP, 7 250cc, 2 125cc)

Photos: Gold & Goose

STARVED of success in recent years, Fausto Gresini's satellite Honda squad enjoyed a mini-revival of fortunes in 2009. The previous season had been the bleakest in nine years in MotoGP management for the former world 125GP champion, the Rimini based squad failing to collect a single podium finish. Two of them in 2009 represented small shoots of recovery, yet the team didn't flourish enough to save either Toni Elias or Alex de Angelis from the axe at the end of the season.

Gresini, who, when absent on the odd occasion, handed management duties to commercial and marketing director Carlo Merlini, has always prided himself on his close association with HRC. Sete Gibernau and Marco Melandri had both been benefactors of Gresini's close bond with Japan, having previously been afforded factory rider status in a satellite team.

The promise of an RC212V close to the spec of the bikes ridden by Repsol Honda pairing Dani Pedrosa and Andrea Dovizioso had convinced Elias to return to the team he had ridden for in 2006 and 2007. But the connection to HRC seemed more distant than ever, and by the end of the season, Elias was biting the hand that fed him, sniping at the lack of any meaningful technical support from the Japanese manufacturer.

HONDA RC212V

Sponsors and Technical Suppliers: San Carlo · Castrol · Bridgestone · Agos · Domino · Berner · Hilterapia · Leo Vince · Nissin · Tenax · TFC · Galileo · ZEX

Fuel: 21-litres · *Wheelbase:* 1440mm

Engine: Liquid-cooled 799cc, DOHC 16v, 77.5 deg (est) Vee-four. Cast crankcases and steel crankshaft with titanium rods. Pneumatic valve spring operation.

Electronics package: HRC ECU hardware and software to control throttle butterflies, fuelling, ignition timing and traction control.

Chassis: Aluminium beam frame. Aluminium swingarm with Pro Link rear linkage. Fully adjustable 47mm Showa 'Big Piston' forks and fully adjustable Showa rear shock.

Brakes: 2 x 320mm Carbon-carbon front discs with radially mounted four-piston Brembo calipers. 218mm HRC rear disc with a twin piston Brembo caliper.

Tyres: Front 16-5 inch Bridgestone control slick on Marchesini wheel. Rear 16.5 Bridgestone control slick on Marchesini wheel.

Working with crew chief Antonio Jimenez, Elias took a solitary podium at Brno, part of an impressive run of six top-ten finishes in the final ten races, but he didn't keep his job. Reluctant even to consider a switch to World Superbike, he was linked with the new Aspar Ducati squad, but seemed certain to find himself riding in the new Moto2 class, most likely for Gresini. The Italian will run bikes designed and built by Japanese tuning specialist Moriwaki.

On the opposite side of the garage, Alex de Angelis's rookie campaign had been blemished by a series of rash mistakes, and he was regarded as a hothead, drawing strong criticism from some of his peers. His 2009 season was arguably one of the biggest improvements in grand prix racing.

Working again with technical director and crew chief Fabrizio Cecchini, he finished in each of the first 12 races, which included a stunning purple patch mid-season. After only two top tens in the opening eight races, he placed fifth in Germany and fourth at Donington Park. His outstanding result came at the resplendent sporting arena of the Indianapolis Motor Speedway. The San Marino rider claimed a brilliant second, and he'd be fourth again at the technically demanding Phillip Island. But old habits die hard, and he was lucky that Nicky Hayden's common sense overwhelmed his outrage when de Angelis wiped out the Kentucky rider and Colin Edwards at the first corner at Misano.

De Angelis also would not keep his ride, but at least he and Elias were put out of their misery relatively early. One of them clearly had to go when, as early as Assen, Gresini ended a period of intense speculation by confirming that he had won the race to capture the prized signature of Marco Simoncelli. The second berth was taken by Melandri on the eve of the German GP.

The extravagantly Hendrix-maned Italian was an important prize. He had been courted by Pramac Ducati and Monster Yamaha Tech 3, despite a high price tag. Reluctant to lose another promising young talent, HRC intervened. Honda had lost Stoner to run riot at Ducati, while Yamaha had poached Lorenzo long before his premier-class debut in 2008.

Simoncelli signed a lucrative contract direct with HRC, many expressing shock at the inflated fee for a rookie, at a time when rider salaries were expected to plummet to counter the global recession.

Crucially for Gresini, Simoncelli's new deal coincided with the renewal of a title sponsorship agreement with San Carlo. The Italian snack food manufacturer had moved from associate sponsor to lead backer in 2008, and the signing of the instantly recognisable Simoncelli helped negotiations for 2010.

Gresini would also welcome back Marco Melandri who in 2005, while under Gresini's wing, finished second in the world championship.

Above: Director Carlo Merlini stands with Gresini at the team's centre.

Left: Fausto Gresini, himself a former champion.

Photos: Gold & Goose

Above: Toni Elias gave the team a podium at Brno.

Left: Alex de Angelis and crew chief Jimenez confer with their data technician (right).

Photos: Gold & Goose

PRAMAC DUCATI

TEAM STAFF

Paolo CAMPINOTI: Team Principal

Fabiano STERLACCHINI: Technical Director

Felix RODRIGUEZ: Team Co-ordinator

Matteo VITELLO: Communication Manager

MIKA KALLIO/ALEIX ESPARGARO PIT CREW

Fabiano STERLACCHINI: Track Engineer

Michele ANDREINI: Chief Mechanic

Mechanics:

Paul RUIZ

Pedro RIVERA

Leonardo GENA (tyres)

David MASSARIN: Data Engineer

NICCOLÒ CANEPA PIT CREW

Sergio VERBENA: Track Engineer

Michele PERUGINI: Chief Mechanic

Mechanics:

Guglielmi ANDREINI

David LOPEZ CACHEDA

Francesco GALINDO (tyres)

Alberto GIRIBUOLA: Data Engineer

MIKA KALLIO

Born: 8 November, 1982 – Valkeakoski, Finland

GP Starts: 131 (16 MotoGP, 33 250cc, 62 125cc)

GP Wins: 12 (5 250cc, 7 125cc)

NICCOLO CANEPA

Born: 14 May, 1988 – Genoa, Italy

GP Starts: 14 MotoGP

Photos: Gold & Goose

DUCATI'S satellite team underwent yet another name change as it turned to youth and potential to build on a controversial, but promising 2008 campaign.

Having previously been Pramac d'Antin, Team d'Antin Pramac and most recently Alice Ducati, the team would be known as Pramac Racing in 2009. The sudden and unsavoury departure of former Spanish figurehead Luis d'Antin in mid-2008 had seen his name instantly blacklisted. And the loss of Italian telecommunications giant Alice as title sponsor forced Pramac CEO Paolo Campinoti into another rebranding exercise.

Campinoti went under the official title of team principal, but again Pramac was more than just title sponsor. It owned the squad, which quit Madrid for a new Italian base.

The signing of 125 and 250 nearly-man Mika Kallio and the relatively unknown Niccolò Canepa marked a shift in Campinoti's rider recruitment policy. Seasoned campaigners like Alex Barros, Alex Hofmann and Toni Elias had been previous Pramac incumbents. But faith in youth had been as much Ducati's desire as Campinoti's, the Bologna factory being eager to nurture young talent at Pramac with a view to a future move to its factory team.

Kallio would have the benefit of vastly experienced Fabiano Sterlacchini as his crew chief. Sterlacchini was also the technical director, and in addition he would act as a sounding board for Canepa and his

DUCATI DESMOSEDICI D16-09

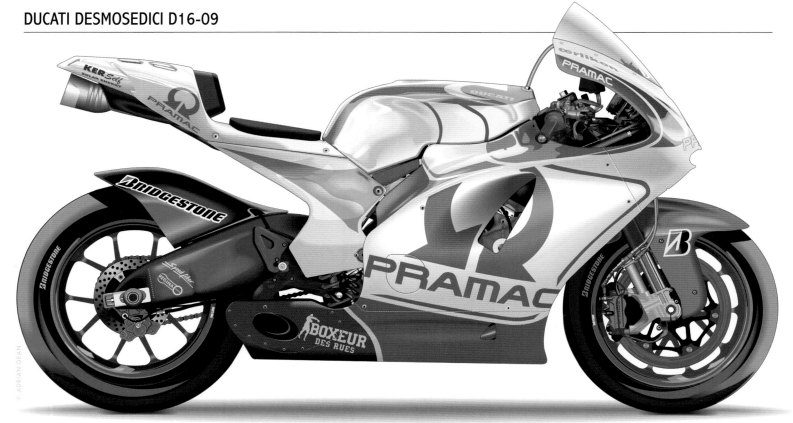

Major Sponsors & Technical Suppliers: Pramac · Kerself · Beta · Regina Chains · Flex · Puma · Bel Ray · Bridgestone

Fuel: 21-litres Wheelbase: N/A

Engine: Liquid-cooled 799cc DOHC 16v, 90 deg Vee-four. Sand-cast crankcases and steel crankshaft with titanium rods. Desmodromic Valve operation.

Electronics package: Marelli MRE ECU hardware and Ducati software to control throttle butterflies, fuelling, ignition timing and traction control.

Chassis: Carbon 'Stressed Airbox' frame attaching in the Vee of the engine. Aluminium/Carbon swingarm with Soft damp rear linkage. Fully adjustable 42mm Ohlins TTx25 forks and fully adjustable Ohlins TTx40TR rear shock,

Brakes: 2 x 320mm Carbon-carbon front discs with radially mounted four-piston Brembo calipers. 200mm rear disc with a twin piston Brembo caliper.

Tyres: Front 16.5-inch Bridgestone control slick on Marchesini wheel. Rear 16.5 Bridgestone control slick on Marchesini wheels.

ALEIX ESPARGARO
Born: 30 July, 1989 – Granoliers, Spain
GP Starts: 71 (4 MotoGP, 44 250cc, 23 125cc)

MICHEL FABRIZIO
Born: 17 September, 1984 – Rome, Italy
GP Starts: 28 (12 MotoGP, 16 125cc)

Below: : Paolo Campinoti.
Photo: Gold & Goose

chief engineer, Marco Rigamonti.

Felix Rodriguez reverted to his familiar role of team co-ordinator, having been elevated into the role of team manager following d'Antin's abrupt exit in 2008.

Pramac certainly benefited from stability, although it would be subjected to yet more upheaval, and once again this would not be self-inflicted disruption.

Deadpan Kallio instantly caught the attention on the finicky GP9 with eighth places in Qatar and Japan. By Assen, he was easily outscoring a woefully out-of-sorts Hayden, but when poised for a brilliant sixth, he crashed on the last lap and was left with a gruesome injury. Most of the top of his wedding-ring finger had been ground away, and he would miss Laguna Seca.

It was a physical issue that nobody could see that would impact on Pramac for the next three races. Casey Stoner's decision to miss Brno, Indianapolis and Misano because of a chronic fatigue issue led to Kallio being seconded to the factory team as the Australian's substitute.

Kallio scored his best rookie-campaign result at Misano with a creditable seventh, and he signed to stay at Pramac for 2010 at the next race in Portugal.

While the Finnish rider was trying to fill the huge void left by Stoner's absence, Campinoti drafted in Michel Fabrizio for Brno, but Ducati's factory World Superbike rider was never remotely competitive, and he retired from the race with a shoulder injury.

Mattia Pasini had tested for Pramac at the post-race test at Brno, and he would do so again in a behind-closed-doors session at Mugello in September. But then came a rags-to-riches story worthy of Hollywood. Aleix Espargaro had started 2009 without a ride, yet he ended it preparing to compete in arguably the highest calibre MotoGP field ever in 2010. The elder brother of the 125 rider replaced Kallio at Indianapolis and Misano, and scored a best of 11th. His Misano result seemed unspectacular, but upon closer inspection, he'd clocked the fifth fastest lap of the race, bested only by Rossi, Lorenzo, Pedrosa and Dovizioso.

Soon after the Portuguese race at Estoril, he was confirmed as Canepa's 2010 replacement.

Canepa's elevation from Ducati test rider in 2008 meant that he came with plenty of experience of the Desmosedici GP9. He was also under the wing of Carlo Pernat, one of the paddock's shrewdest operators. Pernat had managed Max Biaggi at Aprilia, and now had Loris Capirossi and Marco Simoncelli in his stable – so he has an eye for talent. But Canepa's only top tens came in the lottery of the Mugello flag-to-flag clash and the perilously damp conditions at Donington.

Having learned that his contract would not be renewed after Estoril, the Italian didn't race again. A high-speed crash in practice at Phillip Island's mer-

ciless first corner left him with a severe puncture wound to his right forearm.

Espargaro was hauled back again, and he finished 11th and 13th. Canepa signed to join the new Scot Moto2 team two weeks after the season's conclusion.

Above: Canepa debriefs in the box.

Above centre: Kallio would impress from the start.
Photos: Gold & Goose

LCR HONDA

LUCIO Cecchinello's fourth season at the helm of his LCR Honda squad was easily the best since his premier-class debut in 2006, when the Italian unleashed Casey Stoner's precocious talent on MotoGP.

French rider Randy de Puniet scored the Monaco based squad's first rostrum since Stoner, when he completed an unlikely podium behind Andrea Dovizioso and Colin Edwards at the British GP at Donington Park.

And in the midst of a global recession, Cecchinello's budget was saved the pounding it had previously received as de Puniet finally cast off his reputation as a prolific crasher. For the previous three seasons, he had been a one-man demolition squad, having topped the crasher league every year between 2006 and 2008.

His confidence restored by Bridgestone's front tyre, de Puniet scored points in all but two races, although with the exception of his Donington heroics and a spirited ride to fourth at Jerez, for the most part he was a peripheral figure, six times outside the top ten.

Eleventh overall was also the best by an LCR Honda rider since Stoner.

Cecchinello is a highly respected and loyal figure in MotoGP, and his close-knit team remained largely intact from 2008.

Christophe 'Beefy' Bourgignon remained as crew chief, the only notable personnel change being the departure of Hamish Jamieson as chassis and suspension engineer. Former Team Roberts data specialist Brian Harden was also an addition to the squad, in place of Manolo Zafferani.

Cecchinello has also proved himself an astute businessman, and while the credit crunch was sucking money out of the sport, he pulled off a massive investment coup. Most teams were bemoaning the loss of sponsors, or the lack of new ones, in MotoGP. Yet Cecchinello struck a deal with Playboy, one of the most recognisable brands in the world, shortly before the start of the season.

At several races, the famous glamour magazine acted as title sponsor, although strict censorship ruled out deals for Qatar and Malaysia.

When Playboy didn't take up the title sponsor role, Cecchinello turned to a tried and trusted policy for generating revenue. He'd previously showcased a rotation system whereby sponsors could select key markets for which to gain maximum exposure. Radio Monte Carlo, Elettronica Discount and Givi all assumed the role of title sponsor at selected races.

Cecchinello abandoned plans to expand his operation to the new Moto2 class in 2010, instead preferring to dedicate his time and budget to MotoGP. He talked extensively with Marco Melandri and his manager, Alberto Vergani, before signing a new contract with de Puniet during the late summer break in September.

Photos: Gold & Goose

RANDY DE PUNIET

Born: 14 February, 1981 – Maisons Laffitte, France

GP Starts: 183 (70 MotoGP, 80 250cc, 33 125cc)

GP Wins: 5 250cc

TEAM STAFF

Lucio CECCHINELLO: Team Manager
Oscar HARO: PR
Elisa PAVAN: Press Relations and Logistics

RANDY DE PUNIET PIT CREW

Christophe BOURGIGNON: Chief Engineer
Mechanics:
Joan CASAS
Casanovas XAVIER
Chris RICHARDSON
Brian HARDEN: Telemetry
Tomonori SATO: HRC engineer
Ugo GELMI: Tyres
Steve JENKNER: Bridgestone technician

HONDA RCV212V

Major Sponsors and Technical Suppliers: Playboy · Eurobet · Givi · TS · Vision · Elettronica Discount · Dinamica · Elf · VIAR

Fuel: 21-litres · *Wheelbase:* 1440mm

Engine: Liquid-cooled 799cc, DOHC 16v, 77.5 deg (TBC) Vee-four. Cast crankcases and steel crankshaft with titanium rods. Pneumatic valve spring operation.

Electronics package: HRC ECU hardware and software to control throttle butterflies, fuelling, ignition timing and traction control.

Chassis: Aluminium beam frame. Aluminium swingarm with Pro Link rear linkage. Fully adjustable 47mm Showa 'Big Piston' forks and fully adjustable Showa rear shock.

Brakes: 2 x 320mm Carbon-carbon front discs with radially mounted four-piston Brembo calipers. 218mm HRC rear disc with a twin piston Brembo caliper.

Tyres: Front 16-5 inch Bridgestone control slick on Marchesini wheel. Rear 16.5 Bridgestone control slick on Marchesini wheel.

SCOT Honda had proven that a satellite team could still prosper in MotoGP following Dovizioso's eye-catching rookie campaign in 2008. Twelve months later though and the Scot squad had followed Kawasaki and Grupo Francesco Hernandez to become another high profile victim of the global economic crisis, crippled by the financial burden of competing in MotoGP. The bleak economic downturn had ravaged the worldwide construction industry and Italian-based Scot Costruzioni suffered too.

Team owner Cirano Mularoni and new Sporting Director Alberto Martinelli fought a long and tireless battle for survival ... until Mularoni released a statement confirming the demise of his MotoGP squad shortly after the final race.

With Dovizioso gone to the factory team, Mularoni's fight for survival off the track was severely hampered by results on it.

He had courted favour with Honda by signing Japanese rider Yuki Takahashi for 2009. Hirano Yutaka was one of the few survivors of a 2007 merger and subsequent hostile split between Mularoni and JiR boss Gianluca Montiron at the end of 2008, and acted as chief mechanic.

Working under the supervision of Technical Director Emanuele Ventura, it was a baptism of fire for Takahashi. He blotted his copybook in front of HRC hierarchy with a first lap crash at the Twin Ring Motegi. When he did the same at Catalunya, his future was already in doubt.

At the same race that Mularoni had sought to ease the financial woes by signing an unlikely deal with Gabor Talmacsi. The Hungarian former 125 champion had split acrimoniously with "Aspar" Mar-

tinez just three races into a two-year 250 contract. Significantly he had serious financial clout behind him, from Hungarian oil giant MOL.

Honda had been willing to supply parts for both Talmacsi and Takahashi to ride in a two-man squad. But in spite of the MOL investment, the team had resources enough for only one rider, and Takahashi was released before the US GP at Laguna Seca.

Hopes that Talmacsi would galvanise the team's fortunes and attract additional Eastern Europe investment were quickly crushed. The former world 125GP champion did score points in eight of the last nine races, but none of his finishes was higher than 12th in treacherous conditions at Donington Park.

While it was abundantly obvious that Talmacsi was out of his depth, Mularoni and Scot looked certain to sink.

Honda had been willing to support MotoGP by adding a seventh bike for 2010, and new boss Shuhei Nakamoto was sympathetic to Mularoni's plight, extending the order deadline beyond August. At the same time Alex de Angelis, desperate to keep his MotoGP place, came close to finding the necessary investment from the San Marino government. But it fell through, and by the final GP at Valencia Honda's patience had expired. Both de Angelis and fellow Gresini Honda cast off Elias had both failed to unearth the funding needed to secure the ride.

So Scot was out of MotoGP, but had won a pulsating last-ever 250 title with Hiroshi Aoyama. That rider was bound for MotoGP with a new team founded by Swiss 250 Emmi Caffe-Latte team owner Daniel Epp; Mularoni will now focus on a Moto2 effort, with Ventura acting as Project Leader.

SCOT HONDA

Photos: Gold & Goose

GABOR TALMACSI	YUKI TAKAHASHI
Born: 28 May, 1981	Born: 12 July, 1984
Budapest, Hungary	Saitama, Japan
GP Starts: 145 (12 MotoGP,	GP Starts: 73 (7 MotoGP,
3 250cc, 130 125cc	65 250cc, 1 125cc)
GP Wins: 9 125cc	GP Wins: 2 250cc
World Championships: 1 125cc	

TEAM STAFF

Cirano MULARONI : Team manager
Alberto MARTINELLI: Sporting director
Stefano BEDO: Marketing and communications
Raffaelle GIANOLLA: Logistic and Press

YUKI TAKAHASHI/GABOR TALMACSI PIT CREW

Hirano YUTAKA: Chief mechanic
Mechanics: Fabio ROVELLI, Claudio EUSEBI,
Fabio GAROIA
Bernard MARTIGNAC: Data recording
Elena GALLINA: Spare parts
Rafaelle SBROCCA: Tyres and fuel

HONDA RCV212V

Major Sponsors and Technical Suppliers: MOL · Effegibi · GZ Packaging · HRC · Bridgestone

Fuel: 21-litres · *Wheelbase:* 1440mm

Engine: Liquid-cooled 799cc, DOHC 16v, 77.5 deg (TBC) Vee-four. Cast crankcases and steel crankshaft with titanium rods. Pneumatic valve spring operation.

Electronics package: HRC ECU hardware and software to control throttle butterflies, fuelling, ignition timing and traction control.

Chassis: Aluminium beam frame. Aluminium swingarm with Pro Link rear linkage. Fully adjustable 47mm Showa 'Big Piston' forks and fully adjustable Showa rear shock.

Brakes: 2 x 320mm Carbon-carbon front discs with radially mounted four-piston Brembo calipers. 218mm HRC rear disc with a twin piston Brembo caliper.

Tyres: Front 16-5 inch Bridgestone control slick on Marchesini wheel. Rear 16.5 Bridgestone control slick on Marchesini wheel.

HAYATE RACING TEAM

MARCO MELANDRI
Born: 7 August, 1982 – Ravenna, Italy
GP Starts: 190 (114 MotoGP, 47 250cc, 29 125cc)
GP Wins: 22 (5 MotoGP, 10 250cc, 7 125cc)
World Championships: 1 250cc

TEAM STAFF

Andrea DOSOLI (above): Team Manager/Crew Chief

Danilo CASONATO: EFI Engineer

Marcel DUINKER: Suspension Engineer

Robert KLEINHERENBRINK – Parts and Logistics

Jason CORNEY: Workshop/Parts and Logistics

Gerold BUCHER: Telemetry

Jasja BOS – Team Co-ordinator

Mechanics:

Pedro CALVET – First Mechanic

Emanuel BUCHNER

Jerome GALLAND

Alex DUINKER

Photos: Gold & Goose

KAWASAKI ZX-RR 2009

© ADRIAN DEAN

Sponsors & Technical Suppliers: Bridgestone · Akrapovic · NGK · 2D · Magneti Marelli · Regina Chains · MRA motorcycle windshields · Beta · Afam

Fuel: 21-litres · Wheelbase: 1460mm

Engine: Liquid-cooled 798cc DOHC 16v, in line four cylinder. Cast crankcases and steel crankshaft with titanium rods. Pneumatic Valve Spring operation.

Electronics package: Marelli ECU hardware and Kawasaki software to control throttle butterflies, fuelling, ignition timing and traction control.

Chassis: Aluminium beam frame. Aluminium swingarm with Unit-trak. Fully adjustable 42mm Ohlins TTx25 forks and fully adjustable Ohlins TTx36 rear shock,

Brakes: 2 x 314mm Carbon front discs with radially mounted four-piston Brembo calipers. 220mm rear disc with a twin piston Brembo caliper.

Tyres: Front 16.5-inch Bridgestone control slick on JB Magtan wheel. Rear 16.5 Bridgestone control slick on JB Magtan wheel.

THE Hayate Racing Team began the 2009 season (at the 2008 tests) as Kawasaki's full factory MotoGP effort. Two of racing's bigger names, John Hopkins and Marco Melandri, were expected to be part of it.

A flurry of rumours emerged shortly after Christmas, however, that Kawasaki was to quit after six years in MotoGP. And January wasn't even halfway over when Kawasaki made it official. The first high-profile casualty of the global financial meltdown would quit MotoGP with immediate effect.

The dramatic decision sent MotoGP into a state of panic. Kawasaki's withdrawal would see an already wafer-thin grid reduced even further, and it was feared that the decision might be the catalyst for other departures. Dorna CEO Carmelo Ezpeleta flew to Japan for crisis talks, not least to remind Kawasaki that it would face a penalty of close to £20m if it didn't honour its commitment to supply at least two bikes until the end of 2011.

Behind the scenes, competition manager Michael Bartholemy was working frantically on a rescue package. At the same time, tests of the new 2009 machine had gone ahead in Australia, with former rider Olivier Jacque in the testing role. But Kawasaki's management had made up their minds – there would be no going back.

To avoid the hefty financial penalty from Dorna for breach of contract, a compromise was hastily agreed shortly before the start of the season. Kawasaki would supply one of its factory ZX-RR machines and offer technical support for the first couple of races. After that, it would cease to be involved, apart from supplying spare parts for the new team to complete the 17-round season.

It wasn't until the pre-season night test in Qatar that the mystery unravelled. The new team would be known as Hayate Racing and would be run by former Kawasaki staff, all of whom had had their 2009 contracts paid in full when Kawasaki pulled the plug. And the bike would no longer be run in striking green, but in funereal black. Incidentally, Hayate means 'strong wind' or 'hurricane' in Japanese.

Bartholemy had gone and so too had technical manager Naoya Kaneko. Prominent in the Hayate deal was Kawasaki racing director Ichiro Yoda. Unlike in previous years, though, he took a back seat and never spoke to the media. Project leader Yoshimoto Matsuda also retained minimal involvement.

The public face of the team was now Andrea Dosoli. Previously an electronics specialist, he would fill the dual role of crew chief and team manager. Former Kawasaki employee Jasja Bos undertook the role of team co-ordinator.

Hopkins turned down the chance to be the rider and, after a torrid and injury-hit 2008, his career would freefall after a failed move to World Superbikes.

For Melandri, the Kawasaki collapse had piled on the agony. He'd been castigated and written off after a disastrous 2008 with Ducati. Kawasaki had offered him salvation, only for it to be taken away again. He arrived for the Qatar test insisting that he hadn't agreed to ride the bike. He would test at Qatar and Jerez, and then make his decision.

With no alternative to the rebranded Kawasaki, however, he did agree to ride, starting superbly. Two top-six finishes in the first three races were followed by a stunning second in the Le Mans wet-to-dry, flag-to-flag race.

That was as good as it got, though, and for the rest of the season, Melandri would have to be content with a best of seventh, the lack of upgrades stagnating development while every other bike benefited from new parts. Hopes that the early promise would convince Kawasaki into a major rethink were quickly shrugged aside, and at the German GP Melandri agreed to rejoin Gresini Honda.

Dosoli embarked on a fund-raising mission to lease Yamaha engines to keep the Hayate name going. By the end of September, he'd abandoned that ambitious scheme and settled on Hayate entering the new Moto2 600cc four-stroke class.

GRUPO FRANCISCO HERNANDO

AFTER the loss of Kawasaki, the recession hit again in early July with the sudden demise of the new Grupo Francisco Hernando Ducati squad after just eight races.

Formed at the end of 2008 in a blaze of publicity, the team was bankrolled by Spanish property tycoon Francisco Hernando, and heralded a surprise return to racing for former factory Honda, Suzuki and Ducati rider Sete Gibernau, out of racing at the end of an injury-ravaged 2006.

At the helm was highly respected 125GP stalwart Pablo Nieto and his brother Gelete, sons of legendary Spanish racer Angel Nieto.

The season started in confusion, particularly surrounding the title sponsor.

At the start Gibernau's GP9 was emblazoned with logos of Equatorial Guinea, a tiny nation in West Africa. The former Spanish colony is run by dictator Teodoro Obiang Nguema Mbasogo, described by various human rights organisations as among the worst abusers of in Africa, and such a collaboration seemed bizarre in the extreme.

Without any official reason, the logos disappeared early in the season. Then a once booming Spanish property market was crippled by the financial turndown, and Hernando shut the team down with immediate effect after the American MotoGP race in Laguna Seca.

Not even the legendary Nieto name nor Gibernau's marketing clout in Spain could find fresh investment. Gibernau had struggled to recapture the form that once made him the chief nemesis of Valentino Rossi, and did not score a single top ten finish to help with the search for alternative backing.

His best was 11th at Jerez before his left shoulder, severely weakened since the infamous first corner pile-up in Catalunya in 2006, gave way again after a slow speed high-side in Le Mans. He missed the French and Italian races and his last MotoGP action was a crash in Laguna Seca.

STERILGARDA YAMAHA

BEN SPIES wasn't long into a record-breaking rookie World Superbike campaign when it became obvious that Yamaha was infatuated with the Texan, and the company left it to the rider to decide whether to stay in World Superbikes or move to MotoGP.

He decided in early October to join Edwards for an all-Texas line- at Tech 3 in early October, and his influence was such that Yamaha agreed to supply a fifth M1 for the triple American Superbike champion at Valencia.

With the massive reduction in winter testing, Spies was desperate for as much seat time as possible.

It was rumoured that American basketball legend Michael Jordan, who has run his own team in the domestic US series, had bankrolled the deal. It later became apparent that Sterilgarda, an Italian dairy products giant, was financing the majority of it. Sterilgarda had quickly identified Spies's potential and signed up as sponsor of his World Superbike team in May, even though it was already title sponsor of Shane Byrne's Ducati squad.

Spies's race entry was effectively supported by his entire World Superbike crew in Valencia, with Massimo Meregalli at the helm of the squad.

The Valencia race also gave Spies' long-serving crew chief Tom Houseworth and mechanic Greg 'Woody' Wood chance for them to acclimatise to the YZR-M1. Both will be joining Spies in the Tech 3 pit next year, at his behest.

Valencia was Spies' fourth MotoGP appearance – his previous three had been on a factory Suzuki GSV-R - and he distinguished himself with an impressive ride to seventh

HECTOR BARBERA   HIROSHI AOYAMA   ALVARO BAUTISTA

MARCO SIMONCELLI   HECTOR FAUBEL   SHOYA TOMIZAWA

KAREL ABRAHAM   ALEX BALDOLINI   VALENTIN DEBISE

250cc: FINAL CURTAIN

THE 250 class was one of the foundation stones of the original World Championship of 1949. It started 2009 under sentence of death in two years, only for execution to be brought forward by 12 months. Thus, 2009 rather than 2010 was the final year of the classic quarter-litre class.

Considering a grid of just 24, and a big gap between the chosen ones with top-ten potential and the level of some privateers, the elements of a wasting disease were there to see. There was strength at the top end, but very little in depth.

When KTM withdrew at the end of the 2008 season, it left the prospect of an almost all-Aprilia grid. There had been only one Yamaha in 2008, from Indonesia, and the team did not return. Honda's interest and involvement had dwindled in recent years, with just two on the grid in 2008, and then somewhat grudgingly. But Honda obviously felt some obligation (a guilty conscience?) to prevent the class from becoming a one-make series, and boosted numbers to seven. As in recent years, none was a full factory effort; the machines were little changed RS250-Ws.

The rest, all 17 of them, were Aprilias, of widely differing standards and vintages. Nine riders had the latest RSA machines, two of them (those closest to the factory) wearing Gilera badges. The remainder rode previous-generation LE models.

There was a preponderance of Spanish and Italian

spoken in the 250 paddock. Almost half the riders came from those Latin countries, five each. Japan and France had three apiece on the grid; two each from the Czech Republic, Hungary and Switzerland were joined by one Thai and one Russian – technically, Vladimir Leonov was the first Russian in the class, since the few previous entrants had been Soviets.

The youngest in the class, three 17-year-olds, were half the age of the oldest rider. He was Roberto Locatelli (34); the youngest was French Honda rider Valentin Debise, who turned 17 two months before the season began (all ages as at first race).

HONDA

Honda's senior rider was Hiro Aoyama (27), rather surprisingly welcomed back by the manufacturer after three years with KTM, with whom he gained four of his five wins. With the senior team, too: Scot Honda had a strong record in the class with Andrea Dovizioso. His team-mate, up from 125s, was Italian Raffaele de Rosa (22).

Sag Honda had two entries, with Thai hope Ratthapark Wilairot (20) back again, after becoming a top-ten regular in 2008. He would continue to gain strength. His team-mate was experienced ex-125 Spaniard Hector Faubel.

Racing Team Germany ran with 17-year-old Swiss rookie Bastian Chesaux until Misano, when he was replaced

by the younger Aoyama brother, Shuhei, the 24-year-old making a return to GPs. Chesaux took up a second entry on an Aprilia, with the Matteoni team.

The French Team CIP was also a two-rider squad, with a pair of rookies: youngster Debise and an 18-year-old newcomer from Japan, Shoya Tomizawa, who had some promising runs.

GILERA

The defending champion, Marco Simoncelli, had started 2008 without the latest factory machine. For 2009, he was the factory's top rider from the start. The 22-year-old was joined by Locatelli. Both Gileras were to RSA spec.

APRILIA

The highest-profile non-factory team was the large and highly professional Mapfre Aspar team, run by former 80/125cc multi-champion Jorge Martinez (he and his senior staffers would change shirts after the 125 race, where the sponsor was Bancaja). Alvaro Bautista (24) was runner-up in 2008, and the cheerful Spaniard was one of the favourites, on a full RSA. His team-mate was reigning 125 champion Mike di Meglio (21). The Frenchman started the season with an LE model, but was given the use of an RSA from round four, his home GP, onwards.

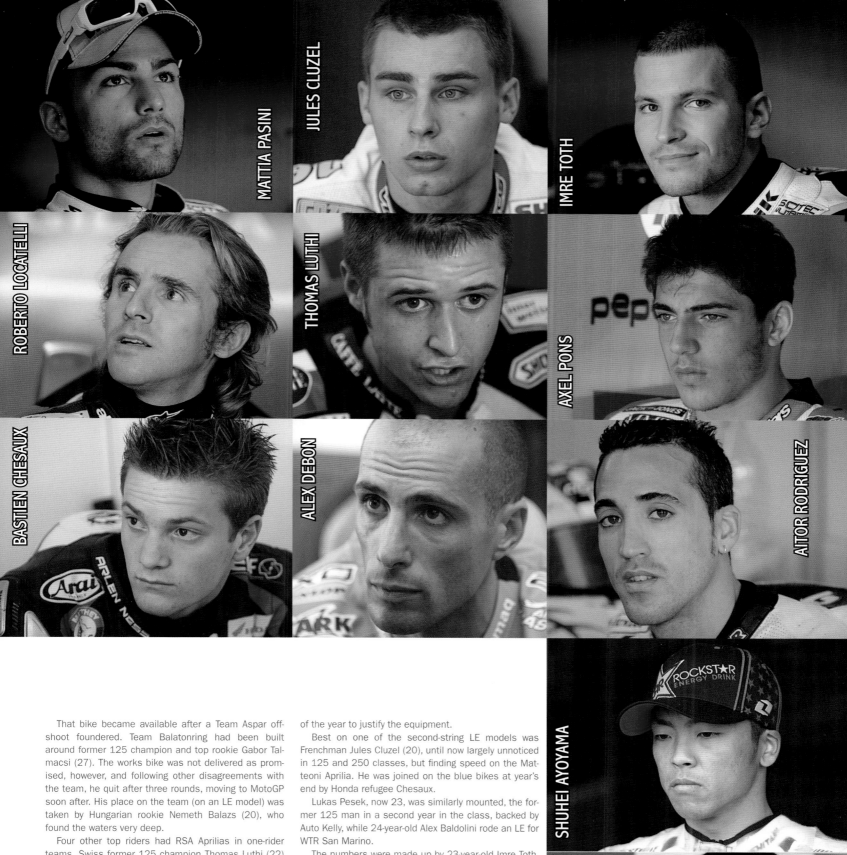

MATTIA PASINI

JULES CLUZEL

IMRE TOTH

ROBERTO LOCATELLI

THOMAS LUTHI

AXEL PONS

BASTIEN CHESAUX

ALEX DEBON

AITOR RODRIGUEZ

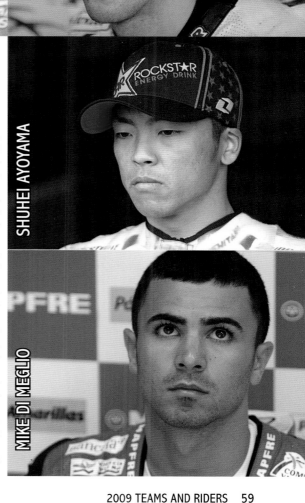

SHUHEI AYOYAMA

MIKE DI MEGLIO

That bike became available after a Team Aspar off-shoot foundered. Team Balatonring had been built around former 125 champion and top rookie Gabor Talmacsi (27). The works bike was not delivered as promised, however, and following other disagreements with the team, he quit after three rounds, moving to MotoGP soon after. His place on the team (on an LE model) was taken by Hungarian rookie Nemeth Balazs (20), who found the waters very deep.

Four other top riders had RSA Aprilias in one-rider teams. Swiss former 125 champion Thomas Luthi (22) was back for a disappointing year with the same Emmi Caffe Latte team. More success awaited Spaniard Hector Barbera (22), with former champion Sito Pons's new Pepe World Pons team.

The third was Italian tough guy Mattia Pasini (23), whose 2008 Polaris World team had been a victim of the credit crisis. He was picked up by Hungarian-run Team Toth, but after struggling financially for most of the year, the squad finally ran out of funds, leaving Pasini to complete the last four races as a semi-independent.

The last potential winner on a top Aprilia was Alex Debon, and the 32-year-old Spaniard only just made it – his one-rider Blusens team found backing at the very last moment from the new Aeropuerto Castello under construction close to his birthplace of Vall d'Uixó.

The last of the RSAs went to Czech rider Karel Abraham (19), who moved up the order somewhat at the end

of the year to justify the equipment.

Best on one of the second-string LE models was Frenchman Jules Cluzel (20), until now largely unnoticed in 125 and 250 classes, but finding speed on the Matteoni Aprilia. He was joined on the blue bikes at year's end by Honda refugee Chesaux.

Lukas Pesek, now 23, was similarly mounted, the former 125 man in a second year in the class, backed by Auto Kelly, while 24-year-old Alex Baldolini rode an LE for WTR San Marino.

The numbers were made up by 23-year-old Imre Toth, son of Team Toth owner, also Imre, and two rookies. One was the son of another team owner: 17-year-old Axel Pons rode alongside Barbera for his father, Sito, a double 250 champion. Vladimir Leonov (21), with Russian backing, joined the German Viesman Team Kiefer.

Two riders were out of luck. Aleix Espargaro (19) was due to ride for the long-standing Campetella team, but it was withdrawn before the first race. The Spaniard rode once as wild-card for Team Balatonring in Germany before being head-hunted as a MotoGP sub at the end of the season. The other was American Stevie Bonsey, up from 125s, but the 19-year-old's Team Madrid also didn't make the first race. While he was recruited to replace Spanish rookie Aitor Rodriguez (24) for the Milar Lucky Juegos team at Catalunya and Assen, that Spanish outfit also promptly ran out of money.

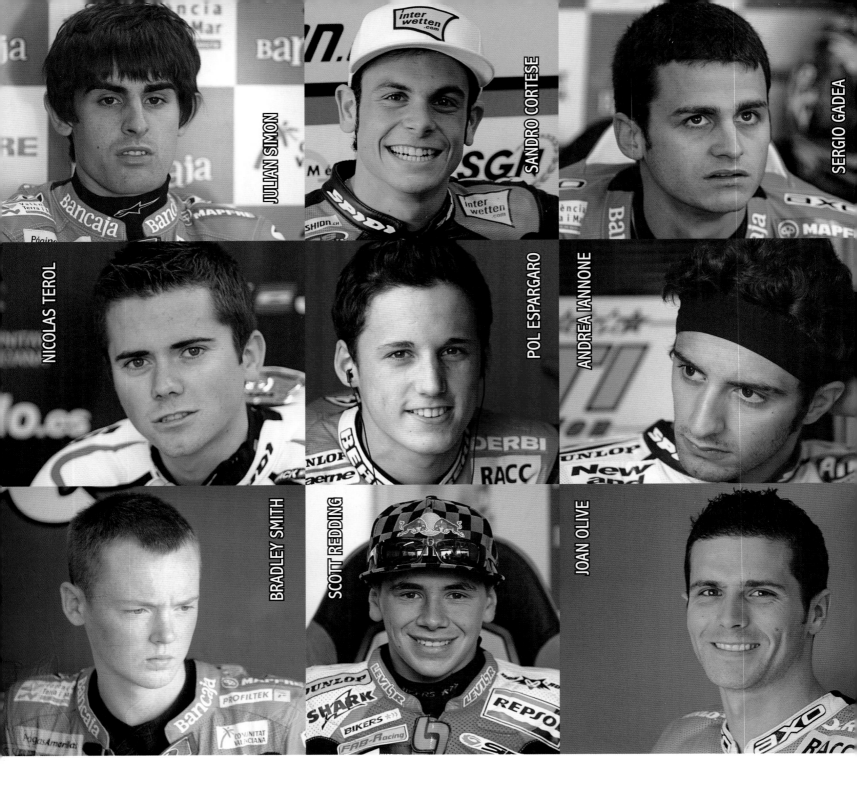

JULIAN SIMON

SANDRO CORTESE

SERGIO GADEA

NICOLAS TEROL

POL ESPARGARO

ANDREA IANNONE

BRADLEY SMITH

SCOTT REDDING

JOAN OLIVE

125cc: STILL BOOMING

IN spite of a cutback here as well by KTM – down from seven machines to just two – and an even greater preponderance of Aprilias and the identical Derbis, the year started with hopes of growing new interest, with the Chinese backed Loncins (née Malaguti, née Honda) now joined by the all-new Maxtra.

The new machine had an engine penned by former Aprilia chief designer and two-stroke luminary Jan Witteveen, a chassis by British specialist Harris Performance, and a team whose figurehead was bike and car racing legend John Surtees, and which was run by ex-Suzuki MotoGP team manager Garry Taylor. The omens were bad, though, for a French company claimed prior rights to the made-up Maxtra name, forcing a late change to Chinese brand Haojue.

What sabotaged the team, however, was the dismal performance of the engine, which was also dangerously unreliable. The effort foundered when backing to source a different (KTM) engine was denied, and the riders were released after five races. Austrian Michael Ranseder

(23) found a berth with the CBC Corse team for the final races, but ex-Red Bull rookie Matthew Hoyle (18) was left in limbo.

This still left a booming grid, with a permanent entry list of 31 surviving the year, frequently swelled by several wild-cards.

The class was very Spanish: nine on the grid, four of whom finished in the top five overall, including first. Italy had five full-timers, Germany four. There would have been four Britons as well, until the departure of Hoyle left three: Bradley Smith, Scott Redding and Danny Webb. The numbers were made up by two each from Japan, Switzerland and France, and singletons from Austria, the Czech Republic, the Netherlands and the USA.

APRILIA/DERBI

As with the 250s, the Aprilia/Derbi ranks covered machines from the latest, expensively fettled skew-disc models to older privateer bikes of varying quality

and provenance.

The best-equipped private teams were on a par with the three-strong Derbi Racing squad. This all-Spanish trio included veteran Joan Olive (24) and Efren Vazquez, still a relative rookie at 22, with one 250 and one 125 season behind him. The strongest was 17-year-old Pol Espargaro, who added two fine wins to a good third season.

The leading team, however, was 'Aspar' Martinez's Bancaja squad: three-strong and set to dominate. Julian Simon (22, from Spain) was back from 250s and KTM; Briton Bradley Smith was in his fourth season, at 18; Spaniard Sergio Gadea (24) was the oldest member. All would win races, and Simon the title.

Another strong Spanish effort came from the Jack & Jones team. Nicolas Terol (20) was at the head, joined from the German GP by rookie Luis Salom (18), also from Spain. He took over from Italian Simone Corsi (21), who switched to the Fontana team at the same time, taking over there from compatriot rookie

Lorenzo Savadori (16).

The Italian Ongetta Team ISPA was four-strong, with Andrea Iannone (19) the ablest rider, while fellow Italian Lorenzo Zanetti (21) was in his fifth year. Japanese rookie Takaaki Nakagami (17) was the third, but German rookie Jonas Folger (15) would prove that he was a rider to watch.

Team Ajo Interwetten was back with the improving German Sandro Cortese (19) and promising Swiss teenager Dominique Aegerter (18), both on Derbis.

The rest were badged Aprilia.

The Viesman Kiefer racing team ran Stefan Bradl (19), but the 2008 race winner would face a difficult season.

From Spain, the Blusens team fielded Spaniard Esteve Rabat (19) and former race winner Scott Redding (16), but the Briton had the worst of the equipment in a year of frequent breakdowns.

Danny Webb (18), in his third season, was with the Dutch De Graaf team, alongside 19-year-old Swiss hope Randy Krummenacher. Dutchman Hugo van den Berg

(18) came and went.

Aprilia numbers were made up by rookies Luca Vitali (17) and Luca Marconi (19), both from Italy for CBC Corse; Johann Zarco (18), from France for WTR San Marino Team; and two rookies for the Matteoni team, firstly Czech Lukas Sembera (16) and at the end France's Quentin Jacquet (18).

HONDA

The two remaining Hondas on the grid were both ridden by rookies. Dutchman Jasper Iwema (19) ran most of the races without distinction, but the marque would be returned to the front by a remarkable rookie, who joined only halfway through the year, and then only now and then. German Marcel Schrotter (18) had made a wildcard debut in 2008, getting in the points at his first attempt. He returned for three races late in the year, riding for former racing hero Toni Mang, and made a big impression – on the front row in Germany and fifth in Valencia.

LONCIN

Chinese branded and Italian based, the Loncin team had a stronger line-up in 2009, with Japanese former race winner Tomoyoshi Koyama (25) joining from KTM. He improved, but did not transform the downbeat results. For most of the year, he was joined by French veteran Alexis Masbou (21); at year's end, Red Bull Rookies Cup winner Jakub Kornfeil (16, Czech Republic) took over.

KTM

Down in size and in the scale of ambitions, what would turn out to be KTM's last involvement with GP racing concentrated on just two entries in the Red Bull backed team, both beginners. Spaniard Marc Marquez (16) was actually in his second season, and was a frequent frontrunner. American Cameron Beaubier (16), fresh from two years in the Red Bull Rookies Cup, would find his GP debut rather more difficult.

Photo: Gold & Goose

MotoGP • 250cc • 125cc

GRANDS PRIX 2009

by MICHAEL SCOTT

QATAR GRAND PRIX

LOSAIL CIRCUIT

Above: Lorenzo's brolly-carrier got wet.
Photo: Martin Heath

Above right: A minute's silence for the Italian earthquake victims. The storm is about to break.

Right: Thumbs-up from Casey. He dominated throughout.

Left: A deserted pit lane in the desert storm.

Main photo: Winner Stoner was simply unbeatable.
Photos: Gold & Goose

Above: Lorenzo heads Dovizioso, his old 250 rival.

Above centre, from top: Gibernau was back for a racing return; Kallio seemed to enjoy his new Ducati; Hayden (on stretcher) not so much.

Top far right: Canepa was straight into MotoGP with no previous experience.

Above far right: Toseland confers with engineer Reynders, who formerly had filled the same role with Edwards.

Right: Dark night, clear visor – the eyes say everything.

Photos: Gold & Goose

HUBRIS is defined as "overweening pride, self-confidence, superciliousness or arrogance", which "leads the protagonist to break a moral law, attempt vainly to transcend normal limitations or ignore a divine warning…with calamitous results."

The ancient desert of Arabia proved that the concept is not all Greek.

To many, simply having a floodlit racetrack where there was not really any pressing need was an act of such vanity that deserved to be punished. The gods obliged, with a biblical storm that struck after both 125 and 250 races had been spoiled by the weather, and precisely as the MotoGP grid lined up for the green light – during, as it happened, a minute's silence for the victims of the recent deadly Abruzzo earthquake. Almost half the annual 50mm average rainfall fell within two hours. Racing was out of the question.

The next day, racing fought back. A proper GP was held, was seen on TV worldwide and counted for full points, as if nothing had happened.

The progress of events between the desert storm that hit with such exact timing and the race the next evening was a frenzy of quick and ultimately correct consultation and decision. Criticism that Dorna did not have a contingency plan in place seemed rather po-faced: it worked out okay in the end.

Everybody already knew – certainly everybody who had read *MOTOCOURSE* after 2008's first floodlit race – that if it rained, a combination of aerial spray and reflected floodlights would make visibility so bad that racing would become impossible. And everybody knew, from previous tests, that sometimes it can rain in the desert.

On race evening, the 125 event had already been interrupted by a shower, and the 250 race had been shortened as a result. The rain had dried fairly quickly, but nobody could have predicted the ferocity of the cloudburst at MotoGP time. So surprising was the

deluge that the first response was just to wait to see if it would all go away. It didn't.

Now came a flurry of decision making in an atmosphere close to panic. As Ezpeleta later explained, once it had become obvious that the track would not dry enough for a delayed race, the first plan had been cancellation. There was loose talk of returning in September, in place of the cancelled Hungarian round, but nobody took it too seriously. A better proposal came from the local federation: to do it all again tomorrow. Teams were canvassed, and while the voting was not unanimous, as IRTA chief Poncharal said, it was overwhelming. Let's stay. Let's race.

The crucial factor came from TV, most especially the Spanish channel TVE, standing by with a raft of presenters, including former champions Alex Criville and Angel Nieto, and a mobile studio. Like the BBC, it had been left high and dry by the flood, scrabbling to fill the allotted schedule. Once they it was agreed that a delayed race would be aired, the die was cast.

Those unfortunates tasked with logistics spent the rest of the night rearranging flights and extending hotel bookings. The rest trundled home not long before dawn to try to get some sleep.

The first race had been preceded by a troubled winter as the words 'Credit' and 'Crunch' assumed almost the same importance as 'Lap' and 'Time'. The banking crisis that struck at the end of 2008 had inspired swift reaction, with the testing calendar slashed – the trip to Australia and one of two to Sepang were cancelled – and an immediate truncation of practice and qualifying, four hours cut back to two-and-a-quarter, with one session less. And there was the new mono-tyre rule. Six riders were switching from Michelin to Bridgestone, while the former Bridgestone riders were adapting from having tyres individually tailored to the new one-size-fits-all constructions and compounds.

The lack of testing made it imperative to get ready

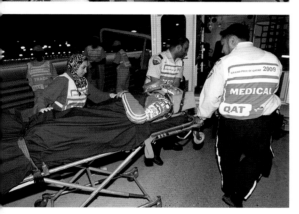

quickly, which some teams clearly did better than others. Fiat Yamaha had showed its usual professionalism, on both sides of the pit barrier, originally installed when the pair was on different tyres. Ducati's all-new carbon-fibre Desmo was up and running, and Stoner – easing himself back in as he recovered from wrist surgery over the winter – dominated the Jerez tests and won the BMW, his fourth. The Suzukis loitered on speed and development, while Hayate/Kawasaki played a surprisingly effective game of catch-up, the team's very existence being in question until the final Qatar tests.

Honda, however, was hampered when Pedrosa crashed hard at the Qatar test, suffering arm fractures and a severe flesh wound to his left knee. He missed the rest of testing and arrived at Qatar still unable to bend his leg fully.

Nor was the tyre transition easy for everybody. Lorenzo was adapting from French to Japanese steadily; likewise Edwards, Dovizioso and a fast de Puniet. Hayden had more than merely tyres to worry about. Toseland was stricken with difficulties, however, precipitating heavy high-side crashes at Qatar and Jerez – a demoralising start to the year.

Kallio and Canepa added an element of novelty, the former to surprisingly good effect – sixth fastest at Jerez tests; the return after two years of Gibernau, who had last raced a 990, had a similar frisson. But there was a dread familiarity in the plight of Hayden, who experienced very similar problems to Melandri in adapting to the very exacting Ducati. Struggling to get into the top 15 times, it was crowned by a thumping 128mph high-side crash in qualifying. He was glad of the 24-hour delay, which gave him twice the recovery time from a bruising and chin-slashing impact.

To the surprise at least of Rossi, for whom – along with tens of thousands of others – Mugello is the race of the year, Qatar won the 25th IRTA Best GP award. "It is best for the quiet of the paddock," quipped the

defending champion, whose usual careful arrangement of fairing stickers was supplemented with one reading "Forza Abruzzo" – other Italian riders wore black armbands.

The Playboy girls and livery, so conspicuous on de Puniet's LCR Honda during Jerez tests, were absent for this race in deference to the hosts, the bike backed instead for one race by Radio Monte Carlo.

Drama in the 250 class had started less than a fortnight before, when defender Simoncelli crashed at the same impromptu motocross track where Rossi sometimes trains and fractured the scaphoid in his right wrist. He turned up at Qatar and ran the first two practice sessions well off the pace, before pulling out.

And records were broken in the 125 race, where rain brought out the red flags after only four laps. Some called it the shortest 125 GP race ever, although that was not so in terms of laps – 125 TTs ran to three laps, nor distance – 2008's five-lap French GP was 20.925km compared with Qatar's 21.52km. It was true, however, in terms of time: 8m 37.245s against 2008's Assen – also five laps – at 9m 04.520s.

In any case, it was short enough not to be worth full points, and only half-scores were awarded to the top 15.

The final verdict after the extraordinary events was that MotoGP had got away with it. But Rossi was in an unequivocal mood. "We should never race at night again," he said, hoping that other keen floodlighters, such as Sepang, would shelve the idea forthwith.

MOTOGP RACE – 22 laps

If the single-tyre rule was expected to encourage closer racing, nobody told Casey Stoner. He dominated every practice, and the whole race, from first corner to the last. The only question concerned the endurance of his post-operative left wrist, which he was favouring with relatively short runs in practice. The answer seemed clear enough: there wasn't much wrong with Casey.

Nor, in the final analysis, was there much wrong with the single tyres, although there had been concerns that the two rears Bridgestone had brought would fall short in terms of endurance: in Stoner's view, the softer of the pair was almost a qualifier, it lasted so few laps. To the relief of all, and a good omen for the rest of the season, while the lap time suffered slightly – Stoner's best was seven-tenths off his own new record set in 2008 – and overall race time was 17.4 seconds longer, the window of performance offered by the new tyres was wider than previously experienced by any of the riders.

Stoner's dominance throughout practice was finally

Rossi, and three laps later Lorenzo got back ahead going into the first corner.

Capirossi had dropped out of touch and was fending off a group led by Edwards from Pedrosa, then Vermeulen, de Angelis and Kallio. At the same corner, a little too much speed saw him fall and slide into the gravel, to become the only non-finisher.

Lorenzo continued to pull clear in a safe lone third, but both Honda riders were finding that the abrupt response of the latest engine was punishing the tyres. Dovizioso began a slow decline, while injured Pedrosa's problems were compounded when an over-ambitious de Angelis collided with him, on his injured side. He saved the near crash, but henceforth fell back quickly. De Angelis was warned afterwards, but suffered no penalty following investigation.

Edwards was on strong form and almost matching Lorenzo's laps in his best smooth style, sweeping past Dovizioso on lap 14 and soon putting a gap on him. Behind, one lap earlier, de Angelis had finally passed Vermeulen; then the Australian came under pressure from rookie Kallio that lasted all the way to the finish.

Next along, Elias had moved forward only slightly from a poor start, passing de Puniet before half-distance. The Frenchman chased for a while, but had given up by the end.

Pedrosa had slowed right up; Gibernau and the cut and battered Hayden were closing rapidly. The Honda was just fast enough to keep ahead, while Hayden was able to deal with the returned Spanish veteran on the last lap.

Melandri came through to 14th from right at the very back, after running off at the first corner at the start of lap two; the final point went to rookie Takahashi, after a lonely and undistinguished debut. Well out of touch, Toseland had run off on lap seven and spent the rest of the time first passing, then failing to escape from yet another rookie, Canepa – a comedown after battling Rossi for fifth on his own debut a year before.

measured at four-tenths, ahead of Rossi and Lorenzo. Dovizioso led row two, his hobbling team-mate, Pedrosa, in 14th. Veterans Capirossi and Edwards were alongside the Italian.

Stoner led the sprint to the first corner, with Capirossi finding a most uncharacteristic spurt to put the Suzuki in second, from row two. Behind the blue bike, Rossi came under immediate attack from Lorenzo and had to spend the rest of the lap lining up to repass his importunate team-mate. A clear portent...

In this way, when they crossed the line first time, Stoner was already well over a second clear of Capirossi, and more than 2.2 seconds ahead of his true rival, Rossi. A decisive gap that Rossi was simply unable to overcome.

Rossi pounced on Capirossi at the start of lap three, but by the end of it, Stoner was 2.8 seconds clear. There followed a remorseless chase, Rossi on the limit as he chipped away little by little. Finally, on lap nine, he reduced the deficit to less than two seconds. But Stoner was circulating steadily and fast, and on lap 11 Rossi's times began to stretch by two- or three-tenths. With the rate of deterioration of his tyres, he settled for second.

It was all a bit processional, but there was more action the further back you went.

Lorenzo, behind the still slowly fading Capirossi, was under pressure from Dovi, who was past both of them by the start of lap four. But he couldn't catch

Above: Dovizioso shows his new colours on his factory-team debut.

Right: Barbera takes the first 250 win.

Far right: Full smiles, but only half points: winner Iannone is flanked by Simon and Cortese.

Below far right: Hope and experience were not enough for the new Haojue team.

Photos: Gold & Goose

Left: From out of the blue – Cluzel leads Barbera, a first for the Frenchman.

Photo: Gold & Goose

250cc RACE – 13 laps

Newcomer Talmacsi started his 250 career by posting fastest time in the first free practice; Simoncelli was three seconds slower and near the back as he nursed his injured right wrist and assessed his chances. By the end of qualifying, he was out, and Bautista had set pole. His nearest rival was Aoyama, back at Honda from the departed KTM team and getting used to just one bike.

Talmacsi ended up sixth; another class rookie and 125 champion, Mike di Meglio, impressed in third, with Barbera on the far end of the front row, still somewhat shaky in his own return from back injury in 2008.

After the 125 farce, they waited and waited for the damp patches to clear. It was dry when the 250s took off, but it was dirty, slippery and scary. The race would go to the brave, for a very surprising result.

Pasini didn't last past the first corner: he was squeezed into the kerb and knocked off, but regained his feet while still sliding to hurl abuse after his departing assailant, Pesek, who had narrowly escaped a similar fate. A little later, the first ever Russian – rather than Soviet – rider, Leonov, flipped over the high side and took Axel Pons down and out, although Leonov remounted.

Barbera led at the end of the lap, but last-minute entry Debon was charging vigorously and took over up front for the next two. But the group of five behind was pushing hard, with the hitherto largely unnoticed Cluzel moving forward within it, the most daring in the conditions.

Accordingly, the Frenchman took the lead on lap six. Barbera tucked up behind, and the pair of them eased away for a lone run to the flag. Cluzel's performance was remarkable: his previous best finish had been tenth. But Barbera had the machinery, the experience and the edge, moving past once more with five laps to go. Cluzel stayed close.

De Rosa had moved steadily through the next pack, and by lap eight had even gained a little breathing space. Behind him, there were ten bikes within 1.2 seconds, Bautista heading Wilairot, Talmacsi, di Meglio, Luthi, Aoyama and Debon, who had run wide with grip problems, dropping from third to tenth in one lap. Then, hard behind, were Locatelli, Faubel and Abraham, who crashed out directly afterwards.

Bautista continued to lead the pursuit to close on de Rosa again, only to have a big moment on the last lap and drop to seventh. In a desperate last-corner scramble, di Meglio took the last rostrum spot, with Aoyama also ahead of his team-mate, de Rosa, and Luthi inches adrift, third to sixth covered by half a second.

Bautista narrowly escaped being swallowed up by Wilairot; Locatelli had dropped away and was alone; Talmacsi held off Faubel to the line. Debon, slithering around, lost another two places to rank rookie Tomizawa and Pesek, the last point going to a lone Baldolini.

125cc RACE – 4 laps

Simon grabbed the first pole of the year, from team-mate Smith, with Iannone and Terol completing the front row.

Lightning was crackling overhead as they lined up for the first race of the year, but nobody expected what would happen next, when a light shower hit after just two laps. It was so unbelievable that race direction waited another three before putting out the red flag, by which time the track was properly, if patchily, wet. It was already too late for Marquez, the first to fall, while Simon had taken the lead on that lap and crashed on the last corner – saved when results were taken from the end of the lap before.

Iannone had led away, while Simon worked his way into second, past Terol and Marquez. The Spaniard took the lead on lap five in anticipation of an early stoppage, only to slide off before it had finished. By then, the race was over.

The pair was already almost five seconds clear of a lively group, led in aggressive style by teen Marquez. The KTM rider was pushing too hard and slipped off out at the back on the fourth lap, giving some warning of changed conditions to those behind.

On the last lap, Cortese pushed through from seventh to third for a first rostrum, taking the prize from Espargaro. Smith also made a dramatic jump forward on the same lap, following the Italian-named German past bright-hope compatriot Jonas Folger and Terol.

But with the top 11 still all up close in spite of the showers, it was something of a lottery. Others in the pack were Bradl, Webb and Rabat. Aegerter headed the next gang, from Gadea, Redding and the rest.

It was an ominously bad start to the season for the all-new Haojue team. Ranseder scraped in at the back, then the qualifying cut was waived, making Hoyle also eligible. An engine seize threw him off during morning warm-up, however, and he was out with hand injuries. Ranseder retired with an engine failure even before the four laps were run. Things would only get worse.

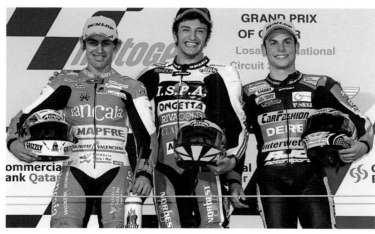

LOSAIL INTERNATIONAL CIRCUIT

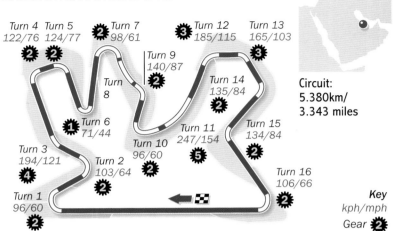

Turn 4 122/76
Turn 5 124/77
Turn 7 98/61
Turn 12 185/115
Turn 13 165/103
Turn 9 140/87
Turn 8
Turn 14 135/84
Turn 6 71/44
Turn 11 247/154
Turn 15 134/84
Turn 3 194/121
Turn 10 96/60
Turn 2 103/64
Turn 16 106/66
Turn 1 96/60

Circuit: 5.380km/ 3.343 miles

Key
kph/mph
Gear

MOTOGP
RACE DISTANCE: 22 laps, 73.545 miles/118.36 km • RACE WEATHER: Dry (air 22°, humidity 79%, track 26°)

Pos.	Rider	Nat.	No.	Entrant	Machine	Tyres	Laps	Time & speed
1	Casey Stoner	AUS	27	Ducati Marlboro Team	Ducati	B	22	42m 53.984s 102.861mph/ 165.539km/h
2	Valentino Rossi	ITA	46	Fiat Yamaha Team	Yamaha	B	22	43m 01.755s
3	Jorge Lorenzo	SPA	99	Fiat Yamaha Team	Yamaha	B	22	43m 10.228s
4	Colin Edwards	USA	5	Monster Yamaha Tech 3	Yamaha	B	22	43m 18.394s
5	Andrea Dovizioso	ITA	4	Repsol Honda Team	Honda	B	22	43m 21.247s
6	Alex de Angelis	RSM	15	San Carlos Honda Gresini	Honda	B	22	43m 23.867s
7	Chris Vermeulen	AUS	7	Rizla Suzuki MotoGP	Suzuki	B	22	43m 27.611s
8	Mika Kallio	FIN	36	Pramac Racing	Ducati	B	22	43m 28.739s
9	Toni Elias	SPA	24	San Carlos Honda Gresini	Honda	B	22	43m 33.465s
10	Randy de Puniet	USA	14	LCR Honda MotoGP	Honda	B	22	43m 36.268s
11	Dani Pedrosa	SPA	3	Repsol Honda Team	Honda	B	22	43m 42.510s
12	Nicky Hayden	USA	69	Ducati Marlboro Team	Ducati	B	22	43m 42.867s
13	Sete Gibernau	SPA	59	Grupo Francisco Hern	Ducati	B	22	43m 46.199s
14	Marco Melandri	ITA	33	Hayate Racing Team	Kawasaki	B	22	43m 50.363s
15	Yuki Takahashi	BRA	72	Scot Racing Team MotoGP	Honda	B	22	43m 54.270s
16	James Toseland	JPN	52	Monster Yamaha Tech 3	Yamaha	B	22	44m 08.962s
17	Nicola Canepa	USA	88	Pramac Racing	Ducati	B	22	44m 09.012s
	Loris Capirossi	ITA	65	Rizla Suzuki MotoGP	Suzuki	B	7	13m 49.501s

Qualifying: Dry
Air: 25° Humidity 41% Track: 25°

	Qualifying	
1	Stoner	1m 55.286s
2	Rossi	1m 55.759s
3	Lorenzo	1m 55.753s
4	Dovizioso	1m 55.997s
5	Capirossi	1m 56.149s
6	Edwards	1m 56.194s
7	de Puniet	1m 56.358s
8	Vermeulen	1m 56.493s
9	de Angelis	1m 56.790s
10	Kallio	1m 56.852s
11	Melandri	1m 56.962s
12	Elias	1m 57.295s
13	Toseland	1m 57.510s
14	Pedrosa	1m 57.729s
15	Gibernau	1m 57.899s
16	Hayden	1m 58.315s
17	Takahashi	1m 58.784s
18	Canepa	1m 58.999s

	Fastest race laps	
1	Stoner	1m 55.844s
2	Rossi	1m 56.093s
3	Dovizioso	1m 56.433s
4	Lorenzo	1m 56.936s
5	Edwards	1m 57.116s
6	Pedrosa	1m 57.121s
7	de Angelis	1m 57.281s
8	Capirossi	1m 57.290s
9	Vermeulen	1m 57.416s
10	Kallio	1m 57.510s
11	Toseland	1m 57.807s
12	Elias	1m 57.849s
13	de Puniet	1m 57.947s
14	Melandri	1m 57.990s
15	Gibernau	1m 58.104s
16	Hayden	1m 58.273s
17	Takahashi	1m 58.665s
18	Canepa	1m 59.170s

Fastest lap: Casey Stoner, on lap 2, 1m 55.844s, 103.887mph/167.190km/h.

Lap record: Casey Stoner, AUS (Ducati), 1m 55.153s, 104.510mph/168.193km/h (2008).

Event best maximum speed: Dani Pedrosa, 210.396mph/338.6km/h (qualifying practice).

Championship Points

1	Stoner	25
2	Rossi	20
3	Lorenzo	16
4	Edwards	13
5	Dovizioso	11
6	de Angelis	10
7	Vermeulen	9
8	Kallio	8
9	Elias	7
10	de Puniet	6
11	Pedrosa	5
12	Hayden	4
13	Gibernau	3
14	Melandri	2
15	Takahashi	1

Constructor Points

1	Ducati	25
2	Yamaha	20
3	Honda	11
4	Suzuki	9
5	Kawasaki	2

Team Points

1	FIAT Yamaha Team	36
2	Ducati Marlboro Team	29
3	San Carlo Honda Gresini	17
4	Repsol Honda Team	16
5	Monster Yamaha Tech 3	13
6	RIZLA Suzuki MotoGP	9
7	Pramac Racing	8
8	LCR Honda MotoGP	6
9	Grupo Francisco Hern	3
10	Hayate Racing Team	2
11	Scot Racing Team MOT	1

Grid order	1	2	3	4	5	6	7	8	9	10	11	12	13	14	15	16	17	18	19	20	21	22	
27 STONER	27	27	27	27	27	27	27	27	27	27	27	27	27	27	27	27	27	27	27	27	27	27	1
46 ROSSI	65	65	46	46	46	46	46	46	46	46	46	46	46	46	46	46	46	46	46	46	46	46	2
99 LORENZO	46	46	65	4	4	4	4	99	99	99	99	99	99	99	99	99	99	99	99	99	99	99	3
4 DOVIZIOSO	99	99	4	65	99	99	99	4	4	4	4	4	4	5	5	5	5	5	5	5	5	4	4
65 CAPIROSSI	4	4	99	99	65	65	65	5	5	5	5	5	5	4	4	4	4	4	4	4	4	5	5
5 EDWARDS	7	7	7	5	5	5	5	3	3	3	7	7	15	15	15	15	15	15	15	15	15		6
14 de PUNIET	14	5	5	7	3	3	3	7	7	7	15	15	7	7	7	7	7	7	7	7	7	7	7
7 VERMEULEN	33	14	3	3	7	7	7	15	15	15	3	36	36	36	36	36	36	36	36	36	36		8
15 de ANGELIS	5	3	14	15	15	15	15	36	36	36	36	3	3	3	3	3	3	24	24	24	24		9
36 KALLIO	3	15	15	36	36	36	14	14	24	24	24	24	24	24	24	24	3	14	14	14	14		10
33 MELANDRI	15	36	36	14	14	14	24	24	14	14	14	14	14	14	14	14	14	3	3	3	3		11
24 ELIAS	36	52	52	52	52	52	24	59	59	59	59	59	59	59	59	59	59	59	59	59	69	12	12
52 TOSELAND	52	24	24	24	24	24	59	69	69	69	69	69	69	69	69	69	69	69	69	69	59	13	13
3 PEDROSA	59	59	59	59	59	59	69	72	72	72	72	72	72	33	33	33	33	33	33	33	33	14	14
59 GIBERNAU	24	69	69	69	69	69	72	88	88	88	33	33	33	33	72	72	72	72	72	72	72	15	15
69 HAYDEN	69	72	72	72	72	72	88	52	33	33	88	88	88	52	52	52	52	52	52	52	52	16	16
72 TAKAHASHI	72	88	88	88	88	88	52	33	52	52	52	52	52	88	88	88	88	88	88	88	88	17	17
88 CANEPA	88	33	33	33	33	33	33																

OFFICIAL TIMEKEEPER

250cc — RACE DISTANCE: 13 laps, 43.458 miles/69.94 km • RACE WEATHER: Dry (air 24°, humidity 41%, track 25°)

Pos.	Rider	Nat.	No.	Entrant	Machine	Laps	Time & Speed
1	Hector Barbera	SPA	40	Pepe World Team	Aprilia	13	26m 50.940s
							(mph/km/h)
							97.117/156.296
2	Jules Cluzel	FRA	16	Matteoni Racing	Aprilia	13	26m 51.766s
3	Mike di Meglio	FRA	63	Mapfre Aspar Team 250cc	Aprilia	13	26m 57.121s
4	Hiroshi Aoyama	JPN	4	Scot Racing Team 250cc	Honda	13	26m 57.549s
5	Raffaele de Rosa	ITA	35	Scot Racing Team 250cc	Honda	13	26m 57.596s
6	Thomas Luthi	SWI	12	Emmi – Caffe Latte	Aprilia	18	26m 57.612s
7	Alvaro Bautista	SPA	19	Mapfre Aspar Team	Aprilia	13	26m 58.548s
8	Ratthapark Wilairot	THA	14	Thai Honda PTT SAG	Honda	13	26m 59.289s
9	Roberto Locatelli	ITA	15	Metis Gilera	Gilera	13	27m 05.972s
10	Gabor Talmacsi	HUN	28	Balaton Racing Team	Aprilia	13	27m 11.288s
11	Hector Faubel	SPA	55	Valencia CF – Honda SAG	Honda	13	27m 11.405s
12	Shoya Tomizawa	JPN	48	CIP Moto - GP250	Honda	13	27m 19.342s
13	Lukas Pesek	CZE	52	Auto Kelly – CP	Aprilia	13	27m 19.846s
14	Alex Debon	ESP	6	Aeropuerto - Castello - Blusens	Aprilia	13	27m 24.719s
15	Alex Baldolini	ITA	25	WTR San Marino Team	Aprilia	13	27m 27.928s
16	Bastien Chesaux	SWI	8	Racing Team Germany	Honda	13	27m 52.670s
17	Imre Toth	HUN	10	Team Toth Aprilia	Aprilia	13	27m 54.452s
18	Vladimir Leonov	RUS	56	Viessmann Kiefer Racing	Aprilia	13	28m 23.325s
19	Aitor Rodriguez	SPA	77	Milar – Juegos Lucky	Aprilia	13	28m 29.692s
	Karel Abraham	CZE	17	Cardion AB Motoracing	Aprilia	7	16m 45.822s
	Axel Pons	SPA	7	Pepe World Team	Aprilia	0	DNF
	Mattia Pasini	ITA	75	Team Toth Aprilia	Aprilia	0	DNF

Fastest lap: Hiroshi Aoyama, on lap 10, 2m 01.752s, 98.845mph/159.077km/h.
Lap record: Alex Debon, SPA (Aprilia), 1m 59.379s, 100.811mph/162.237km/h (2008).
Event best maximum speed: Thomas Luthi, 175.040mph/281.7km/h (race).

Qualifying: Dry — Air: 25° Humidity 37% Ground: 25°

1	Bautista	2m 00.677s
2	Aoyama	2m 00.777s
3	di Meglio	2m 01.113s
4	Barbera	2m 01.174s
5	Faubel	2m 01.636s
6	Talmacsi	2m 01.693s
7	Pasini	2m 01.699s
8	Debon	2m 01.713s
9	Luthi	2m 01.738s
10	Locatelli	2m 01.839s
11	Abraham	2m 01.872s
12	Wilairot	2m 02.062s
13	Cluzel	2m 02.113s
14	de Rosa	2m 02.408s
15	Pesek	2m 02.567s
16	Tomizawa	2m 03.590s
17	Baldolini	2m 03.592s
18	Toth	2m 04.895s
19	Pons	2m 05.240s
20	Leonov	2m 06.329s
21	Chesaux	2m 07.096s
24	Rodriguez, Aitor	2m 07.701s
	Simoncelli	no time

Fastest race laps

1	Aoyama	2m 01.752s
2	di Meglio	2m 02.078s
3	Luthi	2m 02.085s
4	Barbera	2m 02.168s
5	Cluzel	2m 02.214s
6	Bautista	2m 02.433s
7	de Rosa	2m 02.543s
8	Wilairot	2m 02.572s
9	Locatelli	2m 03.054s
10	Abraham	2m 03.393s
11	Talmacsi	2m 03.592s
12	Faubel	2m 03.707s
13	Debon	2m 03.784s
14	Tomizawa	2m 03.956s
15	Pesek	2m 03.999s
16	Toth	2m 05.120s
17	Baldolini	2m 05.276s
18	Chessaux	2m 07.144s
19	Leonov	2m 07.282s
20	Rodriguez, Aitor	2m 09.727s

Championship Points

1	Barbera	25
2	Cluzel	20
3	di Meglio	16
4	Aoyama, Hiroshi	13
5	de Rosa	11
6	Luthi	10
7	Bautista	9
8	Wilairot	8
9	Locatelli	7
10	Talmacsi	6
11	Faubel	5
12	Tomizawa	4
13	Pesek	3
14	Debon	12
15	Baldolini	1

Constructors

1	Aprilia	25
2	Honda	13
3	Gilera	7

125cc — RACE DISTANCE: 4 laps, 13.371 miles/21.52 km • RACE WEATHER: Dry (air 25°, humidity 41%, track 28°) • Race stopped due to rainstorm on 4 laps

Pos.	Rider	Nat.	No.	Entrant	Machine	Laps	Time & Speed
1	Andrea Iannone	ITA	29	Ongetta Team I.S.P.A.	Aprilia	4	8m 37.425s
							(mph/km/h)
							93.067/149.778
2	Julian Simon	SPA	60	Bancaja Aspar Team 125cc	Aprilia	4	8m 37.425s
3	Sandro Cortese	GER	11	Ajo Interwetten	Derbi	4	8m 42.456s
4	Pol Espargaro	SPA	44	Derbi Racing Team	Derbi	4	8m 43.014s
5	Bradley Smith	GB	38	Bancaja Aspar Team 125cc	Aprilia	4	8m 43.895s
6	Jonas Folger	GER	94	Ongetta Team I.S.P.A.	Aprilia	4	8m 43.946s
7	Nicolas Terol	SPA	18	Jack & Jones Team	Aprilia	4	8m 44.016s
8	Stefan Bradl	GER	17	Viessmann Kiefer Racing	Aprilia	4	8m 44.837s
9	Danny Webb	GB	99	Degraaf Grand Prix	Aprilia	4	8m 45.414s
10	Esteve Rabat	SPA	12	Blusens Aprilia	Aprilia	4	8m 45.923s
11	Dominique Aegerter	SWI	77	Ajo Interwetten	Derbi	4	8m 49.477s
12	Sergio Gadea	SPA	33	Bancaja Aspar Team 125cc	Aprilia	4	8m 49.482s
13	Scott Redding	GB	45	Blusens Aprilia	Aprilia	4	8m 49.605s
14	Simon Corsi	ITA	24	Jack & Jones Team	Aprilia	4	8m 50.999s
15	Johann Zarco	FRA	14	WTR San Marino Team	Aprilia	4	8m 51.028s
16	Cameron Beaubier	USA	16	Red Bull KTM Moto Sport	KTM	4	8m 51.138s
17	Efren Vazquez	SPA	7	Derbi Racing Team	Derbi	4	8m 51.415s
18	Joan Olive	SPA	6	Derbi Racing Team	Derbi	4	8m 51.697s
19	Lorenzo Zanetti	ITA	8	Ongetta Team I.S.P.A.	Aprilia	4	8m 52.555s
20	Takaaki Nakagami	JPN	73	Ongetta Team I.S.P.A.	Aprilia	4	8m 55.660s
21	Lorenzo Savadori	ITA	32	Fontana Racing	Aprilia	4	8m 55.847s
22	Randy Krummenacher	SWI	35	Degraaf Grand Prix	Aprilia	4	8m 56.600s
23	Jasper Iwema	NED	53	Racing Team Germany	Honda	4	9m 05.279s
24	Luca Marconi	FRA	87	CBC Corse	Aprilia	4	9m 05.359s
25	Lukas Sembera	CZE	69	Matteoni Racing	Aprilia	4	9m 05.444s
26	Alexis Masbou	FRA	5	Loncin Racing	Loncin	4	9m 05.515s
27	Tomoyoshi Koyama	JPN	71	Loncin Racing	Loncin	4	9m 05.789s
28	Luca Vitali	ITA	10	CBC Corse	Aprilia	4	9m 31.172s
	Marc Marquez	SPA	93	Red Bull KTM Moto Sport	KTM	3	DNF
	Michael Ranseder	AUT	88	Haojue Team	Haojue	3	DNF
dns	Matthew Hoyle	GB	66	Haojue Team	Haojue	–	

Fastest lap: Julian Simon, on lap 2, 2m 06.974s, 94.784mph/152.541km/h.
Lap record: Scott Redding, GB (Aprilia), 2m 05.695s, 95.745mph/154.087km/h (2008).
Event best maximum speed: Danny Webb, GB (Aprilia), 144.717mph/232.9km/h (free practice 2).

Qualifying — Air: 25° Humidity 44% Ground: 26°

1	Simon	2m 06.974s
6	Smith	2m 07.107s
3	Iannone	2m 07.588s
4	Terol	2m 07.781s
5	Cortese	2m 07.835s
6	Gadea	2m 08.147s
7	Bradl	2m 08.148s
8	Espargaro, Pol	2m 08.380s
9	Marquez	2m 08.417s
10	Folger	2m 08.424s
11	Redding	2m 08.681s
12	Olive	2m 08.904s
13	Webb	2m 08.971s
14	Zarco	2m 09.016s
15	Rabat	2m 09.076s
16	Nakagami	2m 09.264s
17	Krummenacher	2m 09.276s
18	Aegerter	2m 09.280s
19	Corsi	2m 09.293s
20	Zanetti	2m 09.702s
21	Vazquez	2m 09.987s
22	Beaubier	2m 10.248s
23	Savadori	2m 10.590s
24	Marconi	2m 11.573s
25	Iwema	2m 11.864s
26	Sembera	2m 11.938s
27	Koyama	2m 12.557s
28	Masbou	2m 12.610s
29	Ranseder	2m 12.676s
30	Vitali	2m 15.014s
31	Hoyle	2m 15.586s

Fastest race laps

1	Simon	2m 06.969s
2	Iannone	2m 07.487s
3	Smith	2m 07.835s
4	Espargaro, Pol	2m 08.455s
5	Cortese	2m 08.514s
6	Marquez	2m 08.551s
7	Terol	2m 08.598s
8	Webb	2m 08.601s
9	Bradl	2m 08.653s
10	Rabat	2m 08.749s
11	Folger	2m 08.854s
12	Olive	2m 09.244s
13	Gadea	2m 09.477s
14	Redding	2m 09.555s
15	Zanetti	2m 09.775s
16	Aegerter	2m 09.813s
17	Zarco	2m 10.137s
18	Vazquez	2m 10.181s
19	Beaubier	2m 10.223s
20	Corsi	2m 10.230s
21	Nakagami	2m 10.452s
22	Krummenacher	2m 10.524s
23	Savadori	2m 10.929s
24	Sembera	2m 13.100s
25	Iwema	2m 13.124s
26	Marconi	2m 13.132s
27	Masbou	2m 13.331s
28	Ranseder	2m 13.516s
11	Koyama	2m 13.552s
31	Vitali	2m 17.249s

Championship Points — Half points awarded for Qatar

1	Iannone	12.5
2	Simon	10
3	Cortese	8
4	Espargaro, Pol	6.5
5	Smith	5.5
6	Folger	5
7	Terol	4.5
8	Bradl	4
9	Webb	3.5
10	Rabat	3
11	Aegerter	2.5
12	Gadea	2
13	Redding	1.5
14	Corsi	1
15	Zarco	0.5

Constructors — Half points awarded for Qatar

1	Aprilia	12.5
2	Derbi	8

Lorenzo had the best of Rossi in a
straight contest – a sign of things to
come.

Photos: Gold & Goose

FIM WORLD CHAMPIONSHIP · ROUND 2

JAPANESE GRAND PRIX

MOTEGI CIRCUIT

THE clouds over the start of the season, both real and allegorical, had hardly dispersed by the time the circus pitched camp at Motegi, an awkward fortnight after the Qatar adventure.

Moving the Japanese race forward in the year, to April from its usual late-September date, brought it right in line for some unpredictable early-spring weather. The rain duly arrived in huge quantities, leaving most of Saturday wasted and official afternoon qualifying sessions eventually cancelled by despairing officials, after the third rescheduling. Grid positions would be taken from the two free practices, in effect from Friday afternoon times.

The figurative storm clouds were exacerbated by the bad weather. Everyone was having trouble getting used to the privations of credit-crunch racing, particularly the single-tyre rule and the cut in practice time. The riders' safety commission used the Friday meeting to ask for more of both, time and rubber. The request to extend practice and qualifying back to hour-long sessions would bear fruit; but there would be no great changes in tyre allocation, with Bridgestone standing firm on the view that the two compound choices they brought to each track would have to do. "It's something strange," said Rossi, "that World Superbike has

more choice than MotoGP." For that series, he said, Pirelli offered four different tyre compounds at each meeting; MotoGP was given just two.

By coincidence, there was a singular tyre problem at this track of repetitive hard braking – a failure that would prove unique over the full season. Pedrosa pulled in after the race with a large sliver of tread missing from his front tyre. The problem had manifested itself several laps from the end, but the tyre had retained its integrity, allowing him to finish on the rostrum. Subsequent investigation by Bridgestone revealed an apparent manufacturing fault: a foreign object within the tread had worked its way out during the course of the race.

The idle Saturday afternoon left more time for talk about the Moto2 class. Dorna was considering more than one tender for engine supply: Honda and Yamaha had put in bids, and there was a surprise offer of rotary engines from Norton. The chassis manufacturers were already busy in Europe, however, knocking up their own prototypes to house, in most cases, a Yamaha engine. Japan turned out to have the inside track, although for Moriwaki to have used anything other than a Honda engine would have run counter to recent co-operation between the long-established

tuning and racing company and HRC. Moriwaki's MD-600 was the first Moto2 prototype to be shown to the Press and an interested paddock, along with a promise to revise the engine mountings to take whatever power unit eventually selected, and an open order book.

On the doom-and-gloom side, there were dark mutterings about threats that MotoGP riders would have only one bike for 2010, Stoner responding with a veiled and subsequently ironic threat to leave the series. "Personally [I'm] thinking about whether we even want to race…in this championship. It's bad enough; the amount of time we get to be on track is not a lot. This is our sport, but we get to do almost nothing." Darker rumours emanated from Britain, where the forthcoming GP was reported to be in double jeopardy, as Donington Park's new operators faced a £2.5m financial suit from owner Wheatcroft, as well as manifold problems with local regulations and major works not yet in progress.

In the big-bike paddock, there were more pressing matters as people got used to what they had, or in some cases, what was wrong with them, in a very limited time. Pedrosa, in the latter category, was two weeks better than Qatar, although far from fully fit,

Left: Vermeulen leads Melandri and Stoner, with Toseland behind. Dry settings were educated guesswork.

Right: Randy de Puniet had his Playboy motifs back.

Below right: The first Moto2 launch: Moriwaki's MD-600.

Below: Honda's half-century of history.

Photos: Gold & Goose

being able to bend his leg more, but still not really enough. Hayden had recuperated from his bruising and stitching at Qatar, but questions were still being asked about Stoner's wrist. He did his best to put them to rest: there was still some lack of movement, but it was more of a hindrance in day-to-day life than while riding, he said. Events would bear him out: his wrist was not the weak link.

Talking of wrists, nor was Simoncelli's fully recovered, the champion able to manage only five or so laps in practice at this track of repeated hard braking before pain got in the way of his concentration.

Machine-wise, Dovizioso was complaining again of the Honda's aggressive way of coming on throttle. As often, this was just one symptom shared by teammate Pedrosa and Elias: the factory-spec chassis had trouble working the new control tyres up to temperature. Pedrosa would get a revised chassis for the next race; Dovi another one race later, but works-bike orphan Elias would have to switch to a production chassis before he could find relief.

Honda had a major anniversary to celebrate: the 50th anniversary of its first entry into GP racing in 1959. Three bikes formed the centrepiece at a celebratory party: the 125 RC-142 on which Naomi

Taniguchi had earned Honda's first point at the Isle of Man in 1959, along with the rider – spry at 73; the 250 RC162 on which Kunimitsu Takahashi had become the company's first Japanese GP winner in 1961; and the first V4 1984 NSR 500, along with Freddie Spencer, Honda's first 500-class champion. The same men rode out at Motegi the next day. The choice of bike for Freddie was quirky, but while largely unsuccessful, the 'upside-down' NSR did sire the most successful 500 motorcycle of all time. Once they put the fuel and exhausts right way up, the NSR evolved to become dominant.

The smallest class's newest enterprise had run into more serious problems. Prior rights owned by a French company had forced Maxtra to change its name to Haojue; now circumstances caused the team to pull out of the weekend prematurely. A continuing spate of engine seizures and piston failures had left them too short of parts to continue after Saturday morning. "It's a question of just what you carry with you to the fly-aways," said team chief Garry Taylor. "We'll be back in Jerez." He was right, but it did not stop growing rumours of alienation from engine designer Jan Witteveen, and the imminent disintegration of the effort.

MOTOGP RACE – 24 laps

Edwards had been fastest in the rain on Saturday morning, but Rossi took pole on Friday afternoon's dry time. Lorenzo and Stoner were alongside, while Vermeulen headed row two, and only then came the American. With everyone desperately short of set-up time, race-morning warm-up would be crucial. But it rained instead, then turned to brilliant sunshine for the race, so they all came to the line with just 45 minutes of dry time behind them. Guesses remained merely educated rather than validated, and with the track ten degrees hotter than on Friday, the softer Bridgestones, which had worked best then, might not go the distance. It was going to be an unpredictable race, lending a welcome air of excitement and uncertainty to the class.

All the same, there was not much unexpected when Rossi went straight into the lead. Vermeulen was in pursuit – until displaced by Pedrosa, after a lightning start from 11th on the grid. Vermeulen would lose another place before the end of the lap, to Lorenzo, who had already got by Stoner. All action.

Pedrosa didn't expect to be up front, given his condition, nor to stay there. Other riders had less pleas-

ant surprises: Stoner would drop back further, battling a front brake vibration, while Edwards was virtually in reverse gear, even holding up his hand to warn other riders as the lap finished. By then, he'd dropped from fifth on the grid to 13th, and was still going backwards. His problem was very new-century: a quirky glitch meant that his bike had reduced-power wet-weather settings, which somehow had failed to reset automatically after the warm-up lap. "I was lucky no-one ran up the back of me," he said.

Up front, Rossi took a small lead as Lorenzo tailed Pedrosa, looking for a way past. His first overtake was promptly rebuffed, but on the third lap, he made his move stick and started to work on a gap to Rossi of just over a second. It took five laps to close it, and one more to move past.

Pedrosa was still right with them, with Dovizioso hanging on impressively half a second or so adrift. Next came a trio led by Vermeulen, and then briefly by Melandri, with Stoner apparently stuck between them. But Vermeulen also had problems: his electronic gearshift system became progressively worse until he was forced to change both up and down manually, which dropped him out of the battle.

Rossi chased Lorenzo hard, but as half-distance passed, his challenge was spent. Set-up problems meant he was losing out under braking, and with no advantage anywhere else to make up for it, as when faced with a rider on a different machine, not even he could do any more. The gap stretched to beyond two seconds on lap 18, by which time Rossi had other problems. Far from fading away, Pedrosa was getting stronger, and the pair engaged in a prolonged dogfight that saw the Spaniard get ahead over the line for one lap, before his front tyre started to feel queasy.

This seemed to spur Rossi on, and he got back ahead with his usual determination before starting to close on Lorenzo once more. It was not enough, however, and although Lorenzo's best lap – well short of the record – had been the 15th, he was able to keep pushing to finish 1.3 seconds clear.

Pedrosa hung on to third for an impressive podium, but it might have been different had Stoner got going quicker. As it was, after finally powering past a determined, but deteriorating, Vermeulen on lap six, it wasn't until after half-distance that he began making inroads on Dovizioso, finally closing the 2.7-second gap to get by on the last lap.

Melandri was next, impressive on the orphan Kawasaki, getting back past Vermeulen in the wake of Stoner, then resisting constant pressure from Capirossi to the finish.

Rookie Kallio was a lone eighth after another strong ride, having started almost at the back. He had gained two places as Edwards fell backwards and then Elias – the Spaniard had stormed up to eighth before running off on lap six and rejoining at the back. Kallio went on to overtake Gibernau, Vermeulen, de Puniet and Toseland over the next eight laps, and then to pull clear. Obviously nobody had told the new boy how difficult overtaking is with the 800s.

Toseland's ninth was no disgrace, having held Vermeulen at bay to the finish; de Puniet was close, and might soon have come under attack from Edwards, whose bike had switched back to the right settings and who also had ignored the no-overtaking principal to get ahead of de Angelis and Canepa, with Elias one lap down. Gibernau had dropped to the back, then fallen and remounted to pit twice before retiring.

250cc RACE – 23 laps

Simoncelli, still troubled by his wrist injury, was on pole anyway on the strength of Friday afternoon's dry-session times, from fired-up home hero Aoyama, Bautista and Pasini.

Aoyama led off the line for an all-action first lap, with Simoncelli taking over only to lose it to Talmacsi, from the second row. By the end of the lap, Simoncelli was in front again.

Aoyama was soon back to second, while another class rookie, di Meglio, passed Pesek for fourth, Pasini close behind. But the real threat was coming from behind. Bautista made his usual bad start and lay eighth after one lap, but began picking up places at once – Pesek and Abraham the next lap, then Pasini, di Meglio and Talmacsi to lie third on lap five.

There was still water streaming across the track at the entry to the second underpass, and Aoyama had already survived a huge moment there – Pons and, on lap six, fourth-placed di Meglio would fall at the

Above: It's no bluebird on Rossi's shoulder.

Right: Pedrosa's tyre was shredded after the race – but he made the rostrum.

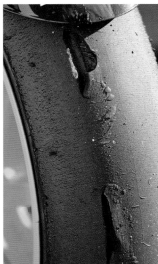

Below right: Where are they? Webb's wet-tyre choice gave him a massive early lead.

Opposite page, from top: Wild-card Shuhei Aoyama heads Czech pair Pesek and Abraham; Locatelli and Cluzel tangled early in the 250 race; damp track, blue skies – Scott Redding contemplates tyre choice for the 125 race.

Photos: Gold & Goose

same spot – giving Simoncelli a lead of better than two seconds. But it was dwindling lap by lap, and on the eighth the pressure pushed him wide and on to the rumble strips. He recovered, but quirkily a rim was cracked and the tyre deflated rapidly. His race was over.

This left Aoyama in the lead, but by barely more than a second. Bautista soon closed up and could see that potentially he was the faster. He was content to bide his time until, thanks to a helpful back-marker, he found an opening into the right at the end of the back straight. He never looked back, pulling away steadily to win by better than five seconds.

Pasini had got past Talmacsi on lap six, and this pair dropped out of touch of the lead and with each other.

If the 41,533 home fans were disappointed that Hiro Aoyama couldn't win, his brother, Shuhei, back in the GP as one of two wild-cards and riding a Harc-Pro Honda, was providing plenty of drama. Riding with the flamboyant style that characterises the breed of Japanese wild-cards, he had qualified 17th and finished lap one 16th. Then he started forging ahead, up to sixth behind Wilairot by half-distance. Among his victims had been Alex Debon, but the Spaniard stayed close, and both were ahead of Wilairot when the Thai rider joined the growing crash list on the 19th lap.

By the finish, the experienced Spaniard was clear again of the younger Aoyama brother for fifth. Pesek was out of touch in seventh, then came Luthi, narrowly ahead of Abraham.

Rookie Tomizawa took a good tenth, while Barbera, in 11th, had never been in the hunt.

Cluzel and Locatelli had crashed out on lap three; later Faubel and Baldolini also paid the price of the tricky conditions. Simoncelli rejoined with a new front wheel to finish one lap down and two places out of the points.

125cc RACE – 20 laps

Iannone claimed pole and made the right tyre gamble in a race that split into two halves as track conditions changed from start to finish.

First out, the 125s got the worst of the sodden warm-up, and a track still very wet in parts for their race. There was standing water under the two bridges, but sunshine prompted most to risk full slicks.

Terol led away, but Webb – on full wets – took over on lap two and galloped clear, almost ten seconds ahead by half-distance. The track was drying fast, and although he sustained his lap times until near the end, those on slicks were up to six seconds a lap faster.

On lap 13, Simon and Espargaro took over, both with cut slick tyres. But Iannone had full slicks and was coming through aggressively, from 12th on lap seven. With four laps left, he pounced on Espargaro, then took Simon on the next lap, resisting his counterattack to set fastest lap on the last for a convincing win.

Bradl had been in the leading group and was still close in fourth, while Marquez had held off Cortese's advance from 17th on lap one. Olive had been outpaced behind, his hands full fending off impressive rookie Folger.

Aegerter had consigned a struggling Smith to tenth; Webb was an eventual 11th. Early wet-tyre front-runners Corsi and Terol dropped to 15th and 17th. Former Red Bull Rookie Savadori, also on wets, enjoyed a moment of glory, running with the leaders until falling on lap three.

TWIN RING MOTEGI

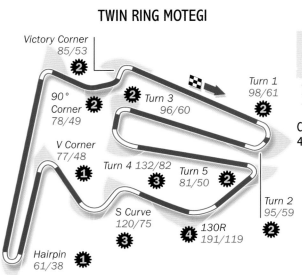

Victory Corner 85/53 **2**

90° Corner 78/49 **2**

Turn 3 96/60 **2**

Turn 1 98/61 **2**

V Corner 77/48 **1**

Turn 4 132/82 **3**

Turn 5 81/50 **2**

Turn 2 95/59 **2**

S Curve 120/75 **3**

130R 191/119 **4**

Hairpin 61/38 **1**

Circuit: 4.801km/2.983 miles

Key
kph/mph
Gear **2**

MOTOGP

RACE DISTANCE: 24 laps, 71.596 miles/115.224 km • RACE WEATHER: Dry (air 22°, humidity 25%, track 31°)

Pos.	Rider	Nat.	No.	Entrant	Machine	Tyres	Laps	Time & speed
1	Jorge Lorenzo	SPA	99	Fiat Yamaha Team	Yamaha	B	24	43m 47.238s 95.886mph/ 157.886km/h
2	Valentino Rossi	ITA	46	Fiat Yamaha Team	Yamaha	B	24	43m 48.542s
3	Dani Pedrosa	SPA	3	Repsol Honda Team	Honda	B	24	43m 51.001s
4	Casey Stoner	AUS	27	Ducati Marlboro Team	Ducati	B	24	43m 52.929s
5	Andrea Dovizioso	ITA	4	Repsol Honda Team	Honda	B	24	44m 56.445s
6	Marco Melandri	ITA	33	Hayate Racing Team	Kawasaki	B	24	44m 17.793s
7	Loris Capirossi	ITA	65	Rizla Suzuki MotoGP	Suzuki	B	24	44m 19.994s
8	Mika Kallio	FIN	36	Pramac Racing	Ducati	B	24	44m 26.654s
9	James Toseland	JPN	52	Monster Yamaha Tech 3	Yamaha	B	22	44m 30.344s
10	Chris Vermeulen	AUS	7	Rizla Suzuki MotoGP	Suzuki	B	24	44m 30.483s
11	Randy de Puniet	USA	14	LCR Honda MotoGP	Honda	B	24	44m 32.072s
12	Colin Edwards	USA	5	Monster Yamaha Tech 3	Yamaha	B	24	44m 33.778s
13	Alex de Angelis	RSM	15	San Carlos Honda Gresini	Honda	B	24	44m 40.763s
15	Nicola Canepa	USA	88	Pramac Racing	Ducati	B	24	44m 09.042s
14	Toni Elias	SPA	24	San Carlos Honda Gresini	Honda	B	24	44m 25.681s
	Sete Gibernau	SPA	59	Grupo Francisco Hernando	Ducati	B	17	41m 40.115s
	Nicky Hayden	USA	69	Ducati Marlboro Team	Ducati	B	0	DNF
	Yuki Takahashi	BRA	72	Scot Racing Team MotoGP	Honda	B	0	DNF

Fastest lap: Jorge Lorenzo, on lap 15, 1m 48.477s, 98.940mph/159.229km/h.
Lap record: Casey Stoner, AUS (Ducati), 1m 47.091s, 104.510mph/161.391km/h (2008).
Event best maximum speed: Dani Pedrosa, 185.665mph/297.8km/h (race).

Qualifying:
*Cancelled - weather conditions**

1	Rossi	1m 48.545s
2	Stoner	1m 48.601s
3	Lorenzo	1m 48.965s
4	Vermeulen	1m 49.382s
5	Edwards	1m 49.697s
6	Capirossi	1m 49.980s
7	Dovizioso	1m 50.030s
8	Melandri	1m 50.123s
9	Elias	1m 50.209s
10	Toseland	1m 50.342s
11	Pedrosa	1m 50.391s
12	Hayden	1m 50.393s
13	Takahashi	1m 50.404s
14	Gibernau	1m 50.538s
15	de Angelis	1m 50.601s
16	de Puniet	1m 50.669s
17	Kallio	1m 51.643s
18	Canepa	1m 51.929s

*Grid positions for the race defined according to best time set from the free practice sessions.
All best times set in free practice 1

Fastest race laps

1	Lorenzo	1m 48.477s
2	Rossi	1m 48.563s
3	Pedrosa	1m 48.602s
4	Stoner	1m 48.635s
5	Dovizioso	1m 48.732s
6	Edwards	1m 49.397s
7	Melandri	1m 49.703s
8	Capirossi	1m 49.727s
9	Kallio	1m 49.816s
10	Vermeulen	1m 49.893s
11	Elias	1m 49.949s
12	de Puniet	1m 50.127s
13	de Angelis	1m 50.141s
14	Gibernau	1m 50.349s
15	Toseland	1m 50.470s
16	Canepa	1m 51.713s

Championship Points

1	Lorenzo	41
2	Rossi	40
3	Stoner	38
4	Dovizioso	22
5	Pedrosa	21
6	Edwards	17
7	Kallio	16
8	Vermeulen	15
9	de Angelis	13
10	Melandri	12
11	de Puniet	11
12	Capirossi	9
13	Elias	7
14	Toseland	7
15	Hayden	4
16	Gibernau	3
17	Canepa	2
18	Takahashi	1

Constructor Points

1	Yamaha	45
2	Ducati	38
3	Honda	27
4	Suzuki	18
5	Kawasaki	12

Team Points

1	FIAT Yamaha Team	81
2	Repsol Honda Team	43
3	Ducati Marlboro Team	42
4	RIZLA Suzuki MotoGP	24
5	Monster Yamaha Tech 3	24
6	San Carlo Honda Gresini	21
7	Pramac Racing	18
8	Hayate Racing Team	12
9	LCR Honda MotoGP	11
10	Grupo Francisco Hernando	3
11	Scot Racing Team MOT	1

Grid order

Grid order	1	2	3	4	5	6	7	8	9	10	11	12	13	14	15	16	17	18	19	20	21	22	23	24	
46 ROSSI	46	46	46	46	46	46	46	46	99	99	99	99	99	99	99	99	99	99	99	99	99	99	99	99	1
27 STONER	3	3	99	99	99	99	99	99	46	46	46	46	46	46	46	46	46	3	46	46	46	46	46	2	2
99 LORENZO	99	99	3	3	3	3	3	3	3	3	3	3	3	3	3	3	46	3	3	3	3	3	3	3
7 VERMEULEN	7	4	4	4	4	4	4	4	4	4	4	4	4	4	4	4	4	4	4	4	4	27	27	4
5 EDWARDS	4	7	33	7	7	27	27	27	27	27	27	27	27	27	27	27	27	27	27	27	27	4	4	5
65 CAPIROSSI	27	33	7	27	27	33	33	33	33	33	33	33	33	33	33	33	33	33	33	33	33	33	33	6
4 DOVIZIOSO	52	27	27	33	33	65	65	65	65	65	65	65	65	65	65	65	65	65	65	65	65	65	65	7
33 MELANDRI	33	52	52	24	24	7	52	52	52	52	52	52	52	52	52	36	36	36	36	36	36	36	36	8
24 ELIAS	65	65	24	65	65	52	7	7	7	14	14	14	14	36	36	52	52	52	52	52	52	52	52	9
52 TOSELAND	24	24	65	52	52	59	59	59	14	7	36	36	36	14	14	14	14	14	14	14	7	7	7	10
3 PEDROSA	59	59	59	59	59	14	14	14	36	59	7	7	7	7	7	7	7	7	7	7	14	14	14	11
69 HAYDEN	14	14	14	14	14	36	36	36	36	58	59	59	15	15	15	15	15	15	15	15	5	5	5	12
72 TAKAHASHI	5	36	36	36	36	15	15	15	15	15	15	15	5	5	5	5	5	5	5	5	15	15	15	13
59 GIBERNAU	36	15	15	15	15	88	88	88	5	5	5	5	88	88	88	88	88	88	88	88	88	88	88	14
15 de ANGELIS	15	88	88	88	88	5	5	5	88	88	88	88	24	24	24	24	24	24	24	24	24	24	24	15
14 de PUNIET	88	5	5	5	5	24	24	24	24	24	24	24	59	59	59	59								
36 KALLIO																								
88 CANEPA																								

59 Pitstop   *24 Lapped rider*

250cc — RACE DISTANCE: 23 laps, 68.613 miles/110.423 km • RACE WEATHER: Dry (air 21°, humidity 33%, track 32°)

Pos.	Rider	Nat.	No.	Entrant	Machine	Laps	Time & Speed
1	Alvaro Bautista	SPA	19	Mapfre Aspar Team	Aprilia	23	44m 06.488s
							(mph/km/h)
							97.117/156.296
2	Hiroshi Aoyama	JPN	4	Scot Racing Team 250cc	Honda	23	44m 12.377s
3	Mattia Pasini	ITA	75	Team Toth Aprilia	Aprilia	23	44m 28.320s
4	Gabor Talmacsi	HUN	28	Balaton Racing Team	Aprilia	23	44m 32.394s
5	Alex Debon	ESP	6	Aeropuerto – Castello – Blusens	Aprilia	23	44m 37.273s
6	Shuhei Aoyama	JPN	73	Harc-Pro	Honda	23	44m 40.276s
7	Lukas Pesek	CZE	52	Auto Kelly – CP	Aprilia	23	44m 43.460s
8	Thomas Luthi	SWI	12	Emmi – Caffe Latte	Aprilia	23	44m 47.506s
9	Karel Abraham	CZE	17	Cardion AB Motoracing	Aprilia	23	44m 48.137s
10	Shoya Tomizawa	JPN	48	CIP Moto – GP250	Honda	23	44m 59.351s
11	Hector Barbera	SPA	40	Pepe World Team	Aprilia	23	45m 07.376s
12	Raffaele de Rosa	ITA	35	Scot Racing Team 250cc	Honda	23	45m 12.835s
13	Imre Toth	HUN	10	Team Toth Aprilia	Aprilia	23	45m 59.637s
14	Kazuki Watanabe	JPN	59	Bardral Racing with SJ-R	Yamaha	22	44m 08.992s
15	Vladimir Leonov	RUS	56	Viessmann Kiefer Racing	Aprilia	22	44m 36.925s
16	Bastien Chesaux	SWI	9	Racing Team Germany	Honda	22	44m 41.786s
17	Marco Simoncelli	ITA	58	Metis Gilera	Gilera	22	44m 59.056s
18	Aitor Rodriguez	SPA	77	Milar – Juegos Lucky	Aprilia	22	45m 22.675s
	Ratthapark Wilairot	THA	14	Thai Honda PTT SAG	Honda	18	DNF
	Alex Baldolini	ITA	25	WTR San Marino Team	Aprilia	17	DNF
	Hector Faubel	SPA	55	Valencia CF – Honda SAG	Honda	6	DNF
	Mike di Meglio	FRA	63	Mapfre Aspar Team 250cc	Aprilia	5	DNF
	Axel Pons	SPA	7	Pepe World Team	Aprilia	3	DNF
	Jules Cluzel	FRA	16	Matteoni Racing	Aprilia	2	DNF
	Roberto Locatelli	ITA	15	Metis Gilera	Gilera	2	DNF

Qualifying: Dry
*Cancelled - weather conditions**

1	Simoncelli	1m 53.093s
2	Aoyama, Hiroshi	1m 53.695s
3	Bautista	1m 53.836s
4	Pasini	1m 53.940s
5	Barbera	1m 54.497s
6	de Rosa	1m 54.584s
7	Talmacsi	1m 54.594s
8	di Meglio	1m 54.595s
9	Locatelli	1m 54.757s
10	Debon	1m 55.103s
11	Pesek	1m 55.158s
12	Wilairot	1m 55.208s
13	Luthi	1m 55.453s
14	Cluzel	1m 55.538s
15	Faubel	1m 55.824s
16	Abraham	1m 55.724s
17	Aoyama, Shuhei	1m 55.929s
18	Baldolini	1m 56.017s
19	Watanabe	1m 57.274s
20	Toth	1m 58.727s
21	Pons	2m 01.044s
22	Leonov	2m 01.447s
23	Chesaux	2m 01.953s
24	Rodriguez, Aitor	2m 03.437s
25	Tomizawa	2m 03.878s

Fastest race laps

1	Bautista	1m 54.047s
2	Aoyama, Hiroshi	1m 54.183s
3	Simoncelli	1m 54.449s
4	Debon	1m 54.639s
5	Pasini	1m 54.809s
6	Talmacsi	1m 54.846s
7	Aoyama, Shuhei	1m 55.225s
8	di Meglio	1m 55.229s
9	Luthi	1m 55.489s
10	Pesek	1m 55.506s
11	Barbera	1m 55.632s
12	Wilairot	1m 55.647s
13	Faubel	1m 55.784s
14	Abraham	1m 55.827s
15	Baldolini	1m 55.831s
16	Tomizawa	1m 55.862s
17	de Rosa	1m 55.963s
18	Locatelli	1m 57.953s
19	Watanabe	1m 58.242s
20	Toth	1m 58.395s
21	Cluzel	1m 58.755s
22	Leonov	1m 59.982s
23	Chessaux	2m 00.196s
24	Pons	2m 00.622s
20	Rodriguez, Aitor	2m 01.752s

Championship Points

1	Bautista	34
2	Aoyama, Hiroshi	33
3	Barbera	30
4	Cluzel	20
5	Talmacsi	19
6	Luthi	18
7	Pasini	16
8	di Meglio	16
9	de Rosa	15
10	Debon	13
11	Pesek	12
12	Aoyama, Shuhei	10
13	Tomizawa	10
14	Wilairot	8
15	Abraham	7
16	Locatelli	7
17	Faubel	5
18	Toth	3
19	Watanabe	2
20	Leonov	1
21	Baldolini	1

Constructors

1	Aprilia	50
2	Honda	33
2	Gilera	7
3	Yamaha	2

Fastest lap: Alvaro Bautista, on lap 20, 1m 54.407s, 96.394mph/151.548km/h.
Lap record: Alvaro Bautista, SPA (Aprilia), 1m 51.412s, 96.394mph/155.132km/h (2008).
Event best maximum speed: Hector Barbera, 161.307mph/259.6km/h (free practice 1).

125cc — RACE DISTANCE: 20 laps, 59.664 miles/96.02 km • RACE WEATHER: Dry (air 17°, humidity 57%, track 28°)

Pos.	Rider	Nat.	No.	Entrant	Machine	Laps	Time & Speed
1	Andrea Iannone	ITA	29	Ongetta Team I.S.PA.	Aprilia	20	42m 23.716s
							(mph/km/h)
							84.439/135.892
2	Julian Simon	SPA	60	Bancaja Aspar Team 125cc	Aprilia	20	42m 25.062s
3	Pol Espargaro	SPA	44	Derbi Racing Team	Derbi	20	42m 28.755s
4	Stefan Bradl	GER	17	Viessmann Kiefer Racing	Aprilia	20	42m 30.620s
5	Marc Marquez	SPA	93	Red Bull KTM Moto Sport	KTM	20	42m 36.777s
6	Sandro Cortese	GER	11	Ajo Interwetten	Derbi	20	42m 38.557s
7	Joan Olive	SPA	6	Derbi Racing Team	Derbi	20	42m 40.136s
8	Jonas Folger	GER	94	Ongetta Team I.S.PA.	Aprilia	20	42m 40.199s
9	Dominique Aegerter	SWI	77	Ajo Interwetten	Derbi	20	42m 51.216s
10	Bradley Smith	GB	38	Bancaja Aspar Team 125cc	Aprilia	20	42m 54.075s
11	Danny Webb	GB	99	Degraaf Grand Prix	Aprilia	20	43m 01.263s
12	Tomoyoshi Koyama	JPN	71	Loncin Racing	Loncin	20	43m 07.572s
13	Esteve Rabat	SPA	12	Blusens Aprilia	Aprilia	20	43m 23.605s
14	Lorenzo Zanetti	ITA	8	Ongetta Team I.S.PA.	Aprilia	20	43m 23.857s
15	Simon Corsi	ITA	24	Jack & Jones Team	Aprilia	20	43m 26.317s
16	Cameron Beaubier	USA	16	Red Bull KTM Moto Sport	KTM	20	43m 26.325s
17	Nicolas Terol	SPA	18	Jack & Jones Team	Aprilia	20	43m 33.583s
18	Randy Krummenacher	SWI	35	Degraaf Grand Prix	Aprilia	20	43m 33.599s
19	Sergio Gadea	SPA	33	Bancaja Aspar Team 125cc	Aprilia	20	43m 38.765s
20	Takaaki Nakagami	JPN	73	Ongetta Team I.S.PA.	Aprilia	20	43m 43.574s
21	Alexis Masbou	FRA	5	Loncin Racing	Loncin	20	43m 07.129s
22	Efren Vazquez	SPA	7	Derbi Racing Team	Derbi	20	44m 16.626s
23	Lukas Sembera	CZE	69	Matteoni Racing	Aprilia	20	44m 30.840s
24	Yuuichi Yanagisawa	JPN	58	18 Grage Racing	Honda	20	44m 31.118s
25	Luca Marconi	FRA	87	CBC Corse	Aprilia	19	42m 36.873s
26	Luca Vitali	ITA	10	CBC Corse	Aprilia	19	42m 36.927s
27	Hiroomi Iwata	JPN	55	Dydo Miu Racing	Honda	19	42m 51.571s
28	Satoru Kamada	JPN	59	Endurance & Osi	Honda	19	44m 14.382s
29	Yuki Oogane	JPN	57	Endurance & Okegawajuku	Honda	18	43m 23.194s
	Yuma Yahagi	JPN	56	Okegawajuku & Endurance	Honda	11	DNF
	Johann Zarco	FRA	14	WTR San Marino Team	Aprilia	10	DNF
	Scott Redding	GB	45	Blusens Aprilia	Aprilia	6	DNF
	Lorenzo Savadori	ITA	32	Fontana Racing	Aprilia	2	DNF
	Jasper Iwema	NED	53	Racing Team Germany	Honda	0	DNF

Qualifying
*Cancelled - weather conditions**

1	Iannone	2m 00.685s
2	Simon	2m 00.037s
3	Bradl	2m 01.029s
4	Rabat	2m 01.372s
5	Terol	2m 01.549s
6	Aegerter	2m 01.565s
7	Smith	2m 01.608s
8	Espargaro, Pol	2m 01.781s
9	Cortese	2m 01.797s
10	Marquez	2m 01.868s
11	Olive	2m 01.947s
12	Gadea	2m 02.333s
13	Webb	2m 02.637s
14	Folger	2m 02.698s
15	Zanetti	2m 02.721s
16	Redding	2m 03.285s
17	Corsi	2m 03.353s
18	Zarco	2m 03.654s
19	Koyama	2m 03.746s
20	Vazquez	2m 03.925s
21	Nakagami	2m 03.967s
22	Krummenacher	2m 04.177s
23	Beaubier	2m 04.424s
24	Savadori	2m 04.442s
25	Masbou	2m 05.015s
26	Yanagisawa	2m 05.081s
27	Yahagi	2m 05.337s
28	Kamada	2m 05.446s
29	Iwata	2m 05.900s
30	Marconi	2m 06.785s
31	Iwema	2m 07.037s
32	Ranseder	2m 07.046s
33	Sembera	2m 07.352s
34	Oogane	2m 07.418s
35	Vitali	2m 08.860s
36	Hoyle	2m 09.282s

Fastest race laps

1	Iannone	2m 01.551s
2	Simon	2m 02.005s
3	Bradl	2m 02.655s
4	Espargaro, Pol	2m 02.773s
5	Cortese	2m 02.826s
6	Folger	2m 03.138s
7	Olive	2m 03.216s
8	Aegerter	2m 03.507s
9	Marquez	2m 03.541s
10	Smith	2m 03.773s
11	Beaubier	2m 04.647s
12	Koyama	2m 04.844s
13	Krummenacher	2m 04.985s
14	Vazquez	2m 05.494s
15	Zanetti	2m 05.691s
16	Rabat	2m 05.922s
17	Webb	2m 07.156s
18	Zarco	2m 07.224s
19	Masbou	2m 08.354s
20	Corsi	2m 08.395s
21	Terol	2m 08.482s
22	Gadea	2m 08.771s
23	Nakagami	2m 09.248s
24	Redding	2m 09.320s
25	Sembera	2m 09.958s
26	Yanagisawa	2m 10.136s
27	Vitali	2m 10.928s
28	Iwata	2m 11.587s
29	Marconi	2m 11.739s
30	Savadori	2m 12.546s
31	Kamada	2m 15.589s
32	Yahagi	2m 18.583s
33	Oogane	2m 19.458s

Championship Points

1	Iannone	37.5
2	Simon	30
3	Espargaro, Pol	22.5
4	Cortese	18
5	Bradl	17
6	Folger	13
7	Smith	11.5
8	Marquez	11
9	Aegerter	9.5
10	Olive	9
11	Webb	8.5
12	Rabat	6
13	Terol	4.5
14	Koyama	4
15	Zanetti	2
16	Gadea	2
17	Corsi	2
18	Redding	1.5
19	Zarco	0.5

Constructors

1	Aprilia	37.5
2	Derbi	24
3	KTM	11
4	Loncin	4

Fastest lap: Andrea Iannone, on lap 20, 2m 01.551s, 88.354mph/142.192km/h.
Lap record: Mika Kallio, FN (KTM), 1m 57.666s, 91.271mph/146.886km/h (2006).
Event best maximum speed: Joan Olive, SPA (Derbi), 138.627mph/223.1km/h (race).

*Grid positions for the race defined according to best time set from the free practice sessions.
All best times set in free practice 1

SPANISH
GRAND PRIX

JEREZ CIRCUIT

Record crowds watched Rossi sneak
past early leader Pedrosa.

Photo: Gold & Goose

TWENTY-three years had elapsed since the first event in the hills outside the sherry capital, and what a change had come upon what is nowadays a showpiece of European racing. Jerez was a crowd-puller from the very start. Back in 1987, I recall factory Yamaha rider Takahiko Taira, in full leathers, running from the access road across open fields to get to morning warm-up in time. He made it and would race to seventh. But Jerez was completely overwhelmed by crowds and traffic, and the roads outside the track remained gridlocked well into the night.

It became normal for paddock people to arrive at the track well before sunrise on race day: as the first rays broke the horizon, the track PA team endeared itself by playing Pink Floyd's 'Dark Side of the Moon' over the speakers. A memorable moment now to be forgotten, because such early arrivals are no longer necessary.

In 2009, organisers claimed a new record crowd – 263,648 for the weekend and 123,340 on race day. You'd never have known it. Sweeping new roads for miles around, massive car parks and, wonder of wonders, a traffic system that really coped. Where once had been a glorious shambles, now the mayhem was carefully controlled, and at Jerez race day ran like clockwork. It's too late for Donington Park, but Silverstone should take careful note.

Thankfully, the weather was benign – at least in that there was no rain all weekend. There were high winds on Saturday, however, causing problems for the smaller bikes especially, as it got under the fairings at full lean: Simoncelli fell three times at the same corner.

With the European season stretching ahead, Honda provided some relief at least for one rider, Pedrosa, in the shape of a new chassis that improved weight transfer, to help work the new control Bridgestones up to temperature. Rossi was still having problems with the tyres too, explaining how he and Stoner had special harder tyres available to them in 2008, and that the new breed meant starting again with settings. He dropped to fourth in final qualifying, but then came another of the team's trade-mark Sunday-morning turn-arounds. Raising the ride height increased the Yamaha's weight transfer and gave more feel into the corners; he took it even further for the race and was proved triumphantly right, taking his first win of the season and the lead in the championship.

In the rule-making mood of the moment, a series of diktats were delivered from the GP Commission meeting. It was confirmed that Honda would supply engines for the Moto2 class, while there was more talk of detail refinement to an apparently firm intention for one bike per rider in 2010. The new rule banning class rookies from factory teams was also modified, with a special exemption for Suzuki, the only factory with no satellite team in which to groom young riders. This immediately reopened speculation that Ben Spies might join the team for 2010, but in fact Suzuki had long since let the promising Texan slip through its fingers, to the benefit of Yamaha.

The confirmation that the control engine for Moto2 would come from Honda – basically the CBR600 unit – had unintentional irony. The company had been largely instrumental in killing off two-strokes, the 250s being the latest victims of a sustained covert campaign. But Honda had kindly – or cynically? – renewed the supply of machines to support the class for its final year. And it was no token support: the Honda won the race and took over the World Championship top spot after a hell of a scrap, the lead changing hands between Bautista and victorious Aoyama three times on the last lap alone. Whatever was so wrong with 250s that they needed to die, clearly it was not the quality of the racing.

Of more immediate significance, while there would be no changes in the tyre allocation – that discussion would have to await Bridgestone's convenience – the riders' pleas for more of a chance to ride their motorcycles was heeded. Practice would remain at three sessions rather than 2008's four, but from the next race at Le Mans, session times would be extended: MotoGP would get an hour each time, while the 125s also benefited from a full hour on Friday, and 45 rather than 30 minutes on Saturday.

This was good news, especially for Hayden, still very much in the same quagmire that had bogged

Left: Hayden was still fighting to get up to speed.

Below: Team-mate Stoner made the rostrum.

Bottom: Ambition foiled as Lorenzo's race ends in the gravel.

Photos: Gold & Goose

down predecessor Melandri. The Italian was enjoying a second top-six in succession, not only on a Kawasaki transformed, but also as proof that he hadn't forgotten how to ride. The American was looking increasingly glum as he tried to puzzle out why team-mate Stoner could qualify the bike 1.5 seconds faster, although at least this time he was ahead of rookie Kallio on the grid. Communication with the team was yet to be clearly established, while the bike was inconsistent. "We improve one thing and something else gets worse," he said. "It's the fast corners that give me most trouble." After heavy crashes at the last two rounds, he was stiff and sore, and plagued with headaches.

At only the third round, rumours were already afoot about rider movements for 2010, Lorenzo being the centre of attention. There were rumours of a big-money offer from Repsol Honda – and the consequent fall-out of where this would leave existing riders Pedrosa and Dovizioso. It was the start of a prolonged who-goes-where silly season that was almost as volatile as the early-season results, and would not be finally resolved until much later in the year.

MotoGP RACE – 27 laps

Rossi blitzed the opening practice, but then fell behind as Lorenzo narrowly shaded Pedrosa for pole, Stoner completing the front row. The defending champion said firmly on Saturday evening that he would be "unable to win", but he would prove himself wrong. He headed row two from the new mature version of de Puniet, who had circulated steadily and fast to be second-best Honda; Capirossi was alongside.

All started cleanly, but it was Pedrosa away up front into turn one, in his usual and preferred jack-rabbit fashion. Immediately he started working on a lead, Stoner chasing, and then Lorenzo, Rossi and de Puniet.

Rossi wasted no time, swooping past Lorenzo as he braked into Angel Nieto corner. The champion's modifications had worked out well, while Lorenzo's settings were less effective in the heat. By lap four, the Spaniard was a second out of touch.

Stoner was harder for Rossi to deal with: it took until lap six before he attacked successfully at the final hairpin, only for Stoner to get him back into turn one. Next time around, Rossi made the same move stick. By now, Pedrosa was 1.3 seconds ahead and looking hard to catch.

Rossi had trimmed the gap to less than a second by lap ten, but Pedrosa opened it up again over the next two. The Honda rider had already given his best, however, and Rossi was getting into his stride: he started to close again, tenth by tenth.

He was on the Honda by lap 17, and Pedrosa – still not fully recovered from injury, of course – offered no resistance to his outbraking move, again at Nieto curve. Rossi pulled away to win by 2.7 seconds.

Stoner had dropped back and was almost three seconds adrift at half-distance, with a similar gap back to Lorenzo. But Lorenzo was at home and in the mood, and he redoubled his efforts when he saw the red bike getting closer. With four laps to go, he was within eight-tenths, but his ambition was his downfall – before getting any closer, he slid off gracefully at

Nieto: "Perhaps the right thing would have been to go more gently, but when you're in front of your fans at home, of course you try your maximum."

De Puniet retained his position as next-best Honda, circulating steadily a long way back, but just clear of pursuers Capirossi, Melandri and Edwards – a strong midfield battle that lasted for much of the race. As the end approached, Melandri was the strongest. He got to the front and stayed there to the flag. Capirossi was a second away, still battling after running wide and letting both by. He passed Edwards, sliding in the higher temperatures, on the last lap, "but there wasn't enough time to get Marco."

Dovizioso, still with the earliest chassis, which was also proving a handful for Elias, had qualified only eighth, but was going strong. He passed Capirossi, Edwards and finally de Puniet for fifth on lap seven, when he ran off the track, rejoining 16th after a buck-ing-bronco ride through the dirt. He picked up speed again, and by the end, he was back up to ninth and closing on the trio ahead at a half a second a lap. He was right on Edwards's heels at the flag; another couple of laps, and he might have passed all three. His last victim had been Elias, fighting to find rear grip.

Vermeulen was three seconds away in tenth, with a familiar Suzuki problem – settings that work in practice can go off quickly when conditions change: "The temperature seemed to affect us more than some others."

A lone 11th was not a bad result for Gibernau, still getting accustomed to an 800 after injury had spoiled his testing, as well as trying to make up for two lost years. His was the second Ducati. Takahashi was next, while Toseland's late braking was enough to hold off de Angelis to the finish.

Hayden trailed in all alone, explaining how an en-forced softer rear tyre choice – "We couldn't get the harder one to work well." – had left him at a disadvantage. The two Pramac Ducati riders had made the same choice, and Kallio had been ahead of Hayden when he pitted on lap 13.

250cc RACE – 26 laps

Debon and his last-minute Aprilia took a clear pole, ahead of Barbera, Simoncelli and Bautista, and the veteran led the pack away. Simoncelli moved past at the start of the second lap, and by the end of it, Bautista and Barbera were also ahead of Debon. And then Aoyama on the following lap – Debon was dropping back, and a big gang piled up behind him, until on lap ten he slid off smoothly at Dry Sack hairpin.

Simoncelli and Bautista were jousting up front, with Barbera holding station a few tenths behind – until lap six, when Aoyama moved past him to attack. The Japanese rider led for the first time on lap 11, and he quickened the pace at once, lap times dropping be-low 1m 44s for the first time. Barbera started to drop away in fourth, and later Simoncelli would admit that he had been taken past his limit. It showed on lap 23: a little slip sent him running wide, dropping him

to fourth to battle to the end with Barbera. Simoncelli reclaimed third on the final lap.

The leading pair was engaged to the very finish. Bautista set a new lap record on the 15th, led from laps 23 to 25 and looked the stronger. Aoyama proved otherwise in a memorable last lap. He attacked into Nieto, with four corners to go. This invited the classic counterattack under braking into the final hairpin, and Bautista took the bait, late on the brakes and running in tight to make the corner sharper for himself, but gaining the lead. Aoyama let him through, relying on a later entry and a faster exit for the run to the line. The tactic worked by 0.132 second.

Simoncelli was 2.7 seconds down, Barbera just six-hundredths behind him.

French privateer Cluzel had qualified an impressive fifth and was heading the gang behind Debon until displaced by di Meglio. At the same time, Pasini was charging through. He'd qualified 15th and finished lap one a place lower, but by the time Debon fell, he was past Cluzel and hounding di Meglio. It took him three laps to get by, and soon afterwards di Meglio had an out-of-saddle moment and lost touch.

Luthi and Talmacsi also overcame Cluzel on his aged Aprilia; Luthi went on ahead to latch on to Pas-ini. On the final lap, he sneaked by, taking fifth by less than a hundredth.

Talmacsi was under pressure from Cluzel to the fin-ish. Locatelli had got past both, only to run wide on the last lap and drop back to a close ninth.

De Rosa seized tenth from the fading di Meglio,

Left: 250 racing at its best: Bautista leads Simoncelli, Barbera and eventual winner Aoyama.

Right: Careful tactics gave jubilant Aoyama a win by inches.

Below right: Aspar delight: Jorge Martinez celebrates his 125 team's one-two finish.

Below: Bradley Smith took a convincing first win: "I'm glad I waited."

Photos: Gold & Goose

also on the last lap; Japanese rookie Tomizawa had another good run, staying ahead of Pesek for 12th. Faubel and Wilairot took the last points.

Abraham joined Debon on the crash list; Debise also fell, but remounted to finish one lap down.

Aoyama's first win of the year avenged his tearful defeat at Motegi and gave him the points lead for the first time.

125cc RACE – 23 laps

Simon was on pole, but Smith led into the first corner. Fellow Briton and deadly rival Redding was second from row two; Simon was third.

Smith led by almost two seconds after one lap. Simon seized second a few corners later, and the pursuit began. He set a new record on lap four, and was barely a second away on lap six when he slid down and out at Dry Sack.

Smith had a ten-second lead and continued to extend it to the flag, in spite of running into electronic shifter problems: the engine died in fifth and he almost crashed, being unable to use that gear thereafter. His first win was at his 50th attempt. "I've waited a long time, but I'm glad I waited," he said.

When Simon fell, Cortese was heading Marquez and Redding, with Gadea, Espargaro and Aegerter closing ahead of a huge gang. Coming through most impressively was rookie Folger: from the back of the grid after crashing in qualifying.

As they started the penultimate lap, Espargaro led a seven-strong group from Marquez, with Folger next, still pushing hard. Too hard: into the final hairpin before starting the last lap, he went down, forcing the hapless Espargaro off the track. Gadea took advantage to lead to the end, from Marquez, Redding, Vasquez and Cortese; Espargaro recovered for a still-close seventh.

Webb was just a couple of seconds behind, nearly caught at the end by scrapping pair Aegerter and Terol, who changed places for the last time on the final lap.

Olive led the next trio, with another close battle for the rest of the points. Iannone had fallen on lap one and rejoined for 19th, and no points. Bradl also crashed out of the top ten.

Haojue's decline continued: Hoyle did not qualify after another seize and crash; Ranseder was left in the pit lane with gear selection failure as the race began.

CIRCUITO DE JEREZ

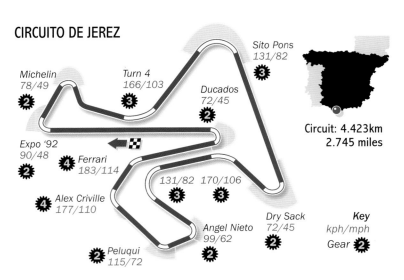

Michelin 78/49 — Gear 2
Turn 4 166/103 — 3
Ducados 72/45 — 2
Sito Pons 131/82 — 3
Expo '92 90/48 — 2
Ferrari 183/114 — 4
131/82 — 3
170/106 — 3
Alex Criville 177/110 — 4
Angel Nieto 99/62 — 2
Dry Sack 72/45 — 2
Peluqui 115/72 — 2

Circuit: 4.423km / 2.745 miles

Key: kph/mph, Gear 2

MOTOGP

RACE DISTANCE: 27 laps, 74.204 miles/119.421 km • **RACE WEATHER:** Dry (air 27°, humidity 31%, track 45°)

Pos.	Rider	Nat.	No.	Entrant	Machine	Tyres	Laps	Time & speed
1	Valentino Rossi	ITA	46	Fiat Yamaha Team	Yamaha	B	27	45m 18.557s 98.264mph/ 158.141km/h
2	Dani Pedrosa	SPA	3	Repsol Honda Team	Honda	B	27	45m 21.257s
3	Casey Stoner	AUS	27	Ducati Marlboro Team	Ducati	B	27	45m 29.064s
4	Randy de Puniet	USA	14	LCR Honda MotoGP	Honda	B	27	45m 50.450s
5	Marco Melandri	ITA	33	Hayate Racing Team	Kawasaki	B	27	45m 51.685s
6	Loris Capirossi	ITA	65	Rizla Suzuki MotoGP	Suzuki	B	27	45m 52.685s
7	Colin Edwards	USA	5	Monster Yamaha Tech 3	Yamaha	B	27	45m 52.978s
8	Andrea Dovizioso	ITA	4	Repsol Honda Team	Honda	B	27	45m 53.182s
9	Toni Elias	SPA	24	San Carlos Honda Gresini	Honda	B	27	46m 01.246s
10	Chris Vermeulen	AUS	7	Rizla Suzuki MotoGP	Suzuki	B	27	46m 03.740s
11	Sete Gibernau	SPA	59	Grupo Francisco Hernando	Ducati	B	17	46m 06.749s
12	Yuki Takahashi	BRA	72	Scot Racing Team MotoGP	Honda	B	27	46m 10.432s
13	James Toseland	JPN	52	Monster Yamaha Tech 3	Yamaha	B	27	46m 12.240s
14	Alex de Angelis	RSM	15	San Carlos Honda Gresini	Honda	B	27	46m 12.498s
15	Nicky Hayden	USA	69	Ducati Marlboro Team	Ducati	B	27	46m 19.794s
16	Nicola Canepa	USA	88	Pramac Racing	Ducati	B	27	46m 29.453s
	Jorge Lorenzo	SPA	99	Fiat Yamaha Team	Yamaha	B	23	DNF
	Mika Kallio	FIN	36	Pramac Racing	Ducati	B	12	DNF

Qualifying: Dry
Air: 26° Humidity: 32% Track: 39°

1	Lorenzo	1m 38.933s
2	Pedrosa	1m 38.984s
3	Stoner	1m 39.415s
4	Rossi	1m 39.642s
5	de Puniet	1m 39.806s
6	Capirossi	1m 39.862s
7	Edwards	1m 39.926s
8	Dovizioso	1m 39.966s
9	Elias	1m 40.112s
10	Vermeulen	1m 40.185s
11	Melandri	1m 40.381s
12	Gibernau	1m 40.440s
13	Takahashi	1m 40.599s
14	Toseland	1m 40.670s
15	de Angelis	1m 40.796s
16	Hayden	1m 40.953s
17	Kallio	1m 41.238s
18	Canepa	1m 41.253s

Fastest race laps

1	Rossi	1m 39.818s
2	Pedrosa	1m 39.836s
3	Stoner	1m 39.855s
4	Lorenzo	1m 40.137s
5	Dovizioso	1m 40.173s
6	de Puniet	1m 40.432s
7	Capirossi	1m 40.775s
8	Melandri	1m 40.929s
9	Takahashi	1m 41.064s
10	Edwards	1m 41.130s
11	Toseland	1m 41.243s
12	Elias	1m 41.259s
13	Vermeulen	1m 41.374s
14	Gibernau	1m 41.457s
15	Kallio	1m 41.582s
16	de Angelis	1m 41.644s
17	Canepa	1m 41.986s
18	Hayden	1m 42.036s

Fastest lap: Valentino Rossi, on lap 4, 1m 39.818s, 99.119mph/159.518km/h.

Lap record: Dani Pedrosa, SPA (Honda), 1m 40.116s, 98.825mph/159.043km/h (2008).

Event best maximum speed: Toni Elias, 172.355mph/277.3km/h (race).

Championship Points

1	Rossi	65
2	Stoner	54
3	Lorenzo	41
4	Pedrosa	41
5	Dovizioso	30
6	Edwards	26
7	de Puniet	24
8	Melandri	23
9	Vermeulen	21
10	Capirossi	19
11	Kallio	16
12	de Angelis	15
13	Elias	15
14	Toseland	10
15	Gibernau	8
16	Takahashi	5
17	Hayden	5
18	Canepa	2

Constructor Points

1	Yamaha	70
2	Ducati	54
3	Honda	47
4	Suzuki	28
5	Kawasaki	23

Team Points

1	FIAT Yamaha Team	106
2	Repsol Honda Team	71
3	Ducati Marlboro Team	59
4	RIZLA Suzuki MotoGP	40
5	Monster Yamaha Tech 3	36
6	San Carlo Honda Gresini	30
7	LCR Honda MotoGP	24
8	Hayate Racing Team	23
9	Pramac Racing	18
10	Grupo Francisco Hern	8
11	Scot Racing Team MOT	5

Grid order

Grid order	1	2	3	4	5	6	7	8	9	10	11	12	13	14	15	16	17	18	19	20	21	22	23	24	25	26	27	
99 LORENZO	3	3	3	3	3	3	3	3	3	3	3	3	3	3	3	3	3	46	46	46	46	46	46	46	46	46	46	1
3 PEDROSA	27	27	27	27	27	46	46	46	46	46	46	46	46	46	46	46	46	3	3	3	3	3	3	3	3	3	3	2
27 STONER	99	46	46	46	46	27	27	27	27	27	27	27	27	27	27	27	27	27	27	27	27	27	27	27	27	27	27	3
46 ROSSI	46	99	99	99	99	99	99	99	99	99	99	99	99	99	99	99	99	99	99	99	99	99	99	14	14	14	14	4
14 de PUNIET	14	14	14	14	4	4	4	14	14	14	14	14	14	14	14	14	14	14	14	14	14	14	14	33	33	33	33	5
65 CAPIROSSI	5	4	4	4	14	14	14	65	65	33	33	33	33	5	5	33	33	33	33	33	33	33	33	5	65	5	65	6
5 EDWARDS	4	5	5	65	65	65	65	33	33	5	5	5	5	33	33	5	5	5	5	5	5	5	5	65	5	65	5	7
4 DOVIZIOSO	65	65	33	5	5	5	5	5	5	65	65	65	65	65	65	65	65	65	65	65	65	65	65	4	4	4	4	8
24 ELIAS	33	33	65	33	33	33	33	72	24	24	24	24	24	24	24	24	24	4	4	4	4	4	4	24	24	24	24	9
7 VERMEULEN	24	24	24	72	72	72	72	24	72	72	72	72	72	72	72	72	4	24	24	24	24	24	24	7	7	7	7	10
33 MELANDRI	72	72	72	24	24	24	24	7	7	7	7	7	7	4	4	7	72	7	7	7	7	7	7	59	59	59	59	11
59 GIBERNAU	59	59	59	59	59	7	7	59	59	59	59	4	4	7	7	4	7	72	72	72	72	72	72	72	72	72	72	12
72 TAKAHASHI	7	36	36	7	7	59	59	36	52	4	4	59	59	59	59	59	59	59	59	59	59	59	59	52	52	52	52	13
52 TOSELAND	36	7	7	36	36	36	36	52	4	52	52	52	52	52	52	52	52	52	52	52	52	52	52	15	15	15	15	14
15 de ANGELIS	15	52	52	52	52	52	52	15	36	15	15	15	15	15	15	15	15	15	15	15	15	15	15	69	69	69	69	15
69 HAYDEN	52	15	15	15	15	15	15	4	15	36	36	36	69	69	69	69	69	69	69	69	69	69	69	88	88	88	88	
36 KALLIO	88	88	88	88	88	88	88	88	69	69	69	69	69	88	88	88	88	88	88	88	88	88	88	88				
88 CANEPA	69	69	69	69	69	69	69	88	88	88	88	88	88															

99 Pitstop

250cc
RACE DISTANCE: 26 laps, 71.456 miles/114.998 km • RACE WEATHER: Dry (air 26°, humidity 31%, track 40°)

Pos.	Rider	Nat.	No.	Entrant	Machine	Laps	Time & Speed
1	Hiroshi Aoyama	JPN	4	Scot Racing Team 250cc	Honda	26	45m 08.805s
							(mph/km/h)
							94.965/152.832
2	Alvaro Bautista	SPA	19	Mapfre Aspar Team	Aprilia	26	45m 08.937s
3	Marco Simoncelli	ITA	58	Metis Gilera	Gilera	26	45m 11.511s
4	Hector Barbera	SPA	40	Pepe World Team	Aprilia	26	45m 11.574s
5	Thomas Luthi	SWI	12	Emmi – Caffe Latte	Aprilia	26	45m 26.751s
6	Mattia Pasini	ITA	75	Team Toth Aprilia	Aprilia	26	45m 26.755s
7	Gabor Talmacsi	HUN	28	Balaton Racing Team	Aprilia	26	45m 35.093s
8	Jules Cluzel	FRA	16	Matteoni Racing	Aprilia	26	45m 35.277s
9	Roberto Locatelli	ITA	15	Metis Gilera	Gilera	26	45m 36.451s
10	Raffaele de Rosa	ITA	35	Scot Racing Team 250cc	Honda	26	45m 41.174s
11	Mike di Meglio	FRA	63	Mapfre Aspar Team 250cc	Aprilia	26	45m 41.422s
12	Shoya Tomizawa	JPN	48	CIP Moto – GP250	Honda	26	45m 43.046s
13	Lukas Pesek	CZE	52	Auto Kelly – CP	Aprilia	26	45m 45.694s
14	Hector Faubel	SPA	55	Valencia CF – Honda SAG	Honda	26	45m 46.042s
15	Ratthapark Wilairot	THA	14	Thai Honda PTT SAG	Honda	26	46m 25.591s
16	Imre Toth	HUN	10	Team Toth Aprilia	Aprilia	26	46m 34.314s
17	Bastien Chesaux	SWI	8	Racing Team Germany	Honda	25	45m 17.952s
18	Aitor Rodriguez	SPA	77	Milar – Juegos Lucky	Aprilia	25	45m 24.420s
19	Vladimir Leonov	RUS	56	Viessmann Kiefer Racing	Aprilia	25	45m 45.476s
20	Valentin Debise	FRA	53	CIP Moto – GP250	Honda	25	46m 27.875s
	Axel Pons	SPA	7	Pepe World Team	Aprilia	22	DNF
	Ivan Maestro	SPA	76	Milar – Juegos Lucky	Aprilia	18	DNF
	Alex Baldolini	ITA	25	WTR San Marino Team	Aprilia	10	DNF
	Alex Debon	ESP	6	Aeropuerto – Castello – Blusens	Aprilia	9	DNF
	Karel Abraham	CZE	17	Cardion AB Motoracing	Aprilia	3	DNF

Fastest lap: Alvaro Bautista, on lap 15, 1m 43.338s, 95.743mph/154.084km/h. (record)
Previous lap record: Marco Simoncelli, ITA (Gilera), 1m 43.546s, 95.551mph/153.775km/h (2008).
Event best maximum speed: Thomas Luthi, Aprilia 154.472mph/248.6 km/h (free practice 2).

Qualifying: Dry
Air: 26° Humidity: 30% Track: 25°

1	Debon	1m 43.028s
2	Barbera	1m 43.317s
3	Simoncelli	1m 43.376s
4	Bautista	1m 43.451s
5	Cluzel	1m 43.521s
6	Aoyama, Hiroshi	1m 43.591s
7	di Meglio	1m 43.792s
8	Luthi	1m 43.864s
9	Faubel	1m 43.891s
10	Talmacsi	1m 44.058s
11	Pesek	1m 44.252s
12	de Rosa	1m 44.484s
13	Wilairot	1m 44.515s
14	Abraham	1m 44.734s
15	Pasini	1m 44.818s
16	Locatelli	1m 44.872s
17	Tomizawa	1m 45.752s
18	Baldolini	1m 45.857s
19	Toth	1m 46.017s
20	Rodriguez, Aitor	1m 47.069s
21	Pons	1m 47.181s
22	Chesaux	1m 47.823s
23	Leonov	1m 48.244s
24	Debise	1m 48.385s
25	Maestro	1m 48.082s
nq	Markham	1m 51.558s

Fastest race laps

1	Bautista	1m 43.338s
2	Aoyama, Hiroshi	1m 43.412s
3	Barbera	1m 43.419s
4	Simoncelli	1m 43.474s
5	Luthi	1m 43.863s
6	Pasini	1m 43.986s
7	Talmacsi	1m 44.134s
8	di Meglio	1m 44.136s
9	Locatelli	1m 44.311s
10	de Rosa	1m 44.347s
11	Cluzel	1m 44.431s
12	Abraham	1m 44.692s
13	Faubel	1m 44.715s
14	Tomizawa	1m 44.748s
15	Debon	1m 44.776s
16	Pesek	1m 44.964s
17	Wilairot	1m 45.633s
18	Baldolini	1m 46.371s
19	Rodriguez, Aitor	1m 46.387s
20	Toth	1m 46.472s
21	Pons	1m 46.547s
22	Chessaux	1m 47.305s
23	Debise	1m 47.885s
24	Maestro	1m 48.039s
25	Leonov	1m 59.982s

Championship Points

1	Aoyama, Hiroshi	58
2	Bautista	54
3	Barbera	43
4	Luthi	29
5	Cluzel	28
6	Talmacsi	28
7	Pasini	26
8	di Meglio	21
9	de Rosa	21
10	Simoncelli	16
11	Pesek	15
12	Locatelli	14
13	Tomizawa	14
14	Debon	13
15	Aoyama, Shuhei	10
16	Wilairot	9
17	Abraham	7
18	Faubel	7
19	Toth	3
20	Watanabe	2
21	Leonov	1
22	Baldolini	1

Constructors

1	Aprilia	70
2	Honda	58
2	Gilera	23
3	Yamaha	2

125cc
RACE DISTANCE: 23 laps, 63.211 miles/101.729 km • RACE WEATHER: Dry (air 24°, humidity 36%, track 34°)

Pos.	Rider	Nat.	No.	Entrant	Machine	Laps	Time & Speed
1	Bradley Smith	GB	38	Bancaja Aspar Team 125cc	Aprilia	23	41m 49.556s
							(mph/km/h)
							84.439/135.892
2	Sergio Gadea	SPA	33	Bancaja Aspar Team 125cc	Aprilia	23	42m 03.080s
3	Marc Marquez	SPA	93	Red Bull KTM Moto Sport	KTM	23	42m 03.109s
4	Scott Redding	GB	45	Blusens Aprilia	Aprilia	23	42m 03.807s
22	Efren Vazquez	SPA	7	Derbi Racing Team	Derbi	23	42m 04.314s
6	Sandro Cortese	GER	11	Ajo Interwetten	Derbi	23	42m 05.101s
7	Pol Espargaro	SPA	44	Derbi Racing Team	Derbi	23	42m 05.112s
8	Danny Webb	GB	99	Degraaf Grand Prix	Aprilia	23	42m 07.328s
9	Dominique Aegerter	SWI	77	Ajo Interwetten	Derbi	23	42m 08.516s
10	Nicolas Terol	SPA	18	Jack & Jones Team	Aprilia	23	42m 08.609s
11	Joan Olive	SPA	6	Derbi Racing Team	Derbi	23	42m 22.036s
12	Esteve Rabat	SPA	12	Blusens Aprilia	Aprilia	23	42m 22.110s
13	Johann Zarco	FRA	14	WTR San Marino Team	Aprilia	23	42m 22.934s
14	Simon Corsi	ITA	24	Jack & Jones Team	Aprilia	23	42m 31.089s
15	Cameron Beaubier	USA	16	Red Bull KTM Moto Sport	KTM	23	42m 33.999s
16	Takaaki Nakagami	JPN	73	Ongetta Team I.S.P.A.	Aprilia	23	42m 34.294s
17	Randy Krummenacher	SWI	35	Degraaf Grand Prix	Aprilia	23	42m 34.490s
18	Lorenzo Zanetti	ITA	8	Ongetta Team I.S.P.A.	Aprilia	23	42m 34.533s
19	Andrea Iannone	ITA	29	Ongetta Team I.S.P.A.	Aprilia	23	42m 45.020s
20	Lukas Sembera	CZE	69	Matteoni Racing	Aprilia	23	42m 54.840s
21	Lorenzo Savadori	ITA	32	Fontana Racing	Aprilia	23	42m 56.976s
22	Alberto Moncayo	SPA	42	Andalucia Aprilia	Aprilia	23	43m 06.381s
23	Luis Salom	SPA	39	SAG – Castrol	Honda	23	43m 14.744s
24	Jasper Iwema	NED	53	Racing Team Germany	Honda	23	43m 18.459s
25	Luca Marconi	FRA	87	CBC Corse	Aprilia	23	43m 18.568s
26	Borja Maestro	SPA	41	Hune Racing Team – TMM	Aprilia	22	42m 28.798s
27	Jordi Dalmau	SPA	31	SAG – Castrol	Honda	22	42m 31.602s
28	Eduard Lopez	SPA	40	TCR Competicion	Aprilia	22	42m 31.771s
	Jonas Folger	GER	94	Ongetta Team I.S.P.A.	Aprilia	21	DNF
	Tomoyoshi Koyama	JPN	71	Loncin Racing	Loncin	21	DNF
	Alexis Masbou	FRA	5	Loncin Racing	Loncin	13	DNF
	Stefan Bradl	GER	17	Viessmann Kiefer Racing	Aprilia	7	DNF
	Julian Simon	SPA	60	Bancaja Aspar Team 125cc	Aprilia	5	DNF
	Luca Vitali	ITA	10	CBC Corse	Aprilia		EXCL
DNS	Michael Ranseder	AUT	88	Haojue Team	Haojue		

Fastest lap: Julian Simon, on lap 5, 1m 47.057s, 92.417mph/148.731km/h. (record)
Lap record: Lukas Pesk, CZE (Derbi), 1m 47.404s, 92.119mph/148.251km/h (2006).
Event best maximum speed: Sandro Cortese, GER (Derbi), 136.701mph/220.000km/h (race).

Qualifying
Air: 24° Humidity 33% Track: 35°

1	Simon	1m 48.237s
2	Smith	1m 48.519s
3	Iannone	1m 48.685s
4	Marquez	1m 48.931s
5	Gadea	1m 48.955s
6	Aegerter	1m 48.237s
7	Redding	1m 49.310s
8	Webb	1m 49.353s
9	Cortese	1m 49.362s
10	Espargaro, Pol	1m 49.400s
11	Olive	1m 49.806s
12	Corsi	1m 49.954s
13	Krummenacher	1m 49.968s
14	Bradl	1m 50.167s
15	Vazquez	1m 50.196s
16	Rabat	1m 50.249s
17	Beaubier	1m 50.256s
18	Terol	1m 50.342s
19	Zarco	1m 50.453s
20	Koyama	1m 50.564s
21	Nakagami	1m 50.781s
22	Savadori	1m 51.098s
23	Sembera	1m 51.542s
24	Iwema	1m 51.605s
25	Moncayo	1m 51.945s
26	Zanetti	1m 52.050s
27	Masbou	1m 52.850s
28	Marconi	1m 53.002s
29	Salom	1m 53.186s
30	Maestro	1m 54.170s
31	Vitali	1m 54.642s
32	Ranseder	1m 54.765s
40	Lopez	1m 55.900s
66	Hoyle	1m 56.300s
31	Dalmau	1m 57.298s
94	Folger	1m 57.508s

Fastest race laps

1	Simon	1m 47.057s
2	Smith	1m 47.252s
3	Espargaro, Pol	1m 48.235s
4	Folger	1m 48.279s
5	Cortese	1m 48.523s
6	Gadea	1m 48.608s
7	Vazquez	1m 48.667s
8	Marquez	1m 48.759s
9	Iannone	1m 48.874s
10	Redding	1m 48.878s
11	Terol	1m 49.051s
12	Aegerter	1m 49.071s
13	Webb	1m 49.118s
14	Bradl	1m 49.179s
15	Corsi	1m 49.274s
16	Zarco	1m 49.332s
17	Rabat	1m 49.374s
18	Krummenacher	1m 49.513s
19	Olive	1m 49.548s
20	Koyama	1m 49.575s
21	Zanetti	1m 49.608s
22	Beaubier	1m 49.859s
23	Nakagami	1m 49.983s
24	Savadori	1m 50.242s
25	Sembera	1m 50.675s
26	Masbou	1m 51.097s
27	Moncayo	1m 51.378s
28	Salom	1m 51.500s
29	Marconi	1m 51.791s
30	Iwema	1m 51.969s
31	Maestro	1m 53.982s
32	Dalmau	1m 54.117s
33	Lopez	1m 54.251s
34	Vitali	1m 54.829s

Championship Points

1	Iannone	37.5
2	Smith	36.5
3	Espargaro, Pol	31.5
4	Simon	30
5	Cortese	28
6	Marquez	27
7	Gadea	22
8	Bradl	17
9	Webb	16.5
10	Aegerter	16.5
11	Redding	14.5
12	Olive	14
13	Folger	13
14	Vazquez	11
15	Terol	10.5
16	Rabat	10
17	Koyama	4
18	Corsi	4
19	Zarco	3.5
20	Zanetti	2
21	Beaubier	1

Constructors

1	Aprilia	62.5
2	Derbi	35
3	KTM	27
4	Loncin	4

FRENCH GRAND PRIX

LE MANS CIRCUIT

Lorenzo, heading Rossi, Pedrosa and Dovizioso, built an unassailable lead by staying out on wet tyres.

Photos: Gold & Goose

Left: Team chief Jorge Martinez shows that the AWOL Talmacsi did have two bikes.

Below left: Will it or won't it? Edwards tries some weather forecasting.

Right: Melandri redeemed: a brilliant and well-judged ride brought second for the Hayate.

Below: Pimp my ride: Bridgestone's new hand-painted whitewalls denoted the softer compound.

Bottom: Nicky Hayden gets to know new crew chief Martinez.

Photos: Gold & Goose

BAD weather struck again and made for a fascinating weekend at Le Mans. The 75,903-strong crowd that braved the conditions was rewarded with a stop-and-go race of huge variety – and another new record for Rossi. For the first time in his career, he came last.

As usual, his progress to that position had been exceptional – and an illustration of how racing rules work.

The race started with a wet track and wet tyres for all, but with the rain having stopped and mechanics warming up dry bikes in the pits. Rossi was losing time to leader Lorenzo and took the gamble: he was first into the pits at the end of lap five, followed by Pedrosa, and first out again, on slicks.

The champion was still cruising when a patch of dark tarmac obscured a lingering damp swathe at Museum. The front tucked and he slid into the gravel. Pedrosa, within sight behind, took warning and made it safely around.

The Yamaha had a snapped gearlever and broken screen. Rossi walked away, then thought of the huge number of crashes in the smaller classes – just 15 125 finishers, from 33 starters. "I thought I might get some points, so I went back and started the bike again," he said.

His other bike was ready again, but with a slick front. The rules obliged it to have at least one tyre that was different from the bike he was bringing to the

pits, preventing the fitting of full slicks and requiring another pit stop for the second change to be made. One last problem: in the rush, the pit-lane speed limiter was forgotten. Rossi broke the limit on his exit and now had to add a ride-through penalty to three pit stops.

If the grand master showed that sometimes even he can get it badly wrong, team-mate Lorenzo demonstrated that it was possible to get it very right: his second win of the year regained him the points lead, and reinforced his growing status, both within Yamaha and in general.

Crazy conditions brought another high point – to Melandri, whose rehabilitation on the orphan Kawasaki/Hayate was completed with a ride to second that was both canny and courageous. It brought hope that Kawasaki, having already relented on pulling out altogether, might further relent on the pledge that there would be no further machine development during the season. Former race chief Ichiro Yoda was in the paddock and echoed the same sentiments: "Maybe some pressure from the Press and the fans will change the situation." But the hopes of upgrades would gradually die over the forthcoming weeks, and after the summer break, it became clear that there would be no further stay of execution either.

Melandri's successor at Ducati was also still a talking point, and the team went through a major reshuffle in its attempts to get Hayden up to speed.

Long-time crew chief Christian Pupulin was shifted to concentrate on data-logging duties, and former Gibernau chief Juan Martinez was brought in as his replacement. For one thing, the Spaniard had a greater command of English. "It's not like he's just going to rub the screen and fix everything, but we started out understanding each other better. I can talk at a more normal speed, and the bike is working better right out of the gate," Nicky said after the first day of practice. It was the start of an improvement, but it would be slow.

It gave Melandri the quote of the weekend: "When I was having trouble with the bike, Ducati sent me to a psychologist. When Nicky has trouble, they give him a new crew chief."

Another Ducati rider was sent straight to the increasingly famous Spanish surgeon, Barcelona based Xavier Mir. It was Gibernau, who high-sided heavily in Saturday morning's free practice and broke his troublesome left collarbone again. This oft-repeated injury dates back to 1993, but he would miss only this and the next race, and it would not be the worst setback to his doomed comeback season.

Political news rumbled on, with more details on Moto2 engine supply. They would come free of charge, issued by Dorna, with strictly controlled specifications. The only adjustments allowed would be to ECU settings, and these would be limited. And the engines would remain sealed, to be maintained by

Honda. At the same time, the spectre of one bike per rider for MotoGP began to recede, as race director Paul Butler explained to *MOTOCOURSE:* "The idea was that manufacturers could build a similar number of bikes to now and put more riders on the grid. But if it doesn't work out, it'll be shelved," he said.

There was shock in the 250 class, where the high-profile new 'satellite' Aspar Balaton team for Hungarian Talmacsi fell apart very publicly after just three races. The absent rider's statement explained firstly that the promise of two bikes for Gabor had not been kept; and secondly that his media rights had been breached by a concocted quote in the team's pre-race press release. This was anodyne enough: that he was "looking forward to the French GP", but by then he had decided not to take part. It might seem a trivial squabble, but Talmacsi is a very big star at home in Hungary and can command generous financial backing from giant Hungarian petro-chemical group MOL. His manager wanted it made clear that his image is not to be trifled with.

An innovation from Bridgestone: whitewall tyres. Or at least a semblance, with a new system introduced to mark the softer of the two options brought to each track with a strip of white around the bead. This had to be done by hand rather than during manufacture, since what was a soft tyre at one track might be the harder option at another.

Racing can be painful, even when you don't crash.

The first brave boy was Toni Elias, straight under the knife after Jerez to solve right-arm pump problems. He had 30 stitches in his forearm. The second was increasingly impressive Thai rider Ratthapark Wilairot, who had gashed the first two fingers on his right hand badly in a domestic accident. He had only the third and fourth fingers for braking.

How Spanish is motorcycle racing? Le Mans was the second GP in a row in which pole in each class went to a Spanish rider.

MotoGP RACE – 28 laps

The first two rows of the grid were covered by less than four-tenths of a second, after a thrilling end to practice that gave the lie to the belief that the lack of qualifying tyres would spoil the spectacle. It had been a full hour, restored at last, and as the final seconds ticked away and the flag dropped with riders still completing their fast laps, the tension mounted. With two minutes left, Stoner led. Then Lorenzo ousted him after the flag. But Pedrosa was still circulating yet faster, and he displaced his younger compatriot by five-thousandths for his first pole of the year, and one of the closest ever.

Rossi headed row two, from Dovizioso and Edwards; at a track where handling is worth more than horsepower, the Suzuki pair of Vermeulen and Capirossi led Melandri on the third.

Left: Pedrosa saw Rossi fall, and avoided the same fate to take third.

Far left: A career first – Rossi comes last.

Left: Takahashi had a lowly battle with Hayden.

Right: Simoncelli's bravery and control in the wet made him untouchable for his first win.

Below: De Puniet's home hopes fell flat.

Bottom right: German rookie Jonas Folger took a surprise second in the 125 race.

Photos: Gold & Goose

Lorenzo lined up in the wrong slot, at one of the markings for a four-row 250/125 grid rather than the three-strong MotoGP front row. Instead of penalising him, as has happened in the past, officials waited until he had wheeled into position.

Conditions could hardly have been worse. Sections of the track were still streaming wet, while others would soon be almost dry.

Pedrosa made his usual lighting getaway and led them up the hill, pursued into the first chicane by Stoner, Lorenzo and Rossi. By the end of the lap, Lorenzo, riding very forcefully for the conditions, had pushed to the front and was starting to pull away rapidly, being better than three seconds clear when Rossi pitted at the end of lap five.

Rossi was second at this point, from Dovizioso and Melandri, with Pedrosa fading in fifth and Stoner already a couple of seconds behind him.

Lorenzo continued to forge ahead, while Rossi began his prolonged series of disasters. Had he stopped too early? It had been the rider's decision, and he thought not: "I had set-up problems in practice and I didn't think I could win. But I could get the podium. The mistake was not the strategy, but the crash. After that, not even the ride-through made any difference."

It was confusing even without all that as riders came into the pits in twos and threes. By the eighth, with about half already changed or changing, Lorenzo was carrying on regardless and seven seconds clear of Dovizioso, also yet to change. Likewise Stoner, five seconds behind that, and Vermeulen, Hayden and Elias.

More significantly, Melandri had changed rubber and was now tenth, but one of the fastest on the track and now ahead of Pedrosa, still getting used to the very erratic surface.

At the end of lap 12, Lorenzo was almost 34 seconds clear, Elias now second, the continued speed of both demonstrating an amazing endurance from the Bridgestone wets. He pitted, emerging still in the lead. Now it was by seven seconds, and it was Melandri in pursuit. Dovi was another nine seconds down before the trio of Stoner, Vermeulen and Pedrosa. It was the last of these who had the most to offer.

With everyone on slicks, the order of the top six didn't change until the last lap, when an uncommonly aggressive ride from Pedrosa saw him hunt down and pounce on Dovizioso at the end of the back straight. Stoner and Vermeulen were spaced out behind.

It was all action further back, Edwards being the leading player. Having run second-last in the early laps as he struggled again with settings, he was 13th after the tyre changes – and slicing through. Quickly past Takahashi and Elias, and then Hayden and de Angelis, he closed on team-mate and sworn enemy Toseland, who was having his best run of the year disputing seventh with Capirossi. The American's attack, up the inside into the daunting turn one, was aggressive and highly effective. Two laps later, he'd closed the 1.3 seconds to Capirossi and slammed passed him too. He was still closing on Vermeulen when the flag cut his progress short.

Toseland finished a lonely ninth; Elias managed to pass and stay ahead of team-mate de Angelis. Hayden, another three seconds away, had his hands full fending off Takahashi. Earlier he'd received tyre marks on his fairing and had been nearly brought down by a crashing Kallio, the only non-finisher. De Puniet was 14th in a home GP disaster. Canepa took the last point. Rossi was two laps away.

And Lorenzo took the points lead again. But it was by just one point, with Rossi and Stoner equal behind, and Pedrosa still close

to fall, displaced from seventh by Pesek: the Czech rider had time to crash out of an early second and rejoin 19th.

All finishers took points, although the rest were little more than mere survivors. Toth was well clear of Leonov; Barbera got back for 11th, one lap down. Abraham also crashed and remounted, while Debise and Markham stayed on to follow along.

125cc RACE – 24 laps

Marquez, 16 in February, took his first pole, just a few days too late to displace Melandri as the youngest ever to take that position in the class. Redding, Terol and coming Swiss youngster Aegerter joined him on the front row; Smith and Simon were on the second.

Conditions were slightly drier than for the 250s, and consequently perhaps even a little trickier. The numbers suggest so: 33 starters, 30 crashers, 15 finishers.

Terol galloped away up front, Simon chasing, with Olive, Marquez and Smith together behind. Simon was closing when he watched Terol fall at the chicane, scrambling back on to rejoin in 25th. One of many adventures of the afternoon.

Not for Simon, however, who now led by almost ten seconds, and who would keep on pulling away to win by almost half a minute, helped by the attrition behind him.

At the end of lap six, the second-placers departed. Olive had got ahead of Marquez, only to fall off right under his wheels, taking them both out and extending Simon's lead to almost 20 seconds.

Smith inherited second, but soon came under threat. Bradl and Folger had managed to dispose of a fading Redding, who soon crashed out, then they got ahead of Smith. But Bradl went down, giving rookie Folger a brilliant second.

Gadea also closed up on Smith and got ahead for the last rostrum spot, by less than a second.

Nakagami was a lone and distant fifth, wheels-down all race long; then came Aegerter, narrowly ahead of Iannone. Both had fallen once, Iannone on the first lap.

Vazquez was alone in eighth; Terol was ninth in spite of a second crash, and Zanetti completed the top ten. Rabat in eleventh was the last rider on the same lap as the leader.

250cc RACE – 26 laps

Bautista's second pole of the year was by almost four-tenths from Simoncelli, while Aoyama and Luthi completed the front row, with fast class rookie di Meglio heading the second row at home.

The race started in streaming wet conditions and stayed more or less wet throughout, hence the high rate of attrition, with 15 crashes – some riders twice – and 14 finishers from 24 starters.

Aoyama led away, only to run wide at Garage Vert before the back straight, dropping to sixth by the end of the lap. He would not play a leading part again.

Simoncelli took over and made the most of a clear track, riding with such smooth daring that nobody could follow. After four laps, he was more than five seconds clear, and he had doubled that after lap ten, eventually winning by 18 seconds. It was a lonely afternoon and mentally tiring, he said, adding, "but it was great."

Only one rider came close to challenging. Pasini had finished lap one in tenth and was passing two or three riders a lap as he charged through. On lap four, he was past Luthi and Faubel for second and pulling away. At this point, he was six seconds away from Simoncelli, but he never would get closer, nor finish that lap, as he slid off, stomping away in disgust.

Luthi managed to get away from battling Spaniards Faubel and Debon, who held each other up as they swapped places. Then Debon was clearly in front and gradually closing. It took until lap 16 for him to catch Luthi, and when he got there he promptly knocked him off: having left his braking too late, he slipped off and his bike skittled the Swiss out of a hitherto safe second. Debon remounted, but only to retire.

This promoted Faubel to second again, now with Locatelli for company, the veteran through from 12th

on lap one. Faubel was too much for him, however, and he finished two seconds down, but back on the rostrum – a popular result.

A long way behind by half-distance, Barbera and Bautista were battling it out, with the former typically aggressive. And it was Barbera who paid the price, falling on the 15th lap to leave Bautista unmolested thereafter.

Wilairot had been running steadily and mainly alone behind them, having passed the fading Aoyama and after companion di Meglio had fallen on the last corner. Fifth was a career best for the already injured rider, well clear of de Rosa. Aoyama had yet further

GRAND PRIX DE FRANCE

17 MAY 2009 • FIM WORLD CHAMPIONSHIP ROUND 4

LE MANS – BUGATTI

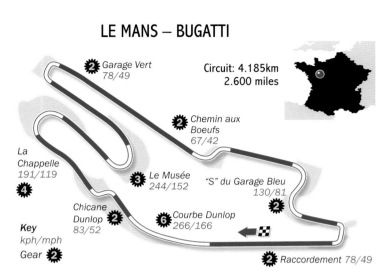

Garage Vert
78/49

Chemin aux
Boeufs
67/42

La
Chappelle
191/119

Le Musée
244/152

"S" du Garage Bleu
130/81

Chicane
Dunlop
83/52

Courbe Dunlop
266/166

Raccordement 78/49

Circuit: 4.185km
2.600 miles

Key
kph/mph
Gear

MotoGP

RACE DISTANCE: 28 laps, 72.812 miles/117.18 km • **RACE WEATHER:** Wet (air 16°, humidity 58%, track 19°)

Pos.	Rider	Nat.	No.	Entrant	Machine	Tyres	Laps	Time & speed
1	Jorge Lorenzo	AUS	99	Fiat Yamaha Team	Yamaha	B	28	47m 52.678s 92.489mph/ 146.848km/h
2	Marco Melandri	ITA	33	Hayate Racing Team	Kawasaki	B	28	48m 10.388s
3	Dani Pedrosa	SPA	3	Repsol Honda Team	Honda	B	28	48m 12.571s
4	Andrea Dovizioso	ITA	4	Repsol Honda Team	Honda	B	28	48m 13.133s
5	Casey Stoner	AUS	27	Ducati Marlboro Team	Ducati	B	28	48m 23.217s
6	Chris Vermeulen	AUS	7	Rizla Suzuki MotoGP	Suzuki	B	28	48m 30.140s
7	Colin Edwards	USA	5	Monster Yamaha Tech 3	Yamaha	B	28	48m 32.869s
8	Loris Capirossi	ITA	65	Rizla Suzuki MotoGP	Suzuki	B	28	48m 38.009s
9	James Toseland	JPN	52	Monster Yamaha Tech 3	Yamaha	B	27	48m 42.985s
10	Toni Elias	SPA	24	San Carlos Honda Gresini	Honda	B	27	48m 45.896s
11	Alex de Angelis	RSM	15	San Carlos Honda Gresini	Honda	B	27	48m 46.228s
12	Nicky Hayden	USA	69	Ducati Marlboro Team	Ducati	B	25	48m 49.325s
13	Yuki Takahashi	BRA	72	Scot Racing Team MotoGP	Honda	B	27	48m 49.366s
14	Randy de Puniet	USA	14	LCR Honda MotoGP	Honda	B	26	49m 03.977s
15	Nicola Canepa	USA	88	Pramac Racing	Ducati	B	25	49m 08.063s
16	Valentino Rossi	JPN	46	Fiat Yamaha Team	Yamaha	B	26	49m 28.685s
nc	Mika Kallio	FIN	36	Pramac Racing	Ducati	B	11	20m 47.302s
dns	Sete Gibernau	SPA	59	Grupo Francisco Hernando	Ducati	B	–	

Fastest lap: Dani Pedrosa, on lap 27, 1m 35.045s, 99.618mph/160.320km/h.

Lap record: Valentino Rossi, ITA (Yamaha), 1m 35.087s, 98.335mph/158.255km/h (2006).

Event best maximum speed: Casey Stoner, 179.3mph/288.5km/h (qualifying practice).

Qualifying: Dry

Air: 18° Humidity 57% Track: 22°

1	Pedrosa	1m 33.974s
2	Lorenzo	1m 33.979s
3	Stoner	1m 34.049s
4	Rossi	1m 34.106s
5	Dovizioso	1m 34.300s
6	Edwards	1m 34.330s
7	Vermeulen	1m 34.676s
8	Capirossi	1m 34.839s
9	Melandri	1m 35.008s
10	de Puniet	1m 35.399s
11	Elias	1m 35.431s
12	Toseland	1m 35.524s
13	Hayden	1m 35.682s
14	Kallio	1m 35.741s
15	Takahashi	1m 35.774s
16	de Angelis	1m 35.785s
17	Canepa	1m 36.136s
	Gibernau	no time

Fastest race laps

1	Pedrosa	1m 51.406s
2	Stoner	1m 52.030s
3	Edwards	1m 52.102s
4	Dovizioso	1m 52.813s
5	Lorenzo	1m 52.327s
6	Vermeulen	1m 52.471s
7	de Angelis	1m 52.681s
8	Elias	1m 52.904s
9	Melandri	1m 52.573s
10	Rossi	1m 53.734s
11	Capirossi	1m 53.774s
12	Takahashi	1m 53.846s
13	Hayden	1m 54.161s
14	de Puniet	1m 54.444s
15	Toseland	1m 54.684s
16	Canepa	1m 55.336s
17	Kallio	1m 55.563s

Championship Points

1	Lorenzo	66
2	Rossi	65
3	Stoner	65
4	Pedrosa	57
5	Melandri	43
6	Dovizioso	43
7	Edwards	35
8	Vermeulen	31
9	Capirossi	27
10	de Puniet	26
11	Elias	21
12	de Angelis	20
13	Toseland	17
14	Kallio	16
15	Hayden	9
16	Gibernau	8
17	Takahashi	8
18	Canepa	3

Constructor Points

1	Yamaha	95
2	Ducati	65
3	Honda	63
4	Kawasaki	20
5	Suzuki	38

Team Points

1	FIAT Yamaha Team	95
2	Repsol Honda Team	131
3	Ducati Marlboro Team	100
4	RIZLA Suzuki MotoGP	58
5	Monster Yamaha Tech	52
6	Hayate Racing Team	20
7	San Carlo Honda Gresini	38
8	LCR Honda MotoGP	20
9	Pramac Racing	19
10	Grupo Francisco Hernando	8
11	Scot Racing Team MOT	8

Grid order

Grid order	1	2	3	4	5	6	7	8	9	10	11	12	13	14	15	16	17	18	19	20	21	22	23	24	25	26	27	28	
3 PEDROSA	99	99	99	99	99	99	99	99	99	99	99	99	99	99	99	99	99	99	99	99	99	99	99	99	99	99	99	99	1
99 LORENZO	3	3	46	46	46	46	4	4	4	4	4	24	33	33	33	33	33	33	33	33	33	33	33	33	33	33	33	33	2
27 STONER	27	46	4	4	4	33	27	27	27	27	27	33	4	4	4	4	4	4	4	4	4	4	4	4	4	4	4	3	3
46 ROSSI	46	27	3	33	33	27	7	7	7	7	7	4	27	3	3	3	3	3	3	3	3	3	3	3	3	3	4	4
4 DOVIZIOSO	4	4	33	3	3	7	69	69	69	24	24	27	7	27	7	7	7	7	27	27	27	27	27	27	27	27	27		5
5 EDWARDS	7	33	7	7	27	69	72	24	24	72	33	7	3	7	27	27	27	27	7	7	7	7	7	7	7	7	7		6
7 VERMEULEN	33	7	27	27	7	52	24	72	72	5	3	52	52	52	52	52	65	65	65	65	65	5	5	5	5	5		7
65 CAPIROSSI	65	65	65	65	65	14	15	5	5	33	69	52	65	65	65	65	52	52	52	52	5	5	65	65	65	65	65		8
33 MELANDRI	14	14	14	52	52	72	5	88	88	69	52	65	69	69	5	5	5	5	5	52	52	52	52	52	52	52			9
14 de PUNIET	52	52	52	14	36	88	33	33	3	36	69	24	15	15	69	15	15	15	24	24	24	24	24	24	24			10
24 ELIAS	24	24	69	69	72	24	33	3	65	65	24	5	5	15	69	69	24	15	15	15	15	15	15	15			11
52 TOSELAND	69	69	72	72	15	5	65	65	52	52	5	72	24	24	24	69	69	69	69	69	69	69	69	69			12
69 HAYDEN	72	72	36	36	14	5	65	52	52	36	5	5	72	72	72	72	72	72	72	72	72	72					13
36 KALLIO	15	36	24	24	24	88	52	36	36	15	88	14	14	14	14	14	14	14	14	14	14	14	14	14			14
72 TAKAHASHI	36	15	15	15	15	3	36	15	15	88	14	88	88	88	88	88	88	88	88	88	88	88	88	88			15
15 de ANGELIS	5	5	5	5	5	65	14	14	14	14	11	46	46	46	46	46	46	46	46	46	46	46	46	46			
88 CANEPA	88	88	88	88	88	46	46	46	46	46	46	46															

99 Pitstop   *46 Lapped rider*

46 Ride through penalty

OFFICIAL TIMEKEEPER

250cc — RACE DISTANCE: 26 laps, 67.611 miles/108.81 km • RACE WEATHER: Wet (air 13°, humidity 82%, track 13°)

Pos.	Rider	Nat.	No.	Entrant	Machine	Laps	Time & Speed
1	Marco Simoncelli	ITA	58	Metis Gilera	Gilera	26	(mph/km/h) 82.071/132.081 49m 07.591s
2	Hector Faubel	SPA	55	Valencia CF – Honda SAG	Honda	26	49m 25.719s
3	Roberto Locatelli	ITA	15	Metis Gilera	Gilera	26	49m 29.233s
4	Alvaro Bautista	SPA	19	Mapfre Aspar Team	Aprilia	26	49m 38.678s
5	Ratthapark Wilairot	THA	14	Thai Honda PTT SAG	Honda	26	49m 58.088s
6	Raffaele de Rosa	ITA	35	Scot Racing Team 250cc	Honda	26	50m 03.957s
7	Lukas Pesek	CZE	52	Auto Kelly – CP	Aprilia	26	50m 23.616s
8	Hiroshi Aoyama	JPN	4	Scot Racing Team 250cc	Honda	26	50m 30.473s
9	Imre Toth	HUN	10	Team Toth Aprilia	Aprilia	26	50m 55.581s
10	Vladimir Leonov	RUS	56	Viessmann Kiefer Racing	Aprilia	26	50m 55.581s
11	Hector Barbera	SPA	40	Pepe World Team	Aprilia	26	49m 08.614s
12	Karel Abraham	CZE	17	Cardion AB Motoracing	Aprilia	25	49m 09.025s
13	Valentine Debise	FRA	53	CIP Moto – GP250	Honda	25	49m 31.243s
14	Toby Markham	GB	54	C&L Racing	Honda	25	50m 01.933s
	Alex Debon	ESP	6	Aeropuerto – Castello – Blusens	Aprilia	21	DNF
	Alex Baldolini	ITA	25	WTR San Marino Team	Aprilia	18	DNF
	Thomas Luthi	SWI	12	Emmi – Caffe Latte	Aprilia	18	DNF
	Mike di Meglio	FRA	63	Mapfre Aspar Team 250cc	Aprilia	10	DNF
	Mattia Pasini	ITA	75	Team Toth Aprilia	Aprilia	4	DNF
	Axel Pons	SPA	7	Pepe World Team	Aprilia	3	DNF
	Aitor Rodriguez	SPA	77	Milar – Juegos Lucky	Aprilia	3	DNF
	Angel Rodriguez	SPA	47	Balatonring Team	Aprilia	2	DNF
	Shoya Tomizawa	JPN	48	CIP Moto – GP250	Honda	1	DNF
	Bastien Chesaux	SWI	8	Racing Team Germany	Honda	0	DNF

Fastest lap: Debon, on lap 16, 1m 51.406s, 84.031mph/135.235km/h.
Lap record: Marco Simoncelli, ITA (Gilera), 1m 39.666s, 93.929mph/151.664km/h (2008).
Event best maximum speed: Bautista, 163.669mph/263.4km/h (free practice 1).

Qualifying: Dry — Air: 18° Humidity 48% Ground: 24°

1	Bautista	1m 38.270s
2	Simoncelli	1m 38.652s
3	Aoyama	1m 38.682s
4	Luthi	1m 38.796s
5	di Meglio	1m 39.003s
6	Debon	1m 39.365s
7	de Rosa	1m 39.367s
8	Pesek	1m 39.381s
9	Locatelli	1m 39.511s
10	Faubel	1m 39.517s
11	Barbera	1m 39.596s
12	Wilairot	1m 39.667s
13	Pasini	1m 39.896s
14	Baldolini	1m 40.066s
15	Abraham	1m 40.462s
16	Rodriguez, Ang	1m 40.620s
17	Tomizawa	1m 40.661s
18	Cluzel	1m 40.852s
19	Toth	1m 41.444s
20	Debise	1m 42.391s
21	Pons	1m 42.654s
22	Leonov	1m 42.812s
23	Chesaux	1m 43.342s
24	Rodriguez, Aitor	1m 44.132s
25	Markham	1m 45.322s

Fastest race laps

1	Debon	1m 51.406s
2	Faubel	1m 52.030s
3	Simoncelli	1m 52.102s
4	Luthi	1m 52.813s
5	Locatelli	1m 52.327s
6	Bautista	1m 52.471s
7	Barbera	1m 52.681s
8	Wilairot	1m 52.904s
9	Baldolini	1m 52.573s
10	Abraham	1m 53.734s
11	de Rosa	1m 53.774s
12	Pesek	1m 53.846s
13	Toth	1m 54.161s
14	di Meglio	1m 54.444s
15	Pasini	1m 54.684s
16	Aoyama	1m 55.336s
17	Debise	1m 55.563s
18	Leonov	1m 55.709s
19	Rodriguez, Ang	1m 56.925s
20	Markham	1m 58.403s
21	Pons	2m 01.042s
22	Rodriguez, Aitor	2m 01.820s

Championship Points

1	Bautista	67
2	Aoyama, Hiroshi	66
3	Barbera	48
4	Simoncelli	41
5	de Rosa	31
6	Locatelli	30
7	Luthi	29
8	Cluzel	28
9	Talmacsi	28
10	Faubel	27
11	Pasini	26
12	Pesek	24
13	di Meglio	21
14	Wilairot	20
15	Tomizawa	14
16	Debon	13
17	Abraham	11
18	Aoyama, Shuhei	10
19	Toth	10
20	Leonov	7
21	Debise	3
22	Markham	2
23	Watanabe	2
24	Baldolini	1

Constructors

1	Aprilia	83
2	Honda	78
3	Gilera	48
4	Yamaha	2

125cc — RACE DISTANCE: 24 laps, 62.410 miles/100.44 km • RACE WEATHER: Wet (air 12°, humidity 83%, track 12°)

Pos.	Rider	Nat.	No.	Entrant	Machine	Laps	Time & Speed
1	Julian Simon	SPA	60	Bancaja Aspar Team 125cc	Aprilia	24	(mph/km/h) 79.439/127.846 47m 08.273s
2	Jonas Folger	GER	94	Ongetta Team I.S.P.A.	Aprilia	24	47m 35.357s
3	Sergio Gadea	SPA	33	Bancaja Aspar Team 125cc	Aprilia	24	47m 39.189s
4	Bradley Smith	GBR	38	Bancaja Aspar Team 125cc	Aprilia	24	47m 39.803s
5	Takaaki Nakagami	JPN	73	Ongetta Team I.S.P.A.	Aprilia	24	48m 17.508s
6	Dominique Aegerter	SWI	77	Ajo Interwetten	Derbi	24	48m 20.496s
7	Andrea Iannone	ITA	29	Ongetta Team I.S.P.A.	Aprilia	24	48m 21.336s
8	Efren Vazquez	SPA	7	Derbi Racing Team	Derbi	24	48m 28.185s
9	Nicolas Terol	SPA	18	Jack & Jones Team	Aprilia	24	48m 48.309s
10	Lorenzo Zanetti	ITA	8	Ongetta Team I.S.P.A.	Aprilia	24	48m 50.973s
11	Esteve Rabat	SPA	12	Blusens Aprilia	Aprilia	24	49m 07.599s
12	Sandro Cortese	GER	11	Ajo Interwetten	Derbi	23	47m 23.157s
13	Jasper Iwema	NED	53	Racing Team Germany	Honda	23	47m 29.445s
14	Gregory di Carlo	FRA	54	Equipe de France	Honda	23	47m 59.484s
15	Randy Krummenacher	SWI	35	Degraaf Grand Prix	Aprilia	22	48m 06.140s
	Lorenzo Savadori	ITA	32	Fontana Racing	Aprilia	16	DNF
	Stefan Bradl	GER	17	Viessmann Kiefer Racing	Aprilia	14	DNF
	Scott Redding	GB	45	Blusens Aprilia	Aprilia	13	DNF
	Tomoyoshi Koyama	JPN	71	Loncin Racing	Loncin	10	DNF
	Luca Vitali	ITA	10	CBC Corse	Aprilia	10	DNF
	Cameron Beaubier	USA	16	Red Bull KTM Moto Sport	KTM	8	DNF
	Lukas Sembera	CZE	69	Matteoni Racing	Aprilia	8	DNF
	Marc Marquez	SPA	93	Red Bull KTM Moto Sport	KTM	8	DNF
	Johann Zarco	FRA	14	WTR San Marino Team	Aprilia	8	DNF
	Sturia Fagerhaug	NOR	50	Red Bull KTM Moto Sport	KTM	6	DNF
	Joan Olive	SPA	6	Derbi Racing Team	Derbi	5	DNF
	Pol Espargaro	SPA	44	Derbi Racing Team	Derbi	5	DNF
	Danny Webb	GB	99	Degraaf Grand Prix	Aprilia	4	DNF
	Steven le Cocquen	FRA	52	Villiers Team Competition	Derbi	4	DNF
	Simon Corsi	ITA	24	Jack & Jones Team	Aprilia	4	DNF
	Alexis Masbou	FRA	5	Loncin Racing	Loncin	2	DNF
	Cyril Carrillo	FRA	36	TJP – TVX Racing	Honda	1	DNF
	Luca Marconi	FRA	87	CBC Corse	Aprilia	0	DNF

Fastest lap: Smith, on lap 24, 1m 56.118s, 00.000mph/129.669km/h.
Lap record: Pol Espargaro, ITA (Gilera), 1m 43.918s, 90.086mph/144.979km/h (2008).
Event best maximum speed: Smith, 136.690mph/223.2km/h (warm up).

Qualifying — Air: 18° Humidity 48% Ground: 24°

1	Marquez	1m 47.080s
2	Redding	1m 47.713s
3	Terol	1m 47.783s
4	Aegerter	1m 47.995s
5	Olive	1m 48.085s
6	Smith	1m 48.115s
7	Simon	1m 48.334s
8	Bradl	1m 48.508s
9	Koyama	1m 49.313s
10	Webb	1m 49.439s
11	Beaubier	1m 49.695s
12	Gadea	1m 50.239s
13	Rabat	1m 50.598s
14	Masbou	1m 50.692s
15	Espargaro, Pol	1m 50.761s
16	Folger	1m 51.001s
17	Krummenacher	1m 51.430s
18	Sembera	1m 51.812s
19	Corsi	1m 52.028s
20	Zanetti	1m 52.443s
21	Savadori	1m 52.684s
22	Le Coquen	1m 53.225s
23	Iannone	1m 53.579s
24	Cortese	1m 54.504s
25	Vazquez	1m 54.640s
26	Marconi	1m 54.739s
27	Carrillo	1m 55.313s
28	di Carlo	1m 56.432s
29	Vitali	1m 56.705s
30	Ranseder	1m 56.846s
31	Iwema	1m 57.807s
32	Ongaro	1m 58.258s
33	Nakagami	1m 58.882s
34	Zarco	1m 59.162s
35	Hoyle	2m 01.457s
36	Fagerhaug	2m 03.768s

Fastest race laps

1	Smith	1m 56.188s
2	Simon	1m 56.331s
3	Gadea	1m 56.281s
4	Folger	1m 56.307s
5	Bradl	1m 56.823s
6	Terol	1m 57.002s
7	Aegerter	1m 57.252s
8	Iannone	1m 57.269s
9	Cortese	1m 57.736s
10	Redding	1m 58.228s
11	Koyama	1m 58.429s
12	Rabat	1m 58.519s
13	Beaubier	1m 58.630s
14	Vazquez	1m 58.763s
15	Zanetti	1m 58.785s
16	Nakagami	1m 58.824s
17	Marquez	1m 59.681s
18	Olive	1m 59.695s
19	Iwema	2m 00.831s
20	Fagerhaug	2m 00.831s
21	Corsi	2m 01.043s
22	Savadori	2m 01.168s
23	Webb	2m 01.398s
24	di Carlo	2m 01.849s
25	Krummenacher	2m 02.034s
26	Espargaro	2m 02.373s
27	Le Cocquen	2m 02.444s
28	Masbou	2m 02.547s
29	Sembera	2m 03.338s
30	Zarco	2m 03.491s
31	Vitali	2m 06.615s

Championship Points

1	Simon	55
2	Smith	49.5
3	Iannone	46.5
4	Gadea	38
5	Folger	33
6	Cortese	32
7	Espargaro, Pol	31.5
8	Marquez	27
9	Aegerter	26.5
10	Vazquez	19
11	Terol	17.5
12	Bradl	17
13	Webb	16.5
14	Rabat	15
15	Redding	14.5
16	Olive	14
17	Nakagami	11
18	Zanetti	8
19	Koyama	4
20	Corsi	4
21	Zarco	3.5
22	Iwema	3
23	di Carlo	2
24	Krummenacher	1
25	Beaubier	1

Constructors

1	Aprilia	87.5
2	Derbi	45
3	KTM	27
4	Loncin	2
5	Honda	3

ITALIAN GRAND PRIX

MUGELLO CIRCUIT

Drag race in the rain. De Puniet, Rossi and Pedrosa are best away, Stoner just behind, Vermeulen prominent, Lorenzo swamped in the pack.
Photo: Gold & Goose

A SECOND successive wet-to-dry race produced a similar event of great variety and excitement: those suggesting that pit stops should be made compulsory were only half facetious. This time there were five different leaders, and another clear winner, the one who timed his tyre change and fast laps exactly right. To the disappointment of the majority of the 81,000-plus capacity crowd, it wasn't Rossi, breaking a run of seven consecutive wins at a circuit he loves. His only consolation was his first ever rostrum in a bike-change race. There was a large enough swathe of red around the Correntaio corner, however, to exult in the fact that it was Casey Stoner's home-grown Ducati. It would be his last untroubled race for a long while.

The Famous Four had already been reduced to three by a mishap suffered by Pedrosa, which came to light after he landed so hard back in the saddle after a slip-and-flick on Saturday that his hip was wrenched severely. Dani was in serious pain again, and with a leg that kept failing to operate, as if the nerve was trapped. "It's like I have a misfire." In fact, the original injury happened while cycle training before the race. There followed a proper heavy tumble on Sunday, and in the following week a fracture and ligament damage were discovered.

By then, Pedrosa had already set a new land-mark: on Friday afternoon, he clocked 349.3km/h (217.0mph), the first time an 800 had exceeded the record set by a first-generation 990. His Honda was 1.9km/h faster than Capirossi's Ducati record, set pre-season in 2003 at Montmelo. Mugello was where MotoGP first cracked 200mph – Regis Laconi's Aprilia in 2003.

Did this, one wondered on a Friday afternoon, comply with the FIM's directive of a weekend in which the federation had espoused green causes, in line with the forthcoming World Environment Day? A document asked the riders to pledge to "avoid using my engine pointlessly". Not a thought many would wish to dwell upon.

Rossi, the obvious hero of the weekend, is known for being lucky. For a second race, Lorenzo seemed set to assume this mantle, as well as the others he seeks to take over. In France, it had been a simple matter of being shifted to the correct grid position. Here it started on the sighting lap, when he slid off inexplicably – he thought. Covered in mud, he managed to get the damaged bike back to the pits. There were seconds to go before the pit exit was formally closed. His team realised it, and frantically sent him out on the spare. He made it by seconds, still muddy when a couple of minutes later he threaded his way through the crowd on the grid to take up his pole position. As he was wiped down, the crew worked frantically to replace the throttle, the complete front brake system and most of the bodywork on his crashed bike, setting it up for a forthcoming change to dry tyres. Disaster narrowly turned into a strong second place.

The other Yamaha needle matched played out to another thrilling climax, and again in favour of Edwards, still fuming about the way Toseland and his former crew chief had conspired behind his back in 2008 to join forces. As at Le Mans, Edwards was uninspiring to start with, then gained massive speed at the end, surging back on his team-mate and sweeping past on the very last lap.

The 250s needed no wet-and-dry to be exciting: the lead changed hands eight times on the last lap alone, with a massively popular victory going to Pasini, whose refusal to give in to the disability of a weakened right arm had become increasingly widely known and admired. Simoncelli, a close second, hugged him afterwards, then was called to the headmaster's office for a spanking. Or the equivalent, the new 'yellow card' system that puts a rider under warning of suspension. Simoncelli and Bautista had collided during a typically fierce battle, and although both had survived, the former was blamed for riding "in an irresponsible manner, causing danger to…Bautista". He was also fined US$5,000 and was outraged. It was

Left: Smeared with gravel dust, but outwardly calm, sighting-lap crasher Lorenzo discusses Plan B with crew chief Ramon Forcada.

Right: Pedrosa's training injuries were exacerbated by a heavy race crash. His title challenge was over.

Below right: Stoner's second clear win was his last good race for months.

Photos: Gold & Goose

normal racing, he insisted, citing other unpunished incidents, like Debon's overtake-attack on Luthi at the previous race, where both had gone down. But race direction had decided it was time for a warning shot, bearing in mind the advent of Moto2 in 2010, and that Simoncelli was an up-and-coming rider who would be in MotoGP for that season. Later in the year, Jorge Lorenzo entered the debate, firmly on the side of law and order. "I did some crazy things and I was punished, and it stopped me," he said.

Again, Moto2 was much on the agenda, IRTA fielding provisional entries for 91 riders from 47 teams when the lists closed during the weekend. With an ideal grid between 34 and 36, "we will have to be pretty ruthless," said IRTA's Mike Trimby, "though some could be smoke and mirrors." Priority would be given to existing 250 teams, a much-trimmed list being due for release in October.

Sadly, but by now not unexpectedly, the Haojue team was absent, and its promises to be back for the next round would come to nothing as the Surtees-patronised England-based team first terminated its engine development contract with Jan Witteveen, then failed to convince its Chinese backers to continue using KTM engines. Far from returning, the team would disband over the coming weeks, its members wearing an expression of highly scrutable dismay.

MotoGP RACE – 23 laps

Another thrilling climax to qualifying: with just over a minute left, Rossi took the lead, but Capirossi was taking a tow and promptly took over. Then, the flag already waiting, Stoner and Lorenzo were each setting fastest section times. Lorenzo was faster, by two-hundredths, for his second pole; Rossi was moved to the second row.

Conditions were fine and warm throughout practice, but it rained on Sunday and warm-up was run in the wet. It dried for the 125s, was sodden for the 250s and was drying quite rapidly when the big bikes lined up, although there were still dark clouds above.

Lorenzo spun up and snaked off the line, his rear tyre smoking as he was swamped. By the time they reached the first corner, Pedrosa was heading Vermeulen, but the boldly ridden blue Suzuki was in the lead before half the lap was done. At the start of the next, Stoner powered past down the straight, Dovizioso a close third, Pedrosa dropping away, with Rossi, Lorenzo, de Puniet and Capirossi in a heap behind him.

On the second lap, Rossi moved past Pedrosa for fourth, the first three still a little way ahead. He closed that over the next couple of laps, by which time the order had changed up front, a fired-up Dovizioso being ahead of Stoner.

Rossi was easily past Vermeulen into third on lap six, and straight past Stoner as well. The Australian was struggling a little with the pace on the drying, but still patchy, surface. He succumbed also to Melandri, inspired by the conditions and his French result. The Kawasaki had been ninth on lap one and had come charging through, passing Lorenzo, Vermeulen and finally Stoner for third by the end of lap seven.

Now it became a game of tactics and deciding when to pit to change to slicks. Toseland, near the back, had taken an early gamble and pitted at the end of lap four, and by the eighth, he was circulating faster than the leaders. This prompted everyone to follow suit, and by the end of lap ten, everyone had called in to switch. The order became slightly easier to follow.

Dovizioso was ahead of Stoner by some three seconds, while Melandri was dropping away, about to lose third to Lorenzo. Capirossi and Rossi were not far adrift, the latter riding very cautiously. Behind him, Vermeulen was having trouble getting heat into his tyres and also losing ground.

It was at this point that Pedrosa crashed on the direction switch at Casanova-Savelli, being thrown

tumbling into the gravel and lying in obvious agony before being stretchered off. He had dropped to tenth by the time he fell.

Up front, Stoner was getting into his stride. He quickly closed on Dovizioso and powered past at the start of lap 14. Capirossi followed him through, and the pair of them started to pull away by more than a second. Then the Ducati briefly lost the lead to the Suzuki – an unlikely scenario, but with good reason. Stoner had run into clutch-slip problems, and when he slackened off the lever, it caused the slipper-clutch settings to go awry. He was straight back ahead, however, as he adjusted rapidly, and from there to the end he pulled away in dominant style.

Capirossi's rostrum hopes would soon be under severe threat. Lorenzo passed Dovizioso on lap 19, Rossi also one lap later. The Spaniard was lapping fastest now, but there weren't enough laps left, although he did get within a second of Stoner. Behind him, Rossi did set fastest lap on the 21st, but he had his hands full keeping Dovizioso behind over the line. Down on power, hapless Capirossi dropped from second to fifth in the last two laps.

Behind, Toseland had come through strongly after his early tyre change, catching de Puniet for a long battle, the pair outpacing Melandri. But they also had trouble coming from behind: for a second race, Edwards had gained speed massively in the closing stages. He dispatched the Frenchman with one lap to go, then pounced on Toseland last time around.

Canepa and Hayden were battling behind him, but the American soon ran into rear brake problems after wearing the pads down in an attempt to control the wheelspin. Vermeulen had dropped behind them, but

was gaining. He passed Hayden with two laps to go, and Melandri on the last.

Far behind, Kallio was fighting with an unhappy Elias, the rookie prevailing narrowly at the finish. De Angelis was a lap down after crashing on his first lap out on dry tyres. Takahashi also crashed out, and with Gibernau absent, there were points for all. And Stoner was back in the lead on points.

250cc RACE – 21 laps

Bautista took pole by a whisker from Simoncelli, with Barbera hardly further behind; Aoyama completed the front row.

Heavy rain struck just before the race, giving time to change tyres, but less to adjust settings – winner Pasini, for example, was riding a 'dry' bike on wet tyres and took time to get going as he adapted to it.

Simoncelli rocketed away, three seconds clear after just one lap of a group: Barbera, Faubel, Aoyama and Bautista, all feeling their way. Pasini was another two places down.

After three laps, Simoncelli's advantage was a gaping 7.3 seconds, but now Pasini was second and Bautista third, both gaining pace and taking whole seconds out of his lead. Bautista got back ahead on lap six, and two laps later all three were together. And on the ninth, it was Bautista in front.

Simoncelli fought back, passing Bautista on the straight only to run wide into the first corner and lose the lead again. Two laps later, a bold attack in the Casanova-Savelli switchback put them on a collision course as he took Bautista by surprise, and both went off into the gravel at high speed. Simoncelli recov-

Left: Pasini, Simoncelli and Bautista laid on a feast for the fans.

Below left: Pasini's fighting win was a popular victory.

Below: 250 rivals Simoncelli *(top)* and Bautista clashed physically once more.

Below right: Two in a row made Smith the most successful Briton for decades.

Photos: Gold & Goose

ered first, losing just over five seconds, Bautista was another four seconds worse off. But Aoyama wasn't close enough to be a worry as both got back up to speed.

Bautista caught Simoncelli with five laps left, Pasini more than 2.5 seconds away. Both were right on the limit, but Bautista was unsighted in the spray and struggling. He kept attacking all the same, until an out-of-the saddle moment forced him to ease off.

Now there were three laps, and Pasini was just 1.3 seconds away from Simoncelli. They started the last lap with the Gilera right on the Aprilia's back wheel.

Simoncelli passed at the end of the straight, but ran wide and was second again. He led once more at the third corner; Pasini at the fourth. And so it went on around the spectacular circuit, the pair changing places eight times in all. But it was Pasini ahead over the line, by just over a tenth, for one of the finest victories of his career. Bautista was 1.3 seconds away, but still extended his points lead over Aoyama.

Almost half a minute away, Luthi had come through from a slow start and had been battling with Barbera, outpacing him by the end to take fourth by less than three seconds.

Aoyama was sixth, three seconds away and never quite in the hunt after Luthi and Barbera got past. Debon had kept him honest, and was still just a second behind. Faubel had fallen back to a lone eighth, with de Rosa and Locatelli completing the top ten. In spite of the conditions, only three riders crashed: Cluzel on lap one, then Pesek and Tomizawa on laps five and six.

The rest were spaced out: Hungarian beginner Balazs Nemeth, drafted into Aspar's Balatonring team to replace deserter Talmacsi, was a lap down, but only one place out of the points and far from last at his first attempt.

125cc RACE – 20 laps

Simon led most of practice, but Smith and Redding snitched ahead by the end. Gadea filled row one; Marquez led the second from Iannone, Zarco and Espargaro.

Morning rain had more or less dried, and all started on slicks for some fraught early laps, with a big gang up front.

The lead group had shrunk to eight when, on lap six, Iannone suddenly slowed and pulled out. Smith was already leading and gained a small advantage, but his attempt to stretch it further meant a couple of slides, so he slacked off to regroup.

Terol and Simon caught up promptly, the rest now losing touch. At half-distance, the first three were together, Terol leading for three laps.

Smith took over again on lap 13, but it would surely go to the flag. Then, with two laps left, Simon began falling away, his engine overheating. With ten seconds to the pursuit, however, he was able to nurse it home.

Terol chased Smith as hard as he could, but "his last lap was just too fast for me". A second win in a row made him the first Briton to win twice in a season since Sheene in 1979 and gave him the points lead.

The next five started the last lap in a mob. Cortese soon left, crashing after tangling with a backmarker, while Redding had a huge moment on the last corner – up in a handstand on the bars. Espargaro got to the flag half a second clear of Marquez; three seconds away, Zarco took sixth, inches ahead of Redding.

Bradl was never quite in the fight, but he saved eighth from Savadori. Cortese was quickly back in the saddle to finish tenth.

Webb crashed out of the front group early on. Vazquez and Olive also tumbled.

GRAN PREMIO D'ITALIA ALICE

31 MAY 2009 • FIM WORLD CHAMPIONSHIP ROUND 5

AUTODROMO INTERNAZIONALE DEL MUGELLO

Scarperia 109/68
Arrabbiata 2 156/97
Palagio 106/66
Correntaio 106/66
Biondetti 1 165/103
Biondetti 2 167/104
Bucine 114/71
Savelli 117/73
San Donato 99/62
Arrabbiata 1 163/101
Materassi 119/74
Luc 11.
Cassanova 114/71
Borgo San Lorenzo 121/75
Poggio Se 119/74

Key
kph/mph
Gear

Circuit 5.245km/3.259 miles

MOTOGP	RACE DISTANCE: 23 laps, 71.596 miles/120.635 km • RACE WEATHER: Wet (air 18°, humidity 66%, track 20°)

Pos.	Rider	Nat.	No.	Entrant	Machine	Tyres	Laps	Time & speed
1	Casey Stoner	AUS	27	Ducati Marlboro Team	Ducati	B	23	45m 41.894s 98.382mph/ 158.331km/h
2	Jorge Lorenzo	SPA	99	Fiat Yamaha Team	Yamaha	B	23	45m 42.895s
3	Valentino Rossi	ITA	46	Fiat Yamaha Team	Yamaha	B	23	45m 43.970s
4	Andrea Dovizioso	ITA	4	Repsol Honda Team	Honda	B	23	45m 44.023s
5	Loris Capirossi	ITA	65	Rizla Suzuki MotoGP	Suzuki	B	23	45m 45.168s
6	Colin Edwards	USA	5	Monster Yamaha Tech 3	Yamaha	B	23	46m 06.345s
7	James Toseland	JPN	52	Monster Yamaha Tech 3	Yamaha	B	23	46m 07.515s
8	Randy de Puniet	USA	14	LCR Honda MotoGP	Honda	B	23	46m 07.940s
9	Nicola Canepa	USA	88	Pramac Racing	Ducati	B	23	46m 13.709s
10	Chris Vermeulen	AUS	7	Rizla Suzuki MotoGP	Suzuki	B	23	46m 16.708s
11	Marco Melandri	ITA	33	Hayate Racing Team	Kawasaki	B	23	46m 16.984s
12	Nicky Hayden	USA	69	Ducati Marlboro Team	Ducati	B	23	46m 21.016s
13	Mika Kallio	FIN	36	Pramac Racing	Ducati	B	23	46m 34.356s
14	Toni Elias	SPA	24	San Carlos Honda Gresini	Honda	B	23	46m 34.372s
15	Alex de Angelis	RSM	15	San Carlos Honda Gresini	Honda	B	22	46m 03.967s
	Dani Pedrosa	SPA	3	Repsol Honda Team	Honda	B	12	DNF
	Yuki Takahashi	BRA	72	Scot Racing Team MotoGP	Honda	B	10	DNF

Fastest lap: Valentino Rossi, on lap 21, 1m 51.186s, 105.523mph/169.823km/h.

Lap record: Casey Stoner, AUS (Ducati), 1m 50.003s, 106.657mph/171.649km/h (2008).

Event best maximum speed: Dani Pedrosa, 217.004mph/349.3km/h (free practice 1).

Qualifying: Dry
Air: 25° Humidity: 22% Track: 42°

1	Lorenzo	1m 48.987s
2	Stoner	1m 49.008s
3	Capirossi	1m 49.121s
4	Rossi	1m 49.148s
5	de Puniet	1m 49.499s
6	Edwards	1m 49.547s
7	Dovizioso	1m 49.648s
8	Pedrosa	1m 50.073s
9	Elias	1m 50.078s
10	Takahashi	1m 50.305s
11	Vermeulen	1m 50.405s
12	de Angelis	1m 50.448s
13	Canepa	1m 50.528s
14	Toseland	1m 50.537s
15	Melandri	1m 50.710s
16	Hayden	1m 50.924s
17	Kallio	1m 51.008s

Fastest race laps

1	Rossi	1m 51.186s
2	Dovizioso	1m 51.187s
3	Stoner	1m 51.310s
4	Lorenzo	1m 51.331s
5	Capirossi	1m 51.980s
6	Edwards	1m 52.179s
7	Toseland	1m 53.233s
8	Canepa	1m 53.361s
9	de Puniet	1m 53.454s
10	Vermeulen	1m 53.473s
11	Hayden	1m 53.710s
12	Melandri	1m 54.033s
13	Elias	1m 54.296s
14	Kallio	1m 54.305s
15	de Angelis	1m 56.863s
16	Pedrosa	1m 58.753s
17	Takahashi	2m 03.081s

Championship Points

3	Stoner	90
2	Lorenzo	86
3	Rossi	81
4	Pedrosa	57
5	Dovizioso	56
6	Melandri	48
7	Edwards	45
8	Capirossi	38
9	Vermeulen	37
10	de Puniet	34
11	Toseland	26
12	Elias	23
13	de Angelis	21
14	Kallio	19
15	Hayden	13
16	Canepa	10
17	Gibernau	8
18	Takahashi	8

Constructor Points

1	Yamaha	115
2	Ducati	90
3	Honda	76
4	Suzuki	49
5	Kawasaki	48

Team Points

1	FIAT Yamaha Team	167
2	Repsol Honda Team	113
3	Ducati Marlboro Team	102
4	RIZLA Suzuki MotoGP	75
5	Monster Yamaha Tech 3	71
6	Hayate Racing Team	48
7	San Carlo Honda Gresini	44
8	LCR Honda MotoGP	34
9	Pramac Racing	29
10	Grupo Francisco Hernando	8
11	Scot Racing Team MOT	8

	Grid order	1	2	3	4	5	6	7	8	9	10	11	12	13	14	15	16	17	18	19	20	21	22	23	
99	LORENZO	7	27	27	4	4	4	4	46	46	33	4	4	4	27	27	27	27	27	27	27	27	27	27	1
27	STONER	27	7	7	27	27	46	46	4	33	46	27	27	27	65	65	65	65	65	65	65	65	99	99	2
65	CAPIROSSI	4	4	4	7	7	27	33	33	99	99	33	65	65	4	4	4	4	4	99	99	99	46	46	3
46	ROSSI	3	46	46	46	46	7	27	99	27	27	99	99	99	99	99	99	99	99	4	4	46	65	4	4
14	de PUNIET	46	3	3	99	33	33	7	7	24	24	65	46	46	46	46	46	46	46	46	4	4	65		5
5	EDWARDS	99	65	99	33	99	99	99	27	36	4	46	33	33	52	52	14	14	52	52	14	52	52	5	6
4	DOVIZIOSO	14	99	33	3	3	3	65	65	72	65	7	52	52	14	14	52	52	14	14	52	14	5	52	7
3	PEDROSA	65	33	65	65	65	65	3	3	4	7	14	14	14	33	33	33	5	5	5	5	14	14		8
24	ELIAS	33	14	14	14	14	24	24	24	7	36	24	7	69	69	69	5	5	88	88	88	88	88		9
72	TAKAHASHI	5	5	5	24	24	14	5	36	65	3	69	69	7	7	5	69	88	33	33	69	33	33	7	10
7	VERMEULEN	24	24	24	5	5	5	15	5	3	69	52	3	5	5	7	88	69	69	69	33	7	7	33	11
15	de ANGELIS	52	69	69	69	15	15	36	15	15	14	3	24	88	88	88	7	7	7	7	7	69	69		12
88	CANEPA	69	15	15	15	69	36	72	72	5	72	36	5	24	24	36	36	36	36	36	36	36	36		13
52	TOSELAND	15	52	36	36	36	69	14	69	69	52	5	88	36	36	24	24	24	24	24	24	24	24		14
33	MELANDRI	72	36	52	72	72	72	69	14	14	5	88	36	15	15	15	15	15	15	15	15	15	15	15	15
69	HAYDEN	36	72	72	88	88	88	52	52	52	88	15	15												
36	KALLIO	88	88	88	52	52	52	88	88	88	15														

33 Pitstop   *15 Lapped rider*

250cc — RACE DISTANCE: 21 laps, 68.613 miles/68.440 km • RACE WEATHER: Wet (air 15°, humidity 76%, track 16°)

Pos.	Rider	Nat.	No.	Entrant	Machine	Laps	Time & Speed
1	Mattia Pasini	ITA	75	Team Toth Aprilia	Aprilia	21	45m 38.391s
							(mph/km/h)
							89.975/144.801
2	Marco Simoncelli	ITA	58	Metis Gilera	Gilera	21	45m 38.508s
3	Alvaro Bautista	SPA	19	Mapfre Aspar Team	Aprilia	21	45m 39.684s
4	Thomas Luthi	SWI	12	Emmi – Caffe Latte	Aprilia	21	46m 02.948s
5	Hector Barbera	SPA	40	Pepe World Team	Aprilia	21	46m 05.405s
6	Hiroshi Aoyama	JPN	4	Scot Racing Team 250cc	Honda	21	46m 08.428s
7	Alex Debon	ESP	6	Aeropuerto – Castello – Blusens	Aprilia	21	46m 09.716s
8	Hector Faubel	SPA	55	Valencia CF – Honda SAG	Honda	21	46m 13.569s
9	Raffaele de Rosa	ITA	35	Scot Racing Team 250cc	Honda	21	46m 23.247s
10	Roberto Locatelli	ITA	15	Metis Gilera	Gilera	21	46m 24.874s
11	Alex Baldolini	ITA	25	WTR San Marino Team	Aprilia	21	46m 27.912s
12	Mike di Meglio	FRA	63	Mapfre Aspar Team 250cc	Aprilia	21	46m 38.930s
13	Karel Abraham	CZE	17	Cardion AB Motoracing	Aprilia	21	47m 02.121s
14	Ratthapark Wilairot	THA	14	Thai Honda PTT SAG	Honda	21	47m 03.910s
15	Imre Toth	HUN	10	Team Toth Aprilia	Aprilia	21	47m 08.788s
16	Balazs Nemeth	HUN	11	Balatonring Team	Aprilia	20	47m 07.283s
17	Axel Pons	SPA	7	Pepe World Team	Aprilia	20	47m 07.373s
18	Bastien Chesaux	SWI	8	Racing Team Germany	Honda	20	47m 07.608s
19	Valentin Debise	FRA	53	CIP Moto – GP250	Honda	20	47m 32.464s
20	Daiel Arcas	SPA	37	Milar – Juegos Lucky	Aprilia	18	46m 39.370s
	Shoya Tomizawa	JPN	48	CIP Moto – GP250	Honda	6	DNF
	Lukas Pesek	CZE	52	Auto Kelly – CP	Aprilia	5	DNF
	Vladimir Leonov	RUS	56	Viessmann Kiefer Racing	Aprilia	4	DNF
	Jules Cluzel	FRA	16	Matteoni Racing	Aprilia	0	DNF

Fastest lap: Marco Simoncelli, on lap 20, 2m 05.830s, 93.242mph/150.059km/h.
Lap record: Alvaro Bautista, SPA (Aprilia), 1m 53.669s, 103.217mph/166.113km/h (2008).
Event best maximum speed: Hector Barbera, 181.813mph/292.6km/h (free practice 1).

Qualifying: Dry — Air: 25° Humidity: 21% Track: 43°

1	Bautista	1m 52.804s
2	Simoncelli	1m 52.818s
3	Barbera	1m 52.842s
4	Aoyama, Hiroshi	1m 53.050s
5	Debon	1m 53.573s
6	Luthi	1m 53.702s
7	Wilairot	1m 53.811s
8	Pasini	1m 53.875s
9	de Rosa	1m 53.941s
10	Locatelli	1m 53.988s
11	Abraham	1m 54.052s
12	Cluzel	1m 54.211s
13	Faubel	1m 55.351s
14	di Meglio	1m 54.363s
15	Pesek	1m 54.375s
16	Tomizawa	1m 54.992s
17	Baldolini	1m 55.461s
18	Toth	1m 56.201s
19	Pons	1m 57.574s
20	Debise	1m 57.699s
21	Leonov	1m 58.464s
22	Nemeth	1m 59.132s
23	Arcas	1m 59.513s
24	Chesaux	1m 59.617s

Fastest race laps

1	Simoncelli	2m 05.830s
2	Bautista	2m 06.083s
3	Pasini	2m 06.436s
4	Luthi	2m 07.903s
5	Barbera	2m 08.407s
6	Debon	2m 08.565s
7	Aoyama, Hiroshi	2m 08.722s
8	Faubel	2m 08.775s
9	Locatelli	2m 08.881s
10	Baldolini	2m 09.235s
11	de Rosa	2m 09.856s
12	di Meglio	2m 10.034s
13	Abraham	2m 11.073s
14	Wilairot	2m 11.435s
15	Toth	2m 11.842s
16	Pesek	2m 13.067s
17	Pons	2m 14.726s
18	Tomizawa	2m 15.159s
19	Chessaux	2m 15.231s
20	Nemeth	2m 15.621s
21	Leonov	2m 18.331s
22	Debise	2m 19.388s
23	Arcas	2m 29.908s

Championship Points

1	Bautista	83
2	Aoyama, Hiroshi	76
3	Simoncelli	61
4	Barbera	59
5	Pasini	51
6	Luthi	42
7	de Rosa	38
8	Locatelli	36
9	Faubel	35
10	Cluzel	28
11	Talmacsi	28
12	di Meglio	25
13	Pesek	24
14	Debon	22
15	Wilairot	22
16	Abraham	14
17	Tomizawa	14
18	Toth	11
19	Aoyama, Shuhei	10
20	Leonov	7
21	Baldolini	6
22	Debise	3
23	Markham	2
24	Watanabe	2

Constructors

		Points
1	Aprilia	108
2	Honda	88
2	Gilera	68
3	Yamaha	2

125cc — RACE DISTANCE: 20 laps, 65.181 miles/104.9 km • RACE WEATHER: Dry (air 18°, humidity 52%, track 19°)

Pos.	Rider	Nat.	No.	Entrant	Machine	Laps	Time & Speed
1	Bradley Smith	GB	38	Bancaja Aspar Team 125cc	Aprilia	20	40m 09.523s
							(mph/km/h)
							97.386/156.728
2	Nicolas Terol	SPA	18	Jack & Jones Team	Aprilia	20	40m 09.739s
2	Julian Simon	SPA	60	Bancaja Aspar Team 125cc	Aprilia	20	40m 16.637s
4	Pol Espargaro	SPA	44	Derbi Racing Team	Derbi	20	40m 21.352s
5	Marc Marquez	SPA	93	Red Bull KTM Moto Sport	KTM	20	40m 21.838s
6	Johann Zarco	FRA	14	WTR San Marino Team	Aprilia	20	40m 24.128s
7	Scott Redding	GB	45	Blusens Aprilia	Aprilia	20	40m 24.828s
8	Stefan Bradl	GER	17	Viessmann Kiefer Racing	Aprilia	20	40m 31.778s
9	Lorenzo Savadori	ITA	32	Fontana Racing	Aprilia	20	40m 31.915s
10	Sandro Cortese	GER	11	Ajo Interwetten	Derbi	20	40m 38.762s
11	Sergio Gadea	SPA	33	Bancaja Aspar Team 125cc	Aprilia	20	40m 45.882s
12	Lorenzo Zanetti	ITA	8	Ongetta Team I.S.P.A.	Aprilia	20	40m 45.967s
13	Randy Krummenacher	SWI	35	Degraaf Grand Prix	Aprilia	20	40m 46.030s
14	Jonas Folger	GER	94	Ongetta Team I.S.P.A.	Aprilia	20	40m 46.104s
15	Takaaki Nakagami	JPN	73	Ongetta Team I.S.P.A.	Aprilia	20	40m 46.159s
16	Esteve Rabat	SPA	12	Blusens Aprilia	Aprilia	20	40m 46.357s
17	Luca Morciano	ITA	61	Junior GP Racing Dream	Aprilia	20	40m 59.393s
18	Simon Corsi	ITA	24	Jack & Jones Team	Aprilia	20	40m 59.942s
19	Dominique Aegerter	SWI	77	Ajo Interwetten	Derbi	20	41m 15.423s
20	Riccardo Moretti	ITA	51	Elligi Racing	Aprilia	20	41m 15.542s
21	Davide Stirpe	ITA	51	CRP Racing	Aprilia	20	41m 29.748s
22	Lukas Sembera	CZE	69	Matteoni Racing	Aprilia	20	41m 31.469s
23	Jasper Iwema	NED	53	Racing Team Germany	Honda	20	41m 52.597s
24	Gennaro Sabatino	ITA	63	Junior GP Racing Dream	Aprilia	19	40m 16.976s
25	Luca Vitali	ITA	10	CBC Corse	Aprilia	19	40m 25.252s
26	Alessandro Tonucci	ITA	62	Junior GP Racing Dream	Aprilia	19	40m 25.563s
	Luca Marconi	FRA	87	CBC Corse	Aprilia	12	DNF
	Danny Webb	GB	99	Degraaf Grand Prix	Aprilia	8	DNF
	Andrea Iannone	ITA	29	Ongetta Team I.S.P.A.	Aprilia	5	DNF
	Joan Olive	SPA	6	Derbi Racing Team	Derbi	5	DNF
	Efren Vazquez	SPA	7	Derbi Racing Team	Derbi	5	DNF
	Tomoyoshi Koyama	JPN	71	Loncin Racing	Loncin	2	DNF
	Alexis Masbou	FRA	5	Loncin Racing	Loncin	1	DNF

Fastest lap: Julian Simon, on lap 8, 1m 58.744s, 98.806mph/159.014km/h.
Lap record: Mike di Meglio, FRA (Derbi), 1m 58.570s, 98.951mph/159.247km/h (2008).
Event best maximum speed: Efren Vazquez, SPA (Derbi), 149.812mph/244.1km/h (race).

Qualifying: Dry — Air: 23° Humidity: 23% Track: 40°

1	Smith	1m 58.134s
2	Redding	1m 58.431s
3	Simon	1m 58.575s
4	Gadea	1m 58.621s
5	Marquez	1m 58.947s
6	Iannone	1m 59.121s
7	Zarco	1m 59.178s
8	Espargaro, Pol	1m 59.186s
9	Cortese	1m 59.358s
10	Webb	1m 59.478s
11	Corsi	1m 59.589s
12	Terol	1m 59.600s
13	Krummenacher	1m 59.726s
14	Rabat	1m 59.974s
15	Vazquez	2m 00.032s
16	Zanetti	2m 00.113s
17	Olive	2m 00.118s
18	Aegerter	2m 00.149s
19	Bradl	2m 00.335s
20	Savadori	2m 00.384s
21	Moretti	2m 00.392s
22	Nakagami	2m 00.445s
23	Folger	2m 00.672s
24	Morciano	2m 01.206s
25	Sembera	2m 01.406s
26	Stirpe	2m 01.425s
27	Tonucci	2m 01.814s
28	Koyama	2m 02.353s
29	Sabatino	2m 02.821s
30	Iwema	2m 03.135s
31	Masbou	2m 03.226s
32	Marconi	2m 04.577s
33	Vitali	2m 05.793s
	Beaubier	no time

Fastest race laps

1	Simon	1m 58.744s
2	Terol	1m 58.819s
3	Smith	1m 59.207s
4	Espargaro, Pol	1m 59.320s
5	Cortese	1m 59.443s
6	Webb	1m 59.463s
7	Marquez	1m 59.556s
8	Redding	1m 59.649s
9	Zarco	1m 59.655s
10	Savadori	1m 59.931s
11	Gadea	2m 00.286s
12	Rabat	2m 00.328s
13	Iannone	2m 00.333s
14	Krummenacher	2m 00.337s
15	Bradl	2m 00.366s
16	Folger	2m 00.371s
17	Olive	2m 00.617s
18	Zanetti	2m 00.675s
19	Vazquez	2m 00.870s
20	Nakagami	2m 00.898s
21	Morciano	2m 01.006s
22	Moretti	2m 01.505s
23	Corsi	2m 01.679s
24	Aegerter	2m 01.905s
25	Stirpe	2m 02.647s
26	Sembera	2m 02.807s
27	Tonucci	2m 03.487s
28	Iwema	2m 03.513s
29	Sabatino	2m 05.372s
30	Koyama	2m 05.372s
31	Marconi	2m 05.846s
32	Vitali	2m 05.951s
33	Masbou	2m 18.541s

Championship Points

1	Smith	74.5
2	Simon	71
3	Iannone	46.5
4	Espargaro, Pol	44.5
5	Gadea	43
6	Marquez	38
7	Cortese	38
8	Terol	37.5
9	Folger	35
10	Aegerter	26.5
11	Bradl	25
12	Redding	23.5
13	Vazquez	19
14	Webb	16.5
15	Rabat	15
16	Olive	14
17	Zarco	13.5
18	Nakagami	12
19	Zanetti	12
20	Savadori	7
21	Koyama	4
22	Krummenacher	4
23	Corsi	4
24	Iwema	3
25	di Carlo	2
26	Beaubier	1

Constructors

		Points
1	Aprilia	112.5
2	Derbi	58
3	KTM	38
4	Loncin	3

CATALUNYA GRAND PRIX

CATALUNYA CIRCUIT

Rossi was at his brilliant bravura best.
His last-corner pass on Lorenzo *(inset top)*
was breathtaking.

Inset above: A moment to savour on
Lorenzo's Land.

Main photo: The Doctor was jubilance
personified.
Photos: Gold & Goose

Above: Montmelo is a slider's paradise. De Angelis shows how.

Left: Gabor Talmacsi found his MotoGP debut sobering.

Below left: Pedrosa was hitting the painkillers again.

Right: Stoner made the rostrum, but was barely strong enough to climb the third step. He was in more trouble than anyone realised.

Photos: Gold & Goose

AT last, after five consecutive bad-weather weekends, bright sunshine put a different complexion on the season. Two events in particular shone forth.

The first was the uplifting race. In spite of growing rider complaints about the 800s, the lack of practice time and testing, and the limitations of control tyres, some people were talking about the best race, or at least the best last lap, they'd ever seen. And never mind that there were just two in it.

A crowd of 88,500, many packed around the natural grandstands of the final loop, watched Rossi at his brilliant bravura best, seizing victory from the jaws of defeat. His last-corner move left Lorenzo looking very much the schoolboy. And it tipped the balance of the championship: now they shared the lead on equal points.

The second important occurrence involved the third rider, who ended the weekend with an identical world championship score – three riders tied after six races. Casey Stoner was fast as usual and finished third after dropping back in the latter part of the race. That he had faded by the end might have had any number of explanations, from some mechanical or settings mismatch to simple tyre wear. Until you saw the state he was in when he arrived in parc fermé. Close to collapse, he slumped on the railings and was helped away to the doctor. Stoner made it to the rostrum, gave some rambling post-race TV interviews and then withdrew to contemplate just why he had been suf-

fering from exhaustion since the afternoon before, and why he had suffered such bad stomach cramps that he had twice dry-retched into his helmet. As yet, nobody had any idea of just how much trouble he was in.

Stoner had started the weekend testy, sounding off about a number of issues. One was the continuing discussions about one bike per rider for 2011, and in particular how to cope with a flag-to-flag wet-dry race like the previous two. One option under discussion was a mandatory two-and-a-half-minute pit stop for all. Even so, he opined, "there's going to be mistakes. There might be wheel nuts left loose... Completely new systems are going to have to be made. More money, more development, more time. I don't see how this is going to fit in."

This was part of a general rant against the current predisposition to make more and more rules, and also the application of them. Anthony West had been given a ride-through penalty for taking the wrong grid slot in 2007; at Le Mans, Lorenzo had been motioned to the right position instead. Then there was the Simoncelli-Bautista incident at Mugello. Simoncelli was fined US$5,000: "I got fined a thousand bloody Euros for holding Dani Pedrosa up on a qualifying lap in 2006. I just don't see where their decisions are coming from. It's the same with all the rules and the changes, it's just not really working."

Rossi was fresh from a first visit to the Isle of Man TT and glowing with it, having followed Ago on a lap

of one of the few places in the world where "you can ride a Yamaha R1 to the limit, and the R1 is a fast bike." He described the race-winning and lap-record heroes he met as "crazy people, and not normal". Coming from him...

The nature of the track's long corners meant it was the first of the year for mixed-compound tyres from Bridgestone: the heat demanded the harder option – "ultra-hard", as they were called.

This also makes it a good track for testing. Or so you must hope, because it is one of just two during the year, with a single day scheduled for the Monday after the race, and another after the Brno race. Some didn't stay on: Tech 3 decided to save the money, while Pedrosa decided to save on the painkiller budget, having already had to spend freely to get through the weekend. Stoner was there to do his duty though. Yamaha didn't have much to test, as it happened, and while Honda had a revised chassis designed for more weight transfer to suit the Bridgestones, Pedrosa actually used that in the race. Only Dovizioso had to wait until Monday – he liked it and set fastest time of the day, ahead of Rossi and Lorenzo. Suzuki had a modified motor, which turned out to make little difference; Kawasaki rider Melandri knew he could expect nothing, and had the misfortune to crash heavily, without injury.

Talmacsi was back and in a new set of leathers – shoehorned into MotoGP thanks to a wedge of Hungarian money from petro-chemical giant MOL. Money was just what the beleaguered Scot team needed, and this was the beginning of a short-lived charade in which the team agreed to expand to two riders, with Talmacsi alongside regular Yuki Takahashi. This was in the hope that Honda would supply them with two more motorcycles, but when the bikes didn't appear, somebody had to go. It was Takahashi, whose first-lap crash – his second of the season – would turn out to be his last attempt, at least for the moment, at MotoGP.

An early start to silly-season rumours scored some hits: Simoncelli was linked to a possible move to Honda; Bautista with Suzuki; while news broke that Yamaha had declined to supply the proposed Aspar team with motorcycles.

The most colourful story of the weekend was no rumour, however. It involved money demands and death threats, and one of the World Championship leaders. Lorenzo had split with manager Dani Amatriain in 2008 after the former racer had run into personal problems. Now Amatriain was demanding recompense, and was detained by police after allegations of death threats made to two of this other former charges, the Espargaro brothers. A sad fall from grace, but reassuringly 'motorbike' in an increasingly sanitised world of racing.

MotoGP RACE – 25 laps

"Pole position is just a number at the end of your career," said Rossi, putting a brave face on losing it to Lorenzo by the blink of an eye. The Yamahas were the class of the field, with Stoner-four tenths down; Dovizioso led row two from Elias and Edwards. Grid numbers were up to 19, with the return of Gibernau – left collarbone freshly replated – and the addition of Talmacsi.

Lorenzo led away, Rossi and Stoner in pursuit; then came de Puniet and the factory Hondas of Pedrosa and Dovizioso. Takahashi was out before half the lap was done, blaming an early braking move by Vermeulen for his crash. A lap later, the first three

were already breaking away, while Pedrosa headed the next trio a second adrift.

The first change came at the start of lap four, as Rossi outbraked Lorenzo into turn one. Stoner was very much with them for the first seven laps, then he started to drop away, slowly at first. It was just the two Yamahas, circulating in close formation, Rossi leading the way.

The next exchange came just after half-distance, Lorenzo moving to the inside under braking at the end of the back straight – the other conventional passing move at this track. Could he break away? No. Rossi was his faithful shadow.

The final skirmishing began as they crossed the line for the 22nd time. Rossi was already out of the draft and alongside, and ahead to outbrake him for the first corner. The next lap, Lorenzo tried to do the same, but Rossi simply refused to concede, easing off on the brakes and almost running on to the grass on the outside to regain control.

Rossi led on to the final lap by 0.095 second as Lorenzo moved so far across to the inside that he actually used the pit lane, seizing the inside line for turn one and slamming the door again in the next corner. On the fourth, Rossi seemed to have passed successfully, but Lorenzo slipped inside again as the older rider ran wide.

One last chance: the end of the back straight. Lorenzo defended the corner perfectly. From here to the line should have been a straightforward run. If not for Rossi.

It takes two to tango, and Lorenzo admitted afterwards that he hadn't defended the last corner as he should have done. After all, it is not thought of as an overtaking place, but he half realised that Rossi might try to change that.

And that's what he did. Opportunism and determination dictated that he must. As Jorge prepared to sweep in triumph on to the finishing straight, his team-mate spurted past on the inside and gained crucial control of the exit. The margin of victory was 0.095 second. The contest had been a classic.

Stoner had been in a world of his own as he fought back the spasm of illness, but unfortunately not in a race of his own. Dovizioso had taken over fourth on lap six, when he was just 1.9 seconds behind Stoner. He'd more than halved that when a slide on lap 15 dropped him back again. He knuckled down once more and, by the end of lap 19, he was on the Ducati's tail. He never did find a way past, Stoner holding him at bay over the line by five-hundredths.

That left Pedrosa engaged with Capirossi, de Puniet having dropped away over the first ten laps. Soon the Frenchman would be under pressure from Edwards, speeding up again as the laps wore on. Kallio was behind after passing Melandri, while Hayden was to and fro with de Angelis. Elias had been in this group, but slid off after losing the front at the notorious La Caixa, at the end of the back straight.

On lap 17, Capirossi took fifth from Pedrosa into turn four. The Spaniard fought back briefly on the next lap, but had to concede, given his pained and fractured con-

dition. "Obviously, 25 laps were very hard," he said.

By the finish, Edwards was still 1.4 seconds behind, having lost too much time in the midfield tussle. De Puniet was alone in eighth; six seconds behind, Kallio was a demoralising 1.7 seconds clear of Hayden's factory Ducati – although tenth was his best result so far.

Vermeulen had taken de Angelis on lap 18 and managed to stay narrowly ahead to the flag; Toseland also had passed the fading Melandri on lap 22, and the returned Gibernau took the last point. Canepa and new boy Talmacsi were ranged out behind.

250cc RACE – 23 laps

Barbera claimed a narrow first pole of the year, ahead of Bautista and Simoncelli, with Luthi alongside on row one, and both Aoyama and Pasini one row behind.

Barbera led away, from Aoyama and Bautista, Simoncelli with them by the end of the lap, and all in a hurry to establish themselves.

Bautista took the lead as they started lap three, with Simoncelli following him through. At the end of the back straight, his swooping line carried him ever closer, but his angle of lean betrayed him and he lost the front wheel, then the back, skating out into the gravel on his back. He rejoined, only to pit in despair after a couple more laps.

Later, Bautista said, "I was never comfortable for the whole race," but nor was he troubled by pursuit.

Left: On the brakes, on the paint, on the limit. Bautista became the first to win two 250 races in 2009.

Below: Simon celebrates a dominant weekend, before it's over.

Bottom: Nico Terol was a beaming second.

Below right: Sympathy? Lucky winner Iannone consoles a shattered Simon.

Photos: Gold & Goose

After nine laps, he'd put a full second on Barbera and kept on stretching for a second win of the year by better than seven.

Pasini had finished lap one seventh, but soon was past Debon, Luthi and the fading Aoyama to take third when Simoncelli fell. He was a second or so behind Barbera, and by half-distance was ready to attack. He dived underneath into La Caixa to lead laps 13 and 14. But Barbera had speed to spare and powered past again down the straight, able gradually to pull away by the finish.

Behind them, Luthi had been caught by Locatelli, who got ahead on lap 13. At the same time, Aoyama had run clear of early intermittent engine problems – "It cut out more than once." – and was closing fast, di Meglio and Debon with him.

Aoyama was flying, and over the last nine laps he easily closed more than three seconds on Pasini to get by on lap 21, then hounded his way up to Barbera, taking second off him on the final lap and hanging on grimly to the line. Later, Barbera told of fighting slides all race long, after switching to softer settings in the cooler morning run.

During all this, Locatelli had crashed on lap 13, then di Meglio had a big moment and ran off the track, rejoining well out of touch. Pasini's fourth was safe; Debon was five seconds down, after passing Luthi with two laps to go.

Wilairot was seventh and all alone, after a strong, uneventful ride.

Cluzel had been heading a strong six-bike battle for eighth when Abraham emerged to take the position, two seconds clear of de Rosa and Faubel. Cluzel went a second down. Pesek and Baldolini were off the back of the group.

Di Meglio was 14th, and temporarily returned American Stevie Bonsey secured one point for 15th in his first ever 250 ride, two-tenths clear of Axel Pons.

Zero points dropped Simoncelli to fifth overall,

while Bautista's lead over Aoyama stretched out a little more. But there were surprises to come in the final battle for the quarter-litre class.

125cc RACE – 22 laps

Simon left having regained the World Championship lead from Smith. But he didn't make it easy on himself. He had dominated practice, started from pole and led almost every lap from the ever-pressing Iannone. At the end of an otherwise perfectly judged race, he rose in his seat in celebration as he crossed the line, comfortably clear of his race-long rival – one lap too soon.

The pair had drawn a little ahead as they exchanged the lead several times, but Simon had been in control, until his unwitting gift made Iannone the first to win three races in the season. He had little sympathy. "That's racing. I've had bad luck in races," he said. Simon was just bemused.

Espargaro had led the first lap and was well in contention on lap six when suddenly he slowed and pulled out, his Derbi's gear-lever snapped off.

The remaining battle for third was intriguing, slimming to four riders by half-distance as erstwhile points leader Smith dropped away. The quartet was still almost side by side as they crossed the line, with Simon also among them after a blazing recovery and swoop through the last corner.

Terol grabbed second by a nose; a photo finish gave third to Gadea from Simon. Marquez and rookie Folger were almost alongside, second to sixth covered by less than three-tenths.

Slow-starting Bradl caught Smith, and held him narrowly behind to the finish.

Cortese prevailed in another big fight for the last points, from Krummenacher and Redding, who had been with the leaders in the early laps. Webb fell back from this group to retire, after suffering painful right-hand injuries in a crash during practice.

GRAN PREMI CINZANO DE CATALUNYA

14 JUNE 2009 • FIM WORLD CHAMPIONSHIP ROUND 6

CIRCUIT DE CATALUNYA

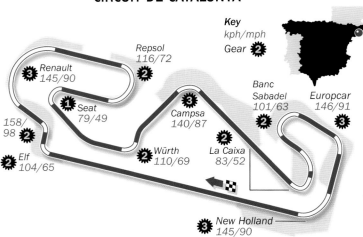

Key
kph/mph
Gear

Repsol 116/72
Renault 145/90
Seat 79/49
Campsa 140/87
Banc Sabadel 101/63
Europcar 146/91
158/98
Elf 104/65
Würth 110/69
La Caixa 83/52
New Holland 145/90

Circuit: 2.937 miles/4.727km

MOTOGP

RACE DISTANCE: 25 laps, 73.430 miles/118.175 km • RACE WEATHER: Dry (air 36°, humidity 12%, track 46°)

Pos.	Rider	Nat.	No.	Entrant	Machine	Tyres	Laps	Time & speed
1	Valentino Rossi	ITA	46	Fiat Yamaha Team	Yamaha	B	25	43m 11.897s 101.990mph/ 164.138km/h
2	Jorge Lorenzo	SPA	99	Fiat Yamaha Team	Yamaha	B	25	43m 11.992s
3	Casey Stoner	AUS	27	Ducati Marlboro Team	Ducati	B	25	43m 20.781s
4	Andrea Dovizioso	ITA	4	Repsol Honda Team	Honda	B	25	43m 20.833s
5	Loris Capirossi	ITA	65	Rizla Suzuki MotoGP	Suzuki	B	25	43m 31.728s
6	Dani Pedrosa	SPA	3	Repsol Honda Team	Honda	B	25	43m 34.079s
7	Colin Edwards	USA	5	Monster Yamaha Tech 3	Yamaha	B	25	43m 35.444s
8	Randy de Puniet	USA	14	LCR Honda MotoGP	Honda	B	25	43m 37.162s
9	Mika Kallio	FIN	36	Pramac Racing	Ducati	B	25	43m 43.694s
10	Nicky Hayden	USA	69	Ducati Marlboro Team	Ducati	B	25	43m 45.490s
11	Chris Vermeulen	AUS	7	Rizla Suzuki MotoGP	Suzuki	B	25	43m 48.580s
12	Alex de Angelis	RSM	15	San Carlos Honda Gresini	Honda	B	25	43m 48.771s
13	James Toseland	JPN	52	Monster Yamaha Tech 3	Yamaha	B	25	43m 51.330s
14	Marco Melandri	ITA	33	Hayate Racing Team	Kawasaki	B	25	43m 56.685s
15	Sete Gibernau	SPA	59	Grupo Francisco Hernando	Ducati	B	25	43m 58.651s
16	Nicola Canepa	USA	88	Pramac Racing	Ducati	B	25	44m 07.770s
17	Gabor Talmacsi	HUN	41	Scot Racing Team MotoGP	Honda	B	25	44m 39.537s
	Toni Elias	SPA	24	San Carlos Honda Gresini	Honda	B	9	DNF
	Yuki Takahashi	BRA	72	Scot Racing Team MotoGP	Honda	B	0	DNF

Fastest lap: Casey Stoner, on lap 2, 1m 42.858s, 105.523mph/166.443km/h.

Lap record: Dani Pedrosa, SPA (Honda), 1m 42.358s, 103.303mph/166.251km/h (2008).

Event best maximum speed: Valentino Rossi, 205.984mph/331.5km/h (race).

Qualifying: Dry
Air: 38° Humidity: 14% Track: 52°

1	Lorenzo	1m 41.947s
2	Rossi	1m 41.987s
3	Stoner	1m 42.426s
4	Dovizioso	1m 42.594s
5	Elias	1m 43.139s
6	Edwards	1m 43.168s
7	de Puniet	1m 43.175s
8	Pedrosa	1m 43.207s
9	Toseland	1m 43.233s
10	Kallio	1m 43.336s
11	Capirossi	1m 43.365s
12	Vermeulen	1m 43.411s
13	Hayden	1m 43.414s
14	de Angelis	1m 43.422s
15	Gibernau	1m 43.714s
16	Takahashi	1m 43.777s
17	Melandri	1m 43.792s
18	Canepa	1m 43.991s
19	Talmacsi	1m 45.833s

Fastest race laps

1	Stoner	1m 42.858s
2	Rossi	1m 42.874s
3	Lorenzo	1m 43.041s
4	Dovizioso	1m 43.276s
5	Capirossi	1m 43.306s
6	Pedrosa	1m 43.335s
7	de Puniet	1m 43.433s
8	Edwards	1m 43.771s
9	Elias	1m 43.779s
10	Melandri	1m 43.836s
11	Kallio	1m 43.883s
12	Toseland	1m 43.898s
13	de Angelis	1m 43.945s
14	Hayden	1m 44.047s
15	Gibernau	1m 44.053s
16	Vermeulen	1m 44.272s
17	Canepa	1m 45.652s
18	Talmacsi	1m 45.652s

Championship Points

1	Rossi	106
2	Lorenzo	106
3	Stoner	106
4	Dovizioso	69
5	Pedrosa	67
6	Edwards	54
7	Melandri	50
8	Capirossi	49
9	de Puniet	42
10	Vermeulen	42
11	Toseland	29
12	Kallio	26
13	de Angelis	25
14	Elias	23
15	Hayden	19
16	Canepa	10
17	Gibernau	9
18	Takahashi	8

Constructor Points

1	Yamaha	140
2	Ducati	106
3	Honda	89
4	Suzuki	60
5	Kawasaki	50

Team Points

1	FIAT Yamaha Team	212
2	Repsol Honda Team	136
3	Ducati Marlboro Team	125
4	RIZLA Suzuki MotoGP	91
5	Monster Yamaha Tech 3	83
6	Hayate Racing Team	50
7	San Carlo Honda Gresini	48
8	LCR Honda MotoGP	42
9	Pramac Racing	36
10	Grupo Francisco Hern	9
11	Scot Racing Team MOT	8

Grid order	1	2	3	4	5	6	7	8	9	10	11	12	13	14	15	16	17	18	19	20	21	22	23	24	25	
99 LORENZO	99	99	99	46	46	46	46	46	46	46	46	46	99	99	99	99	99	99	99	99	99	46	46	46		1
46 ROSSI	46	46	46	99	99	99	99	99	99	99	99	99	46	46	46	46	46	46	46	46	46	99	99	99		2
27 STONER	27	27	27	27	27	27	27	27	27	27	27	27	27	27	27	27	27	27	27	27	27	27	27	27		3
4 DOVIZIOSO	14	3	3	3	3	4	4	4	4	4	4	4	4	4	4	4	4	4	4	4	4	4	4	4		4
24 ELIAS	3	14	14	4	4	3	3	3	3	3	3	3	3	3	3	3	65	65	65	65	65	65	65	65		5
5 EDWARDS	4	4	4	14	65	65	65	65	65	65	65	65	65	65	65	65	3	3	3	3	3	3	3	3		6
14 de PUNIET	65	65	65	65	14	14	14	14	14	14	14	14	14	5	5	5	5	5	5	5	5	5	5	5		7
3 PEDROSA	24	24	24	24	5	5	5	5	5	5	5	5	5	14	14	14	14	14	14	14	14	14	14	14		8
52 TOSELAND	5	5	5	5	24	33	33	36	36	36	36	36	36	36	36	36	36	36	36	36	36	36	36	36		9
36 KALLIO	33	33	33	33	33	24	36	33	33	33	33	33	33	69	69	69	69	69	69	69	69	69	69	69		10
65 CAPIROSSI	36	36	36	36	36	36	24	24	24	69	69	69	69	33	33	15	7	7	7	7	7	7	7	7		11
7 VERMEULEN	69	69	69	69	69	69	15	15	15	15	15	15	15	15	15	7	15	15	15	15	15	15	15	15		12
69 HAYDEN	7	15	15	15	15	15	69	69	69	59	59	7	7	7	7	33	33	33	33	52	52	52	52			13
15 de ANGELIS	15	7	59	59	59	59	59	59	59	7	7	59	59	59	59	52	52	52	52	52	33	33	33	33		14
59 GIBERNAU	52	59	7	52	52	52	52	52	52	52	52	52	52	52	52	59	59	59	59	59	59	59	59	59		15
72 TAKAHASHI	59	52	52	7	7	7	7	7	7	88	88	88	88	88	88	88	88	88	88	88	88	88	88	88		
33 MELANDRI	88	88	88	88	88	88	88	88	88	41	41	41	41	41	41	41	41	41	41	41	41	41	41	41		
88 CANEPA	41	41	41	41	41	41	41	41	41																	
41 TALMACSI																										

250cc — RACE DISTANCE: 23 laps, 67.556 miles/108.721 km • RACE WEATHER: Dry (air 37°, humidity 16%, track 47°)

Pos.	Rider	Nat.	No.	Entrant	Machine	Laps	Time & Speed
1	Alvaro Bautista	SPA	19	Mapfre Aspar Team	Aprilia	23	41m 09.018s
							(mph/km/h)
							98.501/158.522
2	Hiroshi Aoyama	JPN	4	Scot Racing Team 250cc	Honda	23	41m 16.203s
3	Hector Barbera	SPA	40	Pepe World Team	Aprilia	23	41m 16.300s
4	Mattia Pasini	ITA	75	Team Toth Aprilia	Aprilia	23	41m 19.802s
5	Alex Debon	ESP	6	Aeropuerto – Castello – Blusens	Aprilia	23	41m 24.758s
6	Thomas Luthi	SWI	12	Emmi – Caffe Latte	Aprilia	23	41m 24.798s
7	Ratthapark Wilairot	THA	14	Thai Honda PTT SAG	Honda	23	41m 37.672s
8	Karel Abraham	CZE	17	Cardion AB Motoracing	Aprilia	23	41m 40.618s
9	Raffaele de Rosa	ITA	35	Scot Racing Team 250cc	Honda	23	41m 42.778s
10	Hector Faubel	SPA	55	Valencia CF – Honda SAG	Honda	23	41m 42.861s
11	Jules Cluzel	FRA	16	Matteoni Racing	Aprilia	23	41m 43.889s
12	Lukas Pesek	CZE	52	Auto Kelly – CP	Aprilia	23	41m 44.135s
13	Alex Baldolini	ITA	25	WTR San Marino Team	Aprilia	23	41m 48.858s
14	Mike di Meglio	FRA	63	Mapfre Aspar Team 250cc	Aprilia	23	41m 51.839s
15	Stevie Bonsey	USA	51	Milar – Juegos Lucky	Aprilia	23	42m 25.542s
16	Axel Pons	SPA	7	Pepe World Team	Aprilia	20	42m 25.707s
17	Valentin Debise	FRA	53	CIP Moto – GP250	Honda	20	42m 37.844s
18	Balazs Nemeth	HUN	11	Balatonring Team	Aprilia	20	42m 48.506s
19	Bastien Chesaux	SWI	8	Racing Team Germany	Honda	20	42m 56.976s
20	Vladimir Leonov	RUS	56	Viessmann Kiefer Racing	Aprilia	19	41m 34.233s
21	Toby Markham	GB	54	C&L Racing	Honda	19	41m 46.384s
	Imre Toth	HUN	10	Team Toth Aprilia	Aprilia	21	DNF
	Roberto Locatelli	ITA	15	Metis Gilera	Gilera	14	DNF
	Shoya Tomizawa	JPN	48	CIP Moto – GP250	Honda	13	DNF
	Marco Simoncelli	ITA	58	Metis Gilera	Gilera	6	DNF

Fastest lap: Alvaro Bautista, on lap 9, 1m 46.656s, 99.141mph/159.552km/h.
Lap record: Alex de Angelis, RSM (Aprilia), 1m 45.925s, 99.825mph/160.635km/h (2007).
Event best maximum speed: Thomas Luthi, 160.189mph/257.8km/h (race).

250cc — Qualifying: Dry (Air: 37° Humidity: 19% Track: 49°)

1	Barbera	1m 46.749s
2	Bautista	1m 46.908s
3	Simoncelli	1m 46.908s
4	Luthi	1m 47.081s
5	Debon	1m 47.125s
6	Aoyama, Hiroshi	1m 47.166s
7	Pasini	1m 47.225s
8	Faubel	1m 47.379s
9	di Meglio	1m 47.426s
10	Wilairot	1m 47.559s
11	Baldolini	1m 47.596s
12	Abraham	1m 47.725s
13	de Rosa	1m 47.747s
14	Cluzel	1m 47.795s
15	Tomizawa	1m 48.032s
16	Locatelli	1m 48.088s
17	Pesek	1m 48.101s
18	Pons	1m 50.450s
19	Bonsey	1m 50.598s
20	Debise	1m 50.653s
21	Nemeth	1m 50.732s
22	Chesaux	1m 51.229s
23	Toth	1m 51.296s
24	Leonov	1m 52.133s
25	Markham	1m 52.856s

250cc — Fastest race laps

1	Bautista	1m 46.656s
2	Aoyama, Hiroshi	1m 46.750s
3	Pasini	1m 46.835s
4	Barbera	1m 46.863s
5	di Meglio	1m 46.863s
6	Luthi	1m 47.088s
7	Locatelli	1m 47.090s
8	Debon	1m 47.114s
9	Wilairot	1m 47.399s
10	Simoncelli	1m 47.721s
11	Cluzel	1m 47.781s
12	Abraham	1m 47.900s
13	Pesek	1m 47.964s
14	Tomizawa	1m 48.053s
15	de Rosa	1m 48.073s
16	Faubel	1m 48.100s
17	Baldolini	1m 48.268s
18	Bonsey	1m 49.517s
19	Pons	1m 49.797s
20	Debise	1m 50.410s
21	Chessaux	1m 50.562s
22	Nemeth	1m 50.632s
23	Toth	1m 50.795s
24	Leonov	1m 51.606s
25	Markham	1m 52.793s

250cc — Championship Points

1	Bautista	108
2	Aoyama, Hiroshi	96
3	Barbera	75
4	Pasini	64
5	Simoncelli	61
6	Luthi	52
7	de Rosa	45
8	Faubel	41
9	Locatelli	36
10	Cluzel	33
11	Debon	33
12	Wilairot	31
13	Talmacsi	28
14	Pesek	28
15	di Meglio	27
16	Abraham	22
17	Tomizawa	14
18	Toth	11
19	Aoyama, Shuhei	10
21	Baldolini	9
20	Leonov	7
22	Debise	3
23	Markham	2
24	Watanabe	2
25	Bonsey	1

250cc — Constructors

		Points
1	Aprilia	133
2	Honda	108
2	Gilera	68
3	Yamaha	2

125cc — RACE DISTANCE: 20 laps, 64.618 miles/103.994 km • RACE WEATHER: Dry (air 30°, humidity 19%, track 37°)

Pos.	Rider	Nat.	No.	Entrant	Machine	Laps	Time & Speed
1	Andrea Iannone	ITA	29	Ongetta Team I.S.P.A.	Aprilia	22	41m 10.494s
							(mph/km/h)
							94.161/151.539
2	Nicolas Terol	SPA	18	Jack & Jones Team	Aprilia	22	41m 12.824s
3	Sergio Gadea	SPA	33	Bancaja Aspar Team 125cc	Aprilia	22	41m 45.882s
4	Julian Simon	SPA	60	Bancaja Aspar Team 125cc	Aprilia	22	41m 12.825s
5	Marc Marquez	SPA	93	Red Bull KTM Moto Sport	KTM	22	41m 12.850s
6	Jonas Folger	GER	94	Ongetta Team I.S.P.A.	Aprilia	22	41m 13.025s
7	Stefan Bradl	GER	17	Viessmann Kiefer Racing	Aprilia	22	41m 21.289s
8	Bradley Smith	GB	38	Bancaja Aspar Team 125cc	Aprilia	22	41m 21.318s
9	Sandro Cortese	GER	11	Ajo Interwetten	Derbi	22	41m 25.478s
10	Randy Krummenacher	SWI	35	Degraaf Grand Prix	Aprilia	22	41m 25.583s
11	Scott Redding	GB	45	Blusens Aprilia	Aprilia	22	41m 26.921s
12	Esteve Rabat	SPA	12	Blusens Aprilia	Aprilia	22	41m 27.009s
13	Johann Zarco	FRA	14	WTR San Marino Team	Aprilia	22	41m 37.949s
14	Joan Olive	SPA	6	Derbi Racing Team	Derbi	22	41m 38.206s
15	Takaaki Nakagami	JPN	73	Ongetta Team I.S.P.A.	Aprilia	22	41m 38.905s
16	Simon Corsi	ITA	24	Jack & Jones Team	Aprilia	22	41m 44.191s
17	Tomoyoshi Koyama	JPN	71	Loncin Racing	Loncin	22	41m 53.075s
18	Cameron Beaubier	USA	16	Red Bull KTM Moto Sport	KTM	22	41m 59.341s
19	Alberto Moncayo	SPA	42	Andalucia Aprilia	Aprilia	22	42m 00.026s
20	Dominique Aegerter	SWI	77	Ajo Interwetten	Derbi	22	42m 00.266s
21	Jasper Iwema	NED	53	Racing Team Germany	Honda	22	42m 13.160s
22	Sturla Fagerhaug	NOR	50	Red Bull KTM Moto Sport	KTM	22	42m 25.709s
23	Johnny Rosell	SPA	43	Blusens BQR	Aprilia	22	42m 32.062s
24	Luca Marconi	FRA	87	CBC Corse	Aprilia	22	42m 48.413s
25	Jordi Dalmau	ITA	31	SAG-Castrol	Honda	21	41m 47.580s
26	Luca Vitali	ITA	10	CBC Corse	Aprilia	20	42m 12.575s
	Lorenzo Savadori	ITA	32	Fontana Racing	Aprilia	16	DNF
	Luis Salom	SPA	39	SAG-Castrol	Honda	11	DNF
	Danny Webb	GB	99	Degraaf Grand Prix	Aprilia	11	DNF
	Lorenzo Zanetti	ITA	8	Ongetta Team I.S.P.A.	Aprilia	10	DNF
	Pol Espargaro	SPA	44	Derbi Racing Team	Derbi	5	DNF
	Alexis Masbou	FRA	5	Loncin Racing	Loncin	5	DNF
	Lukas Sembera	CZE	69	Matteoni Racing	Aprilia	4	DNF
	Efren Vazquez	SPA	7	Derbi Racing Team	Derbi	1	DNF

Fastest lap: Marc Marquez, on lap 7, 1m 51.175s, 95.110mph/153.006km/h.
Lap record: Randy Krummenacher, SWI (KTM), 1m 50.732s, 95.492mph/153.679km/h (2007).
Event best maximum speed: Andrea Iannone, ITA (Aprilia), 147.513mph/237.4km/h (race).

125cc — Qualifying: Dry (Air: 38° Humidity: 14% Track: 51°)

1	Simon	1m 51.448s
2	Espargaro, Pol	1m 51.468s
3	Folger	1m 51.787s
4	Krummenacher	1m 51.804s
5	Gadea	1m 51.824s
6	Terol	1m 51.958s
7	Smith	1m 52.209s
8	Iannone	1m 52.384s
9	Bradl	1m 52.432s
10	Redding	1m 52.536s
11	Webb	1m 52.548s
12	Marquez	1m 52.616s
13	Zarco	1m 52.782s
14	Cortese	1m 52.832s
15	Koyama	1m 52.935s
16	Olive	1m 52.943s
17	Rabat	1m 53.120s
18	Aegerter	1m 53.156s
19	Zanetti	1m 53.265s
20	Vazquez	1m 53.266s
21	Nakagami	1m 53.301s
22	Beaubier	1m 53.382s
23	Corsi	1m 53.553s
24	Savadori	1m 53.593s
25	Moncayo	1m 54.141s
26	Rosell	1m 54.407s
27	Iwema	1m 54.618s
28	Fagerhaug	1m 54.847s
29	Sembera	1m 54.858s
30	Masbou	1m 55.319s
31	Marconi	1m 55.555s
32	Salom	1m 56.117s
33	Vitali	1m 57.423s
34	Dalmau	1m 58.961s

125cc — Fastest race laps

1	Marquez	1m 51.175s
2	Terol	1m 51.532s
3	Folger	1m 51.576s
4	Iannone	1m 51.641s
5	Simon	1m 51.648s
6	Redding	1m 51.660s
7	Gadea	1m 51.710s
8	Bradl	1m 51.723s
9	Rabat	1m 51.758s
10	Espargaro, Pol	1m 51.867s
11	Smith	1m 51.877s
12	Krummenacher	1m 51.950s
13	Cortese	1m 52.105s
14	Zarco	1m 52.347s
15	Nakagami	1m 52.392s
16	Savadori	1m 52.709s
17	Olive	1m 52.712s
18	Zanetti	1m 52.750s
19	Beaubier	1m 52.836s
20	Corsi	1m 52.841s
21	Webb	1m 52.853s
22	Koyama	1m 53.126s
23	Aegerter	1m 53.445s
24	Moncayo	1m 53.498s
25	Fagerhaug	1m 53.784s
26	Iwema	1m 53.941s
27	Rosell	1m 54.620s
28	Marconi	1m 55.548s
29	Vitali	1m 56.934s
30	Salom	1m 57.111s
31	Sembera	1m 57.369s
32	Dalmau	1m 57.794s
33	Masbou	1m 58.674s
34	Vazquez	2m 00.243s

125cc — Championship Points

	Rider	Points
1	Simon	84
2	Smith	82.5
3	Iannone	71.5
4	Gadea	59
5	Terol	57.5
6	Marquez	49
7	Folger	45
8	Cortese	45
9	Espargaro, Pol	44.5
11	Bradl	34
11	Redding	28.5
12	Aegerter	26.5
13	Vazquez	19
14	Rabat	19
15	Zarco	16.5
16	Webb	16.5
17	Olive	16
18	Nakagami	13
19	Zanetti	12
20	Krummenacher	10
21	Savadori	7
21	Koyama	4
23	Corsi	4
24	Iwema	3
25	di Carlo	2
26	Beaubier	1

125cc — Constructors

		Points
1	Aprilia	112.5
2	Derbi	58
3	KTM	38
4	Loncin	3

One hundred up, and still counting.
Rossi's banner showed every one of his
century of wins.
Photo: Gold & Goose

DUTCH TT

ASSEN CIRCUIT

ROSSI'S century of wins was a landmark, and if he'd have preferred to unfurl his post-race banner at home in Mugello, Assen would do just as well. The track may be only half of what it was, but this most historic venue still has a magisterial air.

The celebrations were ecstatic, a capacity crowd of 96,000 sharing in the history. Rossi has dominated 500cc, 990cc and 800cc, and he had given another masterful display to underline the lesson he'd taught Lorenzo at Barcelona. This was the last of 100 pictures on the celebratory banner that his fan club unwound by the track; the first had been on a 125, at Brno in 1996. It was a great moment. And it had to atone for the fact that the race itself, up front at least, had been another procession.

The emasculation of the classic track in 2006 seriously undercut its reputation as the university of motorcycle racing. It remains a centre of higher education, however, and had an important lesson to teach in 2009. It came on the fast left-handed Ruskenhoek at the end of the new section behind the paddock, and was dictated in the stuttering tones of electronic engine control mechanisms, triggered by wheelspin to drop sparks and cut power. And there was even a student protest: hanging over the fence on the far side of the track was a banner that read "No more traction control".

Barcelona had been so exciting that it escaped notice that the thrill had come from just two guys on identical bikes, which, on that weekend, had been able to turn near-identical lap times. This weekend, the ultimate lap times of each rider were not so close, and the first five places were all follow-my-leader.

Electronic traction control plays a key role in post-two-stroke/post-990 racing. The peaky engines lack mid-range compared with the 990s. This section of track, like the other new sections, has little banking, and the bikes are on their sides for a long time with the throttle open. In such circumstances, the popping and banging is more reminiscent of a tractor race than MotoGP.

The riders enjoy it no more than the spectators, but there seems to be no way around it with the 800cc formula. "Without traction control, these things'd be unrideable – like a light switch," opined Stoner, whose reputation for relying heavily on electronics was undermined still further by team-mate Hayden. "A lot of people said that last year, but if we do a lap overlay, my throttle's wide open more than his," the American explained. "It's not as it looks from the outside: that he just twists the grip and goes. The secret at times is using less throttle, especially the last seven or eight per cent of the throttle, right when the pumping comes in. I don't believe he relies on the electronics at all."

Pedrosa extinguished any remaining chance of rejoining the title battle, crashing out in a front-end failure that was closely echoed a bit later by team-mate Dovizioso. An unpromising debut for the latest chassis, of which Dani had two and Dovi only one. And Stoner's health problems continued during the

Right: Rossi had Lorenzo gasping this time.

Below: The electronics of racing.

Bottom: Student protest at the University of Motorcycle Racing.
Photos: Gold & Goose

weekend, another reason for a processional race, culminating again in a brave third. He made the rostrum, but afterwards went directly to the medical centre, where he was put on a saline drip. The year was assuming its shape: now it was between the two Yamahas, which for a third race had taken the top two slots.

With Edwards coming fourth, the M1 was very much the bike to ride. Marco Simoncelli, however, passed up the opportunity, becoming the first 250 rider to sign for class promotion, with the satellite Gresini Honda team. This was regarded as something of a coup: Suzuki had also been after the quick and charismatic rider. His decision sparked a fresh round of speculation as to who might take the Tech 3 seat in 2010. Sixth-placed Toseland might have taken his best finish of the season, but the rumour mill already had him out of a ride. This would turn out to be correct.

Again, Rossi was smilingly enjoying the latest round of Ferrari F1 rumours, which linked him with a three-car team in the short-lived proposed FOTA breakaway championship. It was, he said, "something to talk about in the café". Similar rumours were that Dorna chief Carmelo Ezpeleta had been approached to run the new series.

The latest in the seemingly almost weekly round of new rules and regulations came as welcome news: plans for a single-bike future for MotoGP had been cancelled, along with another proposal to cut the GP weekend down to two days. The reason, explained race director Butler, was a lack of response from

the manufacturers to hopes that this new rule might encourage them to support more teams.

One bike was more than Mattia Pasini had as 250 practice got under way. Alleging non-payment of lease fees by his Hungarian-owned Team Toth, Aprilia had impounded his motorcycles after the Barcelona race and given them back without the crucial electronic dashboard. This was returned only after a bank transfer had been safely received in Italy – in time for him to get out on track after the other riders had already completed ten laps.

Tyre news: this was the first race in which a shift in regulations came into play, allowing riders to bias their pre-selected tyre choice in favour of one or another of the two compounds brought to each track. Previously, it had been equal numbers of each; now they could choose an extra of the preferred compound, and get one less of the other. It turned out to make little difference. And at the yellow tyre compound, Dunlop was confirmed as sole tyre supplier to 2010's Moto2, after Michelin had lost interest.

Aleix Espargaro made a GP return, taking over the Balatonring 250 for two races and making an impressive run. It was the start of something bigger for the hitherto jobless Spaniard.

For two riders, it was the weekend of the 20-second penalty. One was Elias, whose last-corner indiscretion in a raucous pack disputing sixth was deemed worthy of punishment, dropping him from eighth to 12th; the other was 125 rider Terol, who was punished for a last-lap near-accident, going from second to fifth as a consequence.

MotoGP RACE – 26 laps

Rossi and Lorenzo straddled Pedrosa on the front row; Stoner led the second. As usual, it was Pedrosa who surged into the lead in the first corner, tailed by Rossi and Stoner. Lorenzo was slow away and behind Vermeulen and Edwards.

As they ran out of the ultra-slow first section on to what remains of the Veenslang, Rossi pushed past Pedrosa into the lead, only for Stoner to take both of them under brakes at the end of the back straight to lead lap one.

But when Rossi passed him back, taking a tighter line into the ever-tightening start of lap two, that was that.

Lorenzo took Edwards on lap one, and Vermeulen at the start of the next. Now the front four started to open a gap, and on lap four Lorenzo moved inside Pedrosa going into the Stekkenwal right-hander. Pedrosa tried to fight back for the rest of that lap and on the way into the first corner of the next, only for the front wheel to fold underneath him as he tipped it in. His race was over, but at least for once he escaped injury, he said.

Now there were three, and on the same lap Lorenzo made the final change in order, slipping past Stoner at the end of the back straight. Rossi had 1.4 seconds on him, and took two-tenths on the next lap. From then on, the gap wavered, but never got smaller than that; over the last eight or so, it stretched inexorably. Rossi won his 100th GP on the back wheel, by a five-second margin.

Stoner's lap times had been increasing from the fourth lap as fatigue struck once again. By half-distance, he was almost eight seconds adrift, with a similar cushion behind him. Looking pale and glum on the rostrum, he slipped away forthwith for immediate treatment, issuing a statement later. "I've taken every kind of supplement and vitamin tablet you can think of, but nothing seems to have worked, so it is obviously something we need to have looked at closer. I can't keep going like this," he said.

Over the first six laps, first Dovizioso and then Edwards found their way past Vermeulen, riding his cleanest to try to keep the Suzuki close to the pace. These two were separated by more than a second, and Dovizioso closed only slowly on Stoner. Then he did exactly the same as Pedrosa, the front tucking under going into the first corner, at the start of lap 11.

Edwards was now fourth and circulated there to the end, bemoaning a lack of front-end grip that prevented him from attacking. Vermeulen had lost touch with him before half-distance, but was equally untroubled from behind for his best result of the year.

The battle for sixth was enthralling and unresolved until the final yards.

The group, led at first by Hayden, also included Toseland, Kallio, Capirossi, de Puniet and de Angelis. And, after 14 laps, a charging Elias, who had run off on the first lap and finished it in last place.

Toseland took over up front for a long spell from lap eight, and then Kallio for a couple of laps. Hayden, already battling with a loose left handlebar, dropped to the back of the group after sliding wide under braking

Cortese took a career-first pole, a hundredth ahead of Simon, but it was Terol in the lead at the end of lap one, exchanging the position with Iannone a couple of times before settling there from laps five to 12.

On the sixth, Simon had moved into second, with Gadea third. Iannone and Smith completed the lead group, about to lose touch.

Gadea took the lead on lap 12, then ran wide on the 15th and dropped to third. There was more minor shuffling as the end drew nigh, then tactics took a hand. As they started the last lap, Gadea's pit board read "SIMON FIRST": he had to concede to his team-mate. But at the end of the back straight, Terol dived under Simon for the lead, only to have to pick up. Simon was pushed on to the grass, but Terol made the slip road at undiminished speed, rejoining head-long and almost hitting new leader Gadea.

They crossed the line in that order, Simon almost a second down. A true gentleman, he wouldn't blame Terol and climbed off the bike with a smile. Race direction took a different view, docking Terol 20 seconds and promoting Simon to second.

That also put Smith on the rostrum, narrowly the victor of a fierce battle with Iannone and giving him a hard stare over his shoulder as he crossed the line – payback for the Italian's habitual mid-race gurning.

Terol ended up just clear of a gang disputing sixth, which came to blows at the chicane: Marquez ran off and put Espargaro into the gravel. Bradl took it, inches clear of rookie Folger, Corsi, Espargaro and Marquez. Olive had been victim of another muddle in this group earlier in the lap and was less than two seconds back in 11th; Rabat had crashed out of it earlier.

Cortese also crashed; Webb was knocked off on lap one; unlucky Redding had another breakdown for a third non-finish.

at the end of the back straight. Meanwhile, de Angelis gradually dropped off the back, sliding too much to sustain the pace.

They were still all together and mauling one another as they started the final lap, Kallio in front, from Toseland, Elias, de Puniet, Capirossi and Hayden, all covered by less than one second.

Kallio didn't make the finish, sliding off at high speed at the entrance to the very fast last left, Ramshoek, and suffering serious finger injuries when his left hand was trapped by the handlebar. The rest piled into the chicane braking area in a jumble, Elias making a far too impetuous dive down the inside. He ran off the outside of the track, taking Capirossi with him, and by the time they got to the line, it was Toseland from de Puniet, Elias and Hayden, all within half a second, the discommoded Capirossi less than a second behind.

Elias's move earned the punishment of a 20-second penalty, which dropped him from eighth to 12th, behind not only de Angelis, but also Melandri, whose own race had never really got going after he'd been pushed wide in the early laps.

Gibernau was a lone 13th; Canepa finally prevailed in a long battle with Takahashi over the final points. Wide-eyed Talmacsi was miles behind.

250cc RACE – 24 laps

Barbera took his second successive pole by almost two-tenths, Aoyama alongside, then Bautista and Simoncelli, with Aleix Espargaro heading the second row in his first 250 ride of the season.

Espargaro started well and even led briefly, but by the end of lap one, he was fifth, behind Simoncelli, Barbera, Bautista and Debon. Behind him, Aoyama and di Meglio were pushing hard, the Frenchman up to fourth on lap three, but Aoyama took over three laps later.

Now Simoncelli was in control, while Barbera was battling with Bautista for second. At half-distance, the lead was more than a second. At the same time, Aoyama was about to pass Barbera to harry Bautista, while di Meglio was more than a second adrift and fading. Two seconds behind him, Espargaro was engaged with Locatelli and Wilairot.

From laps 12 to 15, the order stayed the same, but the gaps did not. Simoncelli had run into grip problems, and the two behind were inching ever closer. Then on lap 16, both were past him: Bautista took the lead at Ramshoek, the fast left before the final chicane; Aoyama into the chicane.

Aoyama's first attack came at the looping Strubben, but he ran wide. On the next lap, he outbraked Bautista at De Bult and made it stick. Now the leaders took off together, Simoncelli struggling to keep the pace so that Barbera, barely a second behind, started to close rapidly.

Up front, the Honda led, Bautista planning his attack. He chose the chicane at the end of the penultimate lap, but it went badly wrong half-way through the corner. Bautista was so much faster that he couldn't avoid slamming into the back of Aoyama – so hard that his bike somersaulted and the front tyre came off the rim. Later he suggested that his rival had deliberately backed off, but in fact Aoyama had braked so late that he was on a much slower line.

Miraculously, he stayed on board, the right-hand low-level exhaust bent and dangling, and the mudguard doubled over and scraping on the tyre. His lead of eight seconds was halved over the final lap.

The incident was crucial to the championship: the win gave him the points lead. "My position begins to become interesting," he said.

Barbera first passed Simoncelli in the chicane at the end of lap 20, but Simoncelli passed him back next time around. They were still scrapping when they made contact at the start of the 22nd lap, Simoncelli getting the worst of it to run wide, losing three seconds.

Espargaro took a fine fourth, holding Locatelli at bay, while Debon had dropped back by the flag. Both Abraham and Faubel had passed the fading Wilairot, and the Thai rider had his hands full saving ninth from a pressing de Rosa.

Di Meglio had slipped a long way back in 11th, blaming a too-soft tyre choice; the rest of just 16 finishers were spaced out behind.

Tomizawa, Cluzel, Pasini and Luthi had crashed out, the last two together while battling for tenth, Luthi again the innocent victim. Later they were joined by Chesaux; Bonsey, back for a second race, retired.

Above: Moment of impact as Bautista slams into Aoyama's Honda.
Photo: Gold & Goose

Insets: Bautista's bike was ruined, but he escaped injury, while Aoyama limped on to win.
Photos: Martin Heath

Left: Gadea wins, with Terol keeping a frustrated Simon behind. Penalties would change the outcome.

Top left: The battle at the back – Gibernau (59) will leave Takahashi behind by the end.

Photos: Gold & Goose

TT ASSEN

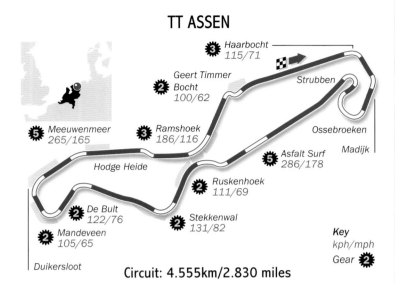

3 Haarbocht 115/71

Geert Timmer Bocht 100/62

Strubben

Ossebroeken

Madijk

5 Meeuwenmeer 265/165

3 Ramshoek 186/116

Asfalt Surf 286/178

Hodge Heide

2 Ruskenhoek 111/69

Key
kph/mph
Gear ⚙2

2 De Bult 122/76

2 Stekkenwal 131/82

2 Mandeveen 105/65

Duikersloot

Circuit: 4.555km/2.830 miles

MOTOGP

RACE DISTANCE: 26 laps, 73.520 miles/118.430 km • **RACE WEATHER:** Dry (air 24°, humidity 48%, track 30°)

Pos.	Rider	Nat.	No.	Entrant	Machine	Tyres	Laps	Time & speed
1	Valentino Rossi	ITA	46	Fiat Yamaha Team	Yamaha	B	26	42m 14.611s 104.520mph/ 168.210km/h
2	Jorge Lorenzo	SPA	99	Fiat Yamaha Team	Yamaha	B	26	42m 19.979s
3	Casey Stoner	AUS	27	Ducati Marlboro Team	Ducati	B	26	42m 37.727s
4	Colin Edwards	USA	5	Monster Yamaha Tech 3	Yamaha	B	26	42m 43.725s
5	Chris Vermeulen	AUS	7	Rizla Suzuki MotoGP	Suzuki	B	26	42m 48.216s
6	James Toseland	JPN	52	Monster Yamaha Tech 3	Yamaha	B	26	42m 53.958s
7	Randy de Puniet	USA	14	LCR Honda MotoGP	Honda	B	26	42m 54.154s
8	Nicky Hayden	USA	69	Ducati Marlboro Team	Ducati	B	26	42m 54.434s
9	Loris Capirossi	ITA	65	Rizla Suzuki MotoGP	Suzuki	B	26	42m 55.284s
10	Alex de Angelis	RSM	15	San Carlos Honda Gresini	Honda	B	26	43m 00.621s
11	Marco Melandri	ITA	33	Hayate Racing Team	Kawasaki	B	25	43m 12.388s
12	Toni Elias	SPA	24	San Carlos Honda Gresini	Honda	B	26	43m 14.385s
13	Sete Gibernau	SPA	59	Grupo Francisco Hernando	Ducati	B	26	43m 19.977s
14	Niccolo Canepa	USA	88	Pramac Racing	Ducati	B	26	43m 24.508s
15	Yuki Takahashi	JPN	72	Scot Racing Team MotoGP	Honda	B	26	43m 24.541s
16	Gabor Talmacsi	HUN	41	Scot Racing Team MotoGP	Honda	B	26	43m 39.710s
	Mika Kallio	FIN	36	Pramac Racing	Ducati	B	25	DNF
	Andrea Dovizioso	ITA	4	Repsol Honda Team	Honda	B	10	DNF
	Dani Pedrosa	SPA	3	Repsol Honda Team	Honda	B	4	DNF

Fastest lap: Valentino Rossi, on lap 4, 1m 36.558s, 105.524mph/169.825km/h (record).
Previous Lap record: Casey Stoner, AUS (Ducati), 1m 36.738s, 104.929mph/168.867km/h (2008).
Event best maximum speed: Dani Pedrosa, 167.708mph/296.9km/h (qualifying practice).

Qualifying: Dry
Air: 23° Humidity: 56% Track: 28°

1	Rossi	1m 36.025s
2	Pedrosa	1m 36.110s
3	Lorenzo	1m 36.393s
4	Stoner	1m 36.633s
5	Edwards	1m 36.760s
6	Capirossi	1m 36.953s
7	Vermeulen	1m 37.194s
8	Dovizioso	1m 37.237s
9	Toseland	1m 37.323s
10	de Puniet	1m 37.473s
11	de Angelis	1m 37.637s
12	Kallio	1m 37.749s
13	Hayden	1m 37.759s
14	Melandri	1m 37.948s
15	Elias	1m 38.136s
16	Gibernau	1m 38.453s
17	Canepa	1m 38.605s
18	Takahashi	1m 38.619s
19	Talmacsi	1m 39.407s

Fastest race laps

1	Rossi	1m 36.558s
2	Lorenzo	1m 36.755s
3	Stoner	1m 36.903s
4	Pedrosa	1m 36.918s
5	Dovizioso	1m 37.262s
6	Edwards	1m 37.375s
7	Vermeulen	1m 37.613s
8	de Puniet	1m 37.883s
9	de Angelis	1m 37.904s
10	Kallio	1m 37.909s
11	Toseland	1m 37.934s
12	Capirossi	1m 37.941s
13	Elias	1m 37.955s
14	Hayden	1m 38.200s
15	Melandri	1m 38.487s
16	Canepa	1m 38.873s
18	Takahashi	1m 39.126s
19	Talmacsi	1m 39.318s

Championship Points

1	Rossi	131
2	Lorenzo	126
3	Stoner	122
4	Dovizioso	69
5	Pedrosa	67
6	Edwards	67
7	Capirossi	55
8	Melandri	54
9	Vermeulen	53
10	de Puniet	51
11	Toseland	39
12	Elias	31
13	de Angelis	30
14	Kallio	26
15	Hayden	26
16	Canepa	12
17	Gibernau	12
18	Takahashi	9

Constructor Points

1	Yamaha	165
2	Ducati	122
3	Honda	98
4	Suzuki	71
5	Kawasaki	54

Team Points

1	FIAT Yamaha Team	257
2	Ducati Marlboro Team	148
3	Repsol Honda Team	136
4	RIZLA Suzuki MotoGP	108
5	Monster Yamaha Tech 3	106
6	San Carlo Honda Gresini	61
7	Hayate Racing Team	54
8	LCR Honda MotoGP	51
9	Pramac Racing	38
10	Grupo Francisco Hernando	12
11	Scot Racing Team	9

Grid order	1	2	3	4	5	6	7	8	9	10	11	12	13	14	15	16	17	18	19	20	21	22	23	24	25	26	
46 ROSSI	27	46	46	46	46	46	46	46	46	46	46	46	46	46	46	46	46	46	46	46	46	46	46	46	46	46	1
3 PEDROSA	46	27	27	27	99	99	99	99	99	99	99	99	99	99	99	99	99	99	99	99	99	99	99	99	99	99	2
99 LORENZO	3	3	3	99	27	27	27	27	27	27	27	27	27	27	27	27	27	27	27	27	27	27	27	27	27	27	3
27 STONER	7	99	99	3	4	4	4	4	4	4	5	5	5	5	5	5	5	5	5	5	5	5	5	5	5	5	4
5 EDWARDS	99	7	7	7	7	5	5	5	5	5	7	7	7	7	7	7	7	7	7	7	7	7	7	7	7	7	5
65 CAPIROSSI	5	5	5	4	5	7	7	7	7	7	52	52	52	52	52	36	36	52	52	52	52	52	52	52	36	52	6
7 VERMEULEN	4	4	4	5	69	69	69	52	52	52	36	36	36	36	36	52	52	36	36	36	36	36	36	36	52	14	7
4 DOVIZIOSO	69	69	69	69	52	52	52	69	69	36	69	69	69	14	14	14	14	14	69	69	24	24	24	24	24		8
52 TOSELAND	14	14	52	52	65	65	65	65	36	69	14	14	14	15	69	69	69	69	14	14	24	65	65	14	14	69	9
14 de PUNIET	33	33	65	65	15	15	15	36	14	14	15	15	15	69	15	15	65	65	65	24	65	14	14	65	65	65	10
15 de ANGELIS	65	65	15	15	36	36	36	14	15	15	65	65	65	65	24	24	24	65	24	14	69	69	69	69	15	15	11
36 KALLIO	52	52	36	36	14	14	14	15	65	65	24	24	24	24	15	15	15	15	15	15	15	15	15	15	33		12
69 HAYDEN	15	15	14	14	24	24	24	24	24	24	33	33	33	33	33	33	33	33	33	33	33	33	33	59			13
33 MELANDRI	36	36	33	24	33	33	33	33	33	33	88	88	88	88	59	59	59	59	59	59	59	59	59	88			14
24 ELIAS	41	41	41	33	88	88	88	88	88	88	72	59	59	59	88	88	88	88	88	88	72	72	72	72			15
59 GIBERNAU	88	88	88	88	41	41	72	72	72	72	59	72	72	72	72	72	72	72	72	72	88	88	88	41			
88 CANEPA	59	24	24	41	72	72	41	41	41	59	41	41	41	41	41	41	41	41	41	41	41	41	41	41			
72 TAKAHASHI	72	72	72	72	59	59	59	59	59	41																	
41 TALMACSI	24	59	59	59																							

250cc — RACE DISTANCE: 24 laps, 67.928 miles/109.320 km • RACE WEATHER: Dry (air 22°, humidity 63%, track 26°)

Pos.	Rider	Nat.	No.	Entrant	Machine	Laps	Time & Speed
1	Hiroshi Aoyama	JPN	4	Scot Racing Team 250cc	Honda	24	40m 44.008s
							(mph/km/h)
							100.057/161.027
2	Hector Barbera	SPA	40	Pepe World Team	Aprilia	24	40m 48.432s
3	Marco Simoncelli	ITA	58	Metis Gilera	Gilera	24	40m 54.347s
4	Aleix Espargaro	ESP	41	Balatonring Team	Aprilia	24	40m 55.391s
5	Roberto Locatelli	ITA	15	Metis Gilera	Gilera	14	40m 55.604s
6	Alex Debon	ESP	6	Aeropuerto – Castello – Blusens	Aprilia	24	40m 58.273s
7	Karel Abraham	CZE	17	Cardion AB Motoracing	Aprilia	24	41m 01.990s
8	Hector Faubel	SPA	55	Valencia CF – Honda SAG	Honda	24	41m 03.020s
9	Ratthapark Wilairot	THA	14	Thai Honda PTT SAG	Honda	24	41m 04.934s
10	Raffaele de Rosa	ITA	35	Scot Racing Team 250cc	Honda	24	41m 05.041s
11	Mike di Meglio	FRA	63	Mapfre Aspar Team 250cc	Aprilia	24	41m 16.136s
12	Lukas Pesek	CZE	52	Auto Kelly – CP	Aprilia	24	41m 25.337s
13	Alex Baldolini	ITA	25	WTR San Marino Team	Aprilia	24	41m 49.329s
14	Valentin Debise	FRA	53	CIP Moto – GP250	Aprilia	24	41m 56.459s
15	Imre Toth	HUN	10	Team Toth Aprilia	Aprilia	23	40m 52.181s
16	Vladimir Leonov	RUS	56	Viessmann Kiefer Racing	Aprilia	23	40m 59.230s
	Alvaro Bautista	SPA	19	Mapfre Aspar Team	Aprilia	22	DNF
	Bastien Chesaux	SWI	8	Racing Team Germany	Honda	19	DNF
	Axel Pons	SPA	7	Pepe World Team	Aprilia	16	DNF
	Toby Markham	GB	54	C&L Racing	Honda	14	DNF
	Stevie Bonsey	USA	80	Milar – Juegos Lucky	Aprilia	13	DNF
	Mattia Pasini	ITA	75	Team Toth Aprilia	Aprilia	13	DNF
	Thomas Luthi	SWI	12	Emmi – Caffe Latte	Aprilia	10	DNF
	Jules Cluzel	FRA	16	Matteoni Racing	Aprilia	5	DNF
	Shoya Tomizawa	JPN	48	CIP Moto – GP250	Aprilia	0	DNF

Fastest lap: Hiroshi Aoyama, on lap 8, 1m 40.706s, 101.177mph/162.830km/h.
Lap record: Alvaro Bautista, ESP (Aprilia), 1m 40.340s, 101.547mph/163.424km/h (2008).
Event best maximum speed: Bautista, 159.257mph/256.3km/h (free practice 1).

Qualifying: Dry — Air: 23° Humidity: 56% Track: 28°

1	Barbera	1m 40.019s
2	Aoyama, Hiroshi	1m 40.192s
3	Bautista	1m 40.210s
4	Simoncelli	1m 40.320s
5	Espargaro, Aleix	1m 40.796s
6	Debon	1m 40.830s
7	de Rosa	1m 41.023s
8	Pasini	1m 41.005s
9	di Meglio	1m 41.072s
10	Pesek	1m 41.190s
11	Wilairot	1m 41.235s
12	Locatelli	1m 41.347s
13	Faubel	1m 41.462s
14	Abraham	1m 41.533s
15	Luthi	1m 41.545s
16	Tomizawa	1m 42.038s
17	Cluzel	1m 42.628s
18	Bonsey	1m 42.679s
19	Baldolini	1m 43.075s
20	Pons	1m 43.470s
21	Debise	1m 43.635s
22	Toth	1m 43.913s
23	Chesaux	1m 44.704s
24	Leonov	1m 44.743s
25	Markham	1m 46.758s

Fastest race laps

1	Aoyama, Hiroshi	1m 40.706s
2	Barbera	1m 40.748s
3	Simoncelli	1m 40.814s
4	di Meglio	1m 40.873s
5	Bautista	1m 40.901s
6	Debon	1m 41.278s
7	Locatelli	1m 41.370s
8	Wilairot	1m 41.378s
9	Pasini	1m 41.488s
10	Abraham	1m 41.556s
11	Luthi	1m 41.573s
12	Espargaro, Aleix	1m 41.589s
13	de Rosa	1m 41.610s
14	Faubel	1m 41.660s
15	Baldolini	1m 41.786s
16	Cluzel	1m 41.889s
17	Pesek	1m 41.951s
18	Debise	1m 43.562s
19	Pons	1m 43.856s
20	Chessaux	1m 44.094s
21	Bonsey	1m 44.193s
22	Toth	1m 45.294s
23	Leonov	1m 45.782s
24	Markham	1m 46.271s

Championship Points

	Rider	Points
1	Aoyama, Hiroshi	121
2	Bautista	108
3	Barbera	95
4	Simoncelli	77
5	Pasini	64
6	Luthi	52
7	de Rosa	51
8	Faubel	49
9	Locatelli	47
10	Debon	43
11	Wilairot	38
12	Cluzel	33
13	di Meglio	32
14	Pesek	32
15	Abraham	31
16	Talmacsi	28
17	Tomizawa	14
18	Espargaro, Aleix	13
19	Toth	12
20	Baldolini	12
21	Aoyama, Shuhei	10
22	Leonov	7
23	Debise	3
24	Markham	2
25	Watanabe	2
26	Bonsey	1

Constructors

		Points
1	Aprilia	133
2	Honda	108
2	Gilera	68
3	Yamaha	2

125cc — RACE DISTANCE: 22 laps, 62.267 miles/100.210 km • RACE WEATHER: Dry (air 21°, humidity 65%, track 24°)

Pos.	Rider	Nat.	No.	Entrant	Machine	Laps	Time & Speed
1	Sergio Gadea	SPA	33	Bancaja Aspar Team 125cc	Aprilia	22	39m 07.577s
							(mph/km/h)
							95.486/153.671
2	Julian Simon	SPA	60	Bancaja Aspar Team 125cc	Aprilia	22	39m 08.478s
3	Bradley Smith	GB	38	Bancaja Aspar Team 125cc	Aprilia	22	39m 19.933s
4	Andrea Iannone	ITA	29	Ongetta Team I.S.P.A.	Aprilia	22	39m 19.977s
5	Nicolas Terol*	SPA	18	Jack & Jones Team	Aprilia	22	39m 27.655s
6	Stefan Bradl	GER	17	Viessmann Kiefer Racing	Aprilia	22	39m 28.045s
7	Jonas Folger	GER	94	Ongetta Team I.S.P.A.	Aprilia	22	39m 28.332s
8	Simon Corsi	ITA	24	Fontana Racing	Aprilia	22	39m 28.840s
9	Pol Espargaro	SPA	44	Derbi Racing Team	Derbi	22	39m 29.135s
10	Marc Marquez	SPA	93	Red Bull KTM Moto Sport	KTM	22	39m 29.518s
11	Joan Olive	SPA	6	Derbi Racing Team	Derbi	22	39m 31.182s
12	Efren Vazquez	SPA	7	Derbi Racing Team	Derbi	22	39m 35.983s
13	Dominique Aegerter	SWI	77	Ajo Interwetten	Derbi	22	40m 07.889s
14	Marvin Fritz	GER	85	LHF-Project Racing	Honda	22	40m 07.932s
15	Lorenzo Zanetti	ITA	8	Ongetta Team I.S.P.A.	Aprilia	22	40m 08.192s
16	Luis Salom	SPA	39	SAG-Castrol	Honda	22	40m 08.206s
17	Takaaki Nakagami	JPN	73	Ongetta Team I.S.P.A.	Aprilia	22	40m 08.574s
18	Michael van der Mark	NED	82	Dutch Racing Team	Honda	22	40m 08.607s
19	Jasper Iwema	NED	53	Racing Team Germany	Honda	22	40m 16.372s
20	Lukas Sembera	CZE	69	Matteoni Racing	Aprilia	22	40m 16.652s
21	Johann Zarco	FRA	14	WTR San Marino Team	Aprilia	22	40m 22.394s
22	Karel Pesek	CZE	86	Pesek Team	Derbi	22	40m 38.306s
23	Luca Marconi	FRA	87	CBC Corse	Aprilia	22	40m 53.821s
24	Pepijn Bijsterbosch	NED	83	Racing Team Bijsterbosch	Honda	21	39m 11.712s
26	Luca Vitali	ITA	10	CBC Corse	Aprilia	21	39m 17.393s
	Esteve Rabat	SPA	12	Blusens Aprilia	Aprilia	11	DNF
	Tomoyoshi Koyama	JPN	71	Loncin Racing	Loncin	9	DNF
	Cameron Beaubier	USA	16	Red Bull KTM Moto Sport	KTM	5	DNF
	Sandro Cortese	GER	11	Ajo Interwetten	Derbi	4	DNF
	Randy Krummenacher	SWI	35	Degraaf Grand Prix	Aprilia	1	DNF
	Lorenzo Savadori	ITA	32	Fontana Racing	Aprilia	1	DNF
	Scott Redding	GB	45	Blusens Aprilia	Aprilia	1	DNF
	Alexis Masbou	FRA	5	Loncin Racing	Loncin	1	DNF
	Danny Webb	GB	99	Degraaf Grand Prix	Aprilia	0	DNF

*includes 20 second penalty
Fastest lap: Julian Simon, on lap 3, 1m 45.537s, 96.546mph/155.376km/h.
Lap record: Sergio Gadea, ESP (Aprilia), 1m 45.098s, 96.949mph/156.025km/h (2006).
Event best maximum speed: Danny Webb, GB (Aprilia), 137.198mph/220.8km/h (qualifying).

Qualifying: Dry — Air: 22° Humidity: 58% Track: 25°

1	Cortese	1m 45.430s
2	Simon	1m 45.441s
3	Terol	1m 45.644s
4	Bradl	1m 45.679s
5	Smith	1m 45.712s
6	Iannone	1m 45.911s
7	Corsi	1m 45.956s
8	Espargaro, Pol	1m 46.063s
9	Gadea	1m 46.125s
10	Marquez	1m 46.164s
11	Olive	1m 46.188s
12	Rabat	1m 46.214s
13	Webb	1m 46.278s
14	Krummenacher	1m 46.681s
15	Vazquez	1m 46.812s
16	Zarco	1m 46.888s
17	Redding	1m 47.087s
18	Folger	1m 47.311s
19	Aegerter	1m 47.341s
20	Beaubier	1m 47.728s
21	Savadori	1m 47.728s
22	Salom	1m 47.933s
23	Zanetti	1m 48.217s
24	van der Mark	1m 48.505s
25	Fritz	1m 48.510s
26	Iwema	1m 48.664s
27	Nakagami	1m 48.777s
28	Masbou	1m 48.784s
29	Pesek, Karel	1m 48.801s
30	Sembera	1m 49.513s
31	Marconi	1m 49.863s
32	Koyama	1m 49.922s
33	Vitali	1m 51.578s
34	Bijsterbosch	1m 51.811s
	outside 107%	
dnq	Pouw	1m 54.484s

Fastest race laps

1	Simon	1m 45.537s
2	Gadea	1m 45.797s
3	Terol	1m 45.799s
4	Iannone	1m 46.232s
5	Smith	1m 46.240s
6	Marquez	1m 46.253s
7	Folger	1m 46.449s
8	Zarco	1m 46.459s
9	Rabat	1m 46.507s
10	Vazquez	1m 46.530s
11	Cortese	1m 46.550s
12	Espargaro, Pol	1m 46.631s
13	Olive	1m 46.743s
14	Corsi	1m 46.760s
15	Bradl	1m 46.977s
16	Zanetti	1m 47.778s
17	Fritz	1m 47.878s
18	Nakagami	1m 47.947s
19	Aegerter	1m 48.279s
20	Sembera	1m 48.379s
21	Salom	1m 48.444s
22	van der Mark	1m 48.511s
23	Iwema	1m 48.671s
24	Koyama	1m 48.889s
25	Beaubier	1m 49.332s
26	Pesek	1m 49.789s
27	Bijsterbosch	1m 49.898s
28	Marconi	1m 50.038s
29	Vitali	1m 50.644s
30	Krummenacher	1m 55.517s
31	Savadori	1m 57.057s
32	Redding	1m 57.140s
33	Masbou	2m 21.302s

Championship Points

	Rider	Points
1	Simon	104
2	Smith	98.5
3	Iannone	84.5
4	Gadea	84
5	Terol	68.5
6	Marquez	55
7	Folger	54
8	Espargaro, Pol	51.5
9	Cortese	45
10	Bradl	44
11	Aegerter	29.5
12	Redding	28.5
13	Vazquez	23
14	Olive	21
15	Rabat	19
16	Zarco	16.5
16	Webb	16.5
18	Nakagami	13
19	Zanetti	13
20	Corsi	12
21	Krummenacher	10
22	Savadori	7
23	Koyama	4
24	Iwema	3
25	Fritz	2
26	di Carlo	2
27	Beaubier	1

Constructors

		Points
1	Aprilia	162.5
2	Derbi	72
3	KTM	55
4	Honda	5
5	Loncin	4

UNITED STATES GRAND PRIX

LAGUNA SECA CIRCUIT

Jack rabbit Pedrosa won the start again
— and the finish. He was never headed.
Stoner, Elias, Rossi, Lorenzo, Dovizioso
and the rest follow.

Photo: Gold & Goose

No matter what happens at Laguna, it is frequently quite extraordinary, but not always pleasant – one remembers a string of crashes and injuries over the years. Many other events are quite unfamiliar at what is marginally the shortest and most certainly the giddiest circuit of the whole year.

They range from losing your bike for the rest of the session if you crash at one of several inaccessible places – as happened to Vermeulen and Toseland – to the emotional rendition of the national anthem for a large and lively crowd of more than 46,000 as the bikes waited on the grid.

Well, it was the day after Independence Day – a date thrust upon unwilling organisers to avoid a clash with F1 – and although Hayden had easily his best ride and result so far in his first Ducati year, it was a far cry from his wins in 2005 and 2006. Nor was an understeering Colin Edwards among the front pack. Nor were there American wild-cards: in 2008, Suzuki

had entered Ben Spies, and Kawasaki Jamie Hacking, but in 2009, Spies had gone to Yamaha and SBK, while Kawasaki was barely supporting one rider, let alone any holidaymakers.

Crashes in practice and qualifying again made the headlines. Notable victims included Lorenzo, trying to improve on what was already pole position, and Stoner, as well as Vermeulen and Toseland. Stoner escaped unhurt, but Lorenzo suffered a fracture in his left foot and a separation of his right collarbone. Attending the post-practice Press conference in a wheelchair, he was ready to race once again with fresh and painful injuries.

The worry was the nature of the crashes, especially experienced by the first two: nasty flicking high-siders that started early in the corner when the throttle was closed, rather than sliding out when it was cracked open. For the first time, this demonstrated a worrying weakness in the control Bridgestone tyres. As Lorenzo

said, "it is a little bit dangerous", but only in certain conditions, it seemed: Stoner blamed himself for forgetting that "these tyres can take a bit of warming up"; Lorenzo's crew believed the right side of his tyre had cooled while he had been following slower riders for a lap or more. But the Bridgestones' greatest asset had always been an ability to work over a wide range of temperatures, so what had gone wrong? The answer was clear to Rossi and other riders: this is a track that needs dual-compound tyres. They would urge Bridgestone to bring such tyres in 2010.

Stoner may have walked away from the crash, but he had other problems. Doctors were now debating whether he had contracted Epstein-Barr virus, or was suffering from post-viral stress syndrome (ME). A full round of tests was scheduled in San Francisco at race-seasoned Dr Art Ting's surgery for the following week. To this was added arm pump, which struck on Friday, for the first time in his road-racing career,

Left: Toseland rocks the crowd on his Yamaha (keyboard).

Far left: Rossi got this close to complacent Pedrosa on the last corner.

Left: Lorenzo's qualifying high-side left him in the hands of the medics again.

Centre row, left to right: Rossi Day is have-a-nice-day in Monterey; the Pramac team's message to Kallio; sacked Takahashi gives his side of the story; bemused champions Lawson, Roberts and Rainey wonder where Rossi went.

Below: Stoner catches up with old GP travelling companion Chaz Davies.

Photos: Gold & Goose

he said, "though I've had it motocrossing". It set the tone for another trying weekend.

There was fevered and unconvincing explanation from Scot Honda as to why Yuki Takahashi had been dumped, with Gabor Talmacsi taking over as sole rider. One such was that he had aggravated back injuries by falling at Catalunya, but the Japanese rider turned up at Laguna in person to deny this. Eventually, the truth was acknowledged. As everybody knew, Team Scot needed money badly, and Talmacsi had come along with a fistful of MOL petro-dollars. But requests to Honda to supply another pair of bikes had fallen on deaf ears, so Yuki had to go.

Kallio was also missing: his Assen crash had ground down one of the fingers of his left hand, and he was recovering from the gruesome injury.

The weekend was attended by the usual razzamatazz, a lot of it thanks to Yamaha USA, which always celebrates the event in style. It was joined in this by Monterey County, which officially appointed 5th July as Valentino Rossi Day.

One celebration of past world champions was all inclusive: although Agostini was absent, every other Yamaha world champion – Roberts, Lawson, Rainey and Rossi – was present. Instead of a track parade in open Cadillacs or some such, Yamaha had arranged a three-lap kart race. The plan was for all four to circulate in close formation for the pictures, then go for it – if they so chose – on the last lap. But while Rossi respects history, his mischievous side got the better of him. He hared from the start at such pace that the others were left looking across at one another, quite bemused. Not even Lawson, a highly accomplished kart racer, could catch him.

Rossi was in high spirits generally after his Assen win, joking about how he enjoyed the jet lag of California "because it gives me a chance to lie in bed longer", and suggesting that he had three or four more years of bike racing left in him, that he intended to spend them with Yamaha. This tune would change…

There were the usual farcical muddles. One involved Toseland, who qualified and dogged around at the back, but still was given a ride-through penalty for the minutest of jump starts. On the hectic gallop, gathering it up out of the last corner and aiming at the difficult turn one just under the bridge, James didn't see the warning and rode on, eventually being given the black flag of disqualification.

Another was vaguely related and potentially more serious, at the same time illustrating the growing gulf between US and GP racing. The national support races were run under the local jurisdiction of the new AMA Pro Racing Group owners. As well as producing a raft of new regulations and categories that had re-drawn the landscape, the group had also introduced a new safety-car system. It was deployed for the headline American Superbike race, already restarted once after a crash.

The second time, just after the start, there was a major tangle as they piled into the second corner, the tight left Andretti hairpin. Three riders went down and debris littered the track. The car came out promptly, to wait near the end of the pit straight. But, like Toseland, riders in the heat of navigating the technicalities at that point on the lap failed to see the warning flags and, until the last minute, the car. Then came the spectacle of the car frantically trying to get up to speed to catch the leaders, most of whom had come piling past, some only narrowly missing it. After that, the race was stopped. "I'm not going to pretend it was successful," said Pro-Racing spokesman Colin Fraser, adding that in future a pace-bike would be

used instead. MotoGP officials watched events unfold in growing dismay. "We have put in a lot of time and effort, especially at Laguna, to get marshalling up to standard, but with just over a minute for the lap, it is difficult," said race director Butler, who would have red-flagged the race immediately.

MotoGP RACE – 32 laps

Lorenzo's lap time before his slam-dunk crash was enough to defend pole position from Rossi's assault, by less than two-tenths; Stoner was a whisker behind. A trio of Hondas filled the second row, Pedrosa from Dovizioso from Elias. Hayden, with a special livery promoting a Nicky Hayden Replica street Ducati, was eighth, on row three.

Rossi led from the middle of the front row, only to see the familiar orange of flyweight Pedrosa surging past from behind, taking the lead into the daunting turn one. Stoner pushed past as well, only for Rossi to dive under him again into the Corkscrew, evoking memories of 2008's great battle.

Elias and Dovizioso were next, with slow-starter Lorenzo mixed up with Edwards and Hayden in the early corners. By the end of the lap, Dovi was up to fourth, with Lorenzo behind him, while both Hayden and Capirossi were ahead of Edwards.

The first four started to pull clear on only the second lap as Stoner moved back into second, passing Rossi's Yamaha around the outside of turn one. The pair were chasing Pedrosa hard, but could make no real impression; Dovi was clinging on the back, until on lap seven the front end tucked again, as at Assen, into the left-hand turn five, leaving the rider looking somewhat astonished at the rapidity of it all. This promoted Lorenzo, who had outpaced Elias, to fourth, less than two seconds off the lead. Whatever the pain, and later he described it as "terrible", it wasn't slowing him down much.

After ten laps, Pedrosa was almost a second clear, and that would grow to better than three seconds by half-distance after a string of immaculate laps that

were faster than his own qualifying time, although still short of the record. Rossi's handling was beginning to improve as the fuel load lightened, but try as he might he couldn't reverse the trend. Nor could he shake off Stoner – until after 20 laps, the Ducati slowed as his left arm "just kept folding under me".

Next time around, Lorenzo was past him – and still less than two seconds off Rossi. Twelve laps left, and although there hadn't been any overtaking for a long while, the issue was not settled. He had his sights set.

Over the next laps, he gradually hunted Rossi down and finally attacked at the end of lap 27, outbraking the Italian on the approach to the tight final turn. But it was flawed, and he was left wrestling for control while Rossi dived safely for the apex and turned up the wick to prevent any repetition, although Lorenzo continued to harry.

This, in turn, started to close Rossi on Pedrosa. He was still 1.57 seconds behind as they started the last lap, but Pedrosa had slackened off, running 1m 23.368s to Rossi's 1m 22.139s, and as they approached the end of it, Rossi "went down the hill like a crazy man" to try to take advantage of the Spaniard's complacency. He failed by just 0.344 second. A relieved-looking Pedrosa dedicated his thanks to not only his team, but also "the many doctors I have passed through in the last year". It was Honda's first win for more than a year, the last having been gained by the same rider at Catalunya in June of 2008.

An exciting finish, in spite of the static positions. Behind the leaders, attrition had whittled away at the numbers: Capirossi had crashed out on lap four while hounding Hayden for seventh, Talmacsi also on the same lap while third from last. Two laps later, Dovizioso had fallen early on the lap, then Gibernau at the end of it, in the last corner, while lying 12th.

There was one more to go: Toseland had jumped the start, albeit very narrowly, and the organisers had been signalling him in for a ride-through penalty, but he hadn't seen the instruction. Nor did he see the subsequent black flag, until lap ten: he pulled in next time around.

When Dovi fell, Elias had dropped back from Lorenzo and into the hands of Hayden, who had an acute case of home GP fever and produced by far his best performance of the season on the wilful Ducati. The American was past on lap eight and gradually inched away. In the closing laps, the Spaniard came back at him, but Nicky wasn't about to surrender. Fourteenth in the first free practice, he said that the thought of "just running around my home race in the back, not even competitive, literally had me sick in my stomach Friday night." Electronic changes had reversed the trend, determination had done the rest.

Edwards had a lonely race and a lonely finish in seventh, comfortably clear of Vermeulen, but complaining of difficulty in turning in throughout the race. In turn, the Suzuki rider had been caught up behind de Puniet in the early laps, the Frenchman using the softer rear tyre; by the time he had got past him and Melandri by lap nine, he was consigned to a following role.

De Puniet was alone in ninth, struggling for grip over the last ten laps. Melandri dropped back to tenth and a long battle with de Angelis, who was ahead for laps 23 to 28, but eight-tenths behind when it mattered. Canepa, the last finisher, was a long way back and on the verge of being lapped.

Advantage Rossi in the championship, but Pedrosa's win lessened the blow to his closer rivals.

Above: The giddying plunge of the Corkscrew: Vermeulen heads Gibernau, Toseland, Talmacsi and de Angelis on lap three.

Left: Edwards was cheerful before the race, Hayden apprehensive. He would redeem himself.

Far left: A strong sixth was best so far for Elias, on the Gresini 'factory' bike.

Photos: Gold & Goose

LAGUNA SECA

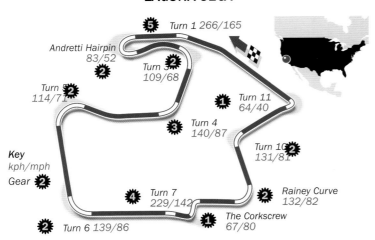

Turn 1 266/165

Andretti Hairpin 83/52

Turn 3 109/68

Turn 9 114/71

Turn 11 64/40

Turn 4 140/87

Turn 10 131/81

Key
kph/mph
Gear

Turn 7 229/142

Rainey Curve 132/82

The Corkscrew 67/80

Turn 6 139/86

Circuit 3.610km/2.243 miles

MOTOGP
RACE DISTANCE: 26 laps, 71.780 miles/115.520 km • RACE WEATHER: Dry (air 22°, humidity 43%, track 42°)

Pos.	Rider	Nat.	No.	Entrant	Machine	Tyres	Laps	Time & speed
1	Dani Pedrosa	SPA	3	Repsol Honda Team	Honda	B	32	44m 01.611s 97.824mph/ 157.433km/h
2	Valentino Rossi	ITA	46	Fiat Yamaha Team	Yamaha	B	32	44m 01.924s
3	Jorge Lorenzo	SPA	99	Fiat Yamaha Team	Yamaha	B	32	44m 03.506s
4	Casey Stoner	AUS	27	Ducati Marlboro Team	Ducati	B	32	44m 14.012s
5	Nicky Hayden	USA	69	Ducati Marlboro Team	Ducati	B	32	44m 23.243s
6	Toni Elias	SPA	24	San Carlos Honda Gresini	Honda	B	32	44m 23.621s
7	Colin Edwards	USA	5	Monster Yamaha Tech 3	Yamaha	B	32	44m 31.781s
8	Chris Vermeulen	AUS	7	Rizla Suzuki MotoGP	Suzuki	B	32	44m 34.437s
9	Randy de Puniet	USA	14	LCR Honda MotoGP	Honda	B	32	44m 41.905s
10	Marco Melandri	ITA	33	Hayate Racing Team	Kawasaki	B	32	44m 49.608s
11	Alex de Angelis	RSM	15	San Carlos Honda Gresini	Honda	B	32	44m 50.576s
12	Niccolo Canepa	USA	88	Pramac Racing	Ducati	B	32	45m 20.111s
	Andrea Dovizioso	ITA	4	Repsol Honda Team	Honda	B	6	DNF
	Sete Gibernau	SPA	59	Grupo Francisco Hernando	Ducati	B	6	DNF
	Loris Capirossi	ITA	65	Rizla Suzuki MotoGP	Suzuki	B	3	DNF
	Gabor Talmacsi	HUN	41	Scot Racing Team MotoGP	Honda	B	3	DNF
EXC	James Toseland	JPN	52	Monster Yamaha Tech 3	Yamaha	B	10	missed ride thru pen

Fastest lap: Dani Pedrosa, on lap 15, 1m 29.928s, 98.566mph/158.627km/h (record).

Previous Lap record: Casey Stoner, AUS (Ducati), 1m 21.488s, 99.098mph/159.483km/h (2008).

Event best maximum speed: Valentino Rossi, 164.663mph/265.000km/h (race).

Qualifying: Dry
Air: 21° Humidity: 44% Track: 46°

1	Lorenzo	1m 21.678s
2	Rossi	1m 21.845s
3	Stoner	1m 21.910s
4	Pedrosa	1m 21.113s
5	Dovizioso	1m 22.135s
6	Elias	1m 22.146s
7	Edwards	1m 22.490s
8	Hayden	1m 22.540s
9	Vermeulen	1m 22.633s
10	Capirossi	1m 22.662s
11	Melandri	1m 22.842s
12	de Angelis	1m 23.004s
13	Gibernau	1m 23.106s
14	de Puniet	1m 23.147s
15	Toseland	1m 23.390s
16	Canepa	1m 23.912s
17	Talmacsi	1m 24.528s

Fastest race laps

1	Pedrosa	1m 21.928s
2	Rossi	1m 21.944s
3	Lorenzo	1m 21.951s
4	Stoner	1m 22.083s
5	Dovizioso	1m 22.179s
6	Elias	1m 22.665s
7	Hayden	1m 22.703s
8	Vermeulen	1m 22.796s
9	Edwards	1m 22.878s
10	de Puniet	1m 22.981s
11	de Angelis	1m 23.024s
12	Melandri	1m 23.242s
13	Gibernau	1m 23.342s
14	Toseland	1m 23.530s
15	Capirossi	1m 23.756s
16	Canepa	1m 24.192s
19	Talmacsi	1m 24.301s

Championship Points

1	Rossi	151
2	Lorenzo	142
3	Stoner	135
4	Pedrosa	92
5	Edwards	76
6	Dovizioso	69
7	Melandri	61
8	Vermeulen	61
9	de Puniet	58
10	Capirossi	56
11	Toseland	39
12	Hayden	38
12	Elias	37
14	de Angelis	36
15	Kallio	26
16	Canepa	16
17	Gibernau	12
18	Takahashi	9

Constructor Points

1	Yamaha	185
2	Ducati	135
3	Honda	123
4	Suzuki	79
5	Kawasaki	61

Team Points

1	FIAT Yamaha Team	293
2	Ducati Marlboro Team	173
3	Repsol Honda Team	161
4	RIZLA Suzuki MotoGP	117
5	Monster Yamaha Tech 3	115
6	San Carlo Honda Gresini	73
7	Hayate Racing Team	61
8	LCR Honda MotoGP	58
9	Pramac Racing	42
10	Grupo Francisco Hernando	12
11	Scot Racing Team MotoGP	9

Grid order	1	2	3	4	5	6	7	8	9	10	11	12	13	14	15	16	17	18	19	20	21	22	23	24	25	26	27	28	29	30	31	32	
99 LORENZO	3	3	3	3	3	3	3	3	3	3	3	3	3	3	3	3	3	3	3	3	3	3	3	3	3	3	3	3	3	3	3	1	1
46 ROSSI	46	46	27	27	27	27	27	27	27	27	46	46	46	46	46	46	46	46	46	46	46	46	46	46	46	46	46	46	46	46	46	46	2
27 STONER	27	27	46	46	46	46	46	46	46	46	46	27	27	27	27	27	27	27	27	27	99	99	99	99	99	99	99	99	99	99	99	3
3 PEDROSA	4	4	4	4	4	4	99	99	99	99	99	99	99	99	99	99	99	99	99	99	27	27	27	27	27	27	27	27	27	27	27	4
4 DOVIZIOSO	99	99	99	99	99	99	24	69	69	69	69	69	69	69	69	69	69	69	69	69	69	69	69	69	69	69	69	69	69	69	69	5
24 ELIAS	24	24	24	24	24	24	69	24	24	24	24	24	24	24	24	24	24	24	24	24	24	24	24	24	24	24	24	24	24	24	24	6
5 EDWARDS	69	69	69	69	69	69	5	5	5	5	5	5	5	5	5	5	5	5	5	5	5	5	5	5	5	5	5	5	5	5	5	7
69 HAYDEN	65	65	65	5	5	5	33	33	7	7	7	7	7	7	7	7	7	7	7	7	7	7	7	7	7	7	7	7	7	7	7	8
7 VERMEULEN	5	5	5	33	33	33	7	7	33	14	14	14	14	14	14	14	14	14	14	14	14	14	14	14	14	14	14	14	14	14	14	9
65 CAPIROSSI	33	33	33	14	14	7	14	14	14	33	33	33	33	33	33	33	33	33	33	33	15	15	15	15	15	15	15	15	15	15	15	10
33 MELANDRI	7	14	14	7	7	14	52	52	52	52	15	15	15	15	15	15	15	15	15	15	33	33	33	33	33	33	33	33	33	33	33	11
15 de ANGELIS	59	59	7	59	59	59	15	15	15	15	88	88	88	88	88	88	88	88	88	88	88	88	88	88	88	88	88	88	88	88	88	12
59 GIBERNAU	14	7	59	52	52	52	88	88	88	88																						
14 de PUNIET	52	52	52	15	15	15																										
52 TOSELAND	88	41	41	88	88	88																										
88 CANEPA	41	15	15																													
41 TALMACSI	15	88	88																													

52 Pitted

GERMAN GRAND PRIX

SACHSENRING

Rossi leads the gang of four. He would
have to work hard for his fourth win.
Photo: Gold & Goose

ALL together again and back in Europe, prepared for a pair of back-to-back race weekends before the summer break proper. It was business as usual, with another weekend of fine, close racing and very treacherous weather. And all the usual undercurrents were in place – including the announcement of yet more proposed rule changes. These caused the most discussion: a bombshell from Dorna suggested nothing less than Moto1, although they were anxious to avoid calling it that.

Only 12 finishers at the US GP had thrown the problem of the shrinking grid into sharp focus, while the suggestion of one bike per rider had not yielded the hoped-for response from the factories: that they would preserve current production levels to equip more riders.

Here's another idea, said CEO Carmelo Ezpeleta, quite unusually calmly: preserve the prototypes as a dwindling elite, but beef up the grids with second-tier bikes, with 1,000cc production-based engines. Tuning would be carefully controlled to make sure they didn't beat the prototypes, but it would open the class to chassis manufacturers in the same way as Moto2, and fill out the grids nicely with traffic for the leaders to lap.

The full implications are analysed elsewhere, but it became a major talking point, not only for this weekend, but also for the weeks to come. And if the tactics were intended to scare the manufacturers into providing more support, eventually they seemed to be successful.

The grid shrinkage became worse anyway, with the shock withdrawal of Sete Gibernau's team. Controversial sponsor Francesco Hernandez had run into financial trouble with several of his huge property developments, and the money was cut off at source. This left the team high and dry, and Sete back home again, his attempted comeback ill-fated from the start. Another Spanish team also foundered: the 250 Milar-Juegos Lucky squad, ending American 250 rider Stevie Bonsey's second coming very shortly after it had begun.

Stoner was present, but intensive tests in the San Francisco clinic had brought him no closer to an answer to his malaise, nor to any imminent recovery. His increasingly baffled team had clung to reports of "slight anaemia and gastritis", but the rider said they were of no importance, instead raising a spectre himself that everyone else had been avoiding – burnout. "After Laguna, I had one test after another. There were five or six doctors coming up with ideas…they stuck tubes down my throat, into my stomach, did scans…I don't know how much blood they took, but my arm is full of holes. Maybe it's just too many years, too many years of travelling, I've been racing since I was four, I've been in Europe since I was 14, and maybe I've been too relaxed this year, and my body's decided to shut down and say, 'Okay, you're relaxing too much.'"

There were a couple of important technical changes: the factory Honda riders had a revised engine with less peaky performance; while Tech 3 Yamaha benefited from the latest electronics, as already used by Rossi and Lorenzo. It was, said Edwards, "like they sprinkled on some gold dust".

For Hayden, after his storming US GP, the beneficial changes were to neither engine nor chassis, but to his positioning. The seat of his bike was raised by an inch or so, and the handlebars by a bit less than half that (10mm), and also set slightly wider. It improved weight transfer, important to make the tyres work at their best. "But I need a stepladder to get on the bike now," he said.

The weather was fickle – showers on Friday and a downpour on Saturday, then the 250 race interrupted on Sunday. The sodden MotoGP qualifying triggered a spate of crashes, almost all high-siders, nine occurring during the one-hour session. Several were on a slippery patch on the run down the hill into the fourth-gear turn seven. Elias and de Angelis both flipped off there, and then Hayden – straight on to the hapless Canepa, who cushioned his fall. Canepa had already tumbled once in the session, and de Puniet also fell twice, as well as Melandri and Capirossi, all without

Right: Capirossi leads Kallio and Hayden and a typical midfield pack.

Below: Time only to wonder if you've got it wrong. Rossi on the grid with crew chief Burgess and his tyre technician.

Photos: Gold & Goose

serious injury. A battered Vermeulen had a thumping high-side on day one.

In turn, these triggered more complaints about the tyre rules, and in particular Bridgestone's decision to provide just one wet compound and no intermediates. This was the first track for a while where it had supplied mixed-compound dry tyres. Hayden summed it up: "I like the single-tyre rule, but at a track where they give us a dual-compound rear, I would like to have another option of wet tyre."

Both Stoner and Lorenzo were still nursing injuries from Laguna misadventures, while Assen victim Kallio was back, nursing a horrendous left-hand, ring-finger injury and riding somewhat gingerly.

There are always ghosts at the Sachsenring, and one of them wore the familiar green of the old MZ racers that had revolutionised two-stroke performance. The MZ factory is only a few kilometres away and had become moribund, but recently it had been bought by former GP racer Martin Wimmer, who had plans to revive the historic marque. Although he foresaw a return to two-stroke innovation sometime in the future, he was showing a four-stroke single as a candidate for a potential 125 replacement. Powered by a 14,000rpm KTM 250 engine, the bike was ridden on a demonstration lap by another German ex-GP winner, Ralf Waldmann.

Another memory was evocative in a more personal way, when Finnish racing legend Jarno Saarinen was inducted posthumously into the MotoGP Hall of Fame. Saarinen had made a strong start toward becoming the first man to win the 500cc title on a two-stroke in 1973, after two runaway wins on a factory Yamaha, when he was killed in the notorious multiple crash at the 250 Italian GP at Monza. Agostini took the two-stroke honour two years later. Saarinen's widow, Soili, and two of his three brothers, along with riders Anton Mang and Angel Nieto, attended the Sachsenring for a muted, touching ceremony.

MotoGP RACE – 30 laps

Lorenzo seemed in control of the sodden qualifying as the flag fell, but Rossi was already on an attacking lap of such ferocity that he stole pole by an amazing margin of more than half a second. Stoner completed row one, sitting out much of the session to preserve his strength; Hayden led row two in spite of his crash (and an alarming, but survivable, gearbox seize in the morning), his best qualifying spot of the season so far.

Rossi won the dash to the first corner, Pedrosa bursting through from row three to follow him in, from de Puniet, Stoner, de Angelis and Lorenzo. There was plenty of banging and barging. The worst victim was Hayden, up front, but on the outside. He admitted that he had gone in too hot, "but the people inside me were too hot too." He had to pick up and dropped to 14th, being back up to ninth by the end of the lap, but stuck in a close pack.

De Puniet didn't get that far, suffering a spectacular high-side on the fastest corner on the track, which led on to the 'waterfall' plunge.

Stoner was third at the end of lap one, with Dovizioso up to fourth, ahead of Lorenzo, two laps later. That lasted only until lap four, when Dovi started a doomed slide backwards, clearly unable to attack the corners like the others. His front tyre had a fault, although the team discretely blamed "electrical problems" for his eventual retirement.

Stoner was on the move, outbraking Pedrosa at the bottom of the hill on lap five, leaning on Rossi for two laps, then doing the same to him. He would lead for the next ten giddy laps.

Rossi stayed close, and on lap nine Lorenzo took up station behind, having dispatched Pedrosa at the same place. The Honda was starting to lose touch: a second adrift before half-distance, then see-sawing back up again as the race wore on.

The front three were still inches apart. On lap 17, Lorenzo got inside Stoner under braking for the first corner, and the two Fiat Yamahas led the race. The younger rider stalked Rossi steadily; Stoner dropped away slightly, while Pedrosa began closing up again.

Lap 26 was crucial. At the start, both Lorenzo and Pedrosa moved up one place under braking for turn one. At the other end of the lap, at the bottom of

the waterfall, Stoner had a huge moment entering the corner, almost crashing and running wide. Now out of the battle, he suddenly realised that adrenaline had been keeping him going. Stricken once more, but safe in fourth, he dropped back rapidly.

With Pedrosa a close spectator, the double Yamaha display was again in full swing: identikit bikes matched inch for inch, neither rider with an obvious advantage. Then Rossi took control again, with a finely judged attack at the first corner. From there to the end, the pair ran faster than they had all race, Rossi keeping himself just out of reach and riding defensively at the few overtaking spots. Lorenzo attacked to the very end, failing by the narrowest of margins.

De Angelis rode a lonely race to fifth, second Honda home for an uncharacteristically unobtrusive best finish so far.

The following gang had been volatile. Edwards was behind de Angelis at the end of the first lap, then came Capirossi holding up the rest. Hayden, Kallio and Melandri were past him next time around, then Melandri led the trio past Edwards by lap eight, by which time Elias had caught up from a bad start and also was ahead of the American.

Before half-distance, Kallio had left the group with tyre problems. Elias was ahead of Hayden and hounding Melandri. He finally got past with four laps to go to claim sixth; Melandri, Hayden and Edwards were in close order right behind.

Toseland looked as though he might catch Edwards, but then dropped away again in tenth. Capirossi was still losing ground in 11th, with Canepa a lone 12th. Vermeulen – hurting after a heavy high-side in practice – was last for the first nine laps, before finally making his way past Talmacsi and, on the last lap, Kallio as well.

Once again, the battle had gone in Rossi's favour, and he was now 18 points ahead of Lorenzo. At this stage, Stoner was 28 adrift.

250cc RACE – 19 laps

The weather hit at the worst possible time for the 250s – just after the start, and after Wilairot had already eliminated himself and knocked three others down at the first corner. The red flags were out before the lap was half done. When the race began again, it was minus the Thai rider and had been cut by ten laps, but was on a dry track.

Simoncelli was on pole for a second time, with Barbera, Bautista and Aoyama alongside. Abraham led row two, from Pasini and Debon.

Debon galloped away, 1.4 seconds clear after lap one. By then, Simoncelli had barged through to second and was closing gradually. By lap five, he was on him; on the eighth, he slipped ahead under braking for the first corner. At this point, they were almost five seconds clear of the rest, and the pair continued in close formation, without changing order, from there until the flag. But the comfort zone was only temporary.

The chase had been delayed in the early laps by a big moment for Barbera on lap two – he dropped from second to eighth in the process. This left Faubel heading the group, all jostling behind him.

On lap four, Aoyama got past; at the same time, Barbera pushed through to lead the next group and was closing rapidly.

At half-distance, there were five of them: Aoyama, Faubel, Barbera, Bautista and di Meglio. They were not yet making any impression on the leaders, while Pasini was charging up from behind.

On lap 13, doubly unlucky di Meglio slipped off at the bottom of the hill; he remounted, only to pit before the end.

By now, Pasini had caught up and sent Faubel to the back of the group. Soon he was engaged with Bautista and Barbera, getting ahead for a lap or so, only to push a fraction too hard over the brow on the final corner, sliding down and out on lap 17.

As the battle for third intensified, the remaining trio closed rapidly on the leaders, Aoyama using every inch of track to keep the two Spaniards behind. He managed it until the start of the final lap, when Bautista outbraked him at the end of the pit straight and took off after Debon, just over a second ahead. He all but caught him, Aoyama right behind and Barbera still there. First to fifth was covered by just over a second; Faubel was five seconds down.

The next pair was closing by the end and, in his second race of the year, Aleix Espargaro got ahead of Luthi for seventh. They had outpaced a lone de Rosa in ninth, with tenth-placed Locatelli in a strung-out bunch. The next battle was for 13th, won in the closing laps by spirited rookie Tomizawa from Cluzel.

Leonov was the only other crasher, right after the restart; engine problems undermined Abraham's best-ever qualifying, heading row two, and he dropped straight to the back to eventual retirement.

125cc RACE – 27 laps

Canny Simon claimed pole in bad weather, a full second clear of Smith on a weekend when he would drive home his advantage. Marquez was alongside, the front row completed by wide-eyed wild-card Marcel Schrotter, riding for ex-multi-champion Toni Mang in only his second GP.

Smith crashed out early on the first lap after losing the lead to Simon into turn one. He rejoined at the back, only to fall once more while trying to push forward. His hard front tyre, he said, wouldn't get warm enough.

Simon had a soft tyre and went off at breakneck speed. After five of the short laps, he was almost three seconds clear. Eventually, he would win by almost ten. With zero points to Smith, this meant a useful 25-point championship lead.

Terol tried to chase, while Gadea escaped from a gang behind to close up, passing on the seventh for a lone second.

By now, a battling quartet was closing on Terol, being reduced to three when Corsi slid out. On lap 23, Olive, Iannone and Marquez caught the Spaniard.

Iannone had abused his tyres coming through from 22nd on the grid, and he dropped away over the last five laps. The other three scrapped to the final two corners. Olive led on the way in, but when Marquez passed him on the exit, the pair collided. This put Marquez off line and into a high-side in the last corner. Olive survived for third, Terol a close fourth.

Espargaro and Cortese battled for most of the race, and by the end they had caught Iannone, both getting ahead by the finish. Bradl had been with them, but crashed out. Webb beat Aegerter and Koyama for eighth; Redding had another mechanical failure. Iwema, Vazquez and Zarco crashed out together in the first corner. Schrotter was an impressive 12th.

Above: Winner Simoncelli and Debon shake hands after their race-long battle.

Above left: Debon with trophy: it was his best result of the year.

Left: Olive and Iannone lead the chase pack in the early stages.

Top: Bautista leads the 250 pack: Espargaro (41) and Pasini (75) prominent.

Above far left: Stoner struggled home fourth.

Photos: Gold & Goose

ALICE MOTORRAD GRAND PRIX DEUTSCHLAND

19 JULY 2009 • FIM WORLD CHAMPIONSHIP ROUND 9

SACHSENRING GP CIRCUIT

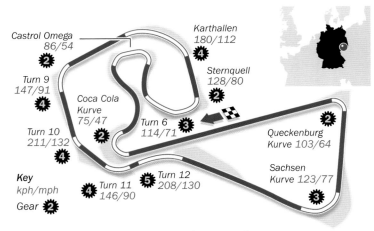

Castrol Omega 86/54 [2]
Karthallen 180/112 [4]
Turn 9 147/91 [4]
Sternquell 128/80 [2]
Coca Cola Kurve 75/47 [2]
Turn 6 114/71 [3]
Turn 10 211/132 [4]
Queckenburg Kurve 103/64 [2]
Sachsen Kurve 123/77 [3]

Key
kph/mph
Gear [2]

Turn 11 146/90 [4]
Turn 12 208/130 [5]

Circuit 3.671km/2.281 miles

MOTOGP

RACE DISTANCE: 30 laps, 68.431 miles/110.130 km • RACE WEATHER: Dry (air 19°, humidity 48%, track 27°)

Pos.	Rider	Nat.	No.	Entrant	Machine	Tyres	Laps	Time & speed
1	Valentino Rossi	ITA	46	Fiat Yamaha Team	Yamaha	B	30	41m 21.769s 99.265mph/ 159.752km/h
2	Jorge Lorenzo	SPA	99	Fiat Yamaha Team	Yamaha	B	30	41m 21.868s
3	Dani Pedrosa	SPA	3	Repsol Honda Team	Honda	B	30	41m 24.668s
4	Casey Stoner	AUS	27	Ducati Marlboro Team	Ducati	B	30	41m 31.995s
5	Alex de Angelis	RSM	15	San Carlos Honda Gresini	Honda	B	30	41m 43.291s
6	Toni Elias	SPA	24	San Carlos Honda Gresini	Honda	B	30	41m 52.621s
7	Marco Melandri	ITA	33	Hayate Racing Team	Kawasaki	B	30	41m 53.070s
8	Nicky Hayden	USA	69	Ducati Marlboro Team	Ducati	B	30	41m 53.735s
9	Colin Edwards	USA	5	Monster Yamaha Tech 3	Yamaha	B	30	41m 54.634s
10	James Toseland	JPN	52	Monster Yamaha Tech 3	Yamaha	B	30	42m 05.695s
11	Loris Capirossi	ITA	65	Rizla Suzuki MotoGP	Suzuki	B	30	42m 19.144s
12	Niccolo Canepa	USA	88	Pramac Racing	Ducati	B	30	42m 22.308s
13	Chris Vermeulen	AUS	7	Rizla Suzuki MotoGP	Suzuki	B	30	42m 25.414s
14	Mika Kallio	FIN	36	Pramac Racing	Ducati	B	30	42m 25.924s
15	Gabor Talmacsi	HUN	41	Scot Racing Team MotoGP	Honda	B	29	41m 22.338s
	Andrea Dovizioso	ITA	4	Repsol Honda Team	Honda	B	25	DNF
	Randy de Puniet	USA	14	LCR Honda MotoGP	Honda	B	0	DNF

Qualifying: Wet
Air: 14° Humidity: 88% Track: 16°

1	Rossi	1m 32.520s
2	Lorenzo	1m 33.160s
3	Stoner	1m 33.759s
4	Hayden	1m 34.404s
5	de Angelis	1m 34.490s
6	de Puniet	1m 34.564s
7	Edwards	1m 34.607s
8	Pedrosa	1m 34.725s
9	Capirossi	1m 34.741s
10	Kallio	1m 34.771s
11	Dovizioso	1m 34.892s
12	Vermeulen	1m 34.937s
13	Melandri	1m 34.938s
14	Toseland	1m 35.005s
15	Canepa	1m 36.012s
16	Talmacsi	1m 36.055s
17	Elias	1m 36.531s

Fastest race laps

1	Pedrosa	1m 22.126s
2	Lorenzo	1m 22.209s
3	Rossi	1m 22.231s
4	Stoner	1m 22.272s
5	de Angelis	1m 22.711s
6	Dovizioso	1m 22.790s
7	Elias	1m 22.989s
8	Edwards	1m 23.034s
9	Melandri	1m 23.052s
10	Kallio	1m 23.083s
11	Hayden	1m 23.093s
12	Toseland	1m 23.591s
13	Capirossi	1m 23.772s
14	Canepa	1m 24.023s
15	Vermeulen	1m 24.068s
16	Talmacsi	1m 24.235s

Fastest lap: Dani Pedrosa, on lap 25, 1m 22.126s, 99.989mph/160.918km/h (record).

Previous Lap record: Dani Pedrosa, SPA (Honda), 1m 23.082s, 98.839mph/159.066km/h (2007).

Event best maximum speed: Dani Pedrosa, 178.830mph/287.8km/h (race).

Championship Points

1	Rossi	176
2	Lorenzo	162
3	Stoner	148
4	Pedrosa	108
5	Edwards	83
6	Melandri	70
7	Dovizioso	69
8	Vermeulen	64
9	Capirossi	61
10	de Puniet	58
11	de Angelis	47
12	Elias	47
13	Hayden	46
14	Toseland	45
15	Kallio	28
16	Canepa	20
17	Gibernau	12
18	Takahashi	9
19	Talmacsi	1

Constructor Points

1	Yamaha	210
2	Ducati	148
3	Honda	139
4	Suzuki	84
5	Kawasaki	70

Team Points

1	FIAT Yamaha Team	338
2	Ducati Marlboro Team	194
3	Repsol Honda Team	177
4	Monster Yamaha Tech 3	128
5	RIZLA Suzuki MotoGP	125
6	San Carlo Honda Gresini	94
7	Hayate Racing Team	70
8	LCR Honda MotoGP	58
9	Pramac Racing	48
10	Grupo Francisco Hernando	12
11	Scot Racing Team	10

Grid order

Grid order	1	2	3	4	5	6	7	8	9	10	11	12	13	14	15	16	17	18	19	20	21	22	23	24	25	26	27	28	29	30	
46 ROSSI	46	46	46	46	46	46	27	27	27	27	27	27	27	27	27	27	46	46	46	46	46	46	46	46	99	99	99	46	46		1
99 LORENZO	3	3	3	3	27	27	46	46	46	46	46	46	46	46	46	46	27	99	99	99	99	99	99	99	46	46	46	99	99		2
27 STONER	27	27	27	27	3	3	3	3	99	99	99	99	99	99	99	99	99	27	27	27	27	27	27	27	3	3	3	3	3		3
69 HAYDEN	99	99	4	99	99	99	99	99	3	3	3	3	3	3	3	3	3	3	3	3	3	3	3	3	27	27	27	27	27		4
15 de ANGELIS	4	4	99	4	4	4	15	15	15	15	15	15	15	15	15	15	15	15	15	15	15	15	15	15	15	15	15	15	15		5
14 de PUNIET	15	15	15	15	15	15	4	4	4	4	4	4	4	4	4	4	33	33	33	33	33	33	33	24	24	24	24	24			6
5 EDWARDS	5	5	5	5	5	33	33	33	33	33	33	33	33	33	33	33	4	24	24	24	24	24	24	33	33	33	33				7
3 PEDROSA	65	36	36	33	33	33	36	36	36	24	24	24	24	24	24	24	24	24	4	4	69	69	69	69	69	69	69	69	69		8
65 CAPIROSSI	69	69	33	36	36	36	5	69	69	36	69	69	69	69	69	69	69	69	69	4	4	5	5	5	5	5	5	5			9
36 KALLIO	36	33	69	69	69	69	69	24	24	69	5	5	5	5	5	5	5	5	5	5	5	4	52	52	52	52	52	52			10
4 DOVIZIOSO	7	65	52	52	52	24	24	5	5	36	52	52	52	52	52	52	52	52	52	52	52	4	65	65	65	65	65				11
7 VERMEULEN	33	24	24	24	24	52	52	52	52	52	36	36	65	65	65	65	65	65	65	65	65	36	88	88	88	88					12
33 MELANDRI	88	52	65	65	65	65	65	65	65	65	65	65	36	36	36	36	36	36	36	36	36	88	36	36	36	7					13
52 TOSELAND	24	7	41	41	41	41	41	88	88	88	88	88	88	88	88	88	88	88	88	88	88	7	7	7	7	36					14
88 CANEPA	52	41	7	88	88	88	88	41	41	7	7	7	7	7	7	7	7	7	7	7	7	41	41	41	41						15
41 TALMACSI	41	88	88	7	7	7	7	7	41	41	41	41	41	41	41	41	41	41	41	41	14	41	41	41	41						
24 ELIAS																															

4 Pitted   41 Lapped rider

250cc — RACE DISTANCE: 19 laps, 43.340 miles/69.749 km • RACE WEATHER: Wet (air 16°, humidity 60%, track 23°)

Pos.	Rider	Nat.	No.	Entrant	Machine	Laps	Time & Speed
1	Marco Simoncelli	ITA	58	Metis Gilera	Gilera	19	27m 11.034s
							(mph/km/h)
							95.659/153.949
2	Alex Debon	ESP	6	Aeropuerto – Castello – Blusens	Aprilia	19	27m 11.513s
3	Alvaro Bautista	SPA	19	Mapfre Aspar Team	Aprilia	19	27m 11.562s
4	Hiroshi Aoyama	JPN	4	Scot Racing Team 250cc	Honda	19	27m 11.900s
5	Hector Barbera	SPA	40	Pepe World Team	Aprilia	19	27m 12.294s
6	Hector Faubel	SPA	55	Honda SAG	Honda	19	27m 17.006s
7	Aleix Espargaro	ESP	41	Balatonring Team	Aprilia	19	27m 19.755s
8	Thomas Luthi	SWI	12	Emmi – Caffe Latte	Aprilia	19	27m 19.796s
9	Raffaele de Rosa	ITA	35	Scot Racing Team 250cc	Honda	19	27m 30.210s
10	Roberto Locatelli	ITA	15	Metis Gilera	Gilera	19	27m 38.984s
11	Alex Baldolini	ITA	25	WTR San Marino Team	Aprilia	19	27m 40.635s
12	Lukas Pesek	CZE	52	Auto Kelly – CP	Aprilia	19	27m 49.333s
13	Shoya Tomizawa	JPN	48	CIP Moto – GP250	Honda	19	28m 02.974s
14	Jules Cluzel	FRA	16	Matteoni Racing	Aprilia	19	28m 03.953s
15	Bastien Chesaux	SWI	8	Racing Team Germany	Honda	19	28m 17.820s
16	Axel Pons	SPA	7	Pepe World Team	Aprilia	19	28m 31.607s
17	Toby Markham	GB	54	C&L Racing	Honda	18	27m 17.661s
18	Imre Toth	HUN	10	Team Toth Aprilia	Aprilia	18	27m 20.889s
19	Joakim Stensmo	SWE	66	Nordgren Racing	Honda	17	28m 09.860s
20	Valentin Debise	FRA	53	CIP Moto – GP250	Honda	15	28m 03.839s
	Mattia Pasini	ITA	75	Team Toth Aprilia	Aprilia	16	DNF
	Mike di Meglio	FRA	63	Mapfre Aspar Team 250cc	Aprilia	16	DNF
	Karel Abraham	CZE	17	Cardion AB Motoracing	Aprilia	8	DNF
	Vladimir Leonov	RUS	56	Viessmann Kiefer Racing	Aprilia	0	
dns	Ratthapark Wilairot	THA	14	Thai Honda PTT SAG	Honda		
dnq	Robin Halen	SWE	67	Promotion Scandinavia AB	Aprilia		
dnq	Marcel Becker	GER	67	Yamaha Road Racing Team	Yamaha		

Fastest lap: Alvaro Bautista, on lap 19, 1m 24.552s, 97.120mph/156.301km/h.
Lap record: Mika Kallio, FIN (KTM), 1m 24.762s, 96.880mph/155.914km/h (2007).
Event best maximum speed: Barbera, 98.957mph/246.5km/h (race).

Qualifying: Wet
Air: 14° Humidity: 89% Track: 16°

1	Simoncelli	1m 32.962s
2	Barbera	1m 33.105s
3	Bautista	1m 34.246s
4	Aoyama, Hiroshi	1m 34.285s
5	Abraham	1m 34.312s
6	Pasini	1m 34.333s
7	Debon	1m 34.632s
8	Faubel	1m 34.660s
9	Espargaro, Aleix	1m 34.718s
10	di Meglio	1m 34.804s
11	Luthi	1m 35.019s
12	Baldolini	1m 35.355s
13	Pesek	1m 35.427s
14	Locatelli	1m 35.673s
15	Cluzel	1m 35.889s
16	Wilairot	1m 36.078s
17	de Rosa	1m 36.097s
18	Tomizawa	1m 36.387s
19	Toth	1m 36.767s
20	Leonov	1m 36.880s
21	Debise	1m 37.633s
22	Markham	1m 37.234s
23	Chesaux	1m 39.234s
	Outside 107%	
dnq	Pons	1m 40.442s
dnq	Halen	1m 41.158s
dnq	Stensmo	1m 42.138s
dnq	Becker	1m 46.868s

Fastest race laps

1	Bautista	1m 24.552s
2	Pasini	1m 24.724s
3	Barbera	1m 24.948s
4	di Meglio	1m 25.014s
5	Aoyama, Hiroshi	1m 25.045s
6	Simoncelli	1m 25.272s
7	Faubel	1m 25.344s
8	Debon	1m 25.430s
9	Espargaro, Aleix	1m 25.431s
10	de Rosa	1m 25.551s
11	Locatelli	1m 25.615s
12	Luthi	1m 25.621s
13	Cluzel	1m 26.662s
14	Baldolini	1m 26.762s
15	Pesek	1m 26.881s
16	Tomizawa	1m 27.288s
17	Pons	1m 28.307s
18	Chessaux	1m 28.386s
19	Debise	1m 29.014s
20	Toth	1m 29.264s
21	Markham	1m 29.723s
22	Stensmo	1m 33.964s
23	Abraham	1m 34.729s

Championship Points

	Rider	Points
1	Aoyama, Hiroshi	134
2	Bautista	124
3	Barbera	106
4	Simoncelli	102
5	Pasini	64
6	Debon	63
7	Luthi	60
8	Faubel	59
9	de Rosa	58
10	Locatelli	53
11	Wilairot	38
12	Pesek	36
13	Cluzel	35
14	di Meglio	32
15	Abraham	31
16	Talmacsi	28
17	Espargaro, Aleix	22
18	Tomizawa	17
19	Baldolini	17
20	Toth	12
21	Aoyama, Shuhei	10
22	Leonov	7
23	Debise	5
24	Markham	2
25	Watanabe	2
26	Chesaux	1
27	Bonsey	1

Constructors

		Points
1	Aprilia	133
2	Honda	108
2	Gilera	68
3	Yamaha	2

125cc — RACE DISTANCE: 27 laps, 61.588 miles/99.117 km • RACE WEATHER: Dry (air 18°, humidity 57%, track 26°)

Pos.	Rider	Nat.	No.	Entrant	Machine	Laps	Time & Speed
1	Julian Simon	SPA	60	Bancaja Aspar Team 125cc	Aprilia	27	39m 57.337s
							(mph/km/h)
							92.484/148.840
2	Sergio Gadea	SPA	33	Bancaja Aspar Team 125cc	Aprilia	27	40m 06.752s
3	Joan Olive	SPA	6	Derbi Racing Team	Derbi	27	40m 14.896s
4	Nicolas Terol	SPA	18	Jack & Jones Team	Aprilia	27	40m 14.924s
5	Pol Espargaro	SPA	44	Derbi Racing Team	Derbi	27	40m 17.077s
6	Sandro Cortese	GER	11	Ajo Interwetten	Derbi	27	40m 18.115s
7	Andrea Iannone	ITA	29	Ongetta Team I.S.P.A.	Aprilia	27	40m 18.245s
8	Danny Webb	GB	99	Degraaf Grand Prix	Aprilia	27	40m 35.558s
9	Dominique Aegerter	SWI	77	Ajo Interwetten	Derbi	27	40m 35.771s
10	Tomoyoshi Koyama	JPN	71	Loncin Racing	Loncin	27	40m 37.422s
11	Randy Krummenacher	SWI	35	Degraaf Grand Prix	Aprilia	27	40m 41.464s
12	Marcel Schrotter	GER	78	Toni – Mang Team	Honda	27	40m 42.388s
13	Luis Salom	SPA	39	Jack & Jones Team	Honda	27	40m 56.941s
14	Cameron Beaubier	USA	16	Red Bull KTM Moto Sport	KTM	27	41m 15.494s
15	Daniel Kartheinninger	GER	79	Freudenberg Racing Team	Honda	27	41m 18.162s
16	Marc Marquez	SPA	93	Red Bull KTM Moto Sport	KTM	27	41m 22.474s
17	Efren Vazquez	SPA	7	Derbi Racing Team	Derbi	27	41m 27.764s
18	Lukas Sembera	CZE	69	Matteoni Racing	Aprilia	27	41m 27.865s
19	Jasper Iwema	NED	53	Racing Team Germany	Honda	26	39m 59.115s
20	Lorenzo Savadori	ITA	32	Fontana Racing	Aprilia	26	40m 12.680s
21	Toni Finsterbusch	GER	71	Freudenberg Racing Team	Honda	26	40m 27.720s
22	Damien Raemy	SWI	80	RBS - Honda Racing	Honda	26	40m 31.349s
23	Johann Zarco	FRA	14	WTR San Marino Team	Aprilia	26	40m 41.311s
24	Luca Marconi	FRA	87	CBC Corse	Aprilia	26	40m 55.828s
	Scott Redding	GB	45	Blusens Aprilia	Aprilia	19	DNF
	Stefan Bradl	GER	17	Viessmann Kiefer Racing	Aprilia	18	DNF
	Takaaki Nakagami	JPN	73	Ongetta Team I.S.P.A.	Aprilia	17	DNF
	Simon Corsi	ITA	24	Fontana Racing	Aprilia	16	DNF
	Jonas Folger	GER	94	Ongetta Team I.S.P.A.	Aprilia	15	DNF
	Michael Ranseder	AUT	88	CBC Corse	Aprilia	8	DNF
	Lorenzo Zanetti	ITA	8	Ongetta Team I.S.P.A.	Aprilia	6	DNF
	Eeki Kuparinen	FIN	81	Ajo Motorsort Jr.	Honda	3	DNF
	Bradley Smith	GB	38	Bancaja Aspar Team 125cc	Aprilia	3	DNF
	Esteve Rabat	SPA	12	Blusens Aprilia	Aprilia	1	DNF
	Alexis Masbou	FRA	5	Loncin Racing	Loncin	1	DNF

Fastest lap: Sergio Gadea, on lap 6, 1m 28.337s, 92.959mph/149.604km/h.
Lap record: Gabot Talmacsi, HUN (Aprilia), 1m 26.909s, 94.487mph/152.062km/h (2007).
Event best maximum speed: Danny Webb, GB (Aprilia), 131.171mph/211.1km/h (race).

Qualifying: Wet
Air: 14° Humidity: 89% Track: 16°

1	Simon	1m 38.671s
2	Smith	1m 39.686s
3	Marquez	1m 40.010s
4	Schrotter	1m 40.486s
5	Terol	1m 40.492s
6	Masbou	1m 40.664s
7	Nakagami	1m 40.828s
8	Vazquez	1m 40.966s
9	Corsi	1m 41.129s
10	Ranseder	1m 41.341s
11	Iwema	1m 41.401s
12	Olive	1m 41.478s
13	Koyama	1m 41.552s
14	Gadea	1m 41.565s
15	Cortese	1m 41.571s
16	Bradl	1m 41.694s
17	Webb	1m 41.714s
18	Zanetti	1m 42.157s
19	Espargaro, Pol	1m 42.174s
20	Sembera	1m 42.532s
21	Folger	1m 42.597s
22	Iannone	1m 42.767s
23	Aegerter	1m 43.151s
24	Redding	1m 43.192s
25	Savadori	1m 43.523s
26	Kartheininger	1m 43.742s
27	Rabat	1m 43.768s
28	Beaubier	1m 43.886s
29	Finsterbusch	1m 44.019s
30	Salom	1m 44.716s
31	Kuparinen	1m 45.155s
32	Marconi	1m 45.358s
	Outside 107%	
	Vitali	1m 45.983s
	Krummenacher	1m 46.959s
	Zarco	1m 47.094s
	Raemy	1m 47.612s

Fastest race laps

1	Gadea	1m 28.337s
2	Simon	1m 28.358s
3	Iannone	1m 28.444s
4	Espargaro, Pol	1m 28.536s
5	Cortese	1m 28.556s
6	Corsi	1m 28.575s
7	Marquez	1m 28.695s
8	Olive	1m 28.706s
9	Terol	1m 28.824s
10	Redding	1m 29.139s
11	Bradl	1m 29.209s
12	Folger	1m 29.332s
13	Webb	1m 29.439s
14	Aegerter	1m 29.475s
15	Ranseder	1m 29.528s
16	Krummenacher	1m 29.529s
17	Koyama	1m 29.641s
18	Schrotter	1m 29.694s
19	Sembera	1m 29.724s
20	Vazquez	1m 30.143s
21	Salom	1m 30.156s
22	Beaubier	1m 30.400s
23	Zarco	1m 30.407s
24	Nakagami	1m 30.420s
25	Iwema	1m 30.544s
26	Smith	1m 30.681s
27	Kartheininger	1m 30.863s
28	Savadori	1m 31.014s
29	Zanetti	1m 31.327s
30	Finsterbusch	1m 31.463s
31	Marconi	1m 31.507s
32	Raemy	1m 31.656s
33	Kuparinen	1m 34.609s
34	Rabat	1m 35.029s
35	Masbou	1m 36.880s

Championship Points

	Rider	Points
1	Simon	129
2	Gadea	104
3	Smith	98.5
4	Iannone	93.5
5	Terol	81.5
6	Espargaro, Pol	62.5
7	Marquez	55
8	Cortese	55
9	Folger	54
10	Bradl	44
11	Olive	37
12	Aegerter	36.5
13	Redding	28.5
14	Webb	24.5
15	Vazquez	23
16	Rabat	19
17	Zarco	16.5
18	Krummenacher	15
19	Nakagami	13
20	Zanetti	13
21	Corsi	12
22	Koyama	10
23	Savadori	7
24	Schrotter	4
25	Salom	3
26	Iwema	3
27	Beaubier	3
28	Fritz	2
26	di Carlo	2
27	Kartheininger	1

Constructors

		Points
1	Aprilia	187.5
2	Derbi	88
3	KTM	57
4	Honda	10
5	Loncin	9

BRITISH
GRAND PRIX

DONINGTON PARK CIRCUIT

Main photo: Rossi and Dovizioso watch as Lorenzo slides out of the lead.

Inset far left: The crowds admire the "Visit Spain" posters from under their umbrellas.

Inset centre: Rossi also crashed, but managed to pick it up and get going again.

Inset below: Dovizioso stayed on board, stayed in front for a first win.

Photos: Gold & Goose

"VISIT Spain", exhorted the trackside banners. Seldom can an invitation have seemed more alluring, as Britain's notorious summer delivered all the weather of the Costa Brava, plus a whole lot more besides, most of which seemed to have come from Norway, or somewhere else very cold. Rain, or the lack of it, disrupted all the racing, and the 125 event was the shortest race ever – more than a kilometre shorter than the Qatar GP.

The final visit to Donington Park had been presaged by doubts that the circuit would be fit to race, after earthworks and a new underpass had compromised run-off at Coppice. Some national meetings had been run with almost half the circuit under yellow caution flags as a consequence – and financial problems and a dispute with the landlords had threatened the whole new enterprise.

The circuit was to be comprehensively rebuilt for Formula One for 2010, but while prophets of doom for that plan eventually would be proved right, the ill-starred old circuit welcomed MotoGP for the

23rd and final time in the usual manner, and just as ready to race.

The weekend began with the Day of Champions – £177,000 was realised, continuing a downward trend from 2008, a thoughtful oil painting by Lorenzo netting £2,300, and Stoner staying away: incomprehensibly, he'd been booed off the stage last time. It continued with the usual uncertain East Midlands summer weather and the usual complaints about the iffy surface. And it ended with only a few regrets as the convoy left the muddy car parks for the last time.

The subtleties and complications of the circuit would be missed, so too (rather surprisingly) would its dual character: one half fast and flowing, the other the opposite in every respect. You need two different bikes, and the challenge for engineering lies in which way to bias the settings.

Not that settings mattered too much for an extraordinary MotoGP race. It wasn't raining, but it wasn't not raining either, with wind blowing moisture around and patches of drizzle settling briefly now and then.

Right: Slip-sliding to second, de Puniet took his best ever MotoGP result.

Below: Toseland's sixth equalled his best, and cheered his loyal fans.
Photos: Gold & Goose

Left: Together at last – on wets, Hayden could match Stoner. But they were a lap behind.

Above, far left: HRC vice president Shuhei Nakamoto, fresh from F1, looks set to enforce the rule. Luckily, Red Bull rookies were exempt.
Photos: Gold & Goose

The track was predominantly dry, and almost everyone chose slicks in spite of the gloomy outlook. Not surprisingly, there were a number of mishaps. Elias was the first to go, on a damp white line, then Lorenzo and then Rossi, both leading at the time. Rossi, his luck holding good again, was able to remount and save 11 points.

Lorenzo had a spirited debate with crew chief Ramon Forcada waiting on the grid: after the sighting lap, the rider had wanted to fit wet tyres. Forcada declined. Only the factory Ducati riders started on wets, and while the gamble might have paid off had it rained properly in the early laps, it was a disastrous decision. Long before the red pair trailed in a lap behind the leaders, observers were questioning the motivation. In Hayden's case, with nothing to lose, the gamble was understandable. But for Stoner? He had a points position to protect. The prudent move would have been to copy the choice of his title rivals, rather than risk all on a throw of the dice.

As surprising was the rider's equanimity after the race. He'd been hoping for a wet race anyway, less stressful in respect of his continuing physical difficulties. And, he said, "there was just a fingernail away from being enough rain. It was wishful thinking, but a calculated risk." Then he was off, he said, to Australia for some rest and recreation, and to consult the doctors who had treated previous injuries about his malaise, and looking forward to it. He wouldn't be

back for almost ten weeks and would miss the next three races.

There were two free weekends before the Czech Republic GP: a rather abbreviated break. Everyone was ready for it. It was fitting in with Formula One, which had spoiled the summer holiday: for the same reason, the MotoGP race was run fully 90 minutes later than usual to avoid a clash with the German car race.

There was much talk about Lorenzo's future; he was keeping Yamaha hanging on, and Honda as well. Not to mention the rest of the paddock: if he were to leave Yamaha, it would throw a big rock into the pool, and many other top riders were still not signed for 2010, including Pedrosa and Dovizioso at Honda, both Suzuki riders and all the satellite riders.

Elsewhere, things were falling into place for the new season. Jorge 'Aspar' Martinez's long-frustrated plans to join MotoGP were at last confirmed: he would field one rider on a Ducati, basically taking over where the defunct Gibernau team had left off. An interesting new position was open, and Aspar wanted Bautista to fill it. But the smiling Alvaro was already in deep with Suzuki, and in the end, it would go to another Spaniard, Hector Barbera.

A blast from the past came from the far end of the 250 pits, where Ralf Waldmann took the place of the Russian Leonov, injured in his Sachsenring prang. Aged 43, twice 250 runner-up Waldie had last raced

in 2003 and was revisiting the scene of his finest win. In 2000, the rain had hit mid-race. Waldmann was 90 seconds behind, but had wet tyres. He caught up to overtake thunderstruck leader Oliver Jacque on the exit from the last corner. In 2009, after qualifying a respectable 20th, he gambled the other way, on slicks with the others on wets. It didn't work, and he slipped off early on, remounting to retire.

More changes: winter testing would be cut still further and rationalised, while the Jerez showpiece would be axed in favour of staying in Malaysia. And an angry rumble from the Superbike paddock, where Infront chief Paolo Flammini threatened legal action in response to the previous week's proposal to run production-based engines in MotoGP. The threat passed unremarked.

So it was goodbye to a track of many and varied memories. "We have lost a great track for motorcycling," said Rossi. "But at least we still have the Playstation to remember it," chipped in Lorenzo.

MotoGP RACE – 30 laps

Most of Friday's first session was lost to rain, but the chance to test wet tyres was welcomed by most, except Stoner, who spent much time preserving his strength in the pits, but was still second. When it mattered, he dropped to fourth, with Rossi ousting Pedrosa from pole and Lorenzo third.

The Ducatis were in trouble from the off: Stoner had dropped to 13th by the end of lap one and continued to lose ground.

Elias took control up front, with a little gap to Lorenzo, Rossi, Dovizioso and fast-away Toseland. By lap three, both Yamahas were ahead of the Spaniard. At the same time, Dovizioso swooped past all three to take the lead. Pedrosa was also moving forward, up to third, ahead of Rossi, a lap later. Rain was spotting, but lap times were unaffected.

Lorenzo took the lead into Redgate as they began lap five, with Pedrosa and Dovizioso bickering behind him, only for Rossi to pass both of them as they swapped again on lap seven. Elias was fifth, but had just got back past Pedrosa at the Old Hairpin on lap eight, when he demonstrated the treachery of the track. Off-line through the next left, he drifted out to the paint and was flicked off almost instantly.

The leading quartet stayed close. Then suddenly the leader was down. He too had touched the paint, under braking for the final hairpin, and fell in a millisecond. He ran to his bike, but the fairing was torn loose and his race over.

The rain was increasing, and Pedrosa saved a near crash at Craner Curves: it was proving impossible for him to keep heat in his tyres. Now he fell into the hands of de Puniet, circulating steadfastly. After a lengthy dispute, the Frenchman would gain firm control.

Rossi and Dovizioso were now line astern and in the lead, Rossi apparently happy to stay in the pioneering role on a surface that was changing lap by lap. He would regret it. On lap 20, going into the Foggy chicane, the rear wheel slipped away, and he was down. In his case, his bike was still rideable, although facing in the wrong direction, and he got back in tenth, losing one more place to Canepa as he regathered himself.

At this point, the fastest on the track was Edwards. He'd finished the first lap 15th and took another six to get the feel of the soft tyres; by half-distance, he was tenth and closing rapidly on the group ahead. He dispatched Melandri and Kallio, and then Capirossi in one lap, and Toseland next time around. Now he was closing on a lone de Angelis. He passed him on lap 21, shortly before both passed the radically slowing Pedrosa.

It even looked as though Edwards might win, because he closed up on de Puniet, promoted to second by the crashes. The Frenchman got the message and also speeded up, closing a gap of ten seconds to leader Dovizioso to less than two. With three laps left, however, he had his hands full with Edwards. The American's first attack lasted half a lap before de Puniet took him back at the first hairpin. Then he waited until the braking zone for the last corner to seize second again by less than a quarter of a second. "That is probably the most mentally draining race ever. Every corner, I would touch the brakes, then think, 'Phew, I got away with it.' I wouldn't wish a race like that on my worst enemy, let alone take part in it," Edwards said, after equalling his best result.

It was de Puniet's first podium of the year, and well earned; likewise, de Angelis, in a far from flamboyant, but effective, fourth.

Four riders had switched to wet bikes: Melandri, then Kallio and both Suzuki men. Rossi stayed on his battered, slick-shod Yamaha and soon was on the charge. He swapped sixth with Pedrosa on lap 25, then set his sights on Toseland, four seconds clear and enjoying the prospect of a best-ever fifth. Until he ran wide and almost crashed on the penultimate lap, losing three seconds and allowing Rossi to get on his tail.

The Italian attacked into the chicane; Toseland passed him straight back on the exit. But Rossi was not to be denied and forced firmly ahead in the final hairpins.

Melandri had been the fastest on wet tyres, rejoining in tenth behind Rossi, then moving through to seventh, ahead of an on-form Canepa. Pedrosa cruised in three seconds behind, still ahead of Kallio. Capirossi's new tyres were no help, and he was 11th; Vermeulen was 13th, behind even Talmacsi, still on slicks. Stoner and Hayden were one lap down.

Eleven points were a handy fillip for Rossi after a bad afternoon, and now he had a one-race margin of 25 points over Lorenzo.

250cc RACE — 27 laps

As often at this track, the 250s were almost as fast as the big bikes, gaining time everywhere except on the tight hairpin section. Barbera was on pole for a third time in four races, ousting Simoncelli, with Aoyama and Debon completing the front row. Bautista crashed twice in qualifying, ending up sixth, next to team-mate di Meglio.

The race was very trying. The track was wet, but the skies clearing. All but Waldmann chose wet tyres, and although some mid-fielders stopped to switch to slicks and then were much faster than the leaders, able to unlap themselves, it was too late to make a difference.

The first lap was busy as one, then another dared to test the grip. Barbera led into Redgate, but by the time they reached the Old Hairpin, Simoncelli was in front and Aoyama pushing through. The Japanese rider attacked at the end of the back straight, passing into the hairpin – and he never saw another rival, although he was overtaken by a couple of riders unlapping themselves after switching tyres near the end.

At first, Debon led the pursuit, chased by Simoncelli and Barbera. But Pasini and Bautista were pushing hard in the tricky going and were ahead of both Spaniards, and of Debon also two laps later.

Bautista looked the strongest, taking second on lap seven, now almost six seconds behind Aoyama, who was both nursing his tyres and trying to escape, a difficult balancing act. The Spaniard was able to leave his companions behind and even close slightly on Aoyama. With ten laps left, he tried again, and he got to within just over two seconds with three laps left. Then he recalled crashing twice the day before and the pain in his arm, and decided to settle for second.

He could afford to slack off again because Pasini and Debon had left the party. Disputing third to and fro, on lap 17 Pasini crashed under braking for the second-last hairpin. Then Debon did exactly the same, at the next corner. Both remounted, Pasini sooner, and he didn't even lose a place. A second or so behind, Simoncelli had got past the accelerating Debon and pulled clear, while the latter found himself under attack by di Meglio. The Frenchman got ahead on the last lap, claiming fifth by half a second.

The rest were mostly widely spaced out, with de Rosa a strong seventh, Barbera three seconds behind, then another gap to Luthi and Faubel, completing the top ten. Cluzel stayed clear of Pesek in a battle for 11th; the remaining points went to Locatelli, Abraham and Tomizawa.

There were only three non-finishers, in spite of the conditions: both Wilairot and Nemeth retired with mechanical problems; Abraham crashed twice, but still finished in the points.

125cc RACE – 5 laps (restarted)

Smith broke out the gingerbread men in his pit to celebrate regaining home pole by a tenth from Marquez. The other Aspar riders completed the front row, Simon ahead of Gadea.

The 125s got the worst of everything, running almost half of the scheduled 25 laps in the dry before rain hit suddenly on lap 14 and people started flying off in all directions. The red flag came out promptly and the race was 'neutralised', counting only for grid positions for a deciding five-lap sprint.

At that point, Espargaro had taken a strong lead from Terol, then Marquez, with Smith and Simon fourth and fifth. For Smith, it turned out to be wasted effort. He led away from the restart, only to crash at Coppice Corner before even completing the first lap. Zero points.

It was also hard on Espargaro, whose set-up for the wet restart was far from satisfactory. He dropped to tenth.

But it could hardly have been better for Simon.

Marquez led the first three laps and was pulling away when he fell entering the chicane. Terol and Corsi had been in pursuit, but the former was losing touch. Corsi's win would be denied by Simon, who pounced early on the last lap and hung on to the finish for his third victory of the year, gaining a comfortable two-race points cushion.

Redding had been sixth in the first leg and was a safe third in the rerun, with Terol and Nakagami next. Behind them, Salom narrowly defeated Zanetti; three seconds back, Aegerter headed the next group, with Vazquez and Espargaro completing the top ten.

Smith remounted for 20th. Webb and Olive were already out after a seven-bike pile-up on the first lap of the first attempt. Cortese, Rabat, Bradl, Iannone, Gadea and Folger were also among the 11 riders who missed the depleted restart.

Above: Bradley Smith's special-brew helmet.

Top: Redding, winner at Donington in 2008, took his only podium.

Above left: Winner in 2000, Ralf Waldmann made a surprise 250 return, at 43.

Left: Aoyama was faultless as he consolidated his title lead.
Photos: Gold & Goose

Opposite page: Andrea Dovizioso looks back to check out his lead.
Photo: Clive Challinor Motorsport Photography

DONINGTON PARK

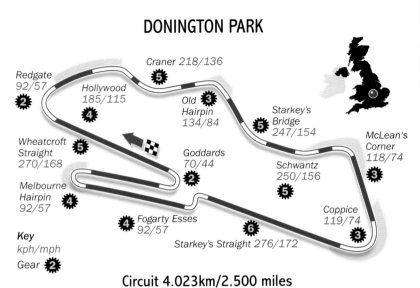

Craner 218/136 **5**

Redgate 92/57 **2**

Hollywood 185/115 **4**

Old Hairpin 134/84 **3**

Starkey's Bridge 247/154 **5**

McLean's Corner 118/74 **3**

Wheatcroft Straight 270/168 **5**

Goddards 70/44 **2**

Schwantz 250/156 **5**

Melbourne Hairpin 92/57 **4**

Coppice 119/74 **3**

Fogarty Esses 92/57 **4**

Starkey's Straight 276/172 **6**

Key
kph/mph
Gear **2**

Circuit 4.023km/2.500 miles

MOTOGP

RACE DISTANCE: 30 laps, 74.993 miles/120.690 km • **RACE WEATHER:** Wet (air 18°, humidity 64%, track 21°)

Pos.	Rider	Nat.	No.	Entrant	Machine	Tyres	Laps	Time & speed
1	Andrea Dovizioso	ITA	4	Repsol Honda Team	Honda	B	30	48m 26.267s 92.893mph/ 149.498km/h
2	Colin Edwards	USA	5	Monster Yamaha Tech 3	Yamaha	B	30	48m 27.627s
3	Randy de Puniet	USA	14	LCR Honda MotoGP	Honda	B	30	48m 27.827s
4	Alex de Angelis	RSM	15	San Carlos Honda Gresini	Honda	B	30	48m 35.225s
5	Valentino Rossi	ITA	46	Fiat Yamaha Team	Yamaha	B	30	48m 47.889s
6	James Toseland	JPN	52	Monster Yamaha Tech 3	Yamaha	B	30	48m 48.732s
7	Marco Melandri	ITA	33	Hayate Racing Team	Kawasaki	B	30	49m 01.551s
8	Niccolo Canepa	USA	88	Pramac Racing	Ducati	B	30	49m 05.036s
9	Dani Pedrosa	SPA	3	Repsol Honda Team	Honda	B	30	49m 08.379s
10	Mika Kallio	FIN	36	Pramac Racing	Ducati	B	30	49m 12.112s
11	Loris Capirossi	ITA	65	Rizla Suzuki MotoGP	Suzuki	B	30	49m 19.457s
12	Gabor Talmacsi	HUN	41	Scot Racing Team MotoGP	Honda	B	30	49m 38.582s
13	Chris Vermeulen	AUS	7	Rizla Suzuki MotoGP	Suzuki	B	30	49m 46.665s
14	Casey Stoner	AUS	27	Ducati Marlboro Team	Ducati	B	29	49m 25.241s
15	Nicky Hayden	USA	69	Ducati Marlboro Team	Ducati	B	29	49m 43.835s
	Jorge Lorenzo	SPA	99	Fiat Yamaha Team	Yamaha	B	8	DNF
	Toni Elias	SPA	24	San Carlos Honda Gresini	Honda	B	7	DNF

Fastest lap: Jorge Lorenzo, on lap 5, 1m 31.554s, 98.293mph/158.188km/h).

Lap record: Dani Pedrosa, SPA (Honda), 1m 28.714s, 101.440mph/163.252km/h (2006).

Event best maximum speed: Dani Pedrosa, 171.436mph/275.9km/h (qualifying practice).

Qualifying: Dry
Air: 21° Humidity: 35% Track: 31°

1	Rossi	1m 28.116s
2	Pedrosa	1m 28.211s
3	Lorenzo	1m 28.402s
4	Stoner	1m 28.446s
5	Dovizioso	1m 28.778s
6	Edwards	1m 28.865s
7	Melandri	1m 29.065s
8	Elias	1m 29.175s
9	Toseland	1m 29.270s
10	de Puniet	1m 29.434s
11	Kallio	1m 29.599s
12	de Angelis	1m 29.600s
13	Vermeulen	1m 30.098s
14	Capirossi	1m 30.153s
15	Hayden	1m 30.268s
16	Canepa	1m 30.572s
17	Talmacsi	1m 31.193s

Fastest race laps

1	Lorenzo	1m 31.554s
2	Rossi	1m 31.741s
3	Pedrosa	1m 31.742s
4	Elias	1m 31.797s
5	Dovizioso	1m 32.150s
6	de Angelis	1m 32.428s
7	Edwards	1m 32.503s
8	de Puniet	1m 32.553s
9	Toseland	1m 32.567s
10	Kallio	1m 32.642s
11	Capirossi	1m 32.769s
12	Melandri	1m 32.981s
13	Canepa	1m 33.505s
14	Vermeulen	1m 33.903s
15	Talmacsi	1m 35.858s
16	Stoner	1m 38.609s
17	Hayden	1m 39.547s

Championship Points

1	Rossi	187
2	Lorenzo	162
3	Stoner	150
4	Pedrosa	115
5	Edwards	103
6	Dovizioso	94
7	Melandri	79
8	de Puniet	74
9	Vermeulen	67
10	Capirossi	66
11	de Angelis	60
12	Toseland	55
13	Hayden	47
14	Elias	47
15	Kallio	34
16	Canepa	28
17	Gibernau	12
18	Takahashi	9
19	Talmacsi	1

Constructor Points

1	Yamaha	230
2	Ducati	164
3	Honda	156
4	Suzuki	89
5	Kawasaki	79

Team Points

1	FIAT Yamaha Team	349
2	Ducati Marlboro Team	209
3	Repsol Honda Team	197
4	Monster Yamaha Tech 3	158
5	RIZLA Suzuki MotoGP	133
6	San Carlo Honda Gresini	107
7	Hayate Racing Team	79
8	LCR Honda MotoGP	74
9	Pramac Racing	62
10	Scot Racing Team	14
11	Grupo Francisco Hernando	12

Grid order	1	2	3	4	5	6	7	8	9	10	11	12	13	14	15	16	17	18	19	20	21	22	23	24	25	26	27	28	29	30	
46 ROSSI	24	24	4	4	99	99	99	99	46	46	46	46	46	46	46	46	46	46	46	4	4	4	4	4	4	4	4	4	4	4	1
3 PEDROSA	99	99	99	99	4	3	46	46	4	4	4	4	4	4	4	4	4	4	4	14	14	14	14	14	14	14	14	14	5	2
99 LORENZO	46	46	3	3	3	4	4	4	3	3	14	3	14	14	3	3	3	14	14	3	3	3	5	5	5	5	5	5	14	3
27 STONER	4	4	24	46	46	46	3	3	14	14	3	14	3	3	14	14	14	3	3	15	5	5	15	15	15	15	15	15	15	4
4 DOVIZIOSO	52	3	46	24	24	24	24	14	15	15	15	15	15	15	15	15	15	15	15	5	15	15	3	52	52	52	52	52	46	5
5 EDWARDS	3	52	52	52	52	14	14	15	65	65	52	52	52	52	52	52	5	5	5	36	36	52	52	3	46	46	46	46	52	6
33 MELANDRI	33	33	33	33	14	52	15	65	52	52	65	65	65	65	65	5	52	36	36	33	33	33	36	46	3	3	3	88	33	33	7
24 ELIAS	14	14	14	14	33	15	52	52	33	36	36	33	33	33	33	65	65	33	33	65	52	88	88	88	88	88	88	3	88	88	8
52 TOSELAND	36	15	15	15	15	33	65	33	36	33	33	36	36	36	36	36	36	52	65	52	88	65	46	33	33	33	33	33	3	3	9
14 de PUNIET	15	36	65	65	65	36	36	36	5	5	5	5	5	5	5	33	33	65	52	88	65	36	33	65	65	36	36	36	36	10
36 KALLIO	65	65	36	36	36	65	33	5	88	88	88	88	88	88	88	88	88	88	46	46	46	65	36	36	65	65	65	65	65	11
15 de ANGELIS	88	88	88	88	88	88	88	88	7	7	7	7	7	7	7	7	7	7	7	41	41	41	41	41	41	41	41	41	41	12
7 VERMEULEN	27	27	5	5	5	5	5	7	41	41	41	41	41	41	41	41	41	41	41	41	41	7	7	7	7	7	7	7	7	13
65 CAPIROSSI	7	5	7	7	7	7	7	41	27	27	69	69	69	69	69	69	69	69	69	69	69	69	69	69	27	27	27	27	27	14
69 HAYDEN	5	7	27	41	41	41	41	27	69	69	27	27	27	27	27	27	27	27	27	27	27	27	27	27	69	69	69	69	69	15
88 CANEPA	69	41	41	27	27	27	27	69																						
41 TALMACSI	41	69	69	69	69	69	69	69																						

7 Pitted   *27 Lapped rider*

250cc — RACE DISTANCE: 27 laps, 67.493 miles/108.621 km • RACE WEATHER: Wet (air 18°, humidity 65%, track 19°)

Pos.	Rider	Nat.	No.	Entrant	Machine	Laps	Time & Speed
1	Hiroshi Aoyama	JPN	4	Scot Racing Team 250cc	Honda	27	45m 17.516s
							(mph/km/h)
							89.411/143.894
2	Alvaro Bautista	SPA	19	Mapfre Aspar Team	Aprilia	27	45m 23.239s
3	Mattia Pasini	ITA	75	Team Toth Aprilia	Aprilia	27	45m 53.677s
4	Marco Simoncelli	ITA	58	Metis Gilera	Gilera	27	45m 54.292s
5	Mike di Meglio	FRA	63	Mapfre Aspar Team 250cc	Aprilia	27	45m 58.934s
6	Alex Debon	ESP	6	Aeropuerto – Castello – Blusens	Aprilia	27	45m 59.454s
7	Raffaele de Rosa	ITA	35	Scot Racing Team 250cc	Honda	27	46m 14.999s
8	Hector Barbera	SPA	40	Pepe World Team	Aprilia	27	46m 17.491s
9	Thomas Luthi	SWI	12	Emmi – Caffe Latte	Aprilia	27	46m 32.368s
10	Hector Faubel	SPA	55	Honda SAG	Honda	27	26m 34.443s
11	Jules Cluzel	FRA	16	Matteoni Racing	Aprilia	27	46m 38.872s
12	Lukas Pesek	CZE	52	Auto Kelly – CP	Aprilia	27	46m 39.181s
13	Roberto Locatelli	ITA	15	Metis Gilera	Gilera	27	46m 47.092s
14	Karel Abraham	CZE	17	Cardion AB Motoracing	Aprilia	26	45m 21.414s
15	Shoya Tomizawa	JPN	48	CIP Moto – GP250	Honda	26	45m 40.123s
16	Alex Baldolini	ITA	25	WTR San Marino Team	Aprilia	26	45m 57.639s
17	Imre Toth	HUN	10	Team Toth Aprilia	Aprilia	26	46m 27.990s
18	Luke Mossey	GBR	64	Sabresport Grand Prix	Aprilia	26	46m 40.616s
19	Valentin Debise	FRA	53	CIP Moto – GP250	Honda	25	45m 18.031s
20	Axel Pons	SPA	7	Pepe World Team	Aprilia	25	45m 39.354s
21	Aitor Rodriguez	SPA	77	Matteoni Racing	Aprilia	25	45m 39.920s
22	Bastien Chesaux	SWI	8	Racing Team Germany	Honda	25	45m 31.526s
23	Toby Markham	GB	54	C&L Racing	Honda	23	45m 30.773s
	Ratthapark Wilairot	THA	14	Thai Honda PTT SAG	Honda	18	DNF
	Ralf Waldmann	GER	95	Viessmann Kiefer Racing	Aprilia	5	DNF
	Balazs Nemeth	HUN	11	Balatonring Team	Aprilia	0	DNF

Fastest lap: Alex Baldolini, on lap 22, 1m 34.963s, 94.764mph/152.509km/h.
Lap record: Marco Simoncelli, I (Gilera), 1m 32.474s, 97.315mph/156.614km/h (2008).
Event best maximum speed: Cluzel, 149.999mph/241.4km/h (qualifying practice).

Qualifying: Dry
Air: 22° Humidity: 34% Track: 35°

1	Barbera	1m 31.802s
2	Simoncelli	1m 31.894s
3	Aoyama, Hiroshi	1m 32.055s
4	Debon	1m 32.268s
5	di Meglio	1m 32.643s
6	Bautista	1m 32.664s
7	Pasini	1m 32.883s
8	Wilairot	1m 33.046s
9	Abraham	1m 33.145s
10	Pesek	1m 33.203s
11	de Rosa	1m 33.218s
12	Luthi	1m 33.360s
13	Locatelli	1m 33.405s
14	Faubel	1m 33.503s
15	Cluzel	1m 33.622s
16	Baldolini	1m 33.768s
17	Tomizawa	1m 33.901s
18	Toth	1m 34.661s
19	Pons	1m 35.351s
20	Waldmann	1m 35.408s
21	Debise	1m 35.600s
22	Nemeth	1m 36.202s
23	Chesaux	1m 36.309s
24	Mossey	1m 37.227s
	Within 107% in free practice 1	
	Markham	1m 38.989s
	Outside 107%	
dnq	Rodriguez	1m 38.638s
dnq	Kenshington	1m 38.657s
dnq	Halen	1m 41.680s

Fastest race laps

1	Baldolini	1m 34.693s
2	Abraham	1m 35.033s
3	Debise	1m 36.816s
4	Chessaux	1m 37.548s
5	Pons	1m 37.716s
6	Aoyama, Hiroshi	1m 38.579s
7	Bautista	1m 38.821s
8	Markham	1m 39.043s
9	Simoncelli	1m 39.401s
10	Pasini	1m 39.436s
11	Debon	1m 39.640s
12	di Meglio	1m 39.784s
13	Luthi	1m 40.540s
14	de Rosa	1m 40.787s
15	Barbera	1m 40.970s
16	Pesek	1m 41.326s
17	Cluzel	1m 41.444s
18	Faubel	1m 41.598s
19	Locatelli	1m 41.725s
20	Tomizawa	1m 41.866s
21	Toth	1m 41.870s
22	Wilairot	1m 43.740s
23	Rodriguez	1m 44.856s
24	Mossey	1m 45.018s
25	Waldmann	1m 46.297s

Championship Points

1	Aoyama, Hiroshi	159
2	Bautista	144
3	Simoncelli	115
4	Barbera	114
5	Pasini	80
6	Debon	73
7	Luthi	67
8	de Rosa	67
9	Faubel	65
10	Locatelli	56
11	di Meglio	43
12	Cluzel	40
13	Pesek	40
14	Wilairot	38
15	Abraham	33
16	Talmacsi	28
17	Espargaro, Aleix	22
18	Tomizawa	17
19	Baldolini	17
20	Toth	12
21	Aoyama, Shuhei	10
22	Leonov	7
23	Debise	5
24	Markham	2
25	Watanabe	2
26	Chesaux	1
27	Bonsey	1

Constructors

1	Aprilia	193
2	Honda	171
2	Gilera	122
3	Yamaha	2

125cc — RACE DISTANCE: 5 laps, 12.498 miles/20.115 km (First race stopped by rain) • RACE WEATHER: Wet (air 17°, humidity 65%, track 20°)

Pos.	Rider	Nat.	No.	Entrant	Machine	Laps	Time & Speed
1	Julian Simon	SPA	60	Bancaja Aspar Team 125cc	Aprilia	5	9m 12.301s
							(mph/km/h)
							81.469/131.113
2	Simon Corsi	ITA	24	Fontana Racing	Aprilia	5	9m 12.691s
3	Scott Redding	GB	45	Blusens Aprilia	Aprilia	5	9m 15.373s
4	Nicolas Terol	SPA	18	Jack & Jones Team	Aprilia	5	9m 18.510s
5	Takaaki Nakagami	JPN	73	Ongetta Team I.S.P.A.	Aprilia	5	9m 21.810s
6	Luis Salom	SPA	39	Jack & Jones Team	Honda	5	9m 23.512s
7	Lorenzo Zanetti	ITA	8	Ongetta Team I.S.P.A.	Aprilia	5	9m 23.873s
8	Dominique Aegerter	SWI	77	Ajo Interwetten	Derbi	5	9m 26.004s
9	Efren Vazquez	SPA	7	Derbi Racing Team	Derbi	5	9m 26.402s
10	Pol Espargaro	SPA	44	Derbi Racing Team	Derbi	5	9m 27.723s
11	Tomoyoshi Koyama	JPN	71	Loncin Racing	Loncin	5	9m 30.206s
12	Joan Olive	SPA	6	Derbi Racing Team	Derbi	5	9m 37.926s
13	Johann Zarco	FRA	14	WTR San Marino Team	Aprilia	5	9m 39.094s
14	Martin Glossop	GBR	91	KRP/Bradley Smith Racing	Honda	5	9m 40.217s
15	Marc Marquez	SPA	93	Red Bull KTM Moto Sport	KTM	5	9m 40.392s
16	Paul Jordan	IRL	92	KRP/Bradley Smith Racing	Honda	5	9m 41.300s
17	Lukas Sembera	CZE	69	Matteoni Racing	Aprilia	5	9m 42.865s
18	Randy Krummenacher	SWI	35	Degraaf Grand Prix	Aprilia	5	9m 46.769s
19	Luca Marconi	FRA	87	CBC Corse	Aprilia	5	9m 51.010s
20	Bradley Smith	GB	38	Bancaja Aspar Team 125cc	Aprilia	5	9m 51.239s
21	Luca Vitali	ITA	10	CBC Corse	Aprilia	5	10m 26.341s
	Jasper Iwema	NED	53	Racing Team Germany	Honda	4	7m 47.187s
	Lorenzo Savadori	ITA	32	Fontana Racing	Aprilia	1	DNF
	Alexis Masbou	FRA	5	Loncin Racing	Loncin	1	DNF
	Michael Ranseder	AUT	88	CBC Corse	Aprilia	1	DNF
DID NOT TAKE PART IN RESTARTED RACE							
	Sandro Cortese	GER	11	Ajo Interwetten	Derbi		
	Esteve Rabat	SPA	12	Blusens Aprilia	Aprilia		
	Cameron Beaubier	USA	16	Red Bull KTM Moto Sport	KTM		
	Stefan Bradl	GER	17	Viessmann Kiefer Racing	Aprilia		
	Andrea Iannone	ITA	29	Ongetta Team I.S.P.A.	Aprilia		
	Sergio Gadea	SPA	33	Bancaja Aspar Team 125cc	Aprilia		
	Karel Pesek	CZE	86	Pesek Team	Derbi		
	James Lodge	GBR	89	KRP/Bradley Smith Racing	Honda		
	Timothy Hastings	GBR	90	KRP/Bradley Smith Racing	Honda		
	Jonas Folger	GER	94	Ongetta Team I.S.P.A.	Aprilia		
	Danny Webb	GB	99	Degraaf Grand Prix	Aprilia		

Fastest lap: Julian Simon, on lap 5, 1m 48.632s, 82.840mph/133.319km/h.
Lap record: Alvaro Bautista, SPA (Aprilia), 1m 37.312s, 92.477mph/148.828km/h (2006).
Event best maximum speed: Sergio Gadea, SPA (Aprilia), 131.482mph/211.6km/h (race, part 1).

Qualifying: Dry
Air: 20° Humidity: 39% Track: 31°

1	Smith	1m 37.442s
2	Marquez	1m 37.573s
3	Simon	1m 37.749s
4	Gadea	1m 37.849s
5	Olive	1m 37.874s
6	Terol	1m 37.989s
7	Espargaro, Pol	1m 38.117s
8	Cortese	1m 38.367s
9	Rabat	1m 38.471s
10	Iannone	1m 38.484s
11	Redding	1m 38.501s
12	Corsi	1m 38.501s
13	Bradl	1m 38.555s
14	Webb	1m 38.570s
15	Folger	1m 38.848s
16	Vazquez	1m 38.879s
17	Ranseder	1m 39.081s
18	Aegerter	1m 39.189s
19	Koyama	1m 39.366s
20	Nakagami	1m 39.393s
21	Krummenacher	1m 39.401s
22	Zanetti	1m 39.407s
23	Zarco	1m 39.533s
24	Salom	1m 40.342s
25	Iwema	1m 40.382s
26	Savadori	1m 40.456s
27	Beaubier	1m 40.509s
28	Masbou	1m 41.086s
29	Pesk	1m 41.129s
30	Lodge	1m 41.571s
31	Glossop	1m 41.778s
32	Sembera	1m 42.080s
33	Marconi	1m 42.426s
34	Hastings	1m 42.473s
35	Jordan	1m 43.393s
	Outside 107%	
	Vitali	1m 45.081s

Fastest race laps

1	Simon	1m 48.632s
2	Redding	1m 48.793s
3	Corsi	1m 49.027s
4	Marquez	1m 49.318s
5	Nakagami	1m 49.702s
6	Zanetti	1m 50.075s
7	Terol	1m 50.174s
8	Salom	1m 50.266s
9	Smith	1m 50.836s
10	Espargaro, Pol	1m 50.955s
11	Vazquez	1m 51.002s
12	Aegerter	1m 51.042s
13	Koyama	1m 51.872s
14	Olive	1m 52.148s
15	Glossop	1m 53.629s
16	Sembera	1m 53.841s
17	Zarco	1m 53.912s
18	Jordan	1m 53.964s
19	Iwema	1m 53.984s
20	Krummenacher	1m 55.368s
21	Marconi	1m 56.018s
22	Savadori	1m 59.584s
23	Vitali	2m 02.839s
24	Masbou	2m 03.751s
25	Ranseder	2m 04.926s

Championship Points

1	Simon	154
2	Gadea	104
3	Smith	98.5
4	Terol	94.5
5	Iannone	93.5
6	Espargaro, Pol	68.5
7	Marquez	56
8	Cortese	55
9	Folger	54
10	Redding	44.5
11	Aegerter	44.5
12	Bradl	44
13	Olive	41
14	Corsi	32
15	Vazquez	30
16	Webb	24.5
17	Nakagami	24
18	Zanetti	13
19	Zarco	19.5
20	Rabat	19
21	Koyama	15
22	Krummenacher	15
23	Salom	13
24	Savadori	7
25	Schrotter	4
26	Iwema	3
27	Beaubier	3
28	Glossop	2
29	Fritz	2
30	di Carlo	2
31	Kartheininger	1

Constructors

1	Aprilia	212.5
2	Derbi	96
3	KTM	58
4	Loncin	15
5	Honda	11

CZECH REPUBLIC GRAND PRIX

BRNO CIRCUIT

After Lorenzo had gone, Rossi was a clear winner, and the title battle seemed over.
Photo: Gold & Goose

THE latest era began at Brno – the first race for the new long-life engines. With a restriction of five sealed engines for the remaining seven rounds, it introduced an element of endurance racing into what had always been an extended sprint. It didn't affect the racing much, but it did and will continue to affect the spectacle in at least one way: no more post-race burnouts for the winner. Must save those motors!

And it affected the riders. Rossi had one word for the feeling of his new power-down, revs-down engine: "Tired." Others were more diplomatic. There had been no change at Honda, said Pedrosa: the engine changes introduced for the German GP already included provision for longer life. And if the responses of the engine had been somewhat tamed, that was all to the good. Hayden said he could "feel no difference" in his Ducati.

Over at Suzuki, they were hoping to have squared the circle: improving endurance at the same time as preserving the rev ceiling and increasing the horsepower, as technical chief Shinichi Sahara told *MOTOCOURSE*. Ironically, Suzuki was the first to fall foul of the rule when Capirossi needed a new engine in Australia, after four races. Never mind that the failure was relatively minor, and could have been fixed by taking off the cam covers and making some adjustments. The cam covers were sealed.

Another peripheral example of engine saving was

to be seen after a crash, the danger being that a running engine would ingest dust or gravel, or pick up air in the oiling system. For practice from now on, cut-off switches would be set to kill the engine the instant a bike went down – but for races, riders would have some 10–20 seconds of grace to give them a chance to pick up the bike and resume.

But engines were not the talking point of the weekend. Not with the news that had broken in the preceding week: Casey Stoner had gone AWOL. Well, not exactly that, but his mystery ailment had got no better, and he had pulled out of this and the next two races. He wouldn't be back until the Portuguese GP at Estoril in October.

Ducati was publicly (and, as it transpired, privately) supportive of his decision to take a mid-season break, to address the troubles that had spoiled his last races. The rest of the paddock was less sympathetic, some identifying his problem as "Rossi-itis". One particular critic was Kevin Schwantz. "I don't know what the medical situation is, but it seems to me in the middle of the championship, you should try and ride around it." Schwantz was famous for doing just that, repeatedly ignoring injuries and fractures that would have kept a normal person in bed.

In the head rider's absence, Kallio was moved up to the factory Marlboro team – "The bike feels not much different," he said – and Brno Superbike winner Michel Fabrizio took the Finn's place at Pramac

Ducati. He would not cover himself with glory, crashing heavily in practice and retiring from the race.

Rider movements for 2010 had been falling into place, but Stoner's unexpected departure threw a big rock in the pool. Would he ever come back? Would he ever be strong again? The memory of the brilliant Freddie Spencer's sudden fall from supremacy was recalled. And in the week after the race, the concerned sponsor showed the depth of disquiet felt within Marlboro and Ducati with a generous bid, estimated at £13m for two years, more than double Yamaha's offer, for Lorenzo to put on the red suit and join the factory team. With Stoner already signed up for 2010, this impinged on Hayden, still waiting to see if he would be kept on. And it spread uncertainty everywhere, with the new prospect of a vacant seat in the factory Yamaha team.

Nothing became clearer when the new president of HRC, Tetsuo Suzuki, called a special meeting to announce that both the Repsol team riders, Pedrosa and Dovizioso, had been signed up for two more years each. This was promptly contradicted by both riders. "We are talking, but nothing is signed," said Pedrosa. It would be many more weeks before both would indeed sign up to stay, but only for one year each.

There was more certainty at the San Carlo team, following the affirmation that new signing Simoncelli would be joined by Melandri. This confirmed a longstanding rumour, and formally put an end to any

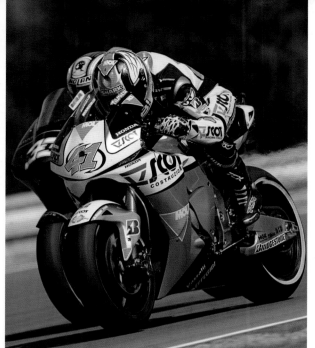

Left: Melandri looks for a way past Talmacsi on lap one, after a slow start.

Far left: Elias and Dovizioso dispute second, with Capirossi hanging on behind.

Below: Kallio took Stoner's vacant slot in the factory Ducati team.

Photos: Gold & Goose

hopes for incumbents de Angelis and Elias. Elias promptly claimed his first rostrum of the year.

It was confirmed that Bautista has definitely shunned Aspar's offer of a Ducati ride in favour of two years with Suzuki. Aspar, rather piqued, gave the spot to Barbera. With Capirossi close to agreement to stay at Suzuki, this in turn put the skids under Vermeulen. The Australian became one of many candidates for the Tech 3 seat, for it was already assumed by all that Toseland's two-year tenure would come to an end. Indeed, the Briton would be heading back to Super-bikes (along with Vermeulen), his second year having been spoiled by a pair of massive crashes pre-season that had left him gun-shy and short of testing.

Brno is a superb circuit for rider and spectators, more than 138,000 of whom were treated to another needle match between Rossi and Lorenzo, so closely matched on speed that the issue would have to be resolved by something else. But this one didn't go to the wire: Lorenzo made a Biaggi-like error when he tried too hard to regain the lead down the hill, leaving a triumphant Rossi alone for the last six laps.

The crash triggered a different kind of pantomime for the fallen Spaniard. He was one of a handful of riders testing airbags for Dainese, and the latest ver-sion – a vest worn inside the leathers – duly inflated as he bounced across the gravel. It had deployed rather later than he'd have preferred, he implied, but what followed was worse. The vest failed to deflate,

as it should have done after a few seconds. Jorge was puffed up like a roly-poly toy, rendering any hopes of a remount at least temporarily void. Even with his leathers unzipped, he made an unintentionally comic figure as he walked away towards the barrier.

This was the second of three races followed by a test, and with such sessions now so rare there was much to be done, even if not a great deal of new equipment. The most significant news was that Honda was to test Öhlins suspension, after decades of using in-house Showa equipment. If the factory team were to switch (and it duly did, although by only one bike at a time), this would put the whole grid on the gold suspension, which had been developed by a Swed-ish company that, for some time, had been owned by Yamaha, but now was independent once again, in the hands of its founder, Kent Öhlin. Asked some time later by *MOTOCOURSE* how it felt to have taken over the top class of racing, he spoke of his unwilling part in yet another monopoly, in a class that should thrive on competition: "To be proud is one thing. To be pleased is another."

MotoGP RACE – 22 laps

Practice saw Lorenzo and Rossi mere hundredths apart on race tyres, but Rossi took the advantage on soft rubber to claim pole – only to crash while trying to improve still further. Neither he nor his bike was dam-

aged. Pedrosa completed the front row, three-tenths down; Elias pushed through to lead the second row, after placing in the top six throughout.

Rossi was still experimenting with settings as the race began, and it would take him a couple of laps to be sure that he had a bike "I could ride as I want". He started well, but as usual Pedrosa out-accelerated him on the run to the first corner. At the third, Rossi smoothly outbraked him, and from there on he was in command.

Lorenzo was third and they stayed close. When Pedrosa started to lose a little ground on the fourth lap, Jorge lined him up at the bottom of the hill and swept past into the next chicane to keep close as the Honda continued to lose touch.

The Yamaha pair traded fastest laps, Lorenzo sev-eral times looking threatening. Later Rossi described how he had resigned himself to another battle to the end. For his part, Lorenzo had decided, having scored no points at Donington, that "today, second would not be good enough".

His move came under brakes into the third corner on lap 17. Now Rossi played the shadow, matching Lorenzo move for move. The resolution came at the same corner next time around. Lorenzo was a little wide on the entry, but he was determined not to leave the door open for Rossi. The effort proved too much for the front tyre, and it slid away gently, but inexora-bly. As one Yamaha skidded out, the other one slipped

safely through to the apex – and on to the chequered flag. Rossi's 102nd win came 13 years almost to the day after his first one at the same circuit in 1996.

Elias had remained best of the rest, chasing the trio, but losing around a second a lap. Dovizioso was close behind, with Capirossi riding rather wildly to stay in touch. His new package was improved, but still lacked acceleration, he said later: he was faster than both the Hondas through the corners, but could never get close enough to take advantage of it.

Dovizioso finally attacked Elias at the same turn three on lap 18; but Elias just kept on coming back as the factory rider wrestled with a sliding front tyre, and he finally got ahead again at the bottom of the hill one lap later. The three were still close over the line.

Behind this, a quartet had been running for the first half of the race: Edwards, Hayden, de Angelis and Kallio, with little in the way of overtaking. Things changed when Hayden found his way past Edwards on lap 14 and upped the pace a little. The Texan followed, but de Angelis was losing touch when an extraordinary incident saw him lose two places on lap 18 – a butterfly had got inside his helmet and was flapping around in front of his eyes.

While de Angelis was so distracted, not only did Kallio squeeze through, but also Melandri, who had picked his way past Toseland and then de Puniet to close up. The Kawasaki was slower than Kallio's factory Ducati on the straights, but was quicker elsewhere, and this tempted Melandri into a desperate move on the last corner. Leaving his braking very late for the wide 90-degree right-hander, he dived to the apex and jammed them on, seizing control of the corner. But Kallio was taking a wider and faster line, and didn't see him until too late. Travelling much faster, he rammed into the back of the Kawasaki, and both went flying. They continued the dispute in the gravel, each blaming the other.

This gave eighth back to de Angelis, while Tose-land had been speeding up at the end, a front-end hopping problem having eased off as the fuel load lightened, and closed to within 1.5 seconds. Along the way, he had passed de Puniet, whose pace was dropping – understandably, since two weeks before, a motocross crash had broken his ankle badly, and he had seven screws in the injury.

Vermeulen was a second adrift, having been boxed in after the start and taken too long to escape. Canepa trailed in, Talmacsi way behind; banged-about Fabrizio had pitted after running a distant last for six laps.

Rossi's win gave him a two-race cushion. It seemed that the title battle was over.

250cc RACE – 20 laps

Aoyama thought he had his first pole of the year, but Simoncelli was still out and riding like the wind, to take his third by three-tenths. Barbera and Debon completed the front row; di Meglio led the second, Bautista on the far end. In between were Locatelli and Pasini.

Luthi and Abraham didn't even make the first corner, the pumped-up home hero running into the back of Luthi on the way in and both falling; Luthi's bike almost broke in two.

Locatelli had led away and for the first couple of laps, pursued by Aoyama, Simoncelli, Debon and Pasini, with Bautista not far behind and heading the next gang.

Soon he was moving forward, Debon doing the opposite – dropping out of the top ten and then pitting to retire after eight laps.

The lead had been back and forth as Locatelli dropped back: Aoyama on lap three, then Barbera, then Simoncelli for two more laps, until Pasini took over the pace from lap seven to ten.

All the while, Bautista had been closing, di Meg-lio with him, although the latter got hung up behind

Left: The brothers Espargaro, Aleix and Pol.

Below: A beaming Terol enjoyed second place.

Photos: Gold & Goose

Left: Pasini hounded Simoncelli all the way to the flag.

Above left: Bautista celebrated third rather too exuberantly, looping on the slow-down lap.

Opposite page: Hayden's fifth showed improving strength. And he was top Ducati for once.

Photos: Gold & Goose

Barbera as Bautista picked his way to a close third at half-distance, ahead of Aoyama, whose bike "felt tired". Di Meglio now took fifth off the fading Barbera and started working on Aoyama, but two laps later he had to run off to avoid hitting the Honda and rejoined a distant 11th.

Now Simoncelli took to the front again. "At first, it was hard to get my rhythm, but later the bike was perfect and I was able to push 100 per cent to the end," he said. His best lap – just short of Lorenzo's 2007 record – was his last, and it was the final straw for his last remaining rival.

Both Pasini and Bautista had gone with him as he pushed away, but the Spaniard soon ran into rear tyre trouble, almost crashing on lap 16, and thereafter settled for third.

Pasini stayed close, just over half a second behind at the flag.

Aoyama was pressed on the last lap by Locatelli, going faster again after dropping back to eighth. He had repassed de Rosa in the process, leaving him in sixth; both were ahead of the still-slowing Barbera in a lone seventh. Cluzel was next, then di Meglio, who had passed the battling SAG Honda team-mates on the way to ninth. They were still just a tenth apart, Faubel ahead of Wilairot.

The rest trailed in, Debise taking the last point off Pons on the final lap.

But the excitement was not over. Bautista celebrated his improving points position with a wheelie on the run up the hill. It went too far, and he sprawled on the track as the bike looped. He was lucky to escape injury, coming up smiling once again.

He was within 12 points of Aoyama; Simoncelli was closing up too. The last 250 battle was gaining tension race by race.

125cc RACE – 19 laps

Iannone took his second pole of the year from Terol. Cortese and Simon completed the first row; Smith led the second from 2008 winner Bradl.

Terol led from start to finish, but under fierce pressure from Iannone and Simon throughout. By the finish, Iannone had dropped away, his front tyre grip gone, but Simon was still less than two-tenths behind.

"I wanted to be sure there were as few riders as possible in the front group," explained Terol, after his first dry win.

Smith had been with the leaders until a big slide and narrow escape dropped him behind Gadea and Vazquez. By the time he'd got ahead again, he was a distant fourth, and would stay there in a surprisingly processional race up front.

There was of course a gang behind, eight-strong at half-distance, now led by Espargaro from Cortese, Gadea, Bradl and rookie Folger.

Bradl took control and escaped, but a mistake on the last lap lost him a full second, letting Espargaro and Cortese past again. Bradl was narrowly ahead of Marquez, then came Gadea, Olive and Zarco, fifth to 11th covered by 1.6 seconds.

Folger had lost touch in 12th; fellow German Schrotter, on his third outing, was 13th and top Honda, taking the place of Vazquez on the last lap.

Corsi retired after running around out of the points; Rabat, Savadori, Zarco and Zanetti were among six to crash.

Terol moved to second overall, ahead of Smith, but Simon's points margin was still better than two races wide.

CARDION AB GRAND PRIX CESKE REPUBLIKY

AUTODROM BRNO

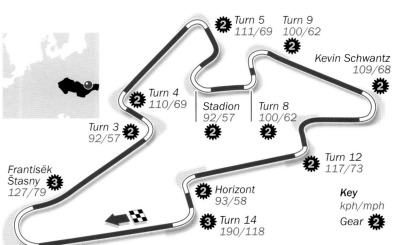

Turn 5 111/69
Turn 9 100/62
Kevin Schwantz 109/68
Turn 4 110/69
Stadion 92/57
Turn 8 100/62
Turn 3 92/57
Turn 12 117/73
Frantisëk Štasny 127/79
Horizont 93/58
Key kph/mph
Turn 14 190/118
Gear

Circuit 5.403km/3.357 miles

MOTOGP

RACE DISTANCE: 22 laps, 73.859 miles/118.866 km • RACE WEATHER: Dry (air 29°, humidity 32%, track 45°)

Pos.	Rider	Nat.	No.	Entrant	Machine	Tyres	Laps	Time & speed
1	Valentino Rossi	ITA	46	Fiat Yamaha Team	Yamaha	B	22	43m 08.991s 102.702mph/ 165.283km/h
2	Dani Pedrosa	SPA	3	Repsol Honda Team	Honda	B	22	43m 20.757s
3	Toni Elias	SPA	24	San Carlos Honda Gresini	Honda	B	22	43m 29.747s
4	Andrea Dovizioso	ITA	4	Repsol Honda Team	Honda	B	22	43m 30.409s
5	Loris Capirossi	ITA	65	Rizla Suzuki MotoGP	Suzuki	B	22	43m 30.529s
6	Nicky Hayden	USA	69	Ducati Marlboro Team	Ducati	B	22	43m 34.535s
7	Colin Edwards	USA	5	Monster Yamaha Tech 3	Yamaha	B	22	43m 34.667s
8	Alex de Angelis	RSM	15	San Carlos Honda Gresini	Honda	B	22	43m 43.100s
9	James Toseland	JPN	52	Monster Yamaha Tech 3	Yamaha	B	22	43m 44.608s
10	Randy de Puniet	USA	14	LCR Honda MotoGP	Honda	B	22	43m 48.815s
11	Chris Vermeulen	AUS	7	Rizla Suzuki MotoGP	Suzuki	B	22	43m 49.767s
12	Niccolo Canepa	USA	88	Pramac Racing	Ducati	B	22	43m 59.652s
13	Gabor Talmacsi	HUN	41	Scot Racing Team MotoGP	Honda	B	22	44m 08.179s
	Mika Kallio	FIN	36	Ducati Marlboro Team	Ducati	B	20	DNF
	Marco Melandri	ITA	33	Hayate Racing Team	Kawasaki	B	20	DNF
	Jorge Lorenzo	SPA	99	Fiat Yamaha Team	Yamaha	B	17	DNF
	Michel Fabrizio	ITA	84	Pramac Racing	Ducati	B	20	DNF

Fastest lap: Jorge Lorenzo, on lap 16, 1m 56.670s, 103.592mph/166.716km/h).

Lap record: Casey Stoner, AUS (Ducati), 1m 57.199s, 103.125mph/165.963km/h (2008).

Event best maximum speed: Dani Pedrosa, 188.026mph/302.6km/h (free practice 2).

Qualifying: Dry
Air: 27° Humidity: 32% Track: 39°

1	Rossi	1m 56.145s
2	Lorenzo	1m 56.195s
3	Pedrosa	1m 56.528s
4	Elias	1m 56.817s
5	Edwards	1m 56.954s
6	Dovizioso	1m 57.108s
7	de Angelis	1m 57.775s
8	Hayden	1m 57.803s
9	Capirossi	1m 57.811s
10	Kallio	1m 57.994s
11	Vermeulen	1m 58.087s
12	Canepa	1m 58.208s
13	de Puniet	1m 58.298s
14	Toseland	1m 58.331s
15	Melandri	1m 58.477s
16	Fabrizio	1m 58.680s
17	Talmacsi	1m 58.749s

Fastest race laps

1	Lorenzo	1m 56.670s
2	Rossi	1m 56.694s
3	Pedrosa	1m 57.228s
4	Elias	1m 57.949s
5	Capirossi	1m 57.964s
6	Dovizioso	1m 57.994s
7	de Angelis	1m 58.056s
8	Kallio	1m 58.105s
9	Hayden	1m 58.110s
10	Edwards	1m 58.140s
11	Melandri	1m 58.153s
12	de Puniet	1m 58.471s
13	Toseland	1m 58.493s
14	Vermeulen	1m 58.775s
15	Canepa	1m 58.835s
16	Talmacsi	1m 58.020s
17	Fabrizio	1m 59.147s

Championship Points

1	Rossi	212
2	Lorenzo	162
3	Stoner	150
4	Pedrosa	135
5	Edwards	112
6	Dovizioso	107
7	de Puniet	80
8	Melandri	79
9	Capirossi	77
10	Vermeulen	72
11	de Angelis	68
12	Elias	63
13	Toseland	62
14	Hayden	57
15	Kallio	34
16	Canepa	32
17	Gibernau	12
18	Takahashi	9
19	Talmacsi	8

Constructor Points

1	Yamaha	255
2	Ducati	184
3	Honda	166
4	Suzuki	100
5	Kawasaki	79

Team Points

1	FIAT Yamaha Team	374
2	Ducati Marlboro Team	242
3	Repsol Honda Team	207
4	Monster Yamaha Tech 3	174
5	RIZLA Suzuki MotoGP	149
6	San Carlo Honda Gresini	131
7	LCR Honda MotoGP	80
8	Hayate Racing Team	79
9	Pramac Racing	66
10	Scot Racing Team	17
11	Grupo Francisco Hernando	12

Grid order	1	2	3	4	5	6	7	8	9	10	11	12	13	14	15	16	17	18	19	20	21	22	
46 ROSSI	46	46	46	46	46	46	46	46	46	46	46	46	46	46	46	46	99	46	46	46	46	46	1
99 LORENZO	3	3	3	99	99	99	99	99	99	99	99	99	99	99	99	99	46	3	3	3	3	3	2
3 PEDROSA	99	99	99	3	3	3	3	3	3	3	3	3	3	3	3	3	3	4	24	24	24	24	3
24 ELIAS	24	24	24	24	24	24	24	24	24	24	24	24	24	24	24	24	24	24	4	4	4	4	4
5 EDWARDS	4	4	4	4	4	4	4	4	4	4	4	4	4	4	4	4	4	65	65	65	65	65	5
4 DOVIZIOSO	65	65	65	65	65	65	65	65	65	65	65	65	65	65	65	65	65	69	69	69	69	69	6
15 de ANGELIS	5	5	5	5	5	5	5	5	5	5	5	5	5	69	69	69	69	5	5	5	5	5	7
69 HAYDEN	69	69	69	69	69	69	69	69	69	69	69	69	69	5	5	5	5	36	36	36	15	15	8
65 CAPIROSSI	15	15	15	15	15	15	15	15	15	15	15	15	15	15	15	15	15	33	33	33	52	52	9
36 KALLIO	36	36	36	36	36	36	36	36	36	36	36	36	36	36	36	36	36	15	15	15	14	14	10
7 VERMEULEN	14	14	14	14	14	14	33	33	33	33	33	33	33	33	33	33	52	52	52	7	7	11
88 CANEPA	52	52	33	33	33	33	14	14	14	14	14	14	14	14	52	52	14	14	14	88	88	12
14 de PUNIET	33	33	52	52	52	52	52	52	52	52	52	52	52	52	14	14	7	7	7	41	41	13
52 TOSELAND	41	41	41	7	7	7	7	7	7	7	7	7	7	7	7	7	88	88	88			
33 MELANDRI	7	7	7	41	41	41	88	88	88	88	88	88	88	88	88	88	41	41	41			
84 FABRIZIO	88	88	88	88	88	88	41	41	41	41	41	41	41	41	41	41						
41 TALMACSI	84	84	84	84	84	84																

84 Pitted

250cc — RACE DISTANCE: 20 laps, 67.493 miles/108.621 km • RACE WEATHER: Wet (air 18°, humidity 65%, track 19°)

Pos.	Rider	Nat.	No.	Entrant	Machine	Laps	Time & Speed
1	Marco Simoncelli	ITA	58	Metis Gilera	Gilera	20	41m 07.174s
							(mph/km/h)
							98.002/157.720
2	Mattia Pasini	ITA	75	Team Toth Aprilia	Aprilia	20	41m 07.174s
3	Alvaro Bautista	SPA	19	Mapfre Aspar Team	Aprilia	20	41m 10.871s
4	Hiroshi Aoyama	JPN	4	Scot Racing Team 250cc	Honda	20	41m 15.236s
5	Roberto Locatelli	ITA	15	Metis Gilera	Gilera	20	41m 16.211s
6	Raffaele de Rosa	ITA	35	Scot Racing Team 250cc	Honda	20	41m 17.360s
7	Hector Barbera	SPA	40	Pepe World Team	Aprilia	20	41m 22.129s
8	Jules Cluzel	FRA	16	Matteoni Racing	Aprilia	20	41m 24.901s
9	Mike di Meglio	FRA	63	Mapfre Aspar Team 250cc	Aprilia	20	41m 25.053s
10	Hector Faubel	SPA	55	Honda SAG	Honda	20	41m 26.448s
11	Ratthapark Wilairot	THA	14	Thai Honda PTT SAG	Honda	20	41m 26.578s
12	Lukas Pesek	CZE	52	Auto Kelly – CP	Aprilia	20	41m 37.122s
13	Shoya Tomizawa	JPN	48	CIP Moto – GP250	Honda	20	41m 43.608s
14	Balazs Nemeth	HUN	11	Balatonring Team	Aprilia	20	42m 23.974s
15	Valentin Debise	FRA	53	CIP Moto – GP250	Honda	20	42m 31.174s
16	Axel Pons	SPA	7	Pepe World Team	Aprilia	20	42m 31.622s
17	Imre Toth	HUN	10	Team Toth Aprilia	Aprilia	20	42m 53.415s
21	Aitor Rodriguez	SPA	77	Matteoni Racing	Aprilia	20	42m 58.955s
22	Vladimir Leonov	RUS	16	Viessmann Kiefer Racing	Aprilia	20	43m 06.284s
	Bastien Chesaux	SWI	8	Racing Team Germany	Honda	12	DNF
	Alex Debon	ESP	6	Aeropuerto – Castello – Blusens	Aprilia	9	DNF
	Alex Baldolini	ITA	25	WTR San Marino Team	Aprilia	6	DNF
	Toby Markham	GB	54	C&L Racing	Honda	1	DNF
	Thomas Luthi	SWI	12	Emmi – Caffe Latte	Aprilia	0	DNF
	Karel Abraham	CZE	17	Cardion AB Motoracing	Aprilia	0	DNF

Fastest lap: Marco Simoncelli, on lap 20, 2m 02.330s, 98.799mph/159.002km/h.
Lap record: Jorge Lorenzo, SPA (Aprilia), 2m 02.229s, 98.825mph/159.043km/h (2007).
Event best maximum speed: Bautista, 159.195mph/256.2km/h (race).

Qualifying: Dry
Air: 26° Humidity: 30% Track: 40°

1	Simoncelli	2m 01.611s
2	Aoyama, Hiroshi	2m 01.961s
3	Barbera	2m 02.064s
4	Debon	2m 02.386s
5	di Meglio	2m 02.426s
6	Locatelli	2m 02.543s
7	Pasini	2m 02.561s
8	Bautista	2m 02.748s
9	de Rosa	2m 02.768s
10	Abraham	2m 02.811s
11	Faubel	2m 02.899s
12	Wilairot	2m 02.921s
13	Luthi	2m 02.932s
14	Cluzel	2m 02.997s
15	Pesek	2m 03.596s
16	Tomizawa	2m 03.951s
17	Baldolini	2m 04.100s
18	Nemeth	2m 05.493s
19	Pons	2m 06.350s
20	Debise	2m 06.571s
21	Chesaux	2m 07.088s
22	Toth	2m 07.130s
23	Leonov	2m 08.362s
24	Rodriguez	2m 08.600s
	Markham	no time

Fastest race laps

1	Simoncelli	2m 02.330s
2	Bautista	2m 02.426s
3	Pasini	2m 02.485s
4	Aoyama, Hiroshi	2m 02.686s
5	di Meglio	2m 02.763s
6	de Rosa	2m 02.862s
7	Locatelli	2m 02.912s
8	Barbera	2m 02.919s
9	Cluzel	2m 03.436s
10	Wilairot	2m 03.481s
11	Debon	2m 03.511s
12	Faubel	2m 03.568s
13	Pesek	2m 03.990s
14	Tomizawa	2m 04.320s
15	Debise	2m 06.036s
16	Pons	2m 06.114s
17	Nemeth	2m 06.248s
18	Baldolini	2m 06.725s
19	Chesaux	2m 06.939s
20	Rodriguez	2m 07.442s
21	Toth	2m 07.559s
22	Leonov	2m 08.121s
23	Markham	2m 19.072s

Championship Points

1	Aoyama, Hiroshi	172
2	Bautista	160
3	Simoncelli	140
4	Barbera	123
5	Pasini	100
6	de Rosa	77
7	Debon	73
8	Faubel	71
9	Locatelli	67
10	Luthi	67
11	di Meglio	50
12	Cluzel	48
13	Pesek	44
14	Wilairot	43
15	Abraham	33
16	Talmacsi	28
17	Espargaro, Aleix	22
18	Tomizawa	21
19	Baldolini	17
20	Toth	12
21	Aoyama, Shuhei	10
22	Leonov	7
23	Debise	6
24	Nemeth	2
25	Markham	2
25	Watanabe	2
26	Chesaux	1
27	Bonsey	1

Constructors

1	Aprilia	213
2	Honda	184
2	Gilera	147
3	Yamaha	2

125cc — RACE DISTANCE: 19 laps, 63.788 miles/102.657 km • RACE WEATHER: Dry (air 26°, humidity 44%, track 35°)

Pos.	Rider	Nat.	No.	Entrant	Machine	Laps	Time & Speed
1	Nicolas Terol	SPA	18	Jack & Jones Team	Aprilia	19	40m 57.378s
							(mph/km/h)
							93.448/150.390
2	Julian Simon	SPA	60	Bancaja Aspar Team 125cc	Aprilia	19	40m 57.546s
3	Andrea Iannone	ITA	29	Ongetta Team I.S.P.A.	Aprilia	19	41m 06.097s
4	Bradley Smith	GB	38	Bancaja Aspar Team 125cc	Aprilia	19	41m 09.821s
5	Pol Espargaro	SPA	44	Derbi Racing Team	Derbi	19	41m 13.384s
6	Sandro Cortese	GER	11	Ajo Interwetten	Derbi	19	41m 13.344s
7	Stefan Bradl	GER	17	Viessmann Kiefer Racing	Aprilia	19	41m 14.483s
8	Marc Marquez	SPA	93	Red Bull KTM Moto Sport	KTM	19	41m 14.485s
9	Sergio Gadea	SPA	33	Bancaja Aspar Team 125cc	Aprilia	19	41m 14.601s
10	Joan Olive	SPA	6	Derbi Racing Team	Derbi	19	41m 14.622s
11	Johann Zarco	FRA	14	WTR San Marino Team	Aprilia	19	41m 14.996s
12	Jonas Folger	GER	94	Ongetta Team I.S.P.A.	Aprilia	19	41m 19.355s
13	Marcel Schrotter	GER	78	Toni Mang Team	Honda	19	41m 31.865s
14	Efren Vazquez	SPA	7	Derbi Racing Team	Derbi	19	41m 31.890s
15	Scott Redding	GB	45	Blusens Aprilia	Aprilia	19	41m 38.936s
16	Danny Webb	GB	99	Degraaf Grand Prix	Aprilia	19	41m 40.476s
17	Randy Krummenacher	SWI	35	Degraaf Grand Prix	Aprilia	19	41m 40.499s
18	Dominique Aegerter	SWI	77	Ajo Interwetten	Derbi	19	41m 40.542s
19	Takaaki Nakagami	JPN	73	Ongetta Team I.S.P.A.	Aprilia	19	41m 40.831s
20	Michael Ranseder	AUT	88	CBC Corse	Aprilia	19	41m 41.295s
21	Tomoyoshi Koyama	JPN	71	Loncin Racing	Loncin	19	41m 48.088s
22	Luigi Morciano	ITA	61	Junior GP Racing Dream	Aprilia	19	42m 07.345s
23	Alessandro Tonucci	ITA	68	Junior GP Racing Dream	Aprilia	19	42m 08.011s
24	Alexis Masbou	FRA	5	Loncin Racing	Loncin	19	42m 32.385s
25	Luca Vitali	ITA	10	CBC Corse	Aprilia	19	42m 36.863s
26	Luca Marconi	FRA	87	CBC Corse	Aprilia	19	42m 37.117s
27	Karel Pesek	CZE	86	Pesek Team	Derbi	19	42m 37.397s
28	Ivan Visak	CRO	68	Team Migomoto	Honda	19	41m 32.489s
29	Ladislav Chmelik	CZE	67	Moto FGR	Honda	18	41m 32.937s
30	Lukas Sembera	CZE	69	Matteoni Racing	Aprilia	18	42m 49.752s
	Simon Corsi	ITA	24	Fontana Racing	Aprilia	12	DNF
	Lorenzo Savadori	ITA	32	Fontana Racing	Aprilia	8	DNF
	Esteve Rabat	SPA	12	Blusens Aprilia	Aprilia	7	DNF
	Luis Salom	SPA	39	Jack & Jones Team	Honda	5	DNF
	Jasper Iwema	NED	53	Racing Team Germany	Honda	1	DNF
	Lorenzo Zanetti	ITA	8	Ongetta Team I.S.P.A.	Aprilia	1	DNF

Fastest lap: Julian Simon, on lap 9, 2m 08.640s, 93.953mph/151.203km/h.
Lap record: Lucio Chechinello, ITA (Aprilia), 2m 07.836s, 94.544mph/152.154km/h (2003).
Event best maximum speed: Joan Olive, SPA (Derbi), 139.000mph/223.7km/h (race).

Qualifying: Dry
Air: 25° Humidity: 34% Track: 39°

1	Iannone	2m 08.171s
2	Terol	2m 08.484s
3	Cortese	2m 08.507s
4	Simon	2m 08.542s
5	Smith	2m 08.957s
6	Bradl	2m 09.184s
7	Gadea	2m 09.240s
8	Espargaro, Pol	2m 09.418s
9	Vazquez	2m 09.434s
10	Zarco	2m 09.462s
11	Olive	2m 09.480s
12	Corsi	2m 09.741s
13	Ranseder	2m 09.962s
14	Salom	2m 10.024s
15	Webb	2m 10.081s
16	Rabat	2m 10.239s
17	Schrotter	2m 10.269s
18	Folger	2m 10.269s
19	Nakagami	2m 10.297s
20	Marquez	2m 10.471s
21	Zanetti	2m 10.500s
22	Redding	2m 10.685s
23	Krummenacher	2m 10.752s
24	Aegerter	2m 10.958s
25	Sembera	2m 11.074s
26	Morciano	2m 11.122s
27	Tonucci	2m 11.332s
28	Iwema	2m 11.387s
29	Pesk	2m 12.123s
30	Savadori	2m 12.286s
31	Masbou	2m 12.303s
32	Marconi	2m 12.482s
33	Koyama	2m 12.840s
34	Vitali	2m 13.176s
35	Chmelik	2m 16.667s

Out of 107%
| | Visak | 2m 18.115s |

Within 107% in free practice
Beaubier

Fastest race laps

1	Simon	2m 08.640s
2	Terol	2m 08.732s
3	Iannone	2m 08.746s
4	Olive	2m 08.951s
5	Cortese	2m 09.007s
6	Marquez	2m 09.016s
7	Espargaro, Pol	2m 09.020s
8	Zarco	2m 09.169s
9	Smith	2m 09.205s
10	Bradl	2m 09.209s
11	Gadea	2m 09.239s
12	Folger	2m 09.249s
13	Rabat	2m 09.487s
14	Schrotter	2m 09.490s
15	Vazquez	2m 09.725s
16	Aegerter	2m 10.375s
17	Nakagami	2m 10.403s
18	Ranseder	2m 10.414s
19	Redding	2m 10.427s
20	Krummenacher	2m 10.642s
21	Webb	2m 10.663s
22	Corsi	2m 10.765s
23	Koyama	2m 10.970s
24	Salom	2m 11.094s
25	Savadori	2m 11.102s
26	Morciano	2m 11.691s
27	Tonucci	2m 11.864s
28	Sembera	2m 12.384s
29	Masbou	2m 12.800s
30	Vitali	2m 12.894s
31	Marconi	2m 13.155s
32	Pesk	2m 13.189s
33	Visak	2m 16.936s
34	Chmelik	2m 17.129s
35	Iwema	2m 21.286s
36	Zanetti	2m 21.435s

Championship Points

1	Simon	174
2	Terol	119.5
3	Smith	111.5
4	Gadea	111
5	Iannone	109.5
6	Espargaro, Pol	79.5
7	Cortese	65
8	Marquez	64
9	Folger	58
10	Bradl	53
11	Olive	47
12	Redding	45.5
13	Aegerter	44.5
14	Corsi	32
15	Vazquez	32
16	Zarco	24.5
17	Webb	24.5
18	Nakagami	24
19	Zanetti	22
20	Rabat	19
21	Koyama	15
22	Krummenacher	15
23	Salom	13
24	Savadori	7
25	Schrotter	7
26	Iwema	3
27	Beaubier	3
28	Glossop	2
29	Fritz	2
30	di Carlo	2
31	Kartheininger	1

Constructors

1	Aprilia	237.5
2	Derbi	107
3	KTM	66
4	Loncin	15
5	Honda	14

FIM WORLD CHAMPIONSHIP • ROUND 12

INDIANAPOLIS GRAND PRIX

INDIANAPOLIS MOTOR SPEEDWAY

Pedrosa's starts just kept getting better, but his lead would not last for long.
Photo: Gold & Goose

THE Indianapolis grand prix circuit loops to and fro within the awe-inspiring banked oval track. It is flat and featureless, with some very slow corners and interesting surface changes. But the run down the straight, shared with the oval and crossing the yard of original bricks at the start-finish line, takes the bikes to almost 200mph, and none of the rest can take away from an impression of grandeur.

It's impossible not to feel the history. A unique kind of history, and a special atmosphere. What could be more unique than Kenny Roberts – not the 2000 world champion, but King Kenny, first US world champion and a legend ever since – taking a run on a motorbike as iconic and as feared as James Dean's 'Little Bastard' Porsche Spyder: the Harley-busting, TZ750-powered, four-cylinder two-stroke dirt bike of 1975.

Based around an already fearsome road-racer, the bike had some 120 horsepower compared with the Harley's 70-odd. The difficulty lay in getting it to the ground. Roberts famously hung on around the soft dirt on the outside of the big corners of the oval, wheels never in line, even on the straights, to beat Harley-Davidson's Corky Keener by inches. After the race, he insisted that the concoction be parked. It was simply too dangerous.

That was across town from the Brickyard, at the Indiana State Fairground, on the awesome Indy Mile circuit. That event had been revived in conjunction with the Indy GP, and on Saturday night it attracted much of the regular paddock to see the spectacle of the race itself, as well as the return of the King. Kenny didn't hang around, either, and climbed off looking rightfully pleased. "I said back then that they didn't pay me enough to ride this thing," he said. "That's still true."

Indy had something to make up to MotoGP, after Hurricane Ike had all but ruined 2008's maiden event there. Once again, the meeting was hit by rain, but only on Friday. And although the crowd was dwarfed by the scale of the stadium, a number of 75,130 was the reward for highly professional promotion and presentation. America at home in America.

Lorenzo responded in his usual studied showman style, adopting a Captain America helmet design. Although he wasn't quite happy: the 'A' was too small, and its wings looked too much like a Honda badge, he believed. His Brno crash was long forgotten: the news was his decision to stay with Yamaha, after retreating to Mallorca to weigh up the lucrative Ducati option. He had changed his mind many times

each day, he said, and "I imagined myself in red". Eventually, however, he opted to stay where he was – although he signed for only one year.

If Rossi was displeased, he didn't show it. "I think Jorge has made the right decision," he said, before again repeating that "I want to end my career with Yamaha". But this was before a cataclysmic weekend, a race in which quite unexpected and deeply disturbing cracks appeared in the Rossi edifice. Pushed to the limit by Lorenzo, he made a most uncharacteristic error. At the next race, he explained to *MOTOCOURSE*: "For me, the bigger problem is the line, because I made a mistake on the turn before. So I came back on the line, but too much, and I braked one-and-a-half metres wider. Maybe there's more dirt, but especially a bigger bump, with a peak. And when I hit the bump, I lost the front."

This crash transformed the championship, halving Rossi's lead at a stroke. He had plenty of time to think about it on the long flight home. By the time he got to Misano for the next race, his attitude to Yamaha, and to Lorenzo, had hardened considerably.

Lorenzo's signing had a big ripple effect. It was some reassurance to Hayden, awaiting confirmation that Ducati would take up his option: for his part, a brilliant ride to third was the best possible contribution to a decision that would go in his favour within days. But it closed a door to Pedrosa, who had been considering a move to Yamaha.

Capirossi also signed with Suzuki, where he would stay to mentor rookie Bautista in 2010, as well as – he insisted with professional confidence – to take advantage of yet another round of promises of improvement from the least successful factory. This had a knock-on effect to Vermeulen, whose tenancy with the team was now definitely at an end. Would he be successful in taking Toseland's place at Tech 3? No: soon it was confirmed that both would be going back to World Superbikes.

Spies was again absent, along with any other wild-cards; Stoner likewise, although Italian magazine *Motosprint* had obtained an interview with the rider, in which he was quoted as saying, "I have not lost my love for bikes and racing, and neither for Ducati." Fatigue had worn him down, he told the magazine. "I felt vulnerable, and found myself in the position of someone doing something he hates. I got to the point that I need rest because the fatigue has become too much to recover as quickly as I should."

His place was filled again by Kallio, while Aleix Espargaro took over the vacant Pramac bike, and made a better fist of it than Fabrizio at Brno, although Spain's youngest-ever MotoGP rider – at 20 – did blot his copybook with a first-lap indiscretion that put both Suzukis and Elias off the track.

There was an increasing volume of complaints about the long-life engines, at least from Yamaha; neither Honda nor Ducati seemed much affected, and Suzuki would find its own problems soon enough. But both satellite team riders were wondering where the horsepower had gone. Rossi put a different twist on the matter, staying indoors for 20 minutes of Friday's first – wet – practice to save the engine. "You are going to see more of this next year," he said.

Nor was there any immediate prospect of restoring grid numbers for 2010: the MSMA had responded to Dorna's 'Moto-1' proposal with a vague offer in principle to make engines available for lease, although only in 2011. According to MSMA spokesman Takenao Tsubouchi, two manufacturers – presumably Honda and Yamaha – had shown firm interest, with more details and a cost structure to follow early in 2010. But when it emerged in the coming month that prices would not be that far short of leasing a whole motorcycle, the idea would come to nothing.

MotoGP RACE – 28 laps

Pedrosa was delighted to have the measure of the Yamahas, fastest in every session, from Friday's wet to the dry qualifying, when his best-ever lap for the circuit put him a half-second clear of Lorenzo. It was his second pole of the year. Rossi just scraped on to the front row at the end, complaining of setting difficulties and narrowly ousting de Angelis.

Pedrosa led away in the usual style, and with half a second in hand at the end of lap one, it looked like he might pull a disappearing act. But Rossi and Lorenzo reeled him in next time around, and the first three pulled quickly clear of Edwards in fourth.

A shemozzle on the first tight corners saw Espargaro take Vermeulen and Elias off the track. Nobody fell, but they lost a lot of time and all rejoined right the back, Elias hindmost.

Opposite, top: A picture for Lorenzo's wall, as nemesis Rossi goes to earth behind him.

Opposite centre, left to right: Aleix Espargaro made a good impression in his MotoGP debut; Earl and Rose Hayden watch their son's progress; King Kenny and the Kong dirt-track Yamaha.
Photos: Gold & Goose

Below: De Angelis atoned for his sins with a career-best second.
Photo: Martin Heath

Left: Nicky Hayden's return to the podium meant deep joy.

Far right: Aoyama leads a pack, from di Meglio, Debon and Pasini (half-hidden), with Bautista (19) lining them up, and Wilairot (14) likewise.

Below: Pedrosa's slip cost him all chance of a podium.

Below right: Smoking in public, Simoncelli celebrates his second successive 250 win.

Bottom: Espargaro, Smith, Corsi – the 125s flash across the line. It was the Spanish youngster's first win.

Photos: Gold & Goose

Pedrosa was fast on the straight and looking hard to pass. Then came disaster as he ran through the slow right-hand turn 15, prelude to the very slow last corner before the run down the front straight. Perhaps the cloud cover had made it cooler, he said, "or perhaps I pushed too much." The front slid away, and although he was quickly back on board, he was in last place. Now it was a Yamaha duel.

Rossi was in front, Lorenzo in position inches behind, pushing and probing. He had set fastest lap of the race on lap four and looked more comfortable, able to hold tighter lines. Clearly there was no escape for Rossi and, as they started lap nine, Lorenzo swept by out of the draft into the long turn one. At the end of that lap, the Spaniard had three-tenths in hand.

Now came Rossi's blunder. He was wide out of the first corner, and off line as he changed direction and braked for the following tight right. He remounted, shaking his head, to circulate for three more laps, only Pedrosa behind him. But his throttle was damaged and his game over.

Lorenzo stretched his advantage at will, winning by almost ten seconds. A signal victory that revitalised the whole view of the championship.

Edwards had been losing more than a second a lap to the leaders, and was more than five adrift when he finally succumbed to de Angelis's persistent attacks on lap six. A couple of laps later, Hayden was also ahead of him and chasing the Honda. Edwards now came under attack by Dovizioso, and was behind him by half-distance.

After lap 18, de Angelis gradually pulled clear, while Edwards was about to drop away rapidly. This secured a career-best second for the San Marinese rider, who had been strong all weekend, and fastest in race-morning warm-up.

That left Hayden with Dovizioso closing relentlessly. But it was by far the American's best ride of the year, and he managed to stay just out of reach for his first rostrum for a year.

A little way behind, Melandri was battling with an on-form Toseland, and generally getting the worse of

it. They were still at it on lap 26, when Melandri suffered a big tumbling crash in the gravel, his lack of front grip finally overcoming his efforts. Toseland was now safe enough in sixth, equalling his best finish of the year.

Next up, Kallio had held off de Puniet in the early laps and then Capirossi for most of the race, until the Suzuki rider reversed the positions with three laps to go.

Ten seconds back came a close trio, led at the last gasp by Elias. He and Vermeulen had come through steadily after their lap-one misadventure, scrapping to and fro all the way. Behind them was the avenging Pedrosa. His bike had not been badly damaged in the spill, and ever since lap ten he'd been whizzing around steadily, half a second or so off lap record pace. He was by far the fastest on the track in the closing stages, and on the last lap he caught the battling pair, getting in between them over the line to consign Vermeulen to 11th.

De Puniet was a lonely 12th, having dropped out of the battle, still in pain from his broken left ankle. Espargaro was next, having caught and outdistanced Talmacsi after half-distance.

Rossi still had an advantage of one race, but he'd demonstrated just how fragile that advantage could be, with five rounds left. As Lorenzo said, "The championship was almost gone, but in one day things have changed a lot."

250cc RACE – 26 laps

There were lots of spills in practice, with Simoncelli falling three times, while Aoyama crashed in morning warm-up – potentially ruinous, with only one bike.

Di Meglio claimed a first-ever 250 pole, narrowly ahead of Aoyama, Simoncelli and Barbera. Cluzel, frequently impressive on his privateer Aprilia, was fastest in the wet, and fifth in the dry, to lead row two.

And it was the Frenchman's light blue bike that came through from the second row to lead the first three laps. The pace was too hot, however, and he

had slipped back to fourth when he slid off on the eighth lap.

Simoncelli had taken over, shadowed by Aoyama. Di Meglio was delayed by a second or so passing Cluzel, and was being chased by Pasini and Debon. All the while, Bautista was catching up, after a typical slow start that saw him finish the first lap barely in the top ten.

Pasini took himself out of the picture on lap five, slipping off, remounting, then retiring. Soon after, Bautista was past Debon and closing on team-mate di Meglio, who was just over a second off the leaders by half-distance. Safely behind, Barbera led the next group from Wilairot and Locatelli, with Pesek and Faubel following closely and ahead of Debon.

Simoncelli now put on a fine display of on-the-limit riding, running a string of ever-faster laps. Aoyama went with him, but with four laps to go, Simoncelli finally broke the tow and escaped. Another new record on lap 24 underlined the point, and he won by just under two seconds. He was the first rider in 2009 to take successive wins, and after a slow start to the year – as in 2008 – the defender was becoming a factor in the championship.

Second-placed Aoyama reported a fraught race, which had included an early collision with an out-of-shape di Meglio and several near crashes on his own account. His consolation was to extend his points lead over Bautista.

The Spaniard had surged past a slowing di Meglio with ten laps to go, but never got close to the leaders.

Barbera had missed a gear off the line to finish lap one 13th, but had charged through to lead the pursuit by lap nine. But the veteran Locatelli was on storming form, passing Wilairot and the Spaniard on successive laps, and then escaping by the end. Wilairot was out, a strong ride and a potential sixth melting away when he broke down with three laps left.

Pesek had lost touch by the finish and was alone in seventh; likewise Faubel, one place behind. Luthi and Abraham completed the top ten, de Rosa alone

behind the latter, there being little change at the back in the latter half of the race. Leonov, the last in the points, was also the final rider on the same lap.

Chesaux crashed out early on; Baldolini fell and got back on for 12th; Debon also crashed out with eight laps to go, after settling in tenth.

125cc RACE – 23 laps

Practice times were very close, Simon taking his fourth pole from Cortese, Terol and Espargaro; Smith led row two.

The race was similarly close, a five-strong thrilling battle raging to the very end.

Terol led into the first corner, and for most of the rest of the race – at least over the line. Iannone was with the front group, but retired after just two laps; Simon had finished the first lap eighth, but was up to fifth by the third lap. There he held a close, but cautious, watching brief of the struggle ahead.

Vazquez had been at the back of the group, but had jumped the start, and his race was ruined by a ride-through penalty.

Smith, Espargaro and Corsi were all over Terol's back wheel, and all stayed there for the inevitable last-lap battle. Espargaro was in front as they started it, and although Smith set a new lap record on the final lap, the Spaniard was in front also at the end of it.

Smith was defending as well as attacking, and his speed allowed him to hold Corsi at bay to the finish. Terol was thoroughly mugged in the final sprint, but nonetheless managed to keep Simon behind him. The first five were across the line in less than five seconds.

Marquez was left behind for sixth, battling to the end with Bradl. Gadea and Olive had been with them, but dropped away, the former fading badly; Olive hung on safely in eighth.

The next trio was also tooth and nail, Nakagami and Aegerter both passing Webb in the last-corners scramble.

INDIANAPOLIS MOTOR SPEEDWAY

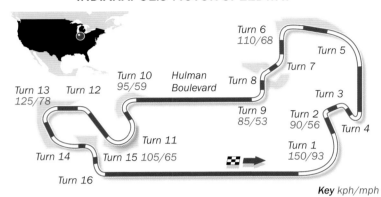

Turn 6 110/68
Turn 5
Turn 7
Turn 10 95/59
Hulman Boulevard
Turn 8
Turn 3
Turn 13 125/78
Turn 12
Turn 9 85/53
Turn 2 90/56
Turn 4
Turn 11
Turn 1 150/93
Turn 14
Turn 15 105/65
Turn 16

Key kph/mph

Circuit 4.216km/2.620 miles

MOTOGP	RACE DISTANCE: 28 laps, 73.351 miles/118.048 km • RACE WEATHER: Dry (air 20°, humidity 35%, track 27°)

Pos.	Rider	Nat.	No.	Entrant	Machine	Tyres	Laps	Time & speed
1	Jorge Lorenzo	SPA	99	Fiat Yamaha Team	Yamaha	B	28	47m 13.592s 93.190mph/ 149.976km/h
2	Alex de Angelis	RSM	15	San Carlos Honda Gresini	Honda	B	28	47m 23.027s
3	Nicky Hayden	USA	69	Ducati Marlboro Team	Ducati	B	28	47m 26.539s
4	Andrea Dovizioso	ITA	4	Repsol Honda Team	Honda	B	28	47m 27.070s
5	Colin Edwards	USA	5	Monster Yamaha Tech 3	Yamaha	B	28	47m 39.846s
6	James Toseland	JPN	52	Monster Yamaha Tech 3	Yamaha	B	28	47m 46.000s
7	Loris Capirossi	ITA	65	Rizla Suzuki MotoGP	Suzuki	B	28	47m 47.992s
8	Mika Kallio	FIN	36	Ducati Marlboro Team	Ducati	B	28	47m 48.448s
9	Toni Elias	SPA	24	San Carlos Honda Gresini	Honda	B	28	47m 58.597s
10	Dani Pedrosa	SPA	3	Repsol Honda Team	Honda	B	28	47m 58.969s
11	Chris Vermeulen	AUS	7	Rizla Suzuki MotoGP	Suzuki	B	28	47m 59.070s
12	Randy de Puniet	USA	14	LCR Honda MotoGP	Honda	B	28	48m 05.886s
13	Aleix Espargaro	SPA	44	Pramac Racing	Ducati	B	28	48m 17.144s
14	Gabor Talmacsi	HUN	41	Scot Racing Team MotoGP	Honda	B	28	48m 28.678s
	Marco Melandri	ITA	33	Hayate Racing Team	Kawasaki	B	25	DNF
	Niccolo Canepa	USA	88	Pramac Racing	Ducati	B	23	DNF
	Valentino Rossi	ITA	46	Fiat Yamaha Team	Yamaha	B	12	DNF

Fastest lap: Jorge Lorenzo, on lap 4, 1m 40.152s, 94.165mph/151.545km/h (record).

Previous lap record: Valentino Rossi, ITA (Yamaha), 1m 49.668s, 85.995mph/138.395km/h (2008).

Event best maximum speed: Alex de Angelis, 204.990mph/323.9km/h (race).

Qualifying: Dry
Air: 27° Humidity: 40% Track: 37°

1	Pedrosa	1m 39.730s
2	Lorenzo	1m 40.236s
3	Rossi	1m 40.609s
4	de Angelis	1m 40.620s
5	Edwards	1m 40.961s
6	Hayden	1m 41.067s
7	Elias	1m 41.283s
8	Dovizioso	1m 41.309s
9	Melandri	1m 41.530s
10	Toseland	1m 41.620s
11	Capirossi	1m 41.742s
12	de Puniet	1m 41.773s
13	Canepa	1m 41.910s
14	Vermeulen	1m 42.038s
15	Kallio	1m 42.250s
16	Espargaro, A	1m 42.577s
17	Talmacsi	1m 42.736s

Fastest race laps

1	Lorenzo	1m 40.152s
2	Pedrosa	1m 40.200s
3	Rossi	1m 40.287s
4	de Angelis	1m 40.862s
5	Hayden	1m 41.041s
6	Dovizioso	1m 41.106s
7	Edwards	1m 41.256s
8	Melandri	1m 41.490s
9	Elias	1m 41.573s
10	Toseland	1m 41.576s
11	Capirossi	1m 41.576s
12	Kallio	1m 41.664s
13	Vermeulen	1m 41.840s
14	de Puniet	1m 41.983s
15	Canepa	1m 42.087s
16	Espargaro, A	1m 42.138s
17	Talmacsi	1m 42.317s

Championship Points

1	Rossi	212
2	Lorenzo	187
3	Stoner	150
4	Pedrosa	141
5	Edwards	123
6	Dovizioso	120
7	de Angelis	88
8	Capirossi	86
9	de Puniet	84
10	Melandri	79
11	Vermeulen	77
12	Hayden	73
13	Toseland	72
14	Elias	70
15	Kallio	42
16	Canepa	32
17	Gibernau	12
18	Talmacsi	10
19	Takahashi	9
20	Espargaro, A	3

Constructor Points

1	Yamaha	280
3	Honda	204
3	Ducati	182
4	Suzuki	109
5	Kawasaki	79

Team Points

1	FIAT Yamaha Team	399
2	Repsol Honda Team	261
2	Ducati Marlboro Team	231
4	Monster Yamaha Tech 3	194
5	RIZLA Suzuki MotoGP	163
6	San Carlo Honda Gresini	158
7	LCR Honda MotoGP	84
8	Hayate Racing Team	79
9	Pramac Racing	69
10	Scot Racing Team	19
11	Grupo Francisco Hernando	12

Grid order	1	2	3	4	5	6	7	8	9	10	11	12	13	14	15	16	17	18	19	20	21	22	23	24	25	26	27	28	
3 PEDROSA	3	3	3	46	46	46	46	46	99	99	99	99	99	99	99	99	99	99	99	99	99	99	99	99	99	99	99	99	1
99 LORENZO	46	46	46	99	99	99	99	99	46	15	15	15	15	15	15	15	15	15	15	15	15	15	15	15	15	15	15	15	2
46 ROSSI	99	99	99	5	5	15	15	15	15	69	69	69	69	69	69	69	69	69	69	69	69	69	69	69	69	69	69	69	3
15 de ANGELIS	5	5	5	15	15	5	5	69	5	5	5	5	4	4	4	4	4	4	4	4	4	4	4	4	4	4	4	4	4
5 EDWARDS	15	15	15	69	69	69	69	69	5	4	4	4	5	5	5	5	5	5	5	5	5	5	5	5	5	5	5	5	5
69 HAYDEN	69	69	69	4	4	4	4	4	52	52	52	52	52	52	52	52	52	52	52	52	52	52	52	52	52	52	52	52	6
24 ELIAS	33	33	33	33	33	52	52	33	33	33	33	33	33	33	33	33	33	33	33	33	33	33	33	33	33	65	65	65	7
4 DOVIZIOSO	4	4	4	52	52	33	33	52	52	36	36	36	36	36	36	36	36	36	36	36	36	36	36	36	65	36	36	36	8
33 MELANDRI	52	52	52	36	36	36	36	36	65	65	65	65	65	65	65	65	65	65	65	65	65	65	65	36	7	7	24		9
52 TOSELAND	14	14	36	14	14	65	65	65	65	14	14	14	14	14	14	14	24	24	24	7	7	7	7	7	24	24	3		10
65 CAPIROSSI	41	41	14	41	65	14	14	14	14	41	88	24	24	24	24	24	7	7	7	24	24	24	24	24	3	3	7		11
14 de PUNIET	88	36	41	65	41	41	41	41	41	88	24	88	88	7	7	7	14	14	14	14	14	14	14	14	14	14	14		12
88 CANEPA	36	65	65	88	88	88	88	88	88	24	41	7	7	88	88	88	88	88	88	88	88	88	3	3	44	44	44		13
7 VERMEULEN	65	88	88	7	7	7	7	24	24	7	7	41	41	44	44	44	44	44	3	3	44	44	44	41	41	41			14
36 KALLIO	7	7	7	44	24	24	24	7	7	44	44	44	44	41	41	41	41	41	3	44	44	41	41						
44 ESPARGARO, A	44	44	44	24	44	44	44	44	46	46	3	3	3	3	3	3	3	3	41	41	41								
41 TALMACSI	24	24	24	3	3	3	3	3	3	3	3	46																	

46 Pitted

250cc

RACE DISTANCE: 26 laps, 68.112 miles/109.616 km • RACE WEATHER: Dry (air 21°, humidity 35%, track 28°)

Pos.	Rider	Nat.	No.	Entrant	Machine	Laps	Time & Speed
1	Marco Simoncelli	ITA	58	Metis Gilera	Gilera	26	45m 43.599s
							(mph/km/h)
							98.002/157.720
2	Hiroshi Aoyama	JPN	4	Scot Racing Team 250cc	Honda	26	45m 45.542s
3	Alvaro Bautista	SPA	19	Mapfre Aspar Team	Aprilia	26	45m 48.260s
4	Mike di Meglio	FRA	63	Mapfre Aspar Team 250cc	Aprilia	26	45m 59.375s
5	Roberto Locatelli	ITA	15	Metis Gilera	Gilera	26	45m 59.074s
6	Hector Barbera	SPA	40	Pepe World Team	Aprilia	26	46m 03.070s
7	Lukas Pesek	CZE	52	Auto Kelly – CP	Aprilia	26	46m 16.408s
8	Hector Faubel	SPA	55	Honda SAG	Honda	26	46m 16.408s
9	Thomas Luthi	SWI	12	Emmi – Caffe Latte	Aprilia	26	46m 32.920s
10	Karel Abraham	CZE	17	Cardion AB Motoracing	Aprilia	26	46m 33.444s
11	Raffaele de Rosa	ITA	35	Scot Racing Team 250cc	Honda	26	46m 37.166s
12	Alex Baldolini	ITA	25	WTR San Marino Team	Aprilia	26	47m 13.316s
13	Valentin Debise	FRA	53	CIP Moto – GP250	Honda	26	47m 21.436s
14	Axel Pons	SPA	7	Pepe World Team	Aprilia	26	47m 30.271s
15	Vladimir Leonov	RUS	56	Viessmann Kiefer Racing	Aprilia	26	47m 30.420s
16	Balazs Nemeth	HUN	11	Balatonring Team	Aprilia	25	46m 09.367s
17	Imre Toth	HUN	10	Team Toth Aprilia	Aprilia	25	46m 38.325s
18	Barrett Long	USA	29	Longetivity Racing	Yamaha	25	47m 03.849s
19	Adam Roberts	CAN	30	Fiat Racing	Yamaha	25	47m 04.092s
	Ratthapark Wilairot	THA	14	Thai Honda PTT SAG	Honda	23	DNF
	Alex Debon	ESP	6	Aeropuerto – Castello – Blusens	Aprilia	18	DNF
	Jules Cluzel	FRA	16	Matteoni Racing	Aprilia	7	DNF
	Mattia Pasini	ITA	75	Team Toth Aprilia	Aprilia	5	DNF
	Bastien Chesaux	SWI	8	Racing Team Germany	Honda	0	DNF
dns	Shoya Tomizawa	JPN	48	CIP Moto – GP250	Honda		

Fastest lap: Mike di Meglio, on lap 19, 1m 44.341s, 89.689mph/144.341km/h.
Lap record: New circuit (no 250cc race run in 2008 due to weather conditions).
Event best maximum speed: Bautista, 171.374mph/275.8km/h (race).

Qualifying: Dry
Air: 27° Humidity: 34% Track: 38°

1	di Meglio	1m 44.341s
2	Aoyama, Hiroshi	1m 44.461s
3	Simoncelli	1m 44.553s
4	Barbera	1m 44.625s
5	Cluzel	1m 44.860s
6	Bautista	1m 44.955s
7	Pasini	1m 45.158s
8	Debon	1m 45.192s
9	Wilairot	1m 45.396s
10	Faubel	1m 45.438s
11	Pesek	1m 45.439s
12	Locatelli	1m 45.560s
13	Baldolini	1m 45.778s
14	Luthi	1m 46.177s
15	de Rosa	1m 46.195s
16	Abraham	1m 46.908s
17	Debise	1m 47.838s
18	Pons	1m 48.458s
19	Toth	1m 48.650s
20	Nemeth	1m 49.143s
21	Leonov	1m 49.807s
22	Chesaux	1m 49.888s
23	Roberts	1m 51.296s
	Outside 107%	
	Long	1m 52.154s
	Within 107% in free practice 1	
	Tomizawa	1m 56.906s

Fastest race laps

1	Simoncelli	1m 44.720s
2	Aoyama, Hiroshi	1m 44.775s
3	di Meglio	1m 44.979s
4	Bautista	1m 45.001s
5	Debon	1m 45.117s
6	Barbera	1m 45.126s
7	Locatelli	1m 45.130s
8	Pasini	1m 45.245s
9	Wilairot	1m 45.325s
10	Cluzel	1m 45.324s
11	Pesek	1m 45.480s
12	Faubel	1m 45.623s
13	Abraham	1m 46.289s
14	Baldolini	1m 46.439s
15	de Rosa	1m 46.425s
16	Luthi	1m 46.600s
17	Debise	1m 47.942s
18	Leonov	1m 48.359s
19	Pons	1m 48.385s
20	Nemeth	1m 49.039s
21	Toth	1m 49.569s
22	Long	1m 51.487s
23	Roberts	1m 51.516s

Championship Points

1	Aoyama, Hiroshi	192
2	Bautista	176
3	Simoncelli	165
4	Barbera	133
5	Pasini	100
6	de Rosa	82
7	Faubel	79
8	Locatelli	78
9	Luthi	74
10	Debon	73
11	di Meglio	63
12	Pesek	53
13	Cluzel	48
14	Wilairot	43
15	Abraham	39
16	Talmacsi	28
17	Espargaro, Aleix	22
18	Tomizawa	21
19	Baldolini	21
20	Toth	12
21	Aoyama, Shuhei	10
22	Debise	9
23	Leonov	8
24	Pons	2
25	Nemeth	2
26	Markham	2
27	Watanabe	2
28	Chesaux	1
29	Bonsey	1

Constructors

1	Aprilia	229
2	Honda	204
2	Gilera	172
3	Yamaha	2

125cc

RACE DISTANCE: 23 laps, 59.631 miles/95.968 km • RACE WEATHER: Dry (air 20°, humidity 40%, track 24°)

Pos.	Rider	Nat.	No.	Entrant	Machine	Laps	Time & Speed
1	Pol Espargaro	SPA	44	Derbi Racing Team	Derbi	23	42m 07.926s
							(mph/km/h)
							85.805/138.091
2	Bradley Smith	GB	38	Bancaja Aspar Team 125cc	Aprilia	23	42m 08.045s
3	Simon Corsi	ITA	24	Fontana Racing	Aprilia	23	42m 08.373s
4	Nicolas Terol	SPA	18	Jack & Jones Team	Aprilia	23	42m 09.538s
5	Julian Simon	SPA	60	Bancaja Aspar Team 125cc	Aprilia	23	42m 09.726s
6	Marc Marquez	SPA	93	Red Bull KTM Moto Sport	KTM	23	42m 27.270s
7	Stefan Bradl	GER	17	Viessmann Kiefer Racing	Aprilia	23	42m 27.283s
8	Joan Olive	SPA	6	Derbi Racing Team	Derbi	23	42m 33.536s
9	Takaaki Nakagami	JPN	73	Ongetta Team I.S.P.A.	Aprilia	23	42m 37.165s
10	Dominique Aegerter	SWI	77	Ajo Interwetten	Derbi	23	42m 37.632s
11	Danny Webb	GB	99	Degraaf Grand Prix	Aprilia	23	42m 38.389s
12	Jonas Folger	GER	94	Ongetta Team I.S.P.A.	Aprilia	23	42m 52.385s
13	Luis Salom	SPA	39	Jack & Jones Team	Honda	23	42m 52.474s
14	Tomoyoshi Koyama	JPN	71	Loncin Racing	Loncin	23	42m 53.253s
15	Sergio Gadea	SPA	33	Bancaja Aspar Team 125cc	Aprilia	23	42m 53.360s
16	Michael Ranseder	AUT	88	CBC Corse	Aprilia	23	42m 53.404s
17	Lorenzo Zanetti	ITA	8	Ongetta Team I.S.P.A.	Aprilia	23	42m 53.923s
18	Sandro Cortese	GER	11	Ajo Interwetten	Derbi	23	43m 01.716s
19	Cameron Beaubier	USA	16	Red Bull KTM Moto Sport	KTM	23	43m 09.104s
20	Esteve Rabat	SPA	12	Blusens Aprilia	Aprilia	23	43m 10.739s
21	Efren Vazquez	SPA	7	Derbi Racing Team	Derbi	23	43m 22.816s
22	Lukas Sembera	CZE	69	Matteoni Racing	Aprilia	23	43m 24.245s
23	Johann Zarco	FRA	14	WTR San Marino Team	Aprilia	23	43m 39.143s
24	Luca Marconi	FRA	87	CBC Corse	Aprilia	23	43m 39.494s
25	Luca Vitali	ITA	10	CBC Corse	Aprilia	23	43m 59.199s
	Andrea Iannone	ITA	29	Ongetta Team I.S.P.A.	Aprilia	20	DNF
	Randy Krummenacher	SWI	35	Degraaf Grand Prix	Aprilia	17	DNF
	Scott Redding	GB	45	Blusens Aprilia	Aprilia	11	DNF
	Alexis Masbou	FRA	5	Loncin Racing	Loncin	7	DNF
	Ben Young	USA	74	Veloce Racing	Aprilia	3	DNF
	Lorenzo Savadori	ITA	32	Fontana Racing	Aprilia	3	DNF
	Miles Thornton	USA	75	Veloce Racing	Aprilia	1	DNF

Fastest lap: Bradley Smith, on lap 23, 1m 49.039s, 86.491mph/139.194km/h (record).
Previous lap record: Stefan Bradl, GER (Aprilia), 1m 50.460s, 85.378mph/137.403km/h (2008).
Event best maximum speed: Esteve Rabat, SPA (Aprilia), 147.699mph/237.7km/h (race).

Qualifying: Dry
Air: 24° Humidity: 43% Track: 31°

1	Simon	1m 49.337s
2	Cortese	1m 49.387s
3	Terol	1m 49.537s
4	Espargaro, Pol	1m 49.577s
5	Smith	1m 49.585s
6	Corsi	1m 49.628s
7	Gadea	1m 49.661s
8	Vazquez	1m 49.703s
9	Marquez	1m 49.852s
10	Olive	1m 49.853s
11	Webb	1m 49.982s
12	Iannone	1m 50.140s
13	Zarco	1m 50.340s
14	Ranseder	1m 50.494s
15	Bradl	1m 50.530s
16	Koyama	1m 50.547s
17	Aegerter	1m 50.721s
18	Savadori	1m 50.728s
19	Nakagami	1m 50.916s
20	Salom	1m 50.006s
21	Folger	1m 51.062s
22	Rabat	1m 51.470s
23	Beaubier	1m 51.527s
24	Zanetti	1m 51.539s
25	Krummenacher	1m 51.546s
26	Redding	1m 51.569s
27	Marconi	1m 52.334s
28	Sembera	1m 52.373s
29	Masbou	1m 52.448s
30	Thornton	1m 53.835s
31	Vitali	1m 54.107s
32	Young	1m 56.451s

Fastest race laps

1	Smith	1m 49.039s
2	Simon	1m 49.148s
3	Terol	1m 49.191s
4	Corsi	1m 49.196s
5	Espargaro, Pol	1m 49.205s
6	Vazquez	1m 49.272s
7	Gadea	1m 49.600s
8	Bradl	1m 49.729s
9	Marquez	1m 49.796s
10	Rabat	1m 50.020s
11	Webb	1m 50.034s
12	Zarco	1m 50.037s
13	Iannone	1m 50.077s
14	Olive	1m 50.090s
15	Aegerter	1m 50.115s
16	Redding	1m 50.121s
17	Nakagami	1m 50.221s
18	Cortese	1m 50.617s
19	Ranseder	1m 50.650s
20	Salom	1m 50.659s
21	Folger	1m 50.757s
22	Zanetti	1m 50.852s
23	Koyama	1m 50.891s
24	Beaubier	1m 51.124s
25	Krummenacher	1m 51.225s
26	Savadori	1m 51.664s
27	Sembera	1m 52.128s
28	Marconi	1m 52.584s
29	Masbou	1m 52.978s
30	Vitali	1m 53.626s
31	Young	1m 57.083s
32	Thornton	2m 05.888s

Championship Points

1	Simon	185
2	Terol	132.5
3	Smith	131.5
4	Gadea	112
5	Iannone	109.5
6	Espargaro, Pol	104.5
7	Marquez	74
8	Cortese	65
9	Folger	62
10	Bradl	62
11	Olive	55
12	Aegerter	50.5
13	Corsi	48
14	Redding	45.5
15	Vazquez	32
16	Nakagami	31
17	Webb	29.5
18	Zarco	24.5
19	Zanetti	22
20	Rabat	19
21	Koyama	17
22	Salom	13
23	Krummenacher	15
24	Savadori	7
25	Schrotter	7
26	Iwema	3
27	Beaubier	3
28	Glossop	2
29	Fritz	2
30	di Carlo	2
31	Kartheininger	1

Constructors

1	Aprilia	257.5
2	Derbi	132
3	KTM	76
4	Loncin	17
5	Honda	14

SAN MARINO GRAND PRIX

MISANO CIRCUIT

Pedrosa and Elias have gone, Rossi is safe and Lorenzo escapes with a bump on the seat as de Angelis triggers mayhem on the first corner. Edwards's bike is sideways, Hayden's horizontal in the background.
Photo: Gold & Goose

MISANO is at the centre of the Rimini holiday coast, whence so many of today's top racers are drawn. But it belongs to Rossi. Close to his home town of Tavullia, for this weekend, it became the centre of the universe.

That Rossi managed to reverse the fortunes of the week before came as a welcome relief to his army of fans, as well as to the rider himself. He arrived in full spate and intending to win, and chastised himself for the amateur-hour error of Indy by changing his 'THE DOCTOR' script for 'THE DONKEY'. In case he should win, he'd also prepared sets of donkey ears for himself and his crew. By the end of the weekend, it seemed pre-destined that they should require them.

Rossi had lit up in another way: he had spent the time between sliding on his backside at Indy and arriving at Misano thinking about Yamaha and the manufacturer signing Lorenzo for 2010. And he was not pleased. He spilled the beans first of all to MOTO-COURSE in an exclusive and incandescent interview.

"I always try to make a great work for developing the bike," he said. "And I usually make the work just for me. But now I am also doing it for my worst enemy. Sincerely, I think I don't deserve this after what I have done for Yamaha. But this is the Yamaha choice…" He would decide his future, he added, in June of 2010.

It was a theme he would develop, and to which Lorenzo would respond. Before too many more weeks, Rossi would not be discouraging an eager Italian Press from linking him with a move to Ducati. Lorenzo, meanwhile, had suggested that in fact it was Rossi who had copied *his* settings.

Contract news was very much the theme. Hayden

was confirmed to stay with Ducati after weeks of growing doubt. "It don't exactly make you feel like a superstar, but that's the business. That's how it is," he said. Both Pedrosa and Dovizioso also confirmed that they would stay another year with the factory Repsol Honda team. The biggest news, however, came from Ben Spies: still not yet Superbike champion, he had signed to spend the next two years with Yamaha. But in which paddock? This was the last piece of the jigsaw.

This was meant to be the last race that Ducati would be without Stoner, but the will-he/won't-he question was still very much in the air. The Kallio/Espargaro switch was in place for a second race, while the Ducati team expressed confidence that Casey would be back at Estoril – but without hard evidence. The only smattering of news to filter out of Australia would come from a local newspaper in the north of Queensland, where Stoner was reported to be relaxing on holiday and having great sport with the local barramundi. In other words, gone fishin'.

Ducati's increasingly revered technical chief, the wheelchair-bound Filippo Preziosi, gave a briefing to describe the benefit wrought by raising the seat height and handlebar position, as well as electronic changes. Previously, unpredictability had led to a costly lack of rider confidence. "When Nicky was at the back, two or three seconds off, it's not because the length of the swing-arm is wrong, it's because he is not believing in the bike, because it is doing something different lap to lap.

"We analysed the data… Nicky was very helpful. We realised that the bike doesn't give confidence to the rider to push, and if he can't push, the tyre won't

warm enough. So it doesn't work at all." Raising the rider meant more weight transfer in both acceleration and braking, which in turn worked the tyres more.

Preziosi also addressed the deeper mystery: why did Stoner not suffer, where Hayden and Melandri before him had done. Firstly, it's because he rode the bike very aggressively from the very first lap, getting heat into the tyres quickly, he explained. But much more important was his innate riding ability.

"I was mistaken when I tried to explain why Casey was so fast in 2007, when our engine was very peaky, and he was using low gearing and high revs. I thought we were lucky because we had found a rider that liked to ride peaky engines. That was my mistake. We were lucky because we found a clever guy. Because as soon as we changed completely, in the middle of 2008, to a very low-rpm, torquier engine, he completely switched his way of using the gearing. I remember in Barcelona, in two laps he completely understood the new behaviour, and he change his riding style and was one second faster. Casey is the opposite of what you read in a lot of papers: they say his performance is because he opens the gas with closed eyes, believing in the traction control. The truth is absolutely the opposite. Even with less TC than the other riders, he can put the bikes and tyres at the optimum spin, very smooth. He does traction with the wrist."

Misano saw the second on-track launch of a Moto2 bike – the first had been the Moriwaki at Motegi, even before the single-engine rule had been decided. The second was from former racer turned chassis engineer Eskil Suter. Others, including the British Harris and the Spanish BQR chassis, were already competing (with Yamaha engines) in the Spanish national championships. In the coming weeks, these would be followed by more from manufacturers in Japan and all around Europe, including Britain's FTR, Kalex from Germany, TSR from Japan and several others.

Honda took the next step in its move from in-house Showa suspension to Öhlins, with Dovizioso using the Swedish suspension on the front and rear of his bike, while Pedrosa stuck with what he knew until the end of the season.

The most dramatic act of the weekend was at the end of a 125 nail-biter. Espargaro seemed to have it won, until a lunatic inside pass on the last corner by Iannone took them both down. Espargaro's bike leapt the barrier, but Iannone's was relatively undamaged, and he ran back to try to get going again, the finish line barely 100 metres away.

Espargaro was incensed, however, and would have none of it. He ran over and smashed his fists down on to the Aprilia's dashboard, which contained crucial electronics. This would stop his assailant. Iannone responded by headbutting the Spaniard – ineffectually, since both still wore helmets – and it was this, along with some unguarded anti-Spanish remarks to Italian TV directly afterwards, that earned the 20-year-old a fine of US$5,000.

MotoGP RACE – 28 laps

Misano had been resurfaced three years before, "and it was bumpy from new," said Rossi. "Now it is even worse." It was forgotten in the white heat at the end of qualifying. With 30 seconds to go, Lorenzo put his name on top; with three seconds left, Pedrosa ousted him by two-tenths. But Rossi was still out, and he aced it, claiming a similar margin for his sixth pole of the year: "It is the most I have had in one season."

As usual, Pedrosa was first away from the line. Elias was in his tracks from the second row, Rossi third. They got through the tight second corner safely. Lorenzo, just behind, only just made it, having received a hefty bump on the seat from Edwards. The American had already knocked Hayden off, himself propelled from behind by the cause of it all, de Angelis. Both Americans had qualified on the second row, and Hayden was so incensed that he had to be physically restrained from getting to grips with de Angelis. Later Edwards said, "De Angelis should be wearing the donkey ears today."

Capirossi and Dovizioso escaped involvement, while the rest picked their way through, Vermeulen again badly delayed to finish the first lap four from the back. De Puniet had also been pushed off and was last by almost ten seconds.

While Elias attacked Pedrosa up front, even nosing in front at one stage, Lorenzo took third off Rossi into the first corner at the start of lap two, the four leaders already pulling away slightly.

On lap four, Rossi started to gain confidence and speed. He passed Lorenzo, and then both Yamahas got ahead of Elias. At the same time, Dovizioso had overtaken Capirossi on lap two and was closing on the leaders. It took him two more laps to clear Elias as well, now just a second behind Lorenzo, but next time around he ran wide and the gap doubled. He would not join the lead group after all.

Pedrosa was now under severe threat from Rossi, but he held him off until lap eight. The pass was clean and convincing, and the reigning champion immediately opened up a small but stable gap.

As half-distance approached, he was more than a second clear, while Lorenzo was stuck behind the Honda. "It has a high corner speed and acceleration, so it was hard," he said. Eventually, Pedrosa made

Above: Ducati's design genius, Filippo Preziosi.

Far left: Melandri leads from Kallio, Talmacsi and Toseland.

Below left: Rossi bore the ass's face on his helmet, after his Indy error.

Below: Hayden had to be restrained from getting physical with de Angelis after their crash.
Photos: Gold & Goose

the little slip he'd been awaiting, running wide on lap 14, and now he was second.

The gap to Rossi was just under 1.5 seconds, and Jorge took a couple more tenths back next lap. Rossi had him covered, though, stretching his legs again with a new record on lap 16. Two laps after that, he was more than 2.5 seconds clear and still gaining. It was in the bag.

Lorenzo had to be content with best of the rest as Pedrosa dropped way behind, safe in third.

By now, fourth was in serious dispute. Capirossi had closed again on Dovizioso, the Suzuki keeping its promise of better performance, at this track anyway. The veteran was also riding like a demon, repeatedly attacking until, on lap 25, he finally made it. Dovi stayed close, however, and used his power advantage to get ahead on the last lap, staying there by just two-tenths.

Their battling meant Elias could stay close, but never close enough to attack.

Kallio was only a couple of seconds behind. He'd got past Melandri on lap six, but couldn't get away. Then, in the later laps, the Italian found his hands full fending off Vermeulen, whose own chances at a track that suited the Suzuki had been spoiled by de Angelis just after the start. He'd finished the first lap 11th, become stuck behind an on-form Toseland for a while, then got ahead just after half-distance. He had closed on Melandri quickly but failed to get by.

Toseland had lost touch by the end, in tenth, well clear of Espargaro. But the rookie had impressed once again in only his second MotoGP ride, setting fifth fastest lap at the mid-point, beaten only by the factory Yamahas and Hondas.

De Puniet had been playing catch-up all race long and finished a lonely 12th; Canepa and Talmacsi trailed in at the back.

Rossi had turned things around. With four races left, he had the advantage once again, and a cushion of more than one race. Under pressure, he was showing his depth. The Donkey was King of the Beasts.

250cc RACE – 26 laps

Pole went to points leader Aoyama, his first of the season, with Barbera less than one hundredth slower, and then Simoncelli – his home even closer to the track than Rossi's. Pasini completed the front row; di Meglio, Debon, Faubel and Bautista filled the second.

They all streamed through the first two tight corners without mishap, Barbera heading Pasini, Aoyama and Simoncelli out into the country. By the time they came back, Pasini was in front, but about to lose the lead to Simoncelli; Aoyama was fourth, behind Barbera, and about to surrender that position to Faubel.

Aoyama would regain that place as Faubel dropped back, but by then Bautista had got ahead of the Japanese, the group now more than two seconds off the leading trio.

Simoncelli led until lap eight, when Pasini displaced him once more. Barbera was still well in the mix, and they were swapping to and fro. Then suddenly Simoncelli was gone. Coming out of one of the tight turns, the back had stepped right out as he opened the throttle and he spun to the ground. Later he blamed failure of his factory Gilera/Aprilia's traction-control system. It was an ultimately fatal blow to his title chances.

That left Pasini to do most of the leading, Barbera being ahead on laps 19 and 20. But as the end approached, the Spaniard found something extra. He

led the last three laps under the most severe pressure from Pasini to win his second race of the year by 0.04 second.

The battle for third was no less enthralling, Aoyama back and forth with team-mates Bautista and di Meglio, and everything to play for.

Bautista missed a gear on lap 17 and dropped to the back of the trio; he was still there as they started the final lap. By the end of it, as they dashed to the line almost three abreast, he was in front again, with Aoyama fourth and di Meglio fifth.

Cluzel had headed the chase group all race long, securing sixth, less than a second ahead of Debon and de Rosa. Faubel was out of touch in ninth; Wilairot had been in the group, but crashed out with five laps left. Luthi was a distant tenth, after getting back ahead of Abraham; a long way behind, Tomizawa shaded Baldolini, who had fallen and got back on in the early stages. Debise was alone in 14th, and Nemeth took the last point-scoring position from Pons on the final lap.

Chesaux crashed out early on; Locatelli after 19 laps, following a long battle with Cluzel.

At this point, the title was in the balance between Aoyama and Bautista, the former's points lead having been cut back to only 12. Simoncelli was fully 40 points adrift – yet he would be the one to come back and challenge at the end.

Above: Eee-Aaw – showman Rossi had the last laugh at home.

Top right: Traction out-of-control as Simoncelli's electronics play him false.

Above right: Barbera was this far in front of Pasini after their fine duel.

Right: Iannone's win-or-bust move goes bust, taking Espargaro with him. Simon slips through inside for the win.

Photos: Gold & Goose

125cc RACE – 23 laps

Smith took pole by less than two-hundredths from Simon. Iannone and Terol completed the front row; Gadea, Espargaro, Marquez and Corsi the second.

Terol was the first leader, then Iannone took control until lap five, a huge group behind them. It was Simon who ousted the Italian, and the pair gradually pulled away. By lap 11, almost half-distance, they were 2.5 seconds clear of a pack of eight, now led again by Terol. Over the line, he was tailed by Espargaro, Bradl, Smith, Marquez, Corsi and Cortese, all over one another.

One rider was particularly noticeable. Espargaro had got away slowly and finished the first lap 13th. Ever since, he had been heading forward, the only one in the gang to be gaining places all the time, and losing none.

Now he was hounding Terol, and both of them catching the leading pair. When Espargaro got ahead with six laps to go, he scythed an interval of 1.3 seconds to nothing in just one lap, taking a new record in the process.

Next time around, he took the lead, and although Iannone grabbed it back as they started the last lap, Espargaro was faster and passed him more or less straight back. He seemed to have done enough as he peeled into the final turn – but for Iannone, it was win or bust. He scythed past on the inside and made for the apex. His speed was far too great, the bike slipped from under him, and straight into Espargaro.

Thus Simon inherited his fourth win of the year, Terol half a second behind. Smith took third, having escaped from a tussle won by Marquez from Cortese. Bradl had dropped behind, with Corsi fading even further. Olive was alone behind him, then rookie Folger prevailed over the next big group, from Webb, Ranseder and the rest.

Gadea crashed out on the first lap; the hapless Redding retired to the pits once again wth his Bluesens Aprilia.

GP CINZANO DI SAN MARINO E RIVIERA DI RIMINI

6 SEPTEMBER 2009 • FIM WORLD CHAMPIONSHIP ROUND 13

MISANO WORLD CIRCUIT

Tramonto 80/50

Rio 80/50

Turn 5

Turn 9

Turn 6

Rimini

Quercia 85/53

Curvone 260/161

Turn 12

Misano

Turn 3

Variante del Parco 125/78

Turn 15

Turn 13

Carro 80/50

Key kph/mph

Circuit 4.226km/2.626 miles

A TAVULLIA VALE C'E' ...

MOTOGP

RACE DISTANCE: 28 laps, 73.525 miles/118.328 km • RACE WEATHER: Dry (air 24°, humidity 32%, track 41°)

Pos.	Rider	Nat.	No.	Entrant	Machine	Tyres	Laps	Time & speed
1	Valentino Rossi	ITA	46	Fiat Yamaha Team	Yamaha	B	28	44m 32.882s 99.028mph/ 159.371km/h
2	Jorge Lorenzo	SPA	99	Fiat Yamaha Team	Yamaha	B	28	44m 35.298s
3	Dani Pedrosa	SPA	3	Repsol Honda Team	Honda	B	28	44m 45.282s
4	Andrea Dovizioso	ITA	4	Repsol Honda Team	Honda	B	28	44m 59.212s
5	Loris Capirossi	ITA	65	Rizla Suzuki MotoGP	Suzuki	B	28	44m 59.421s
6	Toni Elias	SPA	24	San Carlos Honda Gresini	Honda	B	28	45m 01.168s
7	Mika Kallio	FIN	36	Ducati Marlboro Team	Ducati	B	28	45m 03.066s
8	Marco Melandri	ITA	33	Hayate Racing Team	Kawasaki	B	28	45m 04.639s
9	Chris Vermeulen	AUS	7	Rizla Suzuki MotoGP	Suzuki	B	28	45m 04.791s
10	James Toseland	JPN	52	Monster Yamaha Tech 3	Yamaha	B	28	45m 11.229s
11	Aleix Espargaro	SPA	44	Pramac Racing	Ducati	B	28	45m 19.555s
12	Randy de Puniet	USA	14	LCR Honda MotoGP	Honda	B	28	45m 24.923s
13	Niccolo Canepa	USA	88	Pramac Racing	Ducati	B	28	45m 36.080s
14	Gabor Talmacsi	HUN	41	Scot Racing Team MotoGP	Honda	B	28	45m 55.229s
	Alex de Angelis	RSM	15	San Carlos Honda Gresini	Honda	B	0	DNF
	Nicky Hayden	USA	69	Ducati Marlboro Team	Ducati	B	0	DNF
	Colin Edwards	USA	5	Monster Yamaha Tech 3	Yamaha	B	0	DNF

Fastest lap: Valentino Rossi, on lap 16, 1m 34.746s, 99.774mph/160.572km/h (record).

Previous lap record: Valentino Rossi, ITA (Yamaha), 1m 34.904s, 99.609mph/160.305km/h (2008).

Event best maximum speed: Dani Perosa, 173.797mph/279.7km/h (free practice 2).

Qualifying: Dry

Air: 28° Humidity: 19% Track: 37°

1	Rossi	1m 34.338s
2	Pedrosa	1m 34.560s
3	Lorenzo	1m 34.808s
4	Elias	1m 34.907s
5	Edwards	1m 35.184s
6	Hayden	1m 35.223s
7	de Angelis	1m 35.343s
8	Dovizioso	1m 35.492s
9	de Puniet	1m 35.554s
10	Capirossi	1m 35.561s
11	Kallio	1m 35.601s
12	Melandri	1m 35.785s
13	Vermeulen	1m 35.790s
14	Toseland	1m 36.070s
15	Espargaro, A	1m 36.228s
16	Canepa	1m 36.264s
17	Talmacsi	1m 37.091s

Fastest race laps

1	Rossi	1m 34.746s
2	Lorenzo	1m 34.823s
3	Pedrosa	1m 35.115s
4	Dovizioso	1m 35.435s
5	Espargaro, A	1m 35.673s
6	Capirossi	1m 35.680s
7	Vermeulen	1m 35.703s
8	Kallio	1m 35.742s
9	Elias	1m 35.779s
10	Melandri	1m 35.877s
11	de Puniet	1m 35.998s
12	Toseland	1m 36.026s
13	Canepa	1m 36.448s
14	Talmacsi	1m 37.019s

Championship Points

1	Rossi	237
2	Lorenzo	207
3	Pedrosa	157
4	Stoner	150
5	Dovizioso	133
6	Edwards	123
7	Capirossi	97
8	de Angelis	88
9	de Puniet	88
10	Melandri	87
11	Vermeulen	84
12	Elias	80
13	Toseland	78
14	Hayden	73
15	Kallio	51
16	Canepa	35
17	Gibernau	12
18	Talmacsi	12
19	Takahashi	9
20	Espargaro, A	8

Constructor Points

1	Yamaha	305
3	Honda	220
3	Ducati	191
4	Suzuki	120
5	Kawasaki	87

Team Points

1	FIAT Yamaha Team	444
2	Repsol Honda Team	290
2	Ducati Marlboro Team	240
4	Monster Yamaha Tech 3	201
5	RIZLA Suzuki MotoGP	181
6	San Carlo Honda Gresini	168
7	LCR Honda MotoGP	88
8	Hayate Racing Team	87
9	Pramac Racing	77
10	Scot Racing Team	21
11	Grupo Francisco Hernando	12

Grid order

	1	2	3	4	5	6	7	8	9	10	11	12	13	14	15	16	17	18	19	20	21	22	23	24	25	26	27	28	
46 ROSSI	3	3	3	3	3	3	3	46	46	46	46	46	46	46	46	46	46	46	46	46	46	46	46	46	46	46	46	46	1
3 PEDROSA	24	24	24	24	46	46	46	3	3	3	3	3	3	99	99	99	99	99	99	99	99	99	99	99	99	99	99	99	2
99 LORENZO	46	99	99	99	99	99	99	99	99	99	99	99	99	3	3	3	3	3	3	3	3	3	3	3	3	3	3	3	3
24 ELIAS	99	46	46	46	24	4	4	4	4	4	4	4	4	4	4	4	4	4	4	4	4	4	4	65	65	65	4	4	4
5 EDWARDS	65	4	4	4	4	24	24	24	24	24	24	24	24	65	65	65	65	65	65	65	65	65	65	4	4	4	65		5
69 HAYDEN	4	65	65	65	65	65	65	65	65	65	65	65	65	24	24	24	24	24	24	24	24	24	24	24	24	24			6
15 de ANGELIS	33	33	33	33	33	36	36	36	36	36	36	36	36	36	36	36	36	36	36	36	36	36	36	36	36	36	36	36	7
4 DOVIZIOSO	41	36	36	36	36	33	33	33	33	33	33	33	33	33	33	33	33	33	33	33	33	33	33	33	33	33	33	33	8
14 de PUNIET	36	41	41	52	52	52	52	52	52	52	52	52	52	52	7	7	7	7	7	7	7	7	7	7	7	7	7	7	9
65 CAPIROSSI	52	52	52	41	7	7	7	7	7	7	7	7	7	7	52	52	52	52	52	52	52	52	52	52	52	52	52	52	10
36 KALLIO	7	7	7	7	44	44	44	44	44	44	44	44	44	44	44	44	44	44	44	44	44	44	44	44	44	44	44	44	11
33 MELANDRI	44	44	44	44	41	41	41	88	88	88	88	88	14	14	14	14	14	14	14	14	14	14	14	14	14	14	14	14	12
7 VERMEULEN	88	88	88	88	88	88	88	41	41	14	14	88	88	88	88	88	88	88	88	88	88	88	88	88	88	88	88	88	13
52 TOSELAND	14	14	14	14	14	14	14	14	14	41	41	41	41	41	41	41	41	41	41	41	41	41	41	41	41	41	41	41	14
44 ESPARGARO, A																													
88 CANEPA																													
41 TALMACSI																													

250cc — RACE DISTANCE: 26 laps, 68.273 miles/109.876 km • RACE WEATHER: Dry (air 24°, humidity 34%, track 40°)

Pos.	Rider	Nat.	No.	Entrant	Machine	Laps	Time & Speed
1	Hector Barbera	SPA	40	Pepe World Team	Aprilia	26	43m 23.353s
							(mph/km/h)
							94.411/151.940
2	Mattia Pasini	ITA	75	Team Toth Aprilia	Aprilia	26	43m 23.393s
3	Alvaro Bautista	SPA	19	Mapfre Aspar Team	Aprilia	26	43m 25.044s
4	Hiroshi Aoyama	JPN	4	Scot Racing Team 250cc	Honda	26	43m 25.050s
5	Mike di Meglio	FRA	63	Mapfre Aspar Team 250cc	Aprilia	26	43m 25.274s
6	Jules Cluzel	FRA	16	Matteoni Racing	Aprilia	26	43m 32.555s
7	Alex Debon	ESP	6	Aeropuerto – Castello – Blusens	Aprilia	26	43m 33.836s
8	Raffaele de Rosa	ITA	35	Scot Racing Team 250cc	Honda	26	43m 34.713s
9	Hector Faubel	SPA	55	Honda SAG	Honda	26	43m 42.306s
10	Thomas Luthi	SWI	12	Emmi – Caffe Latte	Aprilia	26	43m 47.833s
11	Karel Abraham	CZE	17	Cardion AB Motoracing	Aprilia	26	43m 48.033s
12	Shoya Tomizawa	JPN	48	CIP Moto – GP250	Honda	26	44m 14.874s
13	Alex Baldolini	ITA	25	WTR San Marino Team	Aprilia	26	44m 15.827s
14	Valentin Debise	FRA	53	CIP Moto – GP250	Honda	26	44m 35.028s
15	Balazs Nemeth	HUN	11	Balatonring Team	Aprilia	26	44m 38.866s
16	Axel Pons	SPA	7	Pepe World Team	Aprilia	26	44m 39.019s
17	Vladimir Leonov	RUS	56	Viessmann Kiefer Racing	Aprilia	25	43m 36.763s
18	Imre Toth	HUN	10	Team Toth Aprilia	Aprilia	25	43m 56.557s
19	Aitor Rodriguez	SPA	77	Matteoni Racing	Aprilia	25	44m 01.540s
	Ratthapark Wilairot	THA	14	Thai Honda PTT SAG	Honda	21	DNF
	Roberto Locatelli	ITA	15	Metis Gilera	Gilera	20	DNF
	Toby Markham	GB	54	C & L Racing	Aprilia	15	DNF
	Marco Simoncelli	ITA	58	Metis Gilera	Gilera	12	DNF
	Bastien Chesaux	SWI	8	Racing Team Germany	Honda	3	DNF
	Lukas Pesek	CZE	52	Auto Kelly – CP	Aprilia	2	DNF

Fastest lap: Hiroshi Aoyama, on lap 23, 1m 39.039s, 95.450mph/153.612km/h.
Lap record: Marco Simoncelli, ITA (Gilera) 1m 38.993s, 95.494mph/153.683km/h (2008).
Event best maximum speed: Cluzel, 146.519mph/235.8km/h (free practice 1).

Qualifying: Dry — Air: 31° Humidity: 17% Track: 41°

1	Aoyama, Hiroshi	1m 38.867s
2	Barbera	1m 38.875s
3	Simoncelli	1m 38.038s
4	Pasini	1m 39.068s
5	di Meglio	1m 39.397s
6	Debon	1m 39.416s
7	Faubel	1m 39.602s
8	Bautista	1m 39.825s
9	Locatelli	1m 39.915s
10	Wilairot	1m 39.969s
11	Abraham	1m 39.995s
12	Pesek	1m 40.040s
13	Cluzel	1m 40.066s
14	Luthi	1m 40.128s
15	Baldolini	1m 40.136s
16	de Rosa	1m 40.832s
17	Tomizawa	1m 41.429s
18	Debise	1m 41.903s
19	Nemeth	1m 42.092s
20	Pons	1m 42.158s
21	Chesaux	1m 42.957s
22	Leonov	1m 42.992s
23	Toth	1m 43.079s
24	Markham	1m 43.919s
25	Rodriguez	1m 45.357s

Fastest race laps

1	Aoyama, Hiroshi	1m 39.039s
2	Bautista	1m 39.118s
3	di Meglio	1m 39.257s
4	Barbera	1m 39.281s
5	Pasini	1m 39.309s
6	de Rosa	1m 39.316s
7	Locatelli	1m 39.520s
8	Cluzel	1m 39.526s
9	Simoncelli	1m 39.619s
10	Debon	1m 39.644s
11	Wilairot	1m 39.657s
12	Faubel	1m 39.665s
13	Baldolini	1m 40.185s
14	Luthi	1m 40.193s
15	Abraham	1m 40.321s
16	Nemeth	1m 40.830s
17	Pesek	1m 40.955s
18	Tomizawa	1m 40.972s
19	Pons	1m 41.733s
20	Debise	1m 42.037s
21	Rodriguez	1m 43.653s
22	Leonov	1m 43.759s
23	Chesaux	1m 43.820s
24	Toth	1m 44.140s
25	Markham	1m 45.950s

Championship Points

Pos.	Rider	Points
1	Aoyama, Hiroshi	205
2	Bautista	192
3	Simoncelli	165
4	Barbera	158
5	Pasini	120
6	de Rosa	90
7	Faubel	86
8	Debon	82
9	Luthi	80
10	Locatelli	78
11	di Meglio	74
12	Cluzel	58
13	Pesek	53
14	Abraham	44
15	Wilairot	43
16	Talmacsi	28
17	Tomizawa	25
18	Baldolini	24
19	Espargaro, Aleix	22
20	Toth	12
21	Debise	11
22	Aoyama, Shuhei	10
23	Leonov	8
24	Nemeth	2
25	Pons	2
26	Markham	2
27	Watanabe	2
28	Chesaux	1
29	Bonsey	1

Constructors

Pos.	Constructor	Points
1	Aprilia	254
2	Honda	217
2	Gilera	172
3	Yamaha	2

125cc — RACE DISTANCE: 23 laps, 60.396 miles/97.198 km • RACE WEATHER: Dry (air 23°, humidity 36%, track 28°)

Pos.	Rider	Nat.	No.	Entrant	Machine	Laps	Time & Speed
1	Julian Simon	SPA	60	Bancaja Aspar Team 125cc	Aprilia	23	40m 15.301s
							(mph/km/h)
							85.805/138.091
2	Nicolas Terol	SPA	18	Jack & Jones Team	Aprilia	23	40m 15.874s
3	Bradley Smith	GB	38	Bancaja Aspar Team 125cc	Aprilia	23	40m 20.775s
4	Marc Marquez	SPA	93	Red Bull KTM Moto Sport	KTM	23	40m 24.679s
5	Sandro Cortese	GER	11	Ajo Interwetten	Derbi	23	40m 24.966s
6	Stefan Bradl	GER	17	Viessmann Kiefer Racing	Aprilia	23	40m 27.056s
7	Simon Corsi	ITA	24	Fontana Racing	Aprilia	23	40m 38.345s
8	Joan Olive	SPA	6	Derbi Racing Team	Derbi	23	40m 42.237s
9	Jonas Folger	GER	94	Ongetta Team I.S.P.A.	Aprilia	23	40m 48.152s
10	Danny Webb	GB	99	Degraaf Grand Prix	Aprilia	23	40m 49.740s
11	Michael Ranseder	AUT	88	CBC Corse	Aprilia	23	40m 50.034s
12	Efren Vazquez	SPA	7	Derbi Racing Team	Derbi	23	40m 51.064s
13	Riccardo Moretti	ITA	51	Ellegi Racing	Aprilia	23	40m 51.154s
14	Lorenzo Zanetti	ITA	8	Ongetta Team I.S.P.A.	Aprilia	23	40m 55.238s
15	Dominique Aegerter	SWI	77	Ajo Interwetten	Derbi	23	40m 55.243s
16	Johann Zarco	FRA	14	WTR San Marino Team	Aprilia	23	40m 55.411s
17	Randy Krummenacher	SWI	35	Degraaf Grand Prix	Aprilia	23	41m 14.352s
18	Lukas Sembera	CZE	69	Matteoni Racing	Aprilia	23	41m 14.401s
19	Luigi Morciano	ITA	61	Junior GP Racing Dream	Aprilia	23	41m 15.537s
20	Takaaki Nakagami	JPN	73	Ongetta Team I.S.P.A.	Aprilia	23	41m 16.492s
21	Luis Salom	SPA	39	Jack & Jones Team	Honda	23	41m 18.149s
22	Cameron Beaubier	USA	16	Red Bull KTM Moto Sport	KTM	23	41m 27.115s
23	Jasper Iwema	NED	53	Racing Team Germany	Aprilia	23	41m 27.234s
24	Luca Marconi	FRA	87	CBC Corse	Aprilia	23	41m 27.354s
25	Gabriele Ferro	ITA	65	Grilline Bridgestone Team	Aprilia	23	41m 29.897s
26	Jacub Jantulik	SVK	70	JJ Racing Team	Aprilia	23	41m 44.032s
27	Luca Vitali	ITA	10	CBC Corse	Aprilia	23	41m 44.610s
28	Jakub Kornfeil	CZE	21	Loncin Racing	Loncin	23	41m 45.217s
29	Alessandro Tonucci	ITA	62	Junior GP Racing Dream	Aprilia	22	40m 27.147s
	Andrea Iannone	ITA	29	Ongetta Team I.S.P.A.	Aprilia	22	DNF
	Pol Espargaro	SPA	44	Derbi Racing Team	Derbi	22	DNF
	Tomoyoshi Koyama	JPN	71	Loncin Racing	Loncin	16	DNF
	Esteve Rabat	SPA	12	Blusens Aprilia	Aprilia	15	DNF
	Lorenzo Savadori	ITA	32	Fontana Racing	Aprilia	13	DNF
	Scott Redding	GB	45	Blusens Aprilia	Aprilia	5	DNF
	Sergio Gadea	SPA	33	Bancaja Aspar Team 125cc	Aprilia	0	DNF

Fastest lap: Pol Espargaro, on lap 20, 1m 43.613s, 91.235mph/146.830km/h (record).
Previous lap record: Gabor Talmacsi, HUN (Aprilia), 1m 43.839s, 91.038mph/146.511km/h (2008).
Event best maximum speed: Bradley Smith, GB (Aprilia), 127.070mph/204.5km/h (race).

Qualifying: Dry — Air: 32° Humidity: 18% Track: 36°

1	Smith	1m 43.727s
2	Simon	1m 43.743s
3	Iannone	1m 43.890s
4	Terol	1m 43.987s
5	Gadea	1m 44.062s
6	Espargaro, Pol	1m 44.171s
7	Marquez	1m 44.179s
8	Corsi	1m 44.349s
9	Bradl	1m 44.656s
10	Cortese	1m 44.929s
11	Vazquez	1m 45.116s
12	Rabat	1m 45.157s
13	Webb	1m 45.188s
14	Redding	1m 45.213s
15	Zarco	1m 45.226s
16	Morciano	1m 45.316s
17	Ranseder	1m 45.450s
18	Olive	1m 45.544s
19	Sembera	1m 45.574s
20	Zanetti	1m 45.619s
21	Tonucci	1m 45.687s
22	Nakagami	1m 45.776s
23	Krummenacher	1m 45.791s
24	Aegerter	1m 45.795s
25	Folger	1m 45.868s
26	Moretti	1m 45.932s
27	Koyama	1m 45.948s
28	Beaubier	1m 45.971s
29	Ferro	1m 45.976s
30	Savadori	1m 56.330s
31	Salom	1m 46.352s
32	Marconi	1m 46.536s
33	Iwema	1m 46.664s
34	Jantulik	1m 47.283s
35	Kornfeil	1m 47.699s
36	Vitali	1m 48.014s

Fastest race laps

1	Espargaro, Pol	1m 43.613s
2	Cortese	1m 43.929s
3	Smith	1m 43.962s
4	Iannone	1m 44.026s
5	Terol	1m 44.139s
6	Simon	1m 44.165s
7	Bradl	1m 44.280s
8	Corsi	1m 44.369s
9	Marquez	1m 44.513s
10	Rabat	1m 44.556s
11	Ranseder	1m 44.915s
12	Folger	1m 44.994s
13	Vazquez	1m 45.028s
14	Olive	1m 45.052s
15	Moretti	1m 45.061s
16	Aegerter	1m 45.169s
17	Webb	1m 45.345s
18	Zarco	1m 45.563s
19	Zanetti	1m 45.636s
20	Redding	1m 45.637s
21	Sembera	1m 45.846s
22	Savadori	1m 46.086s
23	Krummenacher	1m 46.105s
24	Morciano	1m 46.136s
25	Tonucci	1m 46.227s
26	Salom	1m 46.467s
27	Iwema	1m 46.507s
28	Koyama	1m 46.689s
29	Marconi	1m 46.710s
30	Beaubier	1m 46.718s
31	Nakagami	1m 46.747s
32	Ferro	1m 46.844s
33	Vitali	1m 47.277s
34	Jantulik	1m 47.304s
35	Kornfeil	1m 47.561s

Championship Points

Pos.	Rider	Points
1	Simon	210
2	Terol	152.5
3	Smith	147.5
4	Gadea	112
5	Iannone	109.5
6	Espargaro, Pol	104.5
7	Marquez	87
8	Cortese	76
9	Bradl	72
10	Folger	69
11	Olive	63
12	Corsi	57
13	Aegerter	51.5
14	Redding	45.5
15	Vazquez	36
16	Webb	35.5
17	Nakagami	31
18	Zarco	24.5
19	Zanetti	24
20	Rabat	19
21	Koyama	17
22	Salom	16
23	Krummenacher	15
24	Savadori	7
25	Schrotter	7
26	Ranseder	5
27	Moretti	3
28	Iwema	3
29	Beaubier	3
30	Glossop	2
31	Fritz	2
32	di Carlo	2
33	Kartheininger	1

Constructors

Pos.	Constructor	Points
1	Aprilia	282.5
2	Derbi	143
3	KTM	89
4	Loncin	17
5	Honda	14

FIM WORLD CHAMPIONSHIP • ROUND 14

PORTUGUESE GRAND PRIX

ESTORIL CIRCUIT

Pale sunshine illuminates re-ascendant moonwalker Lorenzo, his title hopes waxing once more. Stoner was back, strong, and on the rostrum where he belonged.
Photo: Gold & Goose

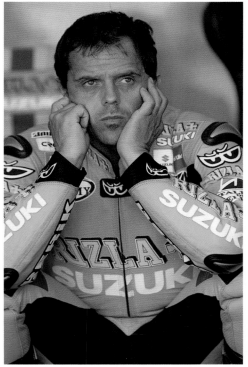

FOR once, in a year of rain, the weather on the Atlantic seaboard was relatively benign, give or take a few blasts of wind and the mist piling up on the hills overlooking the circuit on race morning. A nice change for the riders, and for 45,539 spectators. They did not see an exciting MotoGP race, but they were present at a very important weekend.

Important for the championship, and also for the balance of power at Yamaha, which this weekend teetered heavily in favour of Lorenzo as a pressured Rossi made another very rare mistake. The error was not all his own, but made hand in hand with crew chief Jerry Burgess. Together, they "made a Horlicks" (in Burgess-speak) of the settings, and for once were not able to pull off their usual magic trick of finding a fix in race-morning warm-up, instead going further down a blind alley. "I think we tried to fix the turning problem and set the bike in the wrong direction for rear grip. Today, we suffered a lot," said Rossi. Fourth position was bad enough, but the most hurtful statistic of all was the gap to winner Lorenzo. Most riders are happy when they finish within 30 seconds of the front man. Rossi was 23.5 seconds off his team-mate, riding an identical bike. To him, that was a yawning abyss so deep that you couldn't see the bottom.

The weekend belonged to Jorge. Fiat had commissioned special ice-white livery to celebrate a new Punto launch. Lorenzo recalled that it was 40 years

– and now a few months – since the first moon landing, and commissioned NASA-replica white leathers and space helmet to go with the livery. He was fastest throughout practice and led from lap one to the end, the win giving him the chance to take the tableau further with a post-race moonwalk in the gravel trap.

It also cut Rossi's points advantage once again: now down to 18 points, the smallest it has been since the German GP. One non-finish, and Lorenzo could be in the lead again. He was both optimistic and realistic, saying, "Now the championship is less impossible… but it continues to be very difficult."

It was important also for the return of Stoner. The paddock had been filled with prophecies that his top-flight career might be over. When he only ran 11 laps in Friday afternoon's first practice, questions about endurance went unanswered, but those about speed had been. He was a close fourth, less than eight-tenths off Lorenzo's time, achieved over 27 laps.

Stoner started the weekend with apologies, but no real explanations, promising that even if the fatigue returned, "I'll push myself harder for the last races." His problem had been narrowed down: possibly lactose intolerance, possibly a sodium imbalance; but he was feeling rested and ready to try again.

He finished right back in the mix, strong throughout the race and defiant afterwards, when he pointed out how he had put the doubters – particularly Kevin Schwantz – in their place. "It shows that experience doesn't count for anything," he said, adding more cautiously, "The real test will come in Malaysia in the heat." He would pass that with flying colours.

Stoner's return was a mixed blessing for Hayden, who found his own performance dwarfed once again. "A few races back, I would have been happy with eighth, but anybody with a brain would know that Casey coming back and beating me up, and not only me, would not make you feel great." All this after yet another close encounter with his favourite anti-hero, de Angelis, who had been slipstreaming him down the straight while paying attention to his pit board. He ran right into the back of the Ducati; luckily, neither crashed. "I was doing 274km/h," said a bemused

Hayden, who had been one of the San Marinese's victims at Assen.

Kallio was moved back to the Pramac team, which announced during the weekend that he would stay for another year. At the same time, it had been confirmed that Spies would be taking the second Tech 3 seat, alongside fellow Texan Edwards. This left the other Pramac seat as the final vacancy. Both Elias and de Angelis were eager candidates, while Pasini was another possibility – he had tested with the factory again in the interim. The favoured choice was Vermeulen, but the Australian announced during the weekend that he was quitting MotoGP to join Kawasaki back in World Superbikes. This triggered a decision by Sunday night in favour of team principal Paolo Campinoti's choice, Aleix Espargaro, who had impressed in his substitute rides.

Aoyama had also been on Ducati's shopping list, but there was another surprise: Daniel Epp, the entrepreneur behind Thomas Luthi and the Emmi Caffe Latte 250 team, was to move up to MotoGP with a satellite Honda, and he had secured the services of the 250 title leader. Epp also gained kudos as fairy godmother to Pasini, whose Team Toth hit final meltdown, with both his and team-mate Imre Toth's bikes being repossessed by Aprilia. Pasini missed the first practice altogether, but overnight Epp put together a rescue passage, and the next day he was out on track once more on his own bike, the fairing painted in battleship grey, nominally entered by Globalgest.

A refinement was agreed to the long-life engine rule, specifying a change of punishment. Instead of the rider losing ten points for each extra engine used, the points would be docked from the constructor. The rider would have to start from the back of the grid, for that race only. The riders at least welcomed this: the previous points punishment had left them, as Rossi had said, "with no chance to make up for it".

This weekend was the deadline for release of the provisional entry list for Moto2, and it duly came out – official confirmation that the new class had attracted plenty of interest from far and wide. IRTA chief Mike Trimby said the preferred grid size was "32 to 34, with

Above: Lorenzo was untouchable and did everything right.

Left: Rossi trails his braking foot: he missed the settings and was a disconsolate fourth.

Far left: Engine worries were starting for Loris Capirossi and Suzuki.

Right: The view from Stoner's chair: his return brought out the photographers.

Photos: Gold & Goose

a maximum of 38, plus two wild-cards." The current list numbered 39 riders, with another ten on the reserve list. They were not named, but the teams were. Among them were 12 250 teams, including the leading lights, plus Hayate, Gresini, Tech 3 and Pramac from MotoGP. Team Roberts was also down for two bikes; MZ was on the short reserve list, along with Promoracing – backed by film star Antonio Banderas; the remaining six reserves were for teams that had wanted two riders, but had only been allowed one.

But there was bad news from the smallest class, with confirmation that KTM would withdraw completely.

MotoGP RACE – 28 laps

Lorenzo dominated every session and took his fifth pole of the year. His advantage over Rossi was a quarter of a second, and the only chink in his armour, he said, was that "I have not won a race from pole so far this year." Rossi was troubled in second, complaining of a lack of grip out of the hairpin; Stoner was straight back to the front row, in third. Pedrosa led row two from Edwards and de Puniet.

Once again, Pedrosa had the best speed off the line to lead into the first corner, but by the time they got to the third, Lorenzo was ahead, and that was that for him. Riding with immaculate consistency, he had a lead of six-tenths after one lap, and almost double that next time around. And so he went on.

By then, it was Stoner in second. He had been fourth at the end of lap one, but powered past the sliding Rossi on the way out of the first corner and passed Pedrosa as well next time around. He'd survived a moment that he felt had prevented a possible challenge for the lead as he ran through the fast kink on to the back straight. "I made a small mistake and my right foot came off, and as it hit the tarmac, it spat back up and broke the footrest, so that kept folding up during the race. It was a little difficult for a couple of laps until I got used to it," he explained.

That was the order set until the finish, in a processional race symptomatic of the worst of the character of the 800s. Stoner did close up slightly on Lorenzo, the gap down to 1.3 seconds after seven laps. Then it started to grow again: 2.5 seconds at half-distance, and a yawning 7.4 as they started the final lap.

Pedrosa was still barely three seconds behind Stoner, while Rossi was fully 14 seconds adrift of the Honda. The Spaniard had set fastest lap, a new record, on the 11th.

Fifth-placed Edwards also saw little action, circulating steadily – a bit slower than those ahead, a little faster than those behind.

There was some hand-to-hand combat in the next group, led at first by Capirossi from Hayden, with Kallio and Dovizioso close. By lap three, Elias had caught up and was pushing hard; Toseland tagged on behind, but seesawed a bit at the back of the gang.

Capirossi made a big slip and dropped to ninth on lap five, Kallio taking over for the next two laps – until he crashed out. Now Hayden headed the gang, but Dovizioso got ahead of him on lap seven; Elias followed him past on the next lap.

Dovi was on Öhlins suspension again and had the best pace. He pulled gradually clear, by more than two seconds on lap 16. Soon afterwards, however, Elias, a former winner here, started to close up once more. He got there on lap 23 and swept straight past, staying ahead to the finish – by inches, as Dovizioso made a final vain lunge over the line.

By half-distance, Capirossi had also got ahead of Hayden, but there was trouble to come. On lap 20, he suddenly slowed and cruised to the pits. The official reason was a slick-shift fault that switched the ECU into 'safe' mode, rather than a serious engine problem. Events at the next race suggested this was a smoke screen.

Hayden was now alone in eighth, the challenge from Toseland finally having run out of steam with eight laps to go.

De Puniet had an odd problem as he shifted his weight for the first corner. His boot zip had caught in the fairing and was undone. He spent the next three laps trying to do it up again, dropping to last in the process. Three laps later, he was closing on Vermeulen, who would be promoted to 11th two laps later when de Angelis retired with electrical problems.

The Frenchman caught and eventually passed Vermeulen, who was suffering back pain from a crash during motocross training. De Puniet was also still nursing his ankle injury, so it was a battle of invalids. Vermeulen reversed the positions again on lap 20, and had pulled clear by the end.

A long way back, Melandri had battled with Canepa for almost the whole race, finally taking 12th just two-hundredths ahead. Talmacsi was a distant 14th, losing touch with this pair before half-distance.

250cc RACE – 26 laps

The top three qualified within a tenth: Barbera was narrowly fastest from Bautista – his first front row in five races – and Simoncelli. Aoyama was a couple of tenths down. Debon had a big crash in practice and was stretchered off, but still headed the second row.

Unusually the first race of the day, the 250 contest had only a little more variety in the lead than the MotoGP. Bautista led the first three laps, while Simoncelli made his way up from a bad start, sixth on lap one. But the Gilera rider was up to second on the third lap, and took the lead firmly next time around. From then on, he was secure up front, although still only one second ahead at half-distance. He had more to offer, however, and as the race wore on, he pulled steadily away to win by more than five seconds. His fastest lap, short of the record, was the 17th.

Pole-starter Barbera also got away well and harried Bautista in the early stages. As they started lap five, they managed to push each other wide in the first corner, letting on-form class rookie de Rosa into second.

Later on the same lap, disaster struck Bautista. As

he closed the throttle at the end of the back straight, his engine seized solid and he went tumbling into the gravel.

De Rosa's glory lasted only one more lap before he too crashed – one of eight to go down on the bumpy and difficult track.

By now, di Meglio had caught up impressively, after a storming ride from ninth on lap one, and was pressing Barbera hard. On lap 11, he got ahead for the first time, but the Spaniard fought back and was second again from laps 14 to 19.

Then it was di Meglio again, but there was nothing in it. Di Meglio was ahead as they started the last lap, Barbera in front as they dashed to the line. But his French rival had got a better run out of the last corner and pulled right alongside over the line.

It was a dead heat, but second went to di Meglio, because his best lap had been fractionally faster.

As in practice, Aoyama had never quite been on the pace, lying seventh when Bautista fell. Attrition promoted him to a distant fourth, and there he finished. It was all he could do to stay ahead of the increasingly impressive Cluzel, who had seen off a pressing Wilairot: the improving Thai got ahead mid-race, but lost touch after running wide.

Luthi was seventh after a mainly lonely and undistinguished race; Pasini was eighth. Debon got back up to ninth after staying with the front group in the early laps, running off, then recovering to pass the battling Czech pair of Abraham and Pesek, who were at it to the flag.

Locatelli and Tomizawa also crashed out.

Aoyama was lucky to extend his points lead to 26 over non-scorer Bautista, but Simoncelli was now just two behind the Spaniard as he resumed his end-of-season charge.

125cc RACE – 23 laps

Simon dominated practice and qualifying, with Espargaro and Smith moving up to take the next two places at the end. Smith was nursing badly bruised ankles after a heavy high-side on the first day.

Simon was the first leader, displaced by Terol from laps two to six, the lead group swelling to ten so that when Terol made a small slip, he dropped to sixth, handing a short-lived lead to Smith. The Briton ran wide at the end of the back straight, and as he fought for control on the kerb at the exit, Terol ran into him, falling in the middle of the group. Miraculously, nobody else crashed.

Now Simon led again, and he stretched the gap with increasing authority, more than five seconds ahead at the end of lap 16. He never finished the next lap, however, sliding off all alone, remounting in 13th and gaining one place by the end.

Iannone had tumbled out on lap three, Corsi also on lap eight and Marquez on lap 12, the last two both second at the time. Bradl had faded off the back.

Smith led a gang of three, but Espargaro took over on the last lap to win by almost half a second. Cortese was second, less than two-tenths ahead of Smith, who said, "I must have thought too much about last-lap tactics, and suddenly I was third."

Bradl was fourth. Olive came through to fifth, ahead of Gadea, Rabat, Aegerter and Zarco, with tenth-placed Krummenacher off the back by the end. Webb had been with this group, going for a best-ever finish, only to break down on the last lap. Equally luckless, Redding was just out of the points after suffering a broken swing-arm and consequent crash in the run up to the race.

Above: Dead heat! Di Meglio (nearer the camera) and Barbera could not be separated, even by a photo-finish. A faster lap gave second to di Meglio.

Left: Sandro Cortese's best ever second in the 125 race was his first podium of 2009.

Top left: Pedrosa (third) congratulates Stoner (second) on his blazing return, while doubtless wishing he'd stayed in Australia.

Below: Espargaro, Smith, Cortese – the 125 leaders were this close to the end.

Photos: Gold & Goose

CIRCUITO DO ESTORIL

Key
kph/mph
Gear **2**

Variante 58/36 **1**

3 Turn 8 145/90

Esses 105/65 **2**

Turn 3 74/46 **1**

2 Orelha 87/54

Turn 2 131/82 **2**

5 Recta da Meta 245/153

1 VIP 81/50

Turn 1 76/47 **1**

2 Parabolica Interior 95/59

5 Parabolica 210/131

Circuit 4.182km/2.598 miles

MotoGP

RACE DISTANCE: 28 laps, 72.760 miles/117.096 km • RACE WEATHER: Dry (air 24°, humidity 32%, track 41°)

Pos.	Rider	Nat.	No.	Entrant	Machine	Tyres	Laps	Time & speed
1	Jorge Lorenzo	SPA	99	Fiat Yamaha Team	Yamaha	B	28	45m 35.522s 99.028mph/ 154.001km/h
2	Casey Stoner	AUS	27	Ducati Marlboro Team	Ducati	B	28	45m 41.816s
3	Dani Pedrosa	SPA	3	Repsol Honda Team	Honda	B	28	45m 45.411s
4	Valentino Rossi	ITA	46	Fiat Yamaha Team	Yamaha	B	28	45m 58.950s
5	Colin Edwards	USA	5	Monster Yamaha Tech 3	Yamaha	B	28	46m 08.174s
6	Toni Elias	SPA	24	San Carlos Honda Gresini	Honda	B	28	46m 11.231s
7	Andrea Dovizioso	ITA	4	Repsol Honda Team	Honda	B	28	46m 11.245s
8	Nicky Hayden	USA	69	Ducati Marlboro Team	Ducati	B	28	46m 14.352s
9	James Toseland	JPN	52	Monster Yamaha Tech 3	Yamaha	B	28	46m 19.615s
10	Chris Vermeulen	AUS	7	Rizla Suzuki MotoGP	Suzuki	B	28	46m 28.385s
11	Randy de Puniet	FRA	14	LCR Honda MotoGP	Honda	B	28	46m 31.220s
12	Marco Melandri	ITA	33	Hayate Racing Team	Kawasaki	B	28	46m 40.037s
13	Niccolo Canepa	USA	88	Pramac Racing	Ducati	B	28	46m 40.060s
14	Gabor Talmacsi	HUN	41	Scot Racing Team MotoGP	Honda	B	28	47m 02.821s
	Loris Capirossi	ITA	65	Rizla Suzuki MotoGP	Suzuki	B	8	33m 23.887s
	Alex de Angelis	RSM	15	San Carlos Honda Gresini	Honda	B	20	13m 44.836s
	Mika Kallio	FIN	36	Ducati Marlboro Team	Ducati	B	23	8m 18.517s

Fastest lap: Dani Pedrosa, on lap 11, 1m 36.937s, 96.504mph/155.309km/h (record).

Previous lap record: Jorge Lorenzo, ESP (Yamaha), 1m 37.404s, 96.402mph/160.305km/h (2008).

Event best maximum speed: Canepa, 203.561mph/327.6km/h (free practice 1).

Qualifying: Dry
Air: 28° Humidity: 19% Track: 37°

1	Lorenzo	1m 36.214s
2	Rossi	1m 36.474s
3	Stoner	1m 36.528s
4	Pedrosa	1m 36.702s
5	Edwards	1m 37.142s
6	de Puniet	1m 37.448s
7	Capirossi	1m 37.489s
8	Dovizioso	1m 37.541s
9	Hayden	1m 37.654s
10	Kallio	1m 37.813s
11	de Angelis	1m 37.822s
12	Toseland	1m 37.823s
13	Elias	1m 37.911s
14	Canepa	1m 38.042s
15	Vermeulen	1m 38.342s
16	Melandri	1m 38.538s
17	Talmacsi	1m 39.320s

Fastest race laps

1	Pedrosa	1m 36.937s
2	Lorenzo	1m 36.967s
3	Stoner	1m 37.132s
4	Rossi	1m 37.348s
5	Edwards	1m 37.751s
6	Kallio	1m 37.937s
7	Elias	1m 38.081s
8	Dovizioso	1m 38.161s
9	Hayden	1m 38.168s
10	Capirossi	1m 38.291s
11	Toseland	1m 38.419s
12	de Angelis	1m 38.600s
13	de Puniet	1m 38.746s
14	Vermeulen	1m 38.930s
15	Melandri	1m 39.137s
16	Canepa	1m 39.186s
17	Talmacsi	1m 39.383s

Championship Points

1	Rossi	250
2	Lorenzo	232
3	Pedrosa	173
4	Stoner	170
5	Dovizioso	142
6	Edwards	134
7	Capirossi	97
8	de Puniet	93
9	Melandri	91
10	Elias	90
11	Vermeulen	90
12	de Angelis	88
13	Toseland	85
14	Hayden	81
15	Kallio	51
16	Canepa	38
17	Talmacsi	14
18	Gibernau	12
19	Takahashi	9
20	Espargaro, A	8

Constructor Points

1	Yamaha	330
2	Honda	236
3	Ducati	211
4	Suzuki	126
5	Kawasaki	91

Team Points

1	FIAT Yamaha Team	482
2	Repsol Honda Team	315
3	Ducati Marlboro Team	268
4	Monster Yamaha Tech 3	219
5	RIZLA Suzuki MotoGP	187
6	San Carlo Honda Gresini	178
7	LCR Honda MotoGP	93
8	Hayate Racing Team	91
9	Pramac Racing	80
10	Scot Racing Team	23
11	Grupo Francisco Hernando	12

Grid order	1	2	3	4	5	6	7	8	9	10	11	12	13	14	15	16	17	18	19	20	21	22	23	24	25	26	27	28	
99 LORENZO	99	99	99	99	99	99	99	99	99	99	99	99	99	99	99	99	99	99	99	99	99	99	99	99	99	99	99	99	1
46 ROSSI	3	3	27	27	27	27	27	27	27	27	27	27	27	27	27	27	27	27	27	27	27	27	27	27	27	27	27	27	2
27 STONER	27	27	3	3	3	3	3	3	3	3	3	3	3	3	3	3	3	3	3	3	3	3	3	3	3	3	3	3	3
3 PEDROSA	46	46	46	46	46	46	46	46	46	46	46	46	46	46	46	46	46	46	46	46	46	46	46	46	46	46	46	46	4
5 EDWARDS	5	5	5	5	5	5	5	5	5	5	5	5	5	5	5	5	5	5	5	5	5	5	5	5	5	5	5	5	5
14 DE PUNIET	65	65	65	36	36	69	4	4	4	4	4	4	4	4	4	4	4	4	4	4	4	4	4	24	24	24	24	24	6
65 CAPIROSSI	69	69	69	69	69	4	69	24	24	24	24	24	24	24	24	24	24	24	24	24	24	24	4	4	4	4	4	4	7
4 DOVIZIOSO	36	36	36	65	4	24	24	69	69	69	69	69	69	65	65	65	65	65	69	69	69	69	69	69	69	69	69	69	8
69 HAYDEN	4	4	4	4	65	65	65	65	65	65	65	65	65	69	69	69	69	69	52	52	52	52	52	52	52	52	52	52	9
36 KALLIO	14	24	24	24	24	52	52	52	52	52	52	52	52	52	52	52	52	52	7	7	7	7	7	7	7	7	7	7	10
15 DE ANGELIS	52	52	52	52	52	15	7	7	7	7	7	7	14	14	14	14	7	7	14	14	14	14	14	14	14	14	14	14	11
52 TOSELAND	24	33	15	15	15	7	14	14	14	14	14	14	7	7	7	7	14	14	33	33	33	33	33	33	33	33			12
24 ELIAS	33	15	33	33	7	14	33	33	88	88	88	88	88	88	88	88	88	33	88	88	88	88	88	88	88	88			13
88 CANEPA	41	7	7	7	33	33	41	41	41	33	33	33	33	33	33	33	33	88	65	41	41	41	41	41	41	41			14
7 VERMEULEN	7	41	41	88	14	88	88	88	88	41	41	41	41	41	41	41	41	41	41										
33 MELANDRI	15	88	88	14	88	41	15	15																					
41 TALMACSI	88	14	14	41	41																								

250cc — RACE DISTANCE: 26 laps, 67.562 miles/108.732 km • RACE WEATHER: Dry (air 23°, humidity 62%, track 33°)

Pos.	Rider	Nat.	No.	Entrant	Machine	Laps	Time & Speed
1	Marco Simoncelli	ITA	58	Metis Gilera	Gilera	26	44m 04.298s
							(mph/km/h)
							94.411/148.029
2	Mike di Meglio	FRA	63	Mapfre Aspar Team 250cc	Aprilia	26	44m 09.615s
3	Hector Barbera	SPA	40	Pepe World Team	Aprilia	26	44m 09.615s
4	Hiroshi Aoyama	JPN	4	Scot Racing Team 250cc	Honda	26	44m 16.322s
5	Jules Cluzel	FRA	16	Matteoni Racing	Aprilia	26	44m 18.647s
6	Ratthapark Wilairot	THA	14	Thai Honda PTT SAG	Honda	26	44m 22.554s
7	Thomas Luthi	SWI	12	Emmi – Caffe Latte	Aprilia	26	44m 31.929s
8	Mattia Pasini	ITA	75	Team Globalgest	Aprilia	26	44m 38.965s
9	Alex Debon	ESP	6	Aeropuerto – Castello – Blusens	Aprilia	26	44m 49.708s
10	Karel Abraham	CZE	17	Cardion AB Motoracing	Aprilia	26	44m 50.189s
11	Lukas Pesek	CZE	52	Auto Kelly – CP	Aprilia	26	44m 50.502s
12	Shuhei Aoyama	JPN	73	Racing Team Germany	Honda	26	45m 01.939s
13	Valentin Debise	FRA	53	CIP Moto – GP250	Honda	26	45m 25.607s
14	Alex Baldolini	ITA	25	WTR San Marino Team	Aprilia	26	45m 39.575s
15	Axel Pons	SPA	7	Pepe World Team	Aprilia	25	44m 12.221s
16	Balazs Nemeth	HUN	11	Balatonring Team	Aprilia	25	44m 23.793s
17	Bastien Chesaux	SWI	8	Racing Team Germany	Honda	25	44m 36.584s
18	Imre Toth	HUN	10	Team Toth Aprilia	Aprilia	25	45m 30.295s
19	Christopher Moretti	ITA	88	Matteoni Racing	Aprilia	24	45m 10.459s
	Vladimir Leonov	RUS	56	Viessmann Kiefer Racing	Aprilia	24	42m 24.157s
	Shoya Tomizawa	JPN	48	CIP Moto – GP250	Honda	12	20m 44.573s
	Roberto Locatelli	ITA	15	Metis Gilera	Gilera	9	15m 29.036s
	Raffaele de Rosa	ITA	35	Scot Racing Team 250cc	Honda	7	13m 30.519s
	Alvaro Bautista	SPA	19	Mapfre Aspar Team	Aprilia	4	6m 52.842s
	Hector Faubel	SPA	55	Honda SAG	Honda	4	6m 55.786s

Fastest lap: Marco Simoncelli, on lap 27, 1m 40.863s, 92.747mph/149.263km/h.
Lap record: Alvaro Bautista, SPA (Aprilia) 1m 40.521s, 93.063mph/149.771km/h (2007).
Event best maximum speed: Barbera, 177.090mph/285.0km/h (free practice 2).

Qualifying: Dry
Air: 31° Humidity: 17% Track: 41°

1	Barbera	1m 40.596s
2	Bautista	1m 40.654s
3	Simoncelli	1m 40.684s
4	Aoyama, Hiroshi	1m 40.879s
5	Debon	1m 41.008s
6	de Rosa	1m 41.169s
7	Pasini	1m 41.182s
8	Wilairot	1m 41.190s
9	Cluzel	1m 41.205s
10	di Meglio	1m 41.353s
11	Faubel	1m 41.537s
12	Abraham	1m 41.728s
13	Luthi	1m 41.764s
14	Locatelli	1m 41.794s
15	Aoyama, Shuhei	1m 42.194s
16	Baldolini	1m 42.312s
17	Tomizawa	1m 42.348s
18	Pesek	1m 42.659s
19	Debise	1m 43.427s
20	Pons	1m 43.445s
21	Nemeth	1m 44.305s
22	Leonov	1m 44.583s
23	Chesaux	1m 45.605s
	Not within 107%	
	Moretti	1m 47.971s
	Toth	1m 48.795s

Fastest race laps

1	Simoncelli	1m 40.863s
2	di Meglio	1m 40.961s
3	Barbera	1m 41.169s
4	de Rosa	1m 41.202s
5	Wilairot	1m 41.386s
6	Bautista	1m 41.471s
7	Cluzel	1m 41.569s
8	Aoyama, Hiroshi	1m 41.652s
9	Locatelli	1m 41.759s
10	Luthi	1m 41.843s
11	Faubel	1m 41.934s
12	Pasini	1m 42.139s
13	Debon	1m 42.175s
14	Baldolini	1m 42.218s
15	Tomizawa	1m 42.242s
16	Pesek	1m 42.311s
17	Abraham	1m 42.433s
18	Aoyama, Shuhei	1m 43.003s
19	Debise	1m 43.657s
20	Pons	1m 43.913s
21	Leonov	1m 44.905s
22	Nemeth	1m 45.318s
23	Chesaux	1m 46.085s
24	Moretti	1m 46.532s
25	Toth	1m 47.257s

Championship Points

1	Aoyama, Hiroshi	218
2	Bautista	192
3	Simoncelli	190
4	Barbera	174
5	Pasini	128
6	di Meglio	94
7	de Rosa	90
8	Debon	89
9	Luthi	89
10	Faubel	86
11	Locatelli	78
12	Cluzel	69
13	Pesek	58
14	Wilairot	53
15	Abraham	50
16	Talmacsi	28
17	Baldolini	26
18	Tomizawa	25
19	Espargaro, Aleix	22
20	Aoyama, Shuhei	14
21	Debise	14
22	Toth	12
23	Leonov	8
24	Pons	3
25	Nemeth	3
26	Markham	2
27	Watanabe	2
28	Chesaux	1
29	Bonsey	1

Constructors
1	Aprilia	274
2	Honda	230
3	Gilera	197
4	Yamaha	2

125cc — RACE DISTANCE: 23 laps, 59.767 miles/96.186 km • RACE WEATHER: Dry (air 23°, humidity 36%, track 28°)

Pos.	Rider	Nat.	No.	Entrant	Machine	Laps	Time & Speed
1	Pol Espargaro	SPA	44	Derbi Racing Team	Derbi	22	41m 00.421s
							(mph/km/h)
							87.448/140.735
2	Sandro Cortese	GER	11	Ajo Interwetten	Derbi	23	41m 00.815s
3	Bradley Smith	GB	38	Bancaja Aspar Team 125cc	Aprilia	23	41m 01.002s
4	Stefan Bradl	GER	17	Viessmann Kiefer Racing	Aprilia	23	41m 11.469s
5	Joan Olive	SPA	6	Derbi Racing Team	Derbi	23	41m 17.251s
6	Sergio Gadea	SPA	33	Bancaja Aspar Team 125cc	Aprilia	23	41m 17.591s
7	Esteve Rabat	SPA	12	Blusens Aprilia	Aprilia	23	41m 17.721s
8	Dominique Aegerter	SWI	77	Ajo Interwetten	Derbi	23	41m 17.967s
9	Johann Zarco	FRA	14	WTR San Marino Team	Aprilia	23	41m 18.087s
10	Randy Krummenacher	SWI	35	Degraaf Grand Prix	Aprilia	23	41m 21.799s
11	Takaaki Nakagami	JPN	73	Ongetta Team I.S.P.A.	Aprilia	23	41m 26.733s
12	Julian Simon	SPA	60	Bancaja Aspar Team 125cc	Aprilia	23	41m 31.921s
13	Lorenzo Zanetti	ITA	8	Ongetta Team I.S.P.A.	Aprilia	23	41m 34.615s
14	Jonas Folger	GER	94	Ongetta Team I.S.P.A.	Aprilia	23	41m 35.444s
15	Luis Salom	SPA	39	Jack & Jones Team	Honda	23	41m 54.664s
16	Scott Redding	GB	45	Blusens Aprilia	Aprilia	23	41m 54.753s
17	Jasper Iwema	NED	53	Racing Team Germany	Aprilia	23	42m 03.415s
18	Alberto Moncayo	SPA	42	Andalucia Aprilia	Aprilia	23	42m 03.475s
19	Sturla Fagerhaug	NOR	51	Red Bull KTM Moto Sport	KTM	23	42m 03.482s
20	Johnny Rosell	SPA	43	Blusens BQR	Aprilia	23	42m 24.592s
21	Jacub Jantulik	SVK	70	JJ Racing Team	Aprilia	23	42m 37.800s
22	Luca Vitali	ITA	10	CBC Corse	Aprilia	23	42m 51.011s
23	Quentin Jacquet	FRA	19	Matteoni Racing	Aprilia	23	42m 51.273s
24	Jordi Dalmau	SPA	31	SAG-Castrol	Honda	22	41m 00.641s
25	Jakub Kornfeil	CZE	21	Loncin Racing	Loncin	22	42m 03.732s
	Danny Webb	GB	99	Degraaf Grand Prix	Aprilia	22	39m 30.279s
	Michael Ranseder	AUT	88	CBC Corse	Aprilia	17	30m 47.680s
	Luca Marconi	FRA	87	CBC Corse	Aprilia	13	24m 08.623s
	Marc Marquez	SPA	93	Red Bull KTM Moto Sport	KTM	12	21m 24.202s
	Simon Corsi	ITA	24	Fontana Racing	Aprilia	9	16m 05.713s
	Nicolas Terol	SPA	18	Jack & Jones Team	Aprilia	8	15m 13.862s
	Efren Vazquez	SPA	7	Derbi Racing Team	Derbi	7	12m 34.761s
	Cameron Beaubier	USA	16	Red Bull KTM Moto Sport	KTM	4	7m 23.498s
	Tomoyoshi Koyama	JPN	71	Loncin Racing	Loncin	3	6m 20.383
	Andrea Iannone	ITA	29	Ongetta Team I.S.P.A.	Aprilia	2	3m 40.829

Fastest lap: Sandro Cortese, on lap 11, 1m 45.722, 88.485mph/142.403km/h.
Previous lap record: Gabor Talmacsi, HUN (Aprilia), 1m 45.027s, 89.070mph/143.345km/h (2007).
Event best maximum speed: Cortese (Derbi), 152.541mph/245.6km/h (race).

Qualifying: Dry
Air: 32° Humidity: 18% Track: 36°

1	Simon	1m 45.199s
2	Espargaro, Pol	1m 45.739s
3	Smith	1m 45.775s
4	Marquez	1m 46.056s
5	Bradl	1m 46.056s
6	Terol	1m 46.099s
7	Cortese	1m 46.187s
8	Corsi	1m 46.307s
9	Iannone	1m 46.310s
10	Webb	1m 46.442s
11	Gadea	1m 46.578s
12	Vazquez	1m 46.621s
13	Olive	1m 46.665s
14	Nakagami	1m 46.700s
15	Aegerter	1m 46.704s
16	Zarco	1m 46.821s
17	Rabat	1m 46.884s
18	Krummenacher	1m 47.470s
19	Folger	1m 47.502s
20	Ranseder	1m 47.697s
21	Salom	1m 48.089s
22	Zanetti	1m 48.183s
23	Moncayo	1m 48.232s
24	Redding	1m 48.316s
25	Iwema	1m 48.329s
26	Beaubier	1m 48.465s
27	Fagerhaug	1m 48.588s
28	Koyama	1m 48.764s
29	Marconi	1m 49.256s
30	Kornfeil	1m 49.472s
31	Rosell	1m 49.856s
32	Jacquet	1m 50.031s
33	Jantulik	1m 51.077s
34	Dalmau	1m 51.121s
35	Vitali	1m 51.257s

Fastest race laps

1	Cortese	1m 45.722s
2	Simon	1m 45.860s
3	Corsi	1m 45.887s
4	Marquez	1m 45.933s
5	Vazquez	1m 45.988s
6	Espargaro, Pol	1m 46.004s
7	Smith	1m 46.029s
8	Iannone	1m 46.430s
9	Bradl	1m 44.280s
10	Olive	1m 46.446s
11	Gadea	1m 46.522s
12	Zarco	1m 46.632s
13	Terol	1m 46.638s
14	Aegerter	1m 46.689s
15	Nakagami	1m 46.744s
16	Webb	1m 46.802s
17	Ranseder	1m 46.831s
18	Marconi	1m 46.838s
19	Krummenacher	1m 46.869s
20	Rabat	1m 46.912s
21	Zanetti	1m 47.118s
22	Redding	1m 47.594s
23	Folger	1m 47.677s
24	Salom	1m 48.061s
25	Iwema	1m 48.394s
26	Fagerhaug	1m 48.686s
27	Moncayo	1m 48.699s
28	Koyama	1m 48.775s
29	Beaubier	1m 48.825s
30	Rosell	1m 49.454s
31	Jantulik	1m 49.583s
32	Kornfeil	1m 49.689s
33	Jacquet	1m 50.191s
34	Vitali	1m 50.765s
35	Dalmau	1m 50.826s

Championship Points

1	Simon	214
2	Smith	163.5
3	Terol	152.5
4	Espargaro, Pol	129.5
5	Gadea	122
6	Iannone	109.5
7	Cortese	96
8	Marquez	87
9	Bradl	85
10	Olive	74
11	Folger	71
12	Aegerter	59.5
13	Corsi	57
14	Redding	45.5
15	Nakagami	36
16	Vazquez	36
17	Webb	35.5
18	Zarco	31.5
19	Rabat	28
20	Zanetti	27
21	Krummenacher	21
22	Salom	17
23	Koyama	17
24	Savadori	7
25	Schrotter	7
26	Ranseder	5
27	Moretti	3
28	Iwema	3
29	Beaubier	3
30	Glossop	2
31	Fritz	2
30	di Carlo	2
33	Kartheininger	1

Constructors
1	Aprilia	298.5
2	Derbi	168
3	KTM	89
4	Loncin	17
5	Honda	14

AUSTRALIAN GRAND PRIX

PHILLIP ISLAND

Formation racing down under.
All-Australian comeback kid Stoner
stayed in front all the way.
Photo: Gold & Goose

THE 125 title was decided in Australia, popular Spaniard Julian Simon securing it with another win. The 250 race became closer than ever, after a strange series of events. But for MotoGP, the growing title tension was broken at Phillip Island, by the corner that many riders name as their favourite: the beautiful and daunting turn one.

Approached at top speed, it is one of those places that combines the violence and force of motorcycle racing with the subtlety of touch that marks out the best of the best. The approach is difficult and accuracy is paramount. Errors are punished, often severely: Kenny Roberts Junior is one who knows to his cost.

In 2009, the worst victim, in terms of injury, was Niccolò Canepa: a typical long fast slide in first free practice left him with his right elbow so badly skinned and gashed that he would need skin grafts, and would not complete his rookie season.

For the championship, it was Lorenzo. The previous weekend in Portugal had tipped the balance his way, and he summed it up neatly: "To win the title, I have to win all three races…or at least two. So it is not so easy, but I have this option, and don't have anything to lose. So I am going to try."

Instead, he made one of those mistakes that reveal his relative youth: running impetuously fast into the first corner right after the start, he rammed into the back of Hayden's Ducati, smashing his front brake in the process, and eventually had to abandon ship as, unable to slow down, he ran out of road on the exit. Luckily, his only injury was a cut to his nose.

Rossi didn't win, but second gained him a comfortable 38-point advantage. With just two races left, he was at match point.

Hayden, by the way, after being punted off by Lorenzo, had a wild ride across the grass infield and rejoined way at the back; he never did get out of last place, finishing a lap adrift. It was his second narrow escape at turn one: during practice, he'd had the rear wheel lock on entry, but had managed to save the subsequent disaster.

To the 50,000-plus fans who endured the signature icy winds of the track, which the late Barry Sheene used to call "the gateway to hypothermia", the championship was of minimal interest, compared with the importance of yet another home-grown hero repeating the feats of Gardner and Doohan, and winning his home GP. For the third time in succession. And a proper Aussie battler at that, marking his comeback from the doors of burn-out hell with an emphatic victory. Wearing special home-race Oz-themed white leathers and paint (Hayden had had special livery for his two home GPs, so why shouldn't he?), Casey was certainly back.

Not so much a returning hero, however: Stoner's road-racing career had been in Europe from the start, but he knew enough to smile at complaints about those icy winds, which were present with a vengeance, along with the usual occasional squalls. It was a pity, opined Rossi and others, that the GP was held at this time of year, when the weather at the other end of the season was so much better. Stoner: "At times, this island can throw up the most perfect, beautiful weekend in the world, and other weekends it'll just be horrible, even in the middle of summer. I suppose it's part of its beauty. There's never really a good time to come here."

The weekend started badly for Rossi, with shocking news from home, broken to him as he prepared for the first practice: his estranged stepfather, mother Stefania's third husband, had been found dead by his own hand after a row with his wife. Another trial of strength, of a quite different kind. Suffice to say that he passed the weekend with his usual fortitude, declining to comment on the matter.

It was a punishing weekend for the increasingly beleaguered Suzuki team, at a circuit that has for some years brought out the worst in its bike. First there was the extra engine: Capirossi's breakdown in Portugal had signalled problems – not actually of major components, but in the valve gear: "Taking the cam cover off and fiddling a bit would fix it; it's not a major component. But you're not allowed to take the cam cover off." Thus Suzuki was the first and in fact the only company to fall foul of the engine endurance regulations: punished by the loss of ten constructors'

points and Capirossi being made to start from the back of the grid.

Thing is, he was almost at the back anyway: he'd qualified 13th, while team-mate Vermeulen was 15th, only Talmacsi behind him. But these were still MotoGP prototypes – carbon brakes, Bridgestone mixed-compound tyres – so you'd expect them to be running respectable times, especially on pure qualifying runs. So imagine the red faces when, on the same day, a modified street bike, running under restrictive Australian Superbike rules, went faster. In a race. On Dunlops. Vermeulen's best lap was at 1m 32.338s; Wayne Maxwell's Honda CBR1000RR clocked 1m 32.316s.

The tension was rising in the 250 class, which may have explained the normally calm Aoyama's temper fit in the first practice, when he aimed a kick at Axel Pons as they ran on to the front straight. It was done in full view of the TV cameras, so he could hardly wriggle out of the US$1,000 fine imposed on him by race direction. This disciplinary move came in the wake of an open letter from FIM president Vito Ippolito, addressed to all GP riders and prompted by the finish-line scrap at Misano between 125 combatants Iannone and Espargaro, beseeching them to behave with more decorum and respect.

Team Toth having departed, Pasini's bike was in different colours again: he had dug into his own pocket to help get Paddock GP Racing Team's mechanics and bike to the track. He fell on a damp patch in qualifying, and almost had to fight the marshals to recover his bike and rejoin the fray, to avoid failing to qualify. Then he crashed in the race anyway.

MotoGP RACE – 27 laps

The second practice was hit by bad weather, but by then Stoner was fastest, and he stayed there to claim pole from Rossi by half a tenth, Pedrosa narrowly taking the last spot on the front row from Lorenzo, but both seven-tenths down. It was Lorenzo and his crew chief Forcada's turn to be hunting the right balance.

As per the usual script, Pedrosa got away first, but as they started the second lap both Stoner and Rossi went past, and though the Spaniard tried to hang on for two or three laps, he simply didn't have the pace and settled into third.

Up front, Stoner led and Rossi followed, very closely. With Lorenzo out and the championship in mind, "keeping five per cent", he was unwilling to risk an attack, but ready to stalk the Australian diligently and profit from any errors.

Unfortunately for him, Casey wasn't about to make any; but Rossi enjoyed the track anyway and, watching Stoner slide the rear on the last set of fast lefts, knew that he was doing the same. "This is the last

Above: His master's voice? Rossi speaks, Lorenzo watches his words. Stoner watches both of them.

Left: Suzuki pair Vermeulen and Capirossi. The bike dislikes the track, and it seems the opposite is also true.

Photos: Gold & Goose

track where sliding helps the lap time like four or five years ago," he said. "At other tracks, if you slide, it means you lose time."

The pressure was relentless: Rossi set fastest lap fifth time around – just short of the record – and the gap was seldom more than half a second. Only on one lap, the 21st, was it more than a second, and it closed up again at once – until on the last lap, Rossi finally settled for the runner-up spot.

For Stoner, the win was vindication. "I can't ask for more," he said, thanking everyone from his family to the team for their support. "We definitely made the right decision to take that time off and find our way."

Behind the leaders, de Angelis confounded his critics once again, away clear in fourth from the first lap and continuing to pull away in a lonely, but worthy afternoon's work. Only in the closing laps did he start to come under rather vague pressure from a renascent Colin Edwards, who began closing steadily – but even then it was from a distance, the American three seconds adrift at the flag.

It had been a familiar sort of race for the Texan: a poor start, finishing lap one ninth and taking a few more to pick up his pace. Up one place on lap four, he was with the midfield pack – and past them next time around in the fifth place where he so often finds himself. There he would stay, lonely to the end, but kept honest all the way.

Dovizioso had started better than Edwards, but also took time to get going, losing a place to de Puniet on the second lap, then to Edwards as well. When he did pick up his rhythm, Kallio was in front of him, and it wasn't until three laps into the second half of the race that he got past. He escaped, but it was too late for him to do anything more, and he was alone behind Edwards at the end.

At one point, the battle for seventh involved four riders, Melandri, de Puniet and Elias chasing Kallio. But both the Ducati rider and Elias would run into

different tyre problems. Kallio's front started to slide, while Elias complained of inconsistency with the asymmetrical rear, which had faded so much by the end that he was losing two seconds a lap. "That's just ridiculous," he said.

That left Melandri and de Puniet duking it out; they finished in that order, separated by half a second.

The Suzukis finished in close formation in 11th and 12th, with Talmacsi behind them.

Then came the stragglers, each with a sad story. Toseland was highly disgruntled after being called in for a ride-through penalty for a jumped start – something he denied vociferously. "I feel the decision was incredibly harsh – I've looked at the start on TV and I can't see I've done anything wrong," he said.

Hayden was 15th and last, after his turn-one misadventure – the third time in the season that he had been the innocent victim of a first-lap collision. He had lost more than 20 seconds after riding across the gravel and the grass, and the trip didn't seem to have done his bike much good, because he felt the handling was queasy from then on. He continued to lose time, wondering whether to pull in, especially after he was lapped. "I didn't want to get in anybody's way," he said. It was a disappointment at a favourite track – he still holds the lap record there.

250cc RACE – 18 laps

Aoyama's team-mate, class rookie de Rosa, claimed a career-first pole in an iffy drying qualifying session, with Simoncelli alongside and only then Aoyama. Debon completed the front row; Barbera led the second, Bautista was in tenth, on row three.

Debon led away, but ran off on to the grass before half the lap was down, rejoining right at the back. That handed the lead to Simoncelli, and he would keep it to the end, for a second valuable win in succession. It brought his season total to six, five of them in

the previous seven races. He was beginning to look unstoppable.

It was all the more important for the championship, after a series of events in which the hapless involvement of both riders' team-mates conspired to stop the race early, and put Aoyama seventh.

Barbera went with Simoncelli, de Rosa joining on as Faubel dropped back into a gang of eight disputing fourth. Aoyama seemed stuck in the middle, while Bautista found his way through it to close again on the leaders on lap eight. On the same lap, Pasini crashed out from the back of the chase pack.

Cluzel was at the head of it, and not holding them up either. Then, on lap 13, just after the expected mid-point of a race scheduled for 25 laps, di Meglio got past for a first time; Aoyama, Abraham, Faubel and Wilairot were right behind.

Three laps later, di Meglio passed his privateer compatriot again and on this occasion made it stick for a while. At the same time, with supposedly nine laps to go, Aoyama started to move forward.

As they finished lap 19, he was heading the group in fourth, with team-mate de Rosa over two seconds ahead. But the Scot pit hung out a signal instructing the junior rider to slow down, to give way to Aoyama. And on that lap, fourth became third when Bautista slipped off at the slow hairpin. He got going again almost at once to finish the lap tenth.

But something quite different was unfolding behind them. Coming out of MG hairpin, Simoncelli's team-mate, Locatelli, lying 13th, had a heavy high-side crash, landing apparently unconscious in the middle of the track. The red flags came out at once, and all tactical plans were perforce cancelled.

Results were taken from lap 18, with Barbera and de Rosa second and third. And Aoyama down in seventh, behind Cluzel (who also crashed on lap 19!), di Meglio and Abraham.

Faubel and Wilairot were still close behind; Bautis-

ta was inches ahead of Luthi for tenth, while Pesek was close behind him. Debon came through from the very back to regain 13th.

Simoncelli's win and Aoyama's ill-timed bad luck closed the points gap between the pair to 12. The charismatic Italian was on a roll, while the calculating Japanese was on the back foot. With two races left before the end of the 250 class, it was winding up to a cliff-hanger finish.

125cc RACE – 23 laps

Espargaro was on pole, by almost three-tenths from Terol, Simon and Corsi, all packed close. The important dynamic concerned the championship. Simon had a lead of 50.5 points over Smith, who led row two. All he really needed to do to secure the crown was to finish in front of him.

Smith made him wait until the last lap before he could be sure of doing that.

Espargaro led away, with Corsi nosing ahead a couple of times on the first nine laps. Then Smith took over up front, but with zero security. He was one of a pack of seven, and they shuffled constantly. Simon was playing it cool near the back of it; Vazquez, Iannone and Terol were right in it. And all the while, slow starter Cortese was closing on them, after finishing lap one 17th.

Simon took the lead for the first time on lap 14, and he and Smith started to move away from the fraught and entertaining battle for third. He could concentrate on his last-lap attack, and it couldn't have gone better.

Smith led again three laps later, and Simon tailed him patiently until the last lap. The decisive move came at MG corner, Simon forcing Smith wide as he pushed through on the inside, giving him enough clear air to run to the line without the danger of the Briton drafting past again. The race, and the championship, were won.

Espargaro led the mêlée out of the last corner, but Cortese timed it perfectly to move out of his draft and take the last rostrum spot by a tenth. Corsi, Terol and Vazquez were close behind; Iannone was almost ten seconds adrift, his engine losing power. A long way back, Marquez and Gadea battled to the end. Redding won his fight for 11th, while Webb was a couple of places behind in a big group.

Above: It's turn one, and Lorenzo clobbers hapless Hayden as the rest of the pack piles past.

Top right: The 250 race was stopped after Locatelli crashed in the middle of the track.

Centre right: Rampant 250 winner Simoncelli leads Barbera and Bautista.

Above right: Team owner Aspar Martinez is flanked by new champion Simon and runner-up Smith.

Bottom right: Simon and Smith head Corsi: the Spaniard was fully in control.

Photos: Gold & Goose

Iveco AUSTRALIAN GRAND PRIX

18 OCTOBER 2009 • FIM WORLD CHAMPIONSHIP ROUND 15

PHILLIP ISLAND

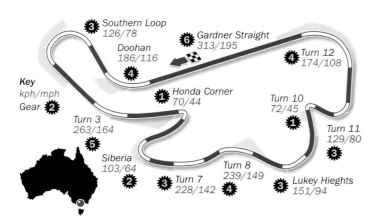

Key
kph/mph
Gear

Southern Loop 126/78
Gardner Straight 313/195
Doohan 186/116
Turn 12 174/108
Honda Corner 70/44
Turn 10 72/45
Turn 3 263/164
Turn 11 129/80
Siberia 103/64
Turn 8 239/149
Turn 7 228/142
Lukey Hieghts 151/94

Circuit 4.448km/2.764 miles

MOTOGP

RACE DISTANCE: 27 laps, 74.624 miles/120.096 km • RACE WEATHER: Dry (air 16°, humidity 45%, track 31°)

Pos.	Rider	Nat.	No.	Entrant	Machine	Tyres	Laps	Time & speed
1	Casey Stoner	AUS	27	Ducati Marlboro Team	Ducati	B	27	40m 56.651s 109.354mph/ 175.989km/h
2	Valentino Rossi	ITA	46	Fiat Yamaha Team	Yamaha	B	27	40m 58.586s
3	Dani Pedrosa	SPA	3	Repsol Honda Team	Honda	B	27	41m 19.269s
4	Alex de Angelis	RSM	15	San Carlos Honda Gresini	Honda	B	27	41m 29.353s
5	Colin Edwards	USA	5	Monster Yamaha Tech 3	Yamaha	B	27	41m 32.536s
6	Andrea Dovizioso	ITA	4	Repsol Honda Team	Honda	B	27	41m 35.133s
7	Marco Melandri	ITA	33	Hayate Racing Team	Kawasaki	B	27	41m 41.112s
8	Randy de Puniet	FRA	14	LCR Honda MotoGP	Honda	B	27	41m 41.592s
9	Mika Kallio	FIN	36	Ducati Marlboro Team	Ducati	B	27	41m.50.996s
10	Toni Elias	SPA	24	San Carlos Honda Gresini	Honda	B	27	41m 57.856s
11	Chris Vermeulen	AUS	7	Rizla Suzuki MotoGP	Suzuki	B	27	42m 02.086s
12	Loris Capirossi	ITA	65	Rizla Suzuki MotoGP	Suzuki	B	27	42m 02.601s
13	Gabor Talmacsi	HUN	41	Scot Racing Team MotoGP	Honda	B	27	42m 14.602s
14	James Toseland	JPN	52	Monster Yamaha Tech 3	Yamaha	B	27	42m 14.636s
15	Nicky Hayden	USA	69	Ducati Marlboro Team	Ducati	B	26	41m 27.127s
	Jorge Lorenzo	SPA	99	Fiat Yamaha Team	Yamaha	B	0	DNF

Fastest lap: Valentino Rossi, on lap 5, 1m 30.085s, 99.774mph/177.752km/h.

Previous lap record: Nicky Hayden, US (Honda), 1m 30.059s, 110.482mph/177.803km/h (2008).

Event best maximum speed: Kallio, 203.871mph/328.01km/h (race).

Qualifying: Dry
Air: 17° Humidity: 52% Track: 32°

1	Stoner	1m 30.341s
2	Rossi	1m 30.391s
3	Pedrosa	1m 31.070s
4	Lorenzo	1m 31.071s
5	Edwards	1m 31.096s
6	de Angelis	1m 31.260s
7	Hayden	1m 31.325s
8	de Puniet	1m 31.380s
9	Kallio	1m 31.384s
10	Dovizioso	1m 31.472s
11	Elias	1m 37.911s
12	Toseland	1m 31.722s
13	Capirossi	1m 31.873s
14	Melandri	1m 32.190s
15	Vermeulen	1m 32.338s
16	Talmacsi	1m 32.752s

Inside 107% in free practice
Canepa

Fastest race laps

1	Rossi	1m 30.085s
2	Stoner	1m 30.092s
3	Pedrosa	1m 30.773s
4	de Angelis	1m 30.826s
5	Edwards	1m 31.273s
6	de Puniet	1m 31.443s
7	Kallio	1m 31.444s
8	Dovizioso	1m 31.570s
9	Melandri	1m 31.649s
10	Toseland	1m 31.666s
11	Elias	1m 31.802s
12	Capirossi	1m 32.555s
13	Hayden	1m 32.607s
14	Talmacsi	1m 32.608s
15	Vermeulen	1m 32.815s

Championship Points

1	Rossi	270
2	Lorenzo	232
3	Stoner	195
4	Pedrosa	189
5	Dovizioso	152
6	Edwards	145
7	de Angelis	101
8	de Puniet	101
9	Capirossi	101
10	Melandri	100
11	Elias	96
12	Vermeulen	95
13	Toseland	87
14	Hayden	82
15	Kallio	58
16	Canepa	38
17	Talmacsi	17
18	Gibernau	12
19	Takahashi	9
20	Espargaro, A	8

Constructor Points

1	Yamaha	350
3	Honda	252
3	Ducati	236
4	Suzuki	121
5	Kawasaki	100

Team Points

1	FIAT Yamaha Team	502
2	Repsol Honda Team	341
2	Ducati Marlboro Team	294
4	Monster Yamaha Tech 3	232
5	San Carlo Honda Gresini	197
6	RIZLA Suzuki MotoGP	196
7	LCR Honda MotoGP	101
8	Hayate Racing Team	100
9	Pramac Racing	87
10	Scot Racing Team	26
11	Grupo Francisco Hernan	12

Grid order

Grid order	1	2	3	4	5	6	7	8	9	10	11	12	13	14	15	16	17	18	19	20	21	22	23	24	25	26	27	
27 STONER	3	27	27	27	27	27	27	27	27	27	27	27	27	27	27	27	27	27	27	27	27	27	27	27	27	27	27	1
46 ROSSI	27	46	46	46	46	46	46	46	46	46	46	46	46	46	46	46	46	46	46	46	46	46	46	46	46	46	46	2
3 PEDROSA	46	3	3	3	3	3	3	3	3	3	3	3	3	3	3	3	3	3	3	3	3	3	3	3	3	3	3	3
99 LORENZO	15	15	15	15	15	15	15	15	15	15	15	15	15	15	15	15	15	15	15	15	15	15	15	15	15	15	15	4
5 EDWARDS	24	24	24	24	5	5	5	5	5	5	5	5	5	5	5	5	5	5	5	5	5	5	5	5	5	5	5	5
15 DE ANGELIS	36	36	36	14	24	14	14	14	14	14	14	14	36	36	36	4	4	4	4	4	4	4	4	4	4	4	4	6
69 HAYDEN	4	14	14	36	14	24	24	4	4	4	4	36	14	4	4	36	33	33	14	14	14	14	33	33	33	33	33	7
14 DE PUNIET	14	4	4	5	36	4	36	24	36	36	36	4	4	14	33	33	14	14	33	33	33	33	14	14	14	14	14	8
36 KALLIO	5	5	5	4	4	33	4	33	33	33	33	33	33	33	14	14	36	36	36	36	36	36	36	36	36	36	36	9
4 DOVIZIOSO	33	52	52	52	33	36	33	36	24	24	24	24	24	24	24	24	24	24	24	24	24	24	24	24	24	24	24	10
24 ELIAS	52	33	33	33	52	52	52	52	52	7	7	7	7	7	7	7	7	7	7	7	7	7	7	7	7	7	7	11
52 TOSELAND	41	41	41	41	7	7	7	7	41	41	41	41	41	41	41	41	41	41	41	65	65	65	65	65	65	65	65	12
33 MELANDRI	7	7	7	7	41	41	41	41	7	65	65	65	65	65	65	65	65	65	65	41	41	41	41	41	41	41	41	13
7 VERMEULEN	65	65	65	65	65	65	65	65	65	52	52	52	52	52	52	52	52	52	52	52	52	52	52	52	52	52	52	14
41 TALMACSI	69	69	69	69	69	69	69	69	69	69	69	69	69	69	69	69	69	69	69	69	69	69	69	69	69	69		15
65 CAPIROSSI																												

250cc — RACE DISTANCE: 18 laps, 49.749 miles/80.064 km • RACE WEATHER: Dry (air 14°, humidity 45%, track 26°)

Pos.	Rider	Nat.	No.	Entrant	Machine	Laps	Time & Speed
1	Marco Simoncelli	ITA	58	Metis Gilera	Gilera	18	28m 17.403s
							(mph/km/h)
							105.512/169.806
2	Hector Barbera	SPA	40	Pepe World Team	Aprilia	18	28m 19.837s
3	Raffaele de Rosa	ITA	35	Scot Racing Team 250cc	Honda	18	28m 20.007s
4	Jules Cluzel	FRA	16	Matteoni Racing	Aprilia	18	28m 29.521s
5	Mike di Meglio	FRA	63	Mapfre Aspar Team 250cc	Aprilia	18	28m 29.595s
6	Karel Abraham	CZE	17	Cardion AB Motoracing	Aprilia	18	28m 29.816s
7	Hiroshi Aoyama	JPN	4	Scot Racing Team 250cc	Honda	18	28m 29.858s
8	Hector Faubel	SPA	55	Honda SAG	Honda	18	28m 30.515s
9	Ratthapark Wilairot	THA	14	Thai Honda PTT SAG	Honda	18	28m 30.963s
10	Alvaro Bautista	SPA	19	Mapfre Aspar Team	Aprilia	18	28m 45.182s
11	Thomas Luthi	SWI	12	Emmi – Caffe Latte	Aprilia	18	28m 45.625s
12	Lukas Pesek	CZE	52	Auto Kelly – CP	Aprilia	18	28m 46.060s
13	Alex Debon	ESP	6	Aeropuerto – Castello – Blusens	Aprilia	18	28m 51.295s
14	Shuhei Aoyama	JPN	73	Racing Team Germany	Honda	18	28m 56.182s
15	Shoya Tomizawa	JPN	48	CIP Moto – GP250	Honda	18	28m 57.932s
16	Balazs Nemeth	HUN	11	Balatonring Team	Aprilia	18	29m 40.603s
17	Bastien Chesaux	SWI	8	Racing Team Germany	Honda	18	29m 41.701s
18	Imre Toth	HUN	10	Team Toth Aprilia	Aprilia	17	28m 40.153s
19	Valentin Debise	FRA	53	CIP Moto – GP250	Honda	17	28m 45.916s
	Roberto Locatelli	ITA	15	Metis Gilera	Gilera	18	28m 47.918s
	Axel Pons	SPA	7	Pepe World Team	Aprilia	16	26m 09.203s
	Alex Baldolini	ITA	25	WTR San Marino Team	Aprilia	15	24m 23.926s
	Mattia Pasini	ITA	75	Team Toth Aprilia	Aprilia	7	11m 11.057s
	Vladimir Leonov	RUS	56	Viessmann Kiefer Racing	Aprilia	7	12m 15.184s

Fastest lap: Raffaele De Rosa, on lap 13, 1m 33.519s, 106.394mph/171.225km/h.
Lap record: Alvaro Bautista, SPA (Aprilia) 1m 32.710s, 107.323mph/172.719km/h (2008).
Event best maximum speed: Luthi, 172.057mph/276.9km/h (race).

Qualifying: Dry
Air: 31° Humidity: 17% Track: 41°

1	de Rosa	1m 33.389s
2	Simoncelli	1m 33.614s
3	Aoyama, Hiroshi	1m 33.633s
4	Debon	1m 33.886s
5	Barbera	1m 33.928s
6	di Meglio	1m 34.030s
7	Wilairot	1m 34.114s
8	Pasini	1m 34.192s
9	Faubel	1m 34.285s
10	Bautista	1m 34.588s
11	Abraham	1m 34.727s
12	Cluzel	1m 34.921s
13	Baldolini	1m 35.016s
14	Pesek	1m 35.018s
15	Luthi	1m 35.374s
16	Aoyama, Shuhei	1m 35.387s
17	Locatelli	1m 36.114s
18	Tomizawa	1m 36.711s
19	Pons	1m 36.860s
20	Leonov	1m 36.901s
21	Nemeth	1m 37.525s
22	Debise	1m 37.984s
23	Toth	1m 38.346s
24	Chesaux	1m 38.893s

Fastest race laps

1	de Rosa	1m 33.519s
2	Bautista	1m 33.520s
3	Barbera	1m 33.614s
4	Simoncelli	1m 33.703s
5	Abraham	1m 33.876s
6	Cluzel	1m 33.962s
7	di Meglio	1m 33.986s
8	Faubel	1m 34.024s
9	Wilairot	1m 34.086s
10	Aoyama, Hiroshi	1m 34.117s
11	Pasini	1m 34.180s
12	Debon	1m 34.342s
13	Luthi	1m 34.944s
14	Locatelli	1m 35.022s
15	Pesek	1m 35.073s
16	Aoyama, Shuhei	1m 35.125s
17	Baldolini	1m 35.221s
18	Tomizawa	1m 35.492s
19	Pons	1m 36.920s
20	Nemeth	1m 37.128s
21	Leonov	1m 37.270s
22	Chesaux	1m 37.833s
23	Debise	1m 38.034s
24	Toth	1m 39.891s

Championship Points

1	Aoyama, Hiroshi	227
2	Simoncelli	215
3	Bautista	198
4	Barbera	194
5	Pasini	128
6	de Rosa	106
7	di Meglio	105
8	Faubel	94
9	Luthi	94
10	Debon	92
11	Cluzel	82
12	Locatelli	78
13	Pesek	62
14	Wilairot	60
15	Abraham	60
16	Talmacsi	28
17	Tomizawa	26
18	Baldolini	26
19	Espargaro, Aleix	22
20	Aoyama, Shuhei	16
21	Debise	14
22	Toth	12
23	Leonov	8
24	Pons	3
25	Nemeth	3
26	Markham	2
27	Watanabe	2
28	Chesaux	1
29	Bonsey	1

Constructors

		Points
1	Aprilia	294
2	Honda	246
3	Gilera	222
4	Yamaha	2

125cc — RACE DISTANCE: 23 laps, 63.568 miles/102.304 km • RACE WEATHER: Dry (air 15°, humidity 45%, track 27°)

Pos.	Rider	Nat.	No.	Entrant	Machine	Laps	Time & Speed
1	Julian Simon	SPA	60	Bancaja Aspar Team 125cc	Aprilia	23	37m 55.798s
							(mph/km/h)
							100.556/161.830
2	Bradley Smith	GB	38	Bancaja Aspar Team 125cc	Aprilia	23	37m 56.111s
3	Sandro Cortese	GER	11	Ajo Interwetten	Derbi	23	37m 57.771s
4	Pol Espargaro	SPA	44	Derbi Racing Team	Derbi	23	37m 57.959s
5	Simon Corsi	ITA	24	Fontana Racing	Aprilia	23	37m 58.128s
6	Nicolas Terol	SPA	18	Jack & Jones Team	Aprilia	23	37m 59.037s
7	Efren Vazquez	SPA	7	Derbi Racing Team	Derbi	23	37m 59.088s
8	Andrea Iannone	ITA	29	Ongetta Team I.S.P.A.	Aprilia	23	38m 08.618s
9	Marc Marquez	SPA	93	Red Bull KTM Moto Sport	KTM	23	38m 18.153s
10	Sergio Gadea	SPA	33	Bancaja Aspar Team 125cc	Aprilia	23	38m 18.400s
11	Scott Redding	GB	45	Blusens Aprilia	Aprilia	23	38m 24.979s
12	Dominique Aegerter	SWI	77	Ajo Interwetten	Derbi	23	38m 24.997s
13	Danny Webb	GB	99	Degraaf Grand Prix	Aprilia	22	38m 25.020s
14	Jonas Folger	GER	94	Ongetta Team I.S.P.A.	Aprilia	23	38m 25.194s
15	Randy Krummenacher	SWI	35	Degraaf Grand Prix	Aprilia	23	38m 25.259s
16	Johann Zarco	FRA	14	WTR San Marino Team	Aprilia	23	38m 25.507s
17	Lorenzo Zanetti	ITA	8	Ongetta Team I.S.P.A.	Aprilia	23	38m 27.049s
18	Takaaki Nakagami	JPN	73	Ongetta Team I.S.P.A.	Aprilia	23	38m 28.280s
19	Luis Salom	SPA	39	Jack & Jones Team	Honda	23	38m 54.131s
20	Michael Ranseder	AUT	88	CBC Corse	Aprilia	23	38m 54.283s
21	Tomoyoshi Koyama	JPN	71	Loncin Racing	Loncin	23	39m 14.815s
22	Jasper Iwema	NED	53	Racing Team Germany	Aprilia	23	39m 19.419s
23	Jakub Kornfeil	CZE	21	Loncin Racing	Loncin	23	39m 19.529s
24	Brad Gross	AUS	97	Gross Racing	Yamaha	22	38m 27.187s
25	Luca Vitali	ITA	10	CBC Corse	Aprilia	22	38m 31.447s
26	Luca Marconi	FRA	87	CBC Corse	Aprilia	22	38m 34.378s
27	Andrew Lawson	AUS	54	Champions Ride Days	Honda	22	38m 54.372s
28	Levi Day	AUS	98	Racetrix / Angelo's Aluminium	Honda	22	39m 20.381s
	Esteve Rabat	SPA	12	Blusens Aprilia	Aprilia	21	34m 58.883s
	Nicky Diles	AUS	96	RSW Racing	Aprilia	7	14m 35.757s
	Stefan Bradl	GER	17	Viessmann Kiefer Racing	Aprilia	2	3m 26.504s
	Joan Olive	SPA	6	Derbi Racing Team	Derbi	2	3m 29.494s
	Cameron Beaubier	USA	16	Red Bull KTM Moto Sport	KTM	2	4m 46.379s

Fastest lap: Sandro Cortese, on lap 16, 1m 37.869s, 101.385mph/163.614km/h.
Lap record: Alvaro Bautista, SPA (Aprilia), 1m 36.927s, 102.653mph/165.204km/h (2008).
Event best maximum speed: Terol (Aprilia), 150.807mph/242.7km/h (race).

Qualifying: Dry
Air: 32° Humidity: 18% Track: 36°

1	Espargaro, Pol	1m 37.770s
2	Terol	1m 38.049s
3	Simon	1m 38.067s
4	Corsi	1m 38.136s
5	Smith	1m 38.155s
6	Marquez	1m 38.292s
7	Cortese	1m 38.552s
8	Iannone	1m 38.568s
9	Olive	1m 38.578s
10	Rabat	1m 38.588s
11	Vazquez	1m 38.663s
12	Bradl	1m 38.890s
13	Zanetti	1m 39.101s
14	Nakagami	1m 39.229s
15	Koyama	1m 39.237s
16	Gadea	1m 39.274s
17	Aegerter	1m 39.354s
18	Beaubier	1m 39.370s
19	Zarco	1m 39.390s
20	Ranseder	1m 39.426s
21	Webb	1m 39.521s
22	Krummenacher	1m 39.596s
23	Folger	1m 39.615s
24	Redding	1m 39.990s
25	Salom	1m 40.545s
26	Iwema	1m 41.646s
27	Kornfeil	1m 42.082s
28	Jacquet	1m 42.965s
29	Vitali	1m 43.436s
30	Savos	1m 44.027s
31	Diles	1m 44.063s
32	Marconi	1m 44.109s
	Outside of 107%	
	Day	1m 44.984s
	Lawson	1m 45.916s
	Mavin	2m 06.661s

Fastest race laps

1	Cortese	1m 37.869s
2	Smith	1m 37.927s
3	Corsi	1m 37.971s
4	Simon	1m 37.978s
5	Iannone	1m 38.091s
6	Vazquez	1m 38.152s
7	Terol	1m 38.245s
8	Espargaro, Pol	1m 38.247s
9	Gadea	1m 38.517s
10	Bradl	1m 38.773s
11	Rabat	1m 38.786s
12	Zanetti	1m 38.868s
13	Marquez	1m 38.902s
14	Webb	1m 38.960s
15	Redding	1m 38.967s
16	Aegerter	1m 39.012s
17	Krummenacher	1m 39.030s
18	Zarco	1m 39.043s
19	Folger	1m 39.098s
20	Nakagami	1m 39.335s
21	Olive	1m 39.696s
22	Ranseder	1m 39.843s
23	Koyama	1m 39.969s
24	Salom	1m 40.300s
25	Kornfeil	1m 41.475s
26	Iwema	1m 41.566s
27	Gross	1m 43.190s
28	Marconi	1m 43.704s
29	Vitali	1m 44.078s
30	Lawson	1m 44.820s
31	Day	1m 45.541s
32	Diles	1m 45.730s
33	Beaubier	1m 47.189s

Championship Points

1	Simon	239
2	Smith	183.5
3	Terol	162.5
4	Espargaro, Pol	142.5
5	Gadea	128
6	Iannone	117.5
7	Cortese	112
8	Marquez	94
9	Bradl	85
10	Olive	74
11	Folger	73
12	Corsi	68
13	Aegerter	63.5
14	Redding	50.5
15	Vazquez	45
16	Webb	38.5
17	Nakagami	36
18	Zarco	31.5
19	Rabat	28
20	Zanetti	27
21	Krummenacher	22
22	Salom	17
23	Koyama	17
24	Savadori	7
25	Schrotter	7
26	Ranseder	5
27	Moretti	3
28	Iwema	3
29	Beaubier	3
30	Glossop	2
31	Fritz	2
30	di Carlo	2
33	Kartheininger	1

Constructors

		Points
1	Aprilia	323.5
2	Derbi	184
3	KTM	96
4	Loncin	17
5	Honda	14

MALAYSIAN GRAND PRIX

SEPANG CIRCUIT

Above: Rossi celebrates World Championship number nine.

Main photo: Stoner, a picture of concentration, gave a solitary masterclass in wet-weather riding.

Photos: Gold & Goose

ROSSI would later describe it as "in some ways, my hardest championship ever". In Malaysia, after another race disrupted by an ill-timed cloudburst, he was mainly interested in the celebrations. He and his scriptwriters had prepared an elaborate, if rather laboured, gag based on the Italian proverb, *"Gallina vecchia fa buon brodo"* (old hens make good soup – or, in other words, don't lay eggs and are fit only for the pot). The charade involved an egg with the number '9' on it, for his ninth title, and something to do with a live chicken, intended to accompany him on his lap of honour. Alas, the hooded bird seemed too moribund to co-operate. Two weeks later, Rossi joked that he had presented it to the circuit operators at Malaysia in exchange for the promise that "they will never kill it".

There was no satay sauce on his championship triumph, however, no race win to underline the prize. For a second race in succession, Stoner was unbeatable, this time with a highly convincing demonstration of wet-weather riding and overall strength. Heavy rain – a veritable monsoon – had delayed the start, but had reduced the punishing heat he had been wondering about. Fatigue was quite absent, and observers were speculating on what might have happened if he hadn't skipped three races, considering his strength since his return. But Stoner wouldn't concern himself with 'what if?', saying later, "If I hadn't taken the break, I wouldn't be able to perform like this now."

Third, with Lorenzo fourth, was good enough for Rossi to kick off a remarkable day for his employers. Over in Europe, at Portimao, Ben Spies would secure the Superbike title, and Cal Crutchlow the 600 Supersport crown. A triple-header for Yamaha in the three most important series. In MotoGP, Fiat Yamaha

had already claimed the team prize, but could not yet confirm the constructors' title, just in case of the freak event that engine replacements at the next GP might knock its score down again, at minus ten points a pop.

Lorenzo congratulated Rossi warmly in *parc fermé*, and paid tribute to his clear victor. Rossi had been "a faster and more complete rider than me in the majority of the races," he said. He could not yet be sure of second in the championship, however. Stoner was now 25 points behind. If the Australian were to win at Valencia and Lorenzo fail to score, they would be equal on points, but Stoner would have five race wins to Lorenzo's four.

There were other battles for the positions, most especially six riders going for seventh: de Angelis, de Puniet, Capirossi, Melandri, Elias and Vermeulen, all covered by just six points. Most prominent was the tussle between team-mates de Angelis and Elias, both still without a MotoGP ride for 2010. De Angelis had heard that his hoped-for backing from the San Marino government would not materialise, perhaps a contribution to a downbeat race. Elias was a little brighter, second Honda rider home, in seventh. They left equal on points.

The arithmetic was also required for the 250s, as fortune swung back to Aoyama, who claimed a win that was both brave and canny, while Simoncelli dropped to third. It stretched his lead in the championship to 21 points.

Meanwhile, Pasini struggled on with his part-self-financed team to yet more misfortune – another race crash. There was money trouble elsewhere near front of the grid. Barbera was in dispute with Pepe World team proprietor Sito Pons and went on strike for the

Left: Second corner, and Dani leads the pack, from Capirossi and Elias. Rossi is losing places behind.

Right: Aleix Espargaro was back on the Pramac Ducati.

Below right: Ducati's Vittorio Guareschi *(far right)* listens in on Stoner's debrief.

Below: The chicken survived, and *'gallina vecchia'* Rossi picked up the egg.

Photos: Gold & Goose

first 20 minutes of the opening free practice, before donning his leathers and going out.

While on the 250s, there was another big crash for Locatelli, already in much discomfort after the high-side that had cut short his Australian GP less than a week before. This one, also in the race, left him with a fractured scaphoid in his right wrist.

Back in MotoGP, fellow Phillip Island victim Canepa was in the pits, but in no state to race: the elder Espargaro brother had been flown in to substitute once again, and once again he impressed, qualifying and finishing within a whisker of team-mate Kallio.

Questions were raised by the presence on the rostrum with Stoner of Vito Guareschi, representing Ducati in place of usual team director Livio Suppo. Guareschi, the factory test rider, had recently been appointed to what was officially a liaison role between riders and factory engineers, for which he was eminently well suited. But rumours were rife that he was being brought in to replace long-term team man Suppo, and the rumours would turn out to be true when Suppo announced his departure from Ducati two weeks later at Valencia. The suppositions made by a vulpine Italian Press, that Suppo had been hounded out after eight years by a hostile Stoner, remained only conjecture. But the mood was rife: this came on the heels of news that Lorenzo's crew chief had resigned (Daniele Romagnoli was seeking a more hands-on job); and that Honda had head-hunted three technicians from the Fiat Yamaha team. The air seemed rich with conspiracy.

The sapping heat and humidity did not affect the riders alone: complaints surfaced again about power-down engines. Rossi suggested that the cold dense air at Phillip Island had restored some sharpness,

making it more obvious now it had gone missing. Stoner loyally insisted that his Ducati had lost no performance.

The race boasted royal patronage to rival that of Spain, in the person of King Mizan Zainel Abidin, Sultan of Terengganu, who presented Stoner with his victory cup. The importance of the event was marked also by a record crowd of more than 60,000.

MotoGP RACE – 21 laps

Rossi laid down a marker – or six of them – in qualifying, with a series of pace-leading laps that culminated in an all-time record, beating his own 2006 990 pole, using Bridgestone's control tyres. His seventh pole of the year, more importantly, was by a margin of well over half a second on his team-mate.

Pedrosa completed the front row; Stoner led the second, almost a second down on Rossi.

The deluge came at just the wrong time, shortly before the sighting lap, the rain so heavy that the track turned into one long puddle. Eventually, the race got under way less than 40 minutes late; the rain was still falling, but now in slightly more manageable quantities. With no practice, wet settings were guesswork.

Lorenzo was already in trouble. Mechanics struggled to start his bike, and by the time he switched to his spare, he was very late out for the sighting lap. Rossi and Toseland were among riders who returned to the pit lane to avoid crossing the start line, thus gaining an extra sighting lap. Lorenzo also pulled back into the pits, getting off the bike as mechanics frantically made adjustments. But now the pit exit was closed: he would have to join the warm-up lap from the pit lane, and start from the back of the grid.

Conditions were streaming wet, but Rossi was brave. Starting from pole, he managed to outdrag Pedrosa to the first corner, only to run wide as most of the rest streamed past on the inside. He finished the first lap tenth, behind Lorenzo. Which put them back on equal footing.

At this point, Stoner was around fifth; afterwards he said he thought his chances of getting through the first turn without being knocked off were rather slim. Accordingly, he immediately set off for the safety of the lead. Before half the lap was done, he had pushed past Capirossi and Elias, and soon dispatched Pedrosa as well. By the end of the lap, his lead was already more than a second. It was almost four next time around, and better than 15 by half-distance. It was a solitary master class in riding in the wet.

Dovizioso had followed Stoner through the mêlée and was third at the end of lap one. Pedrosa was dropping back quickly from the lead, but was proving a hard target for his team-mate. Gradually he closed the gap and was pushing the Spaniard hard by the mid-point of the race. Then, on lap 15, he pushed too hard on the wetter part of the track, and slid off and out. De Puniet had already crashed out, on the second lap.

Elias was leading the pursuit, Capirossi engaged with Hayden behind. But the Yamahas were coming through fast. A daring move by Lorenzo put him past Rossi on the first lap, and the pair began cutting through, Melandri behind them.

By lap four, they had caught Hayden and Capirossi, and were soon past, Lorenzo still ahead. Capirossi dropped away, while Hayden tagged on as best he could.

Lap seven saw both Yamahas ahead of Elias; next time around, Rossi was in front with a smooth move, although a foot off the footrest as he caught a slide through the following corner showed how hard he was trying.

When Dovi fell, Rossi was only two seconds behind the Honda pair and comfortably three ahead of Lorenzo. He did contemplate having a go at Pedrosa, but thought better of it. Now he was on the rostrum, which was all he needed for a proper celebration of his title. As for Pedrosa, he was delighted with his first ever wet-race podium. "I have worked hard to improve in this condition," he said.

Hayden had followed the Yamahas past Elias and pulled safely clear for fifth; for the second half of the race, the Spaniard came under pressure from Vermeulen and Melandri, but the latter dropped away out of touch as Vermeulen got past and pulled well clear ahead, even closing on Hayden by the finish.

Capirossi had slipped back into an entertaining battle for ninth that intensified as the end drew nigh. In the end, he just managed to prevail over Kallio, Espargaro and de Angelis. Edwards had dropped well back from this group, with Talmacsi and a dismayed Toseland trailing in behind.

250cc RACE — 20 laps

Aoyama was on pole, from the increasingly intrusive Cluzel, then di Meglio and Barbera, with Simoncelli on the far end of row two and over a second off the pace.

Conditions were dry and baking hot for the second race, the rain yet to come.

Cluzel led for the first three laps, while Aoyama tussled with Barbera and Simoncelli. Wilairot struggled to hold on to the leaders, while Bautista came through from a moderate start to join in.

Simoncelli took to the front on lap four and stayed there until half-distance. At this stage, Aoyama was right on his back wheel in second, while Cluzel and Barbera were back and forth right behind. Then, on lap 11, the Frenchman was gone, sliding out of the contest.

Left: One hand on the title: 250 winner Aoyama and his Scot team celebrate.

Below left: Smith (38) and Simon once again owned the 125 race.

Far left: The Yamaha rivals came through from the back. Once Rossi got ahead, the positions did not change.

Below: Another 250-class dead heat. This time, second went to Barbera *(right)* from Simoncelli.

Photos: Gold & Goose

It was now that Aoyama started to attack, leading for the first time on lap 11. But Simoncelli fought back vigorously, and over the next three laps they jousted and swapped until the Honda rider showed the pace that had put him on pole, setting new lap records on the 14th and 15th laps to lift him a second clear.

Simoncelli had been looking ragged and tired, and now he lost ground quickly. Barbera was on his back wheel, awaiting his chance. They swapped twice on the penultimate lap, and it came to a battle of lines in the final corner. Barbera stole the inside, but Simoncelli refused to give way, and they drag-raced past the pit wall to cross the line side by side. Times were identical in the second dead heat of the season, and again a photo-finish could not distinguish the winner. This time, the judgement went to Barbera, whose best lap had been faster. In Portugal with di Meglio, it had gone the other way.

Aoyama was jubilant with the points advantage; sportsman Simoncelli hugged him in *parc fermé* and said, "With just one race, the championship is impossible, but I will try anyway in Valencia."

Luthi rode to a storming fourth, pulling through from the back after being forced wide on the second corner. He left team-mates Faubel and Wilairot battling behind, the pair passing Debon on the last lap when he ran wide.

Pesek, Baldolini and Shuhei Aoyama trailed in to complete the top ten, in a race with just 16 finishers from 24 starters.

Bautista lost third overall when he crashed out of fourth place on lap five; team-mate di Meglio also crashed out of the front group early on, while Pasini and Locatelli swelled the crash list, along with Abraham and Tomizawa. De Rosa retired.

125cc RACE – 19 laps

Marquez took a second pole of the season, half a second clear of Simon and Smith. Cortese completed the first row; Terol, still with a slight sniff of second overall, led row two.

Marquez headed the brawl into the first corner, Vazquez nosing ahead briefly, and at the end of the first lap Smith was third, with Simon challenging over the line.

Next time, the new champion was ahead, and by lap four Smith had moved through to join him; from there on, they pulled away from a nine-strong gang to duel to the finish. As in the previous week, Simon showed the speed and race-craft to defeat his rival, but only in the last corner. It was his sixth win, and Smith's fifth successive rostrum. With Terol fifth, it secured second overall for the young English rider, and another one-two for the dominant team.

The battle for third was large and relentless. Youngsters Folger, Marquez and Vazquez played a vital role, along with the more seasoned Cortese, Rabat and Corsi. Terol and Iannone dropped away before one-third distance.

Espargaro took over after the mid-point, gaining a little cushion ahead of the fierce struggle behind.

Both Folger and Vazquez crashed out, as did Corsi, with two laps to go. Terol closed again, along with Gadea, the pair cutting to the head of the group, Gadea ahead for the last two laps. Cortese was next, Rabat a few seconds behind, and then a lone Iannone. Olive won the battle for ninth from Iannone's team-mates, Zanetti and Nakagami.

Bradl was brought down by a high-siding Webb halfway around the first lap; Redding suffered yet another breakdown.

SEPANG INTERNATIONAL CIRCUIT

Langkawi curve
83/52

Genting Curve
140/87

Turn 3
179/112

Turn 5
152/95

Hairpin
72/45

Turn 7
124/77

Pangkor
Laut
Chicane
70/44

KLIA
Curve
127/79

Berjaya Tioman
Corner 63/58

Sunway
Lagoon Corner
87/54

Turn 12
154/96

Kenyir Lake
103/64

Key
kph/mph
Gear

Circuit 5.548km/3.447 miles

MOTOGP

RACE DISTANCE: 21 laps, 72.394 miles/168.508 km • **RACE WEATHER:** Wet (air 27°, humidity 79%, track 22°)

Pos.	Rider	Nat.	No.	Entrant	Machine	Tyres	Laps	Time & speed
1	Casey Stoner	AUS	27	Ducati Marlboro Team	Ducati	B	21	47m 24.435s 91.611mph/ 147.435km/h
2	Dani Pedrosa	SPA	3	Repsol Honda Team	Honda	B	21	47m 39.500s
3	Valentino Rossi	ITA	46	Fiat Yamaha Team	Yamaha	B	21	47m 44.219s
4	Jorge Lorenzo	SPA	99	Fiat Yamaha Team	Yamaha	B	21	47m 60.684s
5	Nicky Hayden	USA	69	Ducati Marlboro Team	Ducati	B	21	48m 03.539s
6	Chris Vermeulen	AUS	7	Rizla Suzuki MotoGP	Suzuki	B	21	48m 05.895s
7	Toni Elias	SPA	24	San Carlos Honda Gresini	Honda	B	21	48m 13.389s
8	Marco Melandri	ITA	33	Hayate Racing Team	Kawasaki	B	21	48m 20.391s
9	Loris Capirossi	ITA	65	Rizla Suzuki MotoGP	Suzuki	B	21	48m 25.137s
10	Mika Kallio	FIN	36	Pramac Racing	Ducati	B	21	48m 25.274s
11	Aleix Espargaro	SPA	44	Pramac Racing	Ducati	B	21	48m 26.489s
12	Alex de Angelis	RSM	15	San Carlos Honda Gresini	Honda	B	21	48m 26.681s
13	Colin Edwards	USA	5	Monster Yamaha Tech 3	Yamaha	B	21	48m 35.612s
14	Gabor Talmacsi	HUN	41	Scot Racing Team MotoGP	Honda	B	21	48m 40.685s
15	James Toseland	JPN	52	Monster Yamaha Tech 3	Yamaha	B	21	49m 15.506s
	Andrea Dovizioso	ITA	4	Repsol Honda Team	Honda	B	14	DNF
	Randy de Puniet	USA	1	LCR Honda MotoGP	Honda	B	1	DNF

Fastest lap: Valentino Rossi, on lap 14, 2m 13.694s, 92.827mph/149.391km/h.

Previous lap record: Casey Stoner, AUS (Ducati), 2m 02.108s, 101.635mph/163.566km/h (2007).

Event best maximum speed: Stoner, 314.600mph/195.483km/h (warm up).

Qualifying: Dry
Air: 34° Humidity: 41% Track: 51°

1	Rossi	2m 00.518s
2	Lorenzo	2m 01.087s
3	Pedrosa	2m 01.254s
4	Stoner	2m 01.455s
5	Capirossi	2m 01.716s
6	Elias	2m 01.918s
7	Hayden	2m 01.980s
8	de Puniet	2m 02.098s
9	Edwards	2m 02.195s
10	de Angelis	2m 02.274s
11	Dovizioso	2m 02.362s
12	Kallio	2m 02.435s
13	Espargaro, A	2m 02.859s
14	Vermeulen	2m 03.032s
15	Melandri	2m 03.088s
16	Toseland	2m 03.528s
17	Talmacsi	2m 03.874s

Fastest race laps

1	Rossi	2m 13.694s
2	Pedrosa	2m 13.765s
3	Stoner	2m 14.120s
4	Lorenzo	2m 14.157s
5	Dovizioso	2m 14.423s
6	Vermeulen	2m 14.820s
7	Hayden	2m 15.258s
8	Melandri	2m 15.678s
9	Capirossi	2m 15.854s
10	Kallio	2m 15.894s
11	Elias	2m 15.958s
12	Espargaro, A	2m 16.158s
13	de Angelis	2m 16.402s
14	Edwards	2m 16.769s
15	Talmacsi	2m 17.072s
16	Toseland	2m 18.824s
17	de Puniet	2m 28.718

Championship Points

1	Rossi	286
2	Lorenzo	245
3	Stoner	220
4	Pedrosa	209
5	Dovizioso	152
6	Edwards	148
7	Melandri	108
8	Capirossi	108
9	de Angelis	105
10	Elias	105
11	Vermeulen	105
12	de Puniet	101
13	Hayden	93
13	Toseland	88
15	Kallio	64
16	Canepa	38
17	Talmacsi	19
18	Espargaro, A	13
19	Gibernau	12
20	Takahashi	9

Constructor Points

1	Yamaha	366
3	Honda	272
3	Ducati	261
4	Suzuki	131
5	Kawasaki	108

Team Points

1	FIAT Yamaha Team	531
2	Repsol Honda Team	361
2	Ducati Marlboro Team	330
4	Monster Yamaha Tech 3	236
5	RIZLA Suzuki MotoGP	213
6	San Carlo Honda Gresini	210
7	Hayate Racing Team	108
8	LCR Honda MotoGP	101
8	Pramac Racing	98
10	Scot Racing Team	28
11	Grupo Francisco Hernan	12

Grid order	1	2	3	4	5	6	7	8	9	10	11	12	13	14	15	16	17	18	19	20	21	
46 ROSSI	27	27	27	27	27	27	27	27	27	27	27	27	27	27	27	27	27	27	27	27	27	1
99 LORENZO	3	3	3	3	3	3	3	3	3	3	3	3	3	3	3	3	3	3	3	3	3	2
3 PEDROSA	4	4	4	4	4	4	4	4	4	4	4	4	4	4	46	46	46	46	46	46	46	3
27 STONER	24	24	24	24	24	24	99	46	46	46	46	46	46	46	99	99	99	99	99	99	99	4
65 CAPIROSSI	14	65	69	69	69	99	46	99	99	99	99	99	99	99	69	69	69	69	69	69	69	5
24 ELIAS	65	69	65	99	99	46	24	69	69	69	69	69	69	69	7	7	7	7	7	7	7	6
69 HAYDEN	69	99	99	65	46	69	69	24	24	24	24	24	24	24	24	24	24	24	24	24	24	7
14 DE PUNIET	99	33	46	46	65	33	33	33	33	33	33	33	7	7	33	33	33	33	33	33	33	8
5 EDWARDS	33	46	33	33	33	65	65	7	7	7	7	7	33	33	36	36	36	36	65	65	65	9
15 DE ANGELIS	46	36	36	36	36	7	7	65	65	15	36	36	36	36	15	15	15	65	15	15	36	10
4 DOVIZIOSO	36	15	15	15	7	15	15	15	15	36	15	15	15	15	65	65	65	15	36	44	15	11
36 KALLIO	15	41	7	7	15	36	36	36	36	65	65	65	5	5	44	44	44	44	44	15		12
44 ESPARGARO	41	7	41	41	5	5	5	5	5	5	5	5	65	65	44	5	5	5	5	5		13
7 VERMEULEN	7	5	5	5	41	41	44	44	44	44	44	44	44	44	41	41	41	41	41	41		14
33 MELANDRI	5	44	44	44	44	44	41	41	41	41	41	41	41	41	52	52	52	52	52	52		15
52 TOSELAND	44	52	52	52	52	52	52	52	52	52	52	52	52	52								
41 TALMACSI	52																					

OFFICIAL TIMEKEEPER

250cc — RACE DISTANCE: 20 laps, 68.947 miles/110.960 km • RACE WEATHER: Dry (air 31°, humidity 49%, track 47°)

Pos.	Rider	Nat.	No.	Entrant	Machine	Laps	Time & Speed
1	Hiroshi Aoyama	JPN	4	Scot Racing Team 250cc	Honda	20	42m 55.689s
							(mph/km/h)
							93.366/155.087
2	Hector Barbera	SPA	40	Pepe World Team	Aprilia	20	43m 02.086s
3	Marco Simoncelli	ITA	58	Metis Gilera	Gilera	20	43m 02.086s
4	Thomas Luthi	SWI	12	Emmi – Caffe Latte	Aprilia	20	43m 10.560s
5	Hector Faubel	SPA	55	Honda SAG	Honda	20	43m 14.866s
6	Ratthapark Wilairot	THA	14	Thai Honda PTT SAG	Honda	20	43m 15.256s
7	Alex Debon	ESP	6	Aeropuerto – Castello – Blusens	Aprilia	20	43m 15.944s
8	Lukas Pesk	CZE	52	Auto Kelly – CP	Aprilia	20	43m 30.250s
9	Alex Baldolini	ITA	25	WTR San Marino Team	Aprilia	20	43m 46.626s
10	Shuhei Aoyama	JPN	73	Racing Team Germany	Honda	20	43m 59.875s
11	Balazs Nemeth	HUN	11	Balatonring Team	Aprilia	20	44m 04.606s
12	Karel Abraham	CZE	17	Cardion AB Motoracing	Aprilia	20	44m 06.305s
13	Valentin Debise	FRA	53	CIP Moto – GP250	Honda	20	44m 13.634s
14	Bastien Chesaux	SWI	8	Racing Team Germany	Honda	20	44m 25.358s
15	Vladimir Leonov	RUS	56	Viessmann Kiefer Racing	Aprilia	20	44m 39.225s
16	Shoya Tomizawa	JPN	48	CIP Moto – GP250	Honda	19	42m 59.560s
	Raffaele de Rosa	ITA	35	Scot Racing Team 250cc	Honda	16	DNF
	Jules Cluzel	FRA	16	Matteoni Racing	Aprilia	11	DNF
	Mattia Pasini	ITA	75	Paddock GP Racing TEam	Aprilia	8	DNF
	Mike di Meglio	FRA	63	Mapfre Aspar Team 250cc	Aprilia	8	DNF
	Alvaro Bautista	SPA	19	Mapfre Aspar Team	Aprilia	6	DNF
	Roberto Locatelli	ITA	15	Metis Gilera	Gilera	5	DNF
	Axel Pons	SPA	7	Pepe World Team	Aprilia	2	DNF
	Imre Toth	HUN	10	Team Toth Aprilia	Aprilia	1	DNF

Fastest lap: Hiroshi Aoyama, on lap 16, 2m 07.597s, 97.263mph/156.530km/h.
Lap record: Alvro Bautitsta, ITA (Aprilia) 2m 08.012s, 96.326mph/156.022km/h (2008).
Event best maximum speed: Luthi. 162.550mph/261.6km/h (free practice 2).

Qualifying: Dry — Air: 34° Humidity: 38% Track: 49°

1	Aoyama, Hiroshi	2m 06.767s
2	Cluzel	2m 07.099s
3	di Meglio	2m 07.232s
4	Barbera	2m 07.301s
5	Bautista	2m 07.371s
6	Wilairot	2m 07.662s
7	Faubel	2m 07.828s
8	Simoncelli	2m 07.916s
9	Luthi	2m 07.949s
10	de Rosa	2m 07.953s
11	Debon	2m 07.998s
12	Pasini	2m 08.159s
13	Locatelli	2m 08.836s
14	Baldolini	2m 08.841s
15	Abraham	2m 08.908s
16	Tomizawa	2m 09.148s
17	Pesek	2m 09.336s
18	Pons	2m 09.392s
19	Aoyama, Shuhei	2m 09.654s
20	Nemeth	2m 11.611s
21	Chesaux	2m 11.941s
22	Debise	2m 12.171s
23	Leonov	2m 12.813s
24	Toth	2m 14.831s

Fastest race laps

1	Aoyama, Hiroshi	2m 07.597s
2	Barbera	2m 08.087s
3	Simoncelli	2m 08.244s
4	Bautista	2m 08.290s
5	Cluzel	2m 08.392s
6	Luthi	2m 08.408s
7	Debon	2m 08.438s
8	Pasini	2m 08.638s
9	di Meglio	2m 08.653s
10	Abraham	2m 08.768s
11	Faubel	2m 08.822s
12	Wilairot	2m 09.079s
13	Pesek	2m 09.594s
14	Tomizawa	2m 09.770s
15	Locatelli	2m 09.781s
16	Baldolini	2m 09.800s
17	Nemeth	2m 10.806s
18	Aoyama, Shuhei	2m 10.837s
19	Debise	2m 10.995s
20	Pons	2m 11.230s
21	Chesaux	2m 11.505s
22	Leonov	2m 12.619s
23	de Rosa	2m 16.677s
24	Toth	2m 27.805s

Championship Points

1	Aoyama, Hiroshi	252
2	Simoncelli	231
3	Barbera	214
4	Bautista	198
5	Pasini	128
6	Luthi	107
7	de Rosa	106
8	di Meglio	105
9	Faubel	105
10	Debon	101
11	Cluzel	82
12	Locatelli	78
13	Wilairot	70
14	Pesek	70
15	Abraham	64
16	Baldolini	33
17	Talmacsi	28
18	Tomizawa	26
19	Espargaro, Aleix	22
20	Aoyama, Shuhei	22
21	Debise	17
20	Toth	12
23	Leonov	9
24	Nemeth	8
25	Chesaux	3
25	Pons	3
27	Markham	2
27	Watanabe	2
29	Bonsey	1

Constructors
1	Aprilia	314
2	Honda	271
2	Gilera	238
3	Yamaha	2

125cc — RACE DISTANCE: 19 laps, 65.499 miles/105.412 km • RACE WEATHER: Dry (air 33°, humidity 44%, track 48°)

Pos.	Rider	Nat.	No.	Entrant	Machine	Laps	Time & Speed
1	Julian Simon	SPA	60	Bancaja Aspar Team 125cc	Aprilia	19	42m 50.916s
							(mph/km/h)
							97.718/147.606
2	Bradley Smith	GB	38	Bancaja Aspar Team 125cc	Aprilia	19	42m 52.030s
3	Pol Espargaro	SPA	44	Derbi Racing Team	Derbi	19	42m 57.209s
4	Sergio Gadea	SPA	33	Bancaja Aspar Team 125cc	Aprilia	19	42m 58.919s
5	Nicolas Terol	SPA	18	Jack & Jones Team	Aprilia	19	42m 59.401s
6	Sandro Cortese	GER	11	Ajo Interwetten	Derbi	19	43m 01.104s
7	Esteve Rabat	SPA	12	Blusens Aprilia	Aprilia	19	43m 06.030s
8	Andrea Iannone	ITA	29	Ongetta Team I.S.PA.	Aprilia	19	43m 13.067s
9	Joan Olive	SPA	6	Derbi Racing Team	Derbi	19	43m 17.304s
10	Lorenzo Zanetti	ITA	8	Ongetta Team I.S.PA.	Aprilia	19	43m 18.029s
11	Takaaki Nakagami	JPN	73	Ongetta Team I.S.PA.	Aprilia	19	43m 18.775s
12	Michael Ranseder	AUT	88	CBC Corse	Aprilia	19	43m 25.754s
13	Randy Krummenacher	SWI	35	Degraaf Grand Prix	Aprilia	19	43m 32.745s
14	Dominique Aegerter	SWI	77	Ajo Interwetten	Derbi	19	43m 33.349s
15	Luis Salom	SPA	39	Jack & Jones Team	Honda	19	43m 42.551s
16	Elly Ilias	MAL	28	Air Asia Team Malaya	Aprilia	19	43m 50.770s
17	Cameron Beaubier	USA	16	Red Bull KTM Moto Sport	KTM	19	43m 58.047s
18	Jasper Iwema	NED	53	Racing Team Germany	Aprilia	19	44m 05.087s
19	Jakub Kornfeil	CZE	26	Loncin Racing	Loncin	19	44m 18.567s
20	Muhmmed Zulfahmi	MAL	23	Air Asia Team Malaya	Yamaha	19	44m 49.695s
21	Blake Leigh-Smith	AUS	47	Degraaf Grand Prix	Honda	19	44m 56.978s
22	Quentin Jaquert	AUS	47	Degraaf Grand Prix	Honda	19	44m 56.978s
	Simon Corsi	ITA	24	Fontana Racing	Aprilia	17	DNF
	Johann Zarco	FRA	14	WTR San Marino Team	Aprilia	17	DNF
	Efren Vazquez	SPA	7	Derbi Racing Team	Derbi	19	DNF
	Luca Marconi	FRA	87	CBC Corse	Aprilia	14	DNF
	Luca Vitali	ITA	10	CBC Corse	Aprilia	13	DNF
	Marc Marquez	SPA	93	Red Bull KTM Moto Sport	KTM	12	DNF
	Scott Redding	GB	45	Blusens Aprilia	Aprilia	10	DNF
	Jonas Folger	GER	94	Ongetta Team I.S.PA.	Aprilia	10	DNF
	Tomoyoshi Koyama	JPN	71	Loncin Racing	Loncin	2	DNF
	Stefan Bradl	GER	17	Viessmann Kiefer Racing	Aprilia	0	DNF
	Danny Webb	GB	99	Degraaf Grand Prix	Aprilia	0	DNF

Fastest lap: Bradley Smith, on lap 7, 2m 14.068s, 92.568mph/148.975km/h.
Previous lap record: Alvaro Bautista, SPA (Aprilia), 2m 13.118s, 93.229mph/150.03km/h (2006).
Event best maximum speed: Corsi, 141.486mph/227.7km/h (race).

Qualifying: Dry — Air: 33° Humidity: 41% Track: 55°

1	Marquez	2m 13.756s
2	Simon	2m 13.811s
3	Smith	2m 14.209s
4	Cortese	2m 14.231s
5	Terol	2m 14.403s
6	Rabat	2m 14.686s
7	Olive	2m 14.816s
8	Webb	2m 14.920s
9	Vazquez	2m 14.975s
10	Folger	2m 14.992s
11	Espargaro, Pol	2m 15.019s
12	Krummenacher	2m 15.219s
13	Iannone	2m 15.282s
14	Zanetti	2m 15.374s
15	Nakagami	2m 15.436s
16	Corsi	2m 15.455s
17	Redding	2m 15.484s
18	Gadea	2m 15.529s
19	Bradl	2m 15.533s
20	Salom	2m 15.951s
21	Aegerter	2m 16.278s
22	Zarco	2m 16.364s
23	Ranseder	2m 16.530s
24	Beaubier	2m 16.533s
25	Ilias	2m 17.952s
26	Koyama	2m 18.384s
27	Iwema	2m 18.572s
28	Kornfeil	2m 18.749s
29	Leiigh-Smith	2m 19.624s
30	Zulfami	2m 19.655s
31	Marconi	2m 19.868s
32	Vitali	2m 21.127s
33	Jaquet	2m 21.148s

Fastest race laps

1	Smith	2m 14.068s
2	Folger	2m 14.105s
3	Espargaro, Pol	2m 14.273s
4	Simon	2m 14.314s
5	Corsi	2m 14.390s
6	Vazquez	2m 14.440s
7	Gadea	2m 14.510s
8	Cortese	2m 14.546s
9	Rabat	2m 14.548s
10	Terol	2m 14.631s
11	Marquez	2m 14.693s
12	Olive	2m 15.071s
13	Iannone	2m 15.079s
14	Zanetti	2m 15.144s
15	Nakagami	2m 15.198s
16	Ranseder	2m 15.793s
17	Zarco	2m 15.909s
18	Krummenacher	2m 16.160s
19	Salom	2m 16.248s
20	Aegerter	2m 16.551s
21	Ilias	2m 16.783s
22	Redding	2m 16.845s
23	Beaubier	2m 17.267s
24	Iwema	2m 17.716s
25	Kornfeil	2m 18.161s
26	Marconi	2m 19.141s
27	Zulfami	2m 20.074s
28	Leigh-Smith	2m 20.457s
29	Vitali	2m 20.870s
30	Jacquet	2m 21.907s
31	Koyama	2m 27.762s

Championship Points

1	Simon	264
2	Smith	203.5
3	Terol	173.5
4	Espargaro, Pol	158.5
5	Gadea	141
6	Iannone	125.5
7	Cortese	122
8	Marquez	94
9	Bradl	85
10	Olive	81
11	Folger	73
12	Corsi	68
13	Aegerter	65.5
14	Redding	50.5
15	Vazquez	45
16	Nakagami	41
17	Webb	38.5
18	Rabat	37
19	Zanetti	33
20	Zarco	31.5
21	Krummenacher	25
22	Salom	18
23	Koyama	17
24	Ranseder	9
25	Savadori	7
26	Schrotter	7
27	Moretti	3
28	Iwema	3
29	Beaubier	3
30	Glossop	2
31	Fritz	2
32	di Carlo	2
33	Kartheininger	1

Constructors
1	Aprilia	348.5
2	Derbi	200
3	KTM	96
4	Loncin	17
5	Honda	14

VALENCIA GRAND PRIX

VALENCIA

The banners are for Rossi and the
Espargaro brothers, but it was Pedrosa
who gave home fans the win they craved.
Photo: Gold & Goose

THEY say that the new season begins the day after the last race. It began a bit sooner for one rider – Ben Spies, fresh from his maiden Superbike title. He arrived in full modest mode to take up his wild-card entry, and then gave the lower MotoGP orders a lesson in overtaking as he moved through from 11th to an eventual seventh. This on a bike he had never ridden before, on carbon brakes for the first time, and on control Bridgestone tyres that were equally new. It didn't stop there: in Tuesday's testing, Spies set fourth fastest time. "Seventh was a good result, but I was still 35 seconds behind the leader," he said.

There was still a last race to get out of the way, in front of Valencia's usual huge and excitable crowds (more than 94,000 on race day). And one championship to be decided – the historic, last ever 250 crown. That played out to maximum effect, the balance swinging first towards Simoncelli, and finally back to Aoyama and his Honda. With elegant irony, the last two-stroke title went to the factory that had played the biggest part in killing off the 250s. Moreover, the two-stroke crown was the only major title that Honda had won not only in 2009, but also for several years.

And it was one last chance for Stoner to show how strongly he had come back. That went pretty well, for the first two days: he was confidently dominant in every session. It went horribly wrong, though, when he crashed on the warm-up lap. While the others made it back to the line, not even sure why the pole slot was empty, Stoner was departing from the trackside, his face as red as his Ducati's new slim-line fairing. Not only was his chance of second overall gone, but also he actually lost third to Pedrosa.

The next day, he was able to laugh about it, but not explain it. He'd hung back as the rest took off, and was still cruising when he ran around the second corner. "I just touched the throttle, and it threw me," he said. "As I hit the ground, I thought, 'That was a stupid mistake,' but I thought about it after that, and I hadn't done anything wrong." He left the question hanging as to whether there had been a tyre or electronic mal-

function; the team's surmise was that the conditions and high wind on the grid had cooled the rear tyre and the track surface, and even though he had weaved on the short straight, it was still too cool.

The incident sparked a discussion on pre-race strategy. Ducati has two variations. In one, the rider dashes out for a high-speed sighting lap on his spare bike, to put heat into the tyres, then pulls into the pit lane in time to switch to his race bike, which he will tour gently to the start line, to save fuel. Mechanics whip the warm and freshly scrubbed tyres off the spare and bring them to the grid to fit to the race bike. The second method entails a single sighting lap on the race bike, at low speed. The rider hangs back for the warm-up lap, then works the tyres hard over the final corners to build up temperature. It was this strategy that caught out Casey at Valencia.

A flurry of end-of-year launches, announcements and debriefs was eclipsed by a comment by Dorna CEO Carmelo Ezpeleta in a TV interview: he confirmed that there was every chance of a switch back to 1000cc when the 800cc tenure expires at the end of 2011, probably to production-based engines. It was a proposal that found great support among the riders, who want the torque and horsepower back, and now increasingly, according to IRTA president Hervé

Poncharal, from the manufacturers. It was a big change of attitude from when the bikes dubbed 'Moto1' were first mooted at the Sachsenring. As Poncharal said, "What was impossible to think of one year ago is now possible."

Two new MotoGP contenders were expected, but only one was present: an all-new Spanish-built V4, already seven months into testing with former now-and-then GP racer Ivan Silva. Nothing of the Inmotec's V4 engine, variable-length intake and pneumatic valve-spring arrangement could be seen when the bike was unveiled with wind-tunnel tested bodywork in place, while power output was said to be "competitive with the current level". The chassis, with carbon-fibre seat/subframe, looked quite conventional; the engine had been designed and developed by the Spanish firm, working with French based Kawasaki tuner and race entrant Akira Technologies. All new, it had an 80-degree vee angle, compared with predecessor Ilmor's 70 degrees. The firm planned a few wild-card entries for 2010, but "we are not a racing team" – the hope was to offer private teams "an alternative to Japan".

Given the 2011 expiry of the 800cc sanction, the venture seemed ill timed, but at least it was there. Another project, the Italian FB Corse, designed by Oral Engineering (actually a down-sized development of a 990cc triple built for BMW, before the company chose Superbike racing instead), had been promised

as a wild-card entry, but there was no substance to the promise.

There were two more new launches for Moto2 – from German firm Kalex and Italian newcomer Rapid Inside, each working exclusively with an established team: Pons and Scot respectively. These joined a large field of chassis on offer from all around the world – some 13 at the last count. They coincided with the finalising of the entry list, bulging at 37. Team Roberts had dropped out, having failed to find finance; one reserve team – the Antonio Banderas backed Promoracing – was in. According to IRTA general secretary Mike Trimby, all but one team had paid the deposit of US$25,000 per rider, "and we are happy that team will pay"; the list was much as before. No riders were named in the official release, "because only about 60 per cent are finalised, and the teams will make their announcement in their own time," said Trimby.

The weekend closed with news that Suzuki's entreaties had borne fruit: MotoGP rookies would be allowed extra testing. New rider Alvaro Bautista was down to join Suzuki factory tester Nobu Aoki in Portugal later in the month; a pre-Christmas outing in Malaysia was also on the cards, Simoncelli and Aoyama being expected to take advantage. The other testing starved riders were not impressed. As Rossi said, "If the rookies want more laps, they should have come to MotoGP four or five years ago."

Above: Chasing Dani: Elias heads Rossi, Lorenzo, Edwards, Hayden and the rest early in the race.

Above left: For once, Rossi almost dressed formally to receive his World Championship trophy.

Left: Edwards ended the year with a strong fourth. Here he leads de Puniet, Hayden and de Angelis.

Photos: Gold & Goose

MotoGP RACE – 30 laps

Practice was blighted by high winds and dominated by Stoner. Pedrosa was next best, a quarter of a second down, and then Lorenzo. Rossi had struggled for grip and was fourth, a diabolical 0.666 second down on pole. This time, his team did find the magic fix on race morning.

Pedrosa was almost caught napping at the start with his visor still up: awaiting Stoner, he assumed that the red-flag man must have made a mistake when he left the grid. He still got away first, however, to lead into the first corner, while Elias burst through from row three to follow him, Rossi, Lorenzo and Edwards behind.

By the end of the lap, Lorenzo was ahead of Rossi, while Pedrosa was already seven-tenths away. This would stretch to more than two seconds at the end of lap three, when Lorenzo got by Elias, followed promptly by Rossi.

They were not to exchange blows, however. A little further around, Lorenzo suffered a big slide and was thrown out of the saddle. He landed rather hard, with two consequences. One was obvious, he crushed his testicles, the other altogether more arcane. The shock of landing inflated his air-bag vest. This time, unlike at Brno, it deflated over the next 30 seconds or so, and the pain between his legs also subsided – but Rossi was ahead and had a cushion of four-tenths that would double next time around.

There was no further change for the top three. Rossi would close a little on Pedrosa, then the Spaniard would stretch away again by a couple of tenths. By half-distance, the lead was almost three seconds, and three laps later more than four. Perversely, as on previous occasions, Puig was signalling his rider with a much smaller gap, anxious to avoid the last-lap relaxation that had almost cost him his other win, at Laguna.

With seven laps left, Lorenzo was just 1.6 behind and pegging away steadily. Rossi got the message:

"I had to switch off my brain and push again." They closed slightly on Pedrosa, but his winning margin was still 2.6 seconds; Lorenzo was just a few tenths behind Rossi.

Elias, afflicted by a heavy head cold, had dropped steadily out of touch. By lap four, he'd been caught by Edwards, who was fending off de Puniet and Hayden. Three laps later, Edwards made a slingshot pass on Elias, and Hayden got in front of de Puniet. Edwards pulled a small gap while de Puniet lost touch, but Hayden and Elias were engaged until the end. The Ducati rider got ahead on lap 13, staying there by three-tenths at the flag.

The next group saw more action. Melandri was in front in the early stages, from de Angelis and Kallio, with Spies dropping behind as he worked to get the feel of the tyres, although he remained ahead of Toseland.

Kallio took over, and the group was closing gradually on de Puniet. Then, just before the mid-point, Melandri ran off, rejoining between Spies and Toseland a little way back.

Dovizioso had qualified a lowly tenth, and started even worse, finishing the first lap 14th. He'd been cutting through ever since, and had caught the group and taken over the lead from Kallio on lap 11.

At the same time, Spies had settled down to some steady fast laps, By the time the group caught de Puniet at half-distance, the new boy had tagged on behind.

His first pass was a gift, when Kallio made a slip and dropped to the back. On the next lap, he overtook de Angelis – now he was getting the feel for it. "In Superbike, you just push past under brakes; with these bikes, you have to plan it a couple of corners earlier." His next victim was de Puniet, on lap 21, and now he had Dovizioso in his sights. Spies was a little apprehensive that if he passed, he might hold up the factory Honda, so he waited four laps before another clean overtake. And managed to stay ahead by better than half a second over the line.

An impressive result, but even more endearing to

his team. By beating Dovizioso, he had secured fifth overall for Edwards, his partner at Tech 3 in 2010. Edwards had one more point; had Spies succumbed, they would have been equal, but the Italian's win at Donington would have secured the position.

Kallio, de Angelis and de Puniet were spaced out behind Spies, with another gap to Toseland in 12th. The Briton was distraught after being so soundly beaten by a rookie on the same bike, and he left the track in some distress.

Espargaro was seven seconds behind, making some progress later by passing Capirossi. It was another dire race for the Suzukis: Vermeulen was never in the mix in his last GP, another five seconds back in 15th. Talmacsi was a further three seconds down, with Melandri fading behind him.

Ultimately, Lorenzo's second overall was not threat-

Left: Aoyama's seventh would have been enough, even if Simoncelli had not crashed. He is the last 250 champion in history.

Below: Barbera became the last 250 race winner.

Photos: Gold & Goose

Above: Simoncelli shrugs it off. At least he was leading when he crashed.

Right: Young guns Marquez (93) and rank rookie Schrotter (78) head the 125 battle for fourth.

Top left: Ben Spies' Yamaha debut was mighty impressive.

Photos: Gold & Goose

ened, for Stoner's no-score actually dropped him to fourth: Pedrosa's second win of the year meant that the Spaniard moved past to secure third. After Edwards and Dovizioso, Elias won the big battle for seventh from team-mate de Angelis.

250cc RACE – 27 laps

The spotlight for the historic last 250 grand prix was firmly on Simoncelli and Aoyama, but home flyer Debon (sponsored by a nearby airport) took the attention in practice, setting pole time near the end and then promptly suffering a seize as he ran into the first corner – a reminder of the dark side of the two-stroke's character. He didn't crash then, but had to bale out at speed before slamming into the barrier after a wild run across the gravel, and was out of the race with broken ribs.

Simoncelli took over the vacant pole, from Barbera and Wilairot (his first front row), with Aoyama promoted to the front row as well, a full half-second slower than Simoncelli.

Tension was peaking as the last ever 250 two-stroke grid filled the air with its unique sound. Barbera led away, pursued at first by Luthi and Aoyama, with Simoncelli fifth, behind Cluzel.

Luthi dropped back almost at once, and it took Simoncelli until lap five to get past Cluzel, by which time Bautista had got ahead of both of them. But Simoncelli had found his rhythm and soon was moving forward in familiar forceful fashion – past Aoyama for second on lap eight and ahead of Barbera next time around.

Aoyama's drama came as they started lap ten. As Barbera braked for the first turn, he almost ran into him, jinking out wide. He wasn't going to make the corner, but as he ran out over the white line, he picked up the bike for a highly fraught long run through the gravel. He narrowly avoided the crash that would have lost the title, and rejoined in 11th. He only needed to stay there – but was his bike damaged?

Simoncelli was firmly in front, but now di Meglio was second after finishing lap one 11th, with Bautista and Barbera right behind.

At half-distance, Barbera was back up to second, while de Rosa had caught up to make a gang of four. Simoncelli had a little gap, but it wouldn't last, as Barbera was about to challenge.

For Simoncelli, it was win or bust, and he almost crashed several times. Finally, he did so on lap 20, leaving Barbera as the last 250 winner. Also, thanks to Simoncelli's crash, he moved up to second overall.

Behind him, Bautista and de Rosa had passed di Meglio, but the fight was close, until the Frenchman slid off on lap 20.

Bautista outpaced de Rosa. Meanwhile, Luthi was back ahead of Cluzel and was closing. A last-lap slip by de Rosa gave the Swiss rider a chance, but the rookie of the year stayed ahead by inches.

Cluzel was left to battle with Wilairot until the Frenchman crashed out with five laps left. By now, Abraham had closed, less than a tenth adrift over the line.

Aoyama was a lone seventh, punching the air in delight at claiming the last ever 250 title. His promotion from 11th had been mainly through attrition, but he had taken Baldolini, who was troubled in the closing laps by Locatelli, fresh off the operating table after crashing in Malaysia.

Tomizawa was tenth. Pons and Pasini retired; Faubel crashed out in the early stages.

Thus Aoyama became the last 250 champion by a comfortable margin. Honda always did make good racing two-strokes, whether the manufacturer liked it or not.

125cc RACE – 24 laps

Simon took a seventh pole, from Corsi, Smith and Marquez. Impressive rookie Marcus Schrotter, in his fourth GP, was on the second row after topping the timesheets several times.

Smith took a flying start and was almost 1.5 seconds clear after the first lap. By then, Simon was second, and by lap five he was on his team-mate, the pair miles ahead of the rest. The end-of-season form of the pair was formidable.

They circulated in formation until lap 20, Smith with a half-second gap as he tried to get away. Instead he almost crashed next lap, letting Simon through.

He closed up again to attack on the last lap. The pair changed places four times, Simon taking his seventh win by two-tenths.

Espargaro had been tenth after lap one, in the thick of a gang of more than a dozen. But he gained places lap by lap, taking third on lap five and almost at once moving clear of the battle to make the spot safe.

At the halfway point, there were still eight riders crawling all over each other for fourth.

Again, Marquez was conspicuous and led on to the last lap. But halfway around, he was knocked flying as they all closed up on one another. At the line, Corsi was fourth, with the amazing Schrotter next, then team-mates Olive and Vazquez, Cortese and Krummenacher, fourth to ninth covered by 1.2 seconds. Tenth-placed Terol had been with them, but lost touch in the closing stages. He did just enough to save third overall from Espargaro. Early points leader Iannone retired on the first lap and lost sixth overall to Cortese.

CIRCUITO DE LA COMUNITAT VALENCIANA

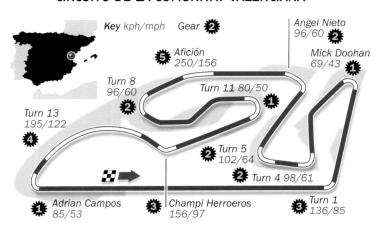

Key kph/mph   Gear 2

Angel Nieto 96/60 2
Aficíon 250/156 5
Mick Doohan 69/43 1
Turn 8 96/60 2
Turn 11 80/50 1
Turn 13 195/122 4
Turn 5 102/64 2
Turn 4 98/61 2
Adrian Campos 85/53 1
Champi Herroeros 156/97 3
Turn 1 136/85 3

Circuit 4.005km/2.488 miles

MOTOGP

RACE DISTANCE: 30 laps, 74.657 miles/120.1505 km • RACE WEATHER: Dry (air 19°, humidity 24%, track 29°)

Pos.	Rider	Nat.	No.	Entrant	Machine	Tyres	Laps	Time & speed
1	Dani Pedrosa	SPA	3	Repsol Honda Team	Honda	B	30	46m 47.553s 95.731mph/ 154.062km/h
2	Valentino Rossi	ITA	46	Fiat Yamaha Team	Yamaha	B	30	46m 50.183s
3	Jorge Lorenzo	SPA	99	Fiat Yamaha Team	Yamaha	B	30	46m 50.466s
4	Colin Edwards	USA	5	Monster Yamaha Tech 3	Yamaha	B	30	47m 20.068s
5	Nicky Hayden	USA	69	Ducati Marlboro Team	Ducati	B	30	47m 22.138s
6	Toni Elias	SPA	24	San Carlos Honda Gresini	Honda	B	30	47m 22.441s
7	Ben Spies	USA	11	Sterilgarda Yamaha Team	Yamaha	B	30	47m 25.259s
8	Andrea Dovizioso	ITA	4	Repsol Honda Team	Honda	B	30	47m 25.917s
9	Mika Kallio	FIN	36	Pramac Racing	Ducati	B	30	47m 30.044s
10	Alex de Angelis	RSM	15	San Carlos Honda Gresini	Honda	B	30	47m 31.242s
11	Randy de Puniet	FRA	14	LCR Honda MotoGP	Honda	B	30	47m 33.571s
12	James Toseland	JPN	52	Monster Yamaha Tech 3	Yamaha	B	30	47m 37.779s
13	Aleix Espargaro	SPA	44	Pramac Racing	Ducati	B	30	47m 44.721s
14	Loris Capirossi	ITA	65	Rizla Suzuki MotoGP	Suzuki	B	30	47m 54.430s
15	Chris Vermeulen	AUS	7	Rizla Suzuki MotoGP	Suzuki	B	30	47m 59.254s
16	Gabor Talmacsi	HUN	41	Scot Racing Team MotoGP	Honda	B	30	48m 01.958s
17	Marco Melandri	ITA	33	Hayate Racing Team	Kawasaki	B	30	48m 20.978s
	Casey Stoner	AUS	27	Repsol Honda Team	Honda	B	0	DNS

Qualifying: Dry		
Air: 22° Humidity: 24% Track: 28°		
1	Stoner	1m 32.256s
2	Pedrosa	1m 32.519s
3	Lorenzo	1m 32.537s
4	Rossi	1m 32.922s
5	Edwards	1m 33.085s
6	Hayden	1m 33.154s
7	de Puniet	1m 33.391s
8	Elias	1m 33.475s
9	Spies	1m 33.539s
10	Dovizioso	1m 33.678s
11	Kallio	1m 33.809s
12	de Angelis	1m 33.844s
13	Capirossi	1m 34.097s
14	Toseland	1m 34.107s
15	Melandri	1m 34.188s
16	Espargaro	1m 34.308s
17	Talmacsi	1m 34.357s
18	Vermeulen	1m 34.537s

Fastest race laps		
1	Pedrosa	1m 32.778s
2	Rossi	1m 32.830s
3	Lorenzo	1m 33.081s
4	Elias	1m 33.717s
5	Edwards	1m 33.736s
6	Hayden	1m 33.865s
7	de Puniet	1m 33.934s
8	de Angelis	1m 33.982s
9	Spies	1m 34.015s
10	Kallio	1m 34.030s
11	Dovizioso	1m 34.050s
12	Capirossi	1m 34.140s
13	Toseland	1m 34.316s
14	Espargaro	1m 34.458s
15	Melandri	1m 34.463s
16	Vermeulen	1m 34.871s
17	Talmacsi	1m 34.919s

Fastest lap: Dani Pedrosa, on lap 10, 1m 32.778s, 96.562mph/155.403km/h.

Lap record: Casey Stoner, AUS (Ducati), 1m 32.582s, 96.767mph/155.732km/h (2008).

Event best maximum speed: Pedrosa, 316.600km/h/196.763km/h (free practice 2).

Championship Points	
1 Rossi	306
2 Lorenzo	261
3 Pedrosa	234
4 Stoner	220
5 Edwards	161
6 Dovizioso	160
7 Elias	115
8 de Angelis	111
9 Capirossi	110
10 Melandri	108
11 de Puniet	106
12 Vermeulen	106
13 Hayden	104
14 Toseland	92
15 Kallio	71
16 Canepa	38
17 Talmacsi	19
18 Espargaro, A	16
19 Gibernau	12
20 Takahashi	9

Constructor Points	
1 Yamaha	386
3 Honda	297
3 Ducati	272
4 Suzuki	133
5 Kawasaki	108

Team Points	
1 FIAT Yamaha Team	567
2 Repsol Honda Team	394
2 Ducati Marlboro Team	341
4 Monster Yamaha Tech 3	253
5 RIZLA Suzuki MotoGP	226
6 San Carlo Honda Gresini	216
7 Hayate Racing Team	108
8 Pramac Racing	108
9 LCR Honda	106
10 Scot Racing Team	28
11 Grupo Francisco Hernan	12

Grid order	1	2	3	4	5	6	7	8	9	10	11	12	13	14	15	16	17	18	19	20	21	22	23	24	25	26	27	28	29	30	
27 STONER	3	3	3	3	3	3	3	3	3	3	3	3	3	3	3	3	3	3	3	3	3	3	3	3	3	3	3	3	3	3	1
3 PEDROSA	24	24	99	46	46	46	46	46	46	46	46	46	46	46	46	46	46	46	46	46	46	46	46	46	46	46	46	46	46	46	2
99 LORENZO	99	99	24	99	99	99	99	99	99	99	99	99	99	99	99	99	99	99	99	99	99	99	99	99	99	99	99	99	99	99	3
46 ROSSI	46	46	46	24	24	24	5	5	5	5	5	5	5	5	5	5	5	5	5	5	5	5	5	5	5	5	5	5	5	5	4
5 EDWARDS	5	5	5	5	5	5	24	24	24	24	24	24	69	69	69	69	69	69	69	69	69	69	69	69	69	69	69	69	69	69	5
69 HAYDEN	14	14	14	14	14	14	69	69	69	69	69	69	24	24	24	24	24	24	24	24	24	24	24	24	24	24	24	24	24	24	6
14 DE PUNIET	69	69	69	69	69	69	14	14	14	14	14	14	14	14	14	4	4	4	4	4	4	4	4	4	11	11	11	11	11	11	7
24 ELIAS	15	15	15	33	33	33	36	36	36	36	4	4	4	4	4	14	14	14	14	14	11	11	11	11	4	4	4	4	4	4	8
11 SPIES	33	33	33	15	15	36	33	4	4	4	36	36	36	36	36	36	11	11	11	11	14	14	14	14	36	36	36	36			9
4 DOVIZIOSO	11	11	11	11	11	15	15	33	33	15	15	15	15	15	15	11	36	36	36	36	36	36	36	36	14	14	15	15			10
36 KALLIO	52	52	36	36	11	11	4	15	11	11	11	11	11	11	11	15	36	36	36	36	36	15	15	15	15	15	14	14			11
15 DE ANGELIS	36	36	52	52	4	4	11	11	11	33	52	52	52	52	52	52	52	52	52	52	52	52	52	52	52	52	52	52			12
65 CAPIROSSI	65	65	65	4	65	52	52	52	52	52	65	65	33	33	44	44	44	44	44	44	44	44	44	44	44	44	44	44			13
52 TOSELAND	4	4	4	65	52	65	65	65	65	65	33	33	65	44	65	65	65	65	65	65	65	65	65	65	65	65	65	65			14
33 MELANDRI	41	41	41	41	41	44	44	44	44	44	44	44	44	65	7	7	7	7	7	7	7	7	7	7	7	7	7	7			15
44 ESPARGARO	7	7	7	44	44	41	41	41	41	41	7	7	7	7	41	41	41	41	41	41	41	41	41	41	41	41	41	41			
41 TALMACSI	44	44	44	7	7	7	7	7	7	7	41	41	41	41	33	33	33	33	33	33	33	33	33	33	33	33	33	33			

250cc — RACE DISTANCE: 27 laps, 67.191 miles/108.135 km • RACE WEATHER: Dry (air 19°, humidity 27%, track 28°)

Pos.	Rider	Nat.	No.	Entrant	Machine	Laps	Time & Speed
1	Hector Barbera	SPA	40	Pepe World Team	Aprilia	27	44m 10.601s
							(mph/km/h)
							91.258/146.867
2	Alvaro Bautista	SPA	19	Mapfre Aspar Team	Aprilia	27	44m 14.264s
3	Raffaele de Rosa	ITA	35	Scot Racing Team 250cc	Honda	27	44m 16.166s
4	Thomas Luthi	SWI	12	Emmi – Caffe Latte	Aprilia	27	44m 16.281s
5	Ratthapark Wilairot	THA	14	Thai Honda PTT SAG	Honda	27	44m 24.202s
6	Karel Abraham	CZE	17	Cardion AB Motoracing	Aprilia	27	44m 24.298s
7	Hiroshi Aoyama	JPN	4	Scot Racing Team 250cc	Honda	27	44m 38.039s
8	Alex Baldolini	ITA	25	WTR San Marino Team	Aprilia	27	44m 45.698s
9	Roberto Locatelli	ITA	15	Metis Gilera	Gilera	27	44m 46.467s
10	Shoya Tomizawa	JPN	48	CIP Moto – GP250	Honda	27	44m 50.777s
11	Shuhei Aoyama	JPN	73	Racing Team Germany	Honda	27	44m 59.696s
12	Lukas Pesek	CZE	52	Auto Kelly – CP	Aprilia	27	45m 03.733s
13	Balazs Nemeth	HUN	11	Balatonring Team	Aprilia	27	45m 16.615s
14	Mike di Meglio	FRA	63	Mapfre Aspar Team 250cc	Aprilia	27	45m 29.293s
15	Valentin Debise	FRA	53	CIP Moto – GP250	Honda	27	45m 29.477s
16	Bastien Chesaux	SWI	8	Racing Team Germany	Honda	26	44m 13.599s
17	Vladimir Leonov	RUS	56	Viessmann Kiefer Racing	Aprilia	26	44m 38.652s
18	William Dunlop	IRL	33	Big Man Racing	Honda	26	45m 34.197s
19	Imre Toth	HUN	10	Team Toth Aprilia	Aprilia	26	45m 42.307s
	Jules Cluzel	FRA	16	Matteoni Racing	Aprilia	23	DNF
	Marco Simoncelli	ITA	58	Metis Gilera	Gilera	20	DNF
	Axel Pons	SPA	7	Pepe World Team	Aprilia	19	DNF
	Mattia Pasini	ITA	75	Paddock GP Racing Team	Aprilia	11	DNF
	Hector Faubel	SPA	55	Honda SAG	Honda	7	DNF

Fastest lap: Hector Barbera, on lap 17, 1m 36.866s, 92.4877mph/148.844km/h.
Lap record: Mika Kallio (KTM) 1m 35.659s, 93.654mph/150.722km/h (2007).
Event best maximum speed: Luthi. 165.595mph/266.5km/h (free practice 2).

Qualifying: Dry — Air: 22° Humidity: 24% Track: 27°

1	Debon	1m 36.116s
2	Simoncelli	1m 36.450s
3	Barbera	1m 36.470s
4	Wilairot	1m 36.563s
5	Aoyama, Hiroshi	1m 36.656s
6	Luthi	1m 36.985s
7	Abraham	1m 37.271s
8	Pasini	1m 37.278s
9	Bautista	1m 37.303s
10	Faubel	1m 37.318s
11	de Rosa	1m 37.365s
12	Baldolini	1m 37.577s
13	Cluzel	1m 37.749s
14	Locatelli	1m 37.811s
15	di Meglio	1m 37.958s
16	Tomizawa	1m 38.085s
17	Pons	1m 38.126s
18	Pesek	1m 38.291s
19	Nemeth	1m 38.737s
20	Aoyama, Shuhei	1m 38.795s
21	Debise	1m 39.283s
22	Leonov	1m 40.371s
23	Chesaux	1m 41.605s
24	Toth	1m 42.416s
25	Dunlop	1m 42.906s

Fastest race laps

1	Barbera	1m 36.866s
2	Simoncelli	1m 36.969s
3	de Rosa	1m 37.090s
4	di Meglio	1m 37.142s
5	Bautista	1m 37.192s
6	Luthi	1m 37.291s
7	Aoyama, Hiroshi	1m 37.351s
8	Wilairot	1m 37.410s
9	Cluzel	1m 37.496s
10	Abraham	1m 37.866s
11	Faubel	1m 38.195s
12	Locatelli	1m 38.259s
13	Baldolini	1m 38.543s
14	Tomizawa	1m 38.717s
15	Aoyama, Shuhei	1m 38.742s
16	Pons	1m 38.935s
17	Pasini	1m 38.972s
18	Pesek	1m 39.044s
19	Nemeth	1m 39.073s
20	Debise	1m 40.102s
21	Chesaux	1m 40.514s
22	Leonov	1m 40.693s
23	Dunlop	1m 42.879s
24	Toth	1m 44.005s

Championship Points

Pos	Rider	Points
1	Aoyama, Hiroshi	261
2	Barbera	239
3	Simoncelli	231
4	Bautista	218
5	Pasini	128
6	de Rosa	122
7	Luthi	120
8	di Meglio	107
9	Faubel	105
10	Debon	101
11	Locatelli	85
12	Cluzel	82
13	Wilairot	81
14	Abraham	74
15	Pesek	74
16	Baldolini	41
17	Tomizawa	32
18	Talmacsi	28
19	Aoyama, Shuhei	27
20	Espargaro, Aleix	22
21	Debise	18
22	Toth	12
23	Nemeth	11
24	Leonov	9
25	Chesaux	3
25	Pons	3
27	Markham	2
27	Watanabe	2
29	Bonsey	1

Constructors

Pos	Make	Points
1	Aprilia	339
2	Honda	287
2	Gilera	245
3	Yamaha	2

125cc — RACE DISTANCE: 24 laps, 59.726 miles/96.12 km • RACE WEATHER: Dry (air 15°, humidity 36%, track 21°)

Pos.	Rider	Nat.	No.	Entrant	Machine	Laps	Time & Speed
1	Julian Simon	SPA	60	Bancaja Aspar Team 125cc	Aprilia	24	41m 17.553s
							(mph/km/h)
							86.784/139.666
2	Bradley Smith	GB	38	Bancaja Aspar Team 125cc	Aprilia	24	41m 17.773s
3	Pol Espargaro	SPA	44	Derbi Racing Team	Derbi	24	41m 29.676s
4	Simon Corsi	ITA	24	Fontana Racing	Aprilia	24	41m 35.130s
5	Marcel Schrotter	GER	78	Toni-Mang Team	Honda	24	41m 35.470s
6	Joan Olive	SPA	6	Derbi Racing Team	Derbi	24	41m 35.887s
7	Efren Vazquez	SPA	7	Derbi Racing Team	Derbi	24	41m 36.005s
8	Sandro Cortese	GER	11	Ajo Interwetten	Derbi	24	41m 36.106s
9	Randy Krummenacher	SWI	35	Degraaf Grand Prix	Aprilia	24	41m 36.284s
10	Nicolas Terol	SPA	18	Jack & Jones Team	Aprilia	24	41m 38.833s
11	Dominique Aegerter	SWI	77	Ajo Interwetten	Derbi	24	41m 41.188s
12	Lorenzo Zanetti	ITA	8	Ongetta Team I.S.P.A.	Aprilia	24	41m 51.922s
13	Luis Salom	SPA	39	Jack & Jones Team	Honda	24	41m 55.503s
14	Takaaki Nakagami	JPN	73	Ongetta Team I.S.P.A.	Aprilia	24	41m 55.643s
15	Johann Zarco	FRA	14	WTR San Marino Team	Aprilia	24	41m 57.596s
16	Sergio Gadea	SPA	33	Bancaja Aspar Team 125cc	Aprilia	24	42m 02.031s
17	Marc Marquez	SPA	93	Red Bull KTM Moto Sport	KTM	24	42m 15.990s
18	Jasper Iwema	NED	53	Racing Team Germany	Aprilia	24	42m 21.367s
19	Albert Moncayo	SPA	42	Andalucia Aprilia	Aprilia	24	42m 25.915s
20	Tomoyoshi Koyama	JPN	71	Loncin Racing	Loncin	24	42m 42.524s
21	Luca Marconi	FRA	87	CBC Corse	Aprilia	23	41m 21.630
	Cameron Beaubier	USA	16	Red Bull KTM Moto Sport	KTM	23	DNF
	Luca Vitali	ITA	10	CBC Corse	Aprilia	21	DNF
	Jonas Folger	GER	94	Ongetta Team I.S.P.A.	Aprilia	17	DNF
	Ivan Maestro	SPA	76	Hune Racing Team-RZT	Aprilia	11	DNF
	Jakub Kornfeil	CZE	21	Loncin Racing	Loncin	9	DNF
	Stefan Bradl	GER	17	Viessmann Kiefer Racing	Aprilia	8	DNF
	Lorenzo Savadori	ITA	32	Junior GP Racing Dream	Aprilia	6	DNF
	Esteve Rabat	SPA	12	Blusens Aprilia	Aprilia	5	DNF
	Scott Redding	GB	45	Blusens Aprilia	Aprilia	5	DNF
	Sturla Fagerhaug	NOR	50	Red Bull KTM Motorsport	KTM	4	DNF
	Michael Ranseder	AUT	88	CBC Corse	Aprilia	3	DNF
	Andrea Iannone	ITA	29	Ongetta Team I.S.P.A.	Aprilia	1	DNF
	Joan Perello	SPA		SAG Castrol	Aprilia	0	DNS

Fastest lap: Julian Simon, on lap 4, 1m 41.650s, 88.134mph/141.839km/h.
Lap record: Hector Faubel, ESP (Aprilia), 1m 39.380s, 90.147mph/145.079km/h (2007).
Event best maximum speed: Espargaro, 142.915mph/230.0km/h (race).

Qualifying: Dry — Air: 22° Humidity: 34% Track: 27°

1	Simon	1m 41.472s
2	Corsi	1m 41.476s
3	Smith	1m 41.830s
4	Marquez	1m 41.991s
5	Olive	1m 42.033s
6	Terol	1m 42.092s
7	Schrotter	1m 42.111s
8	Espargaro, Pol	1m 42.162s
9	Redding	1m 42.233s
10	Cortese	1m 42.246s
11	Rabat	1m 42.307s
12	Vazquez	1m 42.495s
13	Iannone	1m 42.556s
14	Gadea	1m 42.648s
15	Krummenacher	1m 42.767s
16	Bradl	1m 42.769s
17	Beaubier	1m 42.823s
18	Nakagami	1m 42.874s
19	Aegerter	1m 42.913s
20	Folger	1m 42.948s
21	Zarco	1m 43.176s
22	Zanetti	1m 43.441s
23	Ranseder	1m 43.691s
24	Salom	1m 44.081s
25	Iwema	1m 44.264s
26	Joan Perello	1m 44.264s
27	Savadori	1m 44.267s
28	Webb	1m 44.284s
29	Koyama	1m 44.326s
30	Fagerhaug	1m 44.634s
31	Kornfeil	1m 44.979s
32	Maestro	1m 45.136s
33	Marconi	1m 45.530s
34	Moncayo	1m 45.575s
35	Vitali	1m 47.151s

Fastest race laps

1	Simon	1m 41.650s
2	Smith	1m 42.124s
3	Espargaro, Pol	1m 42.512s
4	Cortese	1m 42.546s
5	Corsi	1m 42.546s
6	Schrotter	1m 42.682s
7	Bradl	1m 42.717s
8	Olive	1m 42.739s
9	Krummenacher	1m 42.796s
10	Vazquez	1m 42.853s
11	Terol	1m 42.903s
12	Marquez	1m 42.998s
13	Beaubier	1m 43.053s
14	Zanetti	1m 43.135s
15	Redding	1m 43.144s
16	Folger	1m 43.219s
17	Aegerter	1m 43.247s
18	Gadea	1m 43.258s
19	Rabat	1m 43.280s
20	Salom	1m 43.349s
21	Nakagami	1m 43.547s
22	Zarco	1m 43.591s
23	Iwema	1m 44.465s
24	Savadori	1m 44.606s
25	Moncayo	1m 44.751s
26	Fagerhaug	1m 44.961s
27	Koyama	1m 45.016s
28	Maestro	1m 45.041s
29	Kornfeil	1m 45.149s
30	Marconi	1m 45.944s
31	Vitali	1m 45.683s
32	Ranseder	1m 48.164s
33	Iannone	1m 51.752s

Championship Points

Pos	Rider	Points
1	Simon	289
2	Smith	223.5
3	Terol	179.5
4	Espargaro, Pol	174.5
5	Gadea	141
6	Cortese	130
7	Iannone	125.5
8	Marquez	94
9	Olive	91
10	Bradl	85
11	Corsi	81
12	Folger	73
13	Aegerter	70.5
14	Vazquez	54
15	Redding	50.5
16	Nakagami	43
17	Webb	38.5
18	Rabat	37
19	Zanetti	37
20	Zarco	32.5
21	Krummenacher	32
22	Salom	21
23	Schrotter	18
24	Koyama	17
25	Ranseder	9
26	Savadori	7
27	Moretti	3
28	Iwema	3
29	Beaubier	3
30	Glossop	2
31	Fritz	2
32	di Carlo	2
33	Kartheininger	1

Constructors

Pos	Make	Points
1	Aprilia	373.5
2	Derbi	216
3	KTM	96
4	Honda	25
5	Loncin	17

WORLD CHAMPIONSHIP POINTS 2009

Compiled by PETER McLAREN

2009 MotoGP World Champions

MOTOGP

Position	Rider	Nationality	Machine	Qatar	Japan	Spain	France	Italy	Catalunya	Netherlands	United States	Germany	Great Britain	Czech Republic	Indianapolis	San Marino	Portugal	Australia	Malaysia	Valencia	Points total
1	Valentino Rossi	ITA	Yamaha	20	20	25	-	16	25	25	20	25	11	25	-	25	13	20	16	20	306
2	Jorge Lorenzo	SPA	Yamaha	16	25	-	25	20	20	20	16	20	-	-	25	20	25	-	13	16	261
3	Dani Pedrosa	SPA	Honda	5	16	20	16	-	10	-	25	16	7	20	6	16	16	16	20	25	234
4	Casey Stoner	AUS	Ducati	25	13	16	11	25	16	16	13	13	2	-	-	-	20	25	25	-	220
5	Colin Edwards	USA	Yamaha	13	4	9	9	10	9	13	9	7	20	9	11	-	11	11	3	13	161
6	Andrea Dovizioso	ITA	Honda	11	11	8	13	13	13	-	-	-	25	13	13	13	9	10	-	8	160
7	Toni Elias	SPA	Honda	7	1	7	6	2	-	4	10	10	-	16	7	10	10	6	9	10	115
8	Alex de Angelis	RSM	Honda	10	3	2	5	1	4	6	5	11	13	8	20	-	-	13	4	6	111
9	Loris Capirossi	ITA	Suzuki	-	9	10	8	11	11	7	-	5	5	11	9	11	-	4	7	2	110
10	Marco Melandri	ITA	Kawasaki	2	10	11	20	5	2	5	6	9	9	-	-	8	4	9	8	-	108
11	Randy de Puniet	FRA	Honda	6	5	13	2	8	8	9	7	-	16	6	4	4	5	8	-	5	106
12	Chris Vermeulen	AUS	Suzuki	9	6	6	10	6	5	11	8	3	3	5	5	7	6	5	10	1	106
13	Nicky Hayden	USA	Ducati	4	-	1	4	4	6	8	11	8	1	10	16	-	8	1	11	11	104
14	James Toseland	GBR	Yamaha	-	7	3	7	9	3	10	-	6	10	7	10	6	7	2	1	4	92
15	Mika Kallio	FIN	Ducati	8	8	-	-	3	7	-	-	2	6	-	8	9	-	7	6	7	71
16	Niccolo Canepa	ITA	Ducati	-	2	-	1	7	-	2	4	4	8	4	-	3	3	-	-	-	38
17	Gabor Talmacsi	HUN	Honda	-	-	-	-	-	-	-	-	1	4	3	2	2	2	3	2	-	19
18	Aleix Espargaro	SPA	Ducati	-	-	-	-	-	-	-	-	-	-	-	3	5	-	-	5	3	16
19	Sete Gibernau	SPA	Ducati	3	-	5	-	-	1	3	-	-	-	-	-	-	-	-	-	-	12
20	Ben Spies	USA	Yamaha	-	-	-	-	-	-	-	-	-	-	-	-	-	-	-	-	9	9
21	Yuki Takahashi	JPN	Honda	1	-	4	3	-	-	1	-	-	-	-	-	-	-	-	-	-	9

250cc

Position	Rider	Nationality	Machine	Qatar	Japan	Spain	France	Italy	Catalunya	Netherlands	Germany	Great Britain	Czech Republic	Indianapolis	San Marino	Portugal	Australia	Malaysia	Valencia	Points total
1	Hiroshi Aoyama	JPN	Honda	13	20	25	8	10	20	25	13	25	13	20	13	13	9	25	9	261
2	Hector Barbera	SPA	Aprilia	25	5	13	5	11	16	20	11	8	9	10	25	16	20	20	25	239
3	Marco Simoncelli	ITA	Gilera	-	-	16	25	20	-	16	25	13	25	25	-	25	25	16	-	231
4	Alvaro Bautista	SPA	Aprilia	9	25	20	13	16	25	-	16	20	16	16	16	-	6	-	20	218
5	Mattia Pasini	ITA	Aprilia	-	16	10	-	25	13	-	-	16	20	-	20	8	-	-	-	128
6	Raffaele de Rosa	ITA	Honda	11	4	6	10	7	7	6	7	9	10	5	8	-	16	-	16	122
7	Thomas Luthi	SWI	Aprilia	10	8	11	-	13	10	-	8	7	-	7	6	9	5	13	13	120
8	Mike di Meglio	FRA	Aprilia	16	-	5	-	4	2	5	-	11	7	13	11	20	11	-	2	107
9	Hector Faubel	SPA	Honda	5	-	2	20	8	6	8	10	6	6	8	7	-	8	11	-	105
10	Alex Debon	SPA	Aprilia	2	11	-	-	9	11	10	20	10	-	-	9	7	3	9	-	101
11	Roberto Locatelli	ITA	Gilera	7	-	7	16	6	-	11	6	3	11	11	-	-	-	-	7	85
12	Jules Cluzel	FRA	Aprilia	20	-	8	-	-	5	-	2	5	8	-	10	11	13	-	-	82
13	Ratthapark Wilairot	THA	Honda	8	-	1	11	2	9	7	-	-	5	-	-	10	7	10	11	81
14	Karel Abraham	CZE	Aprilia	-	7	-	4	3	8	9	-	2	-	6	5	6	10	4	10	74
15	Lukas Pesek	CZE	Aprilia	3	9	3	9	-	4	4	4	4	4	9	-	5	4	8	4	74
16	Alex Baldolini	ITA	Aprilia	1	-	-	-	5	3	3	5	-	-	4	3	2	-	7	8	41
17	Shoya Tomizawa	JPN	Honda	4	6	4	-	-	-	-	3	1	3	-	4	-	1	-	6	32
18	Gabor Talmacsi	HUN	Aprilia	6	13	9	-	-	-	-	-	-	-	-	-	-	-	-	-	28
19	Shuhei Aoyama	JPN	Honda	-	10	-	-	-	-	-	-	-	-	-	-	4	2	6	5	27
20	Aleix Espargaro	SPA	Aprilia	-	-	-	-	-	-	13	9	-	-	-	-	-	-	-	-	22
21	Valentin Debise	FRA	Honda	-	-	-	3	-	-	2	-	-	1	3	2	3	-	3	1	18
22	Imre Toth	HUN	Aprilia	-	3	-	7	1	-	1	-	-	-	-	-	-	-	-	-	12
23	Balazs Nemeth	HUN	Aprilia	-	-	-	-	-	-	-	-	2	-	1	-	-	-	5	3	11
24	Vladimir Leonov	RUS	Aprilia	-	1	-	6	-	-	-	-	-	-	1	-	-	-	1	-	9
25	Bastien Chesaux	SWI	Aprilia	-	-	-	-	-	-	-	1	-	-	-	-	-	-	2	-	3
26	Axel Pons	SPA	Aprilia	-	-	-	-	-	-	-	-	-	-	2	-	1	-	-	-	3
27	Toby Markham	GBR	Honda/Aprilia	-	-	-	2	-	-	-	-	-	-	-	-	-	-	-	-	2
28	Kazuki Watanabe	JPN	Yamaha	-	2	-	-	-	-	-	-	-	-	-	-	-	-	-	-	2
29	Stevie Bonsey	USA	Aprilia	-	-	-	-	-	1	-	-	-	-	-	-	-	-	-	-	1

125cc

Position	Rider	Nationality	Machine	Qatar	Japan	Spain	France	Italy	Catalunya	Netherlands	Germany	Great Britain	Czech Republic	Indianapolis	San Marino	Portugal	Australia	Malaysia	Valencia	Points total
1	Julian Simon	SPA	Aprilia	10	20	-	25	16	13	20	25	25	20	11	25	4	25	25	25	289
2	Bradley Smith	GBR	Aprilia	5.5	6	25	13	25	8	16	-	-	13	20	16	16	20	20	20	223.5
3	Nicolas Terol	SPA	Aprilia	4.5	-	6	7	20	20	11	13	13	25	13	20	-	10	11	6	179.5
4	Pol Espargaro	SPA	Derbi	6.5	16	9	-	13	-	7	11	6	11	25	-	25	13	16	16	174.5
5	Sergio Gadea	SPA	Aprilia	2	-	20	16	5	16	25	20	-	7	1	-	10	6	13	-	141
6	Sandro Cortese	GER	Derbi	8	10	10	4	6	7	-	10	-	10	-	11	20	16	10	8	130
7	Andrea Iannone	ITA	Aprilia	12.5	25	-	9	-	25	13	9	-	16	-	-	-	8	8	-	125.5
8	Marc Marquez	SPA	KTM	-	11	16	-	11	11	6	-	1	8	10	13	-	7	-	-	94
9	Joan Olive	SPA	Derbi	-	9	5	-	-	2	5	16	4	6	8	8	11	-	7	10	91
10	Stefan Bradl	GER	Aprilia	4	13	-	-	8	9	10	-	-	9	9	10	13	-	-	-	85
11	Simone Corsi	ITA	Aprilia	1	1	2	-	-	-	8	-	20	-	16	9	-	11	-	13	81
12	Jonas Folger	GER	Aprilia	5	8	-	20	2	10	9	-	-	4	4	7	2	2	-	-	73
13	Dominique Aegerter	SWI	Derbi	2.5	7	7	10	-	-	3	7	8	-	6	1	8	4	2	5	70.5
14	Efren Vazquez	SPA	Derbi	-	-	11	8	-	-	4	-	7	2	-	4	-	9	-	9	54
15	Scott Redding	GBR	Aprilia	1.5	-	13	-	9	5	-	-	16	1	-	-	5	-	-	-	50.5
16	Takaaki Nakagami	JPN	Aprilia	-	-	-	11	1	1	-	-	11	-	7	-	5	-	5	2	43
17	Danny Webb	GBR	Aprilia	3.5	5	8	-	-	-	-	8	-	-	5	6	-	3	-	-	38.5
18	Esteve Rabat	SPA	Aprilia	3	3	4	5	-	4	-	-	-	-	-	-	9	-	9	-	37
19	Lorenzo Zanetti	ITA	Aprilia	-	2	-	6	4	-	1	-	9	-	-	2	3	-	6	4	37
20	Johann Zarco	FRA	Aprilia	0.5	-	3	-	10	3	-	-	3	5	-	-	7	-	-	1	32.5
21	Randy Krummenacher	SWI	Aprilia	-	-	-	1	3	6	-	5	-	-	-	-	6	1	3	7	32
22	Luis Salom	SPA	Aprilia	-	-	-	-	-	-	-	3	10	-	3	-	1	-	1	3	21
23	Marcel Schrotter	GER	Honda	-	-	-	-	-	-	-	4	-	3	-	-	-	-	-	11	18
24	Tomoyoshi Koyama	JPN	Loncin	-	4	-	-	-	-	-	6	5	-	2	-	-	-	-	-	17
25	Michael Ranseder	AUT	Haojue/Aprilia	-	-	-	-	-	-	-	-	-	-	-	5	-	4	-	-	9
26	Lorenzo Savadori	ITA	Aprilia	-	-	-	-	7	-	-	-	-	-	-	-	-	-	-	-	7
27	Riccardo Moretti	ITA	Aprilia	-	-	-	-	-	-	-	-	-	-	-	3	-	-	-	-	3
28	Jasper Iwema	NED	Honda	-	-	-	3	-	-	-	-	-	-	-	-	-	-	-	-	3
29	Cameron Beaubier	USA	KTM	-	-	1	-	-	-	-	2	-	-	-	-	-	-	-	-	3
30	Martin Glossop	GBR	Honda	-	-	-	-	-	-	-	-	2	-	-	-	-	-	-	-	2
31	Marvin Fritz	GER	Honda	-	-	-	-	-	-	2	-	-	-	-	-	-	-	-	-	2
32	Gregory di Carlo	FRA	Honda	-	-	-	2	-	-	-	-	-	-	-	-	-	-	-	-	2
33	Daniel Kartheininger	GER	Honda	-	-	-	-	-	-	-	-	-	-	1	-	-	-	-	-	1

SUPERBIKE WORLD CHAMPIONSHIP

REVIEW OF 2009

By GORDON RITCHIE • Race Reports by OLLIE BARSTOW

Photo: Gold & Goose

CHAMPION PROFILE: BEN SPIES

TEXAS TERROR

by GORDON RITCHIE

THERE has never been a Superbike world champion quite like Ben Spies – which sounds like a bold statement, considering that he is the sixth highly rated American rider to have taken the biggest prize in Superbike.

He entered WSB as an absolute rookie, despite having made three MotoGP starts for Suzuki in 2008. He arrived with a Texas-sized reputation, of course, simply because he had won three AMA titles back to back. And when he was fast in all the WSB winter tests, and on a factory Yamaha, he was an obvious contender – for a few race wins at least.

Turned out he was a lot more than that.

Shy, determined, focused, yet a fish out of American waters in many ways, he went global in WSB. He was full of respect for his rivals, before and after his races, and winning was clearly most important. Victory on Sunday, he said, was all that he worked toward.

For Spies, 2009 was potentially a nightmare season in which to join WSB. There was a new bike to sort, a new manufacturer to deal with, a new team, different tracks, new tyres, a new country of residence, odd languages, lots of unknown rivals, a new engine configuration: all had the potential to flatten his hopes.

Paradoxically, it was also the ideal season to join. All the much-touted apparent strength of his rivals at the start of the season was eroded by their technical problems, injuries and difficulties in developing their new machines fully. In one way or another, all of his perceived rivals had their crosses to bear. Yet Spies was still a worthy champion for a dozen reasons.

Even the mistakes he made seemed like the fast way to learn important lessons, particularly when he just went out and won the next two or three races. No one but Troy Bayliss had had so many no-scores and still won the title, although it would be difficult to imagine two more contrasting riders, with two completely opposite approaches to racing.

Even a month after the Portimao finale, there was still a sense of unreality in the knowledge that Spies really had overcome the 88-point disadvantage to Haga that had threatened to crush him after round six at Kyalami.

Against such overwhelming odds, Spies, his imported American pit-lane pals, Tom and Woody, and his mercurial Italian-based Yamaha factory squad, led by Massimo Meregalli, all held their nerve – and won the title by six points.

Spies had a few obvious people to thank after his winning season, but one rider who would not make his Christmas card list was Mat Mladin. Having to summon up the guts, focus and consistently scary speed required to beat Mladin three times in a row in the AMA series was a remarkable feat. It made Spies at least as much of a winning machine as his all-new cross-plane-crank Yamaha YZF-R1.

It was suggested near season's end that Spies appeared to flatter the new Yamaha a tad. It was a good machine, but not apparently any better than its main rivals. Spies may have won on the Yamaha, but you felt that had he been riding a Ducati, Suzuki, Honda or even an all-new Aprilia, he could still have competed for the title. There can be no higher accolade.

The Texan's MotoGP deal had been signed even before Yamaha saw him wrap up the WSB title in the final race of the year. Although MotoGP Yamaha people may not be concerned with WSB on any level, being the only major manufacturer not to have won

Above: Long tall Texan.

Left: Taming the Yamaha. Spies made history in his maiden World Superbike season.

Photos: Gold & Goose

the riders' championship was nothing short of embarrassing. Even though there was a possibility that Yamaha would ask him to stay until the WSB job was done, he was still allowed to sign for MotoGP in 2010 long before the season ended.

To his credit, he still had the internal motivation to pull off arguably the WSB coup of the century, despite going into the final round ten points down.

His successful rookie WSB championship campaign was a result of his intense focus, adaptability, impeccable preparation and huge talent – and a will to win so strong that it would mark him out as someone special in any era of WSB racing.

2009 TEAMS AND RIDERS

By GORDON RITCHIE

MICHEL FABRIZIO

JAKUB SMRZ

BEN SPIES

LEON HASLAM

TOM SYKES

JONATHAN REA

APRILIA

Aprilia Racing

Aprilia's road-bike and race-bike had been developed in tandem for some time before Aprilia returned to WSB with a full factory team.

Max Biaggi was a race winner and a threat on a consistent basis after mid-season upgrades. His third new bike in three years, this may be the best of them.

Shinya Nakano found his first year in WSB so littered with accidents that eventually he retired from racing altogether. He produced flashes of real ability on occasion and was a welcome sight when in full flow.

The boss on the technical side was Luigi Dall'Igna, who, like most in the garage, was a GP man moving into new territory.

GP 250 champ Marco Simoncelli was a brilliant single-round wild-card at Imola, taking to the podium in one race. New BSB champion Leon Camier came in for the last two rounds and was respectably fast.

BMW

BMW Motorrad Motorsport

A new bunch led by two of the most experienced heads, Troy Corser and Ruben Xaus. The manufacturer that GP racing let slip through the net mounted a serious effort, if only spending bike-level rather than car-level money.

It did bring car-level class to the paddock and its bike was quick on many occasions. Led in the garage by Rainer Bäumel, the team was cosmopolitan in personnel, but Teutonic and serious in organization, adding a dedicated test team mid-season.

Richard Cooper and regular test rider Steve Martin stood in for Xaus when he was injured.

DUCATI

Ducati Xerox Team

Noriyuki Haga was chosen – finally, some would say – to lead the Ducati charge, while younger Italian hope Michel Fabrizio had much expected of him. It went very well for Haga most of the time; Fabrizio was less predictable.

Once more, the team was run by Davide Tardozzi, the most successful team manager ever in this category, but he left immediately after the title had been lost. Ernesto Marinelli looked after the bikes and development again, and took on the role of managing the whole team in Tardozzi's stead.

Team Sterilgarda

Shane Byrne was a lone rider even before the season kicked off, as this team's budget never quite took Alessandro Polita beyond winter testing. Marco Borciani's privateer effort carried on with Sterilgarda money even when Spies and Sykes sported similar logos.

Ducati Guandalini Racing

The team had one potential star in Jakub Smrz, and to start with, one rookie – 2008 Superstock champ Brendan Roberts. Injury in the infamous Monza crash put Roberts out for a while, then Gregorio Lavilla was preferred to the young Aussie. Finally, Matteo Baiocco came in for some races.

WSB riding legend Pierfrancesco Chili was team manager. The squad enjoyed some success, but little money, as a main sponsor pulled out, making it necessary to squeeze the budget to make the final round.

Ducati DFX Corse

Back on Ducatis, DFX looked like it had the potential to be the best privateer, thanks to the experience and early pace of Regis Laconi. His Kyalami

crash and serious neck injury saw both Fonsi Nieto and Lorenzo Lanzi brought in on occasion. A valiant and often effective effort again for team principal Danieli Carli's men, after a few years of hard times with Honda.

HONDA

Hannspree Ten Kate Honda

In reality, this team was three-strong, split into a pairing of Carlos Checa and Jonathan Rea, with Ryuichi Kiyonari running various red, white and blue colours in a self-sponsored effort for Honda, and no Hannspree logos at all.

Ronald Ten Kate oversaw it all, in what was a very busy, but only partially successful year for the official Honda Europe entry.

Hannspree Honda Althea

The Hannspree money left early on, and Briton Tommy Hill left mid-season because of a difference of opinion concerning overall machine set-up. The Honda Althea Racing team then ran its WSS rider Matthieu Lagrive in WSB, except for Magny-Cours, where Flavio Gentile swapped his 600 for Lagrive's Superbike.

Stiggy Racing Honda

This was potentially the best ever WSB opportunity for Leon Haslam, who was the mainstay of the cosmopolitan squad's podium ambitions. Stiggy Racing was the best Honda team at the start.

Johan Stigefelt's financial backers left before the end, but that was some time after the team had brought in jobless John Hopkins in place of original rider Roberto Rolfo. Jake Zemke rode at Miller instead of the oft-injured Hopkins.

Short of money, the team made it to the end with Haslam the lone rider.

FONSI NIETO

MAX BIAGGI

MAX NEUKIRCHNER

SHINYA NAKANO

YUKIO KATAYAMA

RUBEN XAUS

RYUICHI KIYONARI

SHANE BYRNE

TROY CORSER

NORIYUKI HAGA

REGIS LACONI

CARLOS CHECA

Squadra Corse Italia

Vittorio Iannuzzo was a one-man band, often at the back, in the first year for this new Rome based team.

KAWASAKI

Kawasaki World Superbike Racing Team

The official Kawasaki effort was taken over by British based Paul Bird Motorsport for 2009, with experienced World Rally manager Paul Risbridger overseeing a team based on a nucleus of Paul Bird's long-serving technical staff.

Broc Parkes and Makoto Tamada were injured so often, and so harshly, that Stuart Easton, Sheridan Morais and Jamie Hacking all pitched in with rides as subs.

Team Pedercini Kawasaki

It was another good effort from WSB stalwart Lucio Pedercini's men, as Spaniard David Salom and Italian Luca Scassa pitched in some good results for a privateer team on the least-favoured four.

PSG-1 Corse Kawasaki

Pierguido Pagani's former official team stayed in for a while, in blue and white San Marino colours, but first Ayrton Badovini, then Matteo Baiocco were pulled as funds dried up. The team never made it past the home round at Misano.

SUZUKI

Suzuki Alstare

Francis Batta's team endured an incredibly disturbed season. As always a direct Suzuki factory team with some autonomy, it saw early glory crushed by crashes and money disputes with the title sponsor.

Max Neukirchner and Yukio Kagayama started out as regulars, but were repeatedly injured and ended up out of the team. Fonsi Nieto, Blake Young, Karl Muggeridge and then 2010 signing Sylvain Guintoli were brought in to fill the gaps. Giacomo Guidotti was the technical chief once again.

Celani Race

Running machines prepped and fettled by Alstare, the Celani team only received full-spec bikes later in the year. The injured Karl Muggeridge departed mid-season, leaving Alessandro Polita to pick up a ride.

TKR Suzuki Switzerland

Austrian Roland Resch missed some long-haul races on his very private machine, but added some variety and another nationality to the grid when he did ride.

YAMAHA

Yamaha World Superbike Racing Team

Ben Spies was the coup signing of all time; the less-experienced Tom Sykes was injured late in the year, but rode on anyway with typical Yorkshire grit.

Massimo Meregalli oversaw his usual bunch of Monza based Italians, who were joined by Tom Houseworth and 'Woody' Wood from the USA, brought in by Spies to improve communication and make the final pre-flight checks.

The team gained Sterilgarda sponsorship mid-season.

Yamaha France Ipone GMT 94

David Checa was not the force he could have been and was injured to boot. Endurance man Erwan Nigon rode in America, while Shaun Whyte, a Zimbabwean veteran, helped to fund an unexpected run-out for the team at Kyalami.

THE BIKES OF 2009
By GORDON RITCHIE

APRILIA RSV4

BMW S1000RR

DUCATI 1198F09

HONDA CBR1000RR

SUZUKI GSX-R1000K9

KAWASAKI NINJA ZX-10R

YAMAHA YZF-R1

APRILIA RSV4

ONLY those who could not remember the days of the Honda RC30, Bimota YB4, Yamaha R7 and any number of homologation specials made specifically to win WSB (or TT-F1, or World Endurance, or National series for that matter) were misguided enough to think the RSV4 Aprilia an illegal 'MotoGP' bike, no matter how much of Aprilia's combined racing experience went into its design as road-bike and racer.

It was a technical jewel, 999cc worth of 65-degree V4, with ride-by-wire throttle, variable-length inlet trumpets, cassette gearbox, a neat counter-balancer shaft, adjustable chassis and engine position, all right out of the crate.

Add Brembo brakes, Öhlins suspension (although not the absolute newest spec) and Akrapovic exhaust, and go WSB racing. Kind of.

The twin-spar alloy chassis employed both cast and pressed elements, and near the season's end Biaggi was given the right flex for his under-slung swing-arm to reduce chatter without sacrificing torsional stiffness. Three types of rear swing-arm were used during the year. Chain force angle was a critical geometrical element on the thoroughbred Aprilia.

Electronics was also an area of constant focus, with the variable-intake trumpets adding to the complication. Traction control was a constant in the electronics set-up, with other features like wheelie control only coming later.

Power started at a useful 9,000rpm, while peak power came at 14,500, the limiter being set at 15,000. Absolute power was no problem from the start, being as good as the rest at well over 200bhp. It weighed in at 162kg, like the other fours.

BMW S1000RR

ANOTHER all-new bike, but this time a conventional in-line four, at least from the outside. Brembo brakes, Öhlins suspension, a stacked gearbox design, twin-spar alloy chassis – the ingredients were all very familiar.

But low-mass F1-style cam followers, rather than buckets and shims, a claimed 193bhp in standard road trim and a completely home-brewed electronics package, including fly-by-wire throttle, traction and wheelie control, marked out the BMW as a little bit different from the other fours.

Ruben Xaus started out on regular Öhlins equipment, but moved to the more trick TTX Öhlins units toward the end of the year. Three specs of rear swing-arm were used, and OZ magnesium wheels were fitted.

In tuning terms, there were three specifications of engine in 2009. At the start of the season, the race bike had a 14:1 compression ratio, with 80 x 49.7mm bore and stroke engine.

The development path was blazed by several riders, Steve Martin being the mainstay of an effort that relied on its own technology, but racing know-how and set-up came from technical partner Alpha Racing. The original teams charged with improving individual elements were finally amalgamated to work as one entity within a single team after the summer; a test team was created as well.

DUCATI 1198F09

THE powerful 106 x 67.9mm bore and stroke engine of the Ducati was reined in by the same air restrictors any 1200cc twin has to use in WSB, but as critics pointed out, you can't kill class leading torque with air restrictors. In 2009, the Ducati remained at 168kg throughout due to FIM weight handicapping rules.

The factory team claimed that the bike was largely the same as in 2008, but privateers reckoned there was more to the 2009 Ducati Xerox machine than just the fly-by-wire throttle. That on its own was still a useful tool, allowing a greater degree of control under corner exit and downshifting, and particularly when opening the throttle at full lean.

A Marvel 4 EFI, with IWP 162 + IWP 189 twin injectors per cylinder, was used, but on the exhaust side a Termignoni stainless steel 2-1-2 system was chosen, simply because titanium was an unnecessary expense with a 168kg limit to meet.

Factory Öhlins TTX suspension was finally chosen (sometimes) by Haga, who always prefers his suspension to be less high-tech than most.

Brembo brakes, Radial P4X34-38 calipers and 320mm discs were employed with consistency to aid set-up from track to track. For the same reason, one self-designed kit swing-arm was used all year.

Pretty much the same as 2008? Only Ducati's factory team staff really know.

HONDA CBR1000RR

THERE was no new Fireblade for 2009, but with so many different Honda teams, technical solutions to the challenge were varied. One key element of Ten Kate's legendary lone development path finally was left by the wayside this year. Rider pressure and a perceived lack of new factory development WP suspension parts saw Ten Kate join the mass exodus toward Öhlins, this time via Andreani in Italy.

Electronic development, again in conjunction with PI, was carried out as much as possible in-house, but that also proved problematic and led to the electronic controls being wound back to base settings for a time, allowing the team to concentrate on getting the cycle parts set-up properly.

The probable 215bhp from the Ten Kate machines was no longer class-leading, while chassis set-up to eradicate chatter was a constant chore until the Öhlins units arrived and were fettled properly. With three riders, all with different styles and needs, it was not uncommon to see three different swing-arms in use on the same weekend; the best, according to Rea, was the solid looking KR version.

Oral Engineering in Italy partnered the Stiggy Honda team in its tuning quest during its first WSB season, kit swing-arms being used, and Öhlins units allowing the team to make early-season gains on Ten Kate.

KAWASAKI NINJA ZX-10R

ALTHOUGH there was no new Ninja ZX-10R for the all-new factory Kawasaki team, plenty of technical changes were made through the year. Parallel development, with KHI engineers around more often than before, saw some initiatives come from Japan, while other refinements were provided by the team itself.

That made exact technical information difficult to come by.

The odd chassis architecture, a big up-and-over affair curving visibly atop a relatively upright engine, made the Ninja a handful to control, and particularly hard to turn. Add in chatter on some of the tyre constructions available, and all the chassis improvements on the Kawasaki were welcome, if not dramatic developments. Additional engine mounting brackets to change its position were allowed by the rules that permitted parts to be added to the chassis, but not to be removed.

Beautifully made swing-arms, with components machined from solid billet, were universal fitments at the end of the year. Redesigned triple clamps, and experiments with overall geometry, brought improvements, but chassis set-up was a movable target from track to track.

The swing-arms and forks were married to works Showa suspension, and Japanese made Arata exhausts came in a variety of lengths, diameters and protrusions, all designed to centralise mass to some extent.

SUZUKI GSX-R1000K9

A NEW bike, with a stacked gearbox and smaller in all major dimensions, the GSX-R finally came of age in its peer group; the problem was that there was very little continuity of development due to rider injury.

The 2009 bike was still amazingly conventional and, at almost 25-years old, the GSX-R technical lineage is still tethered to the same ideals.

Inside, the engine was even more over-square and had bigger valves than the previous version. It produced 212bhp at 13,300rpm, and featured a 74.5 x 57.3mm bore and stroke. Development included new cams to regain the previous model's pep. The compression ratio was quoted at 13.5:1.

Uniquely, the Suzuki ran twin low-level exhausts, made by Arrow.

The chassis and swing-arm design were all new for 2009, which made some previous data redundant, adding to the complications involved in set-up.

A perceived lack of development in the factory Showa suspension set-up led to the previously improbable addition of Öhlins units to the official machines for the last couple of rounds. They were expected to remain in 2010.

Brembo brakes gave way to Nissin rotors and calipers at the start of the season, at the request of Neukirchner.

YAMAHA YZF-R1

EVEN with the new Aprilia and BMW in the mix, this was the most eagerly anticipated machine in WSB. The biggest departure for the Japanese since Honda's V-twin VTR, the cross-plane-crank R1 fired a bit more like a V-engine than an in-line four, harmonising combustion torque and inertial crankshaft torque. It felt slow, went fast, and had 78 x 55.2mm bore and stroke.

In theory, the uneven firing intervals made the throttle connection far more linear, and it allowed changes of line, even going into corners, without making the machine sit up.

An Akrapovic 4-2-1-2 exhaust came in titanium, and a modified camshaft helped the R1 to reach a power output of more than 215bhp.

Compared to its predecessor, the chassis was made from increasingly complicated parts, and featured Öhlins TTX forks and rear shocks. An electronic steering damper was another feature controlled by the Magneti Marelli electronics system, and was a response to the ban on electronic suspension damping.

Before Aprilia produced its under-slung banana swing-arm, Yamaha already had one, and it was claimed to be 20 per cent stiffer than standard.

New and radical solutions abounded, the fuel tank filler being part of the rider's seat, while the rear fuel cell was actually the rear subframe, which lowered the centre of gravity with a full tank. The whole thing unbolted for servicing. In place of fuel under the dummy tank, there was the airbox, lots of electronics and the injectors.

The bike may not have been a great leap forward, but it was a brave new design in many ways.

Photos: Gold & Goose

PHILLIP ISLAND
ROUND 1 • AUSTRALIA

RACE ONE: PHILIP ISLAND

Haga grabs last gasp victory

NORIYUKI HAGA won a stunning first race of the World Superbike season after a late smattering of rain denied Max Neukirchner victory just two corners from the finish. It was an outstanding performance by both Haga and Neukirchner, up from 13th and 14th on the grid respectively, Neukirchner snatched the lead from Haga at the start of the last lap, but drizzle at the back of the circuit gave him enough of a moment to allow his rival back through. Although the German was close to retaking the lead on the finishing straight, Haga would be classified the winner by just 0.032 second.

It was a race full of drama, many of the expected front-runners falling by the wayside during a frantic opening lap. Haga and Neukirchner took advantage of the chaos around them to end the first circuit second and fifth. Having moved to the front by lap seven, they shadowed one another for the remainder of the race while breaking away from the chasing pack. Twice they swapped positions before Neukirchner appeared to have made the decisive move at the start of the final lap when he slipstreamed his way past.

A combination of damp conditions and rear tyre wear were taking their toll on the Suzuki, however, prompting a massive moment for the German at turn nine and allowing the closely following Haga back through.

Not that Neukirchner was completely finished. He fought back on the exit of turn 12, using his Suzuki's engine power to very nearly nip back ahead on the line. Haga would not be denied though, and the Ducati rider made good on his promise to ignore his lowly starting position and enjoy a 'pressure free' race.

As expected, the closeness of the competition ensured that the order at the end of lap one was very different to how it had started. Confidence among the riders hadn't been helped by the decision to classify the race as 'wet' following a short shower a few minutes before the start.

Nonetheless, the front row got away evenly, with Jonathan Rea snatching the lead going into turn one, ahead of Max Biaggi and pole-sitter Ben Spies. Biaggi and Spies were about to see their races take a turn for the worse, however, when the Italian ran too deep at turn two and was forced to sit up. Spies was caught unawares and was left with nowhere to go but around the outside of the drifting Aprilia, taking a long trip across the grass, the American rejoined the circuit at the very back of the field. Biaggi made a better recovery, but would never get back into the reckoning.

Yamaha's tough start was further compounded when Tom Sykes was delayed by a collision at turn three, which saw Ruben Xaus and Ryuichi Kiyonari come together, the latter falling off his bike and into retirement.

With Spies and Biaggi allowing Rea to make a quick break at the front, the Northern Irishman held on to the top spot for three laps before Haga made

his move on the way down to the first turn. Seemingly keen to protect his tyres and attempt an attack later in the race, Rea began dropping down the order quickly, losing out to Regis Laconi, Neukirchner, Yukio Kagayama Leon Haslam and Michel Fabrizio at just beyond the mid-way stage.

His tactic appeared to be working when Laconi and Haslam paid the price for an inspired start to the race, which had put them in second and fourth briefly. They couldn't sustain their pace to the finish, however, and both were overtaken by a recovering Rea.

Further up the road, Kagayama joined Neukirchner in proving that Suzuki's race pace was substantially better than its qualifying results, battling his way up to third and breaking away from the battle for fourth. Although he didn't have the pace to keep up with the leaders, he did manage his first podium in two years.

Fourth fell to Fabrizio, the Italian fighting back from one of his trademark tardy starts and timing his late-race assault to perfection, pulling away from Rea, Haslam and Laconi in the latter stages.

Rea had to be content with fifth on his full-time WSBK debut, while Haslam held off Laconi for sixth to score good points for the rookie Stiggy Honda team.

Given the hype surrounding Aprilia following qualifying, BMW must have been delighted to have beaten its fellow debutant after Troy Corser finished a fine eighth, the Australian making the most of an aggressive start to the race from 17th on the grid.

This page, from top:
Race-two winner Spies is joined by recently retired hero Troy Bayliss; Badovini's moment of grace before impact; Tom Sykes settled in well for Yamaha; a warm local welcome; Neukirchner, Haga and Kagayama on the race-one rostrum.

Opposite page, top: Haga about to take the lead from Neukirchner.

Far left: Haslam made a strong rostrum start to his year.

Centre left: Race-two battle between Spies and Haga.

Photos: Gold & Goose

Furthermore, Corser made a bit of history by scoring the fastest lap of the race for the brand-new team.

From the front row, Jakub Smrz clung on to a top-ten finish in ninth, ahead of Sykes, who staged an impressive recovery to tenth after his earlier delays had dropped him as low as 18th.

Biaggi held on to 11th in what had been a tougher race than expected for Aprilia, his team-mate Shinya Nakano grabbing a point for 15th. Between them, Carlos Checa had showed signs of his shoulder injury, falling outside the top ten as the race progressed. The Spaniard finished 12th, just ahead of Roberto Rolfo and Tommy Hill, the British rider doing an excellent job to score points on his first WSBK outing.

Elsewhere, Shane Byrne's miserable weekend continued when he crashed out on lap seven, while Spies' recovery was only good enough for 16th.

RACE TWO: PHILIP ISLAND

Spies makes amends with race two win

BEN SPIES took victory in the second race of the season at Phillip Island, after resisting the attentions of a charging Noriyuki Haga. The win did much to make up for the American's disastrous opening race; first place from pole position sealed an otherwise magnificent maiden weekend in World Superbikes for the three-time AMA champion.

Spies' win was notable for the way in which he soaked up pressure from Haga throughout the race. The two potential title rivals indulged in some close, but clean, racing as they swapped the lead on several occasions during the course of the race.

At first the initiative seemed to be with Haga, the Japanese rider having repeated his outstanding start from 13th on the grid to end the first lap in fifth place, before disposing of three more rivals for second by lap four. From there, he immediately set his sights on Spies, who had led the way from turn two after being out-dragged to the first corner by Max Biaggi.

Haga didn't take long to grab his place at the head of the field, passing Spies on the run to turn one at the start of lap five. Despite his rapid rise through the order, however, neither Spies nor Biaggi allowed him to get away. Indeed, the Italian rider put in a fine showing on the new Aprilia RSV-4, staying with the leaders as they broke away from those directly behind.

With the Ducati and Yamaha bikes seemingly favouring different parts of the circuit, the gap between Haga and Spies swung continuously until Spies finally snatched back the lead on lap 11. Even so, it was only good enough for two laps, as a slight error at MG allowed Haga back through.

The Japanese rider even managed to break away from Spies briefly, but he seemed to be suffering the effects of tyre wear during the final laps, which allowed his rival back into contention. In fact, Haga barely posed a threat when Spies attempted a move at the start of lap 18.

Having nursed his tyres better, Spies gradually broke the tow of Haga to come home in front by a comfortable margin, much to the delight of his Yamaha team and his family.

Despite missing out on a double victory, a win and a second place marked a fine start to the year for Haga, particularly when his lowly starting positions are taken into consideration. The results gave him the lead in the championship by a fair margin.

Behind the leaders, the battle for third place proved to be equally engrossing as Biaggi began to fade into the clutches of Michel Fabrizio, Leon Haslam and Regis Laconi. All three had been satisfied to sit on the fringes of the fight at the front until the final few laps, when Fabrizio made his move on Biaggi. Quickly taking advantage, Haslam launched his assault on the Italian too, the pair swapping positions twice before the British rider moved up into fourth.

Haslam wasn't finished though and, as they entered the final lap, latched on to the back of Fabrizio, who, like Haga, also seemed to be experiencing tyre wear issues. The Englishman overtook at turn one, but Fabrizio regained the place at turn two before Haslam finally completed the move at Honda. He held on to the chequered flag, third place and a podium marking a superb return to WSBK competition. Haslam's achievement also suggested that newcomer Stiggy could be a threat to Ten Kate's superiority in the Honda camp.

Laconi enjoyed a stealthy run through the order to fourth, the Frenchman posting his best WSBK results for some time on the DFX Ducati after also overtaking Fabrizio on the final lap.

Biaggi, meanwhile, saw his hopes of a good result on the Aprilia come to nothing when he ran off the circuit on the final lap. Having been swamped by Haslam, Fabrizio and Laconi at Honda, he attempted to regain his position, but in doing so misjudged his braking point and took a trip across the grass. Having snatched the final point in 15th, however, Biaggi showed that the RSV-4 held promise for the season.

After almost winning the first race, Max Neukirchner was a very distant sixth, the German having paid the price for his 14th-place starting position, as he made slow progress through the order. Nonetheless, with his earlier second place, Neurkirchner had done enough to take an early second position in the overall standings.

Jakub Smrz took a second top-ten result of day in seventh, ahead of Yukio Kagayama, while front-row-sitter Jonathan Rea was a disappointing ninth after gradually dropping down the order. It had been a tough race all round for Ten Kate, Rea's team-mates, Carlos Checa and Ryuichi Kiyonari, not faring any better down in 13th and 23rd.

Once again Tom Sykes was forced to make up ground after a poor start, but he did enough to sneak into the top ten, ahead of Ruben Xaus, the Spaniard putting in his most convincing performance on the BMW for five useful points.

Shinya Nakano ran as high as sixth early on before sliding down to 12th, ahead of Checa, the impressive Tommy Hill and the recovering Biaggi. Shane Byrne, meanwhile, left Australia empty handed after crashing for a second time.

LOSAIL
ROUND 2 • QATAR

Above: Biaggi leads Haga, Spies, Byrne, Corser, Sykes and the gang in race two.

Left: Neukirchner (75) would narrowly win this battle for sixth with MotoGP refugee Nakano.

Far left: Corser's new BMW was already close to the pace.

Photos: Gold & Goose

RACE ONE: LOSAIL

Spies snatches victory in Qatar

BEN SPIES swept to victory in the first World Superbike race of 2009 in Qatar, after prevailing in a tense fight with Noriyuki Haga and Max Biaggi. It was a second triumph for the Texan in only three races, and although he won from pole position, he had been forced to work hard for victory after a tardy start had dropped him out of contention initially. In fact, Spies led just four of the 18 laps, the Yamaha rider having been forced to trail Biaggi and Haga for much of the race before making his decisive move for victory in the latter stages.

The American had already admitted that making a good start with the R1 was not easy, and he proved the point when he entered the first corner in fourth position, having been swamped on the outside of the turn. This allowed Biaggi, from third on the grid, to sweep into the lead on the Aprilia, ahead of Haga and Jakub Smrz, the Czech rider having made an uncustomary good start from the front row of the grid.

Spies even ran as low as fifth when Shinya Nakano got the better of him on lap two, and it wasn't until lap five that he made it back through. To his credit though, he did pass Nakano in style, slipstreaming the Japanese rider, and also Smrz, to surge through to third in one go.

Setting off in pursuit of Biaggi and Haga, who had eked out a small gap to the field behind, Spies quickly reeled them in with a series of rapid lap times. Then his progress slowed and he maintained a watching brief in third position for the next eight laps. Meanwhile, Biaggi and Haga embarked on a subtle dice for the lead, and although Haga never really put a determined move on Biaggi, occasionally he got close enough to the Aprilia to show that he was trying.

With the laps ticking down steadily, Spies' hopes of leapfrogging both Haga and Biaggi appeared to dwindle until all three riders entered the long home straight at the end of lap 13, line astern for the first time.

For Haga, it was the ideal opportunity to attempt to slipstream the rapid RSV-4, but for Spies it was an even better chance to capitalise on the draught from both bikes. So when Haga gave up on passing Biaggi, he was caught off guard for long enough to allow Spies to sweep through into second place.

With a new rival to contend with, Biaggi kept up his momentum, but he too was caught unawares when a slight error going into turn six allowed Spies to dive up the inside, forcing the Italian to sit up and scramble back into second position.

Once in the lead, there was no going back for Spies. He used the clear circuit ahead to put in some strong late lap times and forge a gap to Biaggi and Haga, who were still squabbling, but for a less prestigious second place. That battle raged until the chequered flag, Haga finally sweeping past Biaggi at the start of the penultimate lap. The latter replicated the move on the final lap, but he ran wide going into turn one and gifted the place back.

Neither could do anything about Spies though, who wound up a fairly comfortable winner by two seconds, although Haga's decisive second place meant that the gap between them in the standings stood at 15 points in the Japanese rider's favour.

Although disappointed to have ended up third after leading most of the race, Biaggi and Aprilia were delighted to be on the podium so early in their World Superbike endeavour. Furthermore, the joy was compounded when Nakano held on for a similarly impressive fourth position. The former MotoGP rider's cause had been aided when Smrz fell. The Czech rider had appeared to be on course for a career-best result when he crashed from fifth position on the final corner of lap seven.

Smrz wasn't the only rider to suffer problems. Michel Fabrizio had crashed out of seventh position, while Max Neukirchner had endured a spectacular high-side on lap six, having already fallen to the back of the field after a trip across the gravel on lap two. Their mishaps allowed Carlos Checa to record a good top-five result for Ten Kate Honda, the Spaniard having had to work hard for the position as he resisted the attentions of British pair Shane Byrne and Tom Sykes.

Byrne had enjoyed a steady race in sixth position, a considerable improvement on his double DNF in Australia, although Sykes was frustrated because a poor first lap, which had dropped him from fifth to 12th, had prevented him from finishing any better than seventh.

Countrymen Leon Haslam and Jonathan Rea had

Left: Fabrizio goes native.

Below: Biaggi's second race on the Aprilia was a double rostrum.

Photos: Gold & Goose

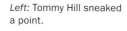

Left: Tommy Hill sneaked a point.

Below: Kiyonari was close to a race-two podium.

Below right: Haga was feeling the heat – from the desert circuit, and newcomer Spies.

Photos: Gold & Goose

enjoyed differing fortunes in the first race, the former having had to battle his way up from outside the top twenty after being one of three riders to run off the track at the start of lap two, the other two being Brendan Roberts and Yukio Kagayama. Nonetheless, a series of quick laps and overtaking manoeuvres put him back in the hunt for a top-ten finish, the Stiggy rider ultimately falling just short in 11th, behind Ryuichi Kiyonari, Troy Corser and Regis Laconi. The last had dropped back after running as high as fifth early on.

Rea, meanwhile, had made swift progress through the order after qualifying a lowly 17th. While he had reached a high of eighth at one point, however, an error in the closing stages dropped him to eventual 12th position, behind Haslam.

Still, with Tommy Hill sneaking another point in 15th, all five British riders were classified inside the points, the Althea rider having finished behind BMW's Ruben Xaus and the sole Kawasaki of Broc Parkes, the Aussie scoring the team's first points of the season in the process.

RACE TWO: LOSAIL

Spies doubles up in Qatar

BEN SPIES completed a double victory in the second round of the championship in Qatar after producing another almost faultless performance. It made for a perfect weekend: a new lap record in Superpole, two race wins and a new race lap record.

Although again Spies didn't lead from the off, he assumed control from lap six before scampering away from the chasing pack and leading home an identical podium trio with Noriyuki Haga and Max Biaggi. He made a better start than in the first race, but nonetheless was beaten to the first corner by Biaggi, while his outside line also allowed Haga to move ahead into second position by turn two.

Having lost out to Spies in the first race, when he had spent too long trying to find his way past Biaggi, Haga made no mistake this time, passing the Italian by the end of the first lap before making a determined effort to get away from his rivals.

Spies took a little longer to dispose of Biaggi, passing on lap four, but he needed just two more laps to catch and pass Haga with a fairly easy draught along the home straight and into turn one. A slight error by Haga in the ensuing lap was enough to break any tow he may have had on the Yamaha, and Spies simply pulled away to a margin of around four seconds.

From that point on, Spies was untroubled to the chequered flag, setting consistent lap times – including a record lap that broke Fonsi Nieto's previ-

ous best – until the final revolution, when he eased off to allow Haga to cross the line around two seconds adrift.

Even so, despite his maximum haul of points, two second places for Haga meant that Spies merely had halved the gap to ten points going into the first of the European rounds at Valencia, where once again he would have to prove that he was a quick learner.

Again, Haga had been made to work hard for second place by an inspired Biaggi, who, despite losing the lead early on in the race, twice had battled his way past the Ducati, including on the final lap. Haga had fought back, however, with only a few corners to go, sweeping back past and consigning Biaggi to the bottom step of the podium again.

On the plus side, Biaggi's brace of points rocketed the Italian up the overall standings to fourth position, while Aprilia was just behind Honda for third in the manufacturers' standings.

Despite the identical podium, the battle for second at least had been a three-way tussle this time, involving Ryuichi Kiyonari, who had put an unnoticed first race behind him to scythe his way up from 12th on the grid. Making up eight positions in just four laps, he had even latched on to the back of the Haga/Biaggi battle, but inexplicably had stalled in that position for the remainder of the race. Nonetheless, fourth represented both his and the Ten Kate Honda team's best result of the season so far.

After a frustrating performance in race one, Tom Sykes had been able to deliver on the promise he had shown throughout the weekend by bringing his Yamaha home a quiet, but well-deserved, fifth. Having made a better start this time, he had diced with Troy Corser and Shane Byrne early on, before settling in the position in which he had started. The consistent beginning to his World Superbike career was rewarded with a move to sixth in the overall standings.

Countryman Byrne didn't fare quite so well, despite having made a marvellous start to jump from eighth on the grid to fourth. He had dropped gradually down the order as the race progressed and finished an eventual 12th.

Travelling in the other direction had been Max Neukirchner, who gave Suzuki something to smile about on an otherwise dismal weekend by finishing sixth from 19th on the grid. The German rider, who was nursing injured arms, had crashed three times during the weekend. He even had the satisfaction of beating Shinya Nakano to the line, by a mere 0.002 second, a result that kept him third in the standings.

Although not quite as quick as Neukirchner, Jonathan Rea also had made good progress through the field from 17th to finish in eighth, ahead of Troy Corser. The Aussie rider had been on the verge of a breakthrough result for the BMW team after somehow battling his way to fifth position from 16th on the grid by the opening split of the race. While he had lapped strongly early on, however, he hadn't been able to sustain the pace to the end of the race. Nonetheless, he came home ninth after beating team-mate Ruben Xaus and Leon Haslam in a blanket finish, the trio being separated by just 0.040 second.

Elsewhere, Carlos Checa was a disappointing 13th after finishing fifth in the first race, ahead of Regis Laconi and Yukio Kagayama. The Japanese rider just edged out Broc Parkes and Jakub Smrz, the front-row-sitter having been forced to start from the pit lane for the second race.

VALENCIA
ROUND 3 • SPAIN

RACE ONE: VALENCIA

Haga wins race one; Spies falls

NORIYUKI HAGA pulled 35 points clear at the top of the championship standings after a race-one victory at Valencia and an accident that sidelined Ben Spies. Superstar rookie Spies, winner of three of the first four races of the season, lost the front of his Yamaha in the fast first turn just before the half-way stage of the race while seeking a way past second-placed Max Neukirchner. Fortunately the American was unharmed, but his R1 was badly damaged after cartwheeling through the Spanish gravel. As always, he would come back strong and fighting.

Haga – who, on the previous day, had claimed that he hadn't been worried by Spies' huge Superpole advantage – was already two seconds clear of the field at the time of the American's accident. The Ducati Xerox star remained out of reach to the finish, eventually claiming his second win of the season by 3.677 seconds from team-mate Michel Fabrizio. In the process, the Japanese rider broke Neil Hodgson's Valencia WSBK race lap record, which had stood since 2003.

Second on the grid Regis Laconi had led the field through turn one, but was demoted by Haga moments later and lost second place to Neukirchner before the end of the lap. The German's Alstare Suzuki then draughted past Haga along the home straight, but the latter regained the lead for the final time with a pass going into turn one of lap three.

Thus Neukirchner was left to defend against Spies, who had dropped from pole to fifth on lap one, but had gained a position when a fast-starting Troy Corser had lost the front of his BMW while holding an impressive fourth on lap two.

AMA champion Spies relegated Laconi's DFX Ducati from third on lap six, but his steady climb through the order got no further. His exit gave Neukirchner a welcome breathing space until Fabrizio began to apply pressure in the closing stages, the Italian successfully diving inside the German with three laps to go.

The last lap began with Fabrizio, Neukirchner and Laconi, in second, third and fourth places respectively, covered by just 0.8 second. Fabrizio, under pressure to obtain results after a double DNF at Qatar, made his 1198 as wide as possible during the final lap, thwarting Neukirchner's hopes of second position.

Almost ten seconds behind Laconi, Stiggy Honda's Leon Haslam had carved his way through the order for fifth position, just ahead of Yukio Kagayama, with Tom Sykes and Max Biaggi having worked their way forward from 17th and 18th on the grid to finish in seventh and eighth places.

BSB champion Shane Byrne took his Sterilgarda Ducati to ninth, while Broc Parkes was a morale boosting tenth on his Paul Bird-run factory Kawasaki. Former Kawasaki MotoGP rider John Hopkins finished his first WSBK race in 11th position on the second Stiggy machine.

Among those joining Spies and Corser on the DNF list were Jonathan Rea, who had tagged another rider and fallen on lap one, and Hannspree Ten Kate team-mate Carlos Checa, who had run off the track on lap four and later retired.

Left: Haga claimed a double win.

Right: A morale-boosting tenth for Broc Parkes.

Below: Spies crashes out of the first race.

Below right: Hopkins replaced Rolfo on the Stiggy Honda; finished 11th.

Bottom right: Neukirchner took a race-one podium.

Bottom: Laconi's satellite Ducati leads Spies, Kagayama and Fabrizio.

Photos: Gold & Goose

Leon Haslam turned his tenth position on the grid into two satisfying fifth-place finishes for Stiggy Honda, while Neukirchner, third behind Haga and Fabrizio in race one, dropped to a disappointing seventh in race two.

Home star Carlos Checa, who had retired from race one, salvaged some pride with sixth in race two for Hannspree Ten Kate Honda.

As in race one, Tom Sykes and Max Biaggi had worked their way forward from an unrepresentative 17th and 18th on the grid, Biaggi claiming eighth position on the lone Aprilia, while Sykes was tenth on the second factory backed Yamaha.

Ryuichi Kiyonari finished between the pair in ninth for Ten Kate, and another BSB champion, Shane Byrne, was 11th.

John Hopkins had made a storming start to sit seventh on the opening lap of race two, but the Stiggy Honda rider appeared to struggle with his CBR1000RR in the closing stages and eventually was shuffled back to 12th position, but only a few seconds from seventh-placed Neukirchner.

In the title standings, Neukirchner was now 30 points behind Spies in third, with Fabrizio fourth, Haslam fifth and Laconi sixth.

RACE TWO: VALENCIA

Haga beats Spies for the double

HAVING HALTED Ben Spies' victory run in the opening race, Noriyuki Haga comprehensively beat the American in a straight fight during race two, taking his first double victory of the season.

After three rounds, Haga and Spies had taken three wins each, but the former's consistency – the Ducati Xerox star had finished first or second in every race –put the Japanese into a solid 40-point title lead over the AMA champion, who had scored no points in race one at Phillip Island in addition to his Valencia DNF.

Once again Spies lost ground from pole at the start of race two, his R1 raising its front wheel too much off the line, but Haga faired little better, and the two title contenders found themselves fourth and fifth during the opening lap, Spies' early attempt to overtake Haga having been firmly rebuffed. The pair then worked their way forward, past Regis Laconi, Michel Fabrizio and Max Neukirchner. Haga hit the front on lap five, with Spies sliding into second soon after.

At that stage, Haga was only 1.2 second ahead of Spies, but the Japanese rider edged ever further away and, despite a slow final lap, crossed the finish line a distant 5.105 seconds in front of the Yamaha rider. Spies in turn faced little pressure from behind, third-placed Fabrizio having his hands full defending the final podium position from Laconi. The Italian claimed the spot by less than 0.2 second from the satellite Ducati rider.

RACE ONE: ASSEN

Spies takes win in dramatic fashion

BEN SPIES won his fourth race of the WSBK season at Assen after snatching victory from Noriyuki Haga's grasp with an outstanding overtaking move just three corners from the chequered flag. The American had looked to be out of contention in third with just a handful of laps remaining, but a late spurt put him on the tail of Haga by the final revolution, whereupon he proceeded to dive down the inside of his rival at the high-speed right-hand kink at turn 15. It was a dramatic finish to an exciting battle for first place that also had included an inspired Leon Haslam.

Spies had fought his way into the reckoning after being removed from the lead spot on lap 13 by a charging Haga. Before that, he had held a comfortable lead, having finally managed to secure a good start from pole position and subsequently resisted the attentions of fast-starting Max Neukirchner. Meanwhile, Haga and Haslam had lost time attempting to overtake third-placed Jakub Smrz.

Once he had passed the Czech rider, Haga rapidly chased down Neukirchner, who was close enough to be pressuring Spies for the lead of the race. While he was able to resist Haga's advances for a short time, however, the German's hopes of victory lasted no longer than lap seven, when he lost the front end of his Suzuki going into the final-corner chicane and went crashing down. Remarkably, the bike became upright again, crossing the second part of the chicane, narrowly avoiding Haslam and ending its trajectory in the tyre barrier.

Despite the delay caused by navigating around Neukirchner's runaway bike, Haslam was undeterred and promptly reeled off a series of excellent lap times, including one that broke Troy Bayliss' race lap record, and he soon found himself on the back of the lead fight.

Spies, meanwhile, was still at the front, but he had his hands full of Haga, who had made his presence felt with a series of feigned moves toward the final corners of the lap.

With Haslam keeping a watching brief in third, Haga chose lap 13 to make his move, prompted by Spies making a slight error on the way out of the long second turn and subsequently running slightly wide into the hairpin. Haga pounced to take the lead, while Haslam eagerly capitalized on Spies' error also to sweep past going into the next corner. Having shown aggressive pace in the early stages of the race, Haga attempted to sprint away, but Haslam stayed with him, shadowing him for several laps.

Meanwhile Spies remained in contention, but appeared to pose no threat to the leading pair until around five laps from the finish, when he began to reel in Haslam, who could not quite find the extra speed he needed to get past Haga.

When Spies did make his move, it came three laps from home as he dipped the Yamaha up the inside of turn eight. Haslam clung on though, staying alongside Spies right up to the turn ten right-hander and attempting to negate his outside line by leaving only just enough room for his rival. Spies persevered, however, and eventually was rewarded with second place.

With just two laps left to catch Haga, who was beginning to struggle with fading tyres, Spies didn't waste any time in latching on to the Ducati, the pair heading into the final revolution nose-to-tail. Even so, when Spies' first attempt to overtake, at the hairpin, failed, it seemed unlikely that he would be able to relieve the experienced Haga of the win. Nonetheless, the American continued to mirror his rival, tucking in behind him and using his Yamaha's sheer pace to catch him unawares at the high-speed turn 15.

Although on the defence immediately, Haga couldn't respond in time before Spies was pulling a wheelie across the finish line to complete what was arguably his finest victory of the season.

Haga was left a rather frustrated second, having shown strong pace throughout the race. Haslam was delighted, however, to have scored his second podium of the season for Stiggy after delivering front-running pace throughout.

With such intense action at the front, it came as no surprise that fourth-placed Tom Sykes was some eight seconds behind at the finish after a very lonely race. The Yamaha rider had run with Haslam in the early stages, but hadn't been able to maintain his pace, although the result did signal a season's best and maintained his run of top-ten finishes.

The battle for fifth had almost been as riveting as that for the lead, with up to five riders swapping positions during the race. Eventually, Max Biaggi had prevailed after fighting his way past Smrz and then Michel Fabrizio. The Italian had shown decent form and eventually pulled away from the tussle.

After having plummeted relatively quickly in the early stages, Smrz had stalked his way back into contention to finish sixth for Guandalini Ducati. Jonathan Rea held on to seventh, the Northern Irishman having shown well in the early stages as he recovered from a poor start, while Regis Laconi and Fabrizio, who had dropped back rapidly in the closing stages, were eighth and ninth. BMW's Troy Corser was tenth to make it five manufacturers inside the top ten.

Elsewhere, Shane Byrne continued to keep his points ticking over in 11th, while Karl Muggeridge scored his first of the season in 12th for Celani Suzuki.

Following his disappointing fall early on, Neukirchner had made a fine recovery, catching and passing the final point scorers, Ruben Xaus and Ryuichi Kiyonari, to finish 13th. His team-mate, Yukio Kagayama, however, was one of a few riders to crash out and stay out, the Japanese rider having been joined on the sidelines by Tommy Hill, Carlos Checa and Shinya Nakano.

Left: An epic overtake gave Spies race one.

Far left: Haga and Spies fight it out.

Below: Scot Stuart Easton took over the injured Parkes' Kawasaki.

Photos: Gold & Goose

Above: Sykes continued his top-ten run.

Left: Kawasaki team chief Paul Bird.

Right: A second rostrum visit for Haslam *(left)* and Haga, a first for Smrz *(right)*.

Photos: Gold & Goose

RACE TWO: ASSEN

Haga eases to victory after Spies DNF

NORIYUKI HAGA stretched his WSBK advantage to 60 points after capitalising on an accident suffered by Ben Spies to win the second race of the day at Assen. The Japanese rider was left with a relatively easy run to the finish line when the American, who had led at the end of the opening lap, went down at the first turn as they entered the second lap.

Although there was a high degree of attrition in the race, with only 17 bikes finishing, there wasn't nearly as much action as in the earlier event, although the 'round two' match of Spies versus Haga had looked promising at the start when they almost swapped paint through the first few corners. While Haga got the better start to move in front on the exit of the first turn, albeit only after Leon Haslam had run wide following a determined attempt to take the lead himself, Spies struck back at the hairpin and dipped back ahead.

Just as the race was shaping up to be another epic tussle between the two title protagonists, however, Spies went down and out at the first turn, landing in the gravel trap while his Yamaha catapulted into the barrier. Looking visibly frustrated by his misfortune, particularly after his headline grabbing performance in the first race, the American was left to watch while Haga steadily moved away from the chasing pack to claim an unhampered fourth win of the season and establish a mammoth lead in the points chase.

With Haga easing away at the front, attention turned instead to the battle for second place, which was led initially by Max Neukirchner, ahead of Haslam, Jakub Smrz and Michel Fabrizio.

After a disappointing ninth in race one, Fabrizio was on the move in the early stages, passing both Smrz and Haslam before displacing Neukirchner with a dive down the inside of the chicane. Caught unawares, the German was forced to sit up and straight-line the corner, which dropped him to the back of the pack. Despite his best efforts, though, Fabrizio could not break away. Haslam and Smrz went with him, and the trio began lapping at a similar pace to Haga, who, by that stage, was several seconds up the road.

Buoyed by his superb run to third in the first race, Haslam kept Fabrizio under significant pressure, hounding the Italian through each bend, but being unable to find his way through. Nonetheless, the Stiggy rider's perseverance paid off when finally he planted a move on lap 13, subsequently resisting Fabrizio's counterattacks to move through and gradually pull away.

Haslam crossed the line just over two seconds behind Haga, second place marking his best-ever WSBK result to date and bringing to a close an outstanding day that also saw him up to third in the overall standings.

The battle for third went down to the wire too, Fabrizio holding the position into the final lap, only for Smrz to get the better of him and record what was also his and Guandalini Ducati's best ever result at WSBK level.

Some way behind, Jonathan Rea received a much needed boost after a run to fifth, the Northern Irishman having recovered from another poor start to come out on top in a heated battle with sole Yamaha rider Tom Sykes. Keeping a watching brief just behind, Carlos Checa was seventh, with Shane Byrne eighth, Neukirchner ninth and Troy Corser tenth. Ruben Xaus followed in 11th after a race-long fight with Yukio Kagayama.

In a race that had seen problems for Spies, Regis Laconi, Karl Muggeridge and Stuart Easton among others, the final three points paying positions fell to Brendan Roberts, Matteo Baiocco and Luca Scassa, all first-time scorers at this level.

RACE ONE: MONZA

Fabrizio victorious after last-corner drama

MICHEL FABRIZIO took his first WSBK victory in the first race at Monza, after Ben Spies lost speed dramatically on the final corner while in the lead. Having led for most of the race, the American looked set for victory as he started the last lap after shaking off the advances of Fabrizio and Noriyuki Haga. He was forced to coast across the finish line in 15th, however, when his Yamaha slowed down suddenly going through the Parabolica, just metres from the finish line. He had run out of fuel.

Despite the fortuitous circumstances surrounding the win, Fabrizio's maiden triumph was worthy, as he had led in the early stages of the race before developing a small gearing problem that had dropped him behind Spies and Haga. Nonetheless, Fabrizio worked his way around the problem and stalked his way back into contention, dicing with team-mate Haga before launching an assault on Spies and passing him for the lead with three laps to go.

Spies struck back one lap later, however, to grab an advantage he thought would be good enough to carry him to the finish line.

Fabrizio still had to work hard for what would become the win, going head-to-head with Haga once again and pulling off an audacious – and crucial – move on him at Ascari with just over a lap to go.

The race itself was a restart, following a terrifying accident that involved five riders at the initial get-away. After contact between several riders, Makoto Tamada and Brendan Roberts were forced on to the grass, where they fell heavily. Roberts' errant Guandalini Ducati continued to skate across the grass, however, sliding into the path of the other riders rounding the first chicane and eliminating Max Neukirchner, who

was leading at that stage. In the process, the German suffered serious injuries to both legs. Further back, Tommy Hill and Troy Corser also came to grief mid-pack, one of the bikes subsequently catching fire.

A lengthy clean-up operation followed, and the race didn't restart for almost an hour. Corser made the restart, but failed to complete the opening lap after crashing at the Parabolica.

Away from the fight for the lead, which quickly became a three-way battle, a spirited tussle between Max Biaggi and Yukio Kagayama eventually went the Italian's way. Despite being promoted to third, however, courtesy of Spies' problem, Biaggi quickly learned that he had been given a 20-second penalty, dropping him to 11th. That meant the podium fell, surprisingly, to Ryuichi Kiyonari, who had put in a marvellous performance on the Ten Kate Honda after a terrible start had left him in 17th position at the end of the opening lap. Nonetheless, the Japanese rider had reeled off a series of consistently quick laps to pick off the competition, although even he was surprised to secure a first podium of the season, having entered the final lap in fifth position.

Countryman Kagayama gave Suzuki something to smile about after Neukirchner's dramatic exit by taking fourth place, ahead of Jonathan Rea, who got the better of former BSB sparring partner Tom Sykes following a race-long duel.

Spies' problems and Biaggi's penalty also played into the hands of Ruben Xaus, who recorded BMW's best WSBK finish so far with a fine seventh, ahead of Regis Laconi and Carlos Checa, while Broc Parkes sneaked a top-ten finish for Kawasaki too.

Biaggi found himself a disgruntled 11th, while Jakub Smrz, Shinya Nakano and Shane Byrne were the remaining riders to jump ahead of Spies as he crept across the finish line.

RACE TWO: MONZA

Spies responds with win as Haga crashes

BEN SPIES avoided a repeat of his race-one disaster by claiming a dominant victory in the second race of the day at Monza, while Noriyuki Haga crashed out. The American led from almost lights to finish, breaking the slipstream to those behind to win by almost three seconds from race-one winner Michel Fabrizio and Ryuichi Kiyonari.

Spies assumed the lead at the second chicane when Haga suddenly dropped back after hitting a bird. Although Yukio Kagayama rallied for the lead initially, the American reeled off a series of relentlessly quick lap times to put a gap between himself and the battle for second.

Haga's race, however, went from bad to worse. Having dropped to 15th position by the end of the opening lap, he was making progress when he committed what was arguably his first error of the year by barrel-rolling out of the race on lap three at the Parabolica. The spectacular accident sent his Ducati Xerox catapulting over the barriers, but luckily Haga emerged unscathed.

Meanwhile, Spies continued to pull away up front, aided by the fact that Kagayama had been given a drive-through penalty that dropped him out of contention.

Behind Spies, the battle for the next three positions enticed the Monza crowd, with Fabrizio, Kiyonari and Jonathan Rea squabbling for second, third and fourth. Initially, Fabrizio held second, but Kiyonari – benefiting from a much better start in this race – was back through on lap seven. Nonetheless, while the Japanese rider managed to escape briefly, Fabrizio gradually reeled him in to snatch the place back on lap 12, resisting the Honda to the finish line.

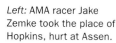

Left: AMA racer Jake Zemke took the place of Hopkins, hurt at Assen.

Right: Sideways Xaus took BMW's first top ten.

Centre left: Luca Scassa celebrates scoring two home points.

Far left: Team-mates? Fabrizio took race one from Haga.

Below left: Kiyonari heads Laconi through the fast corners.

Bottom: Mayhem yards after the start of race one. Erstwhile leader Neukirchner came off worst.

Photos: Gold & Goose

Although he would drop away from the battle ahead of him, Rea held on for his second top-five finish of the day, taking fourth, ahead of Max Biaggi.

The British contingent enjoyed a prosperous race, Tom Sykes and Leon Haslam joining Rea in celebrating strong finishes in sixth and seventh, the latter impressing after starting in 17th.

Another to make big gains on his grid position was Jakub Smrz, who got the better of Ruben Xaus, Carlos Checa and Regis Laconi to secure eighth, the quartet crossing the line almost line astern.

Shinya Nakano and Broc Parkes came home in 12th and 13th, while Luca Scassa got the better of Matteo Baiocco by just three-thousandths of a second in the battle for 14th and 15th.

Elsewhere, an early pit-lane appearance for Shane Byrne left him languishing toward the back of the field, while Tommy Hill had to be content with 16th, having run as high as 11th in the early stages of the race.

In the overall standings, Spies and Haga left Monza almost as they had arrived, with 54 points separating them. The big winner, however, was Fabrizio, who moved up to third place at the expense of Haslam and was just 21 points off Spies.

RACE ONE: KYALAMI

Haga at home in Kyalami race one

NORIYUKI HAGA claimed victory in the opening race of the Kyalami WSBK weekend, fending off Ducati team-mate Michel Fabrizio and Yamaha pole-sitter Ben Spies. Showing little effect of the Monza injuries that he had feared could compromise his performance, the Japanese veteran got the jump at the start, but had to give best to Fabrizio mid-race before returning to the front and making the most of the ensuing battle between the Italian and Spies by building the cushion he needed to secure victory.

Spies and Fabrizio scrapped over second until the American made a mistake and allowed the Ducati back through, while Jonathan Rea kept his nerve to deny a determined Max Biaggi on the run to the flag to round out the top five.

Initially, Spies appeared to have the holeshot, trying to convert his record-equalling sixth straight pole into an early lead, but Haga swept across from the opposite side of the front row to claim the advantage, while the Yamaha rider attempted to fend off the equally fast-starting Biaggi through turns one and two. Fabrizio, meanwhile, tucked into fourth, before quickly picking off the two men ahead of him to leave Xerox Ducati sitting 1-2 at the end of the opening lap.

Initially, Carlos Checa held fifth spot, but soon lost it to Ten Kate team-mate Rea, who had ended the first tour with Shinya Nakano, Jakob Smrz, Sheridan Morais and Yukio Kagayama right behind him. Smrz's presence was not long-lived, however, the Czech disappearing to the rear of the field, but at least he was still running, which is more than could be said for Ruben Xaus, whose race ended on lap two with his BMW buried in the dirt.

Fabrizio, perhaps keen to underline his early weekend dominance, swept to the front a lap later, while Rea followed suit by leading Checa past Biaggi for fourth and fifth. The rest of the British contingent wasn't fairing quite so well, however, poor qualifying positions condemning Leon Haslam and Shane Byrne to tenth and 11th respectively, while a poor start had seen Tom Sykes drop even further back, the Yamaha rider unlucky 13th; Tommy Hill was mired toward the rear of the field.

While Checa and Biaggi traded fifth place on lap nine, Haslam began to make a move, passing Kagayama for ninth as the first ten laps were ticked off and then engaging in a spirited dice with local favourite Morais for eighth, the South African stand-in just managing to keep the place.

Approaching half-way, Haga tired of chasing his team-mate and duly returned his Ducati to the front

of the pack. Almost immediately, Spies appeared to raise his game, the American keen to prevent the points leader from making too much of a break lest he extended the gap between them on paper as well as tarmac. Having to deal with Fabrizio, however, Spies' progress was not dramatic, and Haga increased the distance to the squabbling pair, initially four-tenths, but later growing toward a second.

Having finally disposed of the stubborn Morais, Haslam appeared on course to edge closer to the top six as he unearthed the race pace that the Stiggy team had spoken of after qualifying. The Briton's charge ended almost as soon as it had begun, however, and he was forced to pick himself out of the dirt; he joined Xaus as the race's only DNFs.

Meanwhile, Morais appeared spent, his Kawasaki slipping down the order as Kagayama, Byrne and Sykes all found a way through and into the top ten. Before the end, Gregorio Lavilla and Ryuichi Kiyonari would also demote the South African, who ended the race 13th overall, four seconds clear of the recovering Smrz.

Haga's break also came to nothing, for Fabrizio and Spies had bridged the gap by lap 16, bringing the top three back together. Rea, in fourth, was a long way adrift and with problems of his own as Biaggi came back into play.

Spies finally overcame Fabrizio on lap 17, al-

Left: Haga leads Spies and Rea on the first lap of race two.

Below centre, left to right: Rea made the podium in race two; Laconi's spare Ducati was idle – the Frenchman was badly hurt in practice; Fabrizio and Haga were unbeatable; local Sheridan Morais claimed points on the Kawasaki.

Photos: Gold & Goose

		BEST	LL	SPLIT 1
1	19 SPIES	1'37.288		5
2	84 FABRIZIO	1'37.289		6
3	3 BIAGGI	1'37.466		7
4	41 HAGA	1'37.544		3
5	65 REA	1'37.634		7
6	96 SMRZ	1'37.677		4
7	7 CHECA C.	1'37.940		6
8	66 SYKES	1'38.241		7
9	56 NAKANO			
	91 HASLAM			
	132 MORAIS			
	9 KIYONARI			

Above: Closest ever Superpole: Spies one-thousandth faster than Fabrizio.

Left: South African Shaun Whyte took over the Yamaha France machine.

Photos: Gold & Goose

though the move allowed Haga to pull away again, but then the Italian began to fight back, the pair swapping places twice more on the following lap. The battle was decided once and for all, however, with five laps to run, when Spies made an error on the way out of Yellow Pages that saw him out of the Yamaha's saddle with his right leg flailing as he attempted to ride it out. Although he managed to save the moment, Fabrizio was quick to capitalise, moving smartly past the American and back into P2, this time with a small margin.

By now, Haga was nearly two seconds up the road, and the gap to his team-mate only reduced as the Japanese veteran eased off on the final tour, keen to ensure that he collected his 38th career win and another at Kyalami after a gap of seven years. The cushion at the flag was down to just under a second, Fabrizio refusing to give up the scent of a second win in as many weekends, but the Italian had to make do with another trip to step two of the podium as Spies backed off in third.

Rea, meanwhile, had Biaggi all over the back of his Honda, the Italian determined to return Aprilia to the top four. For lap after lap, the Irishman held firm, but Biaggi appeared to have gained the chance he craved as they headed into the final turn. For all his experience, however, the Roman Emperor carried too much speed into the corner and ran wide on the exit, allowing Rea to sneak back through and claim the position as they flashed across the line.

Behind the top five, Checa, Nakano, Kagayama, Byrne and Sykes rounded out a relatively sedate top ten, although the battles for sixth and ninth remained close to the flag, while Broc Parkes claimed the final point for Kawasaki in 15th after opening a four-second gap to Fonsi Nieto.

RACE TWO: KYALAMI

Haga flies to Kyalami double

A WEEK after being struck by an errant bird at Monza, Noriyuki Haga clinched a double victory in round six of the WSBK championship at Kyalami, fending off Xerox Ducati team-mate Michel Fabrizio on the final lap to ensure that he left South Africa as he arrived – as the only Kyalami winner in the current field.

The Japanese veteran got the holeshot for the second time, but had to give best to pole-sitter Ben Spies in the early stages. Whether the American could have denied the points leader his double – and joined countrymen Colin Edwards and Ben Bostrom as a winner in South Africa – was a moot point, for the Yamaha coughed and died on lap three, allowing Haga back ahead and into a comfortable lead. Jonathan Rea, meanwhile, held off Max Biaggi for much of the race – as he had done in race one – and then survived a late assault from fellow Briton Leon Haslam to claim the final podium spot.

Biaggi appeared to have claimed the advantage heading into turn one, a position he knew he needed to stand a chance of taking Aprilia back to the top of the podium, but, once again, the Italian was shuffled back as the pack rounded the turn, coming out in third spot as both Haga and Spies got the better of him. Then he was pushed back to fourth as Rea also showed his fighting colours.

By the end of the opening lap, Biaggi was ahead of Carlos Checa, Fabrizio, Leon Haslam – the Stiggy Honda rider having made the flying start he missed in race one – Shinya Nakano, Yukio Kagayama and Tom Sykes, who again went backwards off the line.

Before the next tour could be completed, the race had a new leader, Spies having swept past Haga in a bid, no doubt, not to be left behind by the Ducati ace as had happened earlier in the day. The American's hold on proceedings only lasted another lap, however, the Yamaha swinging wide to the left at Continental and slowing as the pole-man realised that something was amiss. He had enough power to get back to the pits, but his day, and his bid to stop Haga extending his points advantage, was over.

Haga gratefully accepted the chance to move back into the lead as Spies joined the clashing Ruben Xaus and Karl Muggeridge on the sidelines. He was immediately able to open a comfortable gap over Rea, who now had Fabrizio, rather than Biaggi, for company. Despite his best defence, the Ulsterman left a Ducati-sized hole on the inside at Westbank on lap four, allowing the Italian through into second spot with only his team-mate between himself and a second WSBK win.

Far from responding and going with Fabrizio, Rea dropped back into Biaggi's clutches, the Aprilia rider bringing Haslam into the equation as the Briton mounted an assault on fourth spot. Neither could make a move stick, however, and the order at the end of ten laps read Haga, Fabrizio, Rea, Biaggi and Haslam, followed by Checa, Nakano, Sykes, Kagayama and Sheridan Morais, the South African again transcending recent Kawasaki performances on his WSBK debut.

With Haga enjoying a comfortable, and apparently unbridgeable, margin to his team-mate, and the battle in the lower reaches of the top hardly befitting the description, all attention fell on the scrap for third. That took a twist as Haslam found a way past Biaggi on lap 13, then proceeded to bang fairings with Rea as he sensed an opportunity to join the Ducati twins on the podium. Both survived the brush, Rea being able to hold on to third spot as the trio continued to circulate as one for a few more laps, and it was the Irishman who emerged the strongest over the longer distance, eventually easing away from his pursuers as the race wore on. Biaggi wasn't done, but Haslam proved to have enough to frustrate the veteran to the flag.

With few moves being made in the field, Kagayama reclaiming eighth from Sykes notwithstanding, and the order closely resembling that of race one, the race appeared to be heading toward a quiet conclusion – until Fabrizio decided to make one last bid for victory.

With Haga keen not to do anything silly on the final tour, the Italian was able to home in on his team-mate, eventually taking sufficient tenths from the gap between them to get close enough to take a look on the way out of Wesbank. Perhaps distracted by back marker Shaun Whyte ahead of them, Haga didn't block Fabrizio, but the Italian carried too much speed into the turn to make the move stick. Undeterred, he gathered himself and launched another assault at the final turn, initially appearing to emerge ahead, until Haga found better drive to the line, completing the third win double in Kyalami's five-round WSBK history.

Rea duly completed the podium on a generally good day for British riders, while Haslam held on to fourth, but needed a little assistance to make it back to parc fermé. Biaggi rounded out the top five for the second time on the day, with Checa, Nakano, Kagayama, Sykes and Jakob Smrz completing the leading ten. Morais, Gregorio Lavilla, Ryuichi Kiyonari, Broc Parkes and Fonsi Nieto were the remaining scorers, while Shane Byrne had joined the list of retirements after seven laps.

Above: Dramatic desert backdrop dwarfs the pack: Spies leads Fabrizio and Checa (7).

Right: Former MotoGP winner Carlos Checa was second in race one.

Centre right: Fabrizio, here heading Biaggi (3) and Rea (65), took two podiums.

Photos: Gold & Goose

RACE ONE: UTAH

Spies wins interrupted Miller opener

BEN SPIES overcame a mid-race restart to score his fifth WSBK win of the season in front of his home fans at Miller Motorsports Park. In a race determined by aggregate results following a red-flag period on lap seven, Spies kept his cool on both occasions to romp away from the field and win by almost ten seconds from Carlos Checa.

Spies led comfortably from the first start, capitalising on his pole position to sling his Yamaha into the lead on the run to the opening bend, while Shinya Nakano made full use of the lengthy straight to catapult from tenth on the grid to second position behind the American. Equally impressive off the line was Noriyuki Haga, who went from ninth to third, ahead of Ryuichi Kiyonari, Broc Parkes and front-row-sitter Checa.

With Spies already putting considerable air between himself and Nakano, the outcome began to look like a foregone conclusion after just a few laps. The American's cause was certainly aided by Haga, whose good getaway only brought an apparent lack of race pace into sharper focus. Indeed, he was down to sixth, behind team-mate Michel Fabrizio, by lap four, and then was faced with the unusual situation of being swamped by the feisty Kawasakis of Parkes and Jamie Hacking. Both men provided considerable entertainment in their run toward the front of the field, belying the bike's previous lack of pace to achieve their aims on lap six and get the better of Haga.

Hacking was on a particular charge, having made his way past Haga, Parkes and Checa by the end of lap six to find himself suddenly in fourth position. His hopes of progressing would come to nothing, however, when the red flag was produced after an accident involving Karl Muggeridge further back. The Australian had lost control of his Celani Suzuki, and with both man and machine stricken on the circuit, the organisers chose to stop the race.

Muggeridge's accident was bad news for Hacking and Parkes, who were moved back to their respective eighth and seventh positions on count-back at the restart, although they gained a position at the expense of Nakano, who had crashed before the race was stopped when he lost the front end of his Aprilia while attempting to defend from Checa. He didn't make the restart.

Following a 20-minute delay, during which Muggeridge was seen making his own way to the ambulance for a check-up at the medical centre, the race was restarted using the aggregate times from the riders' positions at the end of lap six. This meant that Spies held a four-second advantage over Kiyonari, with Checa third in the absence of Nakano, Fabrizio fourth and Haga fifth.

At the lights, Spies got away well again, but he was beaten into the first corner by an equally fast-starting Kiyonari. However, any hope the Japanese rider had of beating Spies was dashed half-way around the lap when Spies pushed his way through and took charge once more.

Another to benefit from the restart was Jonathan Rea, who launched off the line to end the 'first' lap fourth on the road, albeit still eighth in the aggregate standings. Nonetheless, with only his team-mates for company up ahead and running a good pace, it wasn't long before he was scaling the timesheets, moving past those who were getting caught up in a much tighter fight just behind.

A great start for Parkes saw him running fifth, meaning that he briefly held fourth overall, ahead of Fabrizio, Biaggi, Rea, Haga and Hacking. The Australian began to struggle as the race wore on, however, being reined in by Biaggi and Fabrizio before actually being clipped by his team-mate on lap 11 when Hacking attempted an overtaking manoeuvre. The light contact prompted an even more alarming drop down the order, and he would fail to reach the chequered flag.

As the field began to spread out, an unconventional tussle took place for the remaining podium positions behind Spies, Kiyonari clinging on to second position, despite the fact that he was running quite far behind Checa on the road. The former BSB champion held the position until lap 13, when, under pressure from Rea, he made an error at Attitude. He was flung briefly from his seat, but recovered to run behind his team-mates.

Seemingly unable to maintain the pace he had managed at the original start, Kiyonari found himself down to sixth position on the road, behind Biaggi and Fabrizio. Of the two, the latter was his biggest threat for the final podium position on aggregate, and the Italian duly grabbed the spot on the final lap when he managed to slipstream his way past Biaggi and use the clear air to put in a strong late effort.

Top: Haga jumps ship in practice.

Above: AMA racer Jamie Hacking was seventh, Kawasaki's best finish since 2007.

Below: "You again!" Spies and rostrum returnee Rea share congratulations.

Photos: Gold & Goose

Up at the front, though, Spies was cruising to victory for Yamaha, gradually pulling out his advantage over Checa to cross the line four seconds up on the Spaniard, but almost ten seconds in total. Second was the best result of the season so far for Checa, who was comfortably classified ahead of the hard charging Fabrizio. The Italian's last-lap effort helped to keep Spies honest in the battle for second in the standings.

Despite fading away in the closing stages, Kiyonari's strong showing at the original start meant that he could cling on to fourth, less than a second ahead of Rea, who came away with fifth, despite having finished a physical third.

Battling up from 16th on the grid, Biaggi was sixth, the Italian having utilised the outstanding straight-line speed of the Aprilia RSV-4 to pull off some impressive moves along the long home straight.

While he wasn't quite as prolific as he had been in the early stages, seventh position for Jamie Hacking marked Kawasaki's best WSBK finish since Vallelunga 2007. His cause had been aided by a thrilling exchange for eighth position, which had come down to a fight between six riders, the place having changed hands constantly in the final laps. Haga had held on to the spot for most of the race, but the ailing championship leader had been swallowed up by Leon Haslam and Shane Byrne, the latter having recovered from a terrible start that had left him in 16th at the end of the opening lap.

While both men had managed to get the jump on Haga by lap 16, the gulf of time they had needed to make up on the Japanese rider had proved to be too much, and they were forced to contend with tenth and 11th, Haslam ahead of Byrne. Even so, Haga was demoted to ninth at the finish, having been leapfrogged by Jakub Smrz. The Czech rider had made stealthy progress through the field to snatch the position on the final lap.

Elsewhere, Yukio Kagayama finished 12th, ahead of Tom Sykes – his first finish outside the top ten of the season – Gregorio Lavilla and Troy Corser.

RACE TWO: UTAH

Spies does the double on home soil

YAMAHA RIDER Ben Spies completed a double victory on home ground at Miller Motorsports Park to make some headway in cutting Noriyuki Haga's substantial WSBK championship lead. Although he didn't have an interruption to contend with on this occasion, the American was in similarly dominant form, leading from start to finish for his sixth win and second double of the season.

With Haga finishing in eighth, Spies was able to reduce the chasm between himself and the championship leader by 35 points, reducing it to a somewhat more manageable 53.

Having been untouchable during the first race, Spies was the man to beat from the start line, the Texan producing arguably his finest start of the season so far to slingshot into the lead, ahead of fellow front-row-starter Michel Fabrizio.

Just behind, Carlos Checa managed a good getaway from second to slot into third, ahead of Haga and Max Biaggi, the pair doing a fine job of bullying their way to the front of the field from their respective ninth and 16th starting positions.

With a clear track ahead of him, Spies quickly began to assert his authority by pulling away from the pack, although Fabrizio hung on gamely as he attempted to match the Yamaha through the Utah cir-

cuit's twists and turns. He pulled out a gap to those behind him, and the advantage improved on lap four when third-placed Checa went crashing down at the Attitude chicane, putting a frustrating end to what had looked like being his best weekend of the season so far.

Checa's demise left Rea in third position, the Northern Irishman having capitalised on Biaggi's messy attempt to pass Haga for fourth, the pair losing out as the Ten Kate Honda slid through.

While Rea couldn't pull away from the pack, he showed remarkable defensive skill against the rivals queuing up behind him. Haga, Biaggi and Kiyonari all tried to get the better of Rea, but he was able to maintain tight lines and, significantly, get a good drive out of the final corner to counteract any slipstream effect down the lengthy home straight.

Further back, some of the star performers from race one – Shane Byrne, Broc Parkes and Jamie Hacking – were having a tougher time. Byrne ran well in the early stages, but dropped to the back of the field on lap five, while both Kawasaki riders were outside the top twenty at the end of the opening lap. Worse was to follow for Hacking when he clipped the back of Luca Scassa's Pedercini ZX-10R, sending the Italian skyward and out of the race, while the American slipped to the back of the field.

At the front, Haga's attempt at a podium finish began to falter as the race reached the mid-point, and he fell away from Rea, while Kiyonari, a charging Leon Haslam, Jakub Smrz and Shinya Nakano all found their way through eventually.

Of those backed up behind Rea, Haslam made the most prolific progress, forcing Kiyonari to sit up as he dived through to assume fourth position. Indeed, the Stiggy Honda rider looked the most likely candidate to wrestle third from Rea's grasp, which he did momentarily on lap 17, only for the Ten Kate machine to slip back through at the start of lap 18.

Just as Haslam was gearing up for a last-lap challenge to secure a third podium of the season, however, he lost the front end of his machine on the run to Attitude, which put him out of the race, much to his obvious disappointment.

At the same time, Spies crossed the line to celebrate his second win of the day, five seconds up on Fabrizio after the Italian's spirited mid-race assault, during which he had kept the gap to his rival pegged at less than two seconds, faltered toward the end.

Haslam's demise meant that Rea was fairly comfortable as he crossed the line for his second podium in consecutive events, while the outcome also allowed him to overtake Haslam for fourth in the overall standings. He finished ahead of Biaggi and Kiyonari, who also capitalised on the Briton's error to secure top-five results.

Smrz completed a decent weekend in sixth, ahead of Nakano – bandaged up after his race-one accident – and Haga, the championship leader having had his first 'off' weekend of the season.

Tom Sykes kept his finishes ticking over in ninth, up from 21st on the grid, ahead of Byrne, whose charge back through the field would most likely have seen him fighting for the podium but for his earlier delay. The same could be said of Parkes, who had scythed his way past a number of rivals to finish 11th.

A forgettable weekend for Suzuki ended with Yukio Kagayama and Fonsi Nieto finishing line-astern in 12th and 13th, ahead of series returnee Lorenzo Lanzi, while Haslam's late retirement promoted his Stiggy team-mate, Jake Zemke, to 15th and his first WSBK point.

RACE ONE: MISANO

Spies storms to wet-to-dry win at Misano

BEN SPIES took his eighth WSBK victory of the season at Misano after unleashing a searing pace when it mattered most. In the early stages of the race, which had begun in damp conditions, he had looked to be out of contention, Shane Byrne taking the initiative instead and pulling out a huge 15-second gap over his nearest rival. However, as the circuit dried rapidly and the flag-to-flag rule came into effect, the American was mesmerising on his second bike as he quickly caught and passed Byrne to win by a clear eight seconds.

It was an eventful race defined by the tumultuous weather conditions. All the riders had started on treaded rubber, but the arrival of the sun meant that most had swapped their bikes by the mid-point. It didn't take long for drama to strike though, Troy Corser tumbling on the warm-up lap and being unable to make the start – he joined returned-from-injury John Hopkins on the sidelines, the American having decided not to race.

From the start, first-time pole-sitter Jakub Smrz got away well, but he was no match for Byrne, who rocketed into the lead at the opening bend, ahead of the sister Guandalini machine, Spies, Carlos Checa and Michel Fabrizio.

Having experienced a dismal season so far, reigning British Superbike champion Byrne wasted no time in attempting to make amends, at one stage lapping more than a second faster than anyone else on the circuit as he excelled on the treacherous surface.

Despite the slippery conditions, all the riders stayed upright, even if some coped better than others. Among those who scythed their way up the order were Gregorio Lavilla, up to eighth by lap three, and Yukio Kagayama in ninth, although both Aprilia riders found conditions tougher as they slipped out of contention

Meanwhile, Jonathan Rea, who had intended to start in second position before being forced to get away from the pit lane, found himself back in the pit lane when he was given a drive-through penalty.

Up at the front, Byrne continued to extend his advantage at a remarkable rate, having pulled out an 8.6-second advantage over Smrz by lap six. The Czech rider also enjoyed a good gap over Fabrizio, Spies and Checa at this stage.

Haga slipped back rapidly, however, as he continued to struggle with the handling of his Ducati Xerox on the drying tarmac, dropping from sixth to tenth in just one lap. It was apparent that the circuit was beginning to reach a stage where riders could switch to their slick-shod machines.

First to take a punt was Shinya Nakano, who ditched his struggling Aprilia in favour of a new one at the end of lap nine; his progress was watched with great interest by the other teams.

Haga followed suit soon afterwards, kick-starting a flurry of activity in the pit lane as riders switched machines. Spies was the first of the lead riders to change.

Up to that point, the Yamaha rider had slipped to fifth position, behind Checa, the Spaniard having found some remarkable speed to pass the American, Fabrizio and Smrz within two laps to move into second position.

Fabrizio pitted on lap 13, rejoining in front of Spies on his return to the circuit, while Checa and Smrz followed on lap 14. Checa's chances were effectively ended, however, when his Ten Kate Honda refused to fire up, leaving the visibly frustrated Spaniard to lose several seconds as his crew attempted to jump-start him down the pit lane. A similar problem had afflicted Rea earlier.

Eventually, Byrne pitted on lap 15, emerging back on track in a provisional first place, with only Ruben Xaus – yet to pit – ahead of him.

On a levelled playing field, however, Spies set a remarkable pace, lapping considerably quicker than

the riders ahead of him to dispatch Fabrizio and Smrz quickly before destroying Byrne's advantage. With the Sterilgarda machine seemingly unable to sustain the pace it had showed in the damp, Spies simply drove around Byrne to take an effective lead.

Just a few seconds up the road, Xaus was leading for BMW, the first time the German brand had ever headed a WSBK race. The Spaniard had been a marvel in the slippery conditions, scything his way into contention after starting in 18th position. He had been able to pull alongside Jamie Hacking and Leon Haslam too, who had filled the top spots for a brief time as they attempted to make their waning rubber last as long as possible.

It didn't take long for Spies, who was lapping around ten seconds faster than Xaus, to relieve the BMW of the lead, moving ahead on lap 19 and simply romping away over the remaining five laps to claim another superb victory at a circuit he had never visited before.

As the remainder of the pack bore down on him, Xaus lasted until the end of lap 19 before eventually pitting and dropping to the bottom end of the top ten. A drive-through penalty, however, would see him cross the line in 14th position.

Spies cruised across the line to continue his quest to close the gap on Haga, who had managed to battle his way to fifth position after passing Yukio Kagayama on the final lap and having run as low as 19th at one stage. The gap between the two riders in the standings was down to 39 points.

Although disappointed to miss out on the win, Byrne held off Fabrizio and a charging Smrz, who was the fastest rider in the latter stages, to finish as the best Ducati on home ground in second. It was easily his best result on the Sterilgarda Ducati.

Behind Haga, Kagayama had defied his injury woes to finish a heroic sixth, ahead of Rea, who deserved plaudits for producing a good result despite the problems that had plagued him throughout the race.

Tom Sykes prevailed in a lengthy battle with Nakano to finish eighth, the Japanese rider finishing well up on team-mate Max Biaggi in ninth. Matthieu Lagrive rounded out the top ten on his WSBK debut aboard the Althea Honda.

Checa had recovered to a frustrated 11th, ahead of Haslam, who had left it too late to pit, while Biaggi, Xaus and Alessandro Polita, on his return, completed the points paying positions.

Above: Sykes' Yamaha heads Xaus' BMW in race one.

Left: Neukirchner was still *hors de combat.*

Far left: Rea held off the Ducatis for his first Superbike win.

Photos: Gold & Goose

RACE TWO: MISANO

Last-gasp Rea seals maiden WSBK victory

JONATHAN REA became only the fourth different WSBK winner of 2009 after a daring last-lap manoeuvre saw him snatch a maiden victory in the second race at Misano. The Northern Irishman was embroiled in a thrilling race-long exchange with Ducati Xerox duo Michel Fabrizio and Noriyuki Haga, but while the Italian seemed to have stolen the initiative when he moved ahead with only a handful of laps remaining, Rea did not let his rival pull away. Primed for attack, Rea launched his assault at the beginning of the final lap and succeeded in passing Fabrizio at the right-hander before resisting pressure from his rival to the chequered flag.

Prior to that, Rea had led the way for most of the race, the Ten Kate Honda man having got away in a leading pack that initially had consisted of early leader Haga, Fabrizio and Carlos Checa.

Race one winner Ben Spies, however, looked down and out at the end of the opening lap when, arm aloft, he appeared to be slowing down to retire. Dropping to the back of the field with a slipping clutch, the American did his best to get it working again, but was left with plenty of work to do to take points from his championship rival, Haga. His cause wasn't aided by Haga's lead, the Japanese rider having surged up from sixth position on the grid to move ahead into the opening turns, followed by Rea. The Ten Kate Honda – resplendent with its distinctive new Öhlins suspension –proved a match for Haga, however, and Rea duly snatched the lead for the first time in the season on lap four.

Despite his attempts to respond, Haga slipped down to third on lap six when Fabrizio pulled a move on him too. While the pair swapped positions twice on lap ten and then lap 15, Rea worked hard to put some air between himself and the feuding team-mates. Fabrizio, though, safely back in second position again, began to be a significant threat to Rea, quickly latching on to the back of the Honda before diving beneath him at the tight second turn on lap 17.

Fabrizio's hopes of disappearing into the distance for a second career victory, however, didn't materialise, as both Rea and Haga kept him under intense pressure, so much so that Rea momentarily repassed the Italian with just four laps remaining, only for the Ducati rider to squeeze back through.

With just one lap remaining, Fabrizio led with Rea and Haga in close company. Getting a good tow down the home straight, Rea tucked beneath Fabrizio before backing the bike up the inside and holding his line into the ensuing left-hander. While Fabrizio attempted to respond through the remaining corners, Rea was able to hold him off to cross the line for a famous first win.

He joined Spies, Haga and Fabrizio on the winner's list for the season so far. The victory also marked a first for Honda since Ryuichi Kiyonari's triumph at Donington Park in 2008.

Although Fabrizio was disheartened to miss out on victory, second place was his eighth consecutive podium finish, and it kept him in the hunt for overall honours.

Haga crossed the line just behind Fabrizio to finish third, being satisfied rather than happy, his performance having been outpaced by his team-mate throughout the weekend.

Nonetheless, with Spies having been able to claw his way back to only ninth position, the American could only reduce the gap to Haga by five points. The margin stood at 48 points, with the ever-present Fabrizio just seven points further back.

Although he had not achieved the podium spot he had targeted from pole position, two fourth-place finishes marked Jakub Smrz's best weekend at WSBK level. The Czech rider had slipped to seventh at one stage after making a mistake on lap eight, but he had overtaken Shane Byrne and Carlos Checa in the latter stages for another good haul of points.

Checa finished a solid fifth on the second Ten Kate Honda, while Byrne completed a strong weekend for the Sterilgarda Ducati team in sixth.

Tom Sykes and Leon Haslam made it four British riders inside the top eight by taking seventh and eighth, while Spies and Max Biaggi rounded out the top ten, the last enduring a difficult weekend on the Aprilia.

Elsewhere, Suzuki pair Yukio Kagayama and Fonsi Nieto kept their points ticking over in 11th and 12th, ahead of Shinya Nakano, Ryuichi Kiyonari and Gregorio Lavilla.

Above: On his second bike, Spies is about to dispossess long-time leader Byrne.

Left: Smrz was surprise Superpole winner.

Photos: Gold & Goose

DONINGTON PARK
ROUND 9 • GREAT BRITAIN

RACE ONE: DONINGTON PARK

Spies resists Biaggi for Donington win

BEN SPIES held firm in the face of constant pressure from Max Biaggi to claim his ninth WSBK victory of the season in race one at Donington Park, while Biaggi survived a last-lap scare to claim his first podium since round two in Qatar.

Spies and Biaggi had held their grid positions into turn one at the start of the race, while world championship leader Noriyuki Haga had leapt from sixth to third. The Ducati Xerox star stuck with Spies and Biaggi for the opening laps, but then began to fade steadily, dropping from 2.5 seconds adrift by the half-way stage of the 23-lap race to over ten seconds behind at the finish.

Spies officially won by 7.156 seconds, but that was only because Biaggi's engine died as he came out of the Fogarty Esses for the final time. Assuming that he was low on fuel, the Italian frantically rocked his Aprilia RSV-4 from side to side and was rewarded when it sprang back into life, allowing him to claim his third podium of the season.

Prior to the incident, Biaggi had shadowed Spies for the entire race. The former grand prix star had gained ground on the Yamaha rider through the latter part of each lap, while Spies had pulled out a few bike lengths on the exit of the final turn and through Craner Curves.

Having realised that Biaggi was, apparently, going the distance, Spies seemed to have saved a little extra for the last lap and was a relatively safe 0.688

second in front as the lap began. Even without Biaggi's problem, the American seemed to have victory in the bag.

Spies went into race two 39 points behind Haga, who finished a lonely race eight seconds clear of fourth-placed Leon Haslam. The Stiggy Honda rider had earned the top Brit finish by overtaking countryman Shane Byrne with seven laps to go. But the Sterilgarda Ducati rider had refused to be shaken off and was just a few tenths behind Haslam at the line.

Biaggi's Aprilia team-mate, Shinya Nakano, was sixth, while Hannspree Ten Kate Honda's Jonathan Rea had fought his way forward from 12th on the grid to seventh.

John Hopkins had made an impressive return to a track he knew well from MotoGP by guiding his Stiggy machine from 13th on lap one to eighth, a tenth in front of Guandalini's Jakub Smrz, with former BSB champion Ryuichi Kiyonari completing the top ten for Ten Kate Honda.

Carlos Checa and particularly Haga's team-mate, Michel Fabrizio, would have expected much better than 11th and 12th, while BSB leader and Donington wild-card Leon Camier salvaged 13th from 17th on the grid, having been just 21st at the end of lap one.

Camier's Airwaves Yamaha team-mate, James Ellison, crashed out of tenth on lap 14, while fellow Brit Tom Sykes suffered his first non-finish of the year when he fell from his R1 while holding seventh on lap seven. Ellison was okay despite a heavy landing in the gravel, but Sykes headed for the medical centre to have his back examined.

RACE TWO: DONINGTON PARK

Spies doubles up, Haga comes down hard

AMERICAN ROOKIE Ben Spies was just 14 points behind WSBK championship leader Noriyuki Haga after the Yamaha rider romped to his second victory of the day at Donington Park, while Haga suffered a heavy fall.

Spies was the only rider to claim two podium finishes on Sunday, while Max Biaggi, who had been second in race one, fell from the runner-up spot on lap four of race two. The Italian, who had momentarily taken the lead from Spies going into turn one, clashed with Alessandro Polita in his haste to rejoin the race and eventually finished 21st and last for Aprilia.

Haga, a lonely third in race one, held that same position early in race two before being promoted to second by Biaggi's error. But he held the position for less than a lap before crashing heavily going through the fast Coppice turn that leads on to the back straight. It was the same corner where his Ducati Xerox predecessor, Troy Bayliss, had lost the end of his finger in 2007, and Haga was hit repeatedly by his bike as he tumbled roughly to a halt. The Japanese rider was able to walk slowly away, with the support of marshals, but his title lead over Spies had taken an even bigger battering.

The Yamaha star, who had suffered four no-scores of his own so far in the season, rode into the distance to claim his tenth victory of the year by 6.622 seconds, having backed off in the closing stages.

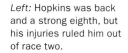

Left: Hopkins was back and a strong eighth, but his injuries ruled him out of race two.

Centre, top to bottom: Wild-cards American Blake Young, and Britons Simon Andrews and Leon Camier, the last sixth in race two.

Below left: James Ellison also scored points.

Far left: Biaggi leads the field into Redgate for race two.

Bottom left: Haslam, here heading Byrne and Nakano, made his home rostrum.

Below right: Smoking Spies celebrates another double.

Photos: Gold & Goose

Five rounds, ten races and a potential 250 points remained before the end of the 2009 season.

Behind Spies, a three-way fight for second between Haga's team-mate, Michel Fabrizio, Stiggy Honda's Leon Haslam and Sterilgarda Ducati's Shane Byrne raged right to the flag – with a third Briton, Tom Sykes, close enough to pounce on any mistakes.

The last lap began with Haslam, Fabrizio, Byrne and Sykes covered by 1.4 seconds and with roughly equal track between them. Haslam rode a mistake-free last lap to equal his best finish of the season to date, while Fabrizio returned to the podium after his lowly race-one score.

Byrne improved a place on his race-one result, while Sykes scored solid points after his first DNF of the season earlier in the day.

British Superbike championship leader Leon Camier fought his way from 17th to sixth for Airwaves Yamaha, while former British Superbike champion Ryuichi Kiyonari narrowly separated Camier from team-mate James Ellison.

Ruben Xaus claimed a welcome ninth for BMW, and wild-card Simon Andrews took an excellent tenth – from 26th on the grid – to finish as the top Kawasaki rider. A bad day for Suzuki saw the top GSX-R1000 of Yuki Kagayama cross the line in 13th position; new team-mate Blake Young was 17th.

Joining Haga and Biaggi in hitting the asphalt were Biaggi's team-mate, Shinya Nakano, who high-sided spectacularly on the exit of the Old Hairpin while holding an early third, plus Carlos Checa, Jakub Smrz and AMA star Jamie Hacking.

Hannspree Ten Kate Honda's Jonathan Rea spun out of sixth at the final turn on lap two before finishing 15th.

John Hopkins, an impressive eighth in only his third WSBK race earlier in the day, hadn't started race two due to pain from his healing injuries.

BRNO
ROUND 10 • CZECH REPUBLIC

RACE ONE: BRNO

Biaggi returns Aprilia to victory circle

MAX BIAGGI took Aprilia to its first victory since returning to the WSBK championship after capitalising on a collision between Ben Spies and Michel Fabrizio during the opening race at Brno. The first World Superbike win for Aprilia since Regis Laconi claimed victory at Imola in 2001, Biaggi's triumph also marked his first since 2007, when he had won at Vallelunga.

Although the Italian was in contention for victory from the start of the race, his cause was undoubtedly aided by a coming together between Fabrizio and Spies on lap four as they disputed the lead. Having recovered from a tardy start, the former was tailing the American as they entered the final corner complex. Fabrizio attempted a move on the inside of his title rival, but he was not quite alongside when an unsuspecting Spies closed the door. The Ducati Xerox folded beneath him, pushing him into the side of the Yamaha and sending them both barrelling out of the race. An incensed Spies, having been denied a perfect opportunity to close on Noriyuki Haga in the standings, vented his frustration on the apologetic Ducati rider. Their demise duly played into the hands of a following Biaggi, who simply moved into the lead of a race he wouldn't lose.

Prior to the collision, Troy Corser had grabbed the everyone's attention in the early stages after sweeping into the lead of the race at the first corner, the Australian capitalising on a season-best grid position of sixth to push ahead of Spies, Jonathan Rea, Fabrizio and Biaggi. He held on to the spot valiantly too, the visibly improved S1000RR proving a match for its rivals in a straight line, while its rider even shrugged off Spies' move for the lead on lap two by snatching it straight back at the very next corner. Unsurprisingly, Spies' second attempt proved more successful, while Fabrizio and Biaggi also dragged themselves through

into second and third.

Despite Corser's impressive start, there was disappointment on the other side of the garage for Ruben Xaus, who suffered a dramatic accident mid-way around the first lap. The Spaniard lost the rear of his BMW before it proceeded to flip end over end across the gravel.

With Lorenzo Lanzi going down on lap three, as well as Spies and Fabrizio's accident, four of the top ten contenders were already out of the race, while an unscheduled pit stop for Tom Sykes also ruled him out.

With Biaggi comfortably in charge, Ten Kate Honda pair Rea and Carlos Checa, up from tenth on the grid, were left to fight over second position, the Spaniard getting the edge on his younger team-mate on lap five.

Further back, all eyes were on Haga, who put in a fine performance as he attempted to capitalise on Spies' unexpected retirement. After rising to eighth position, however, his hopes of avoiding a strenuous race were ended when he became embroiled in an intense tussle for sixth with Leon Haslam, Makoto Tamada and Jakub Smrz.

Having made an excellent start from 17th on the grid, Haslam led the quartet for most of the race, resisting the attentions of first Haga and then Tamada, the returning Japanese rider producing possibly his most convincing ride on the Kawasaki to date. However, all three would fall foul of Smrz, the local favourite being cheered on as he picked his way back up the order from 12th on the grid. Eventually, he passed Haslam three laps from the chequered flag to secure an encouraging sixth-place finish.

Back at the front, despite Checa's best attempts to reel him in, Biaggi was untroubled as he took care to keep the RSV-4 upright through the final turns to claim a marvellous victory for the Italian team. His win made him only the fifth different race winner of the season so far, while it also moved him back up to fourth in the points standings.

Checa finished a lonely second in what had been

one of his most convincing performances to date, while Rea completed a good race for Ten Kate Honda in third, despite having been unable to match his team-mate in terms of race pace.

The battle for fourth came down to an exchange between Corser and Shane Byrne, the Briton having stalked his way back into contention before overtaking the former champion on lap 14. Fourth marked his fifth top-six result in five races.

Despite slipping back in the closing stages, Corser's fifth represented BMW's best-ever result in WSBK. His inspired performance was the best indicator yet of the team's potential at this level.

Behind Smrz in sixth, Haslam was a satisfied seventh, having endured a troublesome weekend so far, although his Stiggy Honda team-mate, John Hopkins, hadn't fared so well when he crashed out while running in tenth position.

Perhaps the most important result of the race, however, was Haga's eighth, the championship leader defying crippling pain in his shoulder and wrist to finish comfortably inside the top ten. Crucially, this added eight points to his margin over Spies, an advantage that now stood at 22 points.

A late charge by Matthieu Lagrive saw him claim his best result yet on the Althea Honda in ninth place, the Frenchman taking advantage of a problem for Tamada in the closing stages to sneak ahead. Nonetheless, Tamada held on for tenth position, his best WSBK finish in 34 races.

Outside the top ten, Fonsi Nieto was a solid 11th on his debut with the DFX Ducati team, the Spaniard just edging out Broc Parkes on the second Kawasaki.

Ryuichi Kiyonari, who had finished inside the top five at Brno in 2008, continued his struggles on the HRC-liveried Ten Kate Honda down in 13th position, just ahead of countryman Yukio Kagayama on the sole Alstare Suzuki. Vittorio Iannuzzo was 15th to score his and the Squadra Corse Italia team's first point of the season.

RACE TWO: BRNO

Spies hits back with Brno victory

BEN SPIES headed into the summer break just seven points behind Noriyuki Haga in the WSBK standings after resisting a late charge by Max Biaggi to win the second race at Brno. The Yamaha rider led to the chequered flag from the second turn, but not before a breathtaking final few laps as he and Biaggi disputed the lead, the American putting on a display of precision riding to deny his rival an opportunity of passing.

The victory went a long way toward making up for Spies' retirement in race one at the hands of Michel Fabrizio, and it put him just a handful of points behind Noriyuki Haga in the standings. The margin could have been even smaller but for Haga's outstanding determination to finish in sixth.

Spies assumed control of the race from early on, taking just one corner to dispatch Troy Corser, the BMW rider once again having got the run down into the first turn from sixth on the grid to lead briefly. The American was promptly followed by Fabrizio and Biaggi, and the trio quickly began to assert their authority over the competition.

Although an error by Fabrizio early on in the race allowed Spies an advantage, both he and countryman Biaggi continued to keep the leader honest, eventually reducing the gap until all three riders were covered by less than a second. However, Spies' cause was aided by Biaggi's persistent attempts to overtake Fabrizio. Indeed, while the Aprilia appeared to have an advan-

tage over the Ducati in a straight line, Biaggi evidently had difficulty in getting the bike stopped in time to complete the manoeuvre. Although he managed to overtake Fabrizio on four occasions, his rival coolly swept back through when he promptly ran wide.

After several laps of harassment, though, Biaggi finally made his move stick with five laps to go. Immediately he set the fastest lap of the race and quickly latched on to the back of Spies to begin his assault on the Yamaha rider. Other than the odd feigned move and close encounters mid-corner, however, Spies was inch perfect and prevented Biaggi from ever getting into a position where he could prise away the lead.

Battling it out until the very final corner, the Italian had to settle for second position behind a delighted Spies, the American putting his race-one devastation behind him as he celebrated across the line.

Behind Biaggi, who had enjoyed his best WSBK weekend in almost two years, Fabrizio was a close third, having run out of laps to try to regain second from his fellow Roman.

Some distance back, Ten Kate Honda was once again the best of the rest, although the positions were reversed, Jonathan Rea leading Carlos Checa across the finish line.

Despite Spies' win, Haga was happy to have emerged from the event with his championship lead still intact after another heroic performance in race two. Moving up inside the top ten from the start, he took on, and beat, Shane Byrne and Troy Corser before holding off Tom Sykes to finish a fine sixth. He now had more than a month to get back to full fitness for the final four rounds of the season.

Following his retirement in race one, Sykes recovered from a poor start to finish exactly where he had started in seventh position, the Briton having managed to fend off a hard charging Byrne and Jakub Smrz, the Czech rider having been cheered on to ninth by his home crowd. Despite having faded as the race wore on, tenth-placed Corser could consider Brno as a breakthrough weekend for BMW.

Unable to match the pace of his team-mate, Aprilia's Shinya Nakano crossed the line in 11th position, ahead of Leon Haslam, who was another to fall away as the race progressed. Matthieu Lagrive, Ryuichi Kiyonari and Lorenzo Lanzi rounded out the points paying positions, having benefited from crashes involving Makoto Tamada and Yukio Kagayama, as well as a retirement for John Hopkins.

Above: At his favourite track, Biaggi took his first win for Aprilia.

Above left: Spies heads Biaggi and Fabrizio in race two.

Right: Pain and suffering for Haga, but a gritty performance gained valuable points.

Below: Corser takes the lead on the best weekend yet for the new BMW.

Photos: Gold & Goose

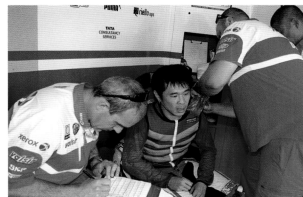

NÜRBURGRING
ROUND 11 • GERMANY

RACE ONE: NÜRBURGRING

Spies edges Haga for crucial 'Ring win

BEN SPIES moved to within two points of the WSBK championship lead after catching, passing and re-sisting Noriyuki Haga to win the opening race at the Nürburgring. The American recovered from an early delay during an exchange with Jonathan Rea to haul himself back into contention and pass his rival mid-way through the race. Haga battled hard to regain control, but save for a failed move three laps from the finish, he was unable to find his way back through. Spies had to work hard for victory, however, after not getting the best of starts from fifth on the grid.

The race had been restarted following a red flag on the original opening lap, prompted after a nasty accident involving John Hopkins and the Kawasakis of Broc Parkes and Makoto Tamada. Hopkins had fallen from his Stiggy Honda and then had been clipped by another bike running off the circuit. Both the American and Tamada had required medical attention, forcing the race to be halted.

At the restart, Haga got away well from pole position, holding off Leon Haslam into the opening turn. The Briton had chosen an opportunistic line around the outside before being baulked and sucked back into the mid-field. Troy Corser inherited the position instead, ahead of Rea and Spies, although both were past the BMW by turn four, when the Northern Irishman dived inside his rival and pulled Spies through.

Behind Corser, Max Biaggi made it five different manufacturers in the top five, while Michel Fabrizio and Fonsi Nieto followed in sixth and seventh, the pair engaging in an enjoyable tussle, ultimately decided in the factory Ducati rider's favour.

At the front, Haga's Ducati was being reeled in by Rea. Meanwhile, Spies had to contend with the attentions of a feisty-looking Corser. Rea's chal-lenge, however, was limited to the odd feigned look at turn one, but Haga seemed more confident on the brakes going into the tight hairpin. This meant that Spies was able to pounce in the same spot on lap five, moving into second, and although the Honda rider struck back with an identical move just a lap later, a mistake at turn three reversed the positions again in Spies' favour.

Eventually, Rea's challenge faded when he ran wide at turn one on lap seven and fell into the clutches of those behind. This freed Spies to begin hunting down Haga, who had moved 1.5 seconds clear as he capitalised on the exchanges behind him.

Nonetheless, Spies immediately signalled his intentions by undercutting Haga's lap times, chipping away at the margin until he was on the back of the 1198 by lap ten. Once there, he wasted no time in stamping his authority, tucking beneath Haga down the back straight before scything his way through under braking for the left-right Esses.

Now able to control the pace out front, Spies attempted to build on his advantage, but Haga was not to be shaken off, matching his moves corner for corner and never falling more than half a second behind. The Japanese rider began pushing again, and a new lap record on lap 15 was indicative of the pressure he was applying to the American. Their tussle was made all the more enticing by the different race lines adopted through turn one, which prompted sharp intakes of breath from the enthralled crowd as they came remarkably close to touching.

After several laps of threatening, Haga eventually got a tow down the home straight, three laps from the close, and pulled alongside Spies to dive into the lead at the hairpin. Nonetheless, the Yamaha rider calmly placed his bike on the inside of his rival as he ran wide, immediately reclaiming the advantage. Haga could do no more, and Spies turned up the pace again to put some air between them. The Ducati rider had to concede on the final lap, dropping back to give Spies a flattering four-second victory.

Several seconds behind, the battle for third raged until the chequered flag, Carlos Checa eventually getting the nod over team-mate Rea, following an impressive route through the pack on the Ten Kate Honda. The Spaniard had started eighth and ran in the same position in the early stages, before gradually picking his way through the order to catch Rea. It marked his third podium of the season.

Rea settled for fourth, more than five seconds ahead of Biaggi, who had fought a race-long battle with Corser, Haslam and Fabrizio. Corser had held fourth for much of the time, but had begun to fade as the race progressed, slipping into the clutches of his rivals and eventually finishing in eighth. This had benefited Haslam, who finished a solid sixth after having fallen from third to eighth at the start on the Stiggy Honda, while Fabrizio was a quiet seventh and watching his slim title hopes sliding away.

Unable to replicate the pace of his team-mate, Tom Sykes was a lonely ninth on the second Yamaha, while fellow Briton Shane Byrne completed the top ten.

The remaining points scorers were Matthieu Lagrive, Karl Muggeridge, Jakub Smrz, Ryuichi Kiyonari and Yukio Kagayama. Briton Richard Cooper had crashed out of 15th position, seven laps into the race.

RACE TWO: NÜRBURGRING

Rea wins, Spies leads, Haga falls

JONATHAN REA won his second career WSBK race at the Nürburgring, but it was Ben Spies who stole the headlines after assuming the championship lead when Noriyuki Haga retired following an accident caused by contact with Rea.

Haga was dicing with Rea for the lead when the pair collided at the opening turn on lap five, the Japa-

nese rider having run wide before coming back on to line just as Rea was attempting to slip back up the inside. While Rea was able to continue, Haga couldn't remain upright and was forced to lay his Ducati Xerox down. Although it was a low-speed accident, he was unable to get going again.

Prior to that, Haga had been distracted by the attentions of Rea and his Ten Kate Honda team-mate, Carlos Checa, both of whom set a blistering pace in the opening laps. Indeed, after the first few bends, Rea had been down in eighth position from second on the grid, but quickly scythed his way back into contention to get on the back of Checa by the end of lap two,

Checa, meanwhile, was applying pressure to Haga and even moved into the lead for the first time in the season on lap three. Both Haga and Rea managed to find their way through on lap four, but the Ducati rider couldn't resist the charging Northern Irishman

Above: A second win for Ulsterman Rea.

Left: Ducati disaster as Haga falls, Fabrizio is forced wide.

Right: Richard Cooper, on injured Xaus' BMW, crashed out of the points.

Above right: Luis Salom, pointless on the Pedercini Kawasaki.

Right: The crucial touch – winner Rea nudges loser Haga.

Bottom: Race-two podium: winner Rea is flanked by Spies and team-mate Checa.

Photos: Gold & Goose

as he swept in front almost straight away. Not to be outdone, Haga used the tow down the home straight at the start of lap five to dive down the inside of the Honda at turn one, the action leading to their coming together.

Haga's fall, in the middle of the circuit, sent the following riders scattering, Michel Fabrizio losing out in particular as he took drastic avoiding action to miss his team-mate. By contrast, Spies was the big winner, since Haga's fall came when he appeared to be struggling for pace.

After a poor start that had left him in seventh, Spies had made no progress before his rival's fall, but he leapt three positions straight away, before going on to dispatch Carlos Checa for third on lap nine at the Esses.

Rea, meanwhile, held a comfortable margin over Leon Haslam, Spies, Checa and Max Biaggi, the Italian recovering from a few 'wide' moments early on to catch and pass Fabrizio and Troy Corser.

While not as prolific in his progress as race one, Spies was still proving to be a contender for the win as he shadowed Haslam in second place, the American eventually getting the better of him under braking at his favoured overtaking spot, the Esses.

Setting off in pursuit of Rea, Spies managed to catch the youngster, but was never close enough to launch anything more than the occasional lunge to unsettle him. Safe in the knowledge that he was the new championship leader, the American pushed hard on the final lap, but had no answer to Rea, who shrugged off the pressure, not only keeping Spies at bay, but also setting a new lap record in the process.

Spies had been forced to play second fiddle, but the result turned his two-point deficit in the championship into an 18-point advantage at a crucial stage in the season, with only six races remaining.

An error by Haslam shortly after Spies had overtaken him promoted Checa to third for his second podium of the day, the Spaniard completing an outstanding weekend for Ronald ten Kate's eponymous team.

Biaggi was another to benefit from a fading Haslam, securing another top-five finish on an Aprilia that had threatened to be off the pace during the initial stages of the weekend. Haslam, meanwhile, had held on for another good result to consolidate his sixth place in the standings.

Although not quite as good as his fifth-place finish in Brno, a sixth and an eighth for Troy Corser marked his and BMW's best combined result of the season, the S1000RR beginning to prove it had the pace – if not the longevity – to challenge at the front of the field.

Having barely featured all weekend, an inspired Ryuichi Kiyonari was a surprising seventh after battling his way up from 18th on the grid, and passing Tom Sykes and Fabrizio in the closing stages. The latter rider had endured a disappointing weekend to all but end his title hopes.

Suzuki had been on for a possible double top-ten finish, which would have been its first since Valencia, but an accident involving Karl Muggeridge had put paid to that. He had been ahead of team-mate Yukio Kagayama up to that point, the Japanese rider inheriting tenth position.

Jakub Smrz had an unusually quiet day and took 11th, while Fonsi Nieto, Broc Parkes, Luca Scassa and Vittorio Iannuzzo completed the points positions, the last scoring his second point of the year.

Meanwhile, British riders Shane Byrne and Richard Cooper had failed to finish after separate crashes.

RACE ONE: IMOLA

Haga fights back for convincing Imola win

NORIYUKI HAGA clawed back significant ground on Ben Spies in the WSBK championship standings after taking an impressive victory in race one at Imola. The Japanese rider delivered a feisty performance to win his first race since Kyalami after snatching the lead on lap 18 and easing to a comfortable margin over Max Biaggi. Spies, meanwhile, could only manage fourth.

Biaggi had led most of the race, the Aprilia rider having taken the lead at the start from sixth on the grid, but while he was able to resist pressure from Haga for almost the entirety of the race, he couldn't quite hold on to the chequered flag.

More significantly, however, Spies was a relatively quiet fourth after never quite having got on terms with the lead fight. He lost 12 points to Haga in the process, cutting his championship advantage to six points.

Although fireworks had been expected off the line with the top four riders in the standings all starting on the front row, it was Biaggi who spoiled their intentions from sixth place, taking the inside line into turn one allowing the RSV-4 to sweep around the inside and grab the advantage. He headed up pole-sitter Michel Fabrizio, Jonathan Rea and Haga, while Spies was baulked going into the first corner after banging panels with Troy Corser's BMW, eventually recovering for fifth.

With the jump on Spies, Haga wasted no time in moving toward the front, passing Nürburgring sparring partner Rea at the final-corner chicane on lap one before putting a bold move on his team-mate at the Variante Alta. Fabrizio appeared not to expect his fellow Ducati rider to attempt a pass there, as he sat up.

Rea's challenge ended on lap three, when he got out of shape over the crest leading down to the Rivazza complex and was forced to straighten up on the tight inside line. With little chance of stopping, he careened across the bows of Fabrizio and Haga, the Japanese rider paying enough attention to back off and allow the Ten Kate Honda to carry on into the gravel trap. Forced to lay the bike down, Rea got going again, albeit in last place.

The lead pack became three when Spies began to lose ground on the front-runners. Seemingly unable to maintain pace, the American was almost three seconds behind after just five laps. Fortunately, there was already a big margin back to fifth, courtesy of Corser, whose strong start from ninth on the grid was flattering to his actual pace. With the Australian backing up Spies' rivals, a large gap opened between fourth and fifth before Leon Haslam was able to get through. He was followed by Shane Byrne and Marco Simoncelli – up to seventh after falling outside the top ten at the start – as Corser trailed off.

Having already impressed with his pace over a single lap on the unknown RSV-4, Simoncelli was proving to be an adept racer as he tackled Byrne and then Haslam. In fifth, his laps were not far off the leaders' times. It all came to a disappointing conclusion on lap ten, however, when he low-sided out of the race at the Tosa left-hander. The corner was problematic for a number of riders, Carlos Checa and Byrne also falling at the same point shortly beforehand.

At the front, Biaggi continued to hold the lead, but was under pressure from Fabrizio, who had defied assumed Ducati Xerox team orders by retaking second from Haga with an opportunistic pass at turn one. Although hampered by a shoulder injury, Fabrizio was very nearly able to capitalise on a mistake made by his countryman on the way out of Tosa, but he could do nothing about the Aprilia's sheer speed. Indeed, the undulating track apparently favoured the compact Aprilia's renowned top speed: no matter how many times Fabrizio or Haga got alongside Biaggi, they could not out-drag him, particularly up the hill.

Even so, it became Haga's turn to try to outfox Biaggi when he swept past Fabrizio on lap eight on the run down to Rivazza. A very similar pass on lap ten would see him pass Biaggi, only for the home favourite to get the crowd on their feet by fighting back straight away into turn one.

With the leading trio tripping over one another, Spies began to haul himself back into the reckoning. Then he started to be backed up by Fabrizio, who later would complain of a clutch problem to go with his painful shoulder. This allowed Haga some margin of error as he attempted to find his way around Biaggi. The Japanese rider remained cool as he sized up his opponent, attempting to unnerve him by getting as close to the rear of the Aprilia as possible.

The actual defining pass, on lap 18, was somewhat of an anti-climax. Biaggi's bike became skittish over the crest out of Acque Minerali, allowing Haga a run at him into the Variante Alta. Despite the Italian's speed, Haga was past before they reached the bend.

With clear air in front and only three laps remaining, Haga began to put the hammer down, quickly pulling a margin over Biaggi, who in turn was being pushed hard by Fabrizio again. Overcoming his less-than-perfect bike and physical condition, Fabrizio got through after getting a better run out of the final chicane with just over a lap to go. Spies attempted to follow, but Biaggi had him covered.

Haga, meanwhile, was cruising to victory, easing across the line to give himself a significant psychological boost and Ducati a much needed victory on home soil.

Hopes of a 1-2, though, were dashed at the final bend, where Biaggi fought back and dived up the inside of Fabrizio to scrape through, holding on to the spot by just a hundredth of a second. Spies, meanwhile, had backed, finishing five seconds behind Haga.

While the drama at the front attracted much attention, there were some very notable performances in the battle for 'best of the rest' status. Fifth eventually fell to Kiyonari, who had battled his way up from

Left: Title rivals Haga and Spies join for a track inspection after concerns about the surface.

Far left: Fabrizio celebrates the win ahead of team-mate Haga.

Below left: Guest star Simoncelli was a popular third.

Below: Biaggi is forced wide by his temporary team-mate.

Below centre: Haga returned to form at Imola.

Bottom: Biaggi led the Ducatis in race one.

Photos: Gold & Goose

14th on the grid for his best result since Miller Motorsports Park. He also scored an important small win over Honda counterpart Haslam after pulling off an identical move to Biaggi by grabbing the position at the very final corner.

Despite the less than favourable conclusion to the race, Haslam was a solid sixth, having started in tenth on the sole Stiggy Honda, although he fell even further back in the championship fight to fourth overall.

Having been in the barriers on lap three, Rea delivered an outstanding recovery ride to finish in seventh and keep his points ticking over. Capitalising on a tight mid-pack, he had overturned a sizeable deficit at the back of the field to lap on the lead pace and force his way forward, scoring a useful nine points.

Despite starting fifth, Jakub Smrz couldn't maintain his form through to the race, settling for eighth position at the finish, ahead of Tom Sykes and Broc Parkes, the Australian reaching the top ten for the first time since Monza. The trio had benefited from a problem experienced by Yukio Kagayama, however, the Japanese rider having started the final lap in eighth place, only to finish in 15th. He also had lost positions to Corser – who had faded as the race wore on – Ruben Xaus, Karl Muggeridge and Matteo Baiocco.

RACE TWO: IMOLA

Fabrizio beats Haga as Spies loses out

DUCATI RIDER Noriyuki Haga retook the lead of the WSBK championship standings, despite having been denied a double victory at Imola by Michel Fabrizio. While many expected team orders to come into play, the Italian managed to catch and overtake his team-mate on lap 13, romping home to a comfortable second career victory on home soil

Although the result meant five fewer points for Haga, he was still able to move ahead of Ben Spies again in the overall standings. The American could only finish fifth after tripping over the feuding Aprilias of Marco Simoncelli and Max Biaggi, a result that put him three points adrift with four races remaining.

Spies' problems began at the start, when a poor get-away from second position dropped him to sixth, behind Michel Fabrizio, who had scythed into the lead from pole, Haga, Biaggi, Shane Byrne and Jonathan Rea.

While an error by Rea at the Bassa chicane on the first lap, when he appeared to catch a bump on the exit, promoted Spies into fifth, a gap was already forming to the top three as Fabrizio, Haga and Biaggi stretched out.

Having complained of problems with his arm in the first race, Fabrizio looked more comfortable in the lead on this occasion as he fought to keep his team-mate at bay. When Haga got a better exit out of Acque Minerali, however, he made his move before reaching Variante Alta to take a lead many assumed he would be able to hold.

Biaggi overtook Fabrizio on the same lap, but the younger Roman fought back on lap five to regain the position. After fending off an additional attempt to pass by Biaggi at Rivazza on lap six, Fabrizio pushed on to try to reduce the margin Haga had quickly built up over him.

Fabrizio was back on the tail of the other Ducati by lap 11 and beginning to apply pressure. Team orders or not, it was clear that the Italian was not prepared to make it easy for his team-mate until he was math-ematically out of the title reckoning – particularly on home soil – and he pulled a move back on Haga going into turn one on lap 13.

After the race, Haga said that the changes he had made to the bike between races weren't working out, and as a result he didn't have a response to Fabrizio's late charge. Although it was anticipated that the Italian would slow to allow Haga back through, he continued to the chequered flag, adding to his maiden triumph at Monza in May.

Fabrizio was delighted to secure a second win on home turf for Ducati, while an unfazed Haga appeared happy to see his team-mate come away with victory. The result doused Rea's brief threat for third in the standings.

Part of Haga's positive mood may have been due to Spies' somewhat laboured fifth-place finish, the Yamaha rider bringing an underwhelming weekend to a close on a disappointing note. His position was gained at Rea's expense, the Northern Irishman having dropped outside the top ten by first going straight on at Tamburello on lap three before doing the same at Variante Bassa two laps later.

Spies had worked hard in an attempt to breach Byrne's staunch defence of fourth place, and his frustration had increased on lap four when Simoncelli had pulled off a fine pass on the exit of Rivazza. Then he had been forced to watch as the Italian had dispatched Byrne at Tosa on lap seven.

Increasingly desperate to get past the Sterilgarda Ducati, Spies and Byrne almost had come together at Tosa on lap ten before the title contender finally made a move stick across the finish line moments later.

Further up the road, having rallied early on in the race, Biaggi had begun to fade into the clutches of his rapidly closing team-mate, Simoncelli, Aprilia's 'guest' rider having been given a good opportunity to put one over on his more experienced counterpart.

However, it took a surprisingly bold move – which Simoncelli later admitted had been a disguised mistake – at the Variante Bassa to get through. Starting from a substantial distance back and braking late, Simoncelli had scrambled through, forcing Biaggi to sit up.

It was Biaggi's tight line into the second part of the chicane, however, that had proved Spies' undoing. He had been able to get on the back of the two Italians as they entered the chicane, but Biaggi had run wide on the exit and into the path of the American, forcing him off into the gravel trap. While the low-speed nature of the incident had allowed Spies to keep his bike upright, it had dropped him back behind Byrne and well off the fight for the podium. Although he had battled to pass Byrne, fifth place and 11 points meant that he was back in the role hunter again, with Magny-Cours and Portimao remaining.

While few riders get away with tackling Biaggi in front of his home crowd, Simoncelli remained a hugely popular podium winner. The future MotoGP rider had proved his worth by lapping on a similar pace to the leaders throughout the race.

Despite having been shown up somewhat by Simoncelli, Biaggi did at least hold on for fourth at the end of an otherwise satisfying day, closing the gap on Rea in the battle for fourth in the points standings. Rea had continued his somewhat erratic ride back through the order, passing Byrne two laps from the end before promptly running wide at Piratella. He managed to secure the spot properly a lap later to finish sixth, ahead of Byrne.

Leon Haslam enjoyed a quiet ride to eighth, ahead of Jakub Smrz and Carlos Checa, while Lorenzo Lanzi, Tom Sykes, Ruben Xaus, Karl Muggeridge and Broc Parkes made up the top fifteen.

MAGNY COURS
ROUND 13 • FRANCE

RACE ONE: MAGNY COURS

Spies edges Haga in final lap thriller

BEN SPIES inched back into the lead of the WSBK championship standings after recovering from a mistake on the final lap of the first race to win at Magny-Cours. The American led from start to finish, but very nearly threw it away at the final time of asking when he ran wide at the 180 bend. While the error allowed Noriyuki Haga into the lead very briefly, the Yamaha rider calmly regained the position to win by just over a tenth of a second.

Haga had been on a charge in the latter stages after having been bottled up behind Max Biaggi for much of the race, but the erstwhile championship leader's lap times had not been quite good enough to snatch victory from his great rival. It meant that the pair swapped positions again in the standings, with Spies two points up on the Japanese rider.

Starting from his tenth pole position of the season, Spies got away well to lead into the sweeping first right-hander, while Biaggi's quick get-away from fourth was hampered by a tighter line into the opening bend. Haga was shuffled down to sixth position through the opening bends, however, although a bit of savvy team play by Ducati Xerox counterpart Michel Fabrizio helped him up to fourth by the end of the first lap.

Haga promptly latched on to the lead group of Spies, Jonathan Rea – who had passed Biaggi at the Adelaide hairpin – and Biaggi, but any hope he may have had of being aided further by his team-mate was dashed by the Italian's difficulty in getting past Leon Haslam. The Briton delayed the Imola winner sufficiently to rule him out of contention for the win.

Any likelihood that Spies' Yamaha team-mate, Tom Sykes, could have any influence on the outcome was also scotched on lap two, when the Briton suffered an accident on the run down to Lycee. He lost the front end of his R1 at high speed, which sent his bike flipping down the track, just missing the Suzuki of Karl Muggeridge.

Up front, Rea and Biaggi traded fastest laps as they attempted to get on terms with Spies, who in turn was maintaining the gap with a series of consistent times. Rea's hope of challenging Spies for victory was ended on lap seven, however, when, after seemingly out-braking himself rather innocuously at Lycee, he rode into the pit lane and retired.

Rea's retirement promoted Biaggi and Haga to second and third, and attention turned to whether the Japanese rider could get past his sparring partner and launch a challenge on Spies. Just as he had demonstrated at Imola, though, Biaggi proved a difficult obstacle for Haga to overcome, the Aprilia's superior pace out of the corners negating the Ducati's seemingly better braking ability. With Spies just beginning to creep away out front, Haga's mid-race assault saw him overlap Biaggi going into the Adelaide hairpin on numerous occasions, only for the RSV-4 to hold its position on the exit of the bend.

Haga was running out of time to make his move, and it was his trademark tight line into the 180 left-hander that eventually saw him past Biaggi, the Italian leaving a Ducati-sized gap on lap 17 that allowed his rival through into second position.

While attempting to fight back at Adelaide hairpin on the very next lap, Biaggi ran on after out-braking himself, freeing Haga to chase down Spies, who had extended his lead to 1.3 seconds.

With just six laps remaining, the Ducati rider, cheered on by team manager Davide Tardozzi from the pit wall, immediately signalled his intentions with a series of quick laps, most notably his record breaking effort on the penultimate revolution. Nonetheless, with Spies also visibly pushing hard to repel any last-lap challenge, it was evident that the American would need to make an error if Haga were to get through.

Remarkably, that is exactly what occurred when Spies missed his apex into 180 and was forced to take a wide line around the bend. Haga pounced, slipping up the inside to snatch the lead. Nonetheless, Spies kept his cool to cut back up the inside of the Japanese rider on the exit of the corner, his superior drive out of the bend putting him back ahead as they sprinted into the high-speed Imola right-left.

Spies and Haga were almost side by side on the long run down to Lycee, but the Yamaha rider got through the bend first, and there was no chance for his rival to take back the position.

It was Spies' 13th win of the season and it put him back into the lead of the standings by a mere two points with only three races remaining.

Having dropped away after his failed attempt at regaining second from Haga, Biaggi settled for third for his and Aprilia's seventh podium finish of the season. The Italian was also able to capitalise on Rea's retirement to take fourth in the points standings.

Having lost touch early on after taking five laps to get past Haslam, Fabrizio hadn't been able to regain any ground on the way to a lonely fourth on the second Ducati.

Haslam crossed the line fifth for the ailing Stiggy Racing team, the Briton's impressive start having allowed him just to hold off Honda counterpart Carlos Checa later on. The Spaniard had made solid progress up the order from 12th on the grid to cross the line in sixth and bring some smiles to the disappointed Ten Kate team.

Suzuki also had reason to be pleased after Yukio Kagayama delivered its best result since Misano with seventh position, the Japanese rider having used his experience of the French circuit to run as high as sixth at one point. He had just managed to hold off Shane Byrne, who had paid the price for a poor start to finish just one position higher than his grid spot, Troy Corser and Jakub Smrz, the quartet having spent much of the race in formation to cross the line just two seconds apart.

The group had included Leon Camier too until three laps from the end of the race, when a technical problem had forced him out on his Aprilia debut.

Above: Aprilia debutant Leon Camier ran well until it let him down.

Top: Biaggi and winner Haga after race two.

Above left: Victory in race one was not enough to regain Spies the points lead.

Below: Haga carves inside Rea in race two.

Photos: Gold & Goose

Camier was one of several riders to retire during the first race: Fonsi Nieto, Broc Parkes, Ryuichi Kiyonari and Muggeridge were all forced out of points paying positions. As a result, Ruben Xaus was a solid 11th on the second BMW; Matteo Baiocco and Luca Scassa produced their best results of the season in 12th and 13th respectively; while David Salom and David Checa scored their first points of the year in 14th and 15th.

RACE TWO: MAGNY COURS

Haga takes advantage as Spies struggles

NORIYUKI HAGA would take a ten-point lead over Ben Spies into the final round of the WSBK championship after cruising to an eighth win of the season at Magny-Cours. Having slipped two points behind the American after he had won the opening race in France, the Ducati rider struck back by taking the lead of race two on the first lap and never looked back. By contrast, Spies endured a troublesome race, quickly falling away from the lead fight to cross the line more than 18 seconds adrift of his rival.

Despite a rather confusing end to the race, when Haga and second-placed Max Biaggi continued racing for a lap beyond the chequered flag, victory for the Japanese rider also meant that Ducati sealed the manufacturer's title one round early.

His challenge for victory in race one having been blunted by a tardy start, Haga made no such mistakes on this occasion from fifth on the grid, moving straight past pole-sitter Spies off the line before muscling his way up to second around the long Estoril right-hander.

Having made an excellent start on the swift Aprilia, it was Biaggi who led as the field braked into the Adelaide hairpin, but having seen how difficult the Italian was to overtake during race one, Haga wasted no time in dispatching his sparring partner, slipping up the inside at 180. Although Spies attempted to follow through, all he achieved was a loss of position to Jonathan Rea.

Despite losing the lead, Biaggi refused to allow Haga to sprint away into the distance, the Brno race winner shadowing him until making an attempt to pass through the Adelaide hairpin on lap five. Haga calmly cut through on the inside on the exit to snatch back the position.

Biaggi made a second attempt around the outside of Haga going into the same bend two laps later, but he failed and the close following Rea slipped through into second.

Determined to make up for his retirement in race one, Rea set about trying to hustle Haga straight away, the Northern Irishman looking confident as he attempted to pull alongside on the exit of Estoril. Nonetheless, Haga stayed firm, his superiority on the brakes preventing Rea from getting anything more than a brief overlap.

From this point on, the pendulum between the top three swung continuously, the gap increasing and shrinking as they either worked together or tripped over one another.

Eventually, Biaggi worked his way back up to second after a late braking manoeuvre on Rea at Lycee, the latter being forced to concede on the tarmac run-off area in a failed attempt to repel his rival. This allowed the Italian one last go at taking the win. Haga kept things very much under control, however, taking the victory by just over a second from Biaggi, who in turn made it a double podium for Aprilia, and Rea in third.

Spies, meanwhile, laboured home in fourth after rapidly dropping off the pace with an apparent problem on his Yamaha R1. Having rallied early on, he was more than two seconds behind the leaders when he began to drop back more noticeably, the visibly frustrated race-one winner finishing well adrift by the chequered flag.

Nonetheless, the result kept Spies within ten points of Haga in the standings. Crucially, this meant that if he were to win both races at Portimao – one of the few circuits on the calendar he knew – and Haga were to finish just behind him in second position, his greater number of wins (a potential 15 to Haga's eight) would see him win the title, despite finishing the season equal on points.

In addition, Spies could not be overhauled by Leon Haslam, who posted his second top-five finish of the day for Stiggy Racing after yet another lonely performance.

Sixth position fell to the rider Haslam was tipped to replace at Suzuki for 2010, Yukio Kagayama. The Japanese rider had produced his most convincing race-day performance since Monza to eventually prevail over Shane Byrne following a race-long battle.

Eighth place for Kagayama's team-mate, Karl Muggeridge, gave the team further reason to be pleased. It was the Australian's first top-ten result with Suzuki and his best finish since Miller Motorsports Park in 2008.

Ninth place was originally set to go the way of Leon Camier, but the young Briton had been eliminated once again by a technical issue, which left him with a bitter double DNF on his debut with the Aprilia team. Instead, Carlos Checa assumed the position, having recovered from an early delay when circumnavigating Michel Fabrizio's fallen Ducati, ahead of Troy Corser and Fonsi Nieto. Ruben Xaus, in 12th, ensured that BMW collected its biggest points haul over a single weekend since entering World Superbikes.

Fabrizio scored three points for 13th after having recovered from a tumble at Adelaide on lap four. The Italian had gone down shortly after overtaking Shane Byrne for sixth. Despite having produced an impressive recovery ride to the points, there was no way he could win the title at Portimao.

Just behind, Matteo Baiocco was a double points scorer for Guandalini Ducati in 14th, while Broc Parkes picked up a single point for himself and Kawasaki at the end of a difficult weekend.

PORTIMÃO
ROUND 14 • PORTUGAL

RACE ONE: PORTIMÃO

Spies puts a hand on title after Haga falls

BEN SPIES would take a 15-point advantage over Noriyuki Haga into the final race of the 2009 World Superbike Championship after cruising to victory in race one at Portimao, while his title rival crashed out of contention. The American fended off the attentions of Max Biaggi and Jonathan Rea to take a comfortable lights-to-flag victory, completing the first half of his original objective to secure the double he needed to guarantee the title.

Now, however, he required only a top-six finish in the final race of the year to ensure that he won the trophy in his maiden season, after Haga had thrown away his advantage with a fall on the seventh lap. The Japanese rider had been in fifth position when he lost the front end of his Ducati Xerox at turn four, forcing him into retirement.

Indeed, the erstwhile championship leader had been making solid progress up the order from his tenth-place starting position, having made a decent getaway to survive the mêlée going into the opening bend and move up to eighth place immediately. Spies had executed the start he needed to get out in front, however, the Yamaha man plunging into the opening turn ahead of Biaggi, Shane Byrne, Rea and Leon Haslam.

With Michel Fabrizio's poor start effectively ruling him out of contention for victory, he quickly dropped behind Haga and shadowed him as his team-mate battled it out with fellow Ducati rider Fonsi Nieto. Far from bowing to expected team orders, however, Nieto put up a staunch defence of sixth position on the DFX machine, holding off Haga until the start of lap two, when he was overtaken through the opening bends. Quickly latching on to the British group of Rea, Byrne – the pair having swapped positions at the start of lap two – and Haslam, Haga had an

even tougher time working his way past, but was gifted fifth when the Stiggy Honda rider ran wide at turn one while under pressure from the Ducati on lap six.

Haga's charge up the order would come to a dramatic halt just a lap later, though, when, as he was pushing hard to catch Byrne, his bike got away from him; man and machine slid forlornly off the circuit as the field swept past. Despite his best efforts, Haga couldn't get going again and was forced to concede.

Yamaha notifyied Spies of Haga's misfortune immediately, and attention turned to the front as Biaggi continued to put pressure on the American. A series of quick laps at the start of the race had helped the pair to put air between themselves and Rea, Biaggi mirroring Spies, even if he never looked close enough to wrest the position from him.

However, when both riders began to experience a slight dip in pace at the halfway stage, it prompted Rea and Byrne to push back into contention, the duo making it a four-way battle by lap 14.

Despite the added attention of his rivals, ultimately Spies would benefit from Biaggi and Rea's feuding, eking out his margin to just over a second.

Rea's best opportunity to pass down the home straight was scuppered by the Aprilia's superior straight-line speed, and it took until lap 16, when Biaggi made an error, before the Ten Kate Honda man could get through into second, giving him a shot at trying to catch Spies. He was almost two seconds behind the leader as they entered the latter stages of the race, but the gap wouldn't come down. Instead, Biaggi slipstreamed past into second place again on lap 19. Not to be outdone, Rea struck back on the penultimate revolution with a daring pass on the Italian at turn two.

That left Spies free to ease to the chequered flag with a 1.6-second advantage over Rea, prompting jubilation in the Yamaha garage as the manufactur-

er now stood on the verge of winning its first ever World Superbike title.

Having been unable to respond to Rea's decisive attack, Biaggi was hounded across the finish line by an inspired Byrne, who put in one of the most convincing rides of his season to come home fourth for Sterilgarda Ducati. The result also meant that he moved up to eighth in the standings at the expense of Tom Sykes, who had withdrawn from the final round with a shoulder injury.

Fabrizio came home a quiet fifth, having been outshone by privateer Ducati rider Byrne, while Leon Camier put in a fine performance to claim sixth on the Aprilia, after working his way up from 13th on the grid.

Mirroring his result on home soil for Airwaves Yamaha at Donington Park, the new British Superbike champion finished ahead of several more experienced riders, including Carlos Checa and Ruben Xaus, both of whom had been front-runners at Portimao in 2008.

In a race of attrition that saw just 14 riders finish on the same lap, several top names failed to see the chequered flag, including Haslam, who crashed out on lap 11 while running in sixth. Jakub Smrz and Yukio Kagayama were others to hit the tarmac during the race. Meanwhile, technical issues cost good results for Sylvain Guintoli, Nieto and Troy Corser.

This meant that several riders posted notable results, including Matthieu Lagrive in ninth for Althea Honda, while Guandalini's Matteo Baiocco secured his first World Superbike top-ten result after winning in a battle with the factory Kawasakis.

Broc Parkes and Makoto Tamada followed in 11th and 12th, ahead of David Salom, David Checa and Luca Scassa, the latter scoring despite finishing four laps off the lead after benefiting from a late retirement by Roland Resch, the Austrian having been on course for his first ever points before a spectacular engine blow-up.

Above: Rookie Spies took the crown at the last gasp.

Above centre: Haga falls, and his championship goes with him.

Top left: Byrne leads Spies, Rea, Biaggi, Haslam and Haga through the scenic fast bends.

Top: Biaggi's Aprilia had gained strength through the year.

Right: Fabrizio's race-two win was an excuse for a Xerox Ducati celebration.

Photos: Gold & Goose

RACE TWO: PORTIMÃO

Spies crowned world superbike champion

BEN SPIES would go to MotoGP as the new World Superbike champion after doing exactly what he needed to do to secure the title in the final race of the season at Portimao. Having dominated the opening race to stretch out a 15-point advantage over Noriyuki Haga, the American produced a comparatively tentative performance, taking the chequered flag in fifth place.

The Ducati rider had rallied hard in the latter stages to finish in second, but it wasn't enough to deny Spies. The two rivals and friends concluded their epic season-long battle separated by just six points.

It was an outstanding weekend for Yamaha, which secured the MotoGP and World Supersport titles on the same day. Spies' win was also a first for the Japanese manufacturer at World Superbike level.

The race itself was won by Michel Fabrizio, the Italian taking his third victory of the season, but the focus from the start was entirely on Spies and Haga.

Following Haga's failure to finish in race one, Spies went into the season finale requiring simply a sixth-place finish, but his hopes of controlling the race from the front were scuppered at the lights when he was beaten to the first corner by Shane Byrne.

Despite a couple of nervy moments through turns two and three, Byrne held it together to lead Spies, Jonathan Rea, Max Biaggi, Leon Haslam and Haga, the 'hunter' already up to sixth from his tenth-place starting position.

Desperate not to become embroiled in a fight for position, Spies appeared to favour a safe approach as he defended from Rea. The Northern Irishman got through on lap three when the American looked over his shoulder, only to have his rival surprise him by passing on the other side. Biaggi briefly followed, although Spies snatched the position back, the Italian going on to overtake again on lap five before promptly running off the circuit and dropping to sixth.

It meant, for the first time in the weekend, that Spies and Haga were together on track, the latter having overtaken Haslam on lap three. Also with them was Fabrizio, who was recovering from a terrible start that had left him outside the top ten through the opening bends.

The Italian was on a charge, however, and was up to fifth, behind Haga, on lap five, just as the Japanese rider was attempting to find a way past Spies. When his first attempt was rebuffed, Fabrizio took advantage and moved past his team-mate.

Fabrizio would go on to relieve Spies of third by lap six, just as Haga was being overtaken by a recovering Biaggi for fifth. The latter's push would take him past Spies just a lap later, the Roman making the pass stick this time.

Haga and Spies were left to dispute fifth, the Japanese rider making his move at turn three on lap eight by dipping beneath his rival and forcing him to sit up. Luckily for Spies, the seven-strong field had already been reduced to six following Haslam's second retirement of the day, his departure leaving a sizeable gap to Leon Camier in seventh.

Back at the front, Byrne was continuing to hold steady in the lead, the Briton showing some fighting spirit to keep Rea behind after the Northern Irishman had nosed ahead briefly on lap five.

After ten laps out front, however, Byrne was overtaken by Rea going into turn one after giving up a slipstream to his rival, the Sterilgarda man being demoted to third a lap later when he was passed by a flying Fabrizio. The Italian's relentless rise up the order continued on lap 14, when he slipped past Rea into the lead, before proceeding to slow the pace down to allow Haga to make up some ground on the front-runners.

The strategy certainly helped Haga, as he took fourth from Biaggi, who made a mistake on lap 15, before getting the better of Byrne for third with just four laps of the race remaining. At the same time, though, Rea had fought his way back into the lead after slipstreaming Fabrizio down the home straight and out-braking him into turn one.

There was a further change of position just behind when another error by Biaggi on the ailing Aprilia allowed Spies up to fifth. Biaggi tried to get past Spies on repeated occasions, only to run off the circuit as he struggled to slow his RSV-4 in time.

As the field headed into the final lap, Rea led Fabrizio over the finish line, but an error out of the final turn allowed the Ducati on to the back of the Honda, the tow proving enough for Fabrizio to get past as they dived down the hill for the last time.

Rea fought back at turn five, but out-braked himself going into the bend, which forced him off the circuit, allowing both Fabrizio and the close following Haga through into first and second.

It meant that Ducati Xerox ended the season with a one-two finish, but that wasn't enough for Haga to keep the title in the team's hands for a second successive season, as just a few seconds behind, Spies was crossing the line in fifth to take the championship in his rookie year.

Spies took the title with 14 race wins, 11 pole positions and 462 points, a record breaking feat that put him 14th on the all-time list after just one season.

A dejected Haga finished as runner-up for the third time in his career (and inside the top three for the seventh time), but he would start as hot favourite for the 2010 title following Spies' defection to MotoGP.

Elsewhere, Rea's final-lap error cost him the chance of passing Biaggi for fourth in the overall standings, the pair settling for third and sixth in the race to give the Italian the advantage at the end of an impressive season for series returnee Aprilia.

Broc Parkes signed off for Kawasaki with two points finishes in 12th, ahead of Matthieu Lagrive, Luca Scassa and David Checa.

WORLD SUPERBIKE CHAMPIONSHIP RESULTS

Race 1: 22 laps, 60.763m/97.790km, Time Of Race: 34m 22.631s, Av speed: 106.047mph/170.677 km/h   **Race 2:** 22 laps, 60.763m/97.790km, Time Of Race: 34m 20.457s, Av speed: 106.165mph/170.857km/h

Pos.	Rider	Nat.	No.	Entrant	Machine	Tyres	Time & Gap	Laps	Pos	Rider	Time & Gap	Laps		Superpole			Points	
1	Noriyuki Haga	JPN	41	Ducati Xerox Team	Ducati 1098R	P		22	1	Ben Spies		22	1	Spies	1m 31.069s	1	Haga	45
2	Max Neukirchner	GER	76	Suzuki Alstare BRUX	Suzuki GSX-R 1000 K9	P	0.032s	22	2	Noriyuki Haga	1.286s	22	2	Biaggi	1m 31.402s	2	Neukirchner	30
3	Yukio Kagayama	JPN	71	Suzuki Alstare BRUX	Suzuki GSX-R 1000 K9	P	5.347s	22	3	Leon Haslam	4.213s	22	3	Rea J	1m 31.596s	3	Haslam	26
4	Michel Fabrizio	ITA	84	Ducati Xerox Team	Ducati 1098R	P	6.587s	22	4	Regis Laconi	4.490s	22	4	Smrz	1m 31.600s	4	Spies	25
5	Jonathan Rea	GB	65	HANNspree Ten Kate Honda	Honda CBR-1000RR	P	8.491s	22	5	Michel Fabrizio	6.045s	22	5	Fabrizio	1m 31.837s	5	Kagayama	24
6	Leon Haslam	GB	91	Stiggy Racing Honda	Honda CBR-1000RR	P	8.523s	22	6	Max Neukirchner	9.947s	22	6	Haslam	1m 32.112s	6	Fabrizio	24
7	Regis Laconi	FRA	16	DFX Corse	Ducati 1098R	P	8.766s	22	7	Jakub Smrz	10.174s	22	7	Checa	1m 32.537s	7	Laconi	22
8	Troy Corser	AUS	11	BMW Motorrad Motorsport	BMW S1000 RR	P	11.589s	22	8	Yukio Kagayama	12.100s	22	8	Laconi	1m 32.649s	8	Rea	18
9	Jakub Smrz	CZE	96	Guandalini Racing	Ducati 1098R	P	11.721s	22	9	Jonathan Rea	12.742s	22	9	Nakano	1m 31.843s	9	Smrz	16
10	Tom Sykes	GB	66	Yamaha WSB	Yamaha YZF R1	P	11.761s	22	10	Tom Sykes	20.061s	22	10	Kiyonari	1m 31.860s	10	Sykes	12
11	Max Biaggi	ITA	3	Aprilia Racing	Aprilia RSV4	P	12.609s	22	11	Ruben Xaus	24.854s	22	11	Kagayama	1m 31.867s	11	Corser	8
12	Carlos Checa	SPA	7	HANNspree Ten Kate Honda	Honda CBR-1000RR	P	19.096s	22	12	Shinya Nakano	25.192s	22	12	Sykes	1m 31.881s	12	Checa, C.	7
13	Roberto Rolfo	ITA	14	Stiggy Racing Honda	Honda CBR-1000RR	P	24.149s	22	13	Carlos Checa	27.162s	22	13	Haga	1m 31.907s	13	Biaggi	6
14	Tommy Hill	GB	33	HANNspree Honda Althea	Honda CBR-1000RR	P	27.416s	22	14	Tommy Hill	29.737s	22	14	Neukirchner	1m 31.916s	14	Xaus	5
15	Shinya Nakano	JPN	56	Aprilia Racing	Aprilia RSV4	P	28.173s	22	15	Max Biaggi	30.036s	22	15	Byrne	1m 32.119s	15	Nakano	5
16	Ben Spies	USA	19	Yamaha WSB	Yamaha YZF R1	P	28.235s	22	16	Roberto Rolfo	38.458s	22	16	Parkes	1m 32.719s	16	Hill	4
17	Brendan Roberts	AUS	24	Guandalini Racing	Ducati 1098R	P	37.348s	22	17	Makoto Tamada	44.453s	22	17	Corser	1m 32.873s	17	Rolfo	3
18	Makoto Tamada	JPN	100	Kawasaki World Superbike	Kawasaki ZX 10R	P	37.401s	22	18	Broc Parkes	45.486s	22	18	Rolfo	1m 32.997s			
19	Ruben Xaus	SPA	111	BMW Motorrad Motorsport	BMW S1000 RR	P	42.614s	22	19	Brendan Roberts	46.198s	22	19	Xaus	1m 33.152s			
20	Luca Scassa	ITA	99	Team Pedercini	Kawasaki ZX 10R	P	1m 35.332s	22	20	Luca Scassa	57.921s	22	20	Hill	1m 33.363s			
21	David Salom	SPA	25	Team Pedercini	Kawasaki ZX 10R	P		20	21	Karl Muggeridge	57.989s	22						
22	Matteo Baiocco	ITA	15	PSG1-1 Corse	Kawasaki ZX 10R	P		14	22	Troy Corser	1m 00.093s	22						
23	Broc Parkes	AUS	23	Kawasaki World Superbike	Kawasaki ZX 10R	P		8	23	Ryuichi Kiyonari	1m 07.820s	22						
24	Vittorio Iannuzzo	ITA	77	Squadra Corse Italia	Honda CBR-1000RR	P		8	24	Matteo Baiocco	1m 21.224s	22						
25	Shane Byrne	GB	67	Sterilgarda	Ducati 1098R	P		7	25	David Salom	1m 21.276s	22						
26	Karl Muggeridge	AUS	31	Celani Race	Suzuki GSX-R 1000 K9	P		4	26	Shane Byrne	DNF	11						
27	Ryuichi Kiyonari	JPN	9	Ten Kate Honda Racing	Honda CBR-1000RR	P		0	27	Vittorio Iannuzzo	DNF	7						

Fastest race lap: Troy Corser on lap 3, 1m 32.726s, 107.231mph/172.573km/h.   Fastest race lap: Noriyuki Haga on lap 3, 1m 32.406s, 107.603mph/173.171km/h.

Lap record: Troy Corser, AUS (Yamaha), 1m 31.826s, 108.823mph/174.260km/h (2007).

Race 1: 18 laps, 60.174m/96.840km, Time Of Race: 36m 06.304s, Av speed: 99.997mph/160.930km/h   **Race 2:** 22 laps, 60.174m/96.840km, Time Of Race: 36m 02.126s, Av speed: 100.190mph/161.241km/h

Pos.	Rider	Nat.	No.	Entrant	Machine	Tyres	Time & Gap	Laps	Pos	Rider	Time & Gap	Laps		Superpole			Points	
1	Ben Spies	USA	19	Yamaha WSB	Yamaha YZF R1	P		18	1	Ben Spies		18	1	Spies	1m 57.280s	1	Haga	85
2	Noriyuki Haga	JPN	41	Ducati Xerox Team	Ducati 1098R	P	1.893s	18	2	Noriyuki Haga	1.274s	18	2	Smrz	1m 57.384s	2	Spies	75
3	Max Biaggi	ITA	3	Aprilia Racing	Aprilia RSV4	P	2.168s	18	3	Max Biaggi	1.622s	18	3	Biaggi	1m 57.694s	3	Neukirchner	40
4	Shinya Nakano	JPN	56	Aprilia Racing	Aprilia RSV4	P	12.061s	18	4	Ryuichi Kiyonari	1.845s	18	4	Haga	1m 57.850s	4	Biaggi	38
5	Carlos Checa	SPA	7	HANNspree Ten Kate Honda	Honda CBR-1000RR	P	12.597s	18	5	Tom Sykes	5.117s	18	5	Sykes	1m 57.878s	5	Haslam	36
6	Shane Byrne	GB	67	Sterilgarda	Ducati 1098R	P	12.971s	18	6	Max Neukirchner	9.512s	18	6	Nakano	1m 58.755s	6	Sykes	32
7	Tom Sykes	GB	66	Yamaha WSB	Yamaha YZF R1	P	13.570s	18	7	Shinya Nakano	9.514s	18	7	Checa	1m 59.090s	7	Rea	30
8	Ryuichi Kiyonari	JPN	9	Ten Kate Honda Racing	Honda CBR-1000RR	P	19.306s	18	8	Jonathan Rea	12.621s	18	8	Byrne	2m 00.021s	8	Laconi	30
9	Troy Corser	AUS	11	BMW Motorrad Motorsport	BMW S1000 RR	P	19.388s	18	9	Troy Corser	13.842s	18	9	Rolfo	1m 58.734s	9	Nakano	27
10	Regis Laconi	FRA	16	DFX Corse	Ducati 1098R	P	20.981s	18	10	Ruben Xaus	13.844s	18	10	Fabrizio	1m 58.919s	10	Kagayama	25
11	Leon Haslam	GB	91	Stiggy Racing Honda	Honda CBR-1000RR	P	21.164s	18	11	Leon Haslam	13.888s	18	11	Laconi	1m 59.044s	11	Fabrizio	24
12	Jonathan Rea	GB	65	HANNspree Ten Kate Honda	Honda CBR-1000RR	P	21.994s	18	12	Shane Byrne	14.913s	18	12	Kiyonari	1m 59.055s	12	Corser	22
13	Ruben Xaus	SPA	111	BMW Motorrad Motorsport	BMW S1000 RR	P	22.917s	18	13	Carlos Checa	15.762s	18	13	Parkes	1m 59.074s	13	Checa	21
14	Broc Parkes	AUS	23	Kawasaki World Superbike	Kawasaki ZX 10R	P	27.218s	18	14	Regis Laconi	15.920s	18	14	Kagayama	1m 59.134s	14	Kiyonari	21
15	Tommy Hill	GB	33	HANNspree Honda Althea	Honda CBR-1000RR	P	31.602s	18	15	Yukio Kagayama	19.565s	18	15	Xaus	1m 59.435s	15	Smrz	16
16	Karl Muggeridge	AUS	31	Celani Race	Suzuki GSX-R 1000 K9	P	33.934s	18	16	Broc Parkes	21.759s	18	16	Corser	1m 59.454s	16	Byrne	14
17	Luca Scassa	ITA	2	Team Pedercini	Kawasaki ZX 10R	P	47.496s	18	17	Jakub Smrz	28.523s	18	17	Rea	1m 59.713s	17	Xaus	14
18	David Salom	SPA	25	Team Pedercini	Kawasaki ZX 10R	P	47.505s	18	18	Karl Muggeridge	40.499s	18	18	Haslam	1m 59.882s	18	Hill	5
19	Matteo Baiocco	ITA	15	PSG1-1 Corse	Kawasaki ZX 10R	P	59.278s	18	19	Brendan Roberts	43.761s	18	19	Neukirchner	1m 59.926s	19	Rolfo	3
20	Vittorio Iannuzzo	ITA	77	Squadra Corse Italia	Honda CBR-1000RR	P	59.295s	18	20	Luca Scassa	44.669s	18	20	Hill	2m 00.108s	20	Parkes	2
21	Brendan Roberts	AUS	24	Guandalini Racing	Ducati 1098R	P	59.338s	18	21	Vittorio Iannuzzo	48.955s	18						
22	Yukio Kagayama	JPN	71	Suzuki Alstare BRUX	Suzuki GSX-R 1000 K9	P	1m 04.008s	18	22	Matteo Baiocco		15						
	Ayrton Badovini	ITA	86	PSG1-1 Corse	Kawasaki ZX 10R	P	DNF	10		Roberto Rolfo	DNF	17						
	Michel Fabrizio	ITA	84	Ducati Xerox Team	Ducati 1098R	P	DNF	7		Michel Fabrizio	DNF	13						
	Jakub Smrz	CZE	96	Guandalini Racing	Ducati 1098R	P	DNF	6		David Salom	DNF	8						
	Max Neukirchner	GER	76	Suzuki Alstare BRUX	Suzuki GSX-R 1000 K9	P	DNF	5		Tommy Hill	DNF	6						
	Roberto Rolfo	ITA	14	Stiggy Racing Honda	Honda CBR-1000RR	P	DNF	3		Ayrton Badovini	DNF	1						

Fastest race lap: Noriyuki Haga on lap 3, 1m 59.511s, 100.699mph/162.060km/h.   Fastest race lap: Ben Spies on lap 6, 1m 59.041s, 101.097mph/162.700km/h.

Lap record: Fonsi Nieto, SPA (Suzuki), 1m 59.156s, 102.240mph/164.540km/h (2008).

Race 1: 23 laps, 57.237m/92.115 km, Time Of Race: 36m 44.766s, Av speed: 93.459mph/150.408km/h

Pos.	Rider	Nat.	No.	Entrant	Machine	Tyres	Time & Gap	Laps
1	Noriyuki Haga	JPN	41	Ducati Xerox Team	Ducati 1098R	P		23
2	Michel Fabrizio	ITA	84	Ducati Xerox Team	Ducati 1098R	P	3.677s	23
3	Max Neukirchner	GER	76	Suzuki Alstare BRUX	Suzuki GSX-R 1000 K9	P	3.959s	23
4	Regis Laconi	FRA	55	DFX Corse	Ducati 1098R	P	4.210s	23
5	Leon Haslam	GB	91	Stiggy Racing Honda	Honda CBR-1000RR	P	13.824s	23
6	Yukio Kagayama	JPN	71	Suzuki Alstare BRUX	Suzuki GSX-R 1000 K9	P	14.562s.	23
7	Tom Sykes	GB	66	Yamaha WSB	Yamaha YZF R1	P	15.155s	23
8	Max Biaggi	ITA	3	Aprilia Racing	Aprilia RSV4	P	16.316s	23
9	Shane Byrne	GB	67	Sterilgarda	Ducati 1098R	P	20.361s	23
10	Broc Parkes	AUS	23	Kawasaki World Superbike	Kawasaki ZX 10R	P	23.878s	23
11	John Hopkins	USA	121	Stiggy Racing Honda	Honda CBR-1000RR	P	30.902s	23
12	Ryuichi Kiyonari	JPN	9	Ten Kate Honda Racing	Honda CBR-1000RR	P	31.298s	23
13	Ruben Xaus	SPA	111	BMW Motorrad Motorsport	BMW S1000 RR	P	32.660s	23
14	Makoto Tamada	JPN	100	Kawasaki World Superbike	Kawasaki ZX 10R	P	42.156s	23
15	Tommy Hill	GB	33	Honda Althea Racing	Honda CBR-1000RR	P	43.040s	23
16	Karl Muggeridge	AUS	31	Celani Race	Suzuki GSX-R 1000 K9	P	45.204s	23
17	Ayrton Badovini	ITA	86	PSG1-1 Corse	Kawasaki ZX 10R	P	52.023s	23
18	Luca Scassa	ITA	99	Team Pedercini	Kawasaki ZX 10R	P	52.474s	23
19	David Salom	SPA	25	Team Pedercini	Kawasaki ZX 10R	P	55.775s	23
20	Matteo Baiocco	ITA	15	PSG1-1 Corse	Kawasaki ZX 10R	P	56.602s	23
	Carlos Checa	SPA	7	HANNspree Ten Kate Honda	Honda CBR-1000RR	P	DNF	21
	David Checa	SPA	94	Yamaha France GMT 94 IP ONE	Yamaha YZF R1	P	DNF	13
	Brendan Roberts	AUS	24	Guandalini Racing	Ducati 1098R	P	DNF	12
	Ben Spies	USA	19	Yamaha WSB	Yamaha YZF R1	P	DNF	9
	Vittorio Iannuzzo	ITA	77	Squadra Corse Italia	Honda CBR-1000RR	P	DNF	9
	Roland Resch	AUT	88	TKR Suzuki Switzerland	Suzuki GSX-R 1000 K9	P	DNF	6
	Jakub Smrz	CZE	96	Guandalini Racing	Ducati 1098R	P	DNF	5
	Troy Corser	AUS	11	BMW Motorrad Motorsport	BMW S1000 RR	P	DNF	1
	Jonathan Rea	GB	65	HANNspree Ten Kate Honda	Honda CBR-1000RR	P	DNF	1

Fastest race lap: Noriyuki Haga on lap 5, 1m 34.862s, 94.441 mph/151.989km/h. (new record)

Previous Lap record: Neil Hodgson, GB (Ducati), 1m 35.007s, 94.297mph/153.702km/h (2003).

Race 2: 23 laps, 57.237m/92.115km, Time Of Race: 36m 46.927s, Av speed: 93.367mph/150.261km/h

Pos	Rider	Time & Gap	Laps		Superpole				Points	
1	Noriyuki Haga		23	1	Spies	1m 33.270s		1	Haga	135
2	Ben Spies	5.105s	23	2	Laconi	1m 33.955s		2	Spies	95
3	Michel Fabrizio	6.386s	23	3	Haga	1m 34.082s		3	Neukirchner	65
4	Regis Laconi	6.573s	23	4	Fabrizio	1m 34.259s		4	Fabrizio	60
5	Leon Haslam	14.075s	23	5	Kagayama	1m 34.755s		5	Haslam	58
6	Carlos Checa	17.333s	23	6	Neukirchner	1m 34.903s		6	Laconi	56
7	Max Neukirchner	19.207s	23	7	Rea	1m 35.056s		7	Biaggi	54
8	Max Biaggi	20.697s	23	8	Checa C.	1m 35.346s		8	Sykes	47
9	Ryuichi Kiyonari	21.015s	23	9	Kiyonari	1m 34.536s		9	Kagayama	35
10	Tom Sykes	22.581s	23	10	Haslam	1m 34.655s		10	Rea	33
11	Shane Byrne	22.604s	23	11	Smrz	1m 34.684s		11	Kiyonari	32
12	John Hopkins	23.952s	23	12	Byrne	1m 34.742s		12	Checa C.	31
13	Jonathan Rea	29.082s	23	13	Parkes	1m 34.823s		13	Nakano	31
14	Jakub Smrz	29.277s	23	14	Corser	1m 34.863s		14	Byrne	26
15	Troy Corser	32.384s	23	15	Roberts	1m 35.082s		15	Corser	23
16	Ruben Xaus	35.125s	23	16	Hopkins	1m 35.251s		16	Smrz	18
17	Broc Parkes	38.344s	23	17	Sykes	1m 35.203s		17	Xaus	17
18	Brendan Roberts	39.161s	23	18	Biaggi	1m 35.204s		18	Hopkins	9
19	Karl Muggeridge	39.374s	23	19	Xaus	1m 35.806s		19	Parkes	8
20	David Checa	49.904s	23	20	Nakano	no time		20	Hill	6
21	David Salom	52.631s	23					21	Rolfo	3
22	Tommy Hill	52.966s	23					22	Tamada	2
23	Vittorio Iannuzzo	53.196s	23							
24	Luca Scassa	53.491s	23							
25	Roland Resch	1m 19.946s	23							
	Yukio Kagayama	DNF	21							
	Matteo Baiocco	DNF	20							
	Makoto Tamada	DNF	11							
	Ayrton Badovini	DNF	7							

Fastest race lap: Noriyuki Haga on lap 3, 1m 34.618s, 94.685mph/152.381km/h.

Race 1: 22 laps, 62.267m/100.210km, Time Of Race: 36m 31.338s, Av speed: 102.295mph/164.628km/h

Pos.	Rider	Nat.	No.	Entrant	Machine	Tyres	Time & Gap	Laps
1	Ben Spies	USA	19	Yamaha WSB	Yamaha YZF R1	P		22
2	Noriyuki Haga	JPN	41	Ducati Xerox Team	Ducati 1098R	P	0.154s	22
3	Leon Haslam	GB	91	Stiggy Racing Honda	Honda CBR-1000RR	P	0.779s	22
4	Tom Sykes	GB	66	Yamaha WSB	Yamaha YZF R1	P	8.775s	22
5	Max Biaggi	ITA	3	Aprilia Racing	Aprilia RSV4	P	11.275s	22
6	Jakub Smrz	CZE	96	Guandalini Racing	Ducati 1098R	P	16.126s	22
7	Jonathan Rea	GB	65	HANNspree Ten Kate Honda	Honda CBR-1000RR	P	19.555s	22
8	Regis Laconi	FRA	16	DFX Corse	Ducati 1098R	P	19.760s	22
9	Michel Fabrizio	ITA	84	Ducati Xerox Team	Ducati 1098R	P	23.006s	22
10	Troy Corser	AUS	11	BMW Motorrad Motorsport	BMW S1000 RR	P	24.285s	22
11	Shane Byrne	GB	67	Sterilgarda	Ducati 1098R	P	13.570s	22
12	Karl Muggeridge	AUS	31	Celani Race	Suzuki GSX-R 1000 K9	P	27.814s	22
13	Max Neukirchner	GER	76	Suzuki Aistare BRUX	Suzuki GSX-R 1000 K9	P	36.962s	22
14	Ruben Xaus	SPA	111	BMW Motorrad Motorsport	BMW S1000 RR	P	39.025s	22
15	Ryuichi Kiyonari	JPN	9	Ten Kate Honda Racing	Honda CBR-1000RR	P	41.505s	22
16	Brendan Roberts	AUS	24	Guandalini Racing	Ducati 1098R	P	41.810s	22
17	Makoto Tamada	JPN	100	Kawasaki World Superbike	Kawasaki ZX 10R	P	50.186s	22
18	Stuart Easton	GB	32	Kawasaki World Superbike	Kawasaki ZX 10R	P	55.567s	22
19	David Checa	SPA	94	Yamaha France GMT 94 IP ONE	Yamaha YZF R1	P	56.425s	22
20	David Salom	SPA	25	Team Pedercini	Kawasaki ZX 10R	P	1m 05.069s	22
21	Roland	AUT	88	TKR Suzuki Switzerland	Suzuki GSX-R 1000 K9	P	1m 37.663s	22
	Luca Scassa	ITA	99	Team Pedercini	Kawasaki ZX 10R	P	DNF	18
	Shinya Nakano	JPN	56	Aprilia Racing	Aprilia RSV4	P	DNF	13
	Vittorio Iannuzzo	ITA	77	Squadra Corse Italia	Honda CBR-1000RR	P	DNF	13
	Matteo Baiocco	ITA	15	PSG1-1 Corse	Kawasaki ZX 10R	P	DNF	12
	Carlos Checa	SPA	7	HANNspree Ten Kate Honda	Honda CBR-1000RR	P	DNF	4
	Yukio Kagayama	JPN	71	Suzuki Aistare BRUX	Suzuki GSX-R 1000 K9	P	DNF	1
	Tommy Hill	GB	33	HANNspree Honda Althea		P	DNF	0

Fastest race lap: Leon Haslam on lap 11, 1m 38.730s, 103.203mph/166.089km/h. (new record)

Previous Lap record: Max Neukirchner, GER (Suzukii) 1m 39.395s, 102.513mph/164.980km/h (2008).

Race 2: 22 laps, 62.267m/100.210km, Time Of Race: 36m 31.712s, Av speed: 102.278mph/164.600km/h

Pos	Rider	Time & Gap	Laps		Superpole				Points (top 25)	
1	Noriyuki Haga		22	1	Spies	1m 37.626s		1	Haga	180
2	Leon Haslam	2.678s	22	2	Smrz	1m 37.765s		2	Spies	120
3	Jakub Smrz	4.603s	22	3	Haslam	1m 38.072s		3	Haslam	94
4	Michel Fabrizio	8.981s	22	4	Haga	1m 38.202s		4	Fabrizio	80
5	Jonathan Rea	12.104s	22	5	Fabrizio	1m 38.215s		5	Neukirchner	75
6	Tom Sykes	14.575s	22	6	Neukirchner	1m 38.353s		6	Sykes	70
7	Carlos Checa	17.449s	22	7	Checa C.	1m 38.640s		7	Biaggi	65
8	Shane Byrne	17.729s	22	8	Sykes	1m 38.790s		8	Laconi	64
9	Max Neukirchner	18.167s	22	9	Kagayama	1m 38.288s		9	Rea	53
10	Troy Corser	25.056s	22	10	Biaggi	1m 38.441s		10	Smrz	44
11	Ruben Xaus	32.617s	22	11	Rea	1m 38.510s		11	Checa C.	40
12	Yukio Kagayama	32.688s	22	12	Laconi	1m 38.521s		12	Kagayama	39
13	Brendan Roberts	37.415s	22	13	Muggeridge	1m 38.802s		13	Byrne	39
14	Matteo Baiocco	55.088s	22	14	Byrne	1m 38.811s		14	Corser	35
15	Luca Scassa	55.325s	22	15	Corser	1m 38.906s		15	Kiyonari	33
16	Regis Laconi	1m 18.514s	22	16	Kiyonari	1m 39.079s		16	Nakano	27
17	Roland Resch	1m 30.780s	22	17	Hill	1m 39.387s		17	Xaus	24
	Tommy Hill	DNF	20	18	Roberts	1m 35.204s		18	Hopkins	9
	Makoto Tamada	DNF	10	19	Nakano	1m 39.569s		19	Parkes	8
	Ryuichi Kiyonari	DNF	7	20	Xaus	1m 39.643s		20	Hill	6
	David Checa	DNF	5					21	Muggeridge	4
	David Salom	DNF	5					22	Roberts	3
	Karl Muggeridge	DNF	3					23	Rolfo	3
	Stuart Easton	DNF	3					24	Tamada	2
	Ben Spies	DNF	1					25	Baiocco	2
	Vittorio Iannuzzo	DNF	1							
	Max Biaggi	DNF	1							

Fastest race lap: Noriyuki Haga on lap 3, 1m 38.680s, 103.255mph/166.173km/h. (new record)

WORLD SUPERBIKE CHAMPIONSHIP RESULTS

Round 5 • MONZA, Italy • 10 May 2009 • 3.599-mile/5.793m circuit • WEATHER: (Race 1 • Dry • Track 45°C • Air 26°C) (Race 2 • Dry • Track 42°C • Air 25°C)

Race 1: 18 laps, 64.793m/104.274km, Time Of Race: 31m 50.758s, Av speed: 122.073mph/196.459km/h

Race 2: 18 laps, 64.793m/104.274km, Time Of Race: 31m 49.252s, Av speed: 122.170mph/196.614km/h

Pos.	Rider	Nat.	No.	Entrant	Machine	Tyres	Time & Gap	Laps	Pos	Rider	Time & Gap	Laps		Superpole			Points (top 25)	
1	Michel Fabrizio	ITA	84	Ducati Xerox Team	Ducati 1098R	P		18	1	Ben Spies		18	1	Spies	1m 44.073s	1	Haga	200
2	Noriyuki Haga	JPN	41	Ducati Xerox Team	Ducati 1098R	P	0.239s	18	2	Michel Fabrizio	2.665s	18	2	Fabrizio	1m 44.270s	2	Spies	146
3	Ryuichi Kiyonari	JPN	9	Ten Kate Honda Racing	Honda CBR-1000RR	P	8.175s	18	3	Ryuichi Kiyonari	2.810s	18	3	Kiyonari	1m 44.642s	3	Fabrizio	125
4	Yukio Kagayama	JPN	71	Suzuki Alstare BRUX	Suzuki GSX-R 1000 K9	P	11.001s	18	4	Jonathan Rea	7.706s	18	4	Neukirchner	1m 44.900s	4	Haslam	103
5	Jonathan Rea	GB	65	HANNspree Ten Kate Honda	Honda CBR-1000RR	P	12.447s	18	5	Max Biaggi	7.863s	18	5	Haga	1m 45.096s	5	Sykes	90
6	Tom Sykes	GB	66	Yamaha WSB	Yamaha YZF R1	P	13.693s	18	6	Tom Sykes	10.383s	18	6	Rea	1m 45.170s	6	Biaggi	81
7	Ruben Xaus	SPA	111	BMW Motorrad Motorsport	BMW S1000 RR	P	39.025s	18	7	Leon Haslam	11.586s	18	7	Biaggi	1m 45.605s	7	Laconi	77
8	Regis Laconi	FRA	16	DFX Corse	Ducati 1098R	P	24.989s	18	8	Jakub Smrz	21.112s	18	8	Kagayama	1m 45.861s	8	Rea	77
9	Carlos Checa	SPA	7	HANNspree Ten Kate Honda	Honda CBR-1000RR	P	26.930s	18	9	Ruben Xaus	22.112s	18	9	Checa C.	1m 45.166s	9	Neukirchner	75
10	Broc Parkes	AUS	23	Kawasaki World Superbike	Kawasaki ZX 10R	P	27.418s	18	10	Carlos Checa	22.261s	18	10	Sykes	1m 45.383s	10	Kiyonari	61
11	Max Biaggi*	ITA	3	Aprilia Racing	Aprilia RSV4	P	27.752s	18	11	Regis Laconi	23.453s	18	11	Corser	1m 45.543s	11	Smrz	56
12	Jakub Smrz	CZE	96	Guandalini Racing	Ducati 1098R	P	29.545s	18	12	Shinya Nakano	32.956s	18	12	Laconi	1m 45.663s	12	Checa C.	53
13	Shinya Nakano	JPN	56	Aprilia Racing	Aprilia RSV4	P	30.952s	18	13	Broc Parkes	37.116s	18	13	Parkes	1m 46.368s	13	Kagayama	52
14	Shane Byrne	GB	67	Sterilgarda	Ducati 1098R	P	31.414s	18	14	Luca Scassa	43.085s	18	14	Xaus	1m 46.571s	14	Byrne	41
15	Ben Spies	USA	19	Yamaha WSB	Yamaha YZF R1	P	36.998s	18	15	Matteo Baiocco	55.088s	18	15	Byrne	1m 46.593s	15	Xaus	40
16	Karl Muggeridge	AUS	31	Celani Race	Suzuki GSX-R 1000 K9	P	42.732s	18	16	Tommy Hill	43.825s	18	16	Nakano	1m 46.928s	16	Corser	35
17	Matteo Baiocco	ITA	15	PSG1-1 Corse	Kawasaki ZX 10R	P	48.835s	18	17	Yukio Kagayama	53.211s	18	17	Haslam	1m 46.250s	17	Nakano	34
18	Jake Zemke	USA	98	Stiggy Racing Honda	Honda CBR-1000RR	P	48.888s	18	18	Shane Byrne*	1m 00.917s	18	18	Scassa	1m 46.372s	18	Parkes	17
19	David Salom	SPA	25	Team Pedercini	Kawasaki ZX 10R	P	50.612s	18	19	David Checa	1m 17.915s	18	19	Muggeridge	1m 46.407s	19	Hopkins	9
20	Tommy Hill	GB	33	Honda Althea Racing	Honda CBR-1000RR	P	51.706s	18	20	Jake Zemke	1m 28.545s	18	20	Smrz	1m 46.522s	20	Hill	6
21	Vittorio Iannuzzo	ITA	77	Squadra Corse Italia	Honda CBR-1000RR	P	55.510s	18	21	David Salom		18				21	Muggeridge	4
22	David Checa	SPA	94	Yamaha France GMT 94 IP ONE	Yamaha YZF R1	P	58.214s	18	21	Roland Resch		17				22	Roberts	3
23	Luca Scassa	ITA	99	Team Pedercini	Kawasaki ZX 10R	P	1m 01.130s	18		Vittorio Iannuzzo	DNF	5				23	Rolfo	3
24	Roland Resch	AUT	88	TKR Suzuki Switzerland	Suzuki GSX-R 1000 K9	P	1m 16.850s	18		Karl Muggeridge	DNF	3				24	Scassa	3
	Leon Haslam	GB	91	Stiggy Racing Honda	Honda CBR-1000RR	P	DNF	17		Noriyuki Haga	DNF	2				25	Baiocco	3
	Troy Corser	AUS	11	BMW Motorrad Motorsport	BMW S1000 RR	P	DNF	0		Troy Corser	DNS							

* Biaggi penalized 20 seconds

* Byrne penalized 20 seconds

Fastest race lap: Michel Fabrizio on lap 9, 1m 45.336s, 123.021mph/197.984km/h. (new record)

Fastest race lap: Ben Spies on lap 6, 1m 45.344s, 123.012mph/197.969km/h.

Previous Lap record: Noriyuki Haga, JPN (Suzuki), 1m 45.882s, 122.387mph/196.963km/h (2008).

Round 6 • KYALAMI, South Africa • 17 May 2009 • 2.658-mile/4.246m circuit • WEATHER: (Race 1 • Dry • Track 25°C • 21°C) (Race 2 • Dry • Track 31°C • Air 20°C)

Race 1: 24 laps, 63.320m/101.904km, Time Of Race: 39m 47.436s, Av speed: 95.480mph/153.660km/h

Race 2: 24 laps, 63.320m/101.904km, Time Of Race: 39m 45.027s, Av speed: 95.577mph/153.816km/h

Pos.	Rider	Nat.	No.	Entrant	Machine	Tyres	Time & Gap	Laps	Pos	Rider	Time & Gap	Laps		Superpole			Points (top 25)	
1	Noriyuki Haga	JPN	41	Ducati Xerox Team	Ducati 1098R	P		24	1	Noriyuki Haga		24	1	Spies	1m 37.288s	1	Haga	250
2	Michel Fabrizio	ITA	84	Ducati Xerox Team	Ducati 1098R	P	0.950s	24	2	Michel Fabrizio	0.322s	24	2	Fabrizio	1m 37.289s	2	Fabrizio	165
3	Ben Spies	USA	19	Yamaha WSB	Yamaha YZF R1	P	3.391s	24	3	Jonathan Rea	8.936s	24	3	Biaggi	1m 37.466s	3	Spies	162
4	Jonathan Rea	GB	65	HANNspree Ten Kate Honda	Honda CBR-1000RR	P	8.914s	24	4	Leon Haslam	10.561s	24	4	Haga	1m 37.544s	4	Haslam	116
5	Max Biaggi	ITA	3	Aprilia Racing	Aprilia RSV4	P	9.019s	24	5	Max Biaggi	10.767s	24	5	Rea	1m 37.634s	5	Rea	106
6	Carlos Checa	SPA	7	HANNspree Ten Kate Honda	Honda CBR-1000RR	P	14.812s	24	6	Carlos Checa	12.413s	24	6	Smrz	1m 37.677s	6	Biaggi	103
7	Shinya Nakano	JPN	56	Aprilia Racing	Aprilia RSV4	P	14.971s	24	7	Shinya Nakano	12.616s	24	7	Checa	1m 37.940s	7	Sykes	103
8	Yukio Kagayama	JPN	71	Suzuki Alstare BRUX	Suzuki GSX-R 1000 K9	P	15.723s	24	8	Yukio Kagayama	14.878s	24	8	Sykes	1m 38.241s	8	Laconi	77
9	Shane Byrne	GB	67	Sterilgarda	Ducati 1098R	P	21.529s	24	9	Tom Sykes	16.225s	24	9	Nakano	1m 37.935s	9	Neukirchner	75
10	Tom Sykes	GB	66	Yamaha WSB	Yamaha YZF R1	P	21.795s	24	10	Jakub Smrz	18.197s	24	10	Haslam	1m 37.988s	10	Checa C.	73
11	Gregorio Lavilla	SPA	36	Guandalini Racing	Ducati 1098R	P	29.872s	24	11	Sheridan Morais	20.629s	24	11	Morais	1m 38.013s	11	Kiyonari	72
12	Ryuichi Kiyonari	JPN	9	Ten Kate Honda Racing	Honda CBR-1000RR	P	34.216s	24	12	Gregorio Lavilla	24.320s	24	12	Kiyonari	1m 38.081s	12	Kagayama	68
13	Sheridan Morais	RSA	132	Kawasaki World Superbike	Kawasaki ZX 10R	P	34.275s	24	13	Ryuichi Kiyonari	24.564s	24	13	Kagayama	1m 38.130s	13	Smrz	64
14	Jakub Smrz	CZE	96	Guandalini Racing	Ducati 1098R	P	38.280s	24	14	Broc Parkes	38.747s	24	14	Byrne	1m 38.171s	14	Nakano	52
15	Broc Parkes	AUS	23	Kawasaki World Superbike	Kawasaki ZX 10R	P	40.855s	24	15	Fonsi Nieto	50.045s	24	15	Xaus	1m 38.194s	15	Byrne	48
16	Fonsi Nieto	SPA	10	Suzuki Alstare BRUX	Suzuki GSX-R 1000 K9	P	44.821s	24	16	David Salom	57.999s	24	16	Lavilla	1m 38.733s	16	Xaus	40
17	Luca Scassa	ITA	99	Team Pedercini	Kawasaki ZX 10R	P	49.142s	24	17	Tommy Hill	1m 05.973s	24	17	Parkes	1m 38.766s	17	Corser	35
18	Karl Muggeridge	AUS	31	Celani Race	Suzuki GSX-R 1000 K9	P	49.702s	24	18	Steve Martin	1m 28.685s	24	18	Scassa	1m 38.779s	18	Parkes	20
19	Tommy Hill	GB	33	Honda Althea Racing	Honda CBR-1000RR	P	50.065s	24	19	Shaun Whyte		23	19	Salom	1m 38.880s	19	Lavilla	9
20	David Salom	SPA	25	Team Pedercini	Kawasaki ZX 10R	P	50.391s	24		Luca Scassa	DNF	14	20	Hill	1m 39.001s	20	Hopkins	9
21	Shaun Whyte	RSA	49	Yamaha France GMT 94 IP ONE	Yamaha YZF R1	P		23		Shane Byrne	DNF	7				21	Morais	8
22	Steve Martin	AUS	17	BMW Motorrad Motorsport	BMW S1000 RR	P		24		Ben Spies	DNF	2				22	Hill	6
	Leon Haslam	GB	91	Stiggy Racing Honda	Honda CBR-1000RR	P	DNF	14		Ruben Xaus	DNF	2				23	Muggeridge	4
	Ruben Xaus	SPA	111	BMW Motorrad Motorsport	BMW S1000 RR	P	39.025s	18		Karl Muggeridge	DNF	1				24	Roberts	3
																25	Rolfo	3

Fastest race lap: Michel Fabrizio on lap 8, 1m 38.548s, 96.380mph/155.108km/h. (new record)

Fastest race lap: Noriyuki Haga on lap 3, 1m 38.577s, 96.351mph/155.063km/h.

Previous Lap record: New Circuit

Race 1: Aggregate of 21 laps, 64.030m/103.047km, Time Of Race: 38m 30.945s, Av speed: 99.747mph/160.527km/h   **Race 2: 21 laps, 64.030m/103.047km, Time Of Race: 38m 25.391s, Av speed: 99.987mph/160.914km/h**

Pos.	Rider	Nat.	No.	Entrant	Machine	Tyres	Time & Gap	Laps	Pos	Rider	Time & Gap	Laps		Superpole			Points (top 25)	
1	Ben Spies	USA	19	Yamaha WSB	Yamaha YZF R1	P		21	1	Ben Spies		21	1	Spies	1m 48.344s	1	Haga	265
2	Carlos Checa	SPA	7	HANNspree Ten Kate Honda	Honda CBR-1000RR	P	9.394s	21	2	Michel Fabrizio	9.080s	21	2	Checa C.	1m 48.908s	2	Spies	212
3	Michel Fabrizio	ITA	84	Ducati Xerox Team	Ducati 1098R	P	12.742s	21	3	Jonathan Rea	14.357s	21	3	Kiyonari	1m 49.243s	3	Fabrizio	201
4	Ryuichi Kiyonari	JPN	9	Ten Kate Honda Racing	Honda CBR-1000RR	P	14.276s	21	4	Max Biaggi	15.636s	21	4	Fabrizio	1m 49.516s	4	Rea	133
5	Jonathan Rea	GB	65	HANNspree Ten Kate Honda	Honda CBR-1000RR	P	14.915s	21	5	Ryuichi Kiyonari	17.156s	21	5	Smrz	1m 49.658s	5	Biaggi	126
6	Max Biaggi	ITA	3	Aprilia Racing	Aprilia RSV4	P	15.461s	21	6	Jakub Smrz	17.546s	21	6	Byrne	1m 49.982s	6	Haslam	122
7	Jamie Hacking	USA	2	Kawasaki World Superbike	Kawasaki ZX 10R	P	22.901s	21	7	Shinya Nakano	19.659s	21	7	Parkes	1m 51.328s	7	Sykes	113
8	Jakub Smrz	CZE	96	Guandalini Racing	Ducati 1098R	P	25.425s	21	8	Noriyuki Haga	23.455s	21	8	Hacking	1m 51.438s	8	Kiyonari	96
9	Noriyuki Haga	JPN	41	Ducati Xerox Team	Ducati 1098R	P	25.870s	21	9	Tom Sykes	30.489s	21	9	Haga	1m 49.515s	9	Checa C.	93
10	Leon Haslam	GB	91	Stiggy Racing Honda	Honda CBR-1000RR	P	26.093s	21	10	Shane Byrne	31.775s	21	10	Nakano	1m 49.528s	10	Smrz	82
11	Shane Byrne	GB	67	Sterilgarda	Ducati 1098R	P	26.181s	21	11	Broc Parkes	33.246s	21	11	Rea	1m 49.541s	11	Laconi	77
12	Yukio Kagayama	JPN	71	Suzuki Alstare BRUX	Suzuki GSX-R 1000 K9	P	29.275s	21	12	Yukio Kagayama	36.758s	21	12	Haslam	1m 49.765s	12	Kagayama	76
13	Tom Sykes	GB	66	Yamaha WSB	Yamaha YZF R1	P	38.365s	21	13	Fonsi Nieto	36.887s	21	13	Kagayama	1m 50.114s	13	Neukirchner	75
14	Gregorio Lavilla	SPA	36	Guandalini Racing	Ducati 1098R	P	39.454s	21	14	Lorenzo Lanzi	37.920s	21	14	Nieto	1m 50.488s	14	Nakano	61
15	Troy Corser	AUS	11	BMW Motorrad Motorsport	BMW S1000 RR	P	39.513s	21	15	Jake Zemke	42.639s	21	15	Scassa	1m 50.987s	15	Byrne	59
16	Fonsi Nieto	SPA	10	Suzuki Alstare BRUX	Suzuki GSX-R 1000 K9	P	48.889s	21	16	Ruben Xaus	42.777s	21	16	Biaggi	1m 51.351s	16	Zaus	40
17	Lorenzo Lanzi	ITA	57	DFX Corse	Ducati 1098R	P	50.747s	21	17	Troy Corser	45.596s	21	17	Lavilla	1m 50.344s	17	Corser	36
18	Jake Zemke	USA	98	Stiggy Racing Honda	Honda CBR-1000RR	P	51.446s	21	18	David Salom	1m 09.237s	21	18	Salom	1m 50.633s	18	Parkes	25
19	Luca Scassa	ITA	99	Team Pedercini	Kawasaki ZX 10R	P	54.472s	21	19	Jamie Hacking	1m 26.703s	21	19	Lanzi	1m 50.868s	19	Lavilla	11
20	David Salom	SPA	25	Team Pedercini	Kawasaki ZX 10R	P	58.525s	21		Leon Haslam	DNF	20	20	Muggeridge	1m 51.004s	20	Hacking	9
21	Ruben Xaus	SPA	111	BMW Motorrad Motorsport	BMW S1000 RR	P	1m 07.572s	21		Gregorio Lavilla	DNF	6				21	Hopkins	9
22	Erwan Nigon	FRA	64	Yamaha France GMT 94 IP ONE	Yamaha YZF R1	P	56.425s	21		Erwan Nigon	DNF	6				22	Morais	8
	Broc Parkes	AUS	23	Kawasaki World Superbike	Kawasaki ZX 10R	P	DNF	20		Carlos Checa	DNF	3				23	Hill	6
	Shinya Nakano	JPN	56	Aprilia Racing	Aprilia RSV4	P	DNF	5		Luca Scassa	DNF	3				24	Muggeridge	4
	Karl Muggeridge	AUS	31	Celani Race	Suzuki GSX-R 1000 K9	P	DNF	5								25	Nieto	4

Fastest race lap: Ben Spies on lap 7, 1m 48.965s, 100.735mph/162.118km/h (new record).   Fastest race lap: Ben Spies on lap 2, 1m 48.768s, 100.918mph/162.412km/h (new record).

Previous Lap record: Carlos Checa, SPA (Honda), 1m 49.703s, 100.058mph/161.028km/h (2008).

Race 1: 24 laps, 63.022m/101.424km, Time Of Race: 45m 02.773s, Av speed: 83.943mph/135.093km/h   **Race 2: 24 laps, 63.022m/101.424km, Time Of Race: 39m 11.204s, Av speed: 96.495mph/155.293km/h**

Pos.	Rider	Nat.	No.	Entrant	Machine	Tyres	Time & Gap	Laps	Pos	Rider	Time & Gap	Laps		Superpole			Points (top 25)	
1	Ben Spies	USA	19	Yamaha WSB	Yamaha YZF R1	P		24	1	Jonathan Rea		24	1	Smrz	1m 35.435s	1	Haga	292
2	Shane Byrne	GB	67	Sterilgarda	Ducati 1098R	P	7.931s	24	2	Michel Fabrizio	0.063s	24	2	Rea	1m 35.609s	2	Spies	244
3	Michel Fabrizio	ITA	84	Ducati Xerox Team	Ducati 1098R	P	11.836s	24	3	Noriyuki Haga	0.457s	24	3	Spies	1m 35.513s	3	Fabrizio	237
4	Jakub Smrz	CZE	96	Guandalini Racing	Ducati 1098R	P	11.886s	24	4	Jakub Smrz	3.635s	24	4	Fabrizio	1m 35.811s	4	Rea	167
5	Noriyuki Haga	JPN	41	Ducati Xerox Team	Ducati 1098R	P	31.670s	24	5	Carlos Checa	4.460s	24	5	Byrne	1m 36.224s	5	Biaggi	135
6	Yukio Kagayama	JPN	71	Suzuki Aistare BRUX	Suzuki GSX-R 1000 K9	P	33.241s	24	6	Shane Byrne	4.538s	24	6	Haga	1m 36.277s	6	Haslam	134
7	Jonathan Rea	GB	65	HANNspree Ten Kate Honda	Honda CBR-1000RR	P	35.772s	24	7	Tom Sykes	12.679s	24	7	Checa C.	1m 36.537s	7	Sykes	130
8	Tom Sykes	GB	66	Yamaha WSB	Yamaha YZF R1	P	41.931s	24	8	Leon Haslam	12.763s	24	8	Kiyonari	1m 36.884s	8	Checa C.	109
9	Shinya Nakano	JPN	56	Aprilia Racing	Aprilia RSV4	P	51.507s	24	9	Ben Spies	13.237s	24	9	Biaggi	1m 36.439s	9	Smrz	108
10	Matthieu Lagrive	FRA	14	Honda Althea Racing	Honda CBR-1000RR	P	59.921s	24	10	Max Biaggi	14.412s	24	10	Haslam	1m 36.510s	10	Kiyonari	98
11	Carlos Checa	SPA	7	HANNspree Ten Kate Honda	Honda CBR-1000RR	P	1m 04.285s	24	11	Yukio Kagayama	20.073s	24	11	Nieto	1m 36.510s	11	Kagayama	91
12	Leon Haslam	GB	91	Stiggy Racing Honda	Honda CBR-1000RR	P	1m 04.658s	24	12	Fonsi Nieto	20.239s	24	12	Nakano	1m 36.682s	12	Byrne	89
13	Max Biaggi	ITA	3	Aprilia Racing	Aprilia RSV4	P	1m 19.822s	24	13	Shinya Nakano	22.351s	24	13	Kagayama	1m 36.916s	13	Laconi	77
14	Ruben Xaus	SPA	111	BMW Motorrad Motorsport	BMW S1000 RR	P	1m 22.412s	24	14	Ryuichi Kiyonari	24.547s	24	14	Sykes	1m 36.978s	14	Neukirchner	75
15	Alessandro Polita	ITA	28	Celani Race	Suzuki GSX-R 1000 K9	P	1m 31.635s	24	15	Gregorio Lavilla	24.696s	24	15	Corser	1m 36.994s	15	Nakano	71
16	Jamie Hacking	JPN	2	Kawasaki World Superbike	Kawasaki ZX 10R	P	1m 39.380s	24	16	Ruben Xaus	25.615s	24	16	Lanzi	1m 37.209s	16	Xaus	42
17	Broc Parkes	AUS	23	Kawasaki World Superbike	Kawasaki ZX 10R	P	1m 42.964s	24	17	Broc Parkes	31.887s	24	17	Lavilla	1m 37.266s	17	Corser	36
18	Fonsi Nieto	SPA	10	Suzuki Alstare BRUX	Suzuki GSX-R 1000 K9	P	1m 43.303s	24	18	Lorenzo Lanzi	34.751s	24	18	Xaus	1m 37.773s	18	Parkes	25
19	Lorenzo Lanzi	ITA	57	DFX Corse	Ducati 1098R	P		23	19	Troy Corser	38.061s	24	19	Parkes	1m 37.281s	19	Lavilla	12
20	Vittorio Iannuzzo	ITA	77	Squadra Corse Italia	Honda CBR-1000RR	P		23	20	Luca Scassa	47.717s	24	20	Hacking	1m 38.441s	20	Hacking	9
21	David Checa	SPA	94	Yamaha France GMT 94 IP ONE	Yamaha YZF R1	P		23	21	Matthieu Lagrive	48.973s	24				21	Hopkins	9
22	Gregorio Lavilla	SPA	36	Guandalini Racing	Ducati 1098R	P		23	22	Jamie Hacking	51.027s	24				22	Morais	8
23	David Salom	SPA	25	Team Pedercini	Kawasaki ZX 10R	P		23	23	Alessandro Polita	52.526s	24				23	Nieto	8
	Roland Resch	AUT	88	TKR Suzuki Switzerland	Suzuki GSX-R 1000 K9	P		23	24	Vittorio Iannuzzo	57.589s	24				24	Lagrive	6
	Luca Scassa	ITA	99	Team Pedercini	Kawasaki ZX 10R	P	DNF	20		Roland Resch	1m 36.359s	24				25	Hill	6
	Matteo Baiocco	ITA	15	PSG1-1 Corse	Kawasaki ZX 10R	P		15		David Salom		19						
	Ryuichi Kiyonari	JPN	9	Ten Kate Honda Racing	Honda CBR-1000RR	P	DNF	0		David Checa		15						
	Troy Corser	AUS	11	BMW Motorrad Motorsport	BMW S1000 RR	P	DNF	0		Matteo Baiocco		5						
dns	John Hopkins	USA	121	Stiggy Racing Honda	Honda CBR-1000RR	P												

Fastest race lap: Jakub Smrz on lap 23, 1m 38.679s, 95.799mph/154.173km/h.   Fastest race lap: Noriyuki Haga on lap 12, 1m 37.135s, 97.321mph/156.623km/h (new record).

Previous Lap record: Troy Corser, AUS (Yamaha), 1m 37.580s, 96.877mph/155.909km/h (2008).

WORLD SUPERBIKE CHAMPIONSHIP RESULTS

Round 9 • **DONINGTON PARK**, Great Britain • 28 June 2009 • 2.500-mile/4.023m circuit • WEATHER: (Race 1 • Dry • Track 25°C • Air 20°C) (Race 2 • Dry • Track 35°C • Air 23°C)

Race 1: 23 laps, 57.494m/92.529km, Time Of Race: **34m 57.230s,** Av speed: **98.693mph/158.831km/h** — **Race 2: 23 laps, 57.494m/92.529km,** Time Of Race: **35m 14.788s,** Av speed: **97.873mph/157.512km/h**

Pos.	Rider	Nat.	No.	Entrant	Machine	Tyres	Time & Gap	Laps	Pos	Rider	Time & Gap	Laps		Superpole			Points (top 25)	
1	Ben Spies	USA	19	Yamaha WSB	Yamaha YZF R1	P		23	1	Ben Spies		23	1	Spies	1m 29.846s	1	Haga	308
2	Max Biaggi	ITA	3	Aprilia Racing	Aprilia RSV4	P	7.156s	23	2	Leon Haslam	6.662s	23	2	Biaggi	1m 30.080s	2	Spies	294
3	Noriyuki Haga	JPN	41	Ducati Xerox Team	Ducati 1098R	P	10.968s	23	3	Michel Fabrizio	6.816s	23	3	Byrne	1m 30.535s	3	Fabrizio	257
4	Leon Haslam	GB	91	Stiggy Racing Honda	Honda CBR-1000RR	P	18.843s	23	4	Shane Byrne	7.349s	23	4	Nakano	1m 30.671s	4	Rea	177
5	Shane Byrne	GB	67	Sterilgarda	Ducati 1098R	P	19.125s	23	5	Tom Sykes	8.145s	23	5	Fabrizio	1m 30.734s	5	Haslam	167
6	Shinya Nakano	JPN	56	Aprilia Racing	Aprilia RSV4	P	21.286s	23	6	Leon Camier	13.463s	23	6	Haga	1m 31.023s	6	Biaggi	155
7	Jonathan Rea	GB	65	HANNspree Ten Kate Honda	Honda CBR-1000RR	P	23.644s	23	7	Ryuichi Kiyonari	15.571s	23	7	Checa C.	1m 31.324s	7	Sykes	141
8	John Hopkins	USA	121	Stiggy Racing Honda	Honda CBR-1000RR	P	32.849s	23	8	James Ellison	16.837s	23	8	Smrz	1m 34.797s	8	Smrz	115
9	Jakub Smrz	CZE	96	Guandalini Racing	Ducati 1098R	P	32.904s	23	9	Ruben Xaus	22.891s	23	9	Haslam	1m 30.159s	9	Checa C.	114
10	Ryuichi Kiyonari	JPN	9	Ten Kate Honda Racing	Honda CBR-1000RR	P	33.192s	23	10	Simon Andrews	30.347s	23	10	Sykes	1m 30.229s	10	Byrne	113
11	Carlos Checa	SPA	7	HANNspree Ten Kate Honda	Honda CBR-1000RR	P	34.535s	23	11	Lorenzo Lanzi	30.622s	23	11	Hopkins	1m 30.272s	11	Kiyonari	113
12	Michel Fabrizio	ITA	84	Ducati Xerox Team	Ducati 1098R	P	35.093s	23	12	Matthieu Lagrive	31.562s	23	12	Rea	1m 30.387s	12	Kagayama	94
13	Leon Camier	GB	22	Airwaves Yamaha	Yamaha YZF R1	P	35.441s	23	13	Yukio Kagayama	32.148s	23	13	Lavilla	1m 30.612s	13	Nakano	81
14	Lorenzo Lanzi	ITA	57	DFX Corse	Ducati 1098R	P	39.034s	23	14	Broc Parkes	32.607s	23	14	Ellison	1m 30.816s	14	Laconi	77
15	Ruben Xaus	SPA	111	BMW Motorrad Motorsport	BMW S1000 RR	P	41.067s	23	15	Jonathan Rea	32.806s	23	15	Corser	1m 30.916s	15	Neukirchner	75
16	Matthieu Lagrive	FRA	14	Honda Althea Racing	Honda CBR-1000RR	P	46.452s	23	16	Luca Scassa	34.269s	23	16	Xaus	1m 31.120s	16	Xaus	50
17	Yukio Kagayama	JPN	71	Suzuki Aistare BRUX	Suzuki GSX-R 1000 K9	P	47.924s	23	17	Blake Young	40.644s	23	17	Camier	1m 31.176s	17	Corser	36
18	Broc Parkes	AUS	23	Kawasaki World Superbike	Kawasaki ZX 10R	P	48.246s	23	18	Gregorio Lavilla	40.956s	23	18	Kagayama	1m 31.215s	18	Parkes	27
19	Luca Scassa	ITA	99	Team Pedercini	Kawasaki ZX 10R	P	50.932s	23	19	David Salom	41.302s	23	19	Lanzi	1m 31.217s	19	Hopkins	17
20	Simon Andrews	GB	117	MSS Colchester Kawasaki	Kawasaki ZX 10R	P	55.032s	23	20	Troy Corser	42.856s	23	20	Kiyonari	1m 31.260s	20	Camier	13
21	Jamie Hacking	JPN	2	Kawasaki World Superbike	Kawasaki ZX 10R	P	55.216s	23	21	Max Biaggi	47.769s	23				21	Lavilla	12
22	Alessandro Polita	ITA	28	Celani Race	Suzuki GSX-R 1000 K9	P	1m 02.758s	23		Vittorio Iannuzzo	DNF	15				22	Lagrive	12
23	David Salom	SPA	25	Team Pedercini	Kawasaki ZX 10R	P	1m 02.997s	23		Roland Resch	DNF	15				23	Hacking	9
24	David Checa	SPA	94	Yamaha France GMT 94 IP ONE	Yamaha YZF R1	P	1m 12.255s	23		Alessandro Polita	DNF	6				24	Lanzi	9
25	Blake Young	USA	79	Suzuki Alstare BRUX	Suzuki GSX-R 1000 K9	P	1m 12.531s	23		Carlos Checa	DNF	5				25	Ellison	8
	Troy Corser	AUS	11	BMW Motorrad Motorsport	BMW S1000 RR	P	DNF	21		David Checa	DNF	5						
	James Ellison	GB	27	Airwaves Yamaha	Yamaha YZF R1	P	DNF	13		Noriyuki Haga	DNF	4						
	Roland Resch	AUT	88	TKR Suzuki Switzerland	Suzuki GSX-R 1000 K9	P	DNF	13		Jakub Smrz	DNF	2						
	Tom Sykes	GB	66	Yamaha WSB	Yamaha YZF R1	P	DNF	13		Shinya Nakano	DNF	1						
	Gregorio Lavilla	SPA	36	Guandalini Racing	Ducati 1098R	P	DNF	7		Jamie Hacking	DNF	1						
	Vittorio Iannuzzo	ITA	77	Squadra Corse Italia	Honda CBR-1000RR	P	DNF	0										

Fastest race lap: Ben Spies on lap 4, 1m 30.575s, 99.356mph/159.898km/h. (new record) — Fastest race lap: Ben Spies on lap 2, 1m 30.631s, 99.295mph/159.800km/h.

Previous Lap record: Troy Bayliss, AUS (Ducati), 1m 31.575s, 98.270mph/158.150km/h (2007).

Round 10 • **BRNO**, Czech Republic • 26 July 2009 • 3.357-mile/5.403m circuit • WEATHER: (Race 1 • Dry • Track 27°C • Air 20°C) (Race 2 • Dry • Track 39°C • Air 23°C)

Race 1: 20 laps, 67.145m/108.060km, Time Of Race: **40m 18.306s,** Av speed: **99.956mph/160.863km/h** — **Race 2: 20 laps, 67.145m/108.060km,** Time Of Race: **40m 15.420s,** Av speed: **100.074mph/161.055km/h**

Pos.	Rider	Nat.	No.	Entrant	Machine	Tyres	Time & Gap	Laps	Pos	Rider	Time & Gap	Laps		Superpole			Points (top 25)	
1	Max Biaggi	ITA	3	Aprilia Racing	Aprilia RSV4	P		20	1	Ben Spies		20	1	Spies	1m 58.868s	1	Haga	326
2	Carlos Checa	SPA	7	HANNspree Ten Kate Honda	Honda CBR-1000RR	P	3.631s	20	2	Max Biaggi	6.662s	20	2	Fabrizio	1m 58.950s	2	Spies	319
3	Jonathan Rea	GB	65	HANNspree Ten Kate Honda	Honda CBR-1000RR	P	9.948s	20	3	Michel Fabrizio	6.816s	20	3	Biaggi	1m 59.055s	3	Fabrizio	273
4	Shane Byrne	GB	67	Sterilgarda	Ducati 1098R	P	12.952s	20	4	Jonathan Rea	7.349s	20	4	Rea	1m 59.740s	4	Rea	206
5	Troy Corser	AUS	11	BMW Motorrad Motorsport	BMW S1000 RR	P	14.599s	20	5	Carlos Checa	8.145s	20	5	Byrne	1m 59.787s	5	Biaggi	200
6	Jakub Smrz	CZE	96	Guandalini Racing	Ducati 1098R	P	19.359s	20	6	Noriyuki Haga	13.463s	20	6	Corser	2m 00.046s	6	Haslam	180
7	Leon Haslam	GB	91	Stiggy Racing Honda	Honda CBR-1000RR	P	19.680s	20	7	Tom Sykes	15.571s	20	7	Xaus	2m 00.096s	7	Sykes	150
8	Noriyuki Haga	JPN	41	Ducati Xerox Team	Ducati 1098R	P	20.731s	20	8	Shane Byrne	16.837s	20	8	Sykes	2m 00.240s	8	Checa C.	145
9	Matthieu Lagrive	FRA	14	Honda Althea Racing	Honda CBR-1000RR	P	21.923s	20	9	Jakub Smrz	22.891s	20	9	Lanzi	1m 59.730s	9	Byrne	134
10	Makoto Tamada	JPN	100	Kawasaki World Superbike	Kawasaki ZX 10R	P	27.807s	20	10	Troy Corser	30.347s	20	10	Checa C.	1m 59.748s	10	Smrz	132
11	Fonsi Nieto	ITA	10	DFX Corse	Ducati 1098R	P	35.263s	20	11	Shinya Nakano	30.622s	20	11	Tamada	1m 59.873s	11	Kiyonari	119
12	Broc Parkes	AUS	23	Kawasaki World Superbike	Kawasaki ZX 10R	P	36.535s	20	12	Leon Haslam	31.562s	20	12	Smrz	2m 00.159s	12	Kagayama	96
13	Ryuichi Kiyonari	JPN	9	Ten Kate Honda Racing	Honda CBR-1000RR	P	38.586s	20	13	Ryuichi Kiyonari	32.148s	20	13	Kagayama	2m 00.223s	13	Nakano	86
14	Yukio Kagayama	JPN	71	Suzuki Aistare BRUX	Suzuki GSX-R 1000 K9	P	40.061s	20	14	Matthieu Lagrive	32.607s	20	14	Haga	2m 00.235s	14	Laconi	77
15	Vittorio Iannuzzo	ITA	77	Squadra Corse Italia	Honda CBR-1000RR	P	40.280s	20	15	Lorenzo Lanzi	32.806s	20	15	Nakano	2m 00.262s	15	Neukirchner	75
16	Luca Scassa	ITA	99	Team Pedercini	Kawasaki ZX 10R	P	40.641s	20	16	Broc Parkes	34.269s	20	16	Lagrive	2m 00.498s	16	Corser	53
17	David Salom	SPA	25	Team Pedercini	Kawasaki ZX 10R	P	1m 10.529s	20	17	Fonsi Nieto	40.644s	20	17	Haslam	2m 00.718s	17	Xaus	50
18	David Checa	SPA	94	Yamaha France GMT 94 IP ONE	Yamaha YZF R1	P	1m 14.874s	20	18	Vittorio Iannuzzo	40.956s	20	18	Kiyonari	2m 00.811s	18	Parkes	31
19	Roland Resch	AUT	88	TKR Suzuki Switzerland	Suzuki GSX-R 1000 K9	P	1m 42.979s	20	19	David Checa	41.302s	20	19	Parkes	2m 03.819s	19	Lagrive	19
20	Milos Cihak	CZE	51	ProRace	Suzuki GSX-R 1000 K9	P	1m 43.111s	20	20	Roland Resch	42.856s	20	20	Hopkins	2m 14.727s	20	Hopkina	17
	Tom Sykes	GB	66	Yamaha WSB	Yamaha YZF R1	P	DNF	19	21	Alessandro Polita	DNF	15				21	Camier	13
	Alessandro Polita	ITA	53	Celani Race	Suzuki GSX-R 1000 K9	P	DNF	14		Luca Scassa	DNF	15				22	Nieto	13
	John Hopkins	USA	121	Stiggy Racing Honda	Honda CBR-1000RR	P	DNF	10		Milos Cihak	DNF	6				23	Lavilla	12
	Shinya Nakano	JPN	56	Aprilia Racing	Aprilia RSV4	P	DNF	8		John Hopkins	DNF	5				24	Hacking	10
Ben Spies		USA	19	Yamaha WSB	Yamaha YZF R1	P	DNF	4		Yukio Kagayama	DNF	5				25	Lanzi	9
	Michel Fabrizio	ITA	84	Ducati Xerox Team	Ducati 1098R	P	DNF	4		David Salom	DNF	4						
	Lorenzo Lanzi	ITA	57	DFX Corse	Ducati 1098R	P	DNF	2		Makoto Tamada	DNF	2						
	Ruben Xaus	SPA	111	BMW Motorrad Motorsport	BMW S1000 RR	P	DNF	0		Ruben Xaus	DNS	0						

Fastest race lap: Michel Fabrizio on lap 4, 2m 00.116s, 100.620mph/161.933km/h. — Fastest race lap: Max Biaggi on lap 15, 1m 59.961s, 100.750mph/162.143km/h (new record).

Previous Lap record: Michel Fabrizio, I (Ducati), 1m 59.979s, 100.735mph/162.118km/h (2008).

Race 1: 20 laps, 63.840m/102.740km, Time Of Race: **39m 04.818s**, Av speed: **98.013mph/157.737km/h** | **Race 2:** 20 laps, 63.840m/102.740km, Time Of Race: **39m 01.561s**, Av speed: **98.149mph157.956km/h**

Pos.	Rider	Nat.	No.	Entrant	Machine	Tyres	Time & Gap	Laps	Pos	Rider	Time & Gap	Laps	Superpole		Points (top 25)	
1	Ben Spies	USA	19	Yamaha WSB	Yamaha YZF R1	P		20	1	Jonathan Rea		20	1	Haga	1m 55.489s	1	Spies	364
2	Noriyuki Haga	JPN	41	Ducati Xerox Team	Ducati 1098R	P	3.850s	20	2	Ben Spies	0.786s	20	2	Rea	1m 55.749s	2	Haga	346
3	Carlos Checa	SPA	7	HANNspree Ten Kate Honda	Honda CBR-1000RR	P	6.990s	20	3	Carlos Checa	4.993s	20	3	Haslam	1m 55.776s	3	Fabrizio	289
4	Jonathan Rea	GB	65	HANNspree Ten Kate Honda	Honda CBR-1000RR	P	7.109s	20	4	Max Biaggi	8.191s	20	4	Fabrizio	1m 55.927s	4	Rea	244
5	Max Biaggi	ITA	3	Aprilia Racing	Aprilia RSV4	P	12.825s	20	5	Leon Haslam	10.907s	20	5	Spies	1m 55.938s	5	Biaggi	224
6	Leon Haslam	GB	91	Stiggy Racing Honda	Honda CBR-1000RR	P	13.243s	20	6	Troy Corser	17.152s	20	6	Corser	1m 56.296s	6	Haslam	201
7	Michel Fabrizio	ITA	84	Ducati Xerox Team	Ducati 1098R	P	14.223s	20	7	Ryuichi Kiyonari	19.473s	20	7	Biaggi	1m 56.440s	7	Checa C.	177
8	Troy Corser	AUS	11	BMW Motorrad Motorsport	BMW S1000 RR	P	14.382s	20	8	Tom Sykes	19.721s	20	8	Checa C.	1m 56.699s	8	Sykes	165
9	Tom Sykes	GB	66	Yamaha WSB	Yamaha YZF R1	P	17.206s	20	9	Michel Fabrizio	22.981s	20	9	Sykes	1m 56.406s	9	Byrne	140
10	Shane Byrne	GB	67	Sterilgarda	Ducati 1098R	P	26.547s	20	10	Yukio Kagayama	24.161s	20	10	Byrne	1m 56.663s	10	Smrz	140
11	Matthieu Lagrive	FRA	14	Honda Althea Racing	Honda CBR-1000RR	P	27.388s	20	11	Jakub Smrz	29.367s	20	11	Nieto	1m 56.670s	11	Kiyonari	130
12	Karl Muggeridge	AUS	31	Suzuki Aistare BRUX	Suzuki GSX-R 1000 K9	P	30.968s	20	12	Fonsi Nieto	30.007s	20	12	Tamada	1m 56.683s	12	Kagayama	103
13	Jakub Smrz	CZE	96	Guandalini Racing	Ducati 1098R	P	31.069s	20	13	Broc Parkes	37.281s	20	13	Kagayama	1m 56.901s	13	Nakano	86
14	Ryuichi Kiyonari	JPN	9	Ten Kate Honda Racing	Honda CBR-1000RR	P	31.188s	20	14	Luca Scassa	47.883s	20	14	Smrz	1m 57.091s	14	Laconi	77
15	Yukio Kagayama	JPN	71	Suzuki Aistare BRUX	Suzuki GSX-R 1000 K9	P	40.165s	20	15	Vittorio Iannuzzo	49.549s	20	15	Parkes	1m 57.098s	15	Neukirchner	75
16	Luca Scassa	ITA	99	Team Pedercini	Kawasaki ZX 10R	P	54.897s	20	16	Matteo Baiocco	49.635s	20	16	Lagrive	1m 57.293s	16	Corser	71
17	David Salom	SPA	25	Team Pedercini	Kawasaki ZX 10R	P	1m 01.958s	20	17	David Salom	1m 19.554s	20	17	Muggeridge	1m 57.515s	17	Xaus	50
18	Roland Resch	AUT	88	TKR Suzuki Switzerland	Suzuki GSX-R 1000 K9	P		19	18	David Checa	1m 22.329s	20	18	Kiyonari	1m 57.522s	18	Parkes	34
	Shinya Nakano	JPN	56	Aprilia Racing	Aprilia RSV4	P	DNF	14		Richard Cooper	DNF	16	19	Hopkins	1m 57.523s	19	Lagrive	24
	Fonsi Nieto	SPA	10	DFX Corse	Ducati 1098R	P	DNF	11		Karl Muggeridge	DNF	13	20	Iannuzzo	1m 59.279s	20	Hopkins	17
	David Checa	SPA	94	Yamaha France GMT 94 IP ONE	Yamaha YZF R1	P	DNF	9		Roland Resch	DNF	13				21	Nieto	17
	Vittorio Iannuzzo	ITA	77	Squadra Corse Italia	Honda CBR-1000RR	P	DNF	6		Shane Byrne	DNF	9				22	Camier	13
	Richard Cooper	GB	47	BMW Motorrad Motorsport	BMW S1000 RR	P	DNF	5		Noriyuki Haga	DNF	4				23	Lavilla	12
	Broc Parkes	AUS	23	Kawasaki World Superbike	Kawasaki ZX 10R	P	DNF	2		Matthieu Lagrive	DNF	1				24	Lanzi	10
	Matteo Baiocco	ITA	15	Guandalini Racing	Ducati 1098R	P	DNF	2	dns	Shinya Nakano						25	Hacking	9
dns	John Hopkins	USA	121	Stiggy Racing Honda	Honda CBR-1000RR	P											
dns	Makoto Tamada	JPN	100	Kawasaki World Superbike	Kawasaki ZX 10R	P											

Fastest race lap: Noriyuki Haga on lap 15, 1m 56.539s, 98.603mph/158.687km/h (record). | Fastest race lap: Jonathan Rea on lap 20, 1m 56.234s, 98.862mph/159.103km/h (new record).

Previous Lap record: Noriyuki Haga, JPN (Yamaha), 1m 56.892s, 98.306mph/158.208km/h (2008).

Race 1: 21 laps, 64.409m/103.656km, Time Of Race: **38m 32.199s**, Av speed: **100.282mph/161.388km/h** | **Race 2:** 21 laps, 64.409m/103.656km, Time Of Race: **38m 23.143s**, Av speed: **100.676mph/162.023km/h**

Pos.	Rider	Nat.	No.	Entrant	Machine	Tyres	Time & Gap	Laps	Pos	Rider	Time & Gap	Laps	Superpole		Points (top 25)	
1	Noriyuki Haga	JPN	41	Ducati Xerox Team	Ducati 1098R	P		21	1	Michel Fabrizio		21	1	Fabrizio	1m 47.735s	1	Haga	391
2	Max Biaggi	ITA	3	Aprilia Racing	Aprilia RSV4	P	2.074s	21	2	Noriyuki Haga	3.592s	21	2	Spies	1m 47.778s	2	Spies	388
3	Michel Fabrizio	ITA	84	Ducati Xerox Team	Ducati 1098R	P	2.190s	21	3	Marco Simoncelli	6.510s	21	3	Rea	1m 47.834s	3	Fabrizio	330
4	Ben Spies	USA	19	Yamaha WSB	Yamaha YZF R1	P	5.438s	21	4	Max Biaggi	7.445s	21	4	Haga	1m 47.885s	4	Rea	263
5	Ryuichi Kiyonari	JPN	9	Ten Kate Honda Racing	Honda CBR-1000RR	P	14.470s	21	5	Ben Spies	14.678s	21	5	Smrz	1m 48.156s	5	Biaggi	257
6	Leon Haslam	GB	91	Stiggy Racing Honda	Honda CBR-1000RR	P	14.685s	21	6	Jonathan Rea	16.396s	21	6	Biaggi	1m 48.665s	6	Haslam	219
7	Jonathan Rea	GB	65	HANNspree Ten Kate Honda	Honda CBR-1000RR	P	26.822s	21	7	Shane Byrne	17.110s	21	7	Byrne	1m 49.092s	7	Checa C.	183
8	Jakub Smrz	CZE	96	Guandalini Racing	Ducati 1098R	P	32.694s	21	8	Leon Haslam	22.502s	21	8	Simoncelli	1m 49.338s	8	Sykes	176
9	Tom Sykes	GB	66	Yamaha WSB	Yamaha YZF R1	P	33.817s	21	9	Jakub Smrz	25.268s	21	9	Corser	1m 48.981s	9	Smrz	155
10	Broc Parkes	AUS	23	Kawasaki World Superbike	Kawasaki ZX 10R	P	34.801s	21	10	David Checa	30.203s	21	10	Haslam	1m 48.992s	10	Byrne	149
11	Troy Corser	AUS	11	BMW Motorrad Motorsport	BMW S1000 RR	P	35.286s	21	11	Lorenzo Lanzi	32.589s	21	11	Lanzi	1m 49.060s	11	Kiyonari	141
12	Ruben Xaus	SPA	111	BMW Motorrad Motorsport	BMW S1000 RR	P	36.442s	21	12	Tom Sykes	36.243s	21	12	Nieto	1m 49.105s	12	Kagayama	104
13	Karl Muggeridge	AUS	31	Suzuki Alstare BRUX	Suzuki GSX-R 1000 K9	P	38.698s	21	13	Ruben Xaus	36.368s	21	13	Checa C.	1m 49.168s	13	Nakano	86
14	Matteo Baiocco	ITA	15	Guandalini Racing	Ducati 1098R	P	42.147s	21	14	Karl Muggeridge	38.809s	21	14	Kiyonari	1m 49.340s	14	Laconi	77
15	Yukio Kagayama	JPN	71	Suzuki Aistare BRUX	Suzuki GSX-R 1000 K9	P	46.510s	21	15	Broc Parkes	42.453s	21	15	Lagrive	1m 49.641s	15	Corser	76
16	Luca Scassa	ITA	99	Team Pedercini	Kawasaki ZX 10R	P	46.628s	21	16	Matteo Baiocco	49.349s	21	16	Sykes	1m 49.681s	16	Neukirchner	75
17	David Checa	SPA	94	Yamaha France GMT 94 IP ONE	Yamaha YZF R1	P	1m 16.121s	21	17	Ryuichi Kiyonari	1m 01.823s	21	17	Kagayama	1m 49.906s	17	Xaus	57
18	David Salom	SPA	25	Team Pedercini	Kawasaki ZX 10R	P	1m 16.398s	21	18	Luca Scassa	1m 51.308s	21	18	Parkes	1m 50.012s	18	Parkes	41
	Vittorio Iannuzzo	ITA	77	Squadra Corse Italia	Honda CBR-1000RR	P	DNF	13		Matthieu Lagrive	DNF	16	19	Xaus	1m 50.152s	19	Lagrive	24
	Marco Simoncelli	ITA	58	Aprilia Racing	Aprilia RSV4	P	DNF	9		David Checa	DNF	14	20	Muggeridge	1m 50.414s	20	Hopkins	17
	Shane Byrne	GB	67	Sterilgarda	Ducati 1098R	P	DNF	8		Yukio Kagayama	DNF	12				21	Nieto	17
	Carlos Checa	SPA	7	HANNspree Ten Kate Honda	Honda CBR-1000RR	P	DNF	7		Fonsi Nieto	DNF	11				22	Simoncelli	16
	Fonsi Nieto	SPA	10	DFX Corse	Ducati 1098R	P	DNF	7		Vittorio Iannuzzo	DNF	9				23	Lanzi	15
	Makoto Tamada	JPN	100	Kawasaki World Superbike	Kawasaki ZX 10R	P	DNF	5		Troy Corser	DNF	4				24	Camier	13
	Luca Conforti	ITA	124	Barni Racing Team	Ducati 1098R	P	DNF	5		David Salom	DNF	3				25	Muggeridge	13
	Matthieu Lagrive	FRA	14	Honda Althea Racing	Honda CBR-1000RR	P	DNF	3	dns	Makoto Tamada								
	Lorenzo Lanzi	ITA	57	DFX Corse	Ducati 1098R	P	DNF	2										

Fastest race lap: Michel Fabrizio on lap 4, 1m 49.282s, 101.036mph/162.603km/h (record). | Fastest race lap: Noriyuki Haga on lap 20, 1m 48.982s, 101.315mph/163.051km/h (new record).

Previous Lap record: New track.

WORLD SUPERBIKE CHAMPIONSHIP RESULTS

Round 13 • Magny Cours, France • 4 October 2009 • 2.741-mile/4.411km circuit • WEATHER: (Race 1 • Dry • Track 19°C • Air 15°C) (Race 2 • Dry • Track 28°C • Air 20°C)

Race 1: 23 laps, 63.040 m/101.453km, **Time Of Race:** 37m 57.110s, **Av speed:** 99.663mph/160.392km/h

Pos.	Rider	Nat.	No.	Entrant	Machine	Tyres	Time & Gap	Laps
1	Ben Spies	USA	19	Yamaha WSB	Yamaha YZF R1	P		23
2	Noriyuki Haga	JPN	41	Ducati Xerox Team	Ducati 1098R	P	0.181s	23
3	Max Biaggi	ITA	3	Aprilia Racing	Aprilia RSV4	P	5.009s	23
4	Michel Fabrizio	ITA	84	Ducati Xerox Team	Ducati 1098R	P	16.347s	23
5	Leon Haslam	GB	91	Stiggy Racing Honda	Honda CBR-1000RR	P	22.622s	23
6	Carlos Checa	SPA	7	HANNspree Ten Kate Honda	Honda CBR-1000RR	P	24.948s	23
7	Yukio Kagayama	JPN	71	Team Suzuki Aistare	Suzuki GSX-R 1000 K9	P	27.144s	23
8	Shane Byrne	GB	67	Sterilgarda	Ducati 1098R	P	27.578s	23
9	Troy Corser	AUS	11	BMW Motorrad Motorsport	BMW S1000 RR	P	28.486s	23
10	Jakub Smrz	CZE	96	Guandalini Racing	Ducati 1098R	P	28.716s	23
11	Ruben Xaus	SPA	111	BMW Motorrad Motorsport	BMW S1000 RR	P	52.680s	23
12	Matteo Baiocco	ITA	15	Guandalini Racing	Ducati 1098R	P	1m 01.372s	23
13	Luca Scassa	ITA	99	Team Pedercini	Kawasaki ZX 10R	P	1m 05.123s	23
14	David Salom	SPA	25	Team Pedercini	Kawasaki ZX 10R	P	1m 05.483s	23
15	David Checa	SPA	94	Yamaha France GMT 94 IP ONE	Yamaha YZF R1	P	1m 05.672s	23
16	Roland Resch	AUT	88	TKR Suzuki Switzerland	Suzuki GSX-R 1000 K9	P	1m 29.284s	23
17	Flavio Gentile	ITA	40	Honda Althea Racing	Honda CBR-1000RR	P		22
	Leon Camier	GBR	22	Aprilia Racing	Aprilia RSV4	P	DNF	20
	Sheridan Morais	RSA	132	Kawasaki World Superbike	Kawasaki ZX 10R	P	DNF	13
	Fonsi Nieto	SPA	10	DFX Corse	Ducati 1098R	P	DNF	12
	Broc Parkes	AUS	23	Kawasaki World Superbike	Kawasaki ZX 10R	P	DNF	10
	Jonathan Rea	GB	65	HANNspree Ten Kate Honda	Honda CBR-1000RR	P	DNF	8
	Vittorio Iannuzzo	ITA	77	Squadra Corse Italia	Honda CBR-1000RR	P	DNF	5
	Ryuichi Kiyonari	JPN	9	Ten Kate Honda Racing	Honda CBR-1000RR	P	DNF	3
	Karl Muggeridge	AUS	31	Team Suzuki Aistare	Suzuki GSX-R 1000 K9	P	DNF	3
	Tom Sykes	GB	66	Yamaha WSB	Yamaha YZF R1	P	DNF	1
	Lorenzo Lanzi	ITA	57	DFX Corse	Ducati 1098R	P	DNF	2

Race 2: 23 laps, 63.040m/101.453km, **Time Of Race:** 38m 00.282s, **Av speed:** 99.524mph/160.169km/h

Pos	Rider	Time & Gap	Laps		Superpole			Points (top 25)
1	Noriyuki Haga		23	1	Spies	1m 37.709s	1	Haga 436
2	Max Biaggi	1.480s	23	2	Rea	1m 38.191s	2	Spies 426
3	Jonathan Rea	6.024s	23	3	Fabrizio	1m 38.196s	3	Fabrizio 346
4	Ben Spies	18.135s	23	4	Biaggi	1m 38.235s	4	Biaggi 293
5	Leon Haslam	21.236s	23	5	Haga	1m 38.365s	5	Rea 279
6	Yukio Kagayama	23.647s	23	6	Haslam	1m 38.625s	6	Haslam 241
7	Shane Byrne	23.701s	23	7	Nieto	1m 38.670s	7	Checa C. 200
8	Karl Muggeridge	24.838s	23	8	Corser	1m 39.114s	8	Sykes 176
9	Carlos Checa	31.455s	23	9	Byrne	1m 38.831s	9	Byrne 166
10	Troy Corser	32.507s	23	10	Smrz	1m 38.844s	10	Smrz 161
11	Fonsi Nieto	37.594s	23	11	Muggeridge	1m 38.851s	11	Kiyonari 141
12	Ruben Xaus	44.727s	23	12	Checa C.	1m 38.924s	12	Kagayama 123
13	Michel Fabrizio	49.782s	23	13	Kagayama	1m 39.148s	13	Corser 89
14	Matteo Baiocco	50.345s	23	14	Sykes	1m 39.361s	14	Nakano 86
15	Broc Parkes	56.209s	23	15	Xaus	1m 39.444s	15	Laconi 77
16	David Salom	58.796s	23	16	Camier	1m 39.703s	16	Neukirchner 75
17	David Checa	1m 00.391s	23	17	Kiyonari	1m 39.816s	17	Xaus 66
18	Roland Resch	1m 20.777s	23	18	Baiocco	1m 39.868s	18	Parkes 42
19	Sheridan Morais	1m 24.318s	23	19	Parkes	1m 39.905s	19	Lagrive 24
	Leon Camier	DNF	15	20	Salom	1m 40.534s	20	Nieto 24
	Luca Scassa	DNF	14				21	Muggeridge 21
	Jakub Smrz	DNF	13				22	Hopkins 17
	Vittorio Iannuzzo	DNF	12				23	Simoncelli 16
	Tom Sykes	DNF	3				24	Lanzi 15
							25	Camier 13

Fastest race lap: Noriyuki Haga on lap 21, 1m 38.619s, 100.053mph/161.020km/h (new record).

Fastest race lap: Jonathan Rea on lap 14, 1m 38.662s, 100.010mph/160.950km/h.

Previous Lap record: Carlos Checa, SPA (Honda), 1m 39.384s, 98.835mph/159.060km/h (2008).

Round 14 • Portimão, Portugal • 25 October 2009 • 2.853-mile.4,592km circuit • WEATHER: (Race 1 • Dry • Track 33°C • Air 28°C) (Race 2 • Dry • Track 42°C • Air 30°C)

Race 1: 22 laps, 62.773m/101.024km, **Time Of Race:** 38m 15.390s, **Av speed:** 98.451mph/158.442km/h

Pos.	Rider	Nat.	No.	Entrant	Machine	Tyres	Time & Gap	Laps
1	Ben Spies	USA	19	Yamaha WSB	Yamaha YZF R1	P		22
2	Jonathan Rea	GB	65	HANNspree Ten Kate Honda	Honda CBR-1000RR	P	1.697s	22
3	Max Biaggi	ITA	3	Aprilia Racing	Aprilia RSV4	P	2.113s	22
4	Shane Byrne	GB	67	Sterilgarda	Ducati 1098R	P	2.757s	22
5	Michel Fabrizio	ITA	84	Ducati Xerox Team	Ducati 1098R	P	14.753s	22
6	Leon Camier	GB	22	Airwaves Yamaha	Yamaha YZF R1	P	20.044s	22
7	Carlos Checa	SPA	7	HANNspree Ten Kate Honda	Honda CBR-1000RR	P	25.634s	22
8	Ruben Xaus	SPA	111	BMW Motorrad Motorsport	BMW S1000 RR	P	31.104s	22
9	Matthieu Lagrive	FRA	22	Honda Althea Racing	Honda CBR-1000RR	P	36.689s	22
10	Matteo Baiocco	ITA	15	Guandalini Racing	Ducati 1098R	P	39.331s	22
11	Broc Parkes	AUS	23	Kawasaki World Superbike	Kawasaki ZX 10R	P	41.827s	22
12	Makoto Tamada	JPN	100	Kawasaki World Superbike	Kawasaki ZX 10R	P	41.882s	22
13	David Salom	SPA	25	Team Pedercini	Kawasaki ZX 10R	P	54.967s	22
14	David Checa	SPA	64	Yamaha France GMT 94 IP ONE	Yamaha YZF R1	P	1m 50.932s	18
15	Luca Scassa	ITA	99	Team Pedercini	Kawasaki ZX 10R	P	DNF	18
	Roland Resch	AUT	88	TKR Suzuki Switzerland	Suzuki GSX-R 1000 K9	P	DNF	19
	Troy Corser	AUS	11	BMW Motorrad Motorsport	BMW S1000 RR	P	DNF	16
	Leon Haslam	GB	91	Stiggy Racing Honda	Honda CBR-1000RR	P	DNF	10
	Jacub Smrz	CZE	96	Guandalini Racing	Ducati 1098R	P	DNF	8
	Sylvan Guintoli	FRA	50	Team Suzuki Aistare	Suzuki GSX-R 1000 K9	P	DNF	8
	Vittorio Iannuzzo	ITA	77	Squadra Corse Italia	Honda CBR-1000RR	P	DNF	7
	Noriyuki Haga	JPN	41	Ducati Xerox Team	Ducati 1098R	P	DNF	6
	Fonsi Nieto	SPA	10	DFX Corse	Ducati 1098R	P	DNF	3
	Yukio Kagayama	JPN	71	Suzuki Aistare BRUX	Suzuki GSX-R 1000 K9	P	DNF	0

Race 2: 22 laps, 62.773m/101.024km, **Time Of Race:** 38m 19.654s, **Av speed:** 98.269mph/158.148km/h

Pos	Rider	Time & Gap	Laps		Superpole			Points (top 25)
1	Michel Fabrizio		22	1	Spies	1m 42.412s	1	Spies 462
2	Noriyuki Haga	1.195s	22	2	Byrne	1m 42.996s	2	Haga 456
3	Jonathan Rea	1.494s	22	3	Fabrizio	1m 43.015s	3	Fabrizio 382
4	Shane Byrne	5.553s	22	4	Rea	1m 43.126s	4	Biaggi 319
5	Ben Spies	5.842s	22	5	Haslam	1m 43.943s	5	Rea 315
6	Max Biaggi	7.374s	22	6	Biaggi	1m 43.714s	6	Haslam 241
7	Leon Camier	9.658s	22	7	Nieto	1m 43.553s	7	Checa C. 209
8	Jacub Smrz	10.4348s	22	8	Corser	1m 44.719s	8	Byrne 192
9	Troy Corser	17.010s	22	9	Smrz	1m 43.240s	9	Sykes 176
10	Sylvan Guintoli	25.509s	22	10	Haga	1m 43.377s	10	Smrz 169
11	Yukio Kagayama	27.195s	22	11	Guintoli	1m 43.406s	11	Kiyonari 141
12	Broc Parkes	34.825s	22	12	Checa C.	1m 43.461s	12	Kagayama 128
13	Matthieu Lagrive	35.135s	22	13	Camier	1m 43.671s	13	Corser 96
14	Luca Scassa	1m 01.842s	22	14	Kagayama	1m 43.717s	14	Nakano 86
15	David Checa	1m 09.782s	22	15	Tamada	1m 44.050s	15	Laconi 77
16	Makoto Tamada	1m 30.818s	22	16	Baiocco	1m 45.439s	16	Neukirchner 75
17	David Salom	DNF	18	17	Lagrive	1m 44.453s	17	Xaus 74
	Matteo Baiocco	DNF	15	18	Parkes	1m 44.458s	18	Parkes 51
	Leon Haslam	DNF	8	19	Xaus	1m 44.483s	19	Lagrive 34
	Carlos Checa	DNF	7	20	Scassa	1m 44.851s	20	Camier 32
	Ruben Xaus	DNF	7				21	Nieto 24
	Fonsi Nieto	DNF	7				22	Muggeridge 21
	Vittorio Iannuzzo	DNF	3				23	Hopkins 17
							24	Baiocco 1
							25	Simoncelli 16

Fastest race lap: Michel Fabrizio on lap 4, 1m 43.529s, 99.218mph/159.677km/h (new record).

Fastest race lap: Michel Fabrizio on lap 8, 1m 43.720s, 99.036mph/159.383km/h.

Previous Lap record: Troy Bayliss, AUSP (Ducati), 1m 43.787s, 98.972mph/159.280km/h (2008).

WORLD SUPERBIKE CHAMPIONSHIP RIDERS POINTS TABLE

Position	Rider	Nationality	Machine	Phillip Island/1	Phillip Island/2	Losail/1	Losail/2	Valencia/1	Valencia/2	Assen/1	Assen/2	Monza/1	Monza/2	Kyalami/1	Kyalami/2	Miller/1	Miller/2	Misano/1	Misano/2	Donington Park/1	Donington Park/2	Brno/1	Brno/2	Nurburgring/1	Nurburgring/2	Imola/1	Imola/2	Magny-Cours/1	Magny-Cours/2	Portimao/1	Portimao/2	Total points
1	Ben Spies	USA	Yamaha	–	25	25	25	–	20	25	–	1	25	16	–	25	25	25	7	25	25	–	25	25	20	13	11	25	13	25	11	462
2	Noriyuki Haga	JPN	Ducati	25	20	20	20	25	25	20	25	20	–	25	25	7	8	11	16	16	–	8	10	20	–	25	20	20	25	–	20	456
3	Michel Fabrizio	ITA	Ducati	13	11	–	–	20	16	7	13	25	20	20	20	16	20	16	20	4	16	–	16	9	7	16	25	13	3	11	25	382
4	Max Biaggi	ITA	Aprilia	5	1	16	16	8	8	11	–	5	11	11	11	10	13	3	6	20	–	25	20	11	13	20	13	16	20	16	10	319
5	Jonathan Rea	GBR	Honda	11	7	4	8	–	3	9	11	11	13	13	16	11	16	9	25	9	1	16	13	13	25	9	10	–	16	20	16	315
6	Leon Haslam	GBR	Honda	10	16	5	5	11	11	16	20	–	9	–	13	6	–	4	8	13	20	9	4	10	11	10	8	11	11	–	–	241
7	Carlos Checa	SPA	Honda	4	3	11	3	–	10	–	9	7	6	10	10	20	–	5	11	5	–	20	11	16	16	–	6	10	7	9	–	209
8	Shane Byrne	GBR	Ducati	–	–	10	4	7	5	5	8	2	–	7	–	5	6	20	10	11	13	13	8	6	–	–	9	8	9	13	13	192
9	Tom Sykes	GBR	Yamaha	6	6	9	11	9	6	13	10	10	10	6	7	3	7	8	9	–	11	–	9	7	8	7	4	–	–	–	–	176
10	Jakub Smrz	CZE	Ducati	7	9	–	–	–	2	10	16	4	8	2	6	8	10	13	13	7	–	10	7	3	5	8	7	6	–	–	8	169
11	Ryuichi Kiyonari	JPN	Honda	–	–	8	13	4	7	1	–	16	16	4	3	13	11	–	2	6	9	3	3	2	9	11	–	–	–	–	–	141
12	Yukio Kagayama	JPN	Suzuki	16	8	–	1	10	–	–	4	13	–	8	8	4	4	10	5	–	3	2	–	1	6	1	–	9	10	–	5	128
13	Troy Corser	AUS	BMW	8	–	7	7	–	1	6	6	–	–	–	–	1	–	–	–	–	–	11	6	8	10	5	–	7	6	–	7	96
14	Shinya Nakano	JPN	Aprilia	1	4	13	9	–	–	–	–	3	4	9	9	–	9	7	3	10	–	–	5	–	–	–	–	–	–	–	–	86
15	Regis Laconi	FRA	Ducati	9	13	6	2	13	13	8	–	8	5	–	–	–	–	–	–	–	–	–	–	–	–	–	–	–	–	–	–	77
16	Max Neukirchner	GER	Suzuki	20	10	–	10	16	9	3	7	–	–	–	–	–	–	–	–	–	–	–	–	–	–	–	–	–	–	–	–	75
17	Ruben Xaus	SPA	BMW	–	5	3	6	3	–	2	5	9	7	–	–	–	2	–	1	7	–	–	–	–	4	3	5	4	8	–	–	74
18	Broc Parkes	AUS	Kawasaki	–	–	2	–	6	–	–	–	6	3	1	2	–	5	–	–	–	2	4	–	–	3	6	1	–	1	5	4	51
19	Matthieu Lagrive	FRA	Honda	–	–	–	–	–	–	–	–	–	–	–	–	–	–	6	–	–	–	4	7	2	5	–	–	–	–	7	3	34
20	Leon Camier	GBR	Yamaha/Aprilia	–	–	–	–	–	–	–	–	–	–	–	–	–	–	–	–	3	10	–	–	–	–	–	–	–	–	10	9	32
21	Fonsi Nieto	SPA	Suzuki/Ducati	–	–	–	–	–	–	–	–	–	–	1	–	3	–	4	–	–	5	–	–	–	4	–	–	–	5	–	–	22
22	Karl Muggeridge	AUS	Suzuki	–	–	–	–	–	–	4	–	–	–	–	–	–	–	–	–	–	–	–	–	–	4	3	2	–	8	–	–	21
23	John Hopkins	USA	Honda	–	–	–	5	4	–	–	–	–	–	–	–	–	–	–	–	–	8	–	–	–	–	–	–	–	–	–	–	17
24	Matteo Baiocco	ITA	Kawasaki/Ducati	–	–	–	–	–	–	–	2	–	1	–	–	–	–	–	–	–	–	–	–	–	2	–	4	2	6	–	–	17
25	Marco Simoncelli	ITA	Aprilia	–	–	–	–	–	–	–	–	–	–	–	–	–	–	–	–	–	–	–	–	–	16	–	–	–	–	–	–	16
26	Lorenzo Lanzi	ITA	Ducati	–	–	–	–	–	–	–	–	–	–	–	–	2	–	2	5	–	1	–	–	–	–	–	–	5	–	–	–	15
27	Makoto Tamada	JPN	Kawasaki	–	–	–	–	2	–	–	–	–	–	–	–	–	–	–	–	–	–	–	–	6	–	–	–	–	–	4	–	12
28	Gregorio Lavilla	SPA	Ducati	–	–	–	–	–	–	–	–	–	–	5	4	2	–	–	1	–	–	–	–	–	–	–	–	–	–	–	–	12
29	Luca Scassa	ITA	Kawasaki	–	–	–	–	–	–	1	–	2	–	–	–	–	–	–	–	–	–	–	–	–	2	–	–	3	–	1	2	11
30	Jamie Hacking	USA	Kawasaki	–	–	–	–	–	–	–	–	–	–	–	–	–	9	–	–	–	–	–	–	–	–	–	–	–	–	–	–	9
31	James Ellison	GBR	Yamaha	–	–	–	–	–	–	–	–	–	–	–	–	–	–	–	–	–	8	–	–	–	–	–	–	–	–	–	–	8
32	Sheridan Morais	RSA	Kawasaki	–	–	–	–	–	–	–	–	–	–	3	5	–	–	–	–	–	–	–	–	–	–	–	–	–	–	–	–	8
33	Sylvain Guintoli	FRA	Suzuki	–	–	–	–	–	–	–	–	–	–	–	–	–	–	–	–	–	–	–	–	–	–	–	–	–	–	–	6	6
34	Simon Andrews	GBR	Kawasaki	–	–	–	–	–	–	–	–	–	–	–	–	–	–	–	–	–	–	–	6	–	–	–	–	–	–	–	–	6
35	Tommy Hill	GBR	Honda	2	2	1	–	1	–	–	–	–	–	–	–	–	–	–	–	–	–	–	–	–	–	–	–	–	–	–	–	6
36	David Salom	SPA	Kawasaki	–	–	–	–	–	–	–	–	–	–	–	–	–	–	–	–	–	–	–	–	–	–	–	–	2	3	–	–	5
37	David Checa	SPA	Yamaha	–	–	–	–	–	–	–	–	–	–	–	–	–	–	–	–	–	–	–	–	–	–	–	–	1	–	2	1	4
38	Brendan Roberts	AUS	Ducati	–	–	–	–	–	–	3	–	–	–	–	–	–	–	–	–	–	–	–	–	–	–	–	–	–	–	–	–	3
39	Roberto Rolfo	ITA	Honda	3	–	–	–	–	–	–	–	–	–	–	–	–	–	–	–	–	–	–	–	–	–	–	–	–	–	–	–	3
40	Vittorio Iannuzzo	ITA	Honda	–	–	–	–	–	–	–	–	–	–	–	–	–	–	–	–	–	–	1	–	–	–	1	–	–	–	–	–	2
41	Alessandro Polita	ITA	Suzuki	–	–	–	–	–	–	–	–	–	–	–	–	–	–	–	1	–	–	–	–	–	–	–	–	–	–	–	–	1
42	Jake Zemke	USA	Honda	–	–	–	–	–	–	–	–	–	–	–	–	1	–	–	–	–	–	–	–	–	–	–	–	–	–	–	–	1

KING CAL
By GORDON RITCHIE

THERE were early signs that the 2009 championship would be contested between more riders than the usual two or three hardy annuals, thanks to pre-season testing and round one in Australia that saw the first five riders home covered by 1.098 seconds.

It was more of a surprise that the final duo to fight for the title were the two new kids, each old rivals from domestic racing in the UK, but each of whom had joined WSS from diametrically opposite directions.

Eventual winner Cal Crutchlow had won the British Supersport crown in 2006, but had arrived in the Yamaha World Supersport team (alongside 2002 champion and seasoned campaigner Fabien Foret) from an official Honda ride in BSB.

Eugene Laverty (Parkalgar Honda) had actually ridden twice as a substitute rider for the official Yamaha WSS squad in 2008, but only in between his regular commitments on an outpaced Aprilia 250 in GPs.

He had seen enough to let him know that WSS was a better career move, in the short term at least, and was snapped up by the British based Portuguese team representing Parkalgar.

The opponents that Crutchlow and Laverty overcame in their combined rookie year were formidable indeed.

Hannspree Ten Kate Honda had the two most recent champions, Andrew Pitt and Kenan Sofuoglu; Stiggy Honda had Anthony West (who made some short-lived but glorious WSS history for himself a couple of years before). Joan Lascorz was on an all-new official Kawasaki Ninja alongside seasoned race winner Katsuaki Fujiwara for the Provec Motocard.com squad. And 500cc GP winner Garry McCoy was on the official BE-1 Triumph Daytona 675 triple. Add in Mark Aitchison and Matthieu Lagrive on the Althea Hondas, plus fast Italians Massimo Roccoli (Intermoto Czech Honda) and Michele Pirro

(Lorenzini by Leoni Yamaha) and just for once a super-strength Superbike class had not been made up at the expense of WSS.

Just to make a full hand of competing factories, the Hoegee Suzuki team brought Barry Veneman and his strong GSX-R600 along as well.

There was no shortage of possibilities, but nobody really foresaw the final outcome of Englishman versus Ulsterman - even after Sofuoglu, Pitt and West had been followed home so closely by Crutchlow and Laverty in Australia.

Another astoundingly close race in Qatar saw the new boys stake their first joint podium claim. Laverty won, Pitt was second, Crutchlow third and Sofuoglu fourth - only 0.711 seconds from his second win of the year.

The return to Europe and some bizarre changing track conditions at Valencia allowed Crutchlow to dance to his first win, just ahead of West, but a telling eight seconds ahead of Sofuoglu. Having waited for Pitt to get going and to do some homework on his slick-track experience, Laverty left it too long and was only ninth. A hard lesson; forget the reputations of the other riders, go for the wins at your own pace.

He didn't have to wait too long, as Assen was his, but in what was becoming an unbelievably combative and close overall contest, Laverty won from Crutchlow and Lascorz, the margin of victory to third place this time only 0.178 seconds. Foret and Sofuoglu were 1.7 and 1.9 seconds back, Pitt a faller as he started losing front-end confidence.

Crutchlow made his Yamaha's engine speed tell at Monza, although one felt by now he could win on his paddock scooter, so much had his peerless pace been brought to bear on the thought processes of his main rivals. Except for Laverty. Lascorz was 2.6 back, with Foret and Laverty absolutely on his tail.

Logically, Kyalami was where Laverty and Crutchlow's lack of track knowledge should have

told against them. But psychologically it was the effective coup de grace from Cal and Eugene, as they attacked for the entire race, and Laverty won by 2.546 seconds from Crutchlow.

Aitchison scored his only podium of the year, but some 17 seconds from the win. Lascorz was right with him and had he and Sofuoglu not clashed on the final lap, Aitchison would surely have been fifth.

Pitt (sixth) and West (eighth) were by now losing all confidence in their Honda front ends, their 2009 machines proving a handful to set up.

Ten Kate had been a force in WSS forever, and Stiggy real high fliers in 2008. So it was a bitter double dose to have both the relatively tiny Parkalgar privateers as well as the Yamaha they used to beat almost routinely suddenly so far ahead.

Sofuoglu, with a fighting reputation on track despite his dearly held and calming religious beliefs, made a partial comeback at Miller, winning ahead of Laverty and Crutchlow, 0.521 seconds covering the top three. Lascorz was fourth, from pole, but 1.833 seconds back. Pitt was a huge 25 seconds behind his team-mate, West 31 seconds adrift and looking lost.

At half season, Crutchlow had 135 points, Laverty 126 and Sofuoglu 108.

A return to Europe and Misano saw Crutchlow edge out Laverty by 0.263 seconds. The next nearest challenger was Roccoli, having his one podium outing, albeit 16 seconds from the win.

Crutchlow had a heavy fall in practice, but still won the Donington round with a broken ankle and five seconds to spare over Lascorz. Garry McCoy and his BE-1 ParkinGO Triumph gave the British producer its first significant world championship podium for over 40 years. Laverty had fallen while in the leading bunch and lost time, finishing fifth, just ahead of Barry Veneman on a George White Ten Kate Honda. His Hoegee team had run out of money after America, leaving no Suzukis in the field.

Above: Eugene Laverty (top) and Cal Crutchlow rewrote everybody's expectations.

Above left: Crutchlow ended up narrowly the winner at his first attempt.

Right: GP winner Anthony West found his Honda difficult to set up.

Below: Belgian Simeon dominated the 1000 Superstock series.

Bottom right: Laverty and Crutchlow battled almost everywhere. Here Laverty is ahead.

Photos: Gold & Goose

Brno was a breeze for Yamaha. Sort of, as Crutchlow's long lead was suddenly cut when his machine stopped, but team-mate Foret took over, winning another thriller by 0.146 seconds from a somehow temporarily rejuvenated West. Lascorz and Fujiwara were third and fourth for Kawasaki, with 0.4 seconds covering the top four. Laverty was only fifth.

In Germany, home of his team even if it was managed by Dutchman Wilco Zeelenberg, Crutchlow was imperious, ten seconds better than Laverty and Lascorz. With testing at any track allowed for WSS riders, unlike their Superbike cousins, Crutchlow, Sofuoglu and Laverty had all been to a regular track day before the German round. A few of these 'tests' were conducted in 2009, a demonstration of the silliness of a rule that allows free testing but in a climate where no proper private tests could be afforded.

At Imola Laverty had the chance to catch up to Crutchlow and did so with second place in an aggregate race, behind Sofuoglu but ahead of Foret.

Crutchlow was out again after a spectacular crash over the top of the exit of Piratella/entrance to Acque Mineral, when his bike found a false neutral thanks to a glitch in its otherwise clever electronic system.

Laverty's inability to capitalise fully was no great problem for him with two rounds to go, as he had cut Crutchlow's lead to a measly two points. With Sofuoglu 57 behind, it was now simply Englishman v Ulsterman.

In France, the pressure told first on Laverty, as he fell by losing the front at the bottom of the hill, remounting to finish 13th. Crutchlow followed Lascorz home by just under a second, the Spanish rider getting a deserved win and into striking range of Sofuoglu for third overall.

At the final round, with 19 points to make up, Laverty worked extra hard on set-up for his Parkalgar team's home race.

His final push to pole and the eventual race win were a little too late to make a difference to his title ambitions, as Crutchlow's fourth place behind Sofuoglu and McCoy gave him the crown.

On balance the deserved overall win for Crutchlow would have come earlier had it not been for some outrageous bad luck, but his team had the final plea-sure of ending Ten Kate and Honda's seven year run of victories in this important showcase for roadgoing machines.

The effective effort by small-scale team Parkalgar, led by ex-GP rider Simon Buckmaster, was only just not quite enough. With Crutchlow they rewrote people's expectations both inside and outside the paddock.

Kudos also for the fighting spirit of Sofuoglu and the overall effort from Kawasaki and Lascorz, who ensured the traditional two-way Honda/Yamaha split should remain a thing of the past.

WSS racing will never be quite the same again, in a good way.

In the Superstock 1000 FIM Cup class Belgium's Xavier Simeon (Ducati Xerox) broke the usual rule that this class goes to the final round, scoring five wins and five second places to finish his season only 25 points from perfect, and 57 points ahead of Claudio Corti (Alstare Suzuki).

Maxime Berger (Ten Kate Honda), Javier Fores (Pedercini Kawasaki) and Sylvain Barrier (Garnier Yamaha) made sure that five different manufacturers would finish inside the top five.

In the Superstock 600 European Championship Englishman Gino Rea (Ten Kate Honda) held off a horde of Yamahas on his Honda, winning one race at Assen and the title by only a single point, from Marco Bussolotti (Yamaha Italia Jr. Trasimeno). The top four, Rea, Bussolotti, Vincent Lonbois and Danilo Petrucci, were all within eight points.

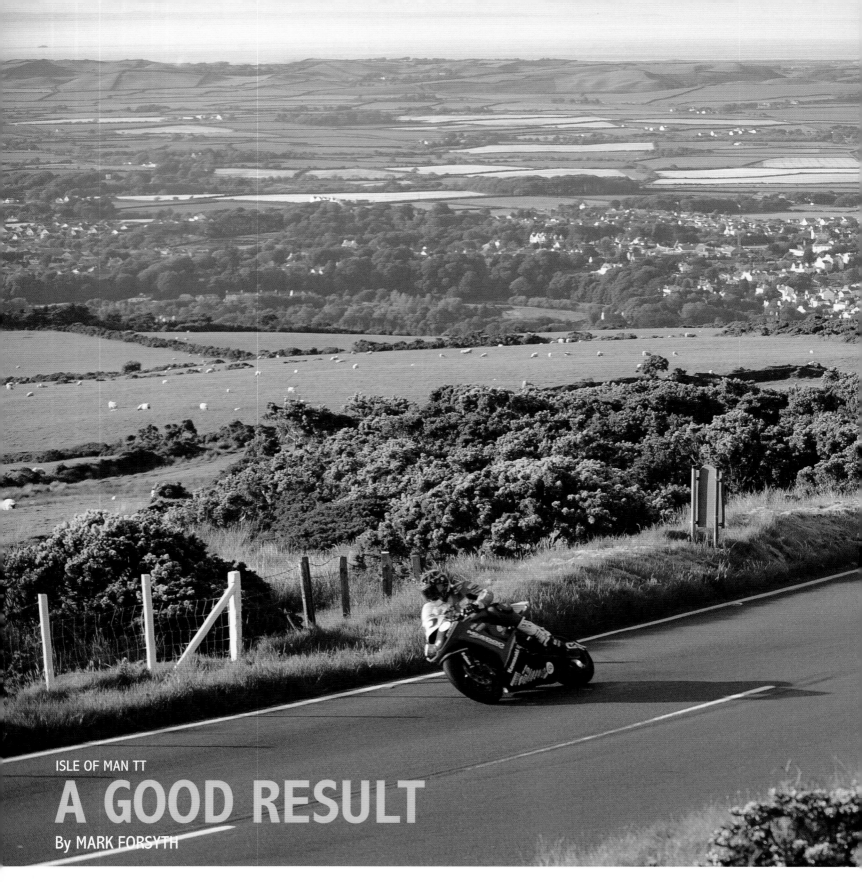

A GOOD RESULT

By MARK FORSYTH

HONDA marked the 50th anniversary of its racing history with a fair degree of serious intent at the 2009 Isle of Man TT. The island holds special significance for the Japanese company, as it marks the spot where the Honda Motor Company first set out its stall back in 1959.

The official HM Plant Honda team wheeled out the big guns, with TT legend John McGuinness and super-talented rookie Steve Plater. If that wasn't enough, Guy Martin and Gary Johnson rode their CBRs for the well-run Hyrdex and Uel Duncan squads respectively. With Keith Amor fielding Hondas for the Wilson Craig outfit, and softly-spoken, but devilishly quick Yorkshireman Ian Hutchinson riding for Padgetts, Honda looked to have all its birthday-party

bases covered. In the three-wheeled corner, the extremely capable Nick Crowe and Mark Cox looked after Honda's outfit interests.

On paper, it looked like a cakewalk before anyone even had turned a wheel. In reality, however, Honda's opposition was formidable.

As practice got under way under distinctly untypical clear blue skies, Honda's worst nightmare began to unfold. The hard charging Antipodean duo of Cameron Donald and Bruce Anstey nudged their Relentless TAS Suzukis into the exclusive 130mph club, and that clearly rattled TT supremo McGuinness. It would get even worse.

On Thursday night, Cameron Donald edged his K9 GSX-R1000 to an all-time unofficial lap record – a

staggering 131.457mph.

"I saw the helicopter following me, so I wondered if I was on a good one, but I didn't look at the clock as I came down [the mountain]. It was a really comfortable lap, too; there's so much grip out there I wouldn't be at all surprised if a few other guys go that fast," said Donald during the post-practice interviews.

Just mentioning this feat to McGuinness that evening drew a reaction that spoke volumes about the kind of event the TT has become. He had been plagued by a misfire in the same session, so had been unable to respond. Looking drawn and pressured, he played down the significance of Donald's lap and quoted the mantra that practice didn't matter; it was the race that counted. You had to

feel sorry for him, though. In an event where you lay your life on the line to bring home the bacon for your sponsors and fans, the last thing you want is extra pressure from someone else. His face told the story: he looked bothered, older than his years.

But McGuinness's stoical pragmatism was to prove absolutely correct and proper. Even though the talk of the paddock, Press room, bars, radio, web forums and newspapers had been of Donald's white-hot pace in the dying minutes of Thursday evening's practice, the TT's unforgiving nature was about to play into McGuinness's hands.

On the next evening – the last practice session before racing was scheduled to begin – Donald

rode his Superstock-specification GSX-R1000 and missed a gear going into Keppel Gate, the quick downhill left-hander before Kate's Cottage. As a result, he ran wide on the exit, on to the grass bank, and lost control, dislocating his shoulder and chipping a vertebrae in the ensuing accident.

The young Aussie was airlifted to Nobles, and it didn't take long for news to filter back that he was out of the 2009 TT. But McGuinness was wrong. Practice did matter. To finish first, first you must finish.

So, with the tattooed, seemingly fearless Donald out of the event, it looked like it might go all HM Plant Honda's way in the big-bike classes. But race week is a long week…

The Island shows its fairest face to Conor Cummings and Adrian Archibald as they round Joey's Bend.
Photo: Gavan Caldwell

SUPERBIKE TT

Practice week's balmy summer conditions were scotched come race day. Saturday broke bleak, windy and wet, giving the organisers little choice but to cancel the proceedings, delaying the start of the Senior TT and Sidecar race until a much sunnier Monday.

Gary Johnson led the race away on his Robinson's Concrete Honda, but by Glen Helen, McGuinness was already two seconds in front of Conor Cummins, with Hutchinson third and Plater reeling in Johnson for fourth. McGuinness passed Johnson on the road going into Ramsey and pulled ahead of Cummins.

McGuinness's blistering 129.799mph opening lap put him five seconds in front. On lap two, he upped the gap, now over Martin, by ten seconds with a flying lap at record pace. His speed, including a pit stop, was 130.442mph! Manxman Cummins encountered trouble at his pit stop and never recovered, eventually suffering engine failure on his McAdoo Kawasaki on the final lap.

By lap three, the running order was McGuinness, Plater and Martin. The gap between Plater and team-mate McGuinness see-sawed for the rest of the six-lap race, but it appeared that when Plater closed the gap, McGuinness was comfortable enough to respond to his pit boards and up the ante in defence.

Watched by a suitably impressed Valentino Rossi, there to ride a much publicised closed-road lap, Mc-

Guinness took the flag, with Plater second and Guy Martin third. For Honda, it was something more of a success, its dominant Fireblade taking control of the first five positions in the first major race of the week.

For McGuinness, it meant much more. A new lap record and his 15th TT win would go some way to helping his employer to celebrate its half-century. "It was a bit dusty and there wasn't much grip out there for the first couple of laps, but I knew I had to go hard from the start, which is what I have done in the past to make a bit of a break," said McGuinness. "The team told me Steve was catching me, so on lap five I had a real good go and was able to cruise on the last lap. I'm over the moon with my 15th TT win, and I can't really believe it. It's about time some of these lads kicked my arse!"

SIDECAR TT – Race One

Veteran Dave Molyneux recorded his 14th TT win an impressive 20 years after his first. The margin of victory was almost a minute, but the Manxman, with passenger Dan Sayle, had inherited the race.

Until half-distance, Nick Crowe and Mark Cox had set the pace, before retiring from the lead at Greeba. Third-placed John Holden retired at Black Dub.

Philip Dongworth and Gary Partridge finished second, Simon Neary and Stuart Bond third. Tragically, Dongworth lost his life at the Southern 100 event a month later.

SUPERSPORT TT – Race One

There was yet more heartbreak for TAS Relentless Suzuki. After 2008's technical infringement exclusion had denied them of a Supersport win, in 2009, its star rider, Bruce Anstey, compounded the misery by running out of fuel.

The Kiwi held a comfortable seven-second lead when his GSXR600 coughed and spluttered to a halt at Brandywell on lap four.

Anstey's downfall was Ian Hutchinson's good fortune, and the Yorkshireman took his Padgetts Honda to the inherited win, with Guy Martin second and a hard charging Keith Amor third.

SUPERSTOCK TT

Hutchinson made it two wins in a day with victory in the Superstock. The Padgetts Honda rider also broke the Superstock lap record, with a best of 129.746mph. Hutchinson's pace served as a startling reminder of just how good the near-stock Superstock bikes have become.

Strangely, the Superstock podium mirrored the earlier Supersport podium, with Hydrex Honda's Guy Martin taking second a little under nine seconds behind Hutchinson, and Scotsman Keith Amor finishing on the final step.

"It's unbelievable. I might ride the Superstock bike on Friday if it can do that," said Hutchinson afterwards.

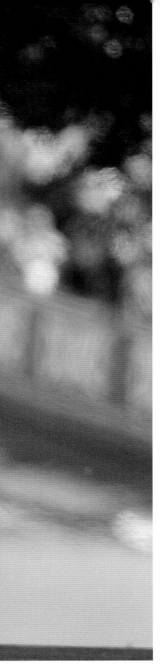

Left: Modern TT master McGuinness flies to victory in the Superbike race, his sole win of the week.

Below: Molyneux and Sale took the honours in the first Sidecar race.

Photos David Collister

Relentless Suzuki's luck didn't improve in the Superstock race, either. 'Mr Superstock' Bruce Anstey retired on lap one at the pits.

SUPERSPORT TT — Race Two

The second Supersport race was a real cliffhanger, where only the brave were rewarded with the spoils of success. Bad weather in the west of the island forced the organisers to postpone the start of the race for two hours. By the time it did get under way, the hailstones may have stopped, but rain in the Glen Helen section still made conditions treacherous and hard to read. Reduced-adhesion flags were being shown from the sixth milestone all the way to Ballaugh Bridge, equating to nearly a third of a lap.

By the end of the first lap, it was clear which riders were prepared to take more chances. Michael Dunlop blasted his Yamaha R6 into an early lead, controlling proceedings from the front in a masterful display of riding in changeable, lethally unpredictable conditions.

Dunlop was never challenged and took the win from Anstey; Conor Cummins gained his first ever TT podium with third .

Guy Martin had been charging hard, but clearly had a problem, as he started to slip down the order. The outspoken Hydrex Honda rider pitted and retired on the third lap with yet another suspected head-gasket failure, his second of the week on the smaller Supersport machine. The unsuspecting pit-lane commentator thrust a microphone under Martin's chin for his reaction to his retirement. To all us radio listeners, it was almost predictable. Martin greeted the question with a flurry of f-shaped expletives and the suggestion that he was just nipping off to deliver a large 'slap' to a certain member of the team. It shouldn't have been a race highlight, but…

Dunlop was clearly delighted with this major victory. "It was my spare bike and all. That's just great.

My dad gave me the knowledge, and he was there on the last lap. It's unbelievable," he said. Touching as well, bearing in mind what the lad's been through.

SIDECAR TT — Race Two

It's unusual for a race to be red-flagged at the Isle of Man, but that's just what happened on the first lap of the second sidecar race. The HM Plant Honda pairing of Nick Crowe and Mark Cox was involved in a high-speed accident at Ballacob on the sixth-gear run up to Ballaugh Bridge.

The cause was allegedly a hare on the racing line; the resulting impact and accident left both rider and passenger in a life threatening condition, and the track blocked by debris and fire. Crowe and Cox were airlifted to Nobles hospital, and the remaining outfits were sent the wrong way around the circuit back to the grandstand area.

Crowe and Cox's disastrous accident not only put a premature end to the second sidecar race of the week, but also curtailed the final Senior practice, due to take place later that evening, such was the damage to that area of the circuit. Witnesses described the scene as like that of a aircraft crash.

SENIOR TT

McGuinness set about the Senior race in a determined fashion. Fresh from his disappointing Supersport result, where he had finished outside the top ten, the 37-year-old wasted no time in breaking free from the chasing pack, setting a new lap record at a stunning 131.578mph as he built a 23-second gap over the pursuing Plater.

But it wasn't to be. McGuinness's chain snapped on the run up to Ramsey on lap four, and the despondent Lancastrian coasted to a halt, bereft of drive.

McGuinness wasn't the only member of the chain gang, Guy Martin's chain shed a link as he entered the pits for a scheduled stop. This time, however, the radio commentator didn't take any chances and gave him a wide berth.

McGuinness had looked unassailable, despite pressure from team-mate Plater. But with McGuinness out, HM Plant Honda's expectations now lay with Plater, and he didn't disappoint, taking the win in the rain shortened race to uphold Honda's birthday honours.

Tellingly, however, two future stars of the island also made a podium appearance. Hutchinson had slid off at Quarter Bridge and, with Martin out, the podium's final two steps were filled by Conor Cummins on his McAdoo ZX-10R Kawasaki and young upstart Gary Johnson on his Robinson Concrete backed Honda. Surely 2010 will see these two riders in contention for race wins as their course experience improves.

The event was marred by the death of 58-year-old campaigner John Crellin, after he lost control of his machine at Mountain Box. Manxman Crellin was an experienced TT rider and a design engineer. Earlier the same day, he was on the rostrum in the zero-emissions TTX race; in an earlier interview, he had said his idea of a perfect day was "a good result from a TT race".

TTX GP

Rob Barber took victory for Team Agni in the first ever TTXGP, a ground-breaking, zero-emissions one-lap sprint, run in two classes: Pro – for battery powered electric racing prototypes, fuel-cell or hydrogen powered machines, and hybrids; and Open – for lower-level electric bikes. There were 20 entrants, all but four in the Pro class, as battery powered prototypes.

In conditions reminiscent of pioneering TT races in the early 1900s, nobody was entirely sure how many of the field would actually make a full lap without having to jump off to push.

But Barber's battery powered GSX-R Suzuki-based machine set an official lap record of 87.434mph – fast enough to silence many critics. Perhaps even more impressive was the fastest recorded speed-trap figure on Sulby Straight: 106.5mph, set by Schoenfelder's XXL Racing Team machine.

Pre-race favourite Barber was leading on the road and on corrected time when he reached Glen Helen, nearly half a minute clear of Shoenfelder, with James McBride in third. By Ballaugh, McBride was in second, only to break down in Ramsey, promoting Schoenfelder back into second with Mark Buckley in third.

The top three remained constant across the

mountain, and Barber crossed the line some three minutes in front of Schoenfelder, with Buckey another 50 seconds in arrears. All three were in the TTX Pro class.

In a distinctly early-20th-century twist, Chris Heath was disqualified and then reinstated as TTX Open class race winner – for not sounding his horn while under red-flag conditions. Chris Petty was second and John Crellin third.

STEAM PACKET LIGHTWEIGHT AND ULTRA-LIGHTWEIGHT TT

To many dyed-in-the-wool enthusiasts, it seems a shame that the two-stroke classes have been overlooked on the Mountain Circuit. Without their shrill cry and exotic odours, the pure race machines weren't able to offer any relief from the monotony of road-bike-based racing during race and practice week.

Instead, for the second year in succession, the 125 and 250cc machines were relegated to the Billown public-road circuit near Castletown – every bit as fast and dangerous, but, at just 4.25 miles long, nowhere near as challenging and much easier to learn quickly.

Ian Lougher, the circuit's outright lap record holder, took three wins to Chris Palmer's one.

BRIGHT SPARKS
The electric motorcycle gets serious

WHEN Rob Barber crossed the line at the end of the first, and only, lap of the 'Electric' TT. a lot of people were very, very impressed. Riding for the low-budget Anglo-Indian Team Agni, Barber was using a virtually standard Suzuki GSX-R750 chassis and rolling gear with two of Cedric Lynch's finest motors bolted on.

Lynch has been racing battery-powered vehicles for years. One of his early car drivers was a young man called Arvind Rabadia. He now runs Agni Motors, the producer of Lynch's latest electric-motor designs.

Lynch motors are like biscuit tins; a typical bike application would have an armature 30mm wide and 200mm in diameter. Fitted with two Agni '95 reinforced' DC motors outside the frame in the cooling wind, the bike had a peak power output of more than 70bhp and a continuous maximum of 42bhp. Power was supplied by Kokam Lithium Ion Polymer batteries weighing 86kg. The power available, monitored by a cheap digital voltage meter strapped to the top fork clamp, was just enough to cover a single lap at a speed in excess of the existing 50cc lap record.

Efficiency is a key. Lynch's motors are about 93-per-cent efficient, which dictates the weight of the batteries needed. People like Lynch bring a spec-tacularly perceptive view to our very conservative speciality, criticising in particular the current restrictions on aerodynamic bodywork, which in turn limit the eventual range.

For those used to petrol fuelled vehicles, the choice of controller – the device that converts the rider's twist-grip input to motive progress – is critical to rider feel and power use. Lynch has very specific preferences. "My favourite controller is a Brusa, from a small firm in Switzerland. They make AC controllers; DC ones are a special order.

"It's nice, because it controls the current. It gives *torque* proportional to how far you turn the throttle. Most of the DC controllers control the *speed* in proportion to the throttle, which is horrible on any vehicle that goes in excess of 10mph.

"On the race bike, we used a Kelly, which allows a choice of voltage or current, but their designers always try to get too clever and stick in micro processors that have faulty logic. The Kelly has a stage where you are coasting and [if] you apply a bit of throttle, it initially holds back, with a slight braking force. Apply a bit more, and it goes back to coasting, then you apply more throttle, and finally it accelerates. The Brusa, though, is very simple, just a nice simple system, which doesn't have any problems." Power is nothing without control.

Neil Spalding

Above: Beaming race winner Steve Plater grapples with the Senior TT Trophy – road-racing's Oscar.

Above left: TT racing at its breathtaking best – the fast run through Kirkmichael.
Photos: Gavan Caldwell

Top: Joey's son Michael returned the Dunlop name to the top of the TT results sheets with a brave Supersport win.

By OLLIE BARSTOW

I F one word were used to describe the 2009 MCE British Superbike Championship, it would be *change*. From welcomes to farewells, bold leaps to sidesteps, surprises to the odd raised eyebrow, there was very little about the 2009 season that could be mistaken for the previous year.

Indeed, change was the recurring theme throughout the season. Yet while rider swaps, injuries and controversies conspired to divert attention from the on-track action, there was always one constant – Leon Camier.

The statistics make for compelling reading. In 26 races, Camier was victorious on 19 occasions, while nine pole positions in 12 events, 18 fastest laps and a winning margin of 136.5 points gave the 23-year-old a series of BSB records.

As the only high-profile rider to have entered a consecutive season with the same team, Camier may have been the cautious title favourite heading into the New Year, but GSE Racing's switch to the pioneering 'big-bang' Yamaha R1 meant that he was no more prepared than his nearest rivals.

There were plenty of new faces in new places as the opening round at Brands Hatch approached. With the leading protagonists from 2008 – Shane Byrne, Leon Haslam, Tom Sykes and Cal Crutchlow – all having left for pastures new, a shortfall of 'big names' threatened to undermine the series' allure.

Nonetheless, the headlines during the off-season should have been enough to whet the appetite of any fan mourning the defection of the 'big four'. These confirmed that reigning champion team GSE Racing would embark on a new chapter by severing its ties with Ducati in favour of a new relationship with Yamaha. That meant that not a single variant of the title winning bike would appear on the grid at the start of 2009.

Byrne's defection also heralded a revised rider line-up for GSE, Camier being joined by James Ellison, whose sterling efforts on the unfancied Hydrex Honda had earned him a plum deal with the Airwaves backed team.

The significance of GSE Racing's bike switch was almost rivalled by Honda and Suzuki's enticing new rider line-ups, following a shake-up over the winter. Haslam and Crutchlow's departure from HM Plant Honda after a single season led the team to look Down Under for its 2009 pairing, luring Josh Brookes from the world stage and British Supersport champion Glen Richards.

Crescent Suzuki, meanwhile, lost its key sponsor in Rizla, which forced it to run to a single bike in 2009, but it gained MotoGP's Sylvain Guintoli. Completing the manufacturer set, Kawasaki entered into a deal with the rebranded MSS Colchester team to sign its top 2008 representative, Simon Andrews,

and endurance racer Julien Da Costa.

Additionally, myriad privateer entrants were waiting in the wings to take their fight to the factories. Yamaha extended its relationship with Rob Mac Racing to run three bikes for Chris Walker, Graeme Gowland and Michael Rutter; Hydrex Honda signed Karl Harris and its Macau GP winner, Stuart Easton; Relentless by TAS Suzuki nabbed Atsushi Watanabe from Crescent and promoted its Supersport racer Ian Lowry; while Buildbase Kawasaki (née Hawk Kawasaki) grew to enter John Laverty and Tristan Palmer.

In all, 20 championship-class riders arrived at the Brands Hatch curtain raiser. All but one were with a new team or on a new bike.

With much of the pre-season testing having taken place behind closed doors – or, in GSE Racing's case, not at all – it wasn't until action got under way officially at the traditional Easter weekend opener at Brands Hatch that there was an opportunity to rank the title contenders.

Even so, few would have anticipated the early running to be made by Harris. The former Yamaha rider settled into his new surroundings at Hydrex Honda with aplomb, however, by topping four of the six practice sessions that preceded the race weekend. Not that this mattered when qualifying came around, though, since he was unable to translate

Left: This was the other riders' usual view of Camier, in his record-breaking season. He'd switched bikes, but not teams.

Below: Stuart Easton plays leader of the pack as the series gets under way at Brands Hatch.

Photos: Clive Challinor

his confident start into anything more than fourth on the grid.

Instead, the spotlight fell on Guintoli, whose stealthy progress through the weekend on the Crescent Suzuki – resplendent in the colours of new backer, Worx – was rewarded with a convincing pole on his competitive Superbike debut, also the first of his career for nine years.

Guintoli duly converted the position into a similarly impressive victory come race day, although he had to work hard for the win after a tardy getaway dropped him to as low as sixth as the field swept into Paddock Hill Bend for the first time. Nonetheless, while his start demonstrated his lack of experience aboard a Superbike, his swift rise through the order on a circuit that offered few overtaking opportunities was more eye-catching than a lights-to-flag victory would have been.

Still, he was helped a little along the way when Harris and Steve Plater – riding the HM Plant Honda after visa irregularities had forced Josh Brookes to skip the opener – fell while battling for the lead, while Richards and Easton faded as they settled for second and third.

While Guintoli had drawn first blood, what followed in race two would ultimately set the tone for the remainder of the season, Camier demonstrating that a lack of testing miles doesn't necessarily hamper a naturally fast machine. A first victory for a bike that GSE team manager Colin Wright insisted was only running at 75 per cent of its potential was an ominous sign of what was to come for Camier's rivals, as he comfortably beat Guintoli and Plater for a fourth career win.

Having obtained valuable performance data, Camier and his Airwaves Yamaha were in even greater form when the series moved on to Oulton Park, where he took pole position and two fairly easy victories.

While bad starts – a recurring theme for Camier in 2009 – would prompt a spirited victory contention from Harris, there was only ever one likely winner. Even so, a pair of second-place finishes for Harris

marked a career high point and went some way to amending for a disappointing opener at Brands Hatch, where he could manage no better than a solitary sixth.

Erstwhile championship leader Guintoli made it identical podiums in both races, while Ellison, Easton and Richards maintained their competitive form from the opener to play a supporting role just behind. The weekend also heralded the first appearance of Brookes, who got his belated chance to sample the rigours of BSB racing with a modest run to tenth.

If his maiden outing could be considered low profile, then his second event at Donington Park would propel him to the other end of the scale after becoming embroiled in a controversial accident with Guintoli, one that would eliminate the Frenchman for much of the season.

They clashed on the sighting lap, and the collision – which was blamed on Brookes – left Guintoli nursing a badly broken leg. It was a substantial loss to the series, particularly after his remarkably quick transition to Superbike racing. Although he would return later in the year, any hopes of a title challenge ended in the Melbourne hairpin gravel trap.

Once again, Airwaves Yamaha was the team to beat, but this time honours were shared between Camier and Ellison. Having swept to victory in race one, Camier was consigned to a lowly 12th in the second after a mysterious technical issue delayed him.

His problems allowed Ellison to celebrate a convincing maiden BSB victory, denying Easton a similar feat. Almost as happy was the man in third, Walker having made a welcome return to the podium after a gutsy ride on the Motorpoint/Henderson backed Yamaha.

Having triumphed in five of the six races thus far, Airwaves Yamaha continued its roll around the fast stretches of the fearsome Thruxton circuit, where Camier resumed his place at the top of the timesheets by securing a second clean sweep.

Poor starts aside, Camier was in devastating form

on the now fully sorted R1, which had successfully avoided many of the teething issues associated with a delayed testing programme. With speed matched by reliability, there was added significance for GSE Racing at Thruxton as Ellison matched Camier move-for-move around the Hampshire track to record a double 1-2 for the clear title favourite.

Guintoli having been forced on to the sidelines, those disputing his role as challenger to the GSE pair became a focal points at Thruxton. The pretenders weren't appearing from the usual sources, however.

With Harris and Richards unable to maintain their momentum from the early stages of the season, Easton emerged as best of the rest with a fourth podium in six races, while his former team, MSS Colchester Kawasaki, had also become a front-runner thanks to Andrews. Indeed, having created a stir with a career-best fourth at Donington Park, Andrews was a podium contender again on the unfancied ZX-10R at Thruxton. He would just miss out, though, settling for another fourth.

Step forward Brookes, who shrugged off the negative publicity surrounding his Donington Park *faux pas* to put in a striking performance in race two, battling his way up to third from ninth on the grid. Displaying a greater affinity with the HM Plant Honda, the Australian's rise to the rostrum was an exciting development for the series.

A return to a happy hunting ground for Camier promptly beckoned with a trip to Norfolk and the Snetterton circuit, scene of his first ever BSB victory in 2008. Another double here lifted his tally to eight victories in just ten races – former team-mate and mentor Byrne had been on seven at this stage of a season that he went on to dominate completely.

Camier delivered with a commanding performance on both occasions. There were even flashes of 'Shakey' in the way he went about his wins, dropping as low as sixth in race one before systematically clawing his way back up the order and passing Easton for the lead.

In race two, triumph followed a first-corner posi-

tion of fifth, Camier being trailed by Ellison to complete another successful day for the seemingly unbeatable GSE team.

Buoyed by his Thruxton display, Brookes was similarly quick at Snetterton as he racked up podiums two and three around the Norfolk circuit, while Superbike rookie Lowry turned a few heads with runs to sixth and fifth on the Relentless Suzuki.

Crossing the border into Scotland for the jaunt to Knockhill, all eyes were on Camier once again to see whether he could make it six in a row. He didn't capture the headlines come the end of qualifying, however, as Brookes emerged fastest from the knockout session.

Comparing the undulating Fife circuit to more familiar Australian venues, Brookes was immediately at home around Knockhill and denied Camier a sixth straight pole. HM Plant Honda also courted headlines for a different reason, however, after a high-speed accident involving Richards left him with a broken leg. Another big name to fall by the wayside, Richards – like Guintoli – wouldn't display the same front-running form on his return later in the year.

Unfortunately for HM Plant, Brookes couldn't capitalise on his position come race day. The former World Superbike rider put up a good fight against Camier, but ultimately was forced to settle for second best. Home favourite Easton rallied hard on the sister Hydrex Honda, but he too was unable to convert early leads in both races into anything more than a second and third. Camier took little time in dispatching the local lad, easing to victories nine and ten, and in doing so, matching Byrne's tally for a whole year with only half of the season completed.

Andrews continued to show impressive pace on the Kawasaki with a fourth and fifth, while Suzuki's unlikely top representative at the end of race two was Tommy Bridewell. On the three-year-old bike last ridden by his late brother, Ollie, who had been tragically killed in an accident at Mallory Park in 2007, Bridewell finished inside the top ten in both races on only his second outing aboard the ageing Team NB machine. He finished ahead of the Worx Crescent

and Relentless Suzuki riders, the result being one of a series of stand-out performances delivered by the Privateer Cup contingent.

Prior to that, all attention on the independent front had been trained on Gary Mason, who was back in BSB with minnow Quay Garage Honda. While his two-year-old machine was far from contemporary, Mason's giant killing antics certainly belied the fact as he qualified on the front row at Thruxton – a first for a privateer entrant – and scored in ten of the first 12 races. With six top-ten results, he held down a similar position in the overall standings, too.

As the season moved into its second half with a trip to Mallory Park, the rider 'merry-go-round' was well in effect, with Michael Rutter landing at SMT Honda, having also completed three events for Suzuki as Guintoli's deputy, and Superstock champion Steve Brogan being promoted to HM Plant's Superbike team as the replacement for Richards. The most notable change, however, was Tommy Hill, who, having lost his Althea Honda ride in the World Championship, was making his return to the domestic scene on the Worx Crescent Suzuki.

Hill didn't waste time in making his presence felt, immediately gelling with the GSX-R1000 to set the pace during free practice. However, while Camier had endured a troublesome weekend to that point, he was still quick enough to deny Hill pole.

Not that qualifying positions mattered come race day, as the notoriously quirky circuit would deliver one of the most controversial rounds in BSB history. Camier was the first to hit problems, his slow start sucking him into the treacherous midfield, where he paid the price when Richard Cooper, who had qualified an outstanding fourth on the Superstock-spec Co-ordit Yamaha, tumbled in front of him. Brought to a halt and forced to touch down, Camier had to wait for the field to stream through before he could circumnavigate the stricken privateer.

With Camier out of contention, the dispute for victory fell to Easton, Hill, Walker and Andrews. Four became three when Easton retired with mechanical problems, leaving the rest to enjoy an entertaining

Left: Bikes and bodies everywhere at Cadwell Park. The six-rider hairpin crash was triggered by Josh Brookes, who was suspended for this second indiscretion.

Below: Ex-MotoGP racer Sylvain Guintoli won the first race, but fell victim to Brookes at the second round, and missed most of the year.

Bottom: BSB veteran Walker on the way to the rostrum in the wet at Mallory: the fans' favourite made the top three only twice.

Photos: Clive Challinor

scrap for the lead.

Unbeknown to them, however, was that Brookes was cutting a determined figure in fourth. The Aussie had endured a dismal weekend thus far, after qualifying towards the back of the grid, but having capitalised on the chaotic opening bend, he was charging up the order.

As the top three tripped over one another, Brookes was now well in the victory equation with several laps remaining. Andrews, meanwhile, was in the lead, having snatched it from Walker, while Hill kept a watching brief in second.

Unfortunately, all three would find themselves in the wrong place at the wrong time when Brookes got it all wrong on a bump while braking for the hairpin. He was catapulted from his CBR1000RR before even reaching the bend, both rider and machine skittling the trio ahead of them in spectacular fashion.

The distraction ahead would catch out John Laverty – heading for a career-best result on the Buildbase Kawasaki – and Karl Harris as well, both being forced to hit the deck in avoidance. With the red flag deployed and the result declared, there was a further shock when Ellison was announced the winner.

Although many had expected the results to be counted back a lap – making Andrews the winner – the rule book states that those not upright at the time of the red flag cannot be counted. Consequently, Andrews, Hill, Walker, Brookes, Laverty and Harris would not be classified. Instead, Ellison, who had negotiated his way through the carnage, was given the victory, while the recovering Camier made it a familiar Airwaves Yamaha 1-2. Motorpoint/Henderson Yamaha's Graeme Gowland looked equally bemused with third.

The fall-out from Brookes' actions was played out on live television, with several team bosses expressing their dismay at his involvement in another detrimental accident. A ban of two rounds ensued.

The second race proved almost as dramatic, as torrid weather conditions forced an early stoppage and the awarding of half-points. Even so, an 11th win of the year for Camier made it a familiar story,

while second for Ellison completed another rewarding day for the team after a poor start. Walker and Laverty made some amends with third and fourth, while Cooper – who made BSB history by becoming the first privateer to lead a race overall – completed a popular top-five finish.

More positive publicity surrounded the next event at Brands Hatch, arranged as a replacement for the canned World Superbike round at the Kent circuit. It was the first ever triple-header event, and it provided a welcome wild-card appearance from the Kawasaki WSBK team, as well as the opportunity to witness Camier rewrite the record books.

Indeed, having established a three-figure advantage over his nearest rival in the overall standings, Camier's title win was no longer in question – it was whether he could surpass Niall Mackenzie's record of 13 victories in a single season.

Broc Parkes was making his presence felt, though, the Aussie on the Paul Bird Motorsport ZX-10R matching Camier's pace throughout the weekend. Launching a victory challenge in all three races, Parkes ultimately would fall just short of getting the edge on his opponent.

Camier's three visits to the top of the podium that weekend would indeed push him past Mackenzie's 12-year-old record, a remarkable feat in itself, but, with nine races remaining, one that was not over yet.

Not even the fearsome Cadwell Park – scene of a horrific leg injury for Camier two years before – could halt his charge. Even the wisps of smoke escaping from the R1 wouldn't prevent him from crossing the line for yet another double... On the other hand,

race officials couldn't ignore it, and with Camier failing to recognise the black and orange flags, he was promptly disqualified.

Ellison was promoted to first for his second fortuitous win of the year, while Easton followed for his second rostrum finish of the weekend. Andrews had reason to celebrate, too, as he inherited a maiden podium for himself and the MSS Colchester team.

Cadwell Park also heralded the welcome return of Guintoli, the Frenchman posting a pair of respectable results as he worked on bolstering his confidence and fitness after almost four months out of action.

Guintoli displaced Hill from the Worx Crescent team, but the latter landed another deal almost straight away at Hydrex, in place of Harris, who had fallen out of favour since his promising start to the season. Reacquainting himself with Honda machinery from Croft onwards, Hill wasn't the only rider in unfamiliar surroundings, for Harris returned to Rob Mac Yamaha, while HM Plant Honda welcomed back its two-time champion Ryuichi Kiyonari for one round only. The latest stand-in for Richards –Brogan, Isle of Man TT legend John McGuinness and former World Supersport Champion Karl Muggeridge all having been charged with the task in recent rounds – Kiyonari joined Brookes, now back from his suspension.

Despite being a former double champion, Kiyonari was not the form man over the weekend, Camier again leading the way with his eighth pole of the season. Still reeling from his Cadwell exclusion and with the title now looming, his unshakeable confidence took another small knock in race one when

an erratic series of moves put him off the track and into a ditch.

He launched into a thrilling fight back around the twisty North Yorkshire circuit, eventually reaching sixth by the chequered flag. His problems gave a long awaited victory to Easton, who fended off the attentions of Ellison and Brookes to record a popular maiden win – the first non-Airwaves Yamaha win since Guintoli had triumphed in the season opener.

Normal service was resumed in race two, when Camier calmly cruised to an unprecedented 16th win, ahead of Easton and Brookes, while Ellison's fourth place opened up a first 'match point' for Camier heading into the penultimate round at Silverstone.

Croft did see the crowning of one champion, though, Mason wrapping up the *Mirror.co.uk Cup* after displaying a level of dominance akin to that of Camier's to win with five races remaining.

Foregone conclusion or not, at least Camier was made to work hard for his title triumph, as Ellison – the only rider capable of wresting the trophy from him – posted his most aggressive performance of the season by dicing for the win with his team-mate. He was duly rewarded with victory in race two, but with Camier – who'd already won a thrilling first encounter – following him across the line, the 2009 British Superbike Championship was decided.

With GSE also wrapping up a fifth team championship, and Yamaha enjoying the first of its many successes, all that remained to be seen was whether Camier could maintain his victory run – now up to 17 –at the Oulton Park season finale.

The fight for the runner-up spot was still being

Left: James Ellison, here leading team-mate Camier and Walker, was reliably the next-best in the series.

Below: Relentless Suzuki's Ian Lowry was fifth overall in his debut BSB season.

Bottom: Simon Andrews (Kawasaki) leads the Suzukis of the returned Guintoli and Lowry at Oulton Park.

Photos: Clive Challinor

disputed by Ellison and Easton, the latter doing his utmost to unsettle an Airwaves Yamaha 1-2 by recording a maiden pole position and winning the first of the weekend's three races. He prevailed in a thrilling last-lap exchange with Camier, which arguably was an altogether more rewarding moment that his debut triumph at Croft.

However, with Ellison – the only rider to score in every race of the season – keeping a watching brief just behind, third in the second race would see him complete a whitewash for GSE, Airwaves and Yamaha. Camier, meanwhile, ended his record breaking season on the ultimate high, adding two more wins to a tally that is likely to prove difficult to beat in the coming years.

The top three having pulled out a substantial advantage over the competition, fourth was more hotly contested, with up to eight riders disputing the

position at one stage. Eventually, Brookes won out, having recovered from his enforced mid-season sabbatical to climb the order with a run of five podiums in the final seven races.

Trailing him in fifth was Lowry, who put in a remarkably stealthy performance on the Relentless Suzuki to emerge ahead of several more fancied – and experienced – rivals, despite failing to make it on to the podium all season.

Injuries and reliability issues conspired to leave Andrews a somewhat unrepresentative sixth overall, marginally ahead of fellow Kawasaki rider Da Costa, the Frenchman having shown greater consistency, if not the same raw pace, as his team-mate.

Despite missing six events, the ever jovial Guintoli scythed his way back up to eighth on his return, ahead of a fading Walker and Laverty, who made it three Kawasakis inside the overall top ten. Meanwhile, Hill finished his part-season 11th after securing a pair of podiums at the final round, while Rutter deserves a special mention for his sheer versatility in riding a Yamaha, Suzuki, Honda, Kawasaki and Ducati at some stage during the season.

As the sun set on another season, attention turned inevitably to the future. Continuing the theme of change into the New Year, BSB 2010 will feature a new 'Evo' category, one that will blur the boundaries between Superbike and Superstock specifications with the intention of bolstering grid numbers.

Furthermore, with a handful of riders, including Camier and Guintoli, destined for the bright lights of World Superbikes, we wait to see who will be making the headlines in 2010 – Neil Hodgson and Yukio Kagayama already have done their bit by confirming their return to the series.

Time will tell, but one thing is certain: 2009 was all about one man, one bike and one team. Camier, Yamaha and GSE Racing have raised the bar – and it's ominously high.

BRITISH SUPERSPORTS

If there was only ever one likely outcome to the 2009 British Superbike Championship, then the Fuchs-Silkolene British Supersport Championship did its bit to keep the fans guessing right up to the final chequered flag.

British Supersports may be a supporting act to Superbikes on the schedule, but four strong manufacturer entrants, a sizeable grid and an enticing combination of experienced hands against youthful exuberance ensured that the level of action would occasionally elevate it to the main stage.

A measure of the competitiveness of the season can be seen in the top four riders: Steve Plater, Billy McConnell, James Westmoreland and Ben Wilson. Representing Honda, Yamaha, Triumph and Kawasaki respectively, all four would taste the winner's champagne at some point in 2009, but only one would emerge triumphant.

Indeed, while this quartet were the stand-out performers of the year, the title challenge was only ever really down to two of them: Plater and McConnell.

Having shown flashes of brilliance on the AIM Yamaha in 2008, Plater was lured to HM Plant Honda to front its new Supersport campaign, while McConnell arrived at the leading MAP Raceways Yamaha team intent on rebuilding his reputation after a disappointing tenure with MSS Discovery Kawasaki in Superbikes.

With odds even at the start of the season, the pair traded continuous blows over the 12 rounds, McConnell drawing first blood by staving off a determined last-lap charge from Plater to win the Brands Hatch opener. Plater struck back with victory at Donington Park, before McConnell won again at Thruxton.

Plater evened things up once more at Snetterton, but crucially McConnell suffered his first DNF, which cost the Aussie 25 points in one swoop. Although he enjoyed better mid-season form, Plater's consistency ensured that the gap couldn't be bettered to less than 11 points as the title battle reached its final-round showdown.

With McConnell needing a win, as well as a first retirement of the year for Plater, the odds were stacked comfortably in the British rider's favour. Unfortunately for McConnell, he was the one to hit problems, letting an early lead slip before cruising into retirement.

His demise ensured that Plater would cross the line as the 2009 Fuchs-Silkolene British Supersport champion, bringing some joy to an HM Plant Honda team that otherwise had endured a fairly dismal year at Superbike level.

McConnell was forced to settle for the runner-up spot, albeit by just five points over a charging Westmoreland in third. The youngster was a revelation during the second half of the season aboard the same Triumph Daytona 675 that had taken Glen Richards to title glory a year before. Winning twice under the self-formed JW Racing banner, Westmoreland was tipped for a title tilt in 2010.

His late surge was enough to push him past Wilson, who contributed to Kawasaki's return to form on the domestic scene with a maiden victory at Knockhill aboard the Gearlink prepared machine.

One of six riders to win a BSS race in 2009, Wilson was joined in the winners' circle by team-mate Chris Martin, who claimed a victory at Mallory Park before ending his season with an accident at the following Brands Hatch round.

Dan Cooper was another to enjoy success after scoring a surprise win at Oulton Park, the Centurion Honda rider mastering treacherous conditions to take victory over several more experienced rivals.

Elsewhere, Ian Hutchinson finished the season seventh, ahead of Rob Mac Racing's Dan Linfoot, who made a fine impression on his Supersport debut by finishing third at Brands Hatch, only for an injury at Snetterton and an early promotion to Superbikes to curtail his involvement. Meanwhile, occasional World Supersport rider Sam Lowes walked away with the Supersport Cup.

In the other categories, the National Superstock Championship was dominated by Alastair Seeley, the Relentless Suzuki rider winning the first nine races to seal the title by Cadwell Park. The National Superstock 600 class was won by Jamie Hamilton, while James Lodge emerged triumphant from the British 125GP Championship.

Above: Dominant Superstock champion Alastair Seeley (Suzuki) sealed the title after winning the first nine races.

Top: A determined Steve Plater (HM Plant Honda) triumphed over Billy McConnell in the final round of a thrilling Supersport championship.
Photos: Clive Challinor

get *your hands* on it...

Fuchs Silkolene has the most **comprehensive range** of high performance motorcycle and motorsport lubricants, developed on the race track to ensure **ultimate performance** and protection.

From **Scooters** to **Superbikes**, weekend rider to full-on racer - **Fuchs Silkolene** is *Your Bike's Adrenaline...*

FUCHS Silkolene

w w w . s i l k o l e n e . c o m

SIDECAR WORLD CHAMPIONSHIP
BROTHERS IN ARMS
By JOHN McKENZIE

SIDECAR racing has oft been the place of respite where traditional filial rivalries are overcome, and brotherly love has given us some great sidecar partnerships over the years – most successfully Tim and Tristan Reeves with back-to-back world titles in 2005 and 2006, and a plethora of top pairings from Switzerland: the Guedels, Egloffs, Zurbruggs and Wyssens spring to mind. The great Steve Webster's earliest races saw his brother Kevin in the chair, and to that long list of distinguished partnerships we can now add Ben and Tom Birchall, crowned 2009 World Sidecar Champions – no relation, by the way, to Simon Birchall, 1990 passenger to Alain Michel, a paddock legend turned successful businessman.

In a dominating season where the Birchall brother's lowest race finish was a third, three wins from seven starts saw them wrest the championship from the hands of Finnish ace Pekka Paivarinta.

The brothers from Mansfield have made stellar progress since beginning their World Championship odyssey in 2005, with ninth as a wild card at Assen. The following season saw a full campaign, posting consistent top-ten finishes, ending the year 13th. In 2007 they muscled their way into championship contention with a final placing of fifth, and scooped up wins in various domestic events including the prestigious Jock Taylor Memorial Trophy.

Last season saw Ben and Tom notch up their first World Championship race win – at Rijeka – to end the season in a fine third overall.

Whilst the pair had certainly shown their hand,

observers could have expected the campaign's main battle to be between 2005/6/7 champion Tim Reeves and 2008 victor Paivarinta.

Reeves had lined up with brother Tris back in the chair, whilst the flying Finn, armed with a new and extensively revised 2009 LCR chassis, had recruited the ubiquitous and evergreen Adolf Hanni.

Seven races at five venues hosted at events as varied as MotoGP, World Endurance Championship and local Superbike Championships confirmed a healthy championship and as ever, close racing.

Round 1 - May 9/10, Schleiz, Germany

The Birchalls got the best of all possible starts with pole position (1'28.434) and a top score in the season opening 11-lap sprint race. Forcing their way into the lead after three laps, they held off Paivarinta throughout the remainder to take a morale-boosting win. Reeves came home third, some 30 seconds down.

For Sunday's 22-lap Gold race, and carrying the 10kg victors' weight penalty, the Birchall brothers battled with Paivarinta/Hanni for the full 22 laps. Birchall had found the front at the midway stage of the race and began to pull clear of the Finn, but backmarkers slowed their charge, allowing Paivarinta to catch up, and eventually regain the lead.

Birchall posted fastest lap (1'28.909) in an effort to get back on terms, but ran out of time. They crossed the line with just a second separating the two outfits. With each team taking a win and a sec-

ond, the championship lead was also shared.

"We lapped the entire field except the three outfits behind us," said Ben. "The outfit ran like a dream, but we didn't have the best of times passing the backmarkers, which really lost the race for us. But they were running their own race, which is fair enough."

Reeves took the third step on the rostrum, three seconds behind.

Round 2 - July 4, Albacete, Spain

After two problematical thirds, Tim Reeves got his 2009 championship challenge firmly back on track with a perfect weekend – pole position, the 20-lap Gold Race win, and a new lap record – and all achieved with 21-year old new boy passenger James Neave, stepping in at a week's notice when brother Tris became unavailable.

With a pole time of 1'34.480 serving notice of intent, Reeves controlled the race from the front. As expected, Birchall and Paivarinta were never out of sight, but at half distance Reeves upped the pace, chalking up a new lap record of 1'34.215, almost one and a half seconds quicker than Steve Abbott's longstanding record, and he was opened up a comfortable lead to cross the line a comfortable 4.712 clear of Paivarinta.

The result gave Neave the rare honour and remarkable statistic of winning his debut World Championship race. He was also the second youngest sidecar passenger winner, after 18-year-old Horst Buckhardt way back in 1957.

Said Reeves: "Schleiz was very much damage limitation. Here was again challenging, but we've come through with flying colours. James agreed to step in for Tristan and I cannot fault him at all – he was simply superb. We'd only done five laps together, at Cadwell Park in the damp."

Cooling problems saw Paivarinta err on the side of safety to ensure some points. Seemingly settling for third behind the Birchalls, he seized a dramatic last corner chance to pip them by two tenths, gaining a four-point title lead.

Remarkably it was Birchall's worst finish of the year. "We battled for the lead over the first ten laps," said Ben, "but at the half way stage we had a slight front tyre problem."

Round 3 - July 19, Sachsenring, Germany

The sidecars were back in the MotoGP paddock but down to one 22-lap race: the sprint giving way to a Red Bull Rookies Cup race. Heavy rain during practice provided an extreme contrast to the baking heat of the opening venues.

Birchall had posted pole at 1'28.155 in the dry first session, and after a typically tough three-way battle, the Mitchells of Mansfield-sponsored brothers managed to establish a lead by the mid-point. Reeves's challenge then took a knock – literally – when a paint exchange with backmarkers left him with a dented fairing and a gearlever that was bent just enough to make down-shifts difficult.

Birchall was able to build up a ten-second advantage, smashing the lap record with a time of 1' 27.706. Paivarinta made up the rostrum.

Reeves commented: "It was a really good, enjoyable race with Ben and he was driving really well so hats off to him. He had an edge on top speed, and whilst I could get by and hold him off on the back part, he would come flying by on the straight."

Wild cards Kurt Hock and Enrico Becker made a

good debut: qualifying fourth, leading the early stages, and finishing eighth.

Birchall now led by five points, but with only nine points covering the top three, an exciting climax to the season was on the cards.

Round 4 - August 22/23, Rijeka, Croatia

With two races and fifty points on the table the season was at the fulcrum. And the balance tipped in the favour of the Birchall brothers, who after their third pole took a second place and a win to give them a 14-point advantage with just one race left.

For Saturday's 11-lap sprint race, in air temperatures of 32 deg C, Birchall and Reeves pulled six seconds out of Paivarinta by mid-race. But Birchall's hopes were dashed when a leaking oil pipe started spraying passenger Tom, giving Reeves just enough advantage to win by 5.7 seconds.

With the 20-lap Gold race on Sunday still to come, there were still only nine points covering the top of the table, and Reeves was just four behind Birchall.

Reeves got another great start, but Birchall forced a way past before the end of the first lap. Then a misfiring ignition slowed Reeves, and after six laps he was fifth. He struggled on, but was forced to pit on lap 13, his hopes of the title disappearing fast.

That left Birchall and Paivarinta at the front, the Mansfield brothers firmly in control, establishing a five-second lead with five laps to go, and extending it to more than 12 seconds at the flag. The result put Birchall into a 14-point lead with just one race to go.

"We are not counting our chickens yet," he said. But all he really had to do at the final round was to follow Paivarinta home.

Round 5 - September 6, Le Mans, France

A footnote in history awaited the eventual victor. If Paivarinta were overturn Birchall's points advantage,

his passenger Adolf Hanni would the oldest in champion history, at 54 years, 97 days on September 6. If the Birchalls held on, Tom would be the youngest, at 22 years, 257 days.

Interesting trivialities aside, it was always going to require a non-finish from Birchall for the Finn to hang on to his title. However we only have to remember Biland versus Webster at Brno back in 1988 to know all things are possible. But with Reeves out of range, it was realistically only Birchall's to lose.

Qualifying was close; Paivarinta sealing pole just 0.07secs ahead of Birchall, with Reeves close in third and desperate for a win now his title hopes were gone.

Paivarinta, faced with a win-or-bust scenario, shot away at the start and held the lead for the full 18 laps.

With Birchall tucked in second place, Reeves began his charge. By lap two he was in the Finn's slipstream. But another four laps in, and the charging Paivarinta had opened a gap to leave Reeves and Birchall battling for second.

By lap nine, Reeves was faltering once more, a broken ignition switch forcing him to pit for a second successive DNF. Birchall tried in vain to reel in Paivarinta, but was still almost nine seconds adrift at the flag.

But the job was done: second gave Birchall the 2009 World Championship by seven points from Paivarinta, with Reeves third after taking two wins, a second and two thirds from the five races he finished.

"It is a fantastic feeling to be the World Champion," said an ecstatic Ben Birchall. "And for Tom to become the youngest ever passenger is the icing on the cake. Neither of us can find the words right now to say how happy we are. We'll celebrate tonight before making our way home and then the hard work will start to prepare for next year." Their winning Suzuki-powered LCR was up for sale, and new machines on order. "We intend to begin a series of tests early in the New Year, for the defence of our World Championship, and also to have another crack at the Isle of Man TT."

Right: Close racing in a strong season – the Reeves brothers lead fast wild cards Hock and Webber at the Sachsenring, with the Moser/Wechselberger outfit chasing hard.

Opposite page, main picture: The Birchall brothers show the style that won their first title.

Opposite page, centre left: Last year's champions Paivarinta and Hanni challenged to the end.

Opposite page, centre right: Driver Ben Birchall (left) and brother Tom wear their medals with pride. At 22, Tom was the youngest-ever champion passenger.

Photos: Mark Walters

ONE HELL OF A YEAR

By PAUL CARRUTHERS

IF Roger Edmondson and the Daytona Motorsports Group set out to bring parity to the AMA Superbike Series, then the case could be made that they were successful. If they'd set out to end Suzuki's domination in the class, then you could say they achieved that as well. And if the ultimate goal was to chase Mat Mladin away from the series – well, then they were successful on all fronts.

But while they could rid the series of its most dominant rider ever, they couldn't stop Mladin from going back to Australia with an unprecedented seventh AMA Superbike Championship in his pocket. Yes, it was that man Mladin again in 2009, the Australian wrapping the title with a round to spare – the first time in his storied career that he'd been able to clinch it before the final round. And, sadly, it will be the last we'll see of him.

At the age of 37, Mladin announced his retirement in 2009. He left as the most successful roadracer in AMA history. It's unlikely that his 82 wins will ever be matched. Ditto his seven titles. Put it this way: the active rider who is second to Mladin on the win list is veteran Aaron Yates, and he has only nine. Oh, and Mladin also has 62 pole positions, another mark likely never to be matched.

Mladin won ten of the 20 rounds of the series in 2009, including seven in a row to start the year. He did so in the first five races on the old model Suzuki – the K8 – but then had to switch to the K9 at Road Atlanta when it was finally in production. He didn't like it as much, but he continued to win. By the Mid-

Ohio round in mid-July, however, Mladin had admitted to losing interest. He was tired of fighting the good fight, and there was no more light at the end of the tunnel. He despised the new regime at DMG, hated what they'd done to the Superbike class and was sickened by their attitude towards track safety.

His results followed suit, and he finished the season with somewhat lacklustre races – for him. But he'd done the necessary work, and all he really had to do was show up and ride to earn his title. And that's what he did – most of the time: he was third and seventh at Mid-Ohio; he sat out the two races at Heartland Park Topeka in Kansas, after deciding the track wasn't safe to race on – he wasn't alone; a second and a ninth came at Virginia International Raceway, where he wrapped up the title; and he ended his AMA career with a crash and a second place at the new venue in New Jersey.

Mladin spilled the beans on the Saturday at Mid-Ohio after finishing third. "The things that are happening in this paddock now and the things that have been overlooked, and the rules and the things that are going on on a daily basis, I've lost interest, pretty much. It's good being in a race with these guys, having a bit of fun and mixing things up, and that gets me going, and fortunately it's all over soon."

Several things pushed Mladin to this point. For starters, just prior to the Mid-Ohio round, DMG homologated the Buell 1125RR for the American Superbike class – a decision that didn't go over well in the paddock. Especially since AMA Pro Racing's

new rules had effectively taken the 'Super' out of Superbike prior to the start of the season.

"The bottom line is it's not legal for Superbike racing," Mladin said at Mid-Ohio. "It's a custom-built racing bike. There's none registered. Nobody can buy and register them on the road, and isn't that part of the rules?" This, and the fact that he felt Yamaha was also receiving preferential treatment in the paddock and on the track, pushed Mladin over the top. He was also not very happy riding the dumbed-down, Superstock-level motorcycles after a career spent fine tuning and honing his skills on the best Superbikes Suzuki could build. Basically, he couldn't be as aggressive on the almost-stock motorcycles, and it zapped a lot of his enthusiasm. Throw in the off-track issues, and it was easy to see why he was over it. It was easy for him to back it down: even after third and seventh at Mid-Ohio, he still led the championship by 126 points.

"I think the stuff we've seen this year will just continue on and maybe get worse," Mladin said. "And it's just nothing that really interests me. It's not fun. That's exactly right. I'm not going to put my life on the line if I'm not having fun. I think I've proven enough over the years that I put it on the line most of the time, and at the moment, it's a struggle. That simple."

It was veteran racer Josh Hayes who picked up the slack. No spring chicken at the age of 34, Hayes' career has been one of ups and downs. Riding for various support teams along the way, he has

won three championships – in Formula Xtreme and Superstock – but he was always overlooked when it came to a full-factory Superbike. He got the chance in 2009 and made the most of it, overshadowing his more famous team-mate, Ben Bostrom, to win seven times.

His first ever Superbike win came in May at Infineon Raceway on the factory R1, and was the first for Yamaha since Anthony Gobert had done likewise in April 2002.

Popular with the fans and his peers, Hayes marched on to second in the title chase and enters the 2010 season as the favourite to win the championship.

If Suzuki is to continue its championship run in 2010, the man most likely to gain it for them is Tommy Hayden. The oldest of the three racing brothers, Tommy ended up third in 2009. Although he failed to take that elusive first Superbike win, his season was one of consistency, and he was 'bridesmaid' seven times. It will be interesting to see how he fares as the lead man in the Yoshimura Suzuki squad for 2010 as he finishes a two-year contract with the team. Most put him down as the rider most likely to challenge Hayes.

Larry Pegram rode his semi-factory backed Ducati to fourth, the only rider other than Mladin and Hayes to win a race – three of them. The first came at Road America, where Pegram used the power advantage of his Ducati 1098R to beat Mladin, giving him a win ten years after he'd last tasted victory, in April 1999.

"So now I'm not a one-hit wonder," Pegram joked after his win.

Pegram's other victories would come in the race Mladin chose to boycott – the series return to Heartland Park Topeka after an 18-year absence. Pegram won twice on the iffy Kansas racetrack after nearly coming to blows with Mladin on the Friday of the race weekend, when the Ohioan tried to tell the Aus-

tralian that the place really wasn't that dangerous. It's worth noting that Heartland Park Topeka is not on the 2010 AMA schedule.

Hayes' Yamaha team-mate, Ben Bostrom, ended the 2008 season fifth in the series standings. Going into the following season, most would have bet on him winning races before Hayes – especially after the former AMA Superbike champion and World Superbike race winner had been so dominant on the Supersport Yamaha R6 in 2008. But by the end of the season, Bostrom was in the shadow of Hayes and probably out of a Superbike ride for 2010. Yamaha likes him, though, so he likely will be moved to the Supersport class (now called Daytona Sport-Bike). Bostrom was no slouch, however, and he did finish second three times on the R1.

It's probably fair to say that Yoshimura Suzuki was looking for better results from Blake Young in his debut season with the team. Young, mentored by Kevin Schwantz, didn't have the season he was hoping for, but still ended up sixth. And he will return with the team for the second year of his contract, joining Tommy Hayden again. Like Bostrom, Young finished second three times, but his season ended with an eighth, a sixth, two sevenths and a ninth, so it wasn't a strong climax. But he's young in more than just name, and many expect him to fight for the 2010 title.

Aaron Yates was seventh on the Michael Jordan Motorsports backed Suzuki GSX-R1000, besting team-mate Geoff May by some 60 points. Yates had two seconds out of six podiums; May's best were three thirds.

Taylor Knapp rode his true privateer Suzuki to an impressive ninth, often beating some of the factory stars. And he mixed in a few rides on the controversial Buell Superbike.

Jake Holden emerged as highest finishing Honda rider, the Corona CBR1000RR mounted Washington State man beating team-mate Neil Hodgson for

Above: Flowing track action at Laguna Seca contrasted with a year of anger, arguments and controversy as the new regime dismantled the traditions of AMA racing.

Right: Mat Mladin was champion for a record seventh time, but was so disenchanted with the Daytona Motorsports Group's management that he quit racing.

Photos: Gold & Goose

tenth overall. Hodgson's season was a complete nightmare. After starting with a second-place finish to Mladin at Daytona, the Briton was injured in a motocross training crash and he missed the next six races, having required shoulder surgery. He returned far from 100 per cent, the best he could muster being fifth in the last round in New Jersey. He was getting stronger, but it was too late, putting paid to his hopes of returning to the AMA Series for 2010. The former World Superbike champion will stay home to compete in the British Superbike series.

DAYTONA SPORTBIKE

The Daytona SportBike class is the favoured class of the DMG and Edmondson, and it shared top billing with the American Superbike class in 2009. The series featured the same number of races (20 at 11 venues) as the Superbike class and was also the headline Daytona 200, which was held under lights for the first time.

The series featured a spec tyre for the first time, and the riders were given fairly average Dunlops initially, with better rubber showing up later in the season, which probably helped ensure parity in the class more than any other factor. Five different riders won races on four different brands of motorcycle – Buell, Yamaha, Suzuki and Honda – and a fifth, Aprilia, was in the mix at a lot of the races.

The title was won by former dirt-tracker Danny Eslick on the factory Buell 1125R, the Oklahoman winning six races on the big twin while often operating under the scrutiny and disparagement of those who believed the Buell and its extra cubic centimetres shouldn't be allowed to compete with the smaller 600s. But in all fairness, Eslick rode the wheels off the bike, coming back from a big hole after being

disqualified from Daytona for passing under a yellow flag. The disqualification carried a five-point penalty, so Eslick actually started the season with a negative points tally.

He bounced back quickly, however, with a double-header sweep of the Auto Club Speedway round in Southern California. He'd win four more times, and when he didn't was always in the hunt, as demonstrated by his four other podium finishes.

In the end, only five points separated Eslick from Yamaha's Josh Herrin, the youngster ending the season on fire with two seconds and four wins in the final six races. If it wasn't for a lacklustre middle season, Herrin would have certainly stormed away with the title, but a 20-race season is a marathon, not a sprint, and Eslick was better in the long run.

It was M4 Suzuki's Martin Cardenas who probably should have won the title. Cardenas, who hails from Colombia, won seven times – one more than Eslick and three more than Herrin. He was dominant through the middle part of the season and looked to be on his way to the title when he crashed during qualifying for the penultimate round at Virginia International Raceway, suffering a broken hand. He would undergo surgery between Virginia and the final round in New Jersey, but was forced to pull out, which dashed his title hopes. Still, his 340 points earned him third in the championship and put him 41 points clear of the man many had pegged as favourite, Jamie Hacking.

With 21 Supersport-class victories (second overall behind Miguel Duhamel), Hacking seemed like the perfect rider to earn the first Daytona SportBike title, but he never came to grips with the spec Dunlops and never got his Attack Kawasaki working the way he wanted. He also joined Mladin in sitting out the Kansas race, opting to jump in his motorhome

and get out of there before something bad happened. In the end, he was fourth in the series point standings, with no wins, but four seconds.

Yamaha didn't re-sign Jason DiSalvo for the '09 season, and he ended up paying for a ride with the M4 Suzuki team alongside Cardenas. DiSalvo was up and down all season, but ended up fifth in the final standings.

The other race winners were Chris Peris and Bostrom. Peris' victory came in the pouring rain at Road America in Wisconsin, the Canadian earning his first ever AMA National win. Bostrom won the two biggest races of the year – and the only two he entered. The first was the season opener under the lights at Daytona, the second was the Laguna Seca final, held in conjunction with the Red Bull US Grand Prix. Bostrom was spectacular in both races, showing that he's the man to beat when he throws his leg over the little Yamaha R6.

Yamaha also found a rising star in Tommy Aquino. The youngster from California blossomed in the latter part of the season with four podium finishes. He will return to the Yamaha team in 2010 with Herrin and possibly Bostrom, while Hayes gets the only Superbike seat in the team.

The other rider who deserves mention is Chaz Davies. After riding for Attack Kawasaki in the previous season, he didn't have a ride for 2009 until Aprilia stepped in. He rode the Italian bike to ninth in the series standings, finishing second twice along the way. But like Hodgson, he will be absent in 2010, expected to ride a Triumph in the World Supersport Championship after faring well in some end-of-season guest rides for the team.

Losing someone like Davies is a blow to the championship. But it's only one of several blows. The 2010 series remains a big question mark.

weren't really sure who had won the race.

It was the first race, and things were already unravelling. And they continued to do so throughout the season, with more grumbling and unhappiness than at any other time in the history of AMA road-racing. The pace car would rear its ugly head again at the Laguna Seca round, the driver basically pulling right into harm's way on the blind crest that is turn one. Fortunately, no one hit the car or crashed while trying to avoid the vehicle, but it led to an ugly confrontation between race officials and racers, in plain view on the front straight.

The comedy of errors would continue. At Mid-Ohio, privateer and perennial back-marker Johnny Rock Page was suspended for holding up the leaders in the first of two American Superbike races. What followed was a confrontation, with AMA head tech man Al Ludington throwing down a profanity-laced tirade at Page, all of which was captured on video and broadcast for all to see on YouTube the week after. Of course, Ludington was suspended by AMA Pro Racing, and he issued a letter of apology to Page and the racing community.

More high-level blunders came at Laguna, where Edmondson announced prematurely that there would be a spec class for 450cc singles – Formula 450s – beginning in 2010. That idea went nowhere, but it did serve to throw more gas on the fire, as most in the paddock were opposed to the class. Then there was the Topeka incident and all the hoopla over the Buells. It all amounted to one hell of a year for AMA racing. And not all of it can be blamed on a failing economy.

But we did get parity, we did see motorcycles other than Suzukis winning the Superbike class, and we did get rid of that damn Mat Mladin…

Left: Tommy Hayden takes over at Suzuki from departing Mladin, who looms over shoulder.

Below left: Danny Eslick's 1125cc Buell prevailed over the 600cc opposition in the new Daytona Sportbike class.

Far left: Veteran Josh Hayes leads team-mate Ben Bostrom in his best Superbike season yet.

Below: Mladin's smoky farewell – better to burn out than fade away.

Photos: Tom Hatniw

For starters, there's no more Mladin. Ben Spies is long gone. Neil Hodgson is gone. And the factory Superbikes are very nearly things of the past. As of this writing, there were only four certain Superbikes for the coming season: Hayes on the factory R1; Hayden and Young on the Yoshimura Suzukis; and Pegram on the Ducati. Honda pulled the plug on its plans (if it actually had any) after meeting with DMG officials and learning that nothing was changing in the rules package for 2010. Kawasaki had no plans to run a Superbike; even the Jordan team was in doubt.

As for the Daytona SportBike class, there won't be much in the way of factory involvement there either, as most of the support teams were still on hold as *MOTOCOURSE* went to press. And the bike that won the championship and caused so much furore along the way? Gone. *Sayonara. Hasta la vista…* Harley-Davidson shocked most of the world with an announcement in October that it was stopping production of Buells. Forever.

AMA: MELTING POT OR MELTDOWN?

WHAT went wrong with AMA Pro Racing in 2009? Where to begin… How about with Daytona? Billed as the Daytona 200 since the bikes raced on the beach, this one only went 193.05 miles because it turned into a debacle.

There were yellow flags, pace cars, scoring snafus and a red flag when the lights for the only night race on the schedule went out. And it was the pace car that basically ruined the race. How? It ended up pulling out in front of the wrong rider, thereby affecting the results. Not to mention the accident that was caused by the car in the first place. It all was a confusing mess; even those in the media centre

MAJOR RESULTS

OTHER CHAMPIONSHIP RACING SERIES WORLDWIDE

Compiled by PETER McLAREN

AMA Championship Road Race Series (Superbike)

DAYTONA INTERNATIONAL SPEEDWAY, Daytona Beach, Florida, 5 March, 43.500 miles/70,006km
1 Mat Mladin (Suzuki); **2** Neil Hodgson (Honda); **3** Tommy Hayden (Suzuki); **4** Larry Pegram (Ducati); **5** Blake Young (Suzuki); **6** Ben Bostrom (Yamaha); **7** Aaron Yates (Suzuki); **8** Josh Hayes (Yamaha); **9** Michael Laverty (Suzuki); **10** Geoff May (Suzuki).

AUTO CLUB SPEEDWAY, Fontana, California, 21–22 March, 43.700 miles/70.328km
Race 1
1 Mat Mladin (Suzuki); **2** Tommy Hayden (Suzuki); **3** Geoff May (Suzuki); **4** Blake Young (Suzuki); **5** Jake Holden (Honda); **6** Josh Hayes (Yamaha); **7** Ben Bostrom (Yamaha); **8** David Anthony (Suzuki); **9** Taylor Knapp (Suzuki); **10** Aaron Gobert (Honda).

Race 2
1 Mat Mladin (Suzuki); **2** Tommy Hayden (Suzuki); **3** Larry Pegram (Ducati); **4** Geoff May (Suzuki); **5** Ben Bostrom (Yamaha); **6** Josh Hayes (Yamaha); **7** Taylor Knapp (Suzuki); **8** David Anthony (Suzuki); **9** Blake Young (Suzuki); **10** Aaron Yates (Suzuki).

ROAD ATLANTA, Braselton, Georgia, 4–5 April, 51.000 miles/82.077km
Race 1
1 Mat Mladin (Suzuki); **2** Tommy Hayden (Suzuki); **3** Geoff May (Suzuki); **4** Blake Young (Suzuki); **5** Josh Hayes (Yamaha); **6** Aaron Yates (Suzuki); **7** Larry Pegram (Ducati); **8** Ben Bostrom (Yamaha); **9** David Anthony (Suzuki); **10** Jake Holden (Honda).

Race 2
1 Mat Mladin (Suzuki); **2** Blake Young (Suzuki); **3** Geoff May (Suzuki); **4** Josh Hayes (Yamaha); **5** Aaron Yates (Suzuki); **6** Tommy Hayden (Suzuki); **7** Taylor Knapp (Suzuki); **8** Ben Bostrom (Yamaha); **9** Jake Holden (Honda); **10** Larry Pegram (Ducati).

BARBER MOTORSPORTS PARK, Leeds, Alabama, 2–3 May, 49.980 miles/80.435km
Race 1
1 Mat Mladin (Suzuki); **2** Blake Young (Suzuki); **3** Ben Bostrom (Yamaha); **4** Tommy Hayden (Suzuki); **5** Josh Hayes (Yamaha); **6** Larry Pegram (Ducati); **7** Geoff May (Suzuki); **8** Jake Holden (Honda); **9** Taylor Knapp (Suzuki); **10** Aaron Yates (Suzuki).

Race 2
1 Mat Mladin (Suzuki); **2** Aaron Yates (Suzuki); **3** Ben Bostrom (Yamaha); **4** Josh Hayes (Yamaha); **5** Geoff May (Suzuki); **6** Larry Pegram (Ducati); **7** Jake Holden (Honda); **8** Tommy Hayden (Suzuki); **9** Taylor Knapp (Suzuki); **10** David Anthony (Suzuki).

INFINEON RACEWAY, Sonoma, California, 16–17 May, 51.040 miles/82.141km
Race 1
1 Josh Hayes (Yamaha); **2** Tommy Hayden (Suzuki); **3** Larry Pegram (Ducati); **4** Aaron Yates (Suzuki); **5** Mat Mladin (Suzuki); **6** Taylor Knapp (Suzuki); **7** David Anthony (Suzuki); **8** Chris Ulrich (Suzuki); **9** Ben Bostrom (Yamaha); **10** Cory Call (Yamaha).

Race 2
1 Mat Mladin (Suzuki); **2** Ben Bostrom (Yamaha); **3** Tommy Hayden (Suzuki); **4** Josh Hayes (Yamaha); **5** Larry Pegram (Ducati); **6** Geoff May (Suzuki); **7** Taylor Knapp (Suzuki); **8** David Anthony (Suzuki); **9** Neil Hodgson (Honda); **10** Ryan Elleby (Yamaha).

ROAD AMERICA, Elkhart Lake, Wisconsin, 6–7 June, 52.000 miles/83.686km
Race 1
1 Mat Mladin (Suzuki); **2** Michael Laverty (Suzuki); **3** Ben Bostrom (Yamaha); **4** Larry Pegram (Ducati); **5** Blake Young (Suzuki); **6** Aaron Yates (Suzuki); **7** Ryan Elleby (Suzuki); **8** David Anthony (Suzuki); **9** Tommy Hayden (Suzuki); **10** Mark Crozier (Suzuki).

Race 2
1 Larry Pegram (Ducati); **2** Mat Mladin (Suzuki); **3** Aaron Yates (Suzuki); **4** Geoff May (Suzuki); **5** Ben Bostrom (Yamaha); **6** Neil Hodgson (Honda); **7** Tommy Hayden (Suzuki); **8** Blake Young (Suzuki); **9** Jake Holden (Honda); **10** David Anthony (Suzuki).

LAGUNA SECA, Monterey, California, 5 July, 41.400 miles/66.627km
1 Mat Mladin (Suzuki); **2** Blake Young (Suzuki); **3** Aaron Yates (Suzuki); **4** Josh Hayes (Yamaha); **5** Ben Bostrom (Yamaha); **6** Neil Hodgson (Honda); **7** Jake Holden (Honda); **8** Tommy Hayden (Suzuki); **9** Geoff May (Suzuki); **10** Larry Pegram (Ducati).

MID-OHIO SPORTS CAR COURSE, Lexington, Ohio, 18–19 July, 50.400 miles/81.111km
Race 1
1 Josh Hayes (Yamaha); **2** Aaron Yates (Suzuki); **3** Mat Mladin (Suzuki); **4** Ben Bostrom (Yamaha); **5** Larry Pegram (Ducati); **6** Tommy Hayden (Suzuki); **7** Blake Young (Suzuki); **8** Geoff May (Suzuki); **9** Jake Holden (Honda); **10** Michael Laverty (Suzuki).

Race 2
1 Josh Hayes (Yamaha); **2** Ben Bostrom (Yamaha); **3** Tommy Hayden (Suzuki); **4** Blake Young (Suzuki); **5** Larry Pegram (Ducati); **6** Michael Laverty (Suzuki); **7** Mat Mladin (Suzuki); **8** Geoff May (Suzuki); **9** Neil Hodgson (Honda); **10** Taylor Knapp (Buell).

HEARTLAND PARK TOPEKA, Topeka, Kansas, 1–2 August, 50.000 miles/80.467km
Race 1
1 Larry Pegram (Ducati); **2** Ben Bostrom (Yamaha); **3** Blake Young (Suzuki); **4** Tommy Hayden (Suzuki); **5** Aaron Yates (Suzuki); **6** Josh Hayes (Yamaha); **7** Jake Holden (Honda); **8** Geoff May (Suzuki); **9** Taylor Knapp (Suzuki); **10** Neil Hodgson (Honda).

Race 2
1 Larry Pegram (Ducati); **2** Tommy Hayden (Suzuki); **3** Josh Hayes (Yamaha); **4** Jake Holden (Honda); **5** Taylor Knapp (Suzuki); **6** Neil Hodgson (Honda); **7** Michael Laverty (Suzuki); **8** Blake Young (Suzuki); **9** Chris Ulrich (Suzuki); **10** Scott Charlton (Suzuki).

VIRGINIA INTERNATIONAL RACEWAY, Alton, Virginia, 15–16 August, 51.750 miles/83.284km
Race 1
1 Josh Hayes (Yamaha); **2** Mat Mladin (Suzuki); **3** Ben Bostrom (Yamaha); **4** Aaron Yates (Suzuki); **5** Tommy Hayden (Suzuki); **6** Blake Young (Suzuki); **7** Jake Holden (Honda); **8** Taylor Knapp (Suzuki); **9** Michael Laverty (Suzuki); **10** Jeff Woods (Suzuki).

Race 2
1 Josh Hayes (Yamaha); **2** Tommy Hayden (Suzuki); **3** Ben Bostrom (Yamaha); **4** Larry Pegram (Ducati); **5** Aaron Yates (Suzuki); **6** Taylor Knapp (Suzuki); **7** Blake Young (Suzuki); **8** Neil Hodgson (Honda); **9** Mat Mladin (Suzuki); **10** Jake Holden (Honda).

NEW JERSEY MOTORSPORTS PARK, Millville, New Jersey, 5–6 September, 51.750 miles/83.284km
Race 1
1 Josh Hayes (Yamaha); **2** Tommy Hayden (Suzuki); **3** Aaron Yates (Suzuki); **4** Ben Bostrom (Yamaha); **5** Larry Pegram (Ducati); **6** Taylor Knapp (Buell); **7** Blake Young (Suzuki); **8** Cory West (Buell); **9** Damian Cudlin (Suzuki); **10** Geoff May (Suzuki).

Race 2
1 Josh Hayes (Yamaha); **2** Mat Mladin (Suzuki); **3** Aaron Yates (Suzuki); **4** Larry Pegram (Ducati); **5** Neil Hodgson (Honda); **6** Jake Holden (Honda); **7** Cory West (Buell); **8** Damien Cudlin (Suzuki); **9** Blake Young (Suzuki); **10** Geoff May (Suzuki).

Final Championship Points

1	Mat Mladin	453
2	Josh Hayes	406
3	Tommy Hayden	373
4	Larry Pegram	347
5	Ben Bostrom	333
6	Blake Young	290

7 Aaron Yates, 290; **8** Geoff May, 234; **9** Taylor Knapp, 207; **10** Jake Holden, 195.

Endurance World Championship

24 HEURES MOTO, Le Mans Bugatti Circuit, France, 18–19 April 2009.
Endurance World Championship, round 1. 727 laps of the 2.600-mile/4.185km circuit, 1890.200 miles/3042.495km
1 Yamaha Austria Racing Team 7, AUT: Igor Jerman/Steve Martin/Gwen Giabbani (Yamaha), 24h 0m 47.964s, 78.728mph/126.700km/h.
2 Honda France, FRA: Steve Plater/Sebastien Charpentier/Matthieu Lagrive (Honda), 722 laps; **3** Suzuki Endurance Racing Team, FRA: Vincent Philippe/Barry Veneman/Guillaume Dietrich (Suzuki), 716 laps; **4** RT Racing Team Moto Virus, ITA: Jean Louis Devoyon/ Raphael Chevre/Frederic Jond (Suzuki), 709 laps; **5** RAC 41 - City Bike, FRA: Gregory Junod/Herve Gantner/Vincent Houssin (Suzuki), 696 laps; **6** Team GSR Kawasaki, FRA: Julien Da Costa/Kenny Foray/Fred Moreira (Kawasaki), 695 laps; **7** Bolliger Team Switzerland, SWI: Horst Saiger/Patric Muff/Rico Penzkofer (Kawasaki), 692 laps; **8** No Limits, ITA: Peter Hickman/Emiliano Bellucci/ Christer Miinin (Suzuki), 685 laps; **9** Amadeus X-One, ITA: Paolo Tessari/Will Gruy/Anthony Dos Santos (Yamaha), 678 laps; **10** RMT 21 Racing Team, GER: Matti Seidel/Christian Zaiser/Shannon Etheridge (Honda), 672 laps; **11** Cross Roads, FRA: Ludovic Loeul/Stephane Paul/ Philippe Durand (KTM), 555 laps.
Fastest lap: Honda France, 1m 38.242s, 95.291mph/153.356km/h, on lap 7.
Championship points: 1 Yamaha Austria Racing Team 7, 35; **2** Honda France, 28; **3** Suzuki Endurance Racing Team, 22; **4** RT Racing Team Moto Virus, 18; **5** RAC 41 - City Bike, 15; **6** Team GSR Kawasaki, 14.

8 HOURS OF OSCHERSLEBEN, Oschersleben Circuit, Germany, 31 May 2009.
Endurance World Championship, round 2. 257 laps of the 2.279-mile/3.667km circuit, 585.703 miles/942.419km
1 Yamaha Austria Racing Team 7, AUT: Igor Jerman/Steve Martin/Gwen Giabbani (Yamaha), 6h 40m 1.383s (race stopped due to weather), 87.834mph/141.355km/h.
2 Amadeus X-One, ITA: Paolo Tessari/Will Gruy/Ayrton Badovini (Yamaha), 253 laps; **3** RT Racing Team Moto Virus, ITA: Jean Louis Devoyon/David Morillon/Frederic Jond (Suzuki), 252 laps; **4** Team 18 Sapeurs Pompiers, FRA: Stéphane Mollinier/David Briere/Jerome Tangre (Suzuki), 252 laps; **5** Bolliger Team Switzerland, SWI: Horst Saiger/Rico Penzkofer/Eric Mizera (Kawasaki), 252 laps; **6** BK Maco Moto Racing Team, SVK: Daniel Ribalta/Andy Meklau/Victor Carrasco (Yamaha), 250 laps; **7** AM Moto Racing Competition, FRA: Sullivan Hernandez/Pierre Guersillon/Fabrice Auger (Suzuki), 250 laps; **8** RMT 21 Racing Team, GER: Olivier Depoorter/ Matti Seidel/Christian Zaiser (Honda), 249 laps; **9** MCS Racing IPONE, ITA: Jure Stibilj/Calvin Hogan/Jordi Almeda (Suzuki), 247 laps; **10** Michelin Power Research Team, FRA: William Costes/Hugo Marchand/Josep Monge (Honda), 246 laps; **11** Motobox Kremer Racing, GER: Achim Steinmacher/Martin Scherrer/Timo Paavilainen (Suzuki), 241 laps; **12** No Limits, ITA: Cedric Tangre/Emiliano Bellucci/Christer Miinin (Suzuki), 234 laps; **13** Racing Team Hepelmann, GER: Hans-Josef Hepelmann/Mike Minnerop/ Reinhard Krächter (Yamaha), 229 laps.
Fastest lap: Yamaha Austria Racing Team 7, 1m 28.502s, 92.686mph/149.163km/h, on lap 30.
Championship points: 1 Yamaha Austria Racing Team 7, 65; **2** RT Racing Team Moto Virus, 37; **3** Amadeus X-One, 34; **4** Honda France, 28; **5** Bolliger Team Switzerland, 26; **6** Suzuki Endurance Racing Team, 22.

8 HOURS OF ALBACETE, Albacete Circuit, Spain, 4 July 2009.
Endurance World Championship, round 3. 292 laps of the 2.199-mile/3.539km circuit, 642.108 miles/1033.388km
1 Yamaha Austria Racing Team 7, AUT: Igor Jerman/Steve Martin/Gwen Giabbani (Yamaha), 8h 0m 25.606s, 80.188mph/129.05km/h.
2 Folch Endurance, SPA: David Checa/ José Manuel LUIS/Daniel RIVAS (Yamaha), 292 laps; **3** Team 18 Sapeurs Pompiers, FRA: Stéphane Mollinier/David Briere/Jerome Tangre (Suzuki), 290 laps; **4** Michelin Power Research Team, FRA: William Costes/Ivan Silva/Josep Monge (Honda), 290 laps; **5** Phase One Endurance, GBR: Damian Cudlin/Alex Cudlin/Pedro Vallcaneras (Yamaha), 289 laps; **6** Bolliger Team Switzerland, SWI: Horst Saiger/Steve Mizera/Rico Penzkofer (Kawasaki), 286 laps; **7** BK Maco Moto Racing Team, SVK: Daniel Ribalta/Jason Pridmore/Victor Carrasco (Yamaha), 284 laps; **8** RT Racing Team Moto Virus, ITA: Jean Louis Devoyon/ Frederic Jond/ Cedric Tangre (Suzuki), 284 laps; **9** No Limits, ITA: Emiliano Bellucci/Christer Miinin/Phil Giles (Suzuki), 281 laps; **10** MCS Racing IPONE, ITA: Jure Stibilj/Ricardo Saseta/Jordi Almeda (Suzuki), 280 laps; **11** Amadeus X-One, ITA: Paolo Tessari/Will Gruy/Ayrton Badovini (Yamaha), 276 laps; **12** AM Moto Racing Competition, FRA: Sullivan Hernandez/Pierre Guersillon/Fabrice Auger (Suzuki), 272 laps.
Fastest lap: Michelin Power Research Team, 1m 32.429s, 85.649mph/137.839km/h, on lap 230.
Championship points: 1 Yamaha Austria Racing Team 7, 95; **2** RT Racing Team Moto Virus, 47; **3** Amadeus X-One, 40; **4** Bolliger Team Switzerland, 38; **5** Honda France, 28; **6** No Limits, 24.

8 HOURS OF SUZUKA, Suzuka Circuit, Japan, 26 July 2009.
Endurance World Championship, round 4. 183 laps of the 3.617-mile/5.821km circuit, 661.911 miles/1065.243km
1 Yoshimura Suzuki with Jomo 12, JPN: Nobuatsu Aoki/Dalsaku Sakai/Kazuki Tokudome (Suzuki), 8h 1m 59.916s, 82.394mph/ 132.60km/h.
2 Trick Star Racing, JPN: Hitoyasu Izutsu/Shinya Takeishi/Ryuji Tsuruta (Kawasaki), 182 laps; **3** Honda Dream RT Sakurai, JPN: Chojun Kamya/Takumi Takahashi (Honda), 182 laps; **4** Yamaha Austria Racing Team 7, AUT: Igor Jerman/Steve Martin/Gwen Giabbani (Yamaha), 181 laps; **5** Plot Faro Panthera, JPN: Osamu Deguchi/Koji Teramoto (Suzuki), 180 laps; **6** Beet Racing, JPN: Katsunori Hasegawa/Syohei Karita/Osamu Nishijima (Kawasaki), 179 laps; **7** Weider DD Boys With A-Style, JPN: Yuta Kodama/Kazuma Tsuda (Honda); 179 laps; **8** Team Plus One & TSR, JPN: Satoru Iwata/Yoshiyuki Sugai/Kazuma Watanabe (Honda), 178 laps; **9** F.C.C. TSR Honda, JPN: Kousuke Akiyoshi/ Shinichi Ito/Yusuke Teshima (Honda), 178 laps; **10** Teluru Honneybee Racing, JPN: Hiroki Noda/Taro Sekiguchi (Honda), 178 laps; **11** BK Maco Moto Racing Team, SVK: Daniel Ribalta/Jason Pridmore (Yamaha), 176 laps; **12** Phase One Endurance, GBR: Damian Cudlin/Graeme Gowland/Pedro Vallcaneras (Yamaha), 176 laps; **13** Team Etching Factory 15, JPN: Koji Adachi/Syogo Takemi/Yasuhiro Usami (Yamaha), 175 laps; **14** Honda Escargo & PGR & Sayyama & H-TECH (E), JPN: Masao Kuboyama/ Naohiro Nakatsuhara (Honda), 175 laps; **15** Honda Dream RT Wakayama, JPN: Minoru Ouchida/Akifumi Yuzaki (Honda), 173 laps.
Fastest lap: F.C.C. TSR Honda, 2m 8.745s, 101.14mph/162.77km/h, on lap 32.
Championship points: 1 Yamaha Austria Racing Team 7, 111; **2** RT Racing Team Moto Virus, 47; **3** Amadeus X-One, 40; **4** Bolliger Team Switzerland, 38; **5** Yoshimura Suzuki with Jomo 12, 30; **6** BK Maco Moto Racing Team, 29.

24 HOURS BOL D'OR, Magny-Cours, France, 12–13 September 2009.
Endurance World Championship, round 5. 815 laps of the 2.741-mile/4.411km circuit, 2233.915 miles/3594.965km
1 Suzuki Endurance Racing Team, FRA: Vincent Philippe/Freddy Foray/Olivier Four (Suzuki), 24h 0m 38.940s, 93.03mph/149.72km/h.

2 Team GSR Kawasaki, FRA: Kenny Noyes/ Kenny Foray/Xavi Fores Querol (Kawasaki), 808 laps; **3** Team 18 Sapeurs Pompiers, FRA: Stéphane Mollinier/David Briere/Jerome Tangre (Suzuki), 793 laps; **4** RAC 41 - City Bike, FRA: Gregory Junod/Greg Black/Vincent Houssin (Suzuki), 793 laps; **5** AM Moto Racing Competition, FRA: Sullivan Hernandez/Pierre Guersillon/ Fabrice Auger (Suzuki), 783 laps; **6** Bolliger Team Switzerland, SWI: Horst Saiger/Eric Mizera/Jose Manuel Luis Rita (Kawasaki), 775 laps; **7** No Limits, ITA: Emiliano Bellucci/Gianfranco Guareschi/Victor Casas (Suzuki), 771 laps; **8** RT Racing Team Moto Virus, ITA: Jean Louis Devoyon/ Frederic Jond/David Morillon (Suzuki), 758 laps; **9** Motobox Kremer Racing, GER: Frank Gaziello/Martin Scherrer/Camille Hedelin (Suzuki), 757 laps; **10** Team World Endurance, SWE: Tobias Andersson/Per Nilsson/Pontus Bergsman (Kawasaki), 747 laps; **11** Slider Endurance, FRA: Mickael Lecouturier/Emmanuel Thuillier/Matthias Kipp (Yamaha), 740 laps; **12** MCS Racing IPONE, ITA: Jure Stibilj/Hogan Calvin/Jordi Almeda (Suzuki), 715 laps; **13** Yamaha Austria Racing Team 7, AUT: Igor Jerman/Steve Martin/Gwen Giabbani (Yamaha), 713 laps; **14** Moto Styl, FRA: Alain Raskin/Fabrice Popot/Marc Guiral (Suzuki), 698 laps.
Fastest lap: Yamaha Austria Racing Team, 1m 41.487s, 97.225mph/156.469km/h, on lap 106.
Championship points: 1 Yamaha Austria Racing Team 7, 115; **2** RT Racing Team Moto Virus, 58; **3** Team 18 Sapeurs Pompiers, 57; **4** Suzuki Endurance Racing Team, 57; **5** Bolliger Team Switzerland, 52; **6** Team GSR Kawasaki, 42.

8 HOURS OF DOHA, Losail Circuit, Qatar, 14 November 2009.
Endurance World Championship, round 6. 226 laps of the 3.343-mile/5.380km circuit, 755.518 miles/1215.88km
1 Yamaha Austria Racing Team 7, AUT: Igor Jerman/Steve Martin/Gwen Giabbani (Yamaha), 8h 1m 32.304s, 94.137mph/151.499km/h.
2 Phase One Endurance, GBR: James Ellison/ Glen Richards/Pedro Vallcaneras (Yamaha), 225 laps; **3** Bolliger Team Switzerland, SWI: Horst Saiger/Eric Mizera/Patric Muff (Kawasaki), 224 laps; **4** Team 18 Sapeurs Pompiers, FRA: Stéphane Mollinier/David Briere/Jerome Tangre (Suzuki), 233 laps; **5** No Limits, ITA: Emiliano Bellucci/Ivan Goi/Victor Casas (Suzuki), 219 laps; **6** RT Racing Team Moto Virus, ITA: Jean Louis Devoyon/ Frederic Jond/David Morillon (Suzuki), 214 laps; **7** Michelin Power Research Team, FRA: William Costes/Hugo Marchand/Josep Monge (Honda), 209 laps; **8** MCS Racing IPONE, ITA: Jure Stibilj/Janez Prosenik/Jordi Almeda (Suzuki), 715 laps.
Fastest lap: Yamaha Austria Racing Team, 2m 2.380s, 98.339mph/158.261km/h, on lap 94.

Final World Championship points

1	Yamaha Austria Racing Team 7, AUT	145
2	Team 18 Sapeurs Pompiers, FRA	73
3	Bolliger Team Switzerland, SWI	71
4	RT Racing Team Moto Virus, ITA	70
5	Suzuki Endurance Racing Team, FRA	57
6	No Limits, ITA	50

7 Team GSR Kawasaki, FRA, 42; **8** Phase One Endurance, GBR, 42; **9** Amadeus X-One, ITA, 40; **10** Michelin Power Research Team, FRA, 34; **11** RAC 41 - City Bike, FRA, 33; **12** AM Moto Racing Competition, FRA, 31; **13** MCS Racing IPONE, ITA, 31; **14** Yoshimura Suzuki with Jomo 12, JPN, 30; **15** BK Maco Moto Racing Team, SVK,

Isle of Man Tourist Trophy Races

ISLE OF MAN TOURIST TROPHY COURSE, 8–12 June 2009. 37.73-mile/60.72km course.
Dainese Superbike TT (6 laps, 226.38 miles/ 364.32km)
1 John McGuinness (1000cc Honda), 1h 46m 7.16s, 127.996mph/205.990km/h.
2 Steve Plater (1000cc Honda), 1h 46m 25.27s; **3** Guy Martin (1000cc Honda), 1h 46m 59.69s; **4** Ian Hutchinson (1000cc Honda), 1h 47m 39.66s; **5** Gary Johnson (1000cc Honda) 1h 47m 43.08s; **6** Adrian Archibald (1000cc Suzuki), 1h 49m 4.24s; **7** Ian Lougher (1000cc Yamaha), 1h 49m 5.63s; **8** Carl Rennie (1000cc Suzuki), 1h 50m 34.63s; **9** Dan Stewart (1000cc Honda), 1h 51m 5.13s; **10** John Burrows (1000cc Suzuki), 1h 51m 45.54s; **11** Mark Miller (1000cc Suzuki), 1h 51m 46.03s; **12** William Dunlop (1000cc Yamaha), 1h 51m 54.06s; **13** Daniel Kneen (1000cc Suzuki), 1h 52m 3.00s; **14** Ian Mackman (1000cc Suzuki), 1h 52m 14.47s; **15** Mats Nilsson (1000cc Yamaha), 1h 52m 24.13s.
Fastest lap: McGuiness, 17m 21.29s, 130.442mph/209.926km/h, on lap 2 (record).

Sure Sidecar Race (3 laps, 113.19 miles/ 182.16km)
1 Dave Molyneux/Dan Sayle (600cc DMR Suzuki), 58m 59.28s, 115.132mph/185.287km/h.
2 Philip Dongworth/Gary Partridge (600cc Ireson Honda), 59m 53.22s; **3** Simon Neary/Stuart Bond (600cc Dynobike Suzuki), 1h 0m 18.86s; **4** Tim Reeves/Patrick Farrance (600cc LCR), 1h 0m 21.88s; **5** Conrad Harrison/Kerry Williams (600cc Shelbourne Honda), 1h 1m 7.95s; **6** Steven Coombes/Paul Knapton (600cc Ireson), 1h 2m 41.59s; **7** Roy Hanks/Dave Wells (600cc DMR Suzuki), 1h 2m 41.59s; **8** Neil Kelly/Jason O'Connor (600cc Ireson Honda), 1h 3m 22.12s; **9** Tony Baker/Fiona Baker-Milligan (600cc Baker Suzuki), 1h 3m 22.12s; **10** Andy Laidlow/James Neave (600cc LCR Suzuki), 1h 4m 21.38s; Dylan Lynch/Aaron Galligan (600cc LCR Yamaha), 1h 4m 22.16s; **12** Francois Leblond/Sylvie Leblond (Shelbourne Suzuki), 1h 4m 59.35s; **13** Mike Cookson/Kris Hibberd (600cc Shelbourne Honda), 1h 5m 12.25s; **14** Kenny Howles/Lee Barrett (600cc MR Equipe Suzuki), 1h 5m 13.22s; **15** Howard Baker/Mike Killingsworth (600cc Shelbourne Honda), 1h 5m, 15.09s.
Fastest lap: Molyneux/Sayle, 19m 30.83s, 116.010mph/186.700km/h, on lap 2.

Relentless Supersport TT Race 1 (4 laps, 150.92 miles/242.88km)
1 Ian Hutchinson (600cc Honda), 1h 12m 56.58s, 124.141mph/199.786km/h.
2 Guy Martin (600cc Honda), 1h 13m 3.39s; **3** Keith Amor (600cc Honda), 1h 13m 4.58s; **4** Steve Plater (600cc Honda), 1h 13m 10.22s; **5** John McGuinness (600cc Honda), 1h 13m 24.20s; **6** Ryan Farquhar (600cc Kawasaki), 1h 13m 38.02s; **7** Ian Lougher (600cc Yamaha), 1h 14m 8.28s; **8** Gary Johnson (600cc Honda), 1h 14m 13.41s; **9** William Dunlop (600cc Yamaha), 1h 14m 20.18s; **10** Conor Cummins (600cc Kawasaki), 1h 14m 30.96s; **11** Daniel Kneen (600cc Yamaha), 1h 14m 52.48s; **12** Mats Nilsson (600cc Yamaha), 1h 15m 7.21s; **13** Roy Richardson (600cc Yamaha), 1h 15m 11.34s; **14** Jimmy Moore (600cc Yamaha), 1h 15m 18.38s; **15** Adrian Archibald (600cc Suzuki), 1h 15m 21.19s.
Fastest lap: Anstey, 17m 53.32s, 126.549mph/ 203.661km/h, on lap 2 (record).

Royal London 360 Superstock TT (4 laps, 150.92 miles/242.88km)
1 Ian Hutchinson (1000cc Honda), 1h 10m 57.54s, 127.612mph/205.372km/h.
2 Guy Martin (1000cc Honda), 1h 11m 6.31s; **3** Keith Amor (1000cc Honda), 1h 11m 14.57s; **4** Steve Plater (1000cc Honda), 1h 11m 39.34s; **5** John McGuinness (1000cc Honda), 1h 11m 57.0s; **6** Conor Cummins (1000cc Kawasaki), 1h 11m 57.28s; **7** Gary Johnson (1000cc Honda), 1h 12m 8.05s; **8** Carl Rennie (1000cc Suzuki), 1h 12m 38.17s; **9** Daniel Stewart (1000cc Yamaha), 1h 13m 10.37s; **10** Daniel Kneen (1000cc Suzuki), 1h 13m 34.62s; **11** William Dunlop (1000cc Yamaha), 1h 13m 45.15s; **12** Mark Miller (1000cc Suzuki), 1h 13m 47.82s; **13** Ian Lougher (1000cc Yamaha), 1h 13m 48.92s; **14** James Hillier (1000cc Kawasaki), 1h 13m 59.32s; **15** Ian Pattinson (1000cc Suzuki), 1h 14m 3.83s.
Fastest lap: Hutchinson, 17m 26.88s, 129.746mph/208.806km/h, on lap 4 (record).

Relentless Supersport TT Race 2 (4 laps, 150.92 miles/242.88km)
1 Michael Dunlop (600cc Yamaha), 1h 14m 34.80s, 121.416mph/195.400km/h.
2 Bruce Anstey (600cc Suzuki), 1h 15m 5.81s; **3** Conor Cummins (600cc Kawasaki), 1h 15m 6.52s; **4** Steve Plater (600cc Honda), 1h 15m 11.20s; **5** Ian Hutchinson (600cc Honda), 1h 15m 50.67s; **6** Ian Lougher (600cc Yamaha), 1h 15m 58.53s; **7** Ryan Farquhar (600cc Kawasaki), 1h 17m 1.68s; **8** Mark Buckley (600cc Yamaha), 1h 17m 15.27s; **9** Carl Rennie (600cc Suzuki), 1h 17m 48.06s; **10** Gary Johnson (600cc Honda), 1h 17m 49.65s; **11** John McGuinness (600cc Honda), 1h 18m 1.47s; **12** Roy Richardson (600cc Yamaha), 1h 18m 4.55s; **13** Michael Rutter (600cc Yamaha), 1h 18m 7.27s; **14** Chris Palmer (600cc Suzuki), 1h 18m 22.0s; **15** Derek Brien (600cc Yamaha), 1h 18m 28.91s.
Fastest lap: Plater, 18m 3.30s, 125.384mph/ 201.786km/h, on lap 4.

Pokerstars Senior TT (6 laps, 226.38 miles/ 364.32km)
1 Steve Plater (1000cc Honda), 1h 45m 53.15s, 128.278mph/206.443km/h.
2 Conor Cummins (1000cc Kawasaki), 1h 46m 12.69s; **3** Gary Johnson (1000cc Honda), 1h 47m 3.37s; **4** Adrian Archibald (1000cc Suzuki), 1h 49m 12.72s; **5** Carl Rennie (1000cc Suzuki), 1h 49m 32.85s; **6** Daniel Stewart (1000cc Honda), 1h 50m 23.19s; **7** Michael Rutter (1000cc Suzuki), 1h 50m 33.08s; **8** John Burrows (1000cc Suzuki), 1h 51m 28.77s; **9** James Hillier (1000cc Kawasaki), 1h 51m 29.24s; **10** Ian Mackman (1000cc Suzuki), 1h 51m 59.20s; **11** Mark Parrett (1000cc Yamaha), 1h 52m 2.86s; **12** Rob Barber (1000cc Suzuki), 1h 52m 48.09s; **13** Paul Owen (1000cc Yamaha), 1h 52m 56.99s; **14** Ian Pattinson (1000cc Suzuki), 1h 53m 16.84s; **15** Chris Palmer (750cc Suzuki), 1h 53m 24.57s.
Fastest lap: McGuinness, 17m 12.30s, 131.578mph/211.754km/h, on lap 2 (record).

British Championships

BRANDS HATCH INDY CIRCUIT, 13 April 2009. 1.199-mile/1.929km circuit.
MCE Insurance British Superbike Championship, rounds 1 and 2 (2 x 30 laps, 35.970 miles/57.870km)
Race 1
1 Sylvain Guintoli (Suzuki) 24m 27.117s, 88.23mph/141.99km/h.
2 Glen Richards (Honda); **3** Stuart Easton (Honda); **4** Leon Camier (Yamaha); **5** James Ellison (Yamaha); **6** Gary Mason (Honda); **7** Simon Andrews (Kawasaki); **8** Jason O'Halloran (Honda); **9** Graeme Gowland (Yamaha); **10** Tristan Palmer (Kawasaki); **11** Julien Da Costa (Kawasaki); **12** John Laverty (Kawasaki); **13** Ian Lowry (Suzuki); **14** Chris Walker (Yamaha); **15** Jon Kirkham (Yamaha).
Fastest lap: Richards, 46.476s, 92.84mph/ 149.41km/h.

Race 2
1 Leon Camier (Yamaha) 23m 25.330s, 92.11mph/148.24km/h.
2 Sylvain Guintoli (Suzuki); **3** Steve Plater (Honda); **4** Stuart Easton (Honda); **5** Glen Richards (Honda); **6** Karl Harris (Honda); **7** James Ellison (Yamaha); **8** Chris Walker (Yamaha); **9** Gary Mason (Honda); **10** Julien Da Costa (Kawasaki); **11** Simon Andrews (Kawasaki); **12** Jason O'Halloran (Honda); **13** John Laverty (Kawasaki); **14** Tristan Palmer (Kawasaki); **15** Graeme Gowland (Yamaha).
Fastest lap: Easton, 46.320s, 93.15mph/ 149.91km/h.
Championship points: 1 Guintoli, 45; **2** Camier, 38; **3** Richards, 31; **4** Easton, 29; **5** Ellison, 20; **6** Mason, 17.

Fuchs-Silkolene British Supersport Championship, round 1 (25 laps, 29.975 miles/ 48.225km)
1 Billy McConnell (Yamaha), 19m 54.680s, 90.29mph/145.31km/h.
2 Steve Plater (Honda); **3** Dan Linfoot (Yamaha); **4** Hudson Kennaugh (Yamaha); **5** Lee Johnston (Yamaha); **6** James Webb (Honda); **7** Craig Fitzpatrick (Yamaha); **8** James Westmoreland (Triumph); **9** Paul Young (Triumph); **10** Sam Lowes (Honda); **11** Tom Grant (Honda); **12** Daniel Cooper (Honda); **13** Jimmy Hill (Yamaha); **14** Ross Walter (Triumph); **15** Dean Hipwell (Yamaha).
Fastest lap: Plater, 47.047s, 91.71mph/ 147.59km/h (record).
Championship points: 1 McConnell, 25; **2** Plater, 20; **3** Linfoot, 16; **4** Kennaugh, 13; **5** Johnson, 11; **6** Webb, 10.

Relentless British 125GP Championship, round 1 (22 laps, 26.378 miles/42.438km)
1 Martin Glossop (Seel Honda), 18m 19.222s, 86.38mph/138.98km/h.
2 Tom Haywood (Honda); **3** Shaun Horsman (Honda); **4** James Lodge (Honda); **5** Paul Jordan (Honda); **6** Connor Behan (Honda); **7** Rob Guiver (Honda); **8** Harry Stafford (Honda); **9** Ryan Saxelby (Honda); **10** Catherine Green (Honda); **11** Edward Rendell (Honda); **12** Philip Wakefield (Honda); **13** Taylor Mackenzie (Honda); **14** Shaun Winfield (Honda); **15** Jon Vincent (Honda).
Fastest lap: Glossop, 49.071s, 87.93mph/ 141.51km/h.
Championship points: 1 Glossop, 25; **2** Haywood, 20; **3** Horsman, 16; **4** Lodge, 13; **5** Jordan, 11; **6** Behan, 10.

OULTON PARK INTERNATIONAL, 4 May 2009. 2.692-mile/4.332km circuit.
MCE Insurance British Superbike Championship, rounds 3 and 4 (2 x 18 laps, 48.456 miles/77.976km)
Race 1
1 Leon Camier (Yamaha) 29m 14.802s, 99.40mph/159.97km/h.
2 Karl Harris (Honda); **3** Sylvain Guintoli (Suzuki); **4** Stuart Easton (Honda); **5** James Ellison (Yamaha); **6** Glen Richards (Honda); **7** Ian Lowry (Suzuki); **8** Jason O'Halloran (Honda); **9** Gary Mason (Honda); **10** Josh Brookes (Honda); **11** Chris Walker (Yamaha); **12** Julien Da Costa (Kawasaki); **13** Jon Kirkham (Yamaha); **14** Atsushi Watanabe (Suzuki); **15** Tristan Palmer (Kawasaki).
Fastest lap: Camier, 1m 36.624s, 100.29mph/ 161.40km/h.

Race 2
1 Leon Camier (Yamaha) 29m 7.389s, 99.83mph/160.66km/h.
2 Karl Harris (Honda); **3** Sylvain Guintoli (Suzuki); **4** James Ellison (Yamaha); **5** Glen Richards (Honda); **6** Ian Lowry (Suzuki); **7** Gary Mason (Honda); **8** Simon Andrews (Kawasaki); **9** Chris Walker (Yamaha); **10** Jason O'Halloran (Honda); **11** Jon Kirkham (Yamaha); **12** Atsushi Watanabe (Suzuki); **13** Martin Jessopp (Honda): **14** David Johnson (Yamaha); **15** Peter Hickman (Yamaha).
Fastest lap: Camier, 1m 36.217s, 100.72mph/ 162.09km/h.
Championship points: 1 Camier, 88; **2** Guintoli, 77; **3** Richards, 52; **4** Harris, 50; **5** Ellison, 44; **6** Easton, 42.

Fuchs-Silkolene British Supersport Championship, round 2 (14 laps, 37.688 miles/ 60.648km)
1 Daniel Cooper (Honda), 25m 59.417s, 87.00mph/140.01km/h.
2 Dennis Hobbs (Yamaha); **3** Ben Wilson (Kawasaki); **4** Dean Hipwell (Yamaha); **5** Craig Fitzpatrick (Yamaha); **6** Tom Grant (Honda); **7** Marty Nutt (Yamaha); **8** Kev Coghlan (Honda); **9** James Westmoreland (Triumph); **10** Billy McConnell (Yamaha); **11** Steve Plater (Honda); **12** Robbie Brown (Yamaha); **13** Ross Walter (Triumph); **14** Mark Cringle (Yamaha); **15** Nick Medd (Yamaha).
Fastest lap: Plater, 1m 41.943s, 95.06mph/ 152.99km/h.
Championship points: 1 McConnell, 31; **2** Cooper, 29; **3** Plater, 25; **4** Fitzpatrick, 20; **5** Hobbs, 20; **6** Linfoot, 16.

Relentless British 125GP Championship, round 2 (12 laps, 32.304 miles/51.984km)
1 Martin Glossop (Seel Honda), 21m 59.348s, 88.14mph/141.85km/h.
2 Rob Guiver (Honda); **3** James Lodge (Honda); **4** Tom Haywood (Honda); **5** Connor Behan (Honda); **6** Tim Hastings (Honda); **7** Ryan Saxelby (Honda); **8** Catherine Green (Honda); **9**

Sam Hornsey (Honda); **10** Peter Sutherland (Aprilia); **11** Philip Wakefield (Honda); **12** Robbie Stewart (Honda); **13** Rob Hodson (Honda); **14** Michael Hill (Honda); **15** Ben Barrett (Honda).
Fastest lap: Horsman, 1m 48.048s, 89.69mph/144.34km/h.
Championship points: 1 Glossop, 50; **2** Haywood, 33; **3** Lodge, 29; **4** Guiver, 29; **5** Behan, 21; Horsman, 16.

DONINGTON PARK GRAND PRIX CIRCUIT, 25 May 2009. 2.500-mile/4.023km circuit.
MCE Insurance British Superbike Championship, rounds 5 and 6 (2 x 20 laps, 50.000 miles/80.460km)
Race 1
1 Leon Camier (Yamaha) 30m 45.324s, 97.54mph/156.98km/h.
2 James Ellison (Yamaha); **3** Stuart Easton (Honda); **4** Glen Richards (Honda); **5** Chris Walker (Yamaha); **6** Karl Harris (Honda); **7** Julien Da Costa (Kawasaki); **8** Ian Lowry (Suzuki); **9** John Laverty (Kawasaki); **10** Graeme Gowland (Yamaha); **11** Jason O'Halloran (Honda); **12** Gary Mason (Honda); **13** Jon Kirkham (Yamaha); **14** Tom Tunstall (Honda); **15** Martin Jessopp (Honda).
Fastest lap: Camier, 1m 31.313s, 98.56mph/158.62km/h.

Race 2
1 James Ellison (Yamaha) 30m 49.102s, 97.34mph/156.65km/h.
2 Start Easton (Honda); **3** Chris Walker (Yamaha); **4** Simon Andrews (Kawasaki); **5** Glen Richards (Honda); **6** Ian Lowry (Suzuki); **7** Gary Mason (Honda); **8** Tristan Palmer (Kawasaki); **9** John Laverty (Kawasaki); **10** Graeme Gowland (Yamaha); **11** Julian Da Costa (Kawasaki); **12** Leon Camier (Yamaha); **13** Jon Kirkham (Yamaha); **14** Peter Hickman (Yamaha); **15** Martin Jessopp (Honda).
Fastest lap: Ellison, 1m 31.680s, 98.16mph/157.97km/h.
Championship points: 1 Camier, 117; **2** Ellison, 89; **3** Easton, 78; **4** Guintoli, 77; **5** Richards, 76; **6** Harris, 60.

Fuchs-Silkolene British Supersport Championship, round 3 (18 laps, 45.000 miles/72.414km)
1 Steve Plater (Honda), 28m 32.260s, 94.61mph/152.26km/h.
2 Dan Linfoot (Yamaha); **3** Billy McConnell (Yamaha); **4** Ben Wilson (Kawasaki); **5** James Webb (Honda); **6** Tom Grant (Honda); **7** Kev Coghlan (Yamaha); **8** James Westmoreland (Triumph); **9** Lee Johnston (Yamaha); **10** Daniel Cooper (Honda); **11** Lee Jackson (Honda); **12** Jack Kennedy (Yamaha); **13** Sam Lowes (Honda); **14** Hudson Kennaugh (Yamaha); **15** Allan Jon Venter (Yamaha).
Fastest lap: Kennaugh, 1m 34.097s, 95.64mph/153.92km/h.
Championship points: 1 Plater, 50; **2** McConnell, 47; **3** Linfoot, 36; **4** Cooper, 35; **5** Wilson, 29; **6** Grant, 25.

Relentless British 125GP Championship, round 3 (7 laps, 17.500 miles/28.161km)
1 Martin Glossop (Seel Honda), 12m 50.620s, 81.75mph/131.56km/h.
2 James Lodge (Honda); **3** Brian Clark (Honda); **4** Taylor Mackenzie (Honda); **5** Lee Costello (Honda); **6** Michal Hill (Honda); **7** Matthew Paulo (Honda); **8** Paul Jordan (Honda); **9** Peter Sutherland (Aprilia); **10** Shaun Horsman (Honda); **11** Tim Hastings (Honda); **12** Jon Vincent (Honda); **13** Adam Blacklock (Honda); **14** Luke Harvey (Honda); **15** Jon McPhee (Honda.
Fastest lap: Glossop, 1m 48.578s, 84.44mph/135.90km/h.
Championship points: 1 Glossop, 75; **2** Lodge, 49; **3** Haywood, 33; **4** Guiver, 29; **5** Horsman, 22; **6** Behan, 21.

THRUXTON, 31 May 2009. 2.356-mile/3.792km circuit.
MCE Insurance British Superbike Championship, rounds 7 and 8 (2 x 20 laps, 47.120 miles/75.840km)
Race 1
1 Leon Camier (Yamaha) 25m 27.557s, 111.04mph/178.70km/h.
2 James Ellison (Yamaha); **3** Stuart Easton (Honda); **4** Simon Andrews (Kawasaki); **5** Michael Rutter (Suzuki); **6** Glen Richards (Honda); **7** Josh Brookes (Honda); **8** John Laverty (Kawasaki); **9** Gary Mason (Honda); **10** Julien Da Costa (Kawasaki); **11** Karl Harris (Honda); **12** Graeme Gowland (Yamaha); **13** Jason O'Halloran (Honda); **14** Atsushi Watanabe (Suzuki); **15** Tom Tunstall (Honda).
Fastest lap: Camier, 1m 15.422s, 112.45mph/180.97km/h.

Race 2
1 Leon Camier (Yamaha) 25m 25.643s, 111.18mph/178.93km/h.
2 James Ellison (Yamaha); **3** Josh Brookes (Honda); **4** Stuart Easton (Honda); **5** Michael Rutter (Suzuki); **6** Simon Andrews (Kawasaki); **7** Glen Richards (Honda); **8** Ian Lowry (Suzuki); **9** Karl Harris (Honda); **10** Julien Da Costa (Kawasaki); **11** John Laverty (Kawasaki); **12** Gary Mason (Honda); **13** Graeme Gowland (Yamaha); **14** Martin Jessopp (Honda); **15** Peter Hickman (Yamaha).
Fastest lap: Camier, 1m 14.933s, 113.18mph/182.15km/h.
Championship points: 1 Camier, 167; **2** Ellison, 129; **3** Easton, 107; **4** Richards, 95; **5** Guintoli, 77; **6** Harris, 72.

Fuchs-Silkolene British Supersport Championship, round 4 (16 laps, 37.696 miles/60.672km)
1 Billy McConnell (Yamaha), 20m 54.401s, 108.18mph/174.10km/h.
2 Steve Plater (Honda); **3** Dan Linfoot (Yamaha); **4** James Westmoreland (Triumph); **5** James Webb (Honda); **6** Ben Wilson (Kawasaki); **7** Paul Young (Triumph); **8** Hudson Kennaugh (Yamaha); **9** Lee Johnston (Yamaha); **10** Joe Dickinson (Honda); **11** Tom Grant (Honda); **12** Robbie Brown (Yamaha); **13** Jack Kennedy (Yamaha); **14** Daniel Cooper (Honda); **15** Lee Jackson (Honda).
Fastest lap: Westmoreland, 1m 17.333s, 109.67mph/176.50km/h (record).
Championship points: 1 McConnell, 72; **2** Plater, 70; **3** Linfoot, 52; **4** Wilson, 39; **5** Cooper, 37; **6** Westmoreland, 36.

Relentless British 125GP Championship, round 4 (14 laps, 32.984 miles/53.088km)
1 Brian Clark (Honda), 19m 22.760s, 102.12mph/164.35km/h.
2 Tom Hasting (Honda); **3** Paul Jordan (Honda); **4** James Lodge (Honda); **5** Shaun Horsman (Honda); **6** Connor Behan (Honda); **7** Rob Guiver (Honda); **8** Adam Blacklock (Honda); **9** Tom Haywood (Honda); **10** Lee Costello (Honda); **11** Ryan Saxelby (Honda); **12** Michael Hill (Honda); **13** Edwards Rendell (Honda); **14** Robbie Stewart (Honda); **15** Catherine Green (Honda).
Fastest lap: Jordan, 1m 21.930s, 103.52mph/166.60km/h.
Championship points: 1 Glossop, 75; **2** Lodge, 62; **3** Clark, 41; **4** Haywood, 40; **5** Guiver, 38; **6** Jordan, 35.

SNETTERTON, 21 June 2009. 1.952-mile/3.141km circuit.
MCE Insurance British Superbike Championship, rounds 9 and 10
Race 1 (18 laps, 35.136 miles/56.538km)
1 Leon Camier (Yamaha) 19m 51.245s, 106.18mph/170.88km/h.
2 Stuart Easton (Honda); **3** Josh Brookes (Honda); **4** James Ellison (Yamaha); **5** Ian Lowry (Suzuki); **6** Chris Walker (Yamaha); **7** Michael Rutter (Suzuki); **8** Karl Harris (Honda); **9** Julien Da Costa (Kawasaki); **10** Simon Andrews (Kawasaki); **11** Graeme Gowland (Yamaha); **12** Jason O'Halloran (Honda); **13** John Laverty (Kawasaki); **14** Jon Kirkham (Yamaha); **15** Tommy Bridewell (Suzuki).
Fastest lap: Camier, 1m 5.464s, 107.34mph/172.75km/h.

Race 2 (22 laps, 42.944 miles/69.102km)
1 Leon Camier (Yamaha) 24m 10.003s, 106.61mph/171.57km/h.
2 James Ellison (Yamaha); **3** Josh Brookes (Honda); **4** Stuart Easton (Honda); **5** John Laverty (Kawasaki); **6** Julien Da Costa (Kawasaki); **7** Ian Lowry (Suzuki); **8** Glen Richards (Honda); **9** Karl Harris (Honda); **10** Jason O'Halloran (Honda); **11** Simon Andrews (Kawasaki); **12** Graeme Gowland (Yamaha); **13** Jon Kirkham (Yamaha); **14** Gary Mason (Honda); **15** Peter Hickman (Yamaha).
Fastest lap: Camier, 1m 5.300s, 107.61mph/173.18km/h.
Championship points: 1 Camier, 217; **2** Ellison, 162; **3** Easton, 140; **4** Richards, 103; **5** Harris, 87; **6** Guintoli, 77.

Fuchs-Silkolene British Supersport Championship, round 5 (13 laps, 25.376 miles/40.833km)
1 Steve Plater (Honda), 14m 53.753s, 102.21mph/164.49km/h.
2 Daniel Cooper (Honda); **3** James Westmoreland (Triumph); **4** Hudson Kennaugh (Yamaha); **5** James Webb (Honda); **6** Craig Fitzpatrick (Yamaha); **7** Ian Hutchinson (Honda); **8** Ben Wilson (Kawasaki); **9** Paul Young (Triumph); **10** Allan Jon Venter (Yamaha); **11** Joe Dickinson (Honda); **12** Robbie Brown (Yamaha); **13** Sam Lowes (Honda); **14** Dean Hipwell (Yamaha); **15** David Paton (Yamaha).
Fastest lap: Plater, 1m 7.713s, 103.77mph/167.01km/h.
Championship points: 1 Plater, 95; **2** McConnell, 72; **3** Cooper, 57; **4** Linfoot, 52; **5** Westmoreland, 52; **6** Wilson, 47.

Relentless British 125GP Championship, round 5 (15 laps, 29.280 miles/47.115km)
1 Paul Jordan (Honda), 18m 44.781s, 93.71mph/150.81km/h.
2 James Lodge (Honda); **3** Tim Hastings (Honda); **4** Tom Haywood (Honda); **5** Martin Glossop (Seel Honda); **6** Brian Clark (Honda); **7** Rob Guiver (Honda); **8** Peter Sutherland (Aprilia); **9** Adam Blacklock (Honda); **10** Ryan Saxelby (Honda); **11** Catherine Green (Honda); **12** Deane Brown (Honda); **13** Taylor Mackenzie (Honda); **14** Edward Rendell (Honda); **15** Jamie Mossey (Honda).
Fastest lap: Lodge, 1m 13.712s, 95.33mph/153.42km/h.
Championship points: 1 Glossop, 86; **2** Lodge, 82; **3** Jordon, 60; **4** Haywood, 53; **5** Clark, 51; **6** Hastings, 51.

KNOCKHILL, 5 July 2009. 1.271-mile/2.046km circuit.
MCE Insurance British Superbike Championship, rounds 11 and 12
Race 1 (33 laps, 41.943 miles/67.518km)
1 Leon Camier (Yamaha) 27m 49.745s, 90.45mph/145.57km/h.
2 Stuart Easton (Honda); **3** Josh Brookes (Honda); **4** Simon Andrews (Kawasaki); **5** James Ellison (Yamaha); **6** Ian Lowry (Suzuki); **7** Chris Walker (Yamaha); **8** Graeme Gowland (Yamaha); **9** Tommy Bridewell (Suzuki); **10** Jason O'Halloran (Honda); **11** Michael Rutter (Suzuki); **12** Peter Hickman (Yamaha); **13** Tom Tunstall (Honda); **14** Atsushi Watanabe (Suzuki); **15** Aaron Zanotti (Honda).
Fastest lap: Camier, 48.884s, 93.62mph/150.67km/h.

Race 2 (30 laps, 38.130 miles/61.380km)
1 Leon Camier (Yamaha) 24m 41.486s, 92.67mph/149.14km/h.
2 Josh Brookes (Honda); **3** James Ellison (Yamaha); **4** Stuart Easton (Honda); **5** Chris Walker (Yamaha); **6** Simon Andrews (Kawasaki); **7** Graeme Gowland (Yamaha); **8** Julien Da Costa (Kawasaki); **9** Tommy Bridewell (Suzuki); **10** Gary Mason (Honda); **11** Tristan Palmer (Kawasaki); **12** Jason O'Halloran (Honda); **13** David Johnson (Yamaha); **14** Peter Hickman (Yamaha); **15** Atsushi Watanabe (Suzuki).
Fastest lap: Camier, 48.893s, 93.60mph/150.63km/h.
Championship points: 1 Camier, 267; **2** Ellison, 189; **3** Easton, 173; **4** Richards, 103; **5** Brookes, 99; **6** Andrews, 92.

Fuchs-Silkolene British Supersport Championship, round 6 (24 laps, 30.504 miles/49.104km)
1 Ben Wilson (Kawasaki), 20m 24.699s, 89.68mph/144.33km/h.
2 James Westmoreland (Triumph); **3** Daniel Cooper (Honda); **4** Billy McConnell (Yamaha); **5** Lee Johnston (Yamaha); **6** Ian Hutchinson (Honda); **7** Tom Grant (Honda); **8** Chris Martin (Kawasaki); **9** Allan Jon Venter (Yamaha); **10** Sam Lowes (Honda); **11** Steve Plater (Honda); **12** Jack Kennedy (Yamaha); **13** Hudson Kennaugh (Yamaha); **14** Craig Fitzpatrick (Yamaha); **15** Joe Dickinson (Honda).
Fastest lap: Westmoreland, 50.359s, 90.88mph/146.26km/h (record).
Championship points: 1 Plater, 100; **2** McConnell, 85; **3** Cooper, 73; **4** Westmoreland, 72; **5** Wilson, 72; **6** Linfoot, 52.

Relentless British 125GP Championship, round 6 (20 laps, 25.420 miles/40.920km)
1 James Lodge (Honda), 18m 12.915s, 83.75mph/134.78km/h.
2 Rob Guiver (Honda); **3** Connor Behan (Honda); **4** Robbie Stewart (Honda); **5** Martin Glossop (Seel Honda); **6** Brian Clark (Honda); **7** Deane Brown (Honda); **8** Lee Costello (Honda); **9** Taylor Mackenzie (Honda); **10** Tom Haywood (Honda); **11** Tim Hastings (Honda); **12** Paul Jordon (Honda); **13** Ryan Saxelby (Honda); **14** Michael Hill (Honda); **15** Philip Wakefield (Honda).
Fastest lap: Glossop, 53.958s, 84.82mph/136.50km/h.
Championship points: 1 Lodge, 107; **2** Glossop, 97; **3** Guiver, 67; **4** Jordan, 64; **5** Clark, 61; **6** Haywood, 59.

MALLORY PARK, 19 July 2009. 1.410-mile/2.269km circuit.
MCE Insurance British Superbike Championship, rounds 13 and 14
Race 1 (22 laps, 31.020 miles/49.918km)
1 James Ellison (Yamaha) 21m 1.786s, 88.50mph/142.43km/h.
2 Leon Camier (Yamaha); **3** Graeme Gowland (Yamaha); **4** Michael Rutter (Honda); **5** Julien Da Costa (Kawasaki); **6** Gary Mason (Honda); **7** Steve Brogan (Honda); **8** Ian Lowry (Suzuki); **9** David Johnson (Yamaha); **10** Tristan Palmer (Kawasaki); **11** Tommy Bridewell (Suzuki); **12** Peter Hickman (Yamaha); **13** Tom Tunstall (Honda); **14** Atsushi Watanabe (Suzuki); **15** Kenny Gilbertson (Kawasaki).
Fastest lap: Ellison, 56.333s, 90.10mph/145.00km/h.

Race 2 (15 laps, 21.150 miles/34.035km)
1 Leon Camier (Yamaha) 15m 34.550s, 81.47mph/131.11km/h.
2 James Ellison (Yamaha); **3** Chris Walker (Yamaha); **4** John Laverty (Kawasaki); **5** Richard Cooper (Yamaha); **6** Michael Rutter (Honda); **7** Karl Harris (Honda); **8** Tommy Hill (Suzuki); **9** Steve Brogan (Honda); **10** Julien Da Costa (Kawasaki); **11** David Johnson (Yamaha); **12** Tristan Palmer (Kawasaki); **13** Graeme Gowland (Yamaha); **14** Peter Hickman (Yamaha); **15** Simon Andrews (Kawasaki).
Fastest lap: Camier, 1m 0.442s, 83.98mph/135.15km/h.
Championship points: 1 Camier, 299.5; **2** Ellison, 224; **3** Easton, 173; **4** Richards, 103; **5** Brookes, 99; **6** Andrews, 92.5.

Fuchs-Silkolene British Supersport Championship, round 7 (25 laps, 35.250 miles/56.725km)
1 Chris Martin (Kawasaki), 25m 20.475s, 83.46mph/134.32km/h.
2 Ben Wilson (Kawasaki); **3** Ian Hutchinson (Honda); **4** Billy McConnell (Yamaha); **5** Brendan Roberts (Yamaha); **6** BJ Toal (Yamaha); **7** Steve Plater (Honda); **8** Daniel Cooper (Honda); **9** Sam Lowes (Honda); **10** Joe Dickinson (Honda); **11** Tom Grant (Honda); **12** Dean Hipwell (Yamaha); **13** Jack Kennedy (Yamaha); **14** Chris Northover (Kawasaki); **15** Marty Nutt (Yamaha).
Fastest lap: McConnell, 58.775s, 86.36mph/138.98km/h.
Championship points: 1 Plater, 109; **2** McConnell, 98; **3** Wilson, 92; **4** Cooper, 81; **5** Westmoreland, 72; **6** Linfoot, 52.

Relentless British 125GP Championship, round 7 (20 laps, 28.200 miles/45.380km)
1 Rob Guiver (Honda), 20m 21.257s, 83.12mph/133.77km/h.
2 James Lodge (Honda); **3** Tim Hasting (Honda); **4** Robbie Stewart (Honda); **5** Shaun Horsman (Honda); **6** Brian Clark (Honda); **7** Adam Blacklock (Honda); **8** Lee Costello (Honda); **9** Corey Lewis (Honda); **10** Michael Hill (Honda); **11** Tom Weeden (Honda); **12** Matthew Paulo (Honda); **13** Shaun Winfield (Honda); **14** Catherine Green (Honda); **15** John McPhee (Honda).
Fastest lap: Behan, 1m 0.347s, 84.11mph/135.36km/h.
Championship points: 1 Lodge, 127; **2** Glossop, 97; **3** Guiver, 92; **4** Hastings, 72; **5** Clark, 71; **6** Jordan, 64.

BRANDS HATCH GP CIRCUIT, 9–10 August 2009. 2.301-mile/3.703km circuit.
MCE Insurance British Superbike Championship, rounds 15, 16 and 17
Race 1 (18 laps, 41.418 miles/66.654km)
1 Leon Camier (Yamaha) 26m 15.747s, 94.61mph/152.26km/h.
2 Broc Parkes (Kawasaki); **3** Stuart Easton (Honda); **4** Karl Muggeridge (Honda); **5** Tommy Hill (Suzuki); **6** James Ellison (Yamaha); **7** John Laverty (Kawasaki); **8** Karl Harris (Honda); **9**

Chris Walker (Yamaha); **10** Julien Da Costa (Kawasaki); **11** Michael Rutter (Kawasaki); **12** Ian Lowry (Suzuki); **13** Gary Mason (Honda); **14** Steve Brogan (Honda); **15** Tristan Palmer (Kawasaki).
Fastest lap: Parkes, 1m 26.568s, 95.68mph/ 153.98km/h.

Race 2 (20 laps, 46.020 miles/74.060km)
1 Leon Camier (Yamaha) 30m 36.823s, 90.18mph/145.13km/h.
2 Broc Parkes (Kawasaki); **3** Stuart Easton (Honda); **4** Tommy Hill (Suzuki); **5** James Ellison (Yamaha); **6** Karl Harris (Honda); **7** Karl Muggeridge (Honda); **8** Steve Brogan (Honda); **9** Graeme Gowland (Yamaha); **10** Sheridan Morais (Kawasaki); **11** Julien Da Costa (Kawasaki); **12** Ian Lowry (Suzuki); **13** John Laverty (Kawasaki); **14** Gary Mason (Honda); **15** Atsushi Watanabe (Suzuki).
Fastest lap: Camier, 1m 26.524s, 95.73mph/ 154.06km/h.

Race 3 (20 laps, 46.020 miles/74.060km)
1 Leon Camier (Yamaha) 29m 5.284s, 94.92mph/152.76km/h.
2 Broc Parkes (Kawasaki); **3** James Ellison (Yamaha); **4** Stuart Easton (Honda); **5** John Laverty (Kawasaki); **6** Karl Muggeridge (Honda); **7** Tommy Hill (Suzuki); **8** Sheridan Morais (Kawasaki); **9** Ian Lowry (Suzuki); **10** Michael Rutter (Kawasaki); **11** Steve Brogan (Honda); **12** Chris Walker (Yamaha); **13** Graeme Gowland (Yamaha); **14** Karl Harris (Honda); **15** Gary Mason (Honda).
Fastest lap: Camier, 1m 26.578s, 95.67mph/ 153.97km/h.
Championship points: **1** Camier, 374.5; **2** Ellison, 261; **3** Easton, 218; **4** Harris, 111.5; **5** Richards, 103; **6** Lowry, 101.

Fuchs-Silkolene British Supersport Championship, round 8 (18 laps, 41.418 miles/ 66.654km)
1 James Westmoreland (Triumph), 27m 50.845s, 89.23mph/143.60km/h.
2 Billy McConnell (Yamaha); **3** Steve Plater (Honda); **4** Ben Wilson (Kawasaki); **5** Ian Hutchinson (Honda); **6** Craig Fitzpatrick (Yamaha); **7** Sam Lowes (Honda); **8** Allan Jon Venter (Yamaha); **9** James Webb (Honda); **10** Jack Kennedy (Yamaha); **11** Robbie Brown (Yamaha); **12** Paul Young (Triumph); **13** Lee Jackson (Honda); **14** BJ Toal (Honda); **15** Dean Hipwell (Yamaha).
Fastest lap: Linfoot, 1m 29.240s, 92.81mph/ 149.37km/h.
Championship points: **1** Plater, 125; **2** McConnell, 118; **3** Wilson, 105; **4** Westmoreland, 97; **5** Cooper, 81; **6** Linfoot, 52.

Relentless British 125GP Championship, round 8 (14 laps, 32.214 miles/51.842km)
1 Rob Guiver (Honda), 22m 24.911s, 86.22mph/138.76km/h.
2 James Lodge (Honda); **3** Adam Blacklock (Honda); **4** Martin Glossop (Seel Honda); **5** Brian Clark (Honda); **6** Robbie Stewart (Honda); **7** Edwards Rendell (Honda); **8** Paul Jordon (Honda); **9** Deane Brown (Honda); **10** Tom Haywood (Honda); **11** Matthew Hoyle (Honda); **12** Taylor Mackenzie (Honda); **13** Harry Stafford (Honda); **14** Tom Weeden (Honda); **15** Michael Hill (Honda).
Fastest lap: Glossop, 1m 34.745s, 87.42mph/ 140.69km/h.
Championship points: **1** Lodge, 147; **2** Guiver, 117; **3** Glossop, 110; **4** Clark, 82; **5** Hastings, 72; **6** Jordon, 72.

CADWELL PARK, 31 August 2009. 2.180-mile/3.508km circuit.
MCE Insurance British Superbike Championship, rounds 18 and 19 (2 x 18 laps, 39.240 miles/63.144km)
Race 1
1 Leon Camier (Yamaha) 26m 38.546s, 88.37mph/142.22km/h.
2 Stuart Easton (Honda); **3** James Ellison (Yamaha); **4** Ian Lowry (Suzuki); **5** Simon Andrews (Kawasaki); **6** Julien Da Costa (Kawasaki); **7** Karl Muggeridge (Honda); **8** Sylvain Guintoli (Suzuki); **9** John Laverty (Kawasaki); **10** Gary Mason (Honda); **11** Chris Walker (Yamaha); **12** John McGuinness (Honda); **13** Tommy Bridewell (Suzuki); **14** Peter Hickman (Yamaha); **15** Karl Harris (Honda).
Fastest lap: Camier, 1m 27.788s, 89.39mph/ 143.86km/h.

Race 2
1 James Ellison (Yamaha) 28m 2.679s, 83.95mph/135.10km/h.
2 Stuart Easton (Honda); **3** Simon Andrews (Kawasaki); **4** Julien Da Costa (Kawasaki); **5** John Laverty (Kawasaki); **6** Chris Walker (Yamaha); **7** Sylvain Guintoli (Suzuki); **8** Karl Harris (Honda); **9** Gary Mason (Honda); **10** Tommy Bridewell (Suzuki); **11** Peter Hickman (Yamaha); **12** Tristan Palmer (Kawasaki); **13** Karl Muggeridge (Honda); **14** Howie Mainwaring (Yamaha); **15** Jon Kirkham (Yamaha).
Fastest lap: Ellison, 1m 27.973s, 89.20mph/ 143.55km/h.
Championship points: **1** Camier, 399.5; **2** Ellison, 302; **3** Easton, 258; **4** Harris, 120.5; **5** Andrews, 119.5; **6** Lowry, 114.

Fuchs-Silkolene British Supersport Championship, round 9 (16 laps, 34.880 miles/ 56.128km)
1 Billy McConnell (Yamaha), 24m 21.701s, 85.90mph/138.24km/h.
2 Steve Plater (Honda); **3** James Westmoreland (Triumph); **4** Allan Jon Venter (Yamaha); **5** Dan Linfoot (Yamaha); **6** Sam Lowes (Honda); **7** Jack Kennedy (Yamaha); **8** Ian Hutchinson (Honda); **9** Marty Nutt (Yamaha); **10** Tom Grant (Honda); **11** Lee Jackson (Honda); **12** James Webb (Honda); **13** Robbie Brown (Yamaha); **14** Paul Young (Triumph); **15** BJ Toal (Honda).
Fastest lap: McConnell, 1m 30.012s, 87.18mph/140.31km/h.
Championship points: **1** Plater, 145; **2** McConnell, 143; **3** Westmoreland, 113; **4** Wilson, 105; **5** Cooper, 81; **6** Linfoot, 63.

Relentless British 125GP Championship, round 9 (8 laps, 17.440 miles/28.064km)
1 Martin Glossop (Seel Honda), 12m 50.478s, 81.48mph/131.13km/h.
2 Deane Brown (Honda); **3** Connor Behan (Honda); **4** Tom Haywood (Honda); **5** Adam Blacklock (Honda); **6** Paul Jordan (Honda); **7** Tim Hastings (Honda); **8** Rob Guiver (Honda); **9** Philip Wakefield (Honda); **10** Jay Lewis (Honda); **11** Ross Walker (Honda); **12** Shaun Horsman (Honda); **13** Catherine Green (Honda); **14** Jon Vincent (Honda); **15** Tom Weeden (Honda).
Fastest lap: Glossop, 1m 35.153s, 82.47mph/ 132.73km/h.
Championship points: **1** Lodge, 147; **2** Glossop, 135; **3** Guiver, 125; **4** Clark, 82; **5** Jordan, 82; **6** Hastings, 81.

CROFT, 13 September 2009. 2.125-mile/ 3.420km circuit.
MCE Insurance British Superbike Championship, rounds 20 and 21 (2 x 20 laps, 42.500 miles/68.400km)
Race 1
1 Stuart Easton (Honda) 27m 6.092s, 94.09mph/151.42km/h.
2 James Ellison (Yamaha); **3** Josh Brookes (Honda); **4** Ryuichi Kiyonari (Honda); **5** Ian Lowry (Suzuki); **6** Leon Camier (Yamaha); **7** Tommy Hill (Honda); **8** Gary Mason (Honda); **9** Julian Da Costa (Kawasaki); **10** Graeme Gowland (Yamaha); **11** Peter Hickman (Yamaha); **12** Tommy Bridewell (Suzuki); **13** John Laverty (Kawasaki); **14** Karl Harris (Yamaha); **15** Howie Mainwaring (Yamaha).
Fastest lap: Camier, 1m 20.350s, 95.20mph/ 153.21km/h.

Race 2
1 Leon Camier (Yamaha) 26m 57.535s, 94.58mph/152.21km/h.
2 Stuart Easton (Honda); **3** Josh Brookes (Honda); **4** James Ellison (Yamaha); **5** Simon Andrews (Kawasaki); **6** Tommy Hill (Honda); **7** Ian Lowry (Suzuki); **8** Gary Mason (Honda); **9** Julien Da Costa (Kawasaki); **10** John Laverty (Kawasaki); **11** Chris Walker (Yamaha); **12** Graeme Gowland (Yamaha); **13** Sylvain Guintoli (Suzuki); **14** Tommy Bridewell (Suzuki); **15** Peter Hickman (Yamaha).
Fastest lap: Camier, 1m 20.097s, 95.51mph/ 153.71km/h.
Championship points: **1** Camier, 434.5; **2** Ellison, 335; **3** Easton, 303; **4** Lowry, 134; **5** Brookes, 131; **6** Andrews, 130.5.

Fuchs-Silkolene British Supersport Championship, round 10 (18 laps, 38.250 miles/ 61.560km)
1 Steve Plater (Honda), 25m 38.321s, 89.51mph/144.05km/h.
2 Billy McConnell (Yamaha); **3** Ben Wilson (Kawasaki); **4** James Westmoreland (Triumph); **5** Ian Hutchinson (Honda); **6** Daniel Cooper (Honda); **7** Dan Linfoot (Yamaha); **8** Marty Nutt (Yamaha); **9** Allan Jon Venter (Yamaha); **10** Jack Kennedy (Yamaha); **11** Lee Johnston (Yamaha); **12** Tom Grant (Honda); **13** BJ Toal (Honda); **14** Lee Jackson (Honda); **15** Joe Dickinson (Honda).
Fastest lap: McConnell, 1m 22.590s, 92.62mph/149.06km/h.
Championship points: **1** Plater, 170; **2** McConnell, 163; **3** Westmoreland, 126; **4** Wilson, 121; **5** Cooper, 91; **6** Linfoot, 72.

Relentless British 125GP Championship, round 10 (14 laps, 29.750 miles/47.880km)
1 Connor Behan (Honda), 20m 47.591s, 85.84mph/138.15km/h.
2 Brian Clark (Honda); **3** Tom Hastings (Honda); **4** Matthew Hoyle (Honda); **5** Deane Brown (Honda); **6** James Lodge (Honda); **7** Adam Blacklock (Honda); **8** Harry Stafford (Honda); **9** Taylor Mackenzie (Honda); **10** Paul Jordan (Honda); **11** Catherine Green (Honda); **12** Ross Walker (Honda); **13** Peter Sutherland (Aprilia); **14** Jon Vincent (Honda); **15** Tom Weeden (Honda).
Fastest lap: Stewart, 1m 27.995s, 86.93mph/ 139.91km/h.
Championship points: **1** Lodge, 157; **2** Glossop, 135; **3** Guiver, 125; **4** Clark, 102; **5** Hastings, 97; **6** Jordan, 88.

SILVERSTONE INTERNATIONAL CIRCUIT, 27 September 2009. 2.213-mile/3.562km circuit.
MCE Insurance British Superbike Championship, rounds 22 and 23
Race 1 (20 laps, 44.260 miles/71.240km)
1 Leon Camier (Yamaha) 28m 55.092s, 91.83mph/147.79km/h.
2 James Ellison (Yamaha); **3** Josh Brookes (Honda); **4** Stuart Easton (Honda); **5** Tommy Hill (Honda); **6** John Laverty (Kawasaki); **7** Sylvain Guintoli (Suzuki); **8** Ian Lowry (Suzuki); **9** Simon Andrews (Kawasaki); **10** Julien Da Costa (Kawasaki); **11** Graeme Gowland (Yamaha); **12** Tommy Bridewell (Suzuki); **13** Glen Richards (Honda); **14** Gary Mason (Honda); **15** Peter Hickman (Yamaha).
Fastest lap: Camier, 1m 25.946s, 92.69mph/ 149.17km/h.

Race 2 (18 laps, 39.834 miles/64.116km)
1 James Ellison (Yamaha) 26m 2.765s, 91.76mph/147.67km/h.
2 Leon Camier (Yamaha); **3** Josh Brookes (Honda); **4** Stuart Easton (Honda); **5** Tommy Hill (Honda); **6** Julien Da Costa (Kawasaki); **7** Simon Andrews (Kawasaki); **8** Sylvain Guintoli (Suzuki); **9** Ian Lowry (Suzuki); **10** Alastair Seeley (Suzuki); **11** Chris Walker (Yamaha); **12** Tommy Bridewell (Suzuki); **13** Peter Hickman (Yamaha); **14** Karl Harris (Honda); **15** Michael Rutter (Ducati).
Fastest lap: Camier, 1m 26.029s, 92.60mph/ 149.02km/h.
Championship points: **1** Camier, 479.5; **2** Ellison, 380; **3** Easton, 329; **4** Brookes, 163; **5** Lowry, 149; **6** Andrews, 146.5.

Fuchs-Silkolene British Supersport Championship, round 11 (18 laps, 39.834 miles/ 64.116km)
1 James Westmoreland (Triumph), 26m 44.949s, 89.35mph/143.79km/h.
2 Steve Plater (Honda); **3** Billy McConnell (Yamaha); **4** Ian Hutchinson (Honda); **5** Tom Grant (Honda); **6** Joe Dickinson (Honda); **7** Jack Kennedy (Yamaha); **8** Daniel Cooper (Honda); **9** Marty Nutt (Yamaha); **10** Hudson Kennaugh (Kawasaki); **11** BJ Toal (Honda); **12** Ross Walter (Triumph); **13** Lee Jackson (Honda); **14** Dean Hipwell (Yamaha); **15** Aaron Walker (Triumph).
Fastest lap: Westmoreland, 1m 28.279s, 90.24mph/145.23km/h.
Championship points: **1** Plater, 190; **2** McConnell, 179; **3** Westmoreland, 151; **4** Wilson, 121; **5** Cooper, 99; **6** Hutchinson, 78.

Relentless British 125GP Championship, round 11 (14 laps, 30.982 miles/49.868km)
1 Rob Guiver (Honda), 22m 10.682s, 83,81mph/134.88km/h.
2 Martin Glossop (Seel Honda); **3** James Lodge (Honda); **4** Taylor Mackenzie (Honda); **5** Brian Clark (Honda); **6** Matthew Hoyle (Honda); **7** Deane Brown (Honda); **8** Paul Jordan (Honda); **9** Harry Stafford (Honda); **10** Tim Hastings (Honda); **11** Tom Haywood (Honda); **12** Catherine Green (Honda); **13** Ian Lougher (Honda); **14** Philip Wakefield (Honda); **15** Shaun Horsman (Honda).
Fastest lap: Glossop, 1m 33.833s, 84.90mph/ 136.64km/h.
Championship points: **1** Lodge, 173; **2** Glossop, 155; **3** Guiver, 150; **4** Clark, 113; **5** Hastings, 103; **6** Jordan, 96.

OULTON PARK INTERNATIONAL, 10–11 October 2009. 2.692-miles/4.332km circuit.
MCE Insurance British Superbike Championship, rounds 24, 25 and 26
Race 1 (12 laps, 32.304 miles/51.984km)
1 Stuart Easton (Honda) 19m 21.434s, 100.13mph/161.14km/h.
2 Leon Camier (Yamaha); **3** Tommy Hill (Honda); **4** James Ellison (Yamaha); **5** Sylvain Guintoli (Suzuki); **6** Simon Andrews (Kawasaki); **7** Julien Da Costa (Kawasaki); **8** Ian Lowry (Suzuki); **9** Chris Walker (Yamaha); **10** John Laverty (Kawasaki); **11** Glen Richards (Honda); **12** Michael Rutter (Ducati); **13** Gary Mason (Honda); **14** Peter Hickman (Yamaha); **15** Tommy Bridewell (Suzuki).
Fastest lap: Ellison, 1m 35.943s, 101.01mph/ 162.56km/h.

Race 2 (16 laps, 43.072 miles/69.312km)
1 Leon Camier (Yamaha) 26m 17.122s, 98.31mph/158.21km/h.
2 Stuart Easton (Honda); **3** James Ellison (Yamaha); **4** Tommy Hill (Honda); **5** Sylvain Guintoli (Suzuki); **6** John Laverty (Kawasaki); **7** Josh Brookes (Honda); **8** Michael Rutter (Ducati); **9** Simon Andrews (Kawasaki); **10** Glen Richards (Honda); **11** Tommy Bridewell (Suzuki); **12** Gary Mason (Honda); **13** Alastair Seeley (Suzuki); **14** Chris Walker (Yamaha); **15** Graeme Gowland (Yamaha).
Fastest lap: Easton, 1m 36.170s, 100.77mph/ 162.17km/h.

Race 3 (12 laps, 32.304 miles/51.984km)
1 Leon Camier (Yamaha) 19m 17.097s, 100.50mph/161.74km/h.
2 Tommy Hill (Honda); **3** Josh Brookes (Honda); **4** Ian Lowry (Suzuki); **5** Sylvain Guintoli (Suzuki); **6** Julien Da Costa (Kawasaki); **7** Chris Walker (Yamaha); **8** Glen Richards (Honda); **9** Tommy Bridewell (Suzuki); **10** Gary Mason (Honda); **11** Graeme Gowland (Yamaha); **12** James Ellison (Yamaha); **13** Tom Tunstall (Honda); **14** Howie Mainwaring (Yamaha); **15** Dan Linfoot (Yamaha).
Fastest lap: Camier, 1m 35.712s, 101.25mph/ 162.95km/h.

Fuchs-Silkolene British Supersport Championship, round 12 (15 laps, 40.380 miles/ 64.980km)
1 Steve Plater (Honda), 24m 59.665s, 96.93mph/155.99km/h.
2 James Westmoreland (Triumph); **3** Ben Wilson (Kawasaki); **4** Hudson Kennaugh (Kawasaki); **5** Lee Johnston (Yamaha); **6** Jack Kennedy (Yamaha); **7** Allan Jon Venter (Yamaha); **8** Marty Nutt (Yamaha); **9** BJ Toal (Honda); **10** Sam Lowes (Honda); **11** Daniel Cooper (Honda); **12** Joe Dickinson (Honda); **13** James Webb (Yamaha); **14** Paul Young (Triumph); **15** Lee Jackson (Honda).
Fastest lap: Westmoreland, 1m 39.052s, 97.84mph/157.45km/h (record).

Relentless British 125GP Championship, round 12 (12 laps, 32.304 miles/51.984km)
1 Brian Clark (Honda), 21m 53.746s, 88.52mph/142.46km/h.
2 Rob Guiver (Honda); **3** Deane Brown (Honda); **4** Adam Blacklock (Honda); **5** Danny Kent (Honda); **6** Connor Behan (Honda); James Lodge (Honda); **8** Paul Jordan (Honda); **9** Tom Haywood (Honda); **10** Ryan Saxelby (Honda); **11** Sam Hornsey (Honda); **12** Catherine Green (Honda); **13** Taylor Mackenzie (Honda); **14** Andy Reid (Honda); **15** Jay Lewis (Yamaha).
Fastest lap: Clark, 1m 48.147s, 89.61mph/ 144.21km/h.

Final British Superbike Championship points

1	Leon Camier	549.5
2	James Ellison	413
3	Stuart Easton	374
4	Josh Brookes	188
5	Ian Lowry	170
6	Simon Andrews	163.5

7 Julien Da Costa, 163; **8** Sylvain Guintoli, 147; **9** Chris Walker, 141; **10** John Laverty, 130.5; **11** Tommy Hill, 127; **12** Glen Richards, 125; **13** Gary Mason, 125; **14** Karl Harris, 124.5; **15** Graeme Gowland, 101.5.

Final British Supersport Championship points

1	Steve Plater	215
2	Billy McConnell	179
3	James Westmoreland	171
4	Ben Wilson	137
5	Daniel Cooper	104
6	Ian Hutchinson	78

7 Dan Linfoot, 72; **8** Tom Grant, 65; **9** Hudson Kennaugh, 58; **10** James Webb, 57; **11** Jack Kennedy, 54; **12** Lee Johnston, 52; **13** Allan Jon Venter, 51; **14** Sam Lowes, 50; **15** Craig Fitzpatrick, 42.

Final British 125GP Championship points

1	James Lodge	182
2	Rob Guiver	170
3	Martin Glossop	155
4	Brian Clark	138
5	Paul Jordan	104
6	Tim Hastings	103

7 Connor Behan, 98; **8** Tom Haywood, 90; **9** Deane Brown, 76; **10** Adam Blacklock, 76; **11** Taylor Mackenzie, 53; **12** Shaun Horsman, 49; **13** Robbie Stewart, 42; **14** Catherine Green, 38; **15** Ryan Saxelby, 36.

Supersport World Championship

PHILLIP ISLAND, Australia, 28 February 2009. 2.762-mile/4.445km circuit.
Supersport World Championship, round 1 (21 laps, 58.002 miles/93.345km)
1 Kenan Sofuoglu, TUR (Honda), 33m 42.156s, 103.260mph/166.180km/h.
2 Andrew Pitt, AUS (Honda); **3** Anthony West, AUS (Honda); **4** Cal Crutchlow, GBR (Yamaha); **5** Eugene Laverty, IRL (Honda); **6** Mark Aitchison, AUS (Honda); **7** Fabien Foret, FRA (Yamaha); **8** Joan Lascorz, SPA (Kawasaki); **9** Massimo Roccoli, ITA (Honda); **10** Gianluca Nannelli, ITA (Triumph); **11** Matthieu Lagrive, FRA (Honda); **12** Michele Pirro, ITA (Yamaha); **13** Barry Veneman, NED (Suzuki); **14** Garry McCoy, AUS (Triumph); **15** Robbin Harms, DEN (Honda).
Fastest lap: Andrew Pitt, AUS (Honda), 1m 35.327s, 104.368mph/167.964km/h.
Championship points: 1 Sofuoglu, 25; **2** Pitt, 20; **3** West, 16; **4** Crutchlow, 13; **5** Laverty, 11; **6** Aitchison, 10.

LOSAIL, Qatar, 14 March 2009. 3.443-mile/5.380km circuit.
Supersport World Championship, round 2 (18 laps, 60.174 miles/96.840km)
1 Eugene Laverty, IRL (Honda), 37m 6.285s, 97.304mph/156.595km/h.
2 Andrew Pitt, AUS (Honda); **3** Cal Crutchlow, GBR (Yamaha); **4** Kenan Sofuoglu, TUR (Honda); **5** Robbin Harms, DEN (Honda); **6** Matthieu Lagrive, FRA (Honda); **7** Garry McCoy, AUS (Triumph); **8** Massimo Roccoli, ITA (Honda); **9** Anthony West, AUS (Honda); **10** Barry Veneman, NED (Suzuki); **11** Michele Pirro, ITA (Yamaha); **12** Miguel Praia, POR (Honda); **13** Joan Lascorz, SPA (Kawasaki); **14** Gianluca Vizziello, ITA (Honda); **15** Mark Aitchison, AUS (Honda).
Fastest lap: Andrew Pitt, AUS (Honda), 2m 2.577s, 98.181mph/158.007km/h (record).
Championship points: 1 Pitt, 40; **2** Sofuoglu, 38; **3** Laverty, 36; **4** Crutchlow, 29; **5** West, 23; **6** Lagrive, 15.

VALENCIA, Spain, 5 April 2009. 2.489-mile/4.005km circuit.
Supersport World Championship, round 3 (23 laps, 57.238 miles/92.115km)
1 Cal Crutchlow, GBR (Yamaha), 38m 15.613s, 89.761mph/144.456km/h.
2 Anthony West, AUS (Honda); **3** Kenan Sofuoglu, TUR (Honda); **4** Mark Aitchison, AUS (Honda); **5** Matthieu Lagrive, FRA (Honda); **6** Michele Pirro, ITA (Yamaha); **8** Barry Veneman, NED (Suzuki); **9** Eugene Laverty, IRL (Honda); **10** Fabien Foret, FRA (Yamaha); **11** Gianluca Vizziello, ITA (Honda); **12** Robbin Harms, DEN (Honda);

13 Andrew Pitt, AUS (Honda); **14** Massimo Roccoli, ITA (Honda); **15** Tata Pradita, INA (Yamaha).
Fastest lap: Cal Crutchlow, GBR (Yamaha), 1m 36.865s, 92.489mph/148.846km/h (record).
Championship points: 1 Crutchlow, 54; **2** Sofuoglu, 54; **3** Laverty, 43; **4** Pitt, 43; **5** West, 43; **6** Lagrive, 25.

ASSEN, Holland, 26 April 2009. 2.830-mile/4.555km circuit.
Supersport World Championship, round 4 (21 laps, 59.437 miles/95.655km)
1 Eugene Laverty, IRL (Honda), 35m 45.160s, 99.747mph/160.528km/h.
2 Cal Crutchlow, GBR (Yamaha); **3** Joan Lascorz, SPA (Kawasaki); **4** Fabien Foret, FRA (Yamaha); **5** Kenan Sofuoglu, TUR (Honda); **6** Mark Aitchison, AUS (Honda); **7** Anthony West, AUS (Honda); **8** Barry Veneman, NED (Suzuki); **9** Robbin Harms, DEN (Honda); **10** Michele Pirro, ITA (Yamaha); **11** Patrik Vostarek, CZE (Honda); **12** Gianluca Nannelli, ITA (Triumph); **13** Massimo Roccoli, ITA (Honda); **14** Katsuaki Fujiwara, JPN (Kawasaki); **15** Garry McCoy, AUS (Triumph).
Fastest lap: Cal Crutchlow, GBR (Yamaha), 1m 40.836s, 101.047mph/162.620km/h (record).
Championship points: 1 Crutchlow, 74; **2** Laverty, 68; **3** Sofuoglu, 65; **4** West, 52; **5** Pitt, 43; **6** Aitchison, 34.

MONZA, Italy, 10 May 2009. 3.600-mile/5.793km circuit.
Supersport World Championship, round 5 (16 laps, 57.594 miles/92.688km)
1 Cal Crutchlow, GBR (Yamaha), 29m 34.605s, 116.836mph/188.020km/h.
2 Joan Lascorz, SPA (Kawasaki); **3** Fabien Foret, FRA (Yamaha); **4** Eugene Laverty, IRL (Honda); **5** Andrew Pitt, AUS (Honda); **6** Katsuaki Fujiwara, JPN (Kawasaki); **7** Michele Pirro, ITA (Yamaha); **8** Garry McCoy, AUS (Triumph); **9** Kenan Sofuoglu, TUR (Honda); **10** Gianluca Nannelli, ITA (Triumph); **11** Franco Battaini, ITA (Triumph); **12** Miguel Praia, POR (Honda); **13** Barry Veneman, NED (Suzuki); **14** Gianluca Vizziello, ITA (Honda); **15** Alessandro Polita, ITA (Suzuki).
Fastest lap: Cal Crutchlow, GBR (Yamaha), 1m 49.728s, 118.097mph/190.059km/h.
Championship points: 1 Crutchlow, 99; **2** Laverty, 81; **3** Sofuoglu, 72; **4** Pitt, 54; **5** West, 52; **6** Lascorz, 47.

KYALAMI, South Africa, 17 May 2009. 2.638-mile/4.246km circuit.
Supersport World Championship, round 6 (23 laps, 60.682 miles/97.658km)
1 Eugene Laverty, IRL (Honda), 39m 6.061s, 93.116mph/149.855km/h.
2 Cal Crutchlow, GBR (Yamaha); **3** Mark Aitchison, AUS (Honda); **4** Joan Lascorz, SPA (Kawasaki); **5** Kenan Sofuoglu, TUR (Honda); **6** Andrew Pitt, AUS (Honda); **7** Garry McCoy, AUS (Triumph); **8** Anthony West, AUS (Honda); **9** Michele Pirro, ITA (Honda); **10** Matthieu Lagrive, FRA (Honda); **11** Michael Laverty, GBR (Honda); **12** Massimo Roccoli, ITA (Honda); **13** Katsuaki Fujiwara, JPN (Kawasaki); **14** Tata Pradita, INA (Yamaha); **15** Danilo Dell'Omo, ITA (Honda).
Fastest lap: Eugene Laverty, IRL (Honda), 1m 41.053s, 93.990mph/151.263km/h (new track).
Championship points: 1 Crutchlow, 119; **2** Laverty, 106; **3** Sofuoglu, 83; **4** Pitt, 64; **5** Lascorz, 60; **6** West, 60.

MILLER MOTORSPORTS, USA, 31 May 2009. 3.049-mile/4.907km circuit.
Supersport World Championship, round 7 (18 laps, 54.883 miles/88.326km)
1 Kenan Sofuoglu, TUR (Honda), 34m 0.510s, 96.828mph/155.830km/h.
2 Eugene Laverty, IRL (Honda); **3** Cal Crutchlow, GBR (Yamaha); **4** Joan Lascorz, SPA (Kawasaki); **5** Fabien Foret, FRA (Yamaha); **6** Garry McCoy, AUS (Triumph); **7** Andrew Pitt, AUS (Honda); **8** Michele Pirro, ITA (Honda); **9** Matthieu Lagrive, FRA (Honda); **10** Anthony West, AUS (Honda);

11 Tata Pradita, INA (Yamaha); **12** Miguel Praia, POR (Honda); **13** Katsuaki Fujiwara, JPN (Kawasaki); **14** Barry Veneman, NED (Suzuki); **15** Gianluca Vizziello, ITA (Honda).
Fastest lap: Kenan Sofuoglu, TUR (Honda), 1m 52.285s, 97.757mph/157.325km/h (new track).
Championship points: 1 Crutchlow, 135; **2** Laverty, 126; **3** Sofuoglu, 108; **4** Pitt, 73; **5** Lascorz, 73; **6** West, 66.

MISANO, Italy, 21 June 2009. 2.623-mile/4.226km circuit.
Supersport World Championship, round 8 (22 laps, 57.770 miles/92.972km)
1 Cal Crutchlow, GBR (Yamaha), 36m 51.032s, 94.061mph/151.377km/h.
2 Eugene Laverty, IRL (Honda); **3** Massimo Roccoli, ITA (Honda); **4** Joan Lascorz, SPA (Kawasaki); **5** Mark Aitchison, AUS (Honda); **6** Katsuaki Fujiwara, JPN (Kawasaki); **7** Anthony West, AUS (Honda); **8** Fabien Foret, FRA (Yamaha); **9** Gianluca Nannelli, ITA (Triumph); **10** Miguel Praia, POR (Honda); **11** Gianluca Vizziello, ITA (Honda); **12** Flavio Gentile, ITA (Honda); **13** Danilo Dell'Omo, ITA (Honda); **14** Arie Vos, NED (Honda); **15** Yannick Guerra, SPA (Yamaha).
Fastest lap: Cal Crutchlow, GBR (Yamaha), 1m 38.868s, 95.615mph/153.878km/h (record).
Championship points: 1 Crutchlow, 160; **2** Laverty, 146; **3** Sofuoglu, 108; **4** Lascorz, 86; **5** West, 75; **6** Pitt, 73.

DONINGTON PARK, Great Britain, 28 June 2009. 2.450-mile/4.023km circuit.
Supersport World Championship, round 9 (22 laps, 54.995 miles/88.506km)
1 Cal Crutchlow, GBR (Yamaha), 34m 15.876s, 96.301mph/154.981km/h.
2 Joan Lascorz, SPA (Kawasaki); **3** Garry McCoy, AUS (Triumph); **4** Kenan Sofuoglu, TUR (Honda); **5** Eugene Laverty, IRL (Honda); **6** Barry Veneman, NED (Honda); **7** Gianluca Vizziello, ITA (Honda); **8** Gianluca Nannelli, ITA (Triumph); **9** Danilo Dell'Omo, ITA (Honda); **10** Andrew Pitt, AUS (Honda); **11** James Westmoreland, GBR (Triumph); **12** Patrik Vostarek, CZE (Honda); **13** Kev Coghlan, GBR (Yamaha); **14** Hudson Kennaugh, RSA (Yamaha); **15** Michele Pirro, ITA (Yamaha).
Fastest lap: Cal Crutchlow, GBR (Yamaha), 1m 32.449s, 97.342mph/156.657km/h (record).
Championship points: 1 Crutchlow, 185; **2** Laverty, 157; **3** Sofuoglu, 121; **4** Lascorz, 106; **5** Pitt, 79; **6** West, 75.

BRNO, Czech Republic, 26 July 2009. 3.357-mile/5.403km circuit.
Supersport World Championship, round 10 (18 laps, 60.431 miles/97.254km)
1 Fabien Foret, FRA (Yamaha), 37m 14.367s, 97.366mph/156.695km/h.
2 Anthony West, AUS (Honda); **3** Joan Lascorz, SPA (Kawasaki); **4** Katsuaki Fujiwara, JPN (Kawasaki); **5** Eugene Laverty, IRL (Honda); **6** Sheridan Morais, RSA (Yamaha); **7** Massimo Roccoli, ITA (Honda); **8** Garry McCoy, AUS (Triumph); **9** Kenan Sofuoglu, TUR (Honda); **10** Andrew Pitt, AUS (Honda); **11** Barry Veneman, NED (Honda); **12** Danilo Dell'Omo, ITA (Honda); **13** Michael Laverty, GBR (Honda); **14** Gianluca Vizziello, ITA (Honda); **15** Jesco Gunther, GER (Honda).
Fastest lap: Cal Crutchlow, GBR (Yamaha), 2m 2.708s, 98.495mph/158.513km/h (record).
Championship points: 1 Crutchlow, 185; **2** Laverty, 168; **3** Sofuoglu, 128; **4** Lascorz, 122; **5** West, 95; **6** Foret, 88.

NÜRBURGRING, Germany, 6 September 2009. 3.192-mile/5.137km circuit.
Supersport World Championship, round 11 (19 laps, 60.648 miles/97.603km)
1 Cal Crutchlow, GBR (Yamaha), 37m 56.481s, 95.907mph/154.348km/h.
2 Eugene Laverty, IRL (Honda); **3** Joan Lascorz, SPA (Kawasaki); **4** Massimo Roccoli, ITA (Honda); **5** Fabien Foret, FRA (Yamaha); **6** Mark Aitchison, AUS (Honda); **7** Andrew Pitt, AUS

(Honda); **8** Garry McCoy, AUS (Triumph); **9** Robbin Harms, DEN (Honda); **10** Danilo Dell'Omo, ITA (Honda); **11** Miguel Praia, POR (Honda); **12** Barry Veneman, NED (Honda); **13** Gianluca Vizziello, ITA (Honda); **14** Kevin Wahr, GER (Triumph); **15** Anthony West, AUS (Honda).
Fastest lap: Cal Crutchlow, GBR (Yamaha), 1m 58.726s, 96.787mph/155.764km/h (record).
Championship points: 1 Crutchlow, 210; **2** Laverty, 188; **3** Lascorz, 138; **4** Sofuoglu, 128; **5** Foret, 99; **6** West, 96.

IMOLA, Italy, 27 September 2009. 3.067-mile/4.936km circuit.
Supersport World Championship, round 12 (19 laps, 58.275 miles/93.784km)
1 Kenan Sofuoglu, TUR (Honda), 35m 51.342s, 97.516mph/156.936km/h.
2 Eugene Laverty, IRL (Honda); **3** Fabien Foret, FRA (Yamaha); **4** Chaz Davies, GBR (Triumph); **5** Garry McCoy, AUS (Triumph); **6** Andrew Pitt, AUS (Honda); **7** Katsuaki Fujiwara, JPN (Kawasaki); **8** Anthony West, AUS (Honda); **9** Miguel Praia, POR (Honda); **10** Danilo Dell'Omo, ITA (Honda); **11** Michele Pirro, ITA (Yamaha); **12** Cristiano Migliorati, ITA; **13** Olivier Four, FRA (Honda); **14** Barry Veneman, NED (Honda); **15** Flavio Gentile, ITA (Honda).
Fastest lap: Cal Crutchlow, GBR (Yamaha), 1m 51.645s, 98.899mph/159.162km/h (new track).
Championship points: 1 Crutchlow, 210; **2** Laverty, 208; **3** Sofuoglu, 153; **4** Lascorz, 138; **5** Foret, 115; **6** West, 104.

MAGNY-COURS, France, 4 October 2009. 2.741-mile/4.411km circuit.
Supersport World Championship, round 13 (19 laps, 52.076 miles/83.809km)
1 Joan Lascorz, SPA (Kawasaki), 32m 21.660s, 96.554mph/155.389km/h.
2 Cal Crutchlow, GBR (Yamaha); **3** Kenan Sofuoglu, TUR (Honda); **4** Anthony West, AUS (Honda); **5** Mark Aitchison, AUS (Honda); **6** Andrew Pitt, AUS (Honda); **7** Katsuaki Fujiwara, JPN (Kawasaki); **8** Massimo Roccoli, ITA (Honda); **9** Matthieu Lagrive, FRA (Honda); **10** Michele Pirro, ITA (Yamaha); **11** Olivier Four, FRA (Honda); **12** Miguel Praia, POR (Honda); **13** Eugene Laverty, IRL (Honda); **14** Kev Coghlan, GBR (Yamaha); **15** Arie Vos, NED (Honda).
Fastest lap: Cal Crutchlow, GBR (Yamaha), 1m 41.407s, 97.302mph/156.593km/h (record).
Championship points: 1 Crutchlow, 230; **2** Laverty, 211; **3** Sofuoglu, 169; **4** Lascorz, 163; **5** West, 117; **6** Foret, 115.

PORTIMAO, Portugal, 25 October 2009. 2.853-mile/4.592km circuit.
Supersport World Championship, round 14 (20 laps, 57.067 miles/91.840km)
1 Eugene Laverty, IRL (Honda), 35m 17.044s, 97.041mph/156.172km/h.
2 Kenan Sofuoglu, TUR (Honda); **3** Garry McCoy, AUS (Triumph); **4** Cal Crutchlow, GBR (Yamaha); **5** Mark Aitchison, AUS (Honda); **6** Michele Pirro, ITA (Yamaha); **7** Chaz Davies, GBR (Triumph); **8** Fabien Foret, FRA (Yamaha); **9** Barry Veneman, NED (Honda); **10** Miguel Praia, POR (Honda); **11** Andrew Pitt, AUS (Honda); **12** Martin Cardenas, COL (Honda); **13** Katsuaki Fujiwara, JPN (Kawasaki); **14** Michael Laverty, GBR (Honda); **15** Kev Coghlan, GBR (Yamaha).
Fastest lap: Joan Lascorz, SPA (Kawasaki), 1m 45.186s, 97.656mph/157.162km/h.

Final World Championship points

1	Cal Crutchlow, GBR	243
2	Eugene Laverty, IRL	236
3	Kenan Sofuoglu, TUR	189
4	Joan Lascorz, SPA	163
5	Fabien Foret, FRA	123
6	Andrew Pitt, AUS	119

7 Anthony West, AUS, 117; **8** Garry McCoy, AUS, 98; **9** Mark Aitchison, AUS, 93; **10** Katsuaki Fujiwara, JPN, 73; **11** Massimo Roccoli, ITA, 70; **12** Michele Pirro, ITA, 70; **13** Barry Veneman, NED, 58; **14** Matthieu Lagrive, FRA, 45; **15** Miguel Praia, POR, 40.